Carl Schurz

Carl Schurz

A Biography

By Hans L. Trefousse

THE UNIVERSITY OF TENNESSEE PRESS / KNOXVILLE

Also by HANS L. TREFOUSSE

Germany and American Neutrality, 1939–1941
Ben Butler: The South Called Him Beast
Benjamin Franklin Wade: Radical Republican from Ohio
The Radical Republicans: Lincoln's Vanguard for Racial Justice
Impeachment of a President: Andrew Johnson, the Blacks, and Reconstruction

FRONTISPIECE: *Carl Schurz (Courtesy of Library of Congress)*

Clothbound editions of University of Tennessee Press books are printed on paper designed for an effective life of at least 300 years, and binding materials are chosen for strength and durability.

Library of Congress Cataloging in Publication Data

Trefousse, Hans Louis.
  Carl Schurz, a biography.

  Bibliography: p.
  Includes index.
    1. Schurz, Carl, 1829-1906. 2. Statesmen—United States—Biography. 3. United States. Congress. Senate—Biography. 4. Legislators—United States—Biography. I. Title.
  E664.S39T7   973.8'092'4[B]   81-3370
  ISBN 0-87049-326-4   AACR2

For Walter and Alberta Albersheim

Preface

Carnegie Hall was crowded on the night of November 21, 1906. An impressive number of people were there; the Honorable Joseph H. Choate, recently ambassador to the Court of St. James, presided. Ex-President Grover Cleveland, President Charles W. Eliot of Harvard, Secretary of the Navy Charles J. Bonaparte, and Booker T. Washington were the main speakers. A sixty-piece orchestra directed by Frank Damrosch furnished the music; the Liederkranz and Arion Society choirs, the songs. But what was most notable was that one of the addresses, delivered by an exchange professor at Harvard, was in German. It was this fact that highlighted the importance of the departed citizen who was honored that night—Carl Schurz, the famous German-American leader who had died six months earlier.

A bridge between Germany and America, a guide across that bridge for millions of immigrants, Carl Schurz had long been America's most celebrated citizen of foreign birth. No matter what his German-American compatriots might think of the varied aspects of his career—of his adventurous escape from the Prussians through a sewer, of his daring rescue of Gottfried Kinkel from Spandau prison, of his controversial service as Union general, Missouri senator, and reforming secretary of the interior, of his many changes of political allegiance, they could always look up to him. Schurz was a German-American who had made it, a fellow countryman who was on intimate terms with presidents, generals, ministers, leading authors, and artists. He showed them how to become good Americans without abandoning their German heritage, how to master the English tongue without giving up the *Muttersprache*. A later generation would have characterized his philosophy as a combination of the idea of the melting pot with that of the retention of ethnicity; in his lifetime, neither term was current but the concepts were applicable, and there was never any doubt where Schurz stood. "Those who would meanly and coldly forget their old mother could not be expected to be faithful to their young bride," he explained in the Senate. Germany was the mother, the mother that had given him life and a great cultural heritage; America was the bride who had given him happiness. The old mother had been unable to provide the freedom he craved, and even when Prince Bismarck later warmly welcomed Schurz in the old homeland, he did not let the honor, if such it was, induce him to return for good. Telling the prince that in a democracy with little government things might go badly in detail but well on the whole, he insisted that in a monarchy with a lot of government they might go well in detail but badly on the whole. What he liked about the United States, he pointed out to Bismarck, was the fact that Americans were self-reliant; they would never have become the energetic people they were had there been a policeman standing at every mud puddle to keep them from stepping into it.

As a role model, then, Schurz made his greatest contributions. It is true that he impressed Abraham Lincoln with his part in 1860 in the success of the new Republican party by allegedly rallying German-Americans to the antislavery cause, that he displayed great courage as a political general during the Civil War, that he wrote a most revealing report about conditions in the South during Reconstruction, and that he earned fame as a senator from Missouri. It is also true that he became one of the principal founders of the Liberal Republican party and added luster to Rutherford B. Hayes's cabinet as secretary of the interior, and that he later became one of the most prominent independents in the country, a reputation which served him in good stead in his long struggle for civil service reform. But none of these accomplishments would earn him more than a subordinate place in the history of his time. All these achievements have often been recounted in detail. Two full-length biographies in English as well as an excellent study of his Americanization appeared within thirty years of his death, and at least four additional lives in German have been published since that time. His great role as a teacher and leader of German-Americans, however, remains to be shown. It was no accident that he wrote his memoirs both in German and in English. A master of both languages, he sought to fuse the advantages of foreign birth and heritage with the privileges of American citizenship. Such a career and such an ideology is of the utmost importance for modern America.

Acknowledgments

My thanks are due above all to Professor and Mrs. Arthur R. Hogue of Indiana University for their hospitality and kindness in making available their extensive collection of Schurz papers. They are wonderful hosts; moreover, Professor Hogue's extensive knowledge of Carl Schurz and his world is indispensable. I should also like to express my gratitude to Mrs. Cissa Morlang of Hamburg, who cooperated so splendidly in sending me Schurz's correspondence with her grandmother, Mrs. Emilie Meyer. Baron Bernard von Friesen of Pembroke, Wales, kindly allowed me to use material shedding light on the Bismarck visit, and Professor Frederick Trautmann of Temple University saved me many long hours by giving me the extensive Schurz material he had collected. Professors Robert A. East and Patrick Riddleberger read the entire manuscript and made valuable suggestions. Many other colleagues have helped me with advice, hospitality, and encouragement. They include Dean Frederick I. Olson of the University of Wisconsin at Milwaukee, Richard Lowitt of Iowa State University, Thomas B. Alexander of Missouri, William E. Parrish of Mississippi State, William Gillette of Rutgers, Harold M. Hyman of Rice, Frederick C. Luebke of Nebraska, Rolf Meyersohn of the City University of New York, Otto Pflanze of Indiana University, and Angel Alcala, Ari Hoogenboom, and Jerome Sternstein of Brooklyn College. Professors William Shank, Helga Feder, and Claire Bowie of the library of the Graduate School of the City University of New York and Harold Jones of the library of Brooklyn College, as well as the staffs of the libraries of Wagner College, the State Historical Society of Wisconsin, and the Houghton Collection at Harvard were especially helpful. All visiting scholars owe a great debt to Watt P. Marchman and his skillful assistants at the Hayes Historical Society, where research is a pleasure. I was also assisted immeasurably by the John Simon Guggenheim Fellowship which I received in 1977–78 and the unfailing support of Dean Nathan Schmukler of Brooklyn College. Finally, I wish to thank my wife, Rashelle F. Trefousse, who knows how much I appreciate her patience, critical faculty, and excellent editorial advice.

Contents

Illustrations

Carl Schurz

I

Youth

ALTHOUGH A FEUDAL CASTLE is not really the proper birthplace for an American statesman, Carl Schurz first saw the light of day at the Gracht, a small château surrounded by a moat at Liblar near Cologne. Of course, as he hastened to point out in his *Reminiscences,* he was not of noble descent; the property belonged to the counts of Wolf-Metternich, feudatories of the former archbishop-electors of Cologne, at whose court they had occupied a distinguished position. But Schurz was the grandson of the count's tenant-in-chief, Heribert Jüssen, whose daughter Marianne had married the local schoolmaster, Christian Schurz. The young couple was still staying with the Jüssens until Christian could establish his own home, and so the future major general, senator from Missouri, and secretary of the interior was born in the outbuildings of the castle. His father christened him Carl Christian.[1]

At the time of Carl's birth on March 2, 1829, most of the feudal arrangements in western Germany were already disappearing. The electoral state had vanished with the French Revolution and the subsequent annexation of the left bank of the Rhine to France, which had introduced the Code Napoleon. After almost twenty years of French rule, the area was ceded to the Kingdom of Prussia, which incorporated it in the newly created Rhine Province and ruled it from faraway Berlin. The peasants had long been free, and the institution of tenant-in-chief, or *Burghalfen,* so called because his share of the crops was one half, was also becoming obsolete. But only the beginnings of the later industrial supremacy of the Rhineland were noticeable. While the count owned the local peat works under the supervision of Carl's uncle Ferdinand, an enterprise which later gave rise to the region's briquette industry, no railroad had as yet penetrated the area. It was farming country—fertile, pleasant, and prosperous.[2]

Certain feudal conventions, however, had not yet been forgotten. While the old count maintained a patriarchal relationship with his tenants, the most important of whom he invited to his great annual hunt, there was still an unbridgeable gap between nobles and commoners. The *Burghalfen* might keep a two-wheeled chaise but not a four-wheeled carriage; his wife and daughters might wear pretty caps or hoods, but no city bonnets. Bonnets and four-wheeled carriages were reserved for the nobility.[3]

Despite these peculiarities, which apparently made a deep impression on little Carl, his childhood seems to have been happy. The castle, partially in baroque style, the outbuildings enclosing on three sides a court which opened on a moat with a stone bridge to the count's living quarters on an island, all surrounded by water and connected to the mainland with drawbridges, provided many opportunities for amusement. The huge garden with its orangery and its statues, the first in the neighborhood to have been laid out in the French style, was inviting, especially since it abounded with peacocks and other fowl, and the count kept wild boars in a pit, which intrigued the child. Dense woods surrounded the village, especially toward the east, where the Ville Hills separated it from neighboring Brühl with its beautiful palace, formerly the electors' summer residence. A pleasant vista of a river valley with little towns and small castles on little islands opened toward the west. Poplar trees, willow groves, and alder trees abounded, and in the far distance, the blue hills of the Eifel Mountains provided a picturesque background. The climate was moderate, the air clear, and life agreeable.[4]

But in the last analysis, it was Carl's family that made his childhood memorable. He was deeply influenced by his grandfather, the *Burghalfen*. A veritable giant of a man, he was a natural leader of enormous physical strength—once on a dare he carried an anvil all through the castle—and Carl learned that leadership paid off. Did not all the people of the village ask his grandfather for advice? Did he not set the pace at the annual village fair, the *Kirmess*? And was he not able at harvest time to hire whatever extra help he needed by simply walking through the village and summoning likely workers? His wife, grandmother Jüssen, was also a person of importance. She prepared the common meals for all the servants, who, after turning around to say their prayers, would sit down on long wooden benches, take their three-pronged forks, and, without speaking a word, eat their common meals from wooden bowls and long, narrow strips of board. Grandfather and his family were respected. The old man adored his grandson, who reciprocated with equal love. And while the old man was not well educated—he was barely able to read and write—he had much common sense. Carl never forgot the disaster that befell the *Burghalfen* when, paralyzed by a stroke, he was confined to his chair with nothing to do but to catch flies.

If grandfather Jüssen was not an intellectual, father Schurz was, or tried to be one. Born into a Rhenish peasant family at Duisdorf near Bonn, he had lost his parents at an early age. After briefly serving in the army in the last campaign against Napoleon, he went to the teachers' seminar at Brühl, where he learned the few skills required of a village schoolmaster and soon started teaching at nearby Liblar. There he married the *Burghalfen*'s daughter and, after the brief period of residence in the castle, moved into a house of his own in the village. Within a few years, his family had grown to four; besides Carl there was another son, Heribert, and two daughters, Anna and Antonia. But teaching at the village school no longer satisfied either his mental or pecuniary needs, and he opened a small hardware store instead.

Business, however, was not Christian Schurz's forte. Happiest when he was puttering in his garden with his birds and flowers, he was fond of books and greatly admired the classical writers. Pictures of Schiller, Goethe, Tasso, Wieland, Körner, and Shakespeare adorned the walls of his living room, and his library

Carl Schurz's Birthplace, Schloss Gracht, Liblar, Germany (Courtesy of German Information Center, 410 Park Avenue, New York 10022)

included works of Rousseau and Voltaire. Determined to provide for his eldest son all the educational opportunities he himself had missed, he decided from the first to prepare him for an academic career. He sought to infuse the love of learning in all his children, and in Carl's case, at least, he was eminently successful.

Mother Schurz's influence was important in a different way. Her rectitude, moral sense, and kindness left a strong legacy for her son, who adored her. Although her spelling was faulty and her insistent religious views less than convincing to him, she imparted to him that powerful sense of right and wrong which always impressed his friends.

In a small German village in the nineteenth century, the family consisted of more than father, mother, and siblings. Uncles, aunts, and cousins were part of it, and while there were few near relatives on the Schurz side, the Jüssen clan was large. Uncle Peter, a former French grenadier and a giant like his father, was the tenant-in-chief of a large estate near the village. Uncle Ferdinand, the supervisor of the peat works, lived in Liblar in comfortable circumstances. A Prussian reserve lieutenant, he was a freethinker, never went to church, and belonged to the Cologne Masonic lodge. The villagers were certain that horrible things went on there, but Uncle Ferdinand did not care. Uncle Jacob, a handsome man of means, was the mayor of the Rhenish city of Jülich, and Uncle Georg, the youngest, tall and good-looking like all of his brothers, eventually took over grandfather's duties at the castle. A brother-in-law, Uncle Rey, lived on a large farm within half an hour's walk from the village. The clan, old and young, often gathered for family affairs, and Uncle Ferdinand's liberal outlook was not lost on the children.

Politics was constantly discussed. Few of the inhabitants of the Rhineland had any great love for their new sovereign, the king of Prussia, since they had only been annexed to that Protestant state in 1815, and the struggles between the government and the archbishop of Cologne excited the neighborhood. General European affairs were also debated, and it is probable that the appalling condition of Gemany did not escape attention. In spite of promises of constitutions during the Wars of Liberation, the forty-odd German princes ruled as petty tyrants, aided and abetted by Count Metternich at Vienna, who feared liberalism and nationalism and used all the means at his disposal to suppress popular demands. A powerless Germanic Confederation had its seat at Frankfurt, but its diet merely reflected the reactionary aspirations of the sovereign members. Nevertheless, liberal stirrings were in the air. The example of France, where two revolutions had taken place within recent memory, and even more that of the United States, was felt everywhere.

For the inhabitants of Liblar, America was truly the promised land. A place where there were no kings, no bishops, and, it was believed, no taxes, was obviously a second Eden. From time to time, Carl saw families of emigrants leave for this earthly paradise, and his father told him that George Washington was the greatest man who had ever lived. Had he not led his country to freedom and then, refusing a crown, taken up the plow again? No matter how inaccurate, this introduction to American history was a lesson young Schurz seemingly took to heart.

Virtually the entire village and neighborhood was Roman Catholic, and the local priest was a man of importance. Carl, however, began to wonder about the clergy at an early age. The priest had taught the children that the only way to go to Heaven was through the Roman Catholic Church. But his father had a Jewish friend named Aaron, a dignified person with a serious face, who, he said, was a good man, better than many a Christian. Was it possible that such an individual was condemned to everlasting hellfire? The boy's sense of justice was outraged. And then the priest took the wrong side in a dispute about the new schoolteacher's alleged seduction of one of his pupils. Schurz's mother, in spite of her constant admonitions to the boy to say his prayers, was most indignant and called the pastor an evil man. The incident did not strengthen Carl's trust in the clergy.

When the boy was barely six, his father took him to the village school. He soon learned to read and write, and when the books in his father's library were too difficult for him, he could find marvelous children's books at the circulating library at nearby Brühl. *Robinson Crusoe* was his favorite, but he also read ancient German legends and a patriotic volume about a soldier in the Wars of Liberation. When he was ill with the measles, his father read Schiller's poems to him. He also introduced him to Lessing's *Nathan the Wise* with its lessons in tolerance.

The elder Schurz gave up his teaching not long after his son entered the school, and because the local institution was too limited, by the time the youngster was nine, he was sent to Brühl to get a better education. He had already taken the long walk across the hills for some time, twice a week in fact, to take piano lessons from the local organist. When his brother Heribert was old enough, he trudged along for his lessons, conveniently scheduled while the local priest introduced Carl to the mysteries of Latin declensions. But Carl did not neglect his music; the Schurzes acquired an old piano without pedals or damper; in spite of its dilapidated condition, it sufficed for finger exercises. The boy eventually became an expert player. For the rest of his life, piano music was a necessity for him, a passion which often helped him in good times and bad.

Schurz's school at Brühl was attached to the teachers' seminary from which his father had graduated. Located in an old Franciscan monastery, it could boast of competent instructors. During the summer months, Carl walked the four miles back and forth from Liblar; in the winter, he boarded with a butcher's widow in town, coming home only on weekends.

It was at Brühl that Carl experienced his first personal tragedy. One day his father arrived unexpectedly during the week; it was obvious that something terrible had happened. His younger brother Heribert had died. Carl, who had been very close to his brother, was disconsolate. Bereft of a walking companion, he took to reading while hiking from Brühl to Liblar. Since his father was an admirer of the German classicist Friedrich Gottlieb Klopstock, the boy managed to read through all twenty cantos of Klopstock's *Messiah*, as well as many less taxing examples of

German literature. But Carl was not a mere bookworm. His mother and father, his family and friends, as well as his books made life agreeable to him, and the sports of the village youths, bird trapping and hiking in the woods, caused him to remember Liblar with pleasure. The village also offered various entertainments, jugglers and players, the annual *Kirmess* with its merrymaking, and the bird shoot on Whitmonday, an event of great importance to the inhabitants. All in all, he enjoyed a sheltered though not pampered youth. Although the village was confining, his parents and uncles provided a view of the outside world. And his father stopped at no sacrifice to make a professor of Carl. The Brühl experience was merely the beginning, for soon he was to enter the Marcellen Gymnasium at Cologne.

Young Schurz was ten when he came to Cologne to enroll in the secondary school of his parents' choice. According to arrangements his father made with a local locksmith for board and lodging, the boy was quartered with the locksmith's son, whose bed he shared. The school was within walking distance, so that Carl could go there every morning while taking in the wonders of the city.[5]

Cologne was then one of the four largest towns of Prussia and the most important center of the Rhineland. Home to some seventy thousand people, it extended in a semicircle along the Rhine, a veritable sea of gables and turrets surmounted by two dozen church towers, including St. Martin with its tall pinnacles, and dominated by the famous but unfinished cathedral, the Dom. Only the choir in the east and that part of the west front on which the towers were to be constructed were completed; the two separate portions were connected by a temporary brick wall, and one of the unfinished towers was topped by a century-old crane from which pieces of lead were suspended. Many of the streets, especially those along the river, were dark and narrow, but the rapid construction of new quarters with villas surrounded by gardens, to say nothing of the introduction of gas lights in the fall of 1841, gave proof of the city's progressive spirit. Art collections, bookstores, museums, and manufacturing establishments abounded. As a whole, Cologne, with its busy streets, myriads of sails crowding the river bank, opulent commercial establishments, and its heavily traveled bridge across the Rhine, was a very lively city. "All is stir, all is life," wrote Victor Hugo, who was greatly impressed by it.[6]

If Hugo was impressed, young Carl must have been overwhelmed by his new surroundings. Cologne had art exhibits, theaters, and libraries; frequent and reasonably priced concerts were easily accessible; and the honor of attending the gymnasium was not lost on the village lad from Liblar.

The school itself was challenging. Offering the usual German gymnasium courses of the nineteenth century, with a heavy emphasis on the classics, Latin, and Greek, the curriculum was tailored to the assumed needs of the sons of upper- and middle-class parents, who were the only ones able to pay the tuition required. Fortunately, Carl had excellent teachers, of whom he remembered especially Heinrich Bone, his mentor in Latin and Greek, who also taught him German composition. Bone emphasized simplicity of style, a lesson his pupil never forgot. Professor Wilhelm Pütz, his history and later German teacher, was also very talented. It was Pütz who introduced him to Goethe, Shakespeare, Calderon, Cervantes, and Tasso. And apparently Pütz's interests were not limited to literature. He taught Carl enough Italian to enable his student to read Silvio Pellico's *My Prison,* an account of the Italian patriot's sufferings at the hands of the Austrians. Schurz decided that history and literature were his favorites, and he excelled in both subjects. He even began to write dramas and poems as well as historical romances.

The locksmith was very kind to his boarder, but his intellectual horizon was limited and he did not own a piano. After a few years Carl, for whom music was indispensable, moved into new quarters, where he was on his own and thus able to receive visitors. Gregarious even then, he had made a number of good friends at school. Among these the most important were Theodore Petrasch, the son of a local civil servant, and Ludwig von Weise, the scion of a Cologne patrician family. Both were a little older than he, but with Petrasch especially Carl established a lifelong friendship. He wrote him long letters when the two friends were separated, exchanging philosophical ideas with him and sharing his joys and delights in literature. It was Petrasch who introduced him to Heine's poetry by lending him the *Book of Songs,* and soon he was completely taken with it. Shakespeare also became a favorite, but Byron left him cold. He considered the romantic poet mediocre.[7]

Although Carl's financial resources were very meager—at the end of his stay in Cologne he received a fellowship and earned some extra money by tutoring—he frequently went to the theater and often attended the imposing Sunday high masses at the cathedral. He was also intrigued by the art museums, where he developed a taste for painting which he retained for the rest of his life.

Vacation time was spent at Liblar, in the midst of the family, and although his many cousins thought him a bit too well brought up, he enthusiastically joined with them in their various pranks. His mother admonished him above all to remember his Heavenly Father. Her religious precepts may not have made a good Catholic of her boy; nevertheless, he appreciated the sentiments behind them.

Father Schurz was exceedingly proud of his son. He liked to show off with him, and so Carl was allowed to play on the church organ at Liblar. For a while, all went well, but one day he treated the congregation to a lively march he had heard on Cologne's parade grounds, and then he confused the church choir by playing in such a way that the singers had to strain to keep up with him. His musical interlude at the Liblar church came to an end, but he earned more fame in his native village by winning the bird-shoot one Whitmonday. It was his first great success.

It was inevitable that the classics were not the only topic of conversation at school. The national liberal spirit which inspired the revolutionaries of 1848 was already very noticeable in the Rhineland, and the boys were affected by vague dreams of a united, liberal Germany. Their ideas were still very romantic, but romanticism was in the air. Even the mercurial king of Prussia, Frederick William IV, was affected by it. Coming to Cologne in 1842 to inaugurate the project of completing the ancient cathedral, he delivered a stirring speech full of medieval allusions and fair promises. The king's words and his deeds were two different things, however, and the reality of Prussian autocracy continued to rest heavily on the population. The easygoing Rhinelanders did not like it.[8]

A gymnasium education usually lasted nine years, at the end of which students were required to take the *Abitur*, a final examination which would enable them to enter the university. But shortly before Schurz's last year at the school, disaster struck the family. His father, who had neither prospered in the hardware business nor in grain speculations, and whose venture in constructing and running an amusement hall had also been unsuccessful, sold his house at Liblar in order to move to Bonn to open a combination boardinghouse and restaurant for students. Before the deal was completed, however, the buyer reneged. When Christian Schurz, who had already established credit on the basis of the projected sale, was unable to pay his notes, one of his creditors put him into debtors' prison. Carl rushed home; it was a dreadful experience to find his father behind bars, and he went to work immediately to help the family settle its affairs. The creditor was persuaded to let Schurz senior out of jail, the family moved to Bonn, and Carl had to leave the gymnasium. But he was able to make an arrangement to finish his studies *in absentia*; in the meantime, he attended lectures at the University of Bonn as a nonmatriculated student.[9]

At first, the prospect of leaving "good old, respectable, stupid Cologne," as he put it, did not seem too bad, especially since Petrasch was already at the University of Bonn and had rented one of the rooms at the Schurzes' new boarding house. But as time went on, the situation in Bonn was less than pleasing. In spite of his strictures, Carl had liked his life at Cologne; the teachers there had befriended him, and as the best student, he had been allowed to take over when the teacher was absent. In contrast, the situation at Bonn was uncertain. The family's boardinghouse, with its main meal at noon, followed by the preparation of take-out food, was not a gold mine. As the students did not pay regularly, the family was still in bad straits. His sister Anna had to leave school altogether; his other sister, Antonia (or, as everyone called her, Toni), continued her education but had to lend a hand in the family business before and after classes. Carl stayed in a small room on the fourth floor, where he prepared for his final examinations and wrote a drama about Ulrich von Hutten. It took some two years before the family was able to afford a better home at Coblenzerstrasse, where there was a garden—a necessity for Christian Schurz—to make the tedium of the new restaurant more bearable.[10]

The city of Bonn with its twelve thousand people was much smaller than Cologne. Situated at a pleasant location some twenty miles up river from the metropolis, with a splendid vista of the Seven Mountains across the Rhine, it had formerly been the residence of the archbishop-electors. Compact, clean, and comfortable, it contained Beethoven's birthplace, but the main attraction was its university, a well-known institution of more than seven hundred students from various parts of the country. Located in the handsome electoral palace, it contained seventeen lecture rooms, some large enough to accommodate three hundred students, a library, one museum of Roman and one of Greek antiquities, an attached hospital, as well as three other buildings for public lectures, the school of anatomy, the observatory, and Poppelsdorf Castle, a splendid palace at the upper end of an imposing avenue flanked by a double row of trees.

The professors, divided into four faculties, were often men of distinction. Earlier renowned for such literary lights as August Wilhelm von Schlegel, the famous translator of Shakespeare, and the historian Barthold Niebuhr, in the early 1840s the university could boast of an especially eminent group of historians and political scientists. Old Ernst Moritz Arndt, the poet of the Wars of Liberation, was still active, and Friedrich Christoff Dahlmann, one of the famous Göttingen Seven, who had been expelled from the university of that city because of their protest against the king of Hanover's unilateral revocation of the constitution, was the great man of the department. Schurz was impressed with the historian Joseph von Aschbach and the classical philologist Friedrich Wilhelm Ritschl, but the one instructor who had the greatest influence on him was Gottfried Kinkel, a young associate professor of German literature and art history who had made a name for himself as a romantic writer and poet. The son of a Protestant minister, he had married the divorced wife of a Catholic bookseller after rescuing her from the waters of the Rhine. Romantic as this courtship was, it scandalized the population and caused him to give up his position as auxiliary pastor of a Protestant congregation at Cologne and to transfer from the faculty of theology to that of philosophy. His wife Johanna, who was an accomplished pianist, provided a most attractive home for him at Poppelsdorf Castle, where his students were frequent visitors.[11]

The students' life at German universities—and Bonn was no exception—excited the envy of those still in secondary school. The infrequent examinations made it possible to attend lectures almost at will, and the free time at the students' disposal was devoted to extracurricular activities. These tended to center on the fraternities, of which the so-called *corps* were somewhat exclusive, aristocratic, and conservative, while others, in the tradition of the *Burschenschaften,* less aristocratic and more liberal, were likely to be centers of progressive activities. Some of these organizations fought the ritual duels which scarred the participants' faces as proof of manliness; others shunned these medieval practices; but all lived according to elaborate codes and traditional customs which lent color to university life. Special uniforms and caps, specific rituals—all these made students proud to be members of the fraternities, and some secretly wore the outlawed national sash of black, red, and gold underneath their clothing. The brothers edited humorous newspapers, spent evenings filled with songs and merriment in local taverns, and convoked regular courts of honor to judge erring members. On weekends, they took long trips into the country and up the river and its neighboring valleys, where they established close contact with the local population, especially the innkeepers, whose favors they sought to obtain credit.[12]

The Frankonia was such an organization, and Carl, who was introduced to it by his friends Petrasch and von Weise, greatly admired it. Unlike some of the *corps*, it did not emphasize beer drinking and duelling. Seeking to attract the more gifted students, it apparently succeeded. Future writers and scientists such as Adolph Strodtmann, a North German who became the biographer of Heinrich Heine, Carl Otto Weber, later a professor of medicine at Heidelberg, Julius Schmidt, a future astronomer, and the archeologist Johannes Overbeck were members, and at first, Carl was overawed. As long as he was still a non-matriculated student he was ineligible for full membership, but when he wrote a piece for the "beer" newspaper which was read aloud at one of the fraternity meetings, his reputation was made, and the brethren appointed him *Möbelwart,* or caretaker of the tavern. As soon as he matriculated, he became a member in full standing and was soon elected one of the judges of the court of honor. He greatly enjoyed the trips, the discussions, and the joyous gatherings in the taverns, and eventually he gained such recognition that he wrote the fraternity's new constitution. His success with the brethren was his first taste of the rewards of politics. The experience did not displease him.[13]

But of course he first had to establish himself by passing the dreaded *Abitur* at the Cologne gymnasium. His desk was cluttered with the *Iliad*, the orations of Isocrates, and Cicero, all of which he studied intensively to prepare for the examination. The pressure of his uncertain status made the first year at Bonn difficult; nevertheless, he found time to attend lectures at the university and to continue his literary activities. His interest in the Reformation had led him to try writing a drama about Ulrich von Hutten; romantic poetry and a novelette, *Richard Wanderer*, also occupied him. *Richard Wanderer* is the epitome of student romanticism; the hero, hopelessly in love but unwanted, eventually sings for his supper and dies a forlorn youth, unrecognized by his beloved. The intensity of Schurz's application was such that he knew whole portions of the *Iliad* by heart, and in August 1847 he finally took the examination.

He did fairly well, considering that he had not attended classes during the last school year. His examiners attested to his good moral character, his industry, especially in the study of languages, and his proficiency in history, geography, and German. In Latin, he would have done better had he attended school to the end; there were still great gaps in his knowledge of Greek and French as well as of mathematics. And while he showed sufficient knowledge of the teachings of the faith, his teachers noted that he did not really display an entirely clear understanding of "the interconnection of religious truths." However, he passed and was fully matriculated at the University of Bonn.[14]

Schurz soon became one of the most popular members of the Frankonia fraternity. An excellent athlete, he took up fencing, not the bloody dueling of rival *corps* which he disdained, but the enjoyable sport. Bowling, hiking, and drinking with his brethren, he himself sometimes felt that perhaps he was a bit too tongue-tied to suit the president of the fraternity, Johannes Overbeck.[15] Forty years later, his companion Friedrich Spielhagen still remembered Schurz as a real "bel homme." Tall, slender, and lean, he cared little for deportment but conducted himself exactly as he pleased. "In relation to the magnificent head covered with a shock of curly, long hair, the face appeared small, almost pinched, especially the lower portion, which towered above the firm, broad forehead like a rock. The light, lively eyes were always framed with glasses which tended to slide down the slightly curved nose, only to be pushed up again with an energetic push of the index finger." But Schurz seemed shy and reserved only at first. He was natural and seemingly had nothing to hide, especially since his marvelous voice made his acquaintances forget the somewhat unattractive face.[16]

It appears that Schurz's early years was a period he could recall with pleasure. Secure in the esteem of his family and friends, successful at school and university, he quickly learned how to overcome his initial shyness. Not even his parents' financial disasters could destroy his firm belief that he had a future. He soon set out to prove it.

II

Revolution

ONE MORNING toward the end of February 1848, Schurz, working hard at his tragedy about Ulrich von Hutten, was sitting in his attic chamber. Suddenly, a friend rushed into the room and berated him for his inactivity. Had he not heard what had happened? The French had driven away Louis Philippe and declared a republic! Schurz threw down his pen, and that was the end of his Ulrich von Hutten. He never touched the manuscript again.[1]

The revolutionary ardor kindled by the overthrow of the July monarchy in France spread like wildfire all over Europe. Especially in Germany, divided into more than thirty-five loosely confederated states with reactionary rulers, pent-up longings for national unity and liberal constitutions could no longer be contained. In Austria and Prussia, the leading members of the Germanic Confederation, as well as in many of the smaller states, revolts flared up. In Vienna, Prince Metternich, the symbol of Austrian reaction, was forced to flee; in Berlin, Frederick William IV, the king of Prussia, after first making promises but then seemingly hesitating, was also unable to resist the general torrent. His troops fired on the crowd and barricades went up in the streets. Finally, yielding to popular resistance, he promised a liberal constitution. Governments everywhere, frightened by the groundswell of liberal opinion, made concessions. Amid such innovations as a Prussian national assembly at Berlin and an all-German parliament at Frankfurt, the seat of the old Germanic Confederation, hopes were high for a new order of things.

At Bonn, as elsewhere, the students were in the forefront of the revolution. With unbounded enthusiasm, they joined the movement for a united fatherland. For a while, classes, lectures, and homework were forgotten; there was a citizen's guard to be manned against imaginary enemies, petitions to be drawn up to reform the government of university and country, and patriotic festivals to be celebrated to mark the dawn of the new era. And when the king of Prussia yielded with vague pledges to work for a new Germany, the excitement knew no bounds. A tremendous procession of citizens, students, and professors, after calling for Arndt, Dahlmann, and other liberals, marched to the central square. Arndt and Dahlmann embraced in public; Kinkel, waving a huge black, red, and gold flag, the colors of liberal Germany, delivered a stirring patriotic speech which made him the hero of the occasion. At night there was a torchlight parade in which Schurz carried one of the flags. Kinkel, generally considered the leader of the radical democratic forces, soon became vice president of the newly formed Central Citizens Assembly.[2]

It did not take long for Schurz to be identified as the romantic professor's chief assistant. As early as March 5, his name appeared on a petition for a general student assembly. A second petition on March 12, this time for a merger with the citizens' guard, also bore his signature. In April, he collaborated with Kinkel in drawing up a democratic party platform, and in an assembly in the second week of May, he delivered his first public address, a speech so impressive that Professor Ritschl, who presided, asked him how old he was and expressed regrets that the nineteen-year-old student was too young to be elected to parliament. But he was not too young to become one of the founding members and secretary of the Democratic Club, of which Kinkel was president. Soon the organization, which on May 31 adopted the name of Democratic Society, published a newspaper, the *Bonner Zeitung*, and Schurz began a lifelong journalistic career.[3]

From the very beginning, however, Schurz's newspaper work was an integral part of his political activities. Rapidly gaining recognition among the students as one of the leaders of the democrats, he often clashed with the opposing Constitutional Society. At first the issue was the incorporation of the students in the general citizens' guard, which his opponents successfully resisted; then the democrats demanded a republic, while the constitutionalists favored the retention of the monarchy. The election of nonradical professors to the Frankfurt Assembly turned Kinkel as well as Schurz into republicans, and the perfidy of Germany's princes in the months to follow did nothing to change their minds, either then or later.[4]

Schurz's opportunity came late in May. After his first speech in the student assembly, he took a hand in an appeal for the election of delegates to the all-German student congress at Eisenach. He himself was not eligible because financial difficulties had forced him to drop his full membership in the Frankonia fraternity, but when the presiding officers of the student assembly were elected and left to attend the meeting, he was chosen provisional presiding officer. Lack of money rather than a deliberate plan to stay at home, as has been asserted, brought him to the forefront.

He put his position to good use. One of the most hated symbols of the old regime was the government representative at the university, and Schurz, at the head of student constituents, marched to the rector's house to present a petition he had framed for the official's removal. The officer in question, Moritz von Bethmann-Hollweg, resigning of his own accord, left the city. Shortly afterward, on July 7, Schurz presided over a democratic meeting which decided to forward to Archduke John, the imperial regent at Frankfurt, a memorial the young revolutionary had been asked to draw up, this time to protest against excessive Junker influence. And on July 13, the democrats scored another success. At a meeting of the Central Citizens Assembly, they defeated a conservative motion to instruct the Bonn deputies at the Frankfurt Assembly to oppose republicanism. Their young leader had made his mark.[5]

Schurz's energy never flagged. Living in his own room outside the city gates, he acquired, in recognition of his new status, a *Leibfuchs*, a freshman placed at his disposal—a delightful young man, he thought. In the company of his friends, he often went hiking to the countryside to spread his democratic ideals among the peasants as well as the townspeople. He spent much time at the Democratic Society, was active in student affairs, and continued to assist Kinkel with the newspaper, of which the professor had become the managing editor in August. He even succeeded in getting along with some of the conservatives, whom he consistently bested in debate.[6] It was all very exciting.

The democrats themselves, however, were divided on the question of socialism. Karl Marx was publishing his *Neue Rheinische Zeitung* at Cologne, and Kinkel too sought to appeal to the underprivileged. Publishing a special paper for them, he also advocated social changes. But neither Marx's radical ideas nor his personality convinced Schurz. He met the famous communist in August when, as the representative of the Bonn society, Schurz attended a democratic congress at Cologne. All of Marx's utterances impressed him as intelligent, logical, and clear; nevertheless, the communist leader was so contemptuous of all who differed with him that every one of his propositions was voted down. Although he himself had attracted attention because of his inflammatory speeches, Schurz determined to treat his opponents differently. Many years later, in his *Reminiscences*, he said nothing about Marx's philosophy, but he did remember the famous revolutionary's insufferable arrogance.[7]

It was evident that in many ways Schurz overshadowed Kinkel, whose talents for leadership were questionable. According to Adolph Strodtmann, Kinkel's admiring biographer, the professor's main assistant was ''a spirited and tireless youth whose searching, keen intellect surpassed even Kinkel's own.'' Ernst von Ernsthausen, who belonged to one of the more conservative student associations, was equally taken with the younger man. ''At first he spoke a lot in abstract phrases which sounded strange to us *corps* students . . . ,'' he wrote, ''but soon his oratory became powerful. He spoke objectively and to the point and showed clearly that he possessed unusual talent.'' Notwithstanding their political differences, the two managed to get along very well.[8]

But in spite of his time-consuming political activities, Schurz did not totally neglect his education. Although it is not now known whether he still attended many lectures, he continued his political studies. One fine summer's day his friend Spielhagen found him walking alone, reading Rousseau's *Contrat Social*. ''Sitôt on peut désobéir impunément, on le peut légitement; et puisque le plus fort a toujours raison, il ne s'agit que de faire en sorte qu'on soit le plus fort,'' he quoted from his reading. But Schurz was not the most powerful one, Spielhagen protested. ''What has not come about may come about,'' was the answer. The young democrat never doubted his destiny.[9]

In September 1848, a second students' congress was to meet in Eisenach in the shadows of the Wartburg, where Luther had translated the Bible and in 1817 the *Burschenschaften* had held their first great festival. Schurz had again called attention to himself by drawing up and forwarding a petition to implement the new liberal local administrative code; he had fully rejoined the Frankonia, of which he was soon elected president, and this time he was a successful candidate for the congress.[10]

His election occurred at a critical time for the revolution. The entire German liberal movement was in a state of great excitement because of the Armistice of Malmö, an agreement which Prussia, under international pressure, had concluded with Denmark. In effect, it nullified the liberal reforms German insurrectionists had introduced into the two duchies of Schleswig and Holstein, which had revolted against their connection with the Danish crown. A brief war in which many revolutionaries received their baptism of fire—Schurz himself had intended to enlist but was dissuaded by Kinkel, who said he needed him—had brought about a new government, now abrogated by the armistice. The agreement was presented to the Frankfurt Assembly, which, after first refusing, finally and with much difficulty ratified it. The result was the outbreak of riots culminating in the assassination of two right-wing deputies, General Hans von Auerswald and Prince Felix Lichnowsky. Only the arrival of troops restored order.[11]

Schurz, who had taken a steamer up the Rhine, arrived at Frankfurt just at this time. It was a bad moment for the democrats; even Kinkel condemned the excesses of his party associates, and Schurz was saddened by the events. He did, however, visit the galleries of historic St. Paul's Church, where the assembly held its sessions, to take a good look at its famous members. Deliberative bodies held a fascination for him.[12]

From Frankfurt he traveled to Eisenach where he met student leaders from all over Germany. The Austrians especially intrigued him—tall, handsome, and greatly favored by the local girls, they had already proven themselves during the March Revolution. But serious business was at hand, and Schurz became involved in drawing up a constitution for all German universities as well as a revolutionary appeal to the German people, which he signed. It was only on the way home, as he was steaming down the Rhine again, that he began to worry. Reactionaries were once more in the ascendancy; for all he knew, an arrest warrant might already have been issued for him.[13]

But the authorities were not especially interested in the students' antics. The revolutionary fervor had reached its crest and was already receding. When in October the Habsburgs reasserted themselves, with the aid of conservative generals and non-German nationality groups, the reactionary princes breathed a little easier. The king of Prussia, whose reluctant liberalism had never been very convincing, now simply sent the national assembly away from Berlin. This drastic action was a direct challenge to the liberals and democrats, and the latter responded by calling for a tax strike. Perhaps the king could still be brought to see reason.[14]

It was again the students, and especially the democratic students, who formed the spearhead of the revolt. A Bonn mass meeting on November 13, electing Kinkel and Schurz presiding officers by acclamation, adopted a memorial asking for a tax strike. The local deputy refused to accept it, but when a few days later the constituent assembly itself voted for the withholding of taxes, a new meeting convened. It set up a committee of public safety consisting of Kinkel, Schurz, and another student, Nathan Pappenheim, which for a few days sought to enforce the strike by attempting to prevent the authorities from collecting the imposts usually levied on the peasants at the city gate. On November 20, when Schurz tried to convince the mayor to cooperate, he noticed that the official was procrastinating, until suddenly the sound of marching troops interrupted the proceedings. A battalion of infantry quickly ended the strike.

Schurz, who had only awaited a signal from Cologne to start a real insurrection, was severely compromised. There were rumors of his impending arrest, but, despite the fact that on December 1 he founded a democratic student society with himself as president, the authorities, fearing a student strike, left him alone. As the rector reported to Berlin, the students believed that one of them, ''the Bonn native named Schurz, a principal leader of the Republicans,'' was to be jailed. Because it was said the arrest was to be carried out illegally, however, even the conservatives sympathized with him. Consequently, when Schurz protested, the academic authorities denied that anything had been planned against him, and the university community calmed down. Although the academic senate was still considering the advisability of bringing charges against him, it finally dropped the matter.[15] The would-be culprit went back to his newspaper articles, to his speeches in the countryside, and to his dreaming. For he thought he had fallen in love.

The object of his affections was a local merchant's daughter, who was reputed to be able to read Shakespeare in the original. Forward as he was with his cronies, in later years Schurz maintained that he had always been shy with girls and that he never even summoned enough courage to speak with his beloved. One night, as he was covering von Flotow's *Martha* for his newspaper, he saw ''Betty,'' as he called her, in the box next to his. It is doubtful that he paid much attention to the opera, although he again did not dare speak to the girl.[16] To what degree this story represents merely the vague recollections of an old man is difficult to determine, but it is certain that in later life, he was anything but reticent, either with persons of his own or the opposite sex.

Schurz's unrequited love did not keep him from his duties at the newspaper. His articles retained their radical flavor and even his friend Petrasch excitedly criticized his ''political vehemence.'' At the turn of the year, the journal changed hands. After a falling-out with the printers, Kinkel made a new arrangement for its publication and renamed it *Neue Bonner Zeitung*. Schurz was kept busier than ever. Given access to the paper's box at the theater, he wrote articles and reviewed operas and plays, a chore he enjoyed tremendously, as he could hardly have afforded the box at the theater on his own. The Greek letter sigma, his signature, appeared more and more frequently.[17]

Before long, Schurz virtually had to take over the newspaper himself. When the king of Prussia decreed a constitution with a two-house legislature, Kinkel was elected to the Second Chamber. Leaving for Berlin in February 1849, he entrusted the paper and the local democratic society to his favorite student, whose name was to appear frequently in the reports of its periodic meetings.

That same month, the democrats of Bonn prepared to celebrate the first anniversary of the fall of Louis Philippe. The authorities forbade all outdoor demonstrations, but Schurz, as student leader and secretary of the Democratic Society, wrote a notice inviting his fellows to a banquet in honor of the occasion. Hundreds of students marched to a local hall decorated with French and German flags. Schurz addressed the audience, toasts were drunk to the friendship of all revolutionary peoples, and the forbidden Polish national anthem was sung. In the days that followed, the authorities punished a number of participants but not the democratic leader, who protested against his fellows' apprehension, albeit without much success. Nevertheless, he boasted to Kinkel that the affair had greatly intensified the zeal of the student body. "I can promise you a mass of petitions for the beginning of the next semester," he wrote. "The whole agitation is rather completely under my control and I shall know how to turn my influence to account. I have become a dreaded person to the university senate, especially since on the occasion of the banquet I spoiled their fun and wriggled out like a serpent. Rector and university court . . . presuppose exceptional judicial knowledge on my part, which is the more gratifying to me inasmuch as they dropped a very dangerous charge against me which they believed themselves unable to sustain."[18]

Schurz's radicalism had become so pronounced that many of his fraternity brothers refused to follow him any longer. He engaged in bitter polemics with opponents, especially in the newspaper, a practice which would become a lifelong habit. And he also took another step that foreshadowed his future political tactics. Unable to sway his old organization, the Frankonia, on March 9 he collaborated with others to found a new one, the Normandie fraternity, which rejoined the parent body only after he was already in exile. As he would explain in later years, his loyalty was to principles, not to organizations.[19]

Now a new problem confronted him. The Prussian army became interested in him and after an examination found him fit and qualified for all branches of the service. He promptly sought help from his friend Petrasch, whose father had some influence with the authorities. Anticipating deferment, he wrote to Kinkel that he hoped to be spared for three years more. Apparently he succeeded.

The threatened induction into the army was not his only difficulty. The newspaper did not pay enough to sustain him, and his private tutoring had also suffered reverses. In desperation, he wrote Kinkel for a raise. Many good citizens would no longer hire him for private lessons for their children, he explained. While some party associates were talking about the destruction of the middle class, he himself had no desire to perish with it.[20]

Schurz's financial embarrassments were soon to be forgotten in the course of more exciting events. The very fact that the Prussian constitution had been imposed from above boded ill for the future. The revolution was not going well, and when early in spring the Frankfurt Assembly offered an imperial crown to Frederick William IV of Prussia, the king disdainfully refused it. Calling it a "pig's crown," not divinely ordained, he rejected the honor as well as the newly drawn imperial constitution.[21]

Schurz was not surprised. He had long ridiculed the idea of establishing a German empire headed by the king of Prussia. Was not Frederick William IV a reactionary, totally out of sympathy with the revolution? The choice would only cause trouble between North and South, he wrote, to say nothing of the exclusion of seven million Germans in Austria. What was needed was an all-German democratic republic.[22]

The Prussian king's refusal to accept the crown led to rebellion in Southern Germany as well as in several Rhenish cities. In order to suppress disorder, the government made preparations for the mobilization of the reserves, plans which the democrats attempted to prevent. Perhaps royal arsenals could be seized and citizens armed; they would then be able to support the all-German constitution rejected by the king.

It was this crisis that finally caused Schurz to participate in armed insurrection. At a meeting of the Bonn citizens' society on May 1, he demanded that the Frankfurt Assembly hold new elections, although he still warned against any premature uprising. On May 6, he spoke from the window of an inn in neighboring Neukirchen to induce the peasants not to obey mobilization orders; thereafter the democratic directory met almost continuously in the back room of Friedrich Kamm's tavern. Finally, on May 10 another assembly convened at Römer Tavern and, on Schurz's motion, decided to recognize as decisive the struggle of the German governments against the National Assembly and to support the latter. Plans were perfected to march on the arsenal at Siegburg, on the other side of the Rhine, to seize the arsenal, and to join the insurrectionists in nearby cities. This harebrained scheme, advocated by Fritz Anneke, a former artillery captain, seemed farfetched even to Kinkel, but he supported it in order not to lose credibility with his followers. When at 10:00 P.M. the professor spoke again, he called on his audience to reassemble at one in the morning and introduced Anneke as commanding officer.

Unlike his mentor, Schurz, knowing what was coming, was in an elated mood. Walking through the dark streets with his friend Friedrich Spielhagen the night before the meeting, he scorned all warnings. Spielhagen thought his companion had made up his mind to risk everything, even to go alone if necessary. Apparently the Siegburg expedition had his complete sanction.

On the evening of May 10, Schurz said goodbye to his family. His father and mother understood; they too were democrats and supported the revolution. Then he rowed across the river to join the motley expedition of some 120 men who had seized the ferryboat. On the road to the arsenal, they were soon overtaken by a detachment of thirty dragoons. Offering no resistance, they scattered; except for a drunken innkeeper's horse which lost its tail to a dragoon's saber, there were no casualties.

Schurz was mortified. After all his planning, after all his preaching, he had made a fool of himself. He had not even destroyed the ferryboat! Bitterly ashamed and desperate, he first made his way to Siegburg, then to Elberfeld, only to see that nowhere in the Rhineland was there still a chance of further military resistance. After hiding briefly in Bonn to pick up his belongings, he decided to wipe out the disgrace by joining the revolutionary army, which had assembled in the Palatinate. Again he took a boat up the Rhine; he stayed for two days at St. Goarshausen, where in Nathan's friendly tavern, the Frankonia's favorite hangout, he said good-bye to his friends and took off for the south. His university career had come to an end.[23]

After leaving St. Goarshausen, Schurz first went to Mainz, where democratic friends told him that Franz Zitz, one of the local party leaders, had gone ahead to the Palatinate to organize his troops. Schurz immediately followed him and traveled to the rebellious province.

The Palatinate was a fertile region on the left bank of the Rhine that had been given to Bavaria in 1815. When the Frankfurt Assembly, notwithstanding the Prussian monarch's rejection of the proffered crown, declared its all-German constitution in force, the population of the Palatinate adhered to the new central government. The refusal of the Bavarian king to do likewise ended his authority in the province, and a provisional regime was established. The inhabitants of the area, together with their neighbors in the Grand Duchy of Baden, where the ruler's flight had placed power in the hands of officials loyal to the Frankfurt Assembly, were the last active supporters of the German revolution. But in spite of Schurz's enthusiastic newspaper accounts for the *Neue Bonner Zeitung* about the great revolutionary spirit, especially at Kirchheimbolanden, the first town he visited, the forces of reaction were already being mobilized against the remaining bastions of liberalism. With the Prussians in the van, powerful armies were concentrating against the revolutionaries. Officers better known for their later service in America in the Union army—men like Louis Blenker, Alexander Schimmel-pfenning, and Franz Sigel—attempted to organize the local troops, but shortages of arms and ammunition made any real resistance problematic.

Schurz had no trouble finding Zitz, who sent him on to Kaiserslautern, where he was reunited with Kinkel. Anneke, now chief of artillery, was also in town and found him a position on his staff, an appointment that carried a lieutenancy with it. Schurz was delighted to be reunited with the professor, with whom he had become so intimate that he addressed him with the familiar *du* rather than the formal *sie*, a most unusual relationship between professor and student. The two comrades took a train to Speyer and then to Neustadt, where Kinkel accepted a post with the

Carl Schurz and Gottfried Kinkel (Courtesy of National Carl Schurz Association, Inc., Philadelphia)

military commission. The professor showed his student letters from home, and the two amateur revolutionaries mused about the sad circumstances that had taken them away from Bonn.

Schurz's duties in the Palatinate were not strenuous. Hostile armies were still at some distance, and the inhabitants, much to his dismay, went about their business as if no great events were impending. The young romantic found it difficult to understand that people could celebrate weddings when the fatherland was in danger. He himself took his task more seriously. On one occasion, he was ordered to arrest a village priest who had kept his parishioners from enlisting in the revolutionary army. Summoning some fifty poorly armed and shabbily uniformed men, he surrounded the manse. The priest was under arrest, he said. The clergyman, amused by the situation, asked his would-be jailer to have a glass of wine with him, retaining Schurz long enough to enable the enraged villagers to come to his aid. The lieutenant, undaunted, took his pistol and held it against the priest's head. Unless the priest would tell the villagers to allow the troops to take him along on official business, Schurz said, he would shoot. The pastor did as he was told; his captor marched away with him, only to tell him later with great amusement that the pistol, which the priest feared might go off at any moment, was not loaded.[24]

But the easy days in the Palatinate soon came to an end. The Prussians were approaching, and the revolutionary army crossed the Rhine to unite with the forces in Baden. Schurz, who in the course of his military duties had learned how to mount a horse, rode into Karlsruhe, the capital of the grand duchy, where he was quartered with the staff in the Zähringer Hof. From his window, he was able to observe the activities on the marketplace, where August von Willich's troops had assembled. "Citizen Kinkel joins the Desançon Company," shouted von Willich, a well-known socialist, and the professor, musket in hand, proudly fell in, to march in the ranks at the right flank. He had finally succeeded in proving his devotion to the cause by enlisting as a private. "The sight captivated me with ominous force," wrote Schurz. "I could not take my eyes off him until, marching in the ranks behind thundering drums, he turned around a corner. Since that time, I have experienced deep devotion as often as his image came to my mind, even though he was my dearest and only friend here. . . ." He saw the professor once more two days later, on June 21, shortly before the engagement at Bruchsal. The two men clasped hands; they were not to meet again until they were both fugitives.[25]

Schurz himself was soon to undergo his first combat experience. On June 23 and 24, he participated in the engagements at Ubstatt and Bruchsal. Believing that an officer ought to set an example of fearlessness, he made a point of sitting straight on his horse as the bullets were whizzing by. A slight flesh wound—a bullet grazed his shin bone—did not disable him, so that he managed to retreat with the revolutionary forces to the Murg River. But then, on June 30, Anneke sent him to the fortress of Rastatt on official business. It was a fateful mission, for when Schurz, after having waited in vain for his commander, sought to ride out of the city to look for him, he found that it was too late. The Prussians had invested the fortress and, willy-nilly, he had to stay.[26]

The trapped lieutenant's situation was hardly a happy one. If the fortress should fall, his comrades might be released after a short period of confinement, but his own future was highly dubious. As a Prussian citizen, he might well be accused of treason and condemned to death. In fact, an order for his arrest in connection with the Siegburg affair had already been published. The police were alerted to look for Carl Schurz, a student of philosophy, twenty years old, 5 feet 11 inches tall, with blond hair and eyebrows, a high forehead, small nose, ordinary mouth, struggling mustache, elongated and somewhat prominent chin, healthy complexion, a slender figure generally wearing glasses.[27] With so precise a description in the enemy's possession, it would be difficult to escape. No mercy could be expected from the Prussian commander, the prince of Prussia, the later Emperor William I, who was known for his ferocious reactionary opinions and was called the "grapeshot prince." Although at first the garrison was cheered by rumors of imminent outside help—Franz Sigel was supposed to be in the vicinity—as time went on it became evident that there was little hope for relief.

Schurz tried to make the best of the situation. Reporting to the governor of Rastatt, Gustav Tiedemann, he was appointed to the staff and given the uniform of a regular lieutenant in the Baden forces. This attire gave him a more military appearance than his improvised free corps outfit had done, but his duties were minimal. He enjoyed the services of his orderly, Adam, who had accompanied him to Rastatt. His main task, aside from frequent tours of inspection, was to keep a sharp lookout from the castle tower, an occupation which gave him an opportunity to familiarize himself with the surrounding countryside. The Black Forest with its wooded slopes to the south, the Rhine valley with its verdant fields and peaceful villages to the north provided a pleasant view. But the most interesting part of the landscape, at least for the lieutenant, was the left bank of the Rhine to the west, French territory, where freedom beckoned. The young staff officers with whom he associated often discussed plans for a sortie in force to reach it.[28]

After some three weeks of siege, during which occasional shelling and a sortie interrupted the routine, the Prussians formally asked the garrison to surrender. All resistance elsewhere had ceased; the situation of Rastatt was hopeless. The Prussians offered to allow two revolutionary officers to accompany them under a flag of truce and see for themselves whether these reports were true. On July 18, Lieutenant Colonel Otto von Corvin and another officer accepted the proposal. When they returned on July 21, the governor summoned the officers to the great hall of the castle to hear the sad news. There was no hope; no other revolutionary forces were still in the field, and the enemy insisted on surrender "at discretion." After another attempt to secure more reasonable terms, on July 23 Tiedemann gave the order to capitulate.[29]

In a state of great excitement, Schurz had already written to his parents and sisters; he also wrote to his fellow students in Bonn. Realizing that his letter might well be his last, he apologized to his parents for the grief he had caused them. But his conscience was clear; he had done his duty. Having just heard the erroneous rumor that Kinkel, who had been captured by the enemy, had been sentenced to death, he ended by asserting that he knew the professor was able to die like a man. "If I could say the same of myself to the same extent," he concluded, "I should at this moment carry my head higher. . . . Farewell, on the day of the capitulation!" For his friends, he had a different message. He admitted that at times he had been too ambitious, yet he explained, "I did not want to be second where I could be first; I did not want to serve where I knew how to command." Although he had acted rashly, he had preserved his personal pride. Then he added, "For the last time I put on belt and sword in order to surrender to the enemy. 'Tis time to bid you farewell. . . ." He gave both letters to his landlord with instructions to mail them as soon as the post office was open again.[30]

In the meantime, orders had been received to begin the surrender. The home guard was to be disarmed at 2:30; the troops led by officers without epaulettes were to march out at 5:30. They were to stack their arms at the glacis and remain at the Prussians' disposal.[31]

Schurz was in a quandary. The capitulation might well spell his doom; he knew better than to believe optimistic rumors that the Prussians would soon release their prisoners. Then a thought flashed through his mind. During his tours of inspection, he had found a sewer near the fortress walls at the Steinmauerner Gate, the exit toward the French border. It led outside to a cornfield and could be entered near a garden hedge. Was it not possible to escape through it, reach the Rhine, and cross into France? Certainly it was worth a try.

The lieutenant and his orderly, who, though not a Prussian, had refused to leave him, immediately made preparations for the escape attempt. Sending Adam to buy some food and several bottles of wine, Schurz put his pistol under his clothes and wrapped a short carbine in his rolled-up cloak, a large dark cape lined with scarlet. He confided his plan to Lieutenant Neustädter, another officer of Prussian origin, who agreed to join him. Then, following the last column of the garrison which was already marching across the marketplace in preparation for the capitulation, the three fugitives turned into a side street and, between one and two in the afternoon, just an hour before the surrender, climbed into the sewer.

Their escape route proved to be a tunnel of masonry made of brick and partially filled with water but large enough to permit them to crawl through it. Hoping to reach the exit after dark, when they might escape unobserved, they rested on a wooden board in the middle of the underground passage.

The hours passed; the noise above indicated that the Prussians had taken over. At nine o'clock, it began to rain heavily. The water in the sewer rose, rats appeared, and the fugitives had to go on. Crawling through the water underneath an iron railing that barred the way, they finally reached the exit, only to find it heavily guarded by Prussian outposts. They had no choice but to turn back. Fortunately, the rain ceased, and after several hours on their wooden plank, where they ate and drank some of the provisions they had taken along, Adam remembered that he had a widowed cousin living in town. She might help. Back they went, out of the sewer until, shortly after three in the morning, they reached a barn which provided temporary shelter. It was located near Adam's cousin's house, where the orderly went in the morning, only to be told that she was unable to help as she expected Prussian soldiers to be quartered there any moment. She did, however, show her unwelcome visitors a ditch where they might hide for a while. From there, they crept into a woodpile. But the cavalrymen had arrived, and the situation seemed almost hopeless, until Schurz saw a workman with tools. Knowing that the laboring population was generally favorably disposed toward the revolution, he asked him for help. His intuition was right; the workman showed him a toolshed with a small loft in which there was just enough room for three men, and the fugitives had another shelter.

But their new hiding place was most uncomfortable. Since it was merely a crawl space under a roof, they had to lie down and barely move lest they be heard; their food had run out, and they were thirsty. Some rainwater helped, but after three days and nights, during which their new friend had failed to come back as he had promised, they decided that they had to get out. Schurz then saw a small house obviously inhabited by another workman. Again trusting his intuition, he sent Neustädter there with money to ask for help. This time, he was more successful. The worker was friendly. He brought them food, told them the outposts outside the city had been withdrawn, and promised to procure a ferry to take them across the Rhine. This was welcome news, and accordingly Schurz made plans once more to attempt the escape through the sewer during the following night.

When the appointed time came, a new difficulty arose. Hussars who had taken the place of the cavalrymen were celebrating, and one of them, right underneath the loft, was making declarations of undying love to a local maiden. The courtship seemed endless; at last, after 10:00 P.M., the couple left, so that Schurz and his two companions were able to run to their new friend's house, where their first hot meal in more than three days awaited them. Then, in the bright moonlit night, they stealthily made for the sewer, which they entered rapidly by taking advantage of the short respite provided by the sentry's turning his back to them as he paced to and fro. Again they crawled through the sewer. After resting for the last time on their bench of wood and dipping underneath the grate, they finally gained the outer exit and beyond it the cornfield, where they found their faithful host, whose name was Augustin Loeffler. Walking briskly with him to the nearby village of Steinmauern, they reached the banks of the Rhine and hired a boat to take them across. After parting from Loeffler, who refused to accept any more money, they were ferried to what they believed was the opposite shore. But to their dismay they discovered that they had been put off on an island still in Baden, though fortunately uninhabited. At daybreak, they signaled to the nearby French bank; a customs official came to call for them, and with joy they tasted their newly-won freedom. Marching off to the nearby town of Selz, Schurz took lodgings at an inn, bathed, and slept for twenty-four hours. On the next day, the innkeeper provided him with a passport of sorts and told him to report to the police at Strasbourg. His life as an exile had begun.[32]

III

Exile

THE BEAUTIFUL ALSATIAN LANDSCAPE, the balmy summer weather, and above all their newly recovered freedom greatly exhilarated the three fugitives. Marching from Selz to Strasbourg on a warm Sunday morning, they were able to see the towers of Rastatt across the river—grim reminders of their lucky escape. In Strasbourg they secured lodging at a hotel known for its friendliness to German revolutionaries. Their troubles, however, were not over. The local police prefect would neither issue them a passport for Switzerland nor permit them to remain. According to orders from the French government, all refugees would have to move to the interior and stay away from the frontiers.

But the police of the Second Republic was not very efficient. Determined to head for Switzerland, where Anneke and other friends had already found refuge, Schurz and Neustädter decided to disregard the prefect and make the attempt. Schurz said good-bye to his orderly, who finally agreed to go home. Then the two remaining fugitives, after visiting and admiring the marvels of the great cathedral, took a train to a station near the Swiss border. Crossing with the aid of a smuggler, they set out for Bern on foot, only to learn on the way that Anneke had moved to Dornachbruck. Schurz parted from Neustädter, retraced his steps, and walked to the small village near Basel.

When he arrived at Dornachbruck, he was to be disappointed again. Anneke and his companions had left for Zurich. Fatigued and almost out of funds, Schurz decided to stay and now for the first time wrote to his parents about his escape. He also asked them to send him some money.[1]

The elder Schurzes had been sorely worried about their son. Hearing of the surrender of Rastatt, Christian hurried to Baden to see whether he could find Carl and save him. He wandered through casemates filled to capacity with prisoners, met the captured Kinkel, but of course was unable to discover a trace of his son. Finally he learned that some refugees had succeeded in crossing to France. Following the lead to Selz, he was told that Carl had indeed been there but had left for the south. With this happy news, he returned to Bonn, where he eventually received the letter from Dornachbruck.[2]

Schurz fully explained his situation. He needed money and a passport fitting his description; with such a document he might settle near the frontier in France or in Belgium. Knowing of his parents' financial stringency, he suggested that they collect money from his friends, possibly in the form of a loan to be repaid when he would be able to publish the diary which he had been keeping.[3]

The reply arrived very quickly. As he lay sick abed at the small inn in Dornachbruck, he suddenly heard the familiar loud voice of his nearsighted and half-deaf friend, Adolph Strodtmann, the odd-looking student who always walked with one shoulder thrust forward because of a wound he had received in the war against the Danes in his native Schleswig; he was later to be known as Kinkel's biographer. Immediately feeling better, Schurz greeted his visitor, who brought him letters and money that friends had collected. On the next day, the two set out for Zurich, where they found Anneke and other refugees, among them Alexander Schimmelpfennig, the future Union general, and Friedrich von Beust, a former Prussian officer who had fought in the revolutionary army. Moving into the house of a baker's widow in the suburbs, Schurz, after recovering from an illness brought on by his fatigue, joined fully in the activities of his fellow refugees.

From the very beginning, however, Schurz disliked his émigré existence. His companions' endless discussions, their incessant jockeying for position in the government to be established, and their unshakable faith in the imminence of success, all seemed unreal to him. Anxious to engage in some regular activity, he began to take up his studies again. Perhaps eventually he would be able to obtain a position as an instructor at the University of Zurich.

The subjects to which he devoted himself were history, especially of the Reformation, and, this time, military science as well. His friends, former officers in the Prussian army, carefully went over the campaigns in Baden with him, studies upon which he sought to rely in later years when attempting to give military advice to Abraham Lincoln. To meet his financial needs, he sold articles to German newspapers like the *Neue Bonner Zeitung*, still published by Mrs. Kinkel, and the *Westdeutsche Zeitung*, edited by the Cologne radical Hermann Becker. At the approach of winter, he moved into the city proper.

The Democratic Society, in which Schurz was active, enabled him to meet most of the important refugees in Switzerland. Perhaps the most remarkable of these was Richard Wagner, but the composer, like Marx, was not popular with his fellow émigrés. He too was too intolerant to please them.[4]

There was still the question of a passport, which Schurz needed even in Switzerland. For a time, he seriously thought of asking for an amnesty. Then, as later, however, he did not want to request favors directly. His escape from Rastatt had given him a good reputation; a petition for amnesty might ruin it. Could not his parents arrange for amnesty without an outright application on his part? He was becoming very impatient.[5]

His restlessness was soon to find an outlet. Although he had managed to escape from the Prussians, his friend Kinkel, who had also been slightly wounded, was taken captive. Court-martialed and tried for treason, he barely escaped being shot. His judges condemned him to life imprisonment, at first in a fortress, but later, after the king reviewed the sentence, in a penitentiary. There he was forced to don prisoners' garb and spin wool, day in and day out. He was even liable to flogging in case of misbehavior.

Kinkel's cruel fate, seemingly made more onerous by the king's "mercy," had created great resentment. Strodtmann wrote a "Spinning Song," for which he was promptly expelled from the university, and when Kinkel was brought back to Cologne to stand trial for the Siegburg affair, the population was highly excited. Spectators lined the streets; the courtroom was crowded, and cheers greeted the prisoner, who defended himself with such a moving speech that he was acquitted. The sentence of life imprisonment for participation in the Baden rebellion, however, still stood. Closely guarded, he was taken back to prison, not to Naugard in Pomerania, where he had already spent some time, but to Spandau near Berlin. In desperation, he tried to escape during the transport, only to run into a pile of wood in the dark. The impact stunned him, and he was quickly recaptured.[6]

Schurz was greatly affected by Kinkel's imprisonment. The injustice of the whole proceeding, the cruelty of the sentence, and the thought of his friend spinning wool in his cell gave him no peace. Therefore, when he received a letter from the professor's wife asking for assistance, he gladly agreed to help. Securing a passport from his cousin Heribert Jüssen, who resembled him, he made preparations to return to Germany. To obtain the addresses of sympathizers, he asked his refugee friends for authority to organize branch societies of their democratic organization. Then he took the train to Frankfurt, reached Coblenz by a circuitous route, transferred to a stage for Bad Godesberg, and walked home to Bonn, where he arrived at his parents' house at three o'clock in the morning. He waited quietly while they were sleeping.

It is easy to imagine the Schurzes' joy upon awakening, when they unexpectedly saw their son. Warned not to broadcast his presence, they quickly prepared a meal for him. Later that morning Mrs. Kinkel stopped by for a visit; without telling anybody about Carl's true mission, the two conspirators perfected their plans. Schurz himself would try to arrange for the professor's escape; details would be left in Schurz's hands, and Mrs. Kinkel and he agreed to communicate with invisible ink. While in Bonn, he also met a number of close friends, among them his fellow student Friedrich Althaus and, for the first time, the then medical student and enthusiastic democrat, Abraham Jacobi, a small man with a leonine head topped with thick, wavy hair; Jacobi was to become his most intimate associate in America. After again fondly gazing at Betty's window—this time she seemed to know about his attentions and sent him flowers—he left again. His next stop was Cologne, where the newspaper publisher Becker—Red Becker, as he was called because of his hair—hid him in an apartment above a restaurant.[7]

In Cologne, too, a large number of people soon learned about Schurz's presence. "Half the city knew it, but no one betrayed him to the police," Mrs. Kinkel boasted.[8] But in view of the excitement engendered by the professor's pending trial, Schurz thought it prudent to disappear from Germany and leave for Paris. Crossing the border with his false passport was not difficult; he would return when the Kinkel trial was over.

It was spring when Schurz saw the French capital for the first time. The city enchanted him. The Temple, the Place de la Bastille, the Hotel de Ville, the Place de la Concorde, the Palais Royal—every corner seemed to recall the stirring events of the great revolution, and the romantic young German was entranced. He met fellow refugees, wrote articles for Becker's newspaper, and awaited a chance to carry out his plans.

Within a month, he returned to Germany. Again he established contact with various sympathizers identified by his Zurich friends. In July he attended a general congress of democrats at Brunswick, where he met fellow revolutionaries from all over the country. Traveling under an assumed name, he tried to make himself as inconspicuous as possible, even seeking the company of government officials to avoid suspicion. Once at Hamm, while sipping coffee at a table with a Prussian lieutenant, he noticed a police officer obviously on the lookout for a suspect. In order to be able to flee if necessary, he moved to another table near the window, a precaution which seemed especially appropriate after he overheard the policeman's description of the culprit, a blond fugitive with glasses. To his relief, the suspense ended quickly when he discovered that the suspect in question was somebody else.

When he came back to Cologne, Johanna Kinkel told him that friends had raised a large sum of money for the professor's rescue. Schurz could embark on his mission. Meeting Jacobi at the railroad station, he started out with him, the fledgling doctor traveling to Schleswig-Holstein, where he wanted to take part in the renewed war for the duchies' independence from Denmark, and Schurz to Berlin, to plot Kinkel's escape. He reached his destination on August 11, after a close call, when a professor from Bonn almost recognized him in the railroad car, only to be thrown off by his apparent lack of concern.[9]

It proved easy to hide in the Prussian capital. Taking lodgings with fraternity brothers at 26 Markgrafenstrasse, he led the life of a dandy, visiting theaters and frequenting restaurants. Unfortunately, he met with an untoward accident shortly after his arrival. Slipping in a public bath, he fell and suffered a severe contusion, which laid him up for more than two weeks. Nevertheless, he was able to carry on. Following up Mrs. Kinkel's leads, he met Dr. Ferdinand Falkenthal, a physician who lived at Moabit and introduced him to an innkeeper at Spandau, Friedrich Krüger. Krüger agreed to help.

Schurz then began to take almost daily trips to Spandau. In the late afternoon, between five and six, after walking along the River Spree to Charlottenburg to avoid taking public transportation, he always hired a one-horse cart to the small city in the center of which the prison was located. If it was too late to return, he stayed at Krüger's inn. Through Krüger he met several prison guards, whom he induced to take letters and food to the professor. But whenever he broached the question of a possible escape, he met with a firm refusal. The guards were retired noncommissioned officers of the Prussian army; much as they sympathized with Kinkel, they were not willing to violate their notions of duty by helping him to flee. Schurz had to try to find more pliable jailers.[10]

In the meantime, the supposed young dandy, amply supplied with funds by Kinkel's friends, continued his visits to places of public entertainment. Although he did not like Berlin as much as Paris because it lacked historical associations and its North German population was not congenial to him, he thoroughly enjoyed its flourishing theaters. Mme. Rachel, the renowned French actress, especially captivated him; he went to see her performances as often as possible. On one of these visits, he ran into his friend Friedrich Althaus, who was greatly astonished at his presence in Germany. When he refused to reveal the real reason for his trip to Berlin, Althaus did not press the matter. But Schurz's appearance startled his companion. "He was elegantly dressed," Althaus remembered, "in top hat, kid gloves, with starched collar and silk neckband . . . , carrying a fashionable cane, and with his gay nonchalance made the impression of a harmless idler rather than that of a revolutionary contemplating ideas dangerous to the government. At that time of abundance in democratic poseurs, no disguise could have kept him more certainly from the observation of the police than that role of a harmless character which he played with such artlessness."[11]

Thus Schurz, still under an assumed name, associated with many liberals in Berlin. Sometimes he was disappointed—the famous Bettina von Arnim, who had previously interceded for Kinkel with the king, refused to help, but neither she nor anyone else betrayed him to the police. One night, however, in the back room of a restaurant, his luck almost ran out. Unexpectedly, a student arrived who had been a police informer in Bonn. He was quickly taken out of the room, but Schurz decided that it might be wise to disappear for a while. Accordingly, he left for Hamburg, where he met new friends, among them the activist writer Malwida von Meysenbug, an aristocratic feminist of great ability, who was to become a close companion.[12]

Late in September, Schurz returned to Berlin. This time, he stayed at Moabit with Dr. Falkenthal. Equipped with a small doctor's bag to be able to pose as the physician's assistant, he resumed his visits to Spandau. Krüger put him in touch with a fourth prison official, but again the turnkey proved uncooperative. At last the innkeeper discovered still another guard, a jailer named Georg Brune, and after some preliminaries, it turned out that Brune was willing to help Kinkel escape. To be sure, he wanted a sum of money to guarantee his family's security, but his request was reasonable. Schurz, impressed by his actions in the Kinkel affair, believed him to be an idealist, yet his previous record was so dubious that he was probably motivated by the proffered bribe as much as by whatever sympathy he might have felt for his prisoner.

Financial backing was now more necessary than ever, and Mrs. Kinkel had seen to it that funds were put at Schurz's disposal. One of the principal contributors was Baroness Marie von Bruiningk, a Baltic noblewoman who thoroughly sympathized with the German revolution. A woman related to the composer Felix Mendelsohn-Bartholdy served as the intermediary; it was at her house that Schurz picked up the money. The baroness alone had given 2,000 thalers.[13]

The plan of escape was simple. Brune was to secure a duplicate of the key to the prison office where the keys to Kinkel's cell were kept, enter the office at night while he was on duty on Kinkel's floor, pick up the keys to the cell, and take the prisoner to the arched gateway where Schurz would take him in hand to lead him outside through a small gate for which he also had duplicate keys. After changing clothes at Krüger's inn, the fugitives would be taken by a relay of drivers to Rostock in Mecklenburg to enable them to sail to England. The Mecklenburg line, offering a certain degree of safety from the Prussian police, was less than fifty miles away, and Schurz traveled along the whole route to arrange for relays of horses. Various ruses might mislead the authorities to look for the fugitives in Hamburg or Bremen.

There was one more difficulty. The prison guard, anxious to provide for his family, demanded the money in advance. For a moment, Schurz hesitated. Could be trust Brune? And what if the money, 400 thalers, disappeared? He would be disgraced for life. But he realized that there was no way out. Before nightfall, he granted the turnkey's request. Kinkel was to be freed in the evening of November 5.

Schurz now completed all his preparations. He alerted the relays and arranged for fellow conspirators to be stationed at strategic corners. At the appointed time, armed with two pistols and a dirk hidden under his cloak, wearing rubbers over his shoes to muffle his steps, he unlocked the small prison gate with his duplicate key, stepped inside the gateway, secured the doors to the office and the commandant's quarters so that they could not be opened from within, and waited.

The minutes passed. Schurz became more and more nervous, but there was no sign of Kinkel or the guard. Something had evidently gone wrong. Finally Brune appeared, utterly dismayed. His plans had misfired. The prison inspector, instead of leaving the cell keys in their usual place, had inadvertently taken them home. Crestfallen, Schurz notified his associates and rode toward Mecklenburg to call off the relays. He would have to wait until Brune was on duty again.

Schurz's dejection did not last long. On the next day, when he saw the guard, he found that Brune could help him that very night. The guard on duty at the top floor of the prison had fallen sick; Brune would offer to take his place. Then he would free Kinkel by lowering him with a rope through a dormer window to the street sixty feet below.

Schurz again alerted Hensel, the wealthy farmer who had volunteered to drive him the first stretch of the road. Again he made his preparations. In order to prevent the noise of falling tiles from giving Kinkel away, he even arranged for a carriage to be driven down the street at full speed at the exact time of the expected descent.

This time the plan worked. Shortly after 11:30 P.M., Brune entered Kinkel's cell. The prisoner was ready, but a wooden railing which divided his sleeping quarters from his work room remained to be opened. Unable to find the key, Brune took an axe and broke the partition. Then he hurried Kinkel to the roof and lowered him to the street, to find Schurz ready to receive him. "This is a bold deed," said the professor; his liberator quickly took him to Krüger's inn, where a birthday

The Spandau Jail (Courtesy of National Carl Schurz Association)

party for one of the prison guards was in progress. While Kinkel was changing from his felon's garb into ordinary clothes, Krüger asked the celebrants whether they would mind if he offered some of their punch to two travelers just arrived from Berlin. The guards were generous, and to his great amusement, their escaped prisoner was toasted with their own liquor. Then the professor and his deliverer stepped into Hensel's carriage and, as quickly as the horses would carry them, left town by way of the Potsdam Gate leading to the west. After following the main highway part of the distance toward Nauen, they turned off on a side road to the north toward Oranienburg, not stopping for thirty-five miles until reaching Gransee, where they had to give the horses some rest. Finally at sunrise they crossed the Mecklenburg line. Driving the horses mercilessly, Hensel stayed on until they came to Neustrelitz, but one of the bays died in the stable of sheer exhaustion.

Sympathizers hurried the two fugitives further, to Neubrandenburg, to Teterow, and Rostock. There, at the White Cross Inn, Moritz Wiggers, a local democratic leader whom Schurz had met at Brunswick, welcomed them. Traveling under the names of Kaiser and Hensel, they were taken to a hotel in the nearby port of Warnemünde. On the next day, Wiggers's friend Ernst Brockelmann, a well-to-do ship owner, gave them a cordial reception at his house, to which they then moved for greater safety. He also promised them a ship to take them to England.

On his long trip, Schurz had had a good opportunity to talk to Kinkel. Aged visibly, his hands chaffed from his descent on the rope, the professor looked pale; but he was in excellent spirits. Overjoyed at his rescue, he related the story of his martyrdom, his attempt to flee on the way back from Cologne, his despair in jail, and his utter dejection at the failure of the first escape attempt. He could not thank his student enough for having risked his life for him. He thought it might be possible to find safety in neighboring Denmark, but in view of that country's relations with the Germanic Confederation—its king was the duke of Holstein, one of the member states—Great Britain seemed safer, even though it would take over a week longer to find a ship for Newcastle. Kinkel's pursuers, however, had already been thrown off the trail. Sympathizers had circulated stories of his appearance at Bremen and Hamburg, and the police were totally ignorant of his whereabouts. So the fugitives settled down to enjoy the Brockelmann family's lavish hospitality.

Finally, on November 17, 1850, the schooner *Kleine Anna* with a cargo of wheat for Newcastle was ready. The professor and his liberator boarded the ship; Brockelmann ordered the captain not to stop in Denmark to pay the sound dues until his return and not to seek refuge in German ports under any circumstances. Slowly they saw the shores of the fatherland disappear in the distance; the *Kleine Anna* made for the open sea, and the fugitives were on the last leg of their journey.[14]

The crossing was difficult. The sea was so rough that Kinkel became desperately seasick, and it took two weeks to reach British waters. Unable to land at Newcastle because of an unfavorable wind, the captain made for Leith, the port of Edinburgh, instead, where the two friends arrived on a Sunday morning. They admired the Scottish capital's architectural treasures, but everything was closed, and small boys made fun of their exotic clothing. It was not until late at night that they finally found an inn. With the aid of some gold pieces, they managed to make themselves understood, although their English was limited to such words as "sherry" and "beefsteak." After obtaining a good meal and shelter for the night, they took the train for London on the next day.[15]

It was only then that the outside world was able to learn part of the true story of Kinkel's sensational escape. While still aboard the *Kleine Anna*, the professor had written letters to his wife and friends. "My savior is Karl," he declared to one of his financial backers. "You were ignorant of this plan, which could be carried out only with loyalty, perseverance, and luck, as well as great intelligence and bold energy, characteristics which, combined with all the magic gifts of charm, that rare youth possesses most abundantly." Filled with pride in his student, he also sent Schurz's parents a letter of gratitude, replete with praise for his liberator. Mrs. Kinkel, too, was overjoyed at Schurz's success. "He has accomplished the impossible," she asserted. "There is no more intelligent, self-sacrificing, and persistent friend than he."[16]

Schurz was not loath to take credit for his exploit. Apologizing for not having told them the true intent of his mission to Germany, he too wrote to his parents from the ship. Soon his fame spread. Fantastic stories of Kinkel's rescue made the rounds—according to one version, Schurz had been disguised as an organ grinder to reconnoiter the professor's prison—and writers of poetry and fiction made the most of the romantic deliverance. These variations of the true story did him no harm. For the sake of the record, however, he apparently wrote down the main facts as soon as he had some leisure, and there can be little doubt that the manuscript was in Wiggers's hands when in 1863 the Mecklenburg democrat published the first full account in a German magazine. That this early fame was good for Schurz's reputation is beyond question; his later career in the United States would have been much more difficult without it.[17]

After a brief stay in London, where they saw the renowned actor William Macready perform in *Macbeth* and *Henry VIII,* Schurz and Kinkel went to Paris. The French capital was then one of the centers of European revolutionary activity, and although Kinkel, whose wife now rejoined him, resolved to establish himself in England, Schurz remained in France. As he wrote to his parents, he would lead a quiet life and devote himself wholly to his studies. In the meantime, he would be able to support himself by writing newspaper articles—he had a contract with the *Rostocker Zeitung*—and send some money to the elder Schurzes as well. His younger sister, Toni, could go to London and stay with the Kinkels, who had invited her.

Of course Schurz never carried out his plan to devote himself wholly to scholarly activities. In order to earn a living, as he had planned, he again made contributions to various German newspapers. He did some studying, visited theaters, concerts, and art museums, but at the same time became involved in the revolutionary activities of his fellow refugees, among whom his newly won fame had given him some standing.

His renewed stay in Paris convinced Schurz that it was time for him to improve his knowledge of French. Accordingly, he took lessons with an impoverished noblewoman who called herself Mme. la Princesse de Beaufort, and by composing little essays on matters of interest to him, which the princess corrected, he became fluent in the language. It was one of his strengths that once he set his mind to learning a foreign tongue he usually succeeded very quickly.

His living arrangements were simple. For a while, he roomed with his friend Strodtmann. The eccentric biographer was so untidy, however, that his quarters were in complete disorder, and when he accidentally burned Schurz's clothes while cooking, the two friends parted amicably. Then Schurz took a room at 17 Quai St. Michel, a house run by an elderly lady with strict views of propriety. He usually ate in cheap restaurants—a socialist cooks' establishment was his favorite—and with a rented piano resumed his musical studies. From time to time the landlady invited him to tea in the salon, and although these visits were boring, they doubtless improved his French.

While Schurz managed to enjoy himself in Paris, not everything in the French capital pleased him. During carnival, he was shocked at the orgy at a ball in the opera, only to discover worse goings-on at a nearby restaurant. Drawn to the galleries of the National Assembly, he did not find the debates inspiring. Nevertheless, he was still hoping for a favorable turn in French politics that might rekindle the revolutionary spirit in Europe.

In the meantime, he had kept in close touch with Kinkel. Warning against a break with the socialists, he alerted the professor to the possibility of their coming to power in France. Then their cooperation would be essential. He wanted his mentor to stay above the factional quarrels in London, but the professor, whom he visited briefly in May, became more and more enmeshed in refugee politics. It proved impossible for Kinkel to follow his disciple's advice and remain aloof.[18]

By spring, Schurz was seriously thinking of moving to London, where he thought he could earn more money. Soon he found out that there were even more compelling reasons for a change of domicile. Paris was gradually becoming unfriendly to foreign revolutionaries; the prince president, Louis Napoleon, was generally believed to be preparing a coup d'état. Moreover, Prussian police officers had been actively pursuing Schurz, focusing attention on him after learning the true identity of Kinkel's liberator. In January 1851, alerting the Prussian envoy in Paris to Schurz's arrival, they erroneously described him as having been condemned to death because of the Siegburg affair and the Baden insurrection. "It is said that he is talked about a lot in Germany because of Kinkel's flight . . . with which he appears to have been connected,'' the message concluded. Although the Prussians thought for a brief time that he had returned to Germany to raise money for the revolutionary cause, they soon learned the truth. Putting pressure on their French colleagues, they met with some success, and late in May, Schurz was arrested. Lodged in jail, he was unable to discover the reason for his confinement for several days. At last, on the fourth day, he was brought before a police official who let him go but politely told him to leave the country.

The prisoner gladly complied. He had already made up his mind to move to London and, during the first days of June, crossed the Channel. On the sixteenth, the Prussian authorities learned that the "well known" Carl Schurz, now described as the chief of and principal intermediary between the revolutionaries in England, France, and Germany, had been expelled from France and had arrived in London.[19]

Schurz had no trouble securing lodging and employment in the British capital. Kinkel had already rented rooms for him at St. John's Wood Terrace, not far from his own house. As it was fashionable at that time to take an interest in German affairs, Schurz found it easy to obtain students willing to pay for German lessons. He settled down to his new routine, and although he later maintained that he knew no English, there is some evidence that he was at least able to communicate with his students.[20]

London in 1851 was a veritable Mecca for refugees. Karl Marx, Giuseppe Mazzini, Louis Blanc, Louis Kossuth, as well as the many German émigrés Schurz knew so well, were all there at one time or another. One of the centers of their many gatherings was the salon kept by Baroness von Bruiningk, who had also left Germany and now became a hostess for her fellow refugees. Schurz often visited the hospitable von Bruiningks. It was they who introduced him to ever larger circles among the fugitives then in England. And Mrs. Kinkel, overjoyed to be able to do something for her husband's deliverer, volunteered to give him piano lessons. He came almost daily to her home to enjoy the family's hospitality.

Because of his loyalty to Kinkel, Schurz became involved in the factional quarrels endemic among the revolutionaries. Not only the Marxists but other radicals with conceptions of the coming struggle different from his own attacked the professor, whose student firmly supported him. At last, urged on by Mazzini, Kinkel reluctantly undertook the mission of raising funds for a loan in America, while Schurz was sent to Switzerland to seek support for the venture.

He left in high spirits. Returning to France without notifying the police, he renewed acquaintances there and in Switzerland, and in September he took a walking tour of the Bernese Alps. His companion was Dr. Wilhelm Löwe, a prominent member of the defunct Frankfurt Assembly, with whom he became very friendly. The scenery—the single peak of the Faulhorn, the magnificent cloud formations, the avalanches—impressed him greatly.

Upon his return to London, Schurz moved in with the Kinkels. The head of the household, who had once again established himself as a lecturer, was still in America, but his wife extended her hospitality to his liberator. Schurz took over the absent professor's political duties—he was one of a deputation of German refugees welcoming Louis Kossuth to London—and, although he did not realize it at the time, Kinkel's liabilities as well. For the trip to America only appeared to be a success. To be sure, wherever he went, the famous fugitive was cordially welcomed. The amount of money he collected, however, was not sufficient for any revolutionary purposes. In addition, his opponents, Armand Gögg, Arnold Ruge, and Joseph Fickler, launched a rival drive for funds to be raised by small weekly or monthly contributions for an immediate world revolution. In disgust, Mazzini complained to Schurz that he could not tell who were the real German revolutionaries.[21]

Schurz became very disillusioned with the project, especially when in December 1851 the French president finally carried out his long-expected coup d'état. Overthrowing the Second Republic, he declared himself consul for ten years, a mere prelude to the reestablishment of the Empire one year later. After some initial hope that the coup would cause a renewed general upheaval in Europe, Schurz realized that counterrevolution had triumphed, at least for the time being. According to his *Reminiscences*, one day in December he met Louis Blanc, the French revolutionary, sitting on a bench in Hyde Park. "Ah, c'est vous, mon jeune ami," Blanc said. "C'est fini, n'est ce pas? C'est fini!" Whether this story is literally true or not—the chronology is certainly wrong because in January he was still hoping for a new uprising—there is no doubt that the failure of the revolution in France was an important factor in Schurz's decision to go to America. As he advised his parents in February 1852, "If no great change has occurred in European conditions by the middle of the year, we have no choice but emigration to America. Such a change of European conditions is not probable so that we have to get used to thoughts of emigration."[22]

The failure of the revolution in Europe was not the only reason for Schurz's opting for life in the United States. Politics was a passion with him, and the impossibility of participating in public life in England, to say nothing of the insufficiency of his income, contributed to his resolve. Whether it was clear to him that the break with the Old World would be permanent is not certain, but in the meantime he had made a commitment which made a new way of earning his livelihood essential.[23] He had fallen in love and was about to be married.

Margarethe Meyer, Schurz's fiancée, was an unusual young woman. The daughter of a wealthy Hamburg cane merchant, she was the youngest of eleven children. Her mother died at her birth, and after at the age of fifteen losing her father also, she was brought up by her siblings, especially her brothers Adolph and Heinrich. Highly attractive, with black hair, a delicate chin, tender mouth, large, brilliant hazel-gray eyes, and a clear complexion, she spoke French and English, played the piano, and sang with a beautiful alto voice that captivated Schurz. She had come to London to help her sister, then expecting a baby, both with the housework and the Froebel kindergarten she was conducting.[24]

When late in 1851 Schurz met Margarethe, she was living in the house of her brother-in-law, Johannes Ronge, a defrocked priest who had left Germany after defying church authorities in a quarrel about the display of the so-called Holy Shroud at Trier. To the dismay of the Meyer brothers, he had fallen in love with their sister, Bertha Traun, who divorced her husband, married Ronge, and left with him for England.

In a fragment for his children, Schurz vividly described his first meeting with his future wife at Ronge's house. "My business was soon disposed of and I rose to go," he wrote,

> when he [Ronge] opened the door and called out into an adjacent room, "Margarethe, come in if you please, here is a gentlemen whom you would probably like to know." A girl of about 18 entered; of stately stature, a dark, curly head, something childlike in her beautiful features, and large, dark, truthful eyes. Ronge presented her to me as his sister-in-law. I had already heard her spoken of in the drawing room of Baroness Bruening, but without paying any attention to it. She had, as she afterwards told me, heard of me as Kinkel's liberator while she was a student at the female high school in Hamburg. As is usual with young girls, she imagined all sorts of romantic things about me, also hoped to become acquainted with me. The meeting had now really come, and it did not pass over without some embarrassment. On her part, because she had in her fancy attributed to me all sorts of great qualities, and therefore been a little afraid of me. On my part, because I had not quite overcome my youthful bashfulness in the presence of women. Our first conversation touched only such ordinary things as common acquaintances, and we parted with the expression of hope that we might meet again. We did indeed meet again; not very soon, but then very often, and [in] not less than a year, I was to be joined to this girl for life.

Schurz met Margarethe—Gredel, as she was called—again at the Bruiningks'. The two fell madly in love, and Schurz courted Gredel throughout the winter of 1851–52. One night early in 1852, wandering through the streets, the two lovers told their life stories to each other. It was raining and she had forgotten her umbrella. The dyes of her green hat were not waterproof, and by the time they reached home, they noticed that she was green all over. That same evening they made a decision. They announced their engagement on the next day.[25]

Their friends were delighted. "Margarethe Meyer, the beautiful girl whom you may still remember . . . has won the jackpot, for she is the fiancée of Karl Schurz, one of the most excellent and noble men whom I know," wrote Malwida von Meysenbug, and her friend Charlotte Voss agreed. As she assured Margarethe's brother, Schurz had made a very good impression on her. "Instead of the eccentric youth and M.'s adoring admirer," she confessed, "I have found a simple, calm, highly understanding and genuine person, whose seriousness by far exceeds his years. His appearance is not handsome but agreeable and marked by tranquil deportment, and the very first conversation with him reveals intelligence and character." She was especially impressed with his behavior toward Margarethe, his open admission of what he was thinking, and his honest recognition of his situation, a poor refugee planning to emigrate to the United States to give lectures in order to have a reliable source of income for his wife. Especially esteemed in England because of his industry—sometimes he gave seven lessons per day—he had entree into many British families. Margarethe, she was sure, was going to marry a "remarkable" man. Everybody was convinced that she would be very happy.[26]

The Meyer family did not share this enthusiasm. Already upset about one sister's marriage to an impecunious revolutionary, they did not cherish the prospect of another refugee brother-in-law. Although they considered themselves liberals, they looked askance at their sister's proposed union with a man without a regular profession or an assured income. After she announced her engagement, her oldest brother Adolph, hoping to convince her to let Carl go to America alone at first, prevailed on Margarethe to return to Germany. Her close companion Charlotte Voss called for her in London; traveling to Hamburg by way of Bonn to meet her future in-laws, she came home.[27]

In the meantime, Schurz, who after Kinkel's return had moved back into his old apartment at St. John's Wood Terrace, was pining away for her and every day impatiently waited for the mailman. In a long letter to his future brother-in-law, he sought to make his position clear and to explain himself. Admitting that he had always lived in modest circumstances, he asserted that he had also known how to make ends meet. The revolution and Kinkel's rescue had interrupted his preparation for an academic career, but he was certain that he would be able to provide decently for his wife-to-be.

The key to his future lay in his plans to go to America. "My nature cannot content itself with the life aims which are contained within my four walls," he wrote. "By and by I might have a good living here in England. But citizenship here, for the alien, is merely formal. The stranger remains a stranger here. Under such circumstances I cannot feel at home. What I am looking for in America is not only personal freedom, but the chance to gain full legal citizenship. If I cannot be the citizen of a free Germany, at least I can be a citizen of free America." Of course there were also many other reasons for his emigrating to the New World. Ever since the Kinkel affair, the Prussian government had been harassing his parents, on one occasion sending soldiers to search the house and inflicting considerable damage. The elder Schurzes had relatives in Wisconsin, where the son wanted to provide for his father and mother. America's large cities would offer many opportunities to deliver lectures until he could find a place to settle down.[28]

Meyer wrote a friendly reply, but he was far from convinced. Schurz tried again. Explaining that he was happy to learn their differences were practical rather than personal, he admitted he could understand that Meyer's views would have to be different from his. But he could not go on teaching declensions and conjugations to unwilling pupils. He would go to America, where, after a few years, he would write a history of the country which would sell on both sides of the Atlantic. As for Margarethe, everything she desired had always been given to her. Thus, never having been compelled to look out for herself, she was unhappy, a condition he could cure by taking her along. To his fiancée, he wrote that he would sail alone if he had to, but he was already so lonesome for her that leaving her in Europe would demolish all his dreams, no matter what her brother was saying. He, Carl, was counting the hours till she came back.[29]

Needless to say, accompanied by her brother, she did return. Carl had his way: the wedding day was set prior to the departure for America. And Meyer made arrangements to let them have a sum of 700 thalers of his sister's inheritance right away.[30]

The wedding took place on July 6, 1852, according to Schurz, at the parish church of St. Marylebone, but according to a contemporary account, in their own house. Telling all acquaintances that they would be at home from twelve to two, they provided for a meal and refreshments—pastries, sandwiches, cakes, pies, and fruits. Margarethe wore a white gown with a broad white sash, a beautiful white veil, and a myrtle wreath with orange blossoms.[31]

So Carl and Gredel were married. Their union was to last for almost a quarter of a century, and there is little doubt that they were deeply in love. Yet Gredel's stubbornness, her jealousy, and her frequent illnesses, perhaps only partially physical and related to her inability ever to feel fully at home in America—in later years, she refused to go to St. Louis—were deeply troublesome for Carl. Conversely, his frequent moves and absences from home were not easy for her. That these domestic difficulties left their mark on him is certain; possibly his egotism, already exaggerated because of his early fame in connection with the rescue of Kinkel, was heightened by his constant need to prove himself to her and to her successful relatives.

Because they could not obtain a passport, they spent their honeymoon in a hired cottage in Hampstead instead. The honeymoon was cut short, however, when within one week, Schurz fell seriously ill. Running a high fever, he could neither swallow properly nor speak. Upon his in-laws' advice, he traveled to Malvern to take a water cure; his bride nursed him, and by the end of the month, he felt better. According to tradition, during his illness he grew by another inch and a half, so that he finally stood more than six feet tall. At any rate, he recovered fully and returned to London.[32]

After coming back, he resumed his plans to leave for the United States. Although Mazzini, for whom he had great respect, urged him to stay to await an imminent uprising in Lombardy, his mind was made up. He would seek his fortune in America. As Margarethe had inherited some 78,557 marks, a considerable sum in 1852, the newlyweds were able to book passage on the comfortable

Margarethe Meyer Schurz (Courtesy of Watertown Historical Society)

packet ship *City of London,* which left Plymouth in August and twenty-eight days later, on September 17, 1852, arrived in New York.[33]

Whether he was aware of it or not, Schurz had broken with Europe.[34] Famous because of his exploits at Rastatt and Spandau and relieved of immediate financial worries, at twenty-three he was able to look forward with optimism to his career in the New World.

IV

America

IT WAS ON A BEAUTIFUL September day that Schurz caught his first glimpse of America, and the sight captivated him. The stately homes and lush hills of Staten Island, then a summer resort for the rich, the steady traffic of small and large boats on the bay, the vista of the great, flag-bedecked city beyond, and the brilliant sky exhilarated the travelers wearied by a four weeks' sea voyage. Even Margarethe, who had taken a dim view of the new country, was pleased.[1]

After landing, the newcomers took a cab to find a hotel. The Astor House and the main hotels on Broadway, the finest in town, were full, but eventually they obtained accommodations in a less splendid establishment at Union Square, at that time the northern end of the city.

The next morning they went sight-seeing. New York in 1852 was a metropolis of 520,000 inhabitants, with 120,000 more across the East River in Brooklyn. Its principal sights were its public buildings—city hall, the customs house, and the churches. Barnum's Museum was the foremost public exhibit, but the new immigrants were not particularly taken with any of these. What interested them most was the spirit of the people, their enterprise, their freedom from constraints, their bustle. And how wonderful it was not to see uniformed guards anywhere! New York was marvelous, Schurz thought, so much more cheerful than London. Broadway might not have the proud magnificence of Regent Street, but with its gorgeous shops, restaurants, and hotels, it approached the elegance of the Paris boulevards. No matter what their backgrounds—he was amazed at the unparalleled racial and ethnic variety—the inhabitants were exuberant and rejoiced in their independence. In spite of its lack of museums and art galleries of note, Schurz saw the city as it was described in the *Visitor's Handbook*, "the grand portal of entrance to the Republic of Freedom."[2]

His positive attitude toward the New World was significant. "If Margarethe occasionally has her little jests with me for thinking every shanty charming," he wrote to Charlotte Voss, "it is only because I am interested in everything that is characteristic."[3] Even though he had not yet broken completely with Europe and his wife continued to long for the Continent all her life, he was determined to become part of the new society, to give it a chance. His eventual success attested to the strength of his resolve.

But Schurz could not enjoy his new surroundings for long. Shortly after he arrived, his wife fell ill. Her health had never been robust, and her indisposition was merely the first of many such interludes that were to mar her entire married life. As her husband anxiously watched over her, his fellow guests tried to do everything they could to make the young stranger comfortable. One evening, when one of them had volunteered to take his place at her sickbed, he walked downstairs to get some air. Dejectedly sitting down on a bench in the park at Union Square, he mused about his fate. The future looked bleak—the new country, his sick wife, his lack of familiarity with the language—what was to become of him? He was very downcast, but he never wavered in his determination to join the mainstream of American life. If anything, his resolve became even more fixed.[4]

His depression did not last long. Margarethe recovered within two weeks, and the young people resumed their planning for the future. America was great; where else would fellow guests have been so friendly to strangers? However, they hardly knew anybody in New York except Anneke. Philadelphia was different. There they had many acquaintances, Germans with whom they could talk. Strodtmann had arrived in Philadelphia to publish a newspaper, and Heinrich Tiedemann, Gustav's brother, practiced medicine there. He would be glad to see a member of the forces who had fought under his brother, the unfortunate commandant of Rastatt, whom the Prussians had executed after the surrender. Moreover, Schurz had been advised to establish a law practice in one of the more important cities of Pennsylvania or Ohio, and he was anxious to start lecturing in Philadelphia. He decided to take a look at the city.[5]

The Schurzes stayed much longer in Philadelphia than they had expected. It was there that Carl took the first serious steps that were to transform him from a German to an American; it was there that he began to take roots in the new country. It was also there that his first child, his daughter Agathe, was born. Most important, it was there that he learned English.

When he had first come to Great Britain, the English language seemed forbidding to him. Its many sibilants, its impure vowels, its entire cadence struck him as unattractive. When he crossed the ocean to America, he struck up conversations with his fellow passengers and learned more during that short time than during his entire stay in England. Now, determined to become part of the new country, he made a deliberate effort to master the language.

This time, there was no impoverished princess to give him lessons. With the aid of a dictionary, he laboriously went through the pages of the Philadelphia *Daily Ledger*—advertisements, insipid articles like "The Joys of Spring" and "The Beauties of Friendship," editorials, news, everything. At the same time, he began reading English novels, Goldsmith, Dickens, Thackeray, Scott. The essays of Macaulay came next, followed by Blackstone and Kent. Finally, he turned to Shakespeare. At the same time, he hit upon the idea of translating the *Junius* letters into German, retranslating them into English, and then comparing his version with the original. The method worked, and although he did not mention it in his memoirs, his positive attitude must have helped him to pick up the language in the streets as well.[6]

Within a few weeks, Schurz was contemplating writing and delivering his planned lectures in English as well as in German. He learned so quickly and so well that, in later years, observers inevitably commented on his skill. Eventually he became one of the most renowned orators in America, and his literary productions, his biography of Henry Clay, for example, are still considered models of clarity. That he spoke without an accent is doubtful; friends sometimes thought so, but opponents never failed to mention the Teutonic cast of his speech. Nevertheless, he became a master of the new language.[7] Realization of his conception of American citizenship was impossible without fluent English, even though he never failed to cherish his mother tongue, and whenever he met or corresponded with a fellow countryman, he insisted on speaking and writing German, the language he also continued to employ in his home.[8] The phrase "melting pot" had not yet been coined, but the idea it represents appealed to him, provided always that it did not also mean the loss of ethnic identity.

In other ways, too, his attitude toward the new country remained entirely favorable. He appreciated the friendliness of the people, the ease with which acquaintances could be made. Even Margarethe, who had been afraid of her reaction to the American "character," was pleasantly surprised. "It is true that we have to miss some things here," he wrote to his brother-in-law, "but nowhere is it easier to miss things than here."

To his friends, too, Schurz enthusiastically reported his experiences. Conceding that democracy in practice was different from democracy in theory, he still insisted that the net effect was positive. Self-government was working, not in the way idealists had imagined it in Europe, but working nonetheless. If conditions sometimes approached a state of anarchy, American practice merely proved how unnecessary many functions of government really were. New York was magnificent, "as bustling as the most animate parts of London," and while Philadelphia was a bit more sedate, the smaller city, too, was impressive. Although he admitted that, as evidenced in their sports, their races, and their wars, Americans manifested a strange indifference to life, he insisted that educated people were able to live as quietly in the United States as anywhere else. Most astonishing was the position of women. Their social liberty unlimited, they could travel alone all over the continent; in fact, a veritable cult of women had developed. There was much that was raw and uncouth, yet the lack of restraint with which individuals were able to pursue their aims was commendable. Labor was free to seek improvement, capital habitually took enormous risks, and everyone enjoyed complete independence. He was much taken by what he saw.[9]

As Schurz became more and more interested in American affairs, European concerns faded somewhat into the background. He had come to the United States with a commission to patch up the quarrel between Kinkel and his opponents. Armand Gögg's group, which favored a universal radical revolution, had proposed the collection of five cents per week to finance the cause, while Kinkel had sold bonds to raise funds for a German democratic revolution. The rival organization was already in decline, especially after the adjournment of the Wheeling Congress of German revolutionaries influenced by Gögg, which had proposed a fantastic program of annexation of all countries to the Union to form a worldwide republic. Nevertheless, the quarrel had raised doubts about the status of Kinkel's fund. In November 1852, after Count Oskar von Reichenbach, an old London acquaintance, had written a letter advocating the return to the donors of the money the professor had collected, Schurz advised Kinkel to make a public statement about the money. But Schurz was vague about his own plans. Some people wanted him to visit Washington to see what could be accomplished there. Perhaps all the talk about the annexation of Cuba might be used for European revolutionary purposes. Pleading unfamiliarity with American conditions, however, he refused to go, at least at that time. While he was anxious to help Krüger, who was being tried for complicity in Kinkel's escape, he was less interested in Europe than before. Gradually, the German revolutionary was becoming an American republican.[10]

Schurz's Americanization was helped by the fact that he enjoyed considerable leisure that winter. His wife, now expecting their first child, was in poor health, and he did not wish to leave her alone. His parents and sisters arrived from Germany; Margarethe helped him with a book on recent history; he practiced English and began to contemplate another volume, a history of the United States. It was delightful to work and plan together, especially as Margarethe, who had been afraid that she would not survive the delivery, quickly recovered after Agathe was born in the spring. Her domestic bliss was complete. "I lack nothing," she wrote to her older sister. "For me, Karl is father, lover, and husband. Those who knew him before are amazed because he seemed so little fitted for family life." He even got up seven times at night when necessary! Carl too was happy. His first year in America was turning out well.[11]

The failure of Kinkel's American efforts also helped Schurz concentrate on the United States rather than Europe. He finally advised the professor to stop agitating the loan question. August von Willich, the socialist revolutionary, had visited Schurz in Philadelphia to propose using the money to establish a German state in America, only to be told that his ideas were purely illusory and would not do any good. Schurz simply believed that no further financial efforts on behalf of the German revolution could succeed. Kossuth's and Kinkel's trips had exhausted all possibilities. It might be possible to interest leading annexationist Democratic statesmen in Germany's cause, but public agitation would have to cease. Although he concluded his letter to Kinkel with the assertion that he was no less attached to the old country in America than he had been in Europe, his advice did not seem to bear out his protestation.[12]

In the meantime, Schurz had given serious thought to the problem of earning a livelihood. Unwilling to live entirely on his wife's money, he made an arrangement with a Philadelphia German named Dümmig, whose retail musical instruments establishment he proposed to expand. The wholesale trade and import business promised to yield good profits. With his brother-in-law Adolph providing some of the necessary funds, Schurz entered upon his first commercial venture in America. Like most of its successors, however, it did not prove very successful. His genius did not extend to business.[13]

But business did not keep the Schurz family from taking long vacations. To escape the summer's heat in Philadelphia, the Schurzes sought relief at Cape May. They enjoyed the resort, especially because of the company of the banker, Jay Cooke, who was to prove a good friend and their financial adviser for years to come. Anxious to find a vacation spot with artistic facilities, however, they rented rooms in Bethlehem, where the Moravian church and the local college had long fostered musical presentations. Bethlehem proved very congenial; it was there that little Agathe (Hans, or Handy, as they called her) first tried to stand on her legs, while the proud parents, dreaming the time away in an old cemetery, read Dickens together.[14]

They returned to the city in the fall. Giving up their house in the suburbs, they moved to the center of town, across from Washington Park. There Agathe could play under her parents' and grandparents' supervision. With Margarethe's health steadily improving, she seemed content, so that the family's adjustment to the new country was made much easier.[15]

During his second winter in America, Schurz turned once more to public affairs. Writing articles about the Crimean War for a New York newspaper, he capitalized on the interest in the new European conflict. With business seemingly flourishing, he had some leisure, and he decided it was time to visit the capital.[16] Perhaps he might gain some insight into the administration's attitude toward the European revolutionary cause.

In 1854 Washington was a raw young city, an uncompleted capital of magnificent distances. The capitol was unfinished; the ministries were housed in nondescript buildings. In later years, Schurz remembered that his first impression of the city had been "rather dismal"; nevertheless, at the time, positive as always about the new country, he wrote that he found Washington fascinating, even pleasing in its own way. How remarkable was the Sunday-like atmosphere—the absence of commercial establishments of any importance accounted for it—how arresting were the delegations of colorfully garbed Indians! Congress intrigued him; compared with the Paulskirche in Frankfurt, the National Assembly in Paris, and the House of Commons in London, it seemed much more representative of its constituency. Its members truly reflected their origins and the habits of the people who had sent them there. No artificiality, no false pomposity set them apart in any way.

To help him carry out his mission, Schurz had letters of introduction to various political leaders. The one who impressed him most favorably was Jefferson Davis, the secretary of war. Dignified and courteous, Davis listened politely to what his visitor had to say, although he remained entirely noncommittal. Senators Richard Brodhead of Pennsylvania and James Shields of Illinois seemed less interesting.

Nevertheless, Schurz believed Shields, an immigrant like himself, might be useful to him. He also met a German-American journalist, Felix Grund, who gave him some pointers about the inner working of Washington politics, and he became acquainted with the poet Sarah Bolton, whose husband was the clerk of one of the congressional committees. "You don't have to be jealous," he reassured his wife, "she is over forty, but her poems are beautiful."[17]

It was obvious that there was little hope for American help for the desired European revolution. "My experience with the President and the Cabinet is, in a word, they have no foreign policy," Schurz concluded, but he was not greatly dismayed. No matter how little he was able to accomplish for Germany, he was much encouraged about his own future in America. "I have just called upon a Senator who seems to be very much interested in me, and to whom my ideas appeal . . . ," he boasted to his wife. "I feel it more and more strongly as I become better acquainted with those who are influencing affairs. Nature has endowed me with a goodly capacity that only awaits an opportunity to make itself useful, and I do not think I am overestimating my value when I say that I would be second to very few here, not now, but in a few years." As he met various politicians, he felt "the old fire of 1848" coursing in his veins again and realized that politics, particularly the solution of universal problems, was his true vocation. "Although the reaction in Europe has thrown me out of my course," he insisted, "you may still see your husband coming into his own."

One morning shortly before he left, his self-esteem received a final boost. A member of Congress who had spent some time with him the night before said to him, "Sir, you have a fair opening before you. You will have a future in this country. I talked about you with my friends and we came to the conclusion that, if you settle in one of the new States, we will meet again in a few years in this city, and then we shall listen to you in the halls of Congress as you now listen to us." Schurz was so impressed that in his German letter to his wife he quoted the remark in English.[18]

Although he arrived in Washington while the Kansas-Nebraska debates were taking place in the House of Representatives, he failed to mention the controversial issue in his letters. Was he embarrassed about his relations with proslavery politicians who were most likely to be interested in foreign ventures? It was only half a century later when he was writing his memoirs that he thought he remembered the debates, specifically those in the Senate. The arrogance of the slaveholders, the forthright stand of their opponents, the deplorable position of their Northern allies, especially of Stephen A. Douglas, all these he thought in retrospect he recalled. In reality, however, he never heard the debates leading to the passage of the Kansas-Nebraska Act in the Senate on March 4, the day he believed he left. He did not even arrive in the city until ten days later, so that, except for the aftermath in the Senate, the only debates he could have witnessed were those in the House.[19]

The great predictions about his future were pleasing, but the reality of the present had to be confronted first. Schurz's expectations about the music business met with disappointment; he needed some new source of income. Convinced of his gifts of persuasion, he made an arrangement with Pennsylvania investors to promote the sale of gas. For this purpose as well as to visit some German acquaintances and to look over the country, in September he left for the West. He described the railroad trip minutely to his wife, the changing landscape once he crossed the Susquehanna, the entry into the mountains, the dense forests, the lonely cabins. Passing through Pittsburgh at three o'clock in the morning, he saw little except the fires lighted in the streets in defense against cholera; he reached Ohio by daybreak. The new country excited him; he even compared the Ohio with the Rhine.

After a brief stop at Cincinnati, he reached Indianapolis, where the Boltons introduced him to Governor Joseph A. Wright. The governor was friendly; he even said he wanted his visitor to settle in the state, and Schurz seriously considered the proposition. He liked the city with its newly laid out streets thronged with men and women on horseback, its attractive public buildings, and its two thousand Germans in their own section. Its future seemed assured. Was it not a good omen that between noon and one o'clock it was possible to see six trains leaving Union Station in different directions? If the gas business developed according to plan, if he could secure the proper patents, at last he would become financially independent, and the irksome monetary relations with the Meyer family would come to an end. Margarethe, too, would find Indianapolis attractive. The Boltons would introduce her to society, and the forthcoming constitutional convention would provide sufficient entertainment for her. He was very optimistic.[20]

For the time being, however, Schurz had to go on. Leaving Indianapolis late in September, he traveled to St. Louis by way of Chicago. Again he described his impressions of the new environment, still in glowing colors, although he admitted that the vast prairie did not seem particularly inviting. He would not like to settle there; Chicago, however, was different.

He arrived in the Windy City late at night. Leaving his baggage at the station, he took a horse-drawn bus to look for a hotel. The only one he was able to find offered a room he had to share with a stranger who looked so unsavory that he refused and walked out again. The streets were deserted; not a soul was in sight. The only living creatures to be seen were the rats living underneath the wooden sidewalks. Finally, totally exhausted, he sat down at the curb and fell asleep. In his ensuing dream, he suddenly saw himself summoned before an assembly of rats. Addressing them in parliamentary language, he apologized for speaking in a language still foreign to him, until he was finally awakened by a passer-by who took him to a cheap hotel. As Chester V. Easum has pointed out, the speech to the rats as he reported it to Margarethe is the first extant sample of Schurz's English. It is well written, except for a few German constructions that mar the free flow of words.[21]

In spite of the bad night and the rats, Chicago fascinated Schurz. The city was developing so fast that its more enterprising citizens were becoming rich merely by growing up with it. Undoubtedly he felt that he too must seize the opportunity of growing up with a city. Chicago was the model; there must be other towns like it.

Schurz's next stop was St. Louis, where he knew some Germans. A short trip brought him to nearby Belleville, Illinois, to visit Friedrich Hecker, the famous German revolutionary and Tiedemann's brother-in-law. The old firebrand had a fever; his choleric temper made it difficult for Schurz to stay long and become better acquainted with the many "Latin farmers," German immigrants better versed in the classics than agriculture, for which the town was famous. After calming Hecker down a bit, he left again for Chicago.

He soon saw more of the West, and the more he saw, the more he liked it. After receiving a letter from his uncle Jacob Jüssen, the former mayor of Jülich, who invited him to visit his new home at Watertown, Wisconsin, Schurz took the night boat to Milwaukee. The experience delighted him. "There is so much here which is grand and beautiful that it well repays one for the expenditure of a little time and some inconvenience," he wrote to Margarethe. "I believe you would quickly lose your dislike for the West if you could once see it. . . . Wherever you direct your gaze, you see something great developing. Grandeur is the first characteristic of all western life." The people were cheerful and open-minded; free of the restraints of the East, they made friends with extraordinary ease.

Wisconsin seemed especially attractive to Schurz. To be sure, Milwaukee had not developed as well as Chicago; the larger city was too near. Moreover, there were too many Germans in Milwaukee, and whenever Germans were forced to live off other Germans in America, they did not do well. But once the territories to the west became states, Milwaukee would come into its own; it would provide a natural outlet for the new states. And the trip to Watertown was most agreeable. The little lakes, the wooded hills, the rapidly developing population—it was just the type of country he liked. Traveling the first seventeen miles by rail, he transferred to a stagecoach on the plank road which took him to his goal.[22]

Schurz did not say much about Watertown when he first visited it. But in spite of his unfavorable remarks about the number of Germans in Milwaukee, the sheer size of the German community in Watertown was something to think about. Immigrants could vote in Wisconsin within one year; the state seemed the perfect base for launching a political career.[23]

When Schurz returned to the East, he found that Margarethe was not well. Her back and chest bothered her, and Carl decided that a change of climate, a trip to Europe, would be beneficial. She had never been enthusiastic about the United States; perhaps a temporary return to the Old World, for which she would always continue to long, would help her recover.

Announcing his intended trip to Kinkel, Schurz sought to explain the political situation in the United States. The aftermath of the Kansas-Nebraska Act, the breakup of the old parties, and the rise of the antislavery and nativist movements had left their mark, so that he could no longer disregard the great issue that was threatening the stability of the Union. Repeating the advice about the revolutionary loan, he now added that nothing could be done for the European revolution until the slaveholders' influence in America had been checked. The mere mention of freedom frightened them.[24]

The Schurzes' trip to Europe was delayed for a while because Carl was now thinking of settling in Watertown after his return. He left Margarethe and the baby in Philadelphia while making arrangements to move his parents and sisters to Wisconson and ultimately decided to accompany them. Reaching Watertown after covering some six miles to the railroad by sleigh, he was again greatly impressed. What he saw strengthened his desire to establish his home there. The town had developed well since his previous visit. Much building was taking place, property values were rising, and he assured his wife that "much can be done here to our great advantage." In addition to its promising business and career prospects, the town seemed to offer an agreeable social life. The winter season had been enlivened by many balls, a German singing society was being organized, and an amateur theater was also in the planning stage. He was certain Watertown was the place for their future happiness.[25]

Just what it was that made Schurz think of Watertown rather than Indianapolis as a proper location for making his fortune is not quite clear. Never a good businessman, he was probably influenced by personal considerations as well as by imagined commercial advantages. The town, some forty-five miles northwest of Milwaukee, was pleasantly located; it contained large numbers of Germans, and members of his family as well as Emil Rothe, his former associate at the Eisenach congress, had already established themselves there. With its nearly ten thousand inhabitants, it was the second-largest city in the state, a town with a seemingly promising future. Schurz determined to grow up with it.[26]

The key to his expectations was a farm located north of the town center, 96 acres of good land and adjacent lots which he thought he could profitably subdivide. The way he figured it, if he could raise the $70 per acre required, within three years he would make $20,000–$25,000, even if immigration declined by one-third. He was convinced the land would yield 12–15 percent per annum and rise in value by 50 percent.[27]

Business was not the only reason for his decision. "After my return from Europe, I expect to go to Wisconsin," he explained to Kinkel. "I transferred some of my business interests there when on my last trip to the West. The German element is powerful in that State, the immigrants being so numerous, and they are striving for political recognition. They only lack leaders that are not bound by the restraints of money-getting. There is the place where I can find a sure, gradually expanding field for my work without truckling to the nativistic elements, and there, I hope, in time, to gain influence that may also become useful to our cause."[28]

His stay in Watertown was cut short. Mrs. Schurz had fallen ill again. Thinking it might be good for her to join her brother Heinrich at Madeira, he told her they were going to Europe for Agathe's health—he did not want to worry her unduly—and in April, the young couple, accompanied by their daughter, took the *Washington* to England.[29]

His trip to Europe in no way lessened his commitment to the United States. Kinkel was wrong to suppose that Schurz was coming back to Europe for good. "I love America. Everything around me vitally interests me; it is no longer strange to me," he declared. He had a horror of the "illusory fussiness" characterizing the life of professional refugees, and although he still avowed his devotion to his old home—Germany's fate, he asserted, was tied up with that of the United States— his lot had really been cast. He was becoming an American.[30]

In London, Schurz revisited all his old acquaintances and friends, Althaus, the Kinkels, Malwida von Meysenbug, and the various international revolutionaries. Only the Ronges caused trouble. Bertha had made false accusations concerning a diamond brooch, a family heirloom; her husband, the eccentric former Catholic priest who had founded his own church, had never been congenial to the freethinking Schurz. All in all, he found that much of the old revolutionary fervor had evaporated. Napoleon III was firmly established on his throne; reaction reigned supreme; and even in London the enthusiasm for Kossuth, whom he saw again, had totally vanished. All these circumstances confirmed his conviction that he had been correct in casting his lot with the rising American West.

It was true that Europe had its advantages. The theatrical performances and concerts were irresistible. Mrs. Kinkel took him to hear Wagner, to whose music she was violently opposed, but before the performance was over, she saw that her warnings had fallen on deaf ears. Schurz was utterly entranced; he remained a Wagnerian for the rest of his life. Not even the artistic life of England, however, not even *Tannhäuser*, could make up for the lack of political opportunities in the United Kingdom.[31]

When Margarethe's health did not improve in London, Carl decided to take her to Malvern, where he himself a few years earlier had benefited so much from the water cure. And instead of Madeira, he urged her family to take her to Switzerland; the mountain climate would do her good. In the meantime, he himself had to return to America. The farm he wanted in Watertown had become available, and he was anxious to buy. His wife could join her family in Germany.[32]

Schurz sailed for the United States on July 6. To leave without his wife was the hardest decision he ever had to make, he complained. But neither the heat—the thermometer stood at 100 degrees in New York—nor his loneliness dampened his enthusiasm for his adopted country. After taking care of some obligations in the East, he hurried to Watertown, where he found his parents in good health, his father puttering in the garden as usual. Only the business he had come for, the purchase of the farm, could not be settled. The owner had left town and would not be back for some time.

The wait convinced Schurz more than ever that he ought to stay in Watertown. Evidence of growth could be seen everywhere. Railroads were being built, and the newspapers predicted that the city would soon be the largest in the interior of the state. He would be able to do very well in Watertown, he assured his wife. With his international reputation, he would soon have an opportunity to occupy a prominent position there. Moreover, given the city's rapid development, he was certain that within five years he would be able to earn $40,000.

How to sell the idea to Margarethe, however, was a problem. To overcome her prejudices against the West, he spent much time describing the beauties of the country, his activities in laying out farms, his hunting trips, and his concern for the crops. So many Germans had made the city their home, he told her, that were it not for the many varied dialects she might think she was in the old country. Even operatic entertainment was available—yes, Watertown offered operatic concerts—and she would not lack company. Strodtmann had just arrived, full of enthusiasm for a free-love community in northern Wisconsin.

In describing the attractions of his new surroundings, Schurz outdid himself. His enthusiasm for America was such that he even thought American farms superior to those run by Germans. The open spaces of Wisconsin, covered with turf, reminded him of the open planted sections in the parks of London. And he had completely changed his mind about Milwaukee. He now considered it the finest American city he had ever seen. Except for his wife's absence, everything appeared perfect.[33]

Late in September he finally settled his business affairs. Buying a farm of 89 acres and several adjacent lots—the total price was $15,700—he took out a mortgage for $8,500. In the expectation of subdividing the lots, he was hopeful of making $50,000 within three years, while his debts would not have to be fully paid until 1861.[34]

But his first love was not business. While laying out his new farm, he heard of the fall of Sevastapol. Europe aflame! The farm, the financial arrangements, all were forgotten as he realized his isolation from the centers of world politics. What would he do if only he were at the head of affairs! "Why must I sit here—a mere nonentity occupied with miserable plans for making money, although my head is full of ideas and the consciousness of inexhaustible strength—while out there momentous decisions are made . . . ," he complained to Margarethe. "To be condemned to sit here and look on!" But of course Watertown did offer some possibilities. It was not long before he was asked to participate in the political campaign of 1855.

Schurz's stay in Watertown that fall was unexpectedly delayed. Just as he was ready to leave, he was incapacitated by an accident. On his way to the farm, his horse stumbled. It fell on his left leg, and for several days he was unable to walk.

While laid up because of his leg, Schurz did a lot of reading. Heine and history occupied much of his time, but, anxious though he was to return to his family, he was still contemplating the future of the city. Its prospects seemed better than ever.

His two sisters had started a millinery establishment; people were making money with amazing speed; and wagon after wagon filled with wheat came to town to find a ready market. Above all, he loved his farm. It was so beautiful. "We are all quite enraptured by the place on the former Jackson farm where we live," he assured Margarethe. "On the left the stream, shining out between tall trees; directly in front of me, the town with its friendly white houses; beyond and to my right, wooded hills and a luscious strip of green meadow land." He was very much encouraged to think that they they would be happy there, much happier than in Europe. Was it not true that the police in Prussia had gone so far as to harass even her?[35]

At last, he was on his legs again, still limping but ready to leave. Delayed by various problems—the threshing machine did not come, contracts for the lots he was leasing had to be signed, and notaries were too busy with the election to transfer the mortgages—he finally returned to Philadelphia early in November. After a new delay occasioned by Dümmig's reluctance to come to terms about the termination of their business association, Schurz was ready to sail. It was high time; he confessed to Margarethe that he was so anxious to be reunited with her and the baby that it cost him an effort of will not simply to forget all his business obligations and depart at once. Finally, on December 17, he arrived in London, where he rejoined his family at the Kinkels' house.[36]

To be reunited with Margarethe was delightful, but her stay in Europe had not helped to improve her physical condition. Pale and coughing, she gave Carl cause for worry. Little Agathe, on the other hand, was doing very well. She was already fluent in both English and German. Heinrich Meyer finally invited the family to join him in Switzerland, a suggestion Schurz welcomed with pleasure. The mountain climate might cure his wife.[37]

While waiting for papers to travel through France, Schurz wrote articles for the British press and again renewed his acquaintances in London. His friend Althaus had recently been widowed, and Schurz sought to console him. He also associated with Malwida von Meysenbug's friend, the Russian revolutionary Alexander Herzen, who considered him "the best of all German emigrants." To Herzen, too, he repeated his commitment to America.[38]

At last in February the necessary papers were ready. The family set out for the Maison-aux-Bains at Montreux, which exceeded all their expectations. As Schurz later wrote of his arrival at the resort, "a scene presented itself which was beyond all description. The moon was the brightest I had ever seen. . . . Before our gaze the lake spread out many miles in extent. A small boat, with sails like swallow's wings, glided lazily over the bright, shimmering water streaks in which the moon mirrored itself. Over . . . on the opposite shore . . . rose the dark mountain walls of Savoy; far to the left gleamed the white peak of the Dent du Midi; directly before us, projected into the lake, was the celebrated castle of Chillon. . . . We held our breaths in ecstasy. . . ." Not wanting to lose a moment of the idyll, they sat down a while before knocking at the door of the hotel.

The vacation was a complete success. Heinrich Meyer turned out to be a good friend. Like his older brother Adolph, he was most congenial, and Schurz developed a close relationship with him and his charming young wife, Emilie. As Margarethe's health improved, the stay in Switzerland became more and more pleasant, so that in later years Schurz would remember it as a perfect interlude. He had rarely been so happy.[39]

But even the joys of Switzerland could not make Schurz forget Watertown. His farm beckoned; a new house was being built according to his specifications. His heart was in America. He returned to London in May, stayed there for a few weeks, and in June sailed for the United States. This time his family accompanied him.[40] He was determined to succeed in his quest for money and fame in Wisconsin.

V

Antislavery and the Beginning of Ethnic Politics

SCHURZ'S TRIP IN 1856 to Europe had not in any way diminished his enthusiasm for America, and especially for the American West. Watertown had caught his fancy. He was certain that the city had a great future. New houses were going up everywhere, streets were being graded, and workmen were kept busy implementing an ordinance of the city council requiring crosswalks to be built of brick or stone. Noting that three railroad lines were under construction, one to Madison, another to Fond du Lac, and a third to Columbus, all scheduled to be opened to traffic by winter, Schurz convinced himself that the town was bound to become an important railroad center. With well-to-do immigrants, ceaseless commercial activity, and the relocation of the county seat in the city, Watertown showed great promise. Not even his disappointment at the failure of the contractor to finish the house he had commissioned prior to his departure could stifle Schurz's optimism about his surroundings.[1]

Schurz's illusions about Watertown made him an enthusiastic booster. He was busily engaged in selling lots, confident that their value would speedily increase. As commissioner for improvements, he attempted to dispose of municipal bonds to his relatives and friends abroad. In addition, he assumed the presidency of an insurance company, was appointed a notary public, and began studying law. Meanwhile his farm provided him with many of the necessities of life. The prototype of a Latin farmer, he resumed the study of classical literature, not merely for its own sake but for its possible bearing on American politics, for he had never given up the idea of a political career.[2]

It was in Watertown that Schurz laid the foundation for his spectacular rise in American politics. He had chosen his residence partially because of the presence of so large a number of Germans in the vicinity, and if his assessment of the city's economic opportunities had been erroneous, his political instincts proved correct. From the very beginning, he realized that his political future in the United States was dependent on his appeal to his fellow countrymen. But the German-Americans, like other immigrants, had generally been loyal Democrats. The party's very name attracted them, and the Whigs had often made common cause with the nativists.[3] This fact created a problem for Schurz. It also gave him his great chance.

When Schurz first arrived in America, he was not hostile to the Democratic party. During his visit to Washington, he sought out leading Democrats, and it was not surprising that in October 1855, Watertown party faithful asked him to deliver a speech for the Democratic incumbent, Governor William A. Barstow. Yet he declined. It was not that he failed to appreciate the honor—"I realize more and more what a wide field is open to me here and that, in a way, I need only grasp the opportunities presenting themselves in order to succeed," he wrote to his wife— but he came to the conclusion that his future did not lie with the Jacksonians.[4] The newly organized Republicans, with their platform of opposition to slavery, or slavery extension, were more to his liking. If the Germans were not yet prepared for a switch in allegiance, he would have to do his best to convert them.

That Schurz was opposed to slavery was natural. As an enthusiastic supporter of the liberal German revolution of 1848, he could hardly have remained immune to the abolitionist fervor then sweeping progressive Europe and the world, especially not as Kinkel's student. The professor was a great admirer of William Wilber- force, the British antislavery activist, and during his trip to the United States had been accused of establishing too intimate a relationship with the abolitionists.[5] Despite Schurz's enthusiasm for America, from the very beginning he deplored the existence of human bondage in the supposed land of freedom. "There is only one shrill discord," he wrote in describing his first impressions of the new country, "and that is slavery in the South." Although in Washington he was still willing to confer with the democratic apologists for the institution, he soon came to the conclusion that "whatever may be the considerations that demand compromise, there can be but one question of freedom" and that the influence of the slave power must be curtailed.[6]

Like most opponents of slavery in the nineteenth century, Schurz was not free from all prejudices. He believed that tropical climates were deleterious to self- government and to the prosperity of Europeans. "I would not like to live in a country that is in the hands of a mixed race of Indians and Spaniards," he warned his brother-in-law, who was considering the advisability of sending a nephew to South America. He considered the people there "lazy through and through" and was convinced that strangers would soon sink to their level. But his prejudices were essentially environmental, and he certainly thought blacks entitled to equal rights. Human slavery was abhorrent to him.[7]

Just when Schurz decided to join the Republican party is difficult to establish. Determined from the very beginning to participate actively in politics, he carried at first letters of introduction to the Democratic leaders long accustomed to obtain the immigrants' allegiance. But while still in Philadelphia, he met the famous Quaker abolitionist Lucretia Mott, who must have reinforced his loathing for slavery, and when in 1854 he traveled to Belleville and met Friedrich Hecker, he probably heard further tirades against the slaveholders. Chester Easum and others have surmised that the visit to Hecker may have helped to convert Schurz to Republicanism. In view of the German revolutionary's ill temper and poor state of health at the time, however, it is doubtful whether he did anything more than strengthen his guest's opinions.[8] It is certain that by January 1855, Schurz was severely condemning the Kansas-Nebraska bill. He denounced it as the result of

Stephen A. Douglas's "unscrupulous ambition," although less than two years earlier, because of his hope for help for the European revolution, he had still shown an interest in the senator's expansionist speeches.[9] The Republican party was organized to oppose the abrogation of the Missouri Compromise confining slavery to territories south of 36°30'; when the party emerged as the principal opponent of the Democrats, who were increasingly identified with the slaveholders, he had no trouble deciding where his loyalties lay.

It was in connection with his work for the Republicans that Schurz developed the technique that was to be his chief contribution to American political life, the appeal to ethnic factors. To be sure, other German-American political leaders, Judge John B. Stallo and Friedrich Hassaurek in Ohio, as well as Francis Hoffman, Friedrich Hecker, and Gustave Koerner in Illinois, had already been active among their countrymen, but none of them succeeded as well as Schurz. He was young, famous because of the liberation of Kinkel, and spoke both English and German fluently. It was an effective combination.

The politics of ethnic appeal had originally been used indiscriminately by the Democrats, and the fact that most immigrants tended to remain loyal to the Jacksonian party made it exceedingly profitable for the small band of German Republicans to use their opponents' techniques against their inventors. They knew that they had to obtain many of their votes from habitual Democrats; the German-Americans were a perfect target for this campaign, and whether or not it succeeded as completely as Schurz and some party leaders imagined made little difference. Every vote counted; the belief that German voters could, and at times did, affect the balance of power was widespread, and what is believed to be true is often more important than what is really true. So astute a politician as Abraham Lincoln subsidized a German newspaper, and as Wisconsin, Illinois, Indiana, and Ohio all had large German minorities and were apparently crucial to Republican success, it was natural that Republican leaders in the Northwest sought to influence as many German-Americans as possible.

Their need was Schurz's great opportunity. Although the persistence of ethnicity in voting behavior had not yet been systematically studied, it was already obvious. And even if the Germans were politically less homogeneous than other immigrant groups, substantial portions of them tended to sympathize with some of Schurz's most deeply held convictions.[10]

When Schurz returned from Europe in the summer of 1856, the presidential campaign was in full progress. The Democrats had nominated James Buchanan on a platform endorsing the Kansas-Nebraska Act; the Know-Nothings, the nativist anti-Catholics, put forward ex-President Millard Fillmore, who was soon to be endorsed by a remnant of the Whigs; and the Republicans, organized only some two years before, chose John C. Frémont, the famous explorer, as their standard-bearer. Their platform denounced "those twin relics of barbarism—Polygamy and Slavery" and advocated their prohibition in the territories.

Schurz had sought to influence the campaign even before he left Europe.

Writing to his Philadelphia friends that a German radical named Dittenhoefer was among the delegates to the Republican national convention in the city, he asked young Fritz Tiedemann, the doctor's son, to ask him to offer a resolution condemning rebellion as treason and treason as a crime. That would show the South not to prattle about legality![11]

After his arrival in Watertown, his participation in the campaign became more personal. Sitting on a dry goods box in front of one of the stores on Main Street, he sought to convince his Democratic fellow countrymen of the errors of their ways, and it was not long before the leaders of the Republican party in Wisconsin heard about the unusual German immigrant in their midst who might be of help to them. The man who launched Schurz's political career in the United States was Louis P. Harvey, a talented manufacturer from Shopiere who took a great interest in educational matters. He was then a member of the state legislature and later governor of the state, a term of office that would be cut short in 1862 when he drowned in the Mississippi River. Approaching Schurz to deliver a speech to the Germans in Jefferson, Harvey first met with objections. According to the speaker's recollections, he was too shy to accept but consented to be present at the meeting. When the proceedings were in full progress, the chairman announced that Carl Schurz of Watertown would speak in German. Whatever the truth of this story—shyness was not one of Schurz's most notable characteristics—Harvey remained his close political collaborator, and soon the newspapers were carrying stories of Schurz's heroism in Kinkel's rescue. Horace Rublee, another Republican politician of note and owner of the Madison *State Journal*, apparently saw to their distribution.

Schurz now began a routine that he was to follow for years to come. Devoting all his spare energy to the campaign, he addressed audiences in all parts of the state. His speeches were generally still in German, but he was becoming well known, and the Republicans discovered that they had enlisted an orator of unusual ability and power. Gustave Koerner, the famous German-American leader from Belleville, was deeply impressed, especially with Schurz's manner and conversation. "He who has once met him will never forget him," the Illinois politician stated. Although Schurz was not yet a citizen and still a newcomer to the Republican ranks—on one occasion, the Milwaukee *Sentinel* referred to him as "Mr. SCHWARTZ of Jefferson"—the party made him its candidate for the assembly. He was beginning to make his mark.[12]

It was inevitable that Schurz's first try for public office would fail. Watertown was Democratic, 1856 was a Democratic year, and he lost by 226 to 174 votes. It was, however, not a bad beginning, especially as the Republicans won in the state. Some of his fellow countrymen might throw stale eggs at him and curse him as a "verdammter Republikaner," but others were beginning to listen to him.[13]

Schurz was proud of his achievements. Describing the excitement of the campaign to his brother-in-law, he stressed America's superiority over the Old World. "You in your decrepit Europe can hardly understand anymore how a great idea can stir up the masses to their depths and how an enthusiastic fight for principles can displace all other interests . . . ," he wrote. "It is the first time in seven years that I have taken part in politics—in a time which arouses even the sleepiest and in a cause which is second to none in the world in reach and greatness." The party of freedom, he was sure, despite its defeat had shown so much strength that it could look forward confidently to future success. And while he thought it was easier to win over native-born Americans to the new idea—he believed the Germans and Irish, by mere force of inertia, were often still "fast anchored" by stupid prejudices—he boasted that Frémont had received upwards of twenty-five thousand German votes in Wisconsin. "As for myself," he concluded, "my brief activity brought me such widespread influence that I shall probably not keep out of official life very long."[14]

Kinkel, too, received a full description of Schurz's involvement in the politics of his new country. Predicting that soon there were going to be only two political organizations in the Union, a Northern antislavery and a Southern proslavery party, he considered it likely that the contradictions within the Democracy might well lead to its breakup during Buchanan's administration. He even considered a clash of arms possible, although he thought the North had little cause for worry. Its material superiority would decide the issue. Above all, he rejoiced over Frémont's victory in Wisconsin. "Much persevering and devoted work was done," he asserted, "and I honestly did my share. During my short activity I gained a relatively great influence and I shall soon have a voice in the affairs of Wisconsin."

Schurz was also proud of his development of oratorical techniques. Obliged to appear a great deal in public, he had worked until his voice and limbs had become more supple, and he was beginning to understand the use of pathos. "I have quite often succeeded in rousing my audience to the fire of enthusiasm," he informed his old teacher, "and I am no longer diffident when I wish to appeal to their sentiment. In short, I have gained courage as an orator, and I hope, should I enter the legislature next year, to be able to accomplish something."[15]

Pride in his activities and imagined success were not the only satisfactions Schurz secured from the campaign. The process of his Americanization had also gone on very rapidly. "I feel more and more that my lot is cast on this side of the ocean," he wrote to Althaus, whom he was trying to induce to come to the United States. His mastery of the English language was fast becoming complete. The foreign tongue no longer troubled him; in many things, he found English even more effective and convenient than German. Karl Schurz of Germany was becoming Carl Schurz of Wisconsin.[16]

It was just about this time that his new house was finished, and it did not take him long to feel comfortable in it. As Claude M. Fuess has pointed out, it was typical of the architecture of the period, "with hideous rococo decorations and no symmetry." Located on a pleasant eminence north of the city, however, it delighted Schurz. "Anything pleasanter than Margarethe's and my suite cannot be

Carl Schurz Home, Watertown, Wisconsin (Courtesy of Watertown Historical Society)

conceived," he wrote to Althaus. "These rooms are on the ground floor, to the right of the corridor. Margarethe usually sits in her light bay window, which is shaded by the veranda roof, with views of the city, the woods, and the hills directly in front of her. My windows, the one directly opposite my writing-table and the other on my left, open upon the yard, the farm buildings, the river, and the woods behind. The rooms are fairly spacious, very high, not without a certain elegance and at the same time liveable and homelike." He was proud of his house, its unhampered view over stream and town and the encircling hills before it and the oak forest with small clearings in the back. The two high rooms on the ground floor were his pride and joy. While Margarethe was taking care of little Agathe in one, he liked to sit at his desk covered with books, especially Blackstone and Kent, in the other. He even enjoyed the fierce snow storms which sang "a many voiced song in the notched pointed arches" of the veranda.[17]

The Schurzes did not lack company in Watertown. Their home was a magnet for visitors from all over the country and from Europe, and they had so many relatives in the vicinity that their social life was very active. Uncle Jacob owned the local Germania House; sister Toni, who had married her cousin Edmund Jüssen, lived in nearby Columbus, and the elder Schurzes had a house downtown at Jones and 2nd streets. Their son could often be seen playing billiards in the Buena Vista House. In spite of his unpopular politics, he was respected as a wealthy and desirable fellow citizen, a reputation he sought to uphold as he and his wife were observed driving through the city in an expensive carriage.

Watertown also offered varied diversions. Its German population had established singing societies as a matter of course; the whole family joined in the performance of various operas, with Schurz doubling as conductor and pianist, and theatrical troupes enlivened the winter season. The Schurzes even gave masked balls at their home, and on frosty mornings neighbors could see lords and ladies, knights, Turks, and pirates sleighing home from the festivities in their exotic costumes.

After moving into her new house, Margarethe, who had been interested in Friedrich Froebel's kindergarten establishments in Germany, sought to found similar institutions in America. Gathering at first members of the Schurz and Jüssen clans, she eventually expanded the experiment, which became one of the first of its kind in the United States. Her own house was too far from the center of town, but her in-laws' home in the city was available, and the first kindergarten was started there.[18]

Early in March, 1857, the Schurzes' second child, another daughter, was born. Like her grandmother, she was called Marianne, although her parents and friends always nicknamed her Pussy. It was a difficult birth; Margarethe almost bled to death, and her health remained frail. The proud father described his new daughter as having the same large eyes as her sister, but he believed that eventually she would be prettier than Handy.[19]

Shortly after Marianne's birth, her father undertook a business trip to the East.

Much to his satisfaction, when he arrived at the Prescott House in New York, the proprietor was so delighted at the presence of so distinguished a guest that at breakfast he brought out a bottle of champagne. Schurz drank it with pleasure. "My fame is now almost seven years old, and in the seventh year it still brings me a bottle of champagne," he mused.

When he returned to Watertown, his wife still had not recovered. Ministering to her needs—he even had to carry her up and down the stairs—he was soon able to report that she was improving. Life became pleasant again, and in later years he would remember his Wisconsin years as his "youth in America." Within a short time, he had the satisfaction of winning his first elective office, alderman for the fifth ward and one of the county supervisors. Exceedingly proud of his success, he reported it in detail to his in-laws in Hamburg.[20]

But he had higher ambitions, and when his friend Harvey held out the possibility of a nomination for lieutenant governor, Schurz was delighted. No matter that he was not yet even an American citizen, a German name for second place on the Republican ticket would constitute a powerful appeal to the ordinarily Democratic German-Americans, and by November his final citizenship papers would make him eligible for office. "I'll write to Harvey that I'll accept the nomination, if he thinks that he'll be able to arrange things in the Republican convention in such a way that I can be sure of obtaining the nomination during the first ballots with a *significant* majority . . . ," he wrote to Margarethe from New York. "I know that Harvey will do everything, and it would not be surprising if on November 5 your husband would be able to introduce himself as Lieutenant Governor of Wisconsin." She would surely be pleased, not least because of the Hamburg clan. "Their eyes will pop and they'll imagine the thing is more than it really is," he added.[21]

The next few months became a period of busy preparation. Active as an alderman on the Common Council's Committees on the Judiciary, Streets and Bridges and the Committee on Schools and Education, he kept his name before the public. And in spite of his declaration to his wife that he would not actively seek office, a ritual statement he was to repeat again and again as long as he was in politics, he arranged for a Republican subsidy for a local German newspaper. After an unsuccessful attempt to take over the Watertown *Anzeiger*, which severed relations with him after one week, he turned to a new journal, the *Volkszeitung*, and secured help for another Republican sheet, the Watertown *Chronicle*. Harvey sought support for Schurz in other parts of the state—Senator James R. Doolittle was one of the converts— and when in August the young Watertown Republican traveled to Madison as a delegate to the state convention, he had reason for optimism.[22]

To become a delegate to the convention at which he served on the committee on nominations had been comparatively easy. Watertown was so solidly Democratic that the few Republicans could be easily influenced. To be recognized throughout the state was more difficult, but Harvey had carefully prepared matters. The Republicans were in need of a German name on the ticket to refute charges of collaboration with the Know-Nothings, and Schurz's revolutionary past in Germany had an appeal to the sizable faction then in revolt against the federal courts in connection with the Joshua Glover fugitive slave case. After a few names had been brought forward as running mates for Alexander W. Randall, the party's choice for governor, Sherman M. Booth, the controversial abolitionist editor famous for his part in the fugitive slave controversy, delivered a ringing speech placing Schurz's name in nomination. Although the delegates hardly knew him, Booth's recital of Schurz's deeds during the German revolution impressed them. Mindful of the party's need for German support, they promptly nominated him.

At first, they were disappointed with their choice. As Schurz came forward, one of the delegates, A. M. Thomson, recalled, "the impression was not favorable. His tall, lank figure and long legs were heightened by his dress, which was seedy, threadbare, and ill fitting. His coat sleeves and his trouser legs were much too short, and his Emersonian nose, adorned with the ever present spectacles, gave him a novel and picturesque appearance." A colleague sitting next to Thomson whispered, "I guess we have done it now for certain." But he soon changed his mind. Schurz had spoken only a few words before he caught the audience's undivided attention. "If the delegates were astounded at his uncouth appearance, they were amazed at his eloquence and the charm and the power of his masterly oratory. When he left the platform he also left the impression upon the mind of everyone present that a man of splendid intellectual abilities had appeared among them, challenging their criticism and winning their admiration."[23]

Schurz made the best of his opportunity. "Mr. President," he said in his acceptance speech, "I am well aware that what little service I have rendered the Republican cause cannot entitle me to so prominent and honorable a position as you have awarded me. I would prefer, for myself, to fight in the ranks as a common soldier. But if this position has been given me, as I believe it has been, as a mark of respect for that solid column of Germans who have joined the Republican cause, in its great effort for the expurgation of slavery in this land, I accept it as such and thank you for it . . . ."[24]

It was not only the ethnic approach which marked Schurz's entrance into state politics. In referring to the expurgation rather than to the limitation of slavery, he clearly sided with the radicals. Considering his revolutionary antecedents in Europe, this identification was not surprising.

The reception of the nomination was not unfavorable. "FOR GOVERNOR, ALEXANDER W. RANDALL, of Milwaukee, FOR LIEUTENANT GOVERNOR, CHARLES SCHURTZ, of Jefferson," proclaimed the Milwaukee *Sentinel*, the leading Republican paper in the state. Admitting that he did not have the pleasure of Schurz's personal acquaintance—his ignorance of the spelling of the name made this very clear—the editor stated that the nominee was known as a "thoroughly educated and accomplished German citizen" who had shown his faith in Republican principles by steady work for their success in "that hotbed of Hunker Democracy," Watertown. Bernard Domschke, the radical German editor of the Milwaukee *Atlas*, predictably welcomed the nomination of his friend. The Madison *State Journal* printed highly fictitious accounts of the rescue of Kinkel, and German papers all over the country expressed their satisfaction. Even the hostile Watertown *Democrat* conceded that the ticket was "moderately respectable as to ability."[25]

But it did not take the Democrats long to find fault. The fact that Schurz's final citizenship papers had not yet come through, although he would be a citizen by the time of his hoped-for induction to office, was a ready-made issue for the opposition journals. They exploited it fully. Accusing the Republicans of utter disregard of constitutional principles by nominating an unnaturalized foreigner, they referred to the candidate as "Shirts," attacked him as a traitor in Germany—a patriot would fight at home, but a rebel would run away, said the Chicago *American*—and finally labeled Kinkel an imposter whom Schurz had let loose on society.[26]

Schurz fought back. He criss-crossed the state, speaking both in English and German in villages and hamlets as well as in the principal cities. He stressed the necessity of refuting Buchanan's notion that slavery was national as well as Douglas's disgraceful doctrines of popular sovereignty. Freedom must be sustained wherever it was endangered. "I don't know whether I have been able to instill into your hearts that deep anxiety for liberty which fills mine," he said at Madison. "You are the spoiled children of fortune. . . . You have grown up nursed by the blessings of self-government, and neither you nor hardly your fathers have seen the day when it was otherwise. . . . But . . . I have seen despotism and felt its scourge." In spite of indications that the Germans were not so easily convinced, he was sanguine about the outcome. After all, the Republicans were in the majority in Wisconsin, and the Democrats had refused to nominate the popular German, Dr. Franz Huebschmann. Schurz thought he would surely win and "then advance at a single leap from the position of alderman in Watertown to that of lieutenant governor of Wisconsin." His Hamburg relatives could be proud of their brother-in-law.[27]

But he was to be disappointed. To be sure, Randall was elected by a narrow margin; Schurz, however, lost to his Democratic opponent, E.D. Campbell, by a mere handful of votes. The onset of the Panic of 1857 and the Republicans' endorsement of black suffrage had reduced the party's vote; the popularity of Schurz's opponent and presumably some lingering nativism had done the rest. For a while he sought to challenge the returns, but the costs were too high and the prospects of success too uncertain. And, as a political associate wrote to him, although he might have been defeated, he had not been politically ruined.

Still, Schurz was very disappointed. Calling his defeat "a disgrace to the name of Wisconsin," he wanted it clearly understood that the Germans had done well. The result would have a bad effect on them; it would be difficult to lead them again. Nevertheless, he himself felt like a man who had done his duty. He was ready to do it again.[28]

In spite of his disappointment, Schurz knew very well that his position was not unfavorable. The party owed him a great debt, and he was determined not to let it forget him. Although he turned down the proffered position of secretary of the state senate, in the summer of 1858 he was happy to accept an appointment to the Board of Regents of the University of Wisconsin. Other honors and emoluments would undoubtedly follow. His political career had been launched.[29]

His electoral defeat was not the only setback Schurz suffered in 1857. The economic downswing which began at that time affected him very badly. Watertown's prospects of rapid development were doomed, and the lots which he had bought on credit at an inflated price proved to be a great burden. Pursued by his creditors, he was unable to discharge his obligations, which continued to cause him trouble until after the Civil War. It is probable that much of Margarethe's money was thus lost, a fact which undoubtedly caused him great anguish. He now had more reason than ever to prove to the Hamburg family that he was somebody. Fortunately, a portion of his wife's inheritance was safely invested in land in Germany—property which was not affected by the panic.[30]

Schurz's straitened economic circumstances led him to seek new sources of income, and he found that one of the best ways of putting his talents to use was to lecture to audiences for pay. The lyceum movement was then in full swing; a mixture between a speakers' bureau and an institute for adult education, it featured prominent lecturers who entertained audiences throughout the country. His first lecture was delivered on January 20, 1858, before the Watertown YMCA. "Democracy and Despotism in France" was his subject, and even the Watertown *Democrat*, which had steadfastly opposed him during the election, gave him favorable publicity. He repeated the lecture in other towns and made use of the opportunity to become better known. Exhausting though it was, lecturing was an activity which he was not to give up for many years to come, but it was only a sideline. In July he turned down an offer of a professorship at the University of Wisconsin on the grounds that leaving Watertown would interfere with his efforts to extricate himself from his business embarrassments.[31]

In spite of his misfortunes, Schurz remained optimistic, at least in his letters to Europe. Because he had held on to his property, he asserted, he had not lost much—a wholly mistaken notion, as it turned out—and he again compared European pessimism with American ebullience. "Never say die" was the American motto, he explained to Kinkel, to whom he detailed his success as a lecturer. He confessed to his old professor of rhetoric that, although he was adept at debate, he would never become a good extemporaneous speaker. When he prepared his material carefully beforehand, however, he was successful. Still, he thought he had gained more friends among the Americans than among the Germans. Too many of the latter were jealous of him.

In his political analyses, he showed considerable foresight. Still convinced that the struggle between slavery and freedom might come to a head during the Buchanan administration, he thought an appeal to arms possible. And since he had become a colonel in the local militia, he was not too perturbed about the eventuality. He had always had a secret liking for military exploits.

It does not seem that the panic had affected his pleasant home life too adversely. Mrs. Schurz was in better health than before her move to Wisconsin, and the Schurz's house was still the center of social life in Watertown. Delighted with his two growing children, Schurz enjoyed his domesticity. His parents had moved in with him. They were living in the old style, grandmother Schurz working in the dairy and grandfather busying himself with his flowers and his garden. The vegetables and fruits he raised came in handy in view of the shortage of money, which for a time reduced the population to virtual barter.[32]

In March, Schurz and his wife traveled east to dispose of some of their real estate. Margarethe stayed in Philadelphia, while Carl sought to conclude his business in New York. When he came back to Philadelphia, he fell ill, so that his return to Wisconsin was delayed. Then, when he finally reached Watertown, first his wife and then he himself were again laid low. He caught the chicken pox, an unpleasant experience for an adult. Fortunately, he recovered fairly rapidly.[33]

Schurz had fully regained his health when he was called upon for another lecture. The Achaean Society of Beloit College invited him to deliver a commencement address, which he gave on July 12 in the old Congregational stone church in Beloit. Entitled "America and Americanism," it emphasized the importance of the American ideal of freedom for the entire world and served to strengthen his reputation as an accomplished orator. The wealthy New York abolitionist Gerrit Smith liked it so much that he invited Schurz to take part in the political campaign of 1858 in the Empire State. He was becoming well known, outside of Wisconsin as well as at home.[34]

Schurz's spreading fame was important to him, not only to satisfy his need for self-esteem, which was never small, but also to help him politically. His loss of the lieutenant governorship had by no means ended his political career. Although in April he was defeated for reelection as supervisor, he was still a member of the Common Council, and he continued to exert influence in the councils of the party. He advised the publication of a strong address to the Republican members of the legislature to define their position "in the great slavery issue with moderation but unequivocally." Such a course would have a great effect on the next campaign, in which nothing ought to be left undone to restore the "impaired ascendancy of the Republicans of Wisconsin." Because he thought the local Republican hopeful for Congress had no chance, he opposed his candidacy and was proven correct when the election returns came in.

The national fate of the party concerned him also. Above all, he was anxious to prevent any endorsement of Douglas, a course of action which had been suggested by some Eastern Republicans after the Little Giant's break with Buchanan.

Douglas's differences with the President about the proposed proslavery Lecompton constitution for Kansas did not impress Schurz. He wholeheartedly supported the Illinois Republicans' refusal to follow Eastern advice and proposed a convention of all Western party members at Chicago to strengthen the organization in Illinois.[35]

The Republicans had to take Schurz seriously. His defeat had so angered the German-Americans that a revolt was brewing in Wisconsin. On August 21 the editors of the state's German Republican newspapers met in Milwaukee to draft resolutions indicting the Randall administration. The Germans had become Republicans because of principle, they asserted in an address drawn up at the occasion, and they did not relish the favor shown to corruption while "true and good men were unceremoniously thrown aside." It was a thinly veiled threat, and Schurz's loyalty to the party was more important for it than ever.

The party did not forget him. When Schurz arrived at the Third District Convention, he was put on the Committee of Resolutions and Credentials. At the state convention in Madison in October, he became chairman of the Committee on Resolutions and signed an address to the people of Wisconsin about the importance of the coming elections. Then, as in the previous year, he sought to rally voters to the ticket by speaking to audiences in English and German. It was a strenuous campaign, especially since he was now in demand outside of Wisconsin as well.[36]

Eighteen fifty-eight was a year of decision in Illinois, where Stephen A. Douglas was fighting against Abraham Lincoln for the retention of his Senate seat. The German element in the state was important; as in Wisconsin, it had largely been Democratic, and a change in its allegiance might well determine the outcome of the election. Accordingly, the state committee asked Schurz for assistance. His speeches might have a good effect. He hastened to accept the invitation.

Schurz's most important address in Illinois that year was a speech at Chicago on September 28 before the Republican Ratification Meeting at Mechanics Hall. His theme was the irrepressible conflict between slavery and freedom, the certainty of victory, and the inevitable doom of the "peculiar institution." Lincoln was right; a house divided against itself could not stand. Was there not already a small antislavery movement in the border states, a portent of things to come? Douglas's sophistries were merely a sham. His doctrine of popular sovereignty, the right of settlers to decide whether a territory should be free or slave, meant that slavery was legal where not prohibited by positive legislation; real popular sovereignty, on the contrary, would favor freedom. Did not the senator know that all previous compromises had failed? The Democratic party was completely controlled by the slaveholders, but time and the spirit of the age was against them, so that a Republican victory was inevitable.

Widely reported and favorably commented upon, the speech greatly enhanced Schurz's prestige. As he assured his friend Althaus, it was read from Maine to Minnesota, reprinted in a million copies, and praised extensively. "If I mention to you the fact that my name has penetrated beyond the borders of Wisconsin and the Western States during the last fight and that I have won a national reputation, I do not speak of this fact boastfully, but because I know that it will give you pleasure," he wrote.[37] Modesty never restrained him.

It was during his trip to Illinois that Schurz first met Abraham Lincoln. After delivering his Chicago speech in English, he traveled to the interior of the state to make several addresses in German. As he later remembered it, shortly before reaching Quincy he noticed a great commotion in the railroad car. Lincoln had come in. "I saw a tall man towering far above those surrounding him," he recalled,

> reaching out a large hand this way and that way to meet other hands eager to grasp his. It was "Old Abe". He seemed to know everybody and everybody knew him. It was like a meeting of old village neighbors. When the first rush subsided, I was introduced to him. There he was, looking down upon me from his altitude of six feet four. A homely, deeply furrowed, swarthy, haggard face, topped with a somewhat battered stovepipe hat; deep-set, melancholy eyes, from time to time illuminated with a merry twinkle; a large mouth with a kind smile; his lank ungainly body clad in a rusty black dress coat with sleeves that might have been a little longer, but the arms so long that one would think the sleeves could not be possibly long enough for them; black pantaloons going down almost to his gigantic feet. On his left arm he carried a gray woolen shawl to do the service of an overcoat. In a somewhat high-pitched but pleasant voice, he began to speak to me as if we had been acquainted a long time, and in a few minutes I felt as if I had actually known him all my life. Nothing could be heartier and more contagious than his laughter.

On the next day, Schurz sat near Lincoln on the platform and with fascination watched the debate with Douglas.[38]

Thus began a relationship that was to be of great importance for Schurz. That he liked Lincoln is beyond question; that the Civil War president reciprocated this feeling is also probable. It is of course not true that the two resembled each other, as has been asserted,[39] but in their mutual aims they were similar. Like Lincoln, Schurz was resolutely opposed to slavery, and if in 1858 he was more radical than his new acquaintance, he was not very far ahead of him. Like Lincoln, he too believed in the power of ideas, the strength of principles. And if Lincoln was not quite as disingenuous as Schurz in disclaiming political artifice, both men knew well how to advance their own interests. The principal differences were Lincoln's consummate skill, his far better sense of timing, and his ability to disregard personal factors.

Schurz completed his speaking engagements in Illinois and returned to Wisconsin to support the Republican ticket. Concentrating on Milwaukee, where the German vote seemed particularly important in the congressional elections, he spoke repeatedly, both in English and in German, for Judge John F. Potter, the party's candidate for the First Congressional District, who later became famous for nearly dueling with Roger Pryor of Virginia. Schurz's efforts were successful, and the party widely credited him and the Germans with the victory. "We are sure every Republican will agree with us," wrote the Milwaukee *Sentinel*, "that . . . to no one is a larger share of the credit due, than to the gifted and eloquent Carl Schurz. He came among us on Saturday and remained till the morning of election day; and in that interval, he wrought wonders. He spoke to meeting after meeting of his German countrymen . . . with a power, eloquence, and effect which proved irresistible." Pointing out that the three wards in question, in which four-fifths of the voters were German, two years earlier had given the Democratic candidate for Congress a majority of 1,652, the paper emphasized that this time that majority had been reduced to a mere 465. It welcomed Schurz to the city and rejoiced that he was about to make his home there.

After the election, at a great meeting in Milwaukee's Albany Hall, Schurz delivered yet another speech. Warning that the Germans were faithful to principles rather than organizations, he predicted that they would immediately desert the party should it prove faithless and sink to the level of corruption he attributed to the Democrats.[40] In some ways, his speech foreshadowed his later appeals to independent voters.

Schurz's newly won fame came at a time when he could make good use of it, not only in politics but also in business. With his financial affairs still in a tangled condition because of his losses in 1857, he was forced to look for new sources of income. After hearing his Chicago address, a number of local citizens asked him to open a law practice in the city; they were even prepared to guarantee him a certain income. When a similar group in Milwaukee matched the offer, he accepted. Henceforth, he would live in the city during the winter while retaining his Watertown house for the summer.[41]

To be admitted to the bar in Jefferson County was an easy matter. A presentation of the application by a Watertown lawyer, "a smile and a nod by the judge, a hand-shake, the signing of a paper, and finally a moderate tipple and a hilarious exchange of lawyers' jokes at the village tavern nearby" was all that was necessary. On January 1, 1859, Schurz entered into a legal partnership with Halbert B. Paine, a radical Republican from Milwaukee, and within a short time the Milwaukee *Sentinel* carried an advertisement for Schurz & Paine, Attorneys at Law, at No. 3, Kneeland's block. How much legal work Schurz actually performed is questionable. On the road most of the time either for lectures or political campaigns, he left most of the day-to-day business to his partner. His name was worth something, however, and Paine remained his friend for life.[42]

The law was not the only way in which Schurz sought to recoup his financial losses. When late in November 1858 the Milwaukee *Atlas*, a radical German weekly, became a daily, he entered into an agreement to write articles for it. In addition, he continued his lecturing, undertaking a trip to New England shortly after he opened his office.[43]

Carl's frequent absences were hard on Margarethe, who was always in a precarious state of health. "I ask you for one thing," he pleaded from his New England trip, "Don't have any sad thoughts *now.* . . . I do want to be good to you and love you as before, and we will get over the hard times as always, and suddenly it will be behind us like a dream." Even though she took an avid interest in her husband's career and sent newspaper clippings of his activities to her relatives in Germany, it was not easy to keep her satisfied in the West, and Schurz was thinking of taking her to Europe again for a cure. It soon became evident, however, that it was impossible to leave. The political situation would not permit him to be absent, nor were conditions in Europe particularly inviting. Immediately after Christmas he read in the newspapers that Kinkel had suffered a terrible blow: Johanna had fallen out of a window and, either deliberately or accidentally, killed herself.[44]

Whatever financial and other misfortunes Schurz may have encountered, his political ambition was undiminished. It was obvious that the Republicans were receptive to his brand of ethnic politics, and it was not long before he was plotting for the next gubernatorial nomination. Carefully approaching Congressman Potter for advice, he pointed out that his name had been mentioned for the office. Should he permit the movement to go on? He had reservations; his friend Harvey might also desire the honor, and he did not wish to compete with him. Moreover, he could neither afford a long struggle nor another defeat, although he was certain that he could "carry the State more easily than most others, provided no side issues are brought up in the contest." As usual, he disavowed any real interest in office. "My political standing is such that I can do without any official station," he asserted. "The thing has only one charm for me, and that is, that a success of this kind would give me a powerful influence on the German population of the northern States, which would tell in 1860." He left no occasion unused to emphasize his value in connection with the German vote.

Among the reasons for Schurz's quest for office were the increasingly vicious attacks upon him. Charges that he was a Prussian spy, an evident attempt to discredit him with German voters, had stung him to the quick. The accusation had first appeared in the Beaver Dam *Democrat*, which sought to prove it by pointing out that his property in Germany had never been confiscated. The brazen lie was too much even for Democratic papers, but it was difficult to discover its author. Some suspected Judge Leonard Mertz of Beaver Dam; Schurz himself, however, believed that Emil Rothe was the culprit, although he was never sure. At any rate, the smear encouraged him to seek higher honors.[45]

Schurz's appeal to the Republicans was enhanced by events in Massachusetts, where the Know-Nothing legislature had proposed a constitutional amendment barring foreign-born citizens from voting for two years after their naturalization. Because many nativists had joined the Republican party, the Democrats spared no effort to identify their opponents with bigotry. Schurz wrote immediately to Edward L. Pierce, later Charles Sumner's biographer, whom he warned that passage of the amendment would cost the party the German vote in the Northwest, without which it could not win in 1860. Pierce and Henry Wilson, Sumner's radical colleague in the Senate, believing that something ought to be done, invited the self-appointed spokesman for the German-Americans to deliver a speech at Faneuil Hall. Asking only that they pay his expenses, which he estimated at $100, he accepted.[46]

The trip to Boston proved to be of great importance to Schurz. It was on this occasion that he met the leading members of the city's intellectual community— Henry Wadsworth Longfellow, Oliver Wendell Holmes, John A. Andrew, Charles Francis Adams, Frank W. Bird, Edwin Percy Whipple, among others— and established his reputation as a fellow reformer and intellectual. "Oh, Boston is a wonderful city, too good to be lived in," he wrote to his wife. His good opinion of the "Hub" was fully reciprocated by his hosts. They in turn were favorably impressed with him.

His speech on April 18 at Faneuil Hall, entitled "True Americanism," was a success. Reprinted widely in leading newspapers, it was well received, at least according to the Republican press. In essence, it was a more polished and shorter restatement of his address at Beloit the previous summer. After a complimentary patriotic opening referring to the sacred associations of the revolutionary shrines in Massachusetts, he defined what he considered the essence of American nationality. As he saw it, it did not "spring from one family, one tribe, one country" but incorporated "the vigorous elements of all civilized nations on earth." This was the difference between Rome and the United States: The Roman Republic protected the rights of citizens; the American, the rights of man. It was a republic of equal rights, "where the title to manhood is the title to citizenship." Slavery was bad not only because of its injustice, but also because of its creation of masters whose freedom of speech was curtailed. He pleaded for complete religious toleration, a position only slightly eroded by some mildly anti-Catholic allusions, called Charles Sumner (the famous antislavery senator struck down by the Southern politician Preston Brooks) a representative of true Americanism, and closed with a ringing reaffirmation of "Liberty and equal rights, one and inseparable."

Schurz was completely satisfied with the results of his effort. "I spoke like a god," he boasted to Margarethe, "and today I cannot get away from the praises of my speech." It had been read with admiration everywhere and had won for him the "whole intelligent world." He also spoke in Springfield, where he stressed the importance to the party of the German vote and then, after making arrangements for further speaking tours, went on to New York. "Do you know what it means to be an intellectual from morning till night and be obliged to say brilliant things?" he complained. "Now I should like a few days' rest and the privilege of being stupid."

In New York, Schurz continued his campaign against the two-year amendment. He saw Horace Greeley, the editor of the New York *Tribune*, whom he urged to publish an address to the people of Massachusetts against the amendment; he tried to enlist other editors and visited William H. Seward, the leading Republican in the Senate, at Auburn to secure his collaboration. When the amendment passed anyway, Schurz once more warned Pierce that the effect would be very serious, at least in the West. Only the complete separation of Massachusetts Republicans from the nativists would suffice to undo the damage. But he really did not have to worry. He had again made a name for himself, and Republicans throughout the North were now thinking of Carl Schurz of Wisconsin as the spokesman for the German-Americans.[47]

Yet, in spite of his rapidly spreading fame, Schurz had already encountered serious problems in his quest for the governorship. The issue of states' rights, then agitating Wisconsin because of the Glover fugitive slave case, had split the Republican party. Sherman M. Booth, who, following the forcible abduction of the fugitive Joshua Glover from the Milwaukee County courthouse, had been taken in custody by the federal court, applied for a writ of habeas corpus to the state supreme court, which freed him on the grounds that the Fugitive Slave Act was unconstitutional. Indicted a second time in January 1855, he was sentenced to one month's imprisonment and a $1,000 fine, only to be released again by a writ of habeas corpus. In 1859, after the Supreme Court of the United States, in *Ableman* v. *Booth*, had decided against the petitioner and Wisconsin decided to defy the mandate, a judicial election took place in the state, with Byron Paine running for Supreme Court justice on the states' rights ticket. Schurz decided to endorse him.[48]

Schurz's involvement in the Glover case was peculiar. His German background might be expected to have turned him against states' rights doctrines—was not the "particularism" of the petty German states one of the causes of the fatherland's troubles? But he was so deeply committed to the antislavery cause, and the injustice to Glover, whom slave catchers had wantonly seized at his house, so upset him that he threw common sense to the winds and on March 24 delivered a ringing speech at Milwaukee's Albany Hall in defense of states' rights. Quoting Calhoun and Jefferson as well as the Virginia and Kentucky resolutions, he announced that centralization and liberty were incompatible. True freedom could be preserved only by the states, he asserted, going so far as to call the federal judiciary an anomaly above the American system. "I will repress that feeling of indignation and burning shame which overcomes me when I hear the clanking of chains in the vaunted Republic of equal rights," he continued, launching a long denunciation of the "inhuman system" and citing Thomas Jefferson on the evils of the power of the Supreme Court. The Paine faction won the election, but important elements of the party were alienated. Timothy O. Howe, formerly Schurz's supporter, to whom he sent his speech for an opinion, thought he had "struck the cause of Republicanism the hardest blow it ever received." Howe became his ardent opponent.[49]

Schurz's participation in the Massachusetts fight against the two-year amendment took place shortly afterward, and while it enhanced his reputation, it also strengthened his enemies' venom. Wisconsin's Democratic papers abused him for having associated with Know-Nothings. The Cincinnati *Enquirer* called him a "renegade German," and the Watertown *Democrat*, emphasizing the anti-Catholic portions of his speech, reprinted the Boston *Courier*'s criticism of his "absurdities, fallacies, and inconsistencies." Even the radical Carl Heinzen, faulting him for not having done more, was not pleased with Schurz's performance. Some Wisconsin Republicans were beginning to doubt the significance of the German vote and inquired whether he would consider various places other than the head of the ticket.[50]

Nevertheless, Schurz decided to make the attempt to displace Randall. In February, the Republicans in the legislature reelected him to the university's Board of Regents; Harvey wrote encouragingly; and Carl Roeser, the editor of the Manitowoc *Demokrat*, took the lead by demanding Schurz's nomination as a fit rebuke to the Know-Nothings.

Governor Randall, anxious to be renominated, now did everything in his power to counteract Schurz's drive. C. C. Washburn, the politically astute member of the famous Republican family, who favored the challenger, nevertheless wrote to Potter that Schurz had better stay off the ticket altogether if he refused any but the top position. The sentiment was to renominate Randall, and there was still a lingering Know-Nothing element which would possibly disappear the following year. Schurz himself contemplated publishing a letter of withdrawal, but Roeser and James H. Paine, Randall's Milwaukee opponent, continued to urge him on. He stayed in the race.[51]

Not even renewed troubles with Margarethe could dissuade her husband from seeking the governship. She was dissatisfied, complained about his letters, and was unhappy about his frequent absences. He sought to reassure her. In the spring he had written to her how happy the seven years of their marriage had been, how satisfied he was when he compared their married life with that of so many others. In July he had chided her for her lack of appreciation of his letters, and in August he reminded her again of his devotion. If he had hurt her, he could not remember what he had written. He had always loved her and nobody could ever mean to him what she meant. But she remained edgy.[52]

In the weeks immediately preceding the convention, Schurz became more and more sanguine. No matter that indications were against him, no matter that he was warned against nativist opposition, he remained hopeful. He disregarded charges that his candidacy was a Democratic trick—the Republicans would be defeated if he were nominated because of nativist defections and equally overwhelmed if he were rejected because of the Germans' disappointment. Trying to convince party leaders that Randall could not be reelected, he stressed the importance of the German vote. Had not German papers outside of the state endorsed his candidacy on the grounds that it would constitute a perfect answer to charges of Know-Nothingism?[53]

When the convention met, it was found that only 48 of 174 delegates favored Schurz, and 20 of these were Germans. Randall was duly renominated. Then the convention unanimously offered the defeated candidate second place on the ticket, but he declined. In a speech thanking his supporters for the intended honor, he promised to continue the fight and to remain loyal to the party's principles.[54]

The aftermath of the convention's actions was ominous for the Republicans. The Germans, furious at the rejection of their favorite, threatened to bolt. Carl Heinzen's *Pionier* called the defeat a second Massachusetts amendment, and for a time the Watertown *Volkszeitung,* now edited by Schurz's associates, refused to endorse the state ticket. As expected, the Democrats were gleeful; stressing the bigoted character of the opposition to Schurz, they pointed out that "German preferences do not easily get recognition from a party which largely consists of stubborn nativists."[55]

For Schurz, this situation presented a real opportunity. If in the midst of general German threats of desertion he could remain loyal, if he could succeed in rallying enough of his disappointed countrymen to the ticket, Randall might not only win but be forever indebted to him. He returned to Milwaukee with great fanfare; at seven o'clock on September 6, fifty-one guns were fired in his honor from the Oneida Street bridge; a huge bonfire was lit in the square; and in the presence of Judge Stallo of Cincinnati, who also spoke, he delivered an appropriate address in English and in German. The convention had made its decision, he said; he could not accept the lower office, but it was the duty of all good Republicans to fight in the ranks.

The party's leaders saw the point. Schurz had long sought funds to keep German Republican papers from going under; now Senator Doolittle actively helped him. Schurz was the endorser of the notes for these papers, Doolittle wrote to Potter; he was an excellent man and must not be allowed to be crushed between the two forces of German and American Know-Nothingism. "Now is the time for the true friends of Carl Schurz to take care of him, and not allow him to [be] sacrificed. He is a man of noble impulses, and the highest order of genius." Apparently the money was raised.[56]

Before Schurz could fully prove his steadfastness in Wisconsin, he received an invitation to campaign in Minnesota. The Republicans in that frontier state were anxious to win over the Germans, and Schurz heeded their summons. He liked the state immensely; Fort Snelling on its cliff overlooking the Mississippi reminded him of the castles on the Rhine, and the raw nature of the country—the impossible roads, primitive conditions, and splendid air—gave him a sense of adventure.

    As in previous campaigns, he succeeded in expanding his contacts. He met
Pennsylvania Republican and later speaker of the House Galusha Grow, in a
small settlement called Lexington, consisting of nothing but a schoolhouse, a
store, and a tavern, where the two visiting statesmen were forced to spend the
night. Trying to figure out a way of procuring something better than the
abominable food the landlord set before them, they went fishing, caught some
fish, and ate it with relish in the morning. He also made the acquaintance of
Morton S. Wilkinson, the Minnesota radical, and encountered Francis P. Blair,
Jr., the representative of the famous Missouri family. No introductions were
necessary; everybody knew "that tremendous Dutchman," as Schurz facetiously
referred to himself, and his speeches met with great favor. Wherever he appeared,
he was welcomed with genuine acclaim; his defeat had only made him more
popular. At St. Anthony he debated his opponent, Emil Rothe, with, as he
thought, considerable success, and the results of the campaign were gratifying.
The Republicans won.

    Pleased with his reception, Schurz took a steamboat back to Wisconsin, an
adventure he was never to forget because he witnessed a race between his boat and
a competitor. When his steamer, with its safety valve tied down, managed to reach
the dock at St. Croix a few minutes before its rival, he was greatly exhilarated by
the experience.[57]

    When he returned to Wisconsin, he found that the Germans were in full revolt.
Leading German Republicans in Manitowoc adopted an address and resolutions
condemning Randall. Threatening a bolt in case the 1860 nominations were not
free of nativist connections, they called for the governor's defeat although they
endorsed the rest of the ticket. They even criticized Schurz for his loyalty to the
party.

    The situation was ready-made for Schurz. Addressing the German Republicans
at Market Hall in Milwaukee, he reminded them that a great victory had just been
won in Minnesota because the Republicans had been united. He personally
resented charges that he had remained steadfast in return for a promise of a seat in
Congress. Stories that a nativist caucus had defeated him at the convention were
also false; had not some Germans been among those who voted for Randall? At
any rate, he was in politics for principle, not for pelf, and, to prepare for the
all-important presidential campaign of 1860, everyone had the duty to refute the
charges of Know-Nothingism and vote for Randall.

    After thus firmly taking his stand, he spoke throughout the state, sometimes in
Harvey's company, sometimes alone. He debated Harrison C. Hobart, the Democratic nominee for governor, at Manitowoc and then at Sheboygan and was
convinced that he had hardly ever experienced "a greater triumph." His
intervention was effective; as the *Pionier am Wisconsin* remarked after his speech
at Sauk City, "So much is certain, that Mr. Schurz has done a lot of good here, and
we even heard German Democrats, who until now have always stood by the
Democratic party, say that they won't vote for the Democratic ticket." German

Republicans who had been hostile to Randall changed their minds, and the governor won his coveted second term. His success was widely attributed to Carl Schurz.[58]

Within the short span of three years, Schurz had succeeded in laying a political base for himself among the Germans of Wisconsin. His fame had spread beyond the state, and the national Republican party had become deeply indebted to him. His manipulation of ethnic politics had paid off handsomely. The reward would not be long in coming.

VI

Victory and Secession

THE FALL AND WINTER of 1859–60 was a period of intense excitement. On October 16, John Brown seized Harper's Ferry. He was quickly overcome, hastily tried, and summarily executed. When church bells rang in Northern towns to mark the event, slaveowners were confirmed in their belief that the old abolitionist had simply carried out the secret designs of the Republican party. Congress was paralyzed for weeks because of the inability of the House of Representatives to elect a speaker; Southerners, threatening secession, called for a federal slave code for the territories. The "irrepressible conflict" between slave and free states was becoming more and more ominous, and, to make matters worse, 1860 was a presidential year. It was obvious that it would be difficult, if not impossible, to avoid a decision on the slavery question.

The crisis facing the nation affected Schurz deeply. He believed in the antislavery cause with all his heart, and with that peculiar mixture of righteousness and self-interest which was so characteristic of him, he considered it his "duty" to rally the Germans to the cause—not merely in Wisconsin, but in the entire country. If at the same time he could accomplish throughout the North what he had already achieved in Wisconsin and become his countrymen's spokesman in national Republican councils, so much the better.

Schurz's rise to national prominence was helped by his frequent appearances on the lecture platform. Forced to replenish his sadly depleted finances, he delivered speeches in many parts of the country. At the end of November he went to Boston, where he lectured on Louis Napoleon and France. Charles Sumner, who had recently returned from Europe after a lengthy period of inactivity after Preston Brooks's attack, was present and complimented the speaker. He was delighted to be back in time to hear the address, he said, but the occasion did not belong to him. It belonged to the distinguished gentleman from Wisconsin, whose speech had been marked "by knowledge, sagacity and elevated sentiment" and had been delivered "with grace and eloquence which may make us all forget that the English tongue was not the language that he spoke in his infancy." It was a handsome compliment, and the senator's friend Pierce thought that "a German who inculcates such noble sentiments and who so nobly vindicates our cause is a perpetual protest against the proscription of foreigners."[1]

Schurz's lecturing kept him in the East for most of the winter. He brought his wife along—she had stayed with the Tiedemanns in Philadelphia—and he carefully looked after his political interests while he was traveling. In Boston, he told friends that N. P. Banks, the speaker of the House, widely suspected of sympathy for the Know-Nothings, could not carry a single Western state. In New York, where he often stayed with his old friend Abraham Jacobi, now a rising pediatrician after an adventurous revolutionary career in Germany, he attended a meeting of the Republican National Committee as a substitute for an absent delegate from Wisconsin. The committee, which met on December 21, decided to hold the next national convention in Chicago.[2] And early in January, he went back to Massachusetts, to Springfield, to deliver a long speech on Douglas and popular sovereignty. The Illinois senator was then the leading presidential hopeful. Considering him a dangerous, unprincipled opponent, Schurz naturally sought to demolish his pretensions at every opportunity.

He came straight to the point. Douglas's doctrine of popular sovereignty was a sham, full of contradictions. His interpretation of the Declaration of Independence reduced that immortal document to a mere "diplomatic dodge" and the sacred Ordinance of 1787 to a minor law passed by a rump Congress. But the senator was mistaken. If he did not care whether slavery was voted up or down, the people did. The slavery question was not a mere wrangle between two political parties for power and spoils. It was "the great struggle between two antagonistic systems of social organization; between advancing civilization and retreating barbarism; between the human conscience and a burning wrong." As long as the moral vitality of the nation was not entirely exhausted, Douglas and his cohorts would "in vain endeavor to reduce the people to that disgusting state of moral indifference" of which he himself was not ashamed to boast. "However degraded some of our politicians may be," Schurz concluded, "the progress of the struggle will show that the popular conscience is still alive, and that the people DO CARE." The speech was so successful that it was widely reprinted.[3]

One of those who liked the Springfield address was Abraham Lincoln, who wrote Schurz a letter of congratulations. The speaker hastened to reply: "You have fought Douglas so long and so well, that you, certainly, are the best man to determine whether I have fought him well also," he wrote. Now that the Little Giant in the aftermath of John Brown's raid had proposed a strong bill to suppress conspiracies to invade any state or territory or assail its institutions—Schurz called it a new "Alien and Sedition law"—he had furnished a great weapon to his opponents. Let them make good use of it.[4]

After this interlude, Schurz returned to his more prosaic lecturing assignments. Sometimes he repeated his talk on France; sometimes he spoke on America in public opinion abroad. He always worked hard preparing his lectures, and apparently he gave his audiences what they wanted. Although because of his financial dependence upon them he worried about his engagements, as he became better known he had little trouble securing more and more.[5]

Once during his lecture trip, he found time to visit his friend Potter in Washington. The congressman took him to the capitol, an experience Schurz never forgot. It was in the midst of the speakership struggle—the House was deadlocked for weeks until it could be organized—and he heard the South Carolina fire-eater, Lawrence Keitt, threaten to break up the Union. The atmosphere was so tense that members of Congress went armed. The crisis was evidently at hand.

The Washington experience only confirmed Schurz's determination to take a prominent part in the coming struggle. Even though on arriving in Philadelphia he found that his wife had fallen sick again and could not travel, he did not stay in the East. Leaving her with his friends, he hurried home alone.[6] The Republican state convention was about to meet and he was not going to miss it.

The Wisconsin Republican convention of 1860 showed how much Schurz's influence in the Badger State had grown. Even though there were only some 12 German delegates of a total of 205, important counties had sent one German each, and the party thought it essential to defer to this prominent element. Accordingly, Schurz became a member of the crucial Committee on Resolutions, from which he reported the planks which interested him, a condemnation of discrimination against the foreign born and an affirmation of the principle of free homesteads for actual settlers. Both were adopted; he himself was elected delegate-at-large to the national convention and became chairman of the Wisconsin delegation.

Schurz's influence was even more astounding in light of the fact that, because of the Glover fugitive slave case, the Republican party in Wisconsin was deeply split between the states' rights and national wings, and he was strongly identified with the former. Chief Justice Edward V. Whiton of the state supreme court had died, so that a new election had become necessary. Luther S. Dixon, who was inclined to recognize the supremacy of the federal judiciary, was one of the aspirants for the highest judicial post; A. D. Smith, who had been involved in a scandal concerning certain railroad bonds, was the other. Schurz was dissatisfied with both. After a vehement debate with T. O. Howe, the later radical senator and postmaster general and then the ablest upholder of federal authority, who did not want the party to endorse any candidates, Schurz secured the convention's nomination of A. Scott Sloan, a states' rights advocate. The maneuver was unsuccessful. Running on an independent ticket, Dixon won, but in spite of the defeat, Schurz maintained his strong position in the party. The belief in the importance of the German vote was pervasive.[7]

Shortly after the close of the convention, Schurz went to Chicago to assist "Long John" Wentworth, the Republican candidate for mayor. Abraham Lincoln was especially anxious to secure the German vote in Illinois, and so the party leaders called on Schurz for help. He spoke to packed houses in English and German; impressed with his reception, he bragged that the "audience fairly trembled with excitement" at his appearance. When the Republicans won, he was convinced that Douglas's chances of a nomination had been wrecked. But should he be chosen anyway, Lincoln would be his natural opponent. Although he was committed to Seward, Schurz had no real objection to such a development.[8] In view of the fact that Lincoln had just delivered his outspoken Cooper Union address, Schurz's sentiments were not surprising.

From Chicago, Schurz again went lecturing. For fifty dollars per speech, he appeared in many towns and cities in Indiana and neighboring states. His schedule was grueling; on March 6, he was in Jacksonville, Illinois; on the 7th, in Terre Haute; on the 8th, in Evansville; and on the 10th, in South Bend; on the 12th, in La Porte; on the 13th, in Indianapolis; on the 14th, in Richmond, and from there he went on to Columbus, Ohio. The trains were bad, the food worse, and the activity somewhat repetitious. But he needed the money, and soon he contracted for further tours to Rochester and New York.

Whether lecturing or not, Schurz did not neglect his political obligations. His trip to Indiana gave him an opportunity to feel the pulse of the German community there. "From what I have seen here I am led to believe that we can turn about 10,000 German votes that were formerly democratic . . . ," he wrote to Potter. "That, it seems to me, is the only way to carry the State." Let the Indiana members of Congress send home copies of his Springfield speech: he himself had already established a statewide system of correspondence which would be in good working order after the convention. He was anxiously looking forward to the presidential campaign.[9]

Schurz's involvement in the maneuvering for the 1860 Republican nomination had begun sometime earlier, when Salmon P. Chase, the radical governor of Ohio, sought to enlist him on his behalf. Chase had taken note of Schurz's speeches during the 1858 campaign; he congratulated Schurz and received a fulsome letter of acknowledgment. But when Schurz did not fully commit himself, Chase tried to woo him through the Wisconsin politician William H. Brisbane. Brisbane stressed Schurz's importance in securing the German vote, which he thought Chase could not afford to neglect. Again and again both the governor and his agent approached Schurz; again and again he seemed friendly, but he never gave an unequivocal answer. Finally, in March of 1860, Chase invited Schurz to visit him at Columbus. During a long interview at his house, he sought again to secure his guest's support, only to be disappointed once more. Schurz remained committed to Seward, whom his state had endorsed.[10]

Schurz's appearance in midwestern cities was always an event in the German community. The halls were crowded long before the speaker arrived. When he finally came, the audience went wild. Lean and supple, with a reddish brown mustache overshadowing the broad line of his mouth, he exuded a youthful magic. Fascinating his listeners with the thoroughly controlled play of his hands and the "fiery and often gripping glance of his eyes," he completely held their attention. As they long remembered, "the conduct of his body was calm and dignified; nevertheless it seemed as if the man had been shivering and bending unobtrusively under the power of the impressive speech."[11] No wonder Republican leaders were anxious to secure his cooperation.

After his visit with Chase, Schurz returned to Wisconsin. He wanted to take part in the judicial election as well as in the Milwaukee municipal campaign, which had given him a chance to secure his partner's nomination for city attorney. His judicial candidate as well as Paine was defeated; nevertheless, the losers did so well that the *Sentinel* headlined the result as "A REPUBLICAN GAIN OF OVER 2,000!! ALL HONOR TO THE GERMANS!" It must have been especially gratifying to read that Carl Schurz and the *Atlas* had "labored long and faithfully to accomplish this end" and that their good work was beginning to "bear handsome fruit."

In the midst of this excitement, the Potter-Pryor affair made Schurz's friend a national hero. Challenged to a duel by Roger A. Pryor of Virginia after an altercation in the House, Potter accepted but chose bowie knives as weapons. Pryor refused to fight on these terms, and the North made merry about the "chivalry's" discomfiture. Genuinely worried about Potter's safety, Schurz was relieved and delighted when the affair was over. "Your constituency has come to the conclusion that you are 'a devil of a fellow,'" he wrote to the congressman. He need no longer worry about his renomination and reelection.

After another speaking tour which took him as far as Rochester—he was now able to get $100 for his appearances in larger cities—Schurz made preparations for his attendance at the Republican National Convention in Chicago. Although pledged to Seward, he was perfectly aware of the New Yorker's problem, the competition of other prominent candidates. He liked the radical Ben Wade of Ohio; nevertheless, he thought Lincoln would be stronger.[12] And he had every right to be optimistic, especially after the Charleston convention, where the Democrats had been unable to nominate anybody because of a Southern bolt. Leaving for Chicago with the Wisconsin delegation, he was determined to make his influence felt.

He reached the convention city on May 13, where Caspar Butz, an Illinois German politician and poet, met him at the depot. Although the city was so crowded with delegates and their retinues that Butz already had four house guests, he extended a cordial invitation not only to Carl but also to Margarethe Schurz. Should she be well enough to travel, she was welcome to stay with Mrs. Butz. "I have been expected with longing," Schurz wrote to his wife with some exaggeration, as some of his countrymen were certainly not too anxious to see him. They had organized a meeting of German-Americans at the Deutsches Haus, possibly to take independent action against nativism and to prevent the nomination of Edward Bates, widely suspected of close ties to the Know-Nothings in Missouri. That Schurz was opposed to any separate action must have been clear to them.

In fact, Schurz's role in the preconvention meeting at the Deutsches Haus was similar to his part in the Wisconsin campaign during the previous summer and fall. Collaborating with Gustave Koerner, he worked to prevent a rupture with the party. And he succeeded. The meeting adjourned with the passage of a series of innocuous resolutions advocating antislavery, homestead, and antinativist planks. The group pledged its support to any candidate favoring these propositions, so that the party was again indebted to the German-American loyalist from Wisconsin.[13]

The Republican National Convention opened on May 16 in the Wigwam, a great hall newly constructed for the event. Schurz, whose name was among those loudly cheered when the roll was called, was appointed Wisconsin's delegate on the committee on resolutions. Together with Preston King of New York, he conducted the permanent chairman, George Ashmun, to the chair—a comical sight, as the tall Schurz and the squat King looked much like Don Quixote and Sancho Panza. It was obvious that the delegates were anxious to honor Schurz; flattery of the Germans was deemed essential.

Assisted by Koerner, in the platform committee Schurz achieved everything he wanted. The platform reported to the convention on May 17 contained not only the expected denunciation of the spread of slavery to the territories, but also a ringing reaffirmation of the rights of the foreign born. Emphasizing the Republican party's opposition to any change in the "naturalization laws or any State legislation by which the rights of citizens hitherto accorded to immigrants from foreign lands shall be abridged or impaired," it pledged "full and efficient protection to the rights of all classes of citizens, whether native or naturalized, both at home or abroad." When David Wilmot of Pennsylvania sought to strike part of this plank to safeguard states' rights, the chairman of the resolutions committee pointed out that it was necessary to retain it because of the foreign-born voters. Wilmot then withdrew his motion; nevertheless, Schurz seized the opportunity to stress the importance of the German vote. As he himself had insisted on the precise wording in question, he reminded the convention of its purpose, to demonstrate unequivocally that the Republican party was unalterably opposed to nativism. Maintaining that 300,000 Germans had already been converted to Republicanism, amid loud cheers he expressed the wish that 300,000 more would find it consistent with their honor to follow suit.

Immediately after this episode, Schurz first became aware of the New York reformer George William Curtis, vibrant, handsome, and idealistic, who was to become his lifelong friend and collaborator. Curtis attracted his attention after the old radical, Joshua R. Giddings, perturbed by the omission of any reference to the great principles of the Declaration of Independence, sought to include them in the platform. Voted down, he had stalked out of the hall, only to be brought back by Curtis's successful renewal of his motion in slightly different form. Schurz was greatly impressed.

The balloting for the party's standard-bearers took place on May 18. The Wisconsin delegation was still pledged to Seward, but even before the voting began, it had become apparent that he had serious competition. Schurz himself was repelled by the politicians in town who were attempting to drum up support for the New Yorker; Thurlow Weed, Seward's friend and mentor, had a sinister reputation, and Horace Greeley, who attended as a delegate from Oregon, was doing everything in his power to defeat his former collaborator.

Schurz tried as long as possible to remain true to his pledge. On behalf of his delegation he seconded William M. Evarts's nomination of Seward and three times cast his delegation's ballots for the New Yorker. Huddled together, the New York, Wisconsin, and Michigan delegates seemed disconcerted as their candidate failed to gain substantial ground. Then, on the third ballot, Lincoln obtained the necessary majority. Bedlam reigned as delegates hastened to join the bandwagon. Finally, after Evarts had risen to make the nomination unanimous, Schurz, speaking for Wisconsin, again seconded the motion. Although his remarks were not as forceful as usual, his disappointment, if such it was, was short-lived. The ticket of Lincoln and Hamlin—Hannibal Hamlin of Maine received the vice presidential nomination—was unobjectionable. In the long run, Schurz was quite satisfied.[14]

He had every reason to be. Not only had his previous encounters convinced him that Lincoln would be an excellent candidate, but it was known that the nominee had publicly denounced the Massachusetts two-year amendment. Lincoln's German newspaper showed that he had a very healthy appreciation of the importance of the German vote. Schurz did not intend to let him forget it.

There was another reason for satisfaction. In 1860, Schurz sympathized with the radical Republicans, and more clearly than many, he recognized that from the radical point of view the nomination was wholly acceptable. "I know Mr. Lincoln," he explained to Charles Sumner. "[I] am sure his administration will very favorably disappoint those who look upon him as a 'conservative' man. His impulses are in the right direction, and I think he has courage enough to follow them."[15]

Schurz wasted no time in establishing working relations with Lincoln. Appointed one of the members of the official notification committee, on the day after the convention he traveled to Springfield to inform the nominee of his selection. He always remembered the trip—the enthusiastic demonstrations at the railroad stations along the way; Lincoln's reception of the committee in his parlor; the bare look of the room: the marble-topped table with a silverplated pitcher of ice water, a Bible or a family photo album on it, and some chairs and a sofa at the walls. Lincoln welcomed the committee in a new black suit of ill-fitting clothes, "his long tawney neck emerging gauntly from his turn-down collar, his melancholy eyes sunken deep in his haggard face." Listening politely to chairman George Ashmun's speech, he responded with a few appropriate remarks. Then he shook each committee member's hand and engaged in small talk. His face now lost its expression of sadness, his eyes lit up, and his charm won over even those of his visitors who had come with misgivings. "Well, we might have done a more brilliant thing, but we could hardly have done a better thing," said William D. Kelley to Schurz as they departed.[16]

A few days later, Schurz followed up his visit with a letter. Frankly acknowledging his previous preference for Seward, he heartily congratulated Lincoln on his triumph. "I feel some delicacy in telling you this," Schurz wrote, "for I do not belong to those worshippers of success whose hearts and minds are readily turned by the changing breezes of fortune. But I deem it my duty to establish between us that confidence which must exist between the head of a party and those who are to fight in the front ranks." Now that he had paid his debts to Seward, his old "chieftain," he was prepared "to do the work of a hundred men" for Lincoln.

Then he turned to practical matters. As a member of the Republican National Committee, to which he had been elected, he proposed the establishment of a speaker's bureau of influential foreign-born citizens to carry the Republican message throughout the country. He was going to set up a regular committee of correspondence to remain in touch with these speakers. And although he intended to do the principal work himself, he would nevertheless see to it that a systematic coverage of the foreign born was not neglected. In fact, he was going to devote his entire time to the campaign.[17]

He was as good as his word. At a ratification meeting in Milwaukee's Albany Hall on May 26, he rendered an account of his performance at Chicago. If Wisconsin had not been pledged to Seward, he said, Lincoln would have been its choice, and he was an excellent candidate. The Republic would be safe with him at the helm. Schurz could guarantee it. Had he not seen the nominee at Springfield? "I do not plead the cause of party discipline," he declared. "That is not one of the deities at whose shrine I worship. It never will be. But must I, born in a foreign land, speak to you of the devotion to the great institutions of your country? Must I entreat you to sacrifice the small whim of personal preference to the greatest cause of this age?" In a grandiloquent peroration, he called upon Wisconsin to stretch out its hand to New York so that it would be known that the two states, which had stood together for Seward in the convention, would be "the first and foremost in the battle for Lincoln and liberty." The speech made a good impression, not only in Wisconsin but also in the East. Schurz was called a "rival of Kossuth," one of Europe's best gifts to America. The Albany *Evening Journal* made use of the occasion to reprint the entire story of his life.[18]

Lincoln answered Schurz's letter on June 18. Apologizing for not writing earlier, he made it clear that he bore no grudge because of Seward. "To the extent of our limited acquaintance, no man stands nearer my heart than yourself," he asserted, inviting Schurz to write him as often as he liked.[19]

Certain of Lincoln's approval, Schurz promptly went about establishing his planned speakers' network. His wide-flung correspondence attests to his efforts from Connecticut to California and the hard work of the Republican National Committee's foreign department. It was the first systematic attempt to corral the ethnic vote.

As he had promised Lincoln, Schurz in fact performed the heavy work himself.

His schedule during the campaign was utterly amazing; traveling over twenty-one thousand miles, he was constantly in demand. His speeches were effective; reprinted in many copies, they served as campaign literature among the Germans. Native-born Americans also appreciated his arguments—"the broadest, the deepest, and most convincing" of the campaign, according to Andrew D. White. And in spite of his grueling schedule, he always maintained his enthusiasm. After all, his efforts not only served a good cause but might also lead to his own political preferment.[20]

Schurz's financial situation remained a serious problem. Because of his losses in 1857, he had to ask the national committee and local agencies for compensation, at least for his expenses, and for many years afterward, his enemies accused him of having campaigned for pay. Technically speaking, they were wrong. They often confused his lectures with his campaign speeches, but in effect, he did receive ample compensation for his expenses. Otherwise, it would have been impossible for him ever to go on the campaign trail.[21]

Schurz's participation in the canvass began early, in July, when he went to New York to meet with the Republican National Committee. At the same time he managed to take care of some university business by visiting the ailing chancellor, Henry Barnard, in Connecticut. On the way back, he stopped off at Cleveland to deliver a German address to a Lincoln ratification meeting. Reminding his fellow countrymen that they had come to America to escape despotism, he told them that they had to oppose the Democratic party. It too supported despotism, because the slaveholders used undemocratic means to gain their ends. But their threats of secession could never be carried out peacefully. True, Southerners were courageous; at the same time, however, they were much weaker than their Northern opponents. Secession would fail; it could neither obtain concessions from the North nor be able to accomplish its purpose. Not one slave could be recovered should the Ohio River ever become an international border.

The address was again widely reported, and the Democrats were becoming uneasy. Conceding that Schurz was a "gentleman of very respectable talents," the Cleveland *Plain Dealer's* correspondent admitted that he could not understand a word of the German speech. But since he considered Schurz's English orations "gigantic pieces of glittering sophistry," he presumed the German speech was no more honest or candid. The Germans disagreed, at least the German Republicans, and invitations to address audiences in various parts of the country came in a steady stream.[22]

Schurz's Cleveland speech was delivered after the Democrats had irrevocably split in Baltimore, where one faction nominated Douglas on a platform of popular sovereignty and the other John Breckinridge on a ticket endorsing a federal slave code for the territories. Because of their opponents' inability to agree—in fact, a fourth ticket headed by John Bell and Edward Everett attempted to disregard the slavery issue altogether—the Republicans' chances for success had greatly improved. Like other opponents of slavery, Schurz was optimistic. His failure to take seriously Southern threats of secession in case of Lincoln's victory showed how gravely he underestimated the great peril confronting the country. As he had said in February, he believed that if the South wanted to dissolve the Union, the day after the Presidential election would be "just one day too late." It was a dangerous illusion.[23]

From Ohio, Schurz traveled to Illinois. Quincy, Peoria, Beardstown, Pekin, Havanna, Belleville—he visited them all, and wherever he appeared, the inevitable processions made his arrival memorable, though he complained about the fuss. He spoke in English and in German, at times assisted by Koerner.[24] Finally, he came to Springfield, where he was received by Lincoln himself.

Schurz was delighted with Old Abe. The candidate did not stand on ceremony. Calling on Schurz shortly after his arrival, Lincoln found the traveler stretched out on the bed and insisted that he remain just as he was. Then the two men talked for two hours, Lincoln discussing the campaign with as much frankness as if he were speaking about a potato crop. Schurz was delighted to find himself appreciated. "Men like you," Lincoln said, "who have real merit and do the work, are always too proud to ask for anything; those who do nothing are always the most clamorous for office. . . . But if I am elected, they will find a tough customer to deal with, and you may depend upon it that I shall know how to distinguish deserving men from the drones." "All right, old Abe," thought Schurz, who reported the conversation verbatim—in English—to his wife.

In the evening, Lincoln asked Schurz to come for supper. Schurz was favorably impressed with the family, with the boys, one of whom insisted on walking around barefoot, and even with the lady of the house. Finding her a fairly good conversationalist, he thought she would adapt very well to the White House. When the time came for the public meeting and the Wide-Awakes arrived to escort the speaker to the hall, Lincoln insisted on coming along. Familiarly greeting acquaintances along the way—"How are you, Dan?" or, "Glad to see you, Ned," or "How do you do, Bill,"—he stayed to listen to the speeches, even the German one, which he could not understand. When it was all over, he shook Schurz's hand—"ouch," the speaker wrote to his wife. "You are an awful fellow," Lincoln said, "I understand your power now." Presenting him with a copy of his debates with Douglas, he invited Schurz to stay with him and bring his wife next time he came to Springfield.[25]

From Illinois, Schurz crossed the Mississippi into Missouri. It was his first appearance in a slave state, and he intended to make the most of the opportunity. He delivered a speech at St. Louis which he entitled "The Doom of Slavery."

He minced no words. The "Irrepressible Conflict," he said, was not a mere quarrel between North and South, but a struggle between two societies, one slave and the other free. In the long run, slavery could not exist without encroaching upon freedom; consequently, it must be contained. As the nineteenth century was the century of progress, could slaveholders really believe that the peculiar institution would last forever? "Slaveholders of America," he explained,

"I appeal to you. Are you really in earnest when you speak of perpetuating slavery? Shall it never cease? Never? Stop and consider where you are and in what day you live." Denouncing Douglas for his subservience to the slaveholders, he again sought to demonstrate the impossibility of secession—the anticipation of a Negro insurrection would paralyze the South, he said—and finally called upon the Republicans of Missouri to maintain the struggle and take the lead in the fight for emancipation. He believed his speech to have been a masterpiece. Many Republicans agreed, especially since it caused the local *Anzeiger des Westens* to urge all Germans to vote the straight Republican ticket.[26]

From St. Louis, Schurz went to Indiana, a state which held its elections in October and was considered crucial. The state committee paid him $200 per week, and he criss-crossed the state assiduously. Except for a short bowling match with his "German brethren," he barely rested, and, as usual, was buoyed up by an unquenchable optimism. "My efforts have been accompanied by the most glittering success," he reported to Margarethe. "I spoke as rarely before, and after our meetings the Democrats regularly circulate to revive their dead and wounded, while the Republicans take the captured prisoners into camp." And just to make sure Lincoln did not forget him, he wrote to Springfield also. The Germans were "coming over in shoals wherever they are judiciously worked with," he bragged. "I think I have succeeded in drawing over a great many wherever I have spoken." He wished he could "multiply" himself "by ten for the next two months."[27]

Schurz's energy was remarkable, especially as the Indiana trip was interrupted by bad news from home. His long absences had been too much for Margarethe, and when he arrived at Evansville, he found an angry letter from her. Accusing him of paying too much attention to other women, she maintained that he kept things from her. He tried to reassure her, but it was obvious that he would have to return soon. And after a brief stop at Monee, Illinois, where his sister Anna had moved, he returned to Wisconsin. How successful he was in calming his wife is questionable. He was still protesting his innocence in November.[28]

In spite of Margarethe's unhappiness, he could not afford to stay home for long. Early in September he went east again, taking a steamer from Detroit to Cleveland. The ship ran into a storm and had to return to Michigan before resuming the voyage, but when the captain found out whom he had aboard, he moved the illustrious passenger into his own stateroom and refused to take any money. Schurz had become famous and enjoyed it enormously.

The high point of the Eastern trip was a speech at Cooper Union in New York. Schurz prepared carefully for it; when he told Governor Edwin D. Morgan that it was going to take more than two hours to deliver, Morgan doubted that any New York audience would stand a speech that long. But Schurz insisted, and the address was again a success. A long indictment of Stephen A. Douglas, his policies, his actions, his ambition, it ended with the same peroration about New York and Wisconsin that Schurz had already used in Milwaukee. The audience liked it, and the speaker was convinced that he had "never spoken as brilliantly as last night." Back home, Horace Rublee also thought the address was the best thing Schurz had ever done "and decidedly the best thing on Douglas that anybody has done."

From New York, Schurz went to Pennsylvania and then once more to Indiana. He was indefatigable, and when at Pittsburgh he heard that five hundred voters might be gained if he came to speak at Erie, he consented, even though the side trip delayed his return to Wisconsin. He simply could not go home when his presence at Erie might prevent the loss of Pennsylvania. Believing that the battle had to be waged and that his part in it was crucial, he felt he had no choice. While everyone around him was exhausted, he boasted to his wife, his powers were undiminished. And the party leaders knew that they owed him something. Aware that Old Abe had not forgotten him, he could look forward to some reward. He had become so well known that his portrait was already being sold in the New York stores.[29]

The night before the favorable results of the October elections were published, Schurz came home to Watertown. The Republican successes greatly cheered him. "Now, o Lord, let thy servant depart in peace," he wrote to Lincoln. "Last night I returned from Indiana. I am almost dead but the telegraph has infused new life in my veins. . . . I feel happy, and I could not help . . . congratulating you and the whole country upon the great news." He was going to leave for New York state at the end of the week, although he thought the remainder of the campaign would be "merely ornamental."[30]

In view of the Republican victories, Schurz did not even have to worry about the ever-increasing attacks on him. They merely proved his effectiveness. If the Democrats misquoted his Springfield remarks by accusing him of maligning the Declaration of Independence, Republican papers could set them straight. In fact, the vicious slurs merely made many of the Germans angry, a result he welcomed. He had deliberately sought to cultivate his countrymen in the October states, even though there were complaints that he did not devote more time to Wisconsin. As he explained to Margarethe, he had to speak where the need was greatest, and that was where he could "assemble the greatest number of Germans."[31]

In the end, he did wind up the campaign in his home state. After another brief trip to the East for speeches in Buffalo, New York, Brooklyn, and New Haven—this time, Margarethe also came east to stay in Philadelphia for the winter—he returned to a great reception in Milwaukee. When he arrived in the afternoon, he was escorted to the Newhall House by the Wide Awakes. Then he spoke in the park, and in the evening a torchlight parade concluded the event.

For the rest of the campaign, he remained in Wisconsin. Speaking in towns and villages in English and in German, he considered the effort a "child's play" in comparison with the work he had performed in Pennsylvania and Indiana. And on election day, he stayed in Milwaukee in order to work at the polls up to the last minute. Then he went to the Chamber of Commerce at the Spring Street bridge to wait for the results.

At first, the reports were unsettling. New York City with its Democratic majority seemed to threaten Republican success in the Empire State. But then the upstate results began to arrive. New York and all the other crucial Northern states were safe for Lincoln. Schurz was jubilant. On the next day, he went home to Watertown to get some sleep.[32]

It was in character that he did not let the great event pass without a letter of congratulations to the President-elect. Asserting that the election constituted a revolution, he assured Lincoln that he had the confidence of the people. All he had to do was to follow his true instincts. In an allusion to the loss of a few electoral votes in New Jersey, Schurz apologized for not having been able to accomplish more in that state. He simply had been too exhausted and was pledged to return to Wisconsin.[33]

A few days later he was back in Milwaukee for a victory celebration at Albany Hall. The party's success was gratifying, but with Southern secessionists threatening to make good their bluster, the situation looked ominous. Addressing himself to the problem of disunion, Schurz said the people had decided that slavery was not national but merely local, and the slaveholders would have to submit. Lincoln had been constitutionally elected; the democratic system depended on the maintenance of the popular will. He for one was certain that it would be sustained. And although a small doubt was beginning to creep into his assertions of the folly and unlikelihood of secession, he was still sanguine about the final outcome.[34]

Just what role the Germans in general and Schurz in particular played in the Republican victory of 1860 has long been a subject of dispute. At the time, Schurz himself and many Republicans, including Lincoln, believed that the German-Americans had come over in large numbers to constitute an important element in the party's success. They demonstrably held the balance of power in Iowa, Minnesota, Illinois, Wisconsin, Indiana, Ohio, Michigan, Pennsylvania, New York, New Jersey, and Connecticut; these states cast all or part of their electoral votes for Lincoln and Hamlin, so that it was easy to conclude that German-American enthusiasm had been decisive. This was not only the conclusion of many contemporaries but also that of subsequent historians. A matter of considerable pride for the German-American community, the crucial contribution of their fellow countrymen to the election of America's greatest president was emphasized by most Germans and German-Americans.[35]

However, the thesis was later challenged. Although admitting that the foreign born participated in the victory, scholars insisted that this contribution was not the determining element. They argued that most of the German Catholics, afraid of nativism, stayed Democratic, and that many of the Protestants, especially the Lutherans, likewise refused to abandon their party. Only the Forty-eighters became Republicans almost to a man; but their influence, in view of the longstanding controversy between the Greens and the Greys, as the newcomers and the older immigrants were called, and the widespread suspicion of their infidel leanings, remained limited.[36]

Nevertheless, the question of Schurz's effectiveness remains significant. It is

Carl Schurz, early 1860s (Courtesy of Library of Congress)

unlikely that, except in Illinois, he succeeded in winning over enough German-Americans to insure Lincoln's triumph; yet this fact is really beside the point. The truth is that at the time, the leaders of the Republican party as well as their opponents were convinced of his decisive influence. And since his career was built on their assumption, he succeeded splendidly. Not long after the election, Abraham Lincoln told the Illinois politician F. A. Hoffmann that he knew the debts he owed to one of the first men of the party and that the Germans would be wholly satisfied in the way Schurz was going to be treated.[37] On February 25, 1862, Charles Sumner declared that without "our German fellow citizens" the Republican cause "would not have triumphed at the last election." And the Milwaukee *Sentinel*, commenting on the October elections, concluded, "much of the victory in Pennsylvania is due to the labor of Carl Schurz." In addition, the violence of the Democrats' attack on Schurz would seem to indicate that they too considered him effective.[38] The old adage that what is thought to be true is more important than what is really true was certainly borne out by Schurz's experiences.

Schurz's political success was gratifying, but his financial problems had become more acute than ever. Answering the accusations that he profited financially from the campaign, he pointed out that after traveling more than twenty-one thousand miles for the Republican party, he received compensation amounting to little more than $1,800; his railroad bill alone totaled $800. His creditors had been hounding him all year, so that it became essential for him to leave home again on a lecture trip. Early in December, after narrowly missing the President-elect in Chicago, he traveled to upstate New York to lecture on American civilization and entertain the snowbound crowds. On the eleventh, he spoke at Tremont Temple in Boston on the theme of free speech, a pointed rebuke to Democratic rowdies who had recently broken up an antislavery meeting there. Other engagements in the vicinity kept him in New England for several weeks.

The lecture trip in the winter of 1860–61, like others, involved hard work. Although Margarethe was well taken care of in Philadelphia, he was not able to see her very often. The separation was difficult for him, especially since he had to spend Christmas Eve without his family, but he could not afford to turn down proffered speaking engagements. Early in the new year, they took him west again, to Ohio, Michigan, Illinois, and Iowa. Connections were uncertain; he found he had to leave Burlington at 5:30 A.M. to cross the frozen Mississippi on foot before dawn in order to catch a train to meet his engagements in Illinois. Frozen river crossings, railroad accidents, raging snowstorms, and nights spent in open fields—it was not an easy existence. In effect, his comparatively settled life in Wisconsin had come to an end.[39]

Schurz's forced preoccupation with his lectures came at a bad time for one so passionately involved in public affairs. The secession crisis had become a reality, despite his refusal to take it seriously. It was useless any longer to remain blind to the emergency confronting the country. There were many who hoped that concessions might still avert the worst, but Schurz remained adamant. He insisted the Republican party must stand firm. Otherwise all his work, all his efforts to convert the Germans, would have been to no purpose.

Like other radical Republicans, Schurz became obsessed with the necessity of keeping the party steadfast. As early as November 30, he wrote to Potter that now that the crisis was upon the country, it was up to the Republicans to make its results final and decisive. "If the North now remains firm," he insisted, "the slave power is done for. We have to choose between a short and a violent crisis and a long, exhausting and dangerous one." Pointing out that common prudence dictated confronting the issue boldly, he advised "meeting treason when and where it is committed" and putting it down "with all the means which manifest destiny has put in our hands." He continued: "My dear Potter, if Slavery in its present form and strength exists in this republic ten years hence, the Republican party will be responsible for it. . . . If no compromise had been made in 1833, we should never again have heard the disunion cry. Let not that mistake be repeated. The future of the country, the repose of the nation, depends on our firmness."⁴⁰

But talk of compromise persisted. First, Buchanan delivered his message declaring that while secession was illegal, the federal government had no real power to do anything about it. Then, as Southern states, with South Carolina in the vanguard, were preparing to secede, a Committee of Thirty-three to adjust sectional differences was appointed in the House. And all the time, Lincoln refused to make a public statement.

Schurz became frantic. If only he did not have to waste his time delivering lectures for pay! If he were a member of Congress, he would tell the Southerners a thing or two! The Republicans must use delaying tactics to prevent any action prior to March 4, when the new president would be inaugurated. Passionately believing in the cause, he repeated his warnings to Potter. Then he wrote directly to Lincoln himself. He did not wish to obtrude, he stated, but he considered it his duty to urge the President-elect to remain steadfast. A compromise would spell the doom of the Republican party. Firmness now would prevent trouble later, and he for one would insist on collecting the revenue no matter what happened in the South. Expressing his utmost confidence in Lincoln, he advised him to include some representatives of the slave states in his cabinet, men like Edward Bates or Henry Winter Davis. "If I ever regretted not being in Congress it is at the present moment," he added. "I have some ideas in the present crisis in my head which if put in the form of a speech would probably strike and startle the minds of a good many." He took this notion so seriously that he asked Potter whether it might not be feasible for some congressman to deliver an address he would write.⁴¹

On December 20, South Carolina seceded. However, there were signs that Republican members of Congress were becoming more resolute. On the Senate floor, Benjamin F. Wade scathingly denounced appeasement and not even the most promising scheme of adjustment, the Crittenden Compromise, proposing by constitutional amendment to divide the nation into slave and free territories along the old Missouri Compromise line, was making much headway. When Lincoln refused to entertain the proposition, the newly created Senate Committee of Thirteen also voted it down.

Schurz was greatly relieved. The danger of the party's degradation was virtually over, he exulted to Margarethe. Lincoln was standing "firm as an oak." But it could not be denied that armed conflict was indeed likely.

The danger of war presaged new perils. The secessionists might attempt to seize Washington, a contingency to which Schurz sought to alert Lincoln. Americans did not believe in plots, he contended, but he knew something about revolutions and was well aware of the purposes of revolutionists. Let the President-elect alert the governors of the Northern states to ready the militia so that secessionists could see the North was determined to prevent a breakup of the Union. In addition, he again suggested collecting the revenue in the South, if necessary aboard a naval vessel. He also wrote in the same vein to several congressmen and to Governor Morgan, the chairman of the Republican National Committee. Perhaps a resolution impeaching the President might divert Congress from further schemes of compromise, he suggested to Potter. What the congressman thought of this suggestion is not known.[42]

The new year brought with it the secession of most of the cotton states, Seward's proposals for compromise, and Buchanan's inability to defend the flag when the *Star of the West* sought to succor beleaguered Fort Sumter. It was a trying time for one as committed as Schurz, who was becoming ever more impatient with the "distasteful" lecture business. He was so anxious to be active on the national stage that between his assignments he found time for a brief visit to Washington. Potter took him to the floor of the House, where on January 21 he heard Thomas Corwin deliver a speech on the state of the Union. He also met the speaker privately, and what he saw did not reassure him.

But he still had reasons for optimism. The papers reported that Lincoln said he had rather die than to purchase the presidency at the price of the surrender of a single plank of the Chicago platform, a course which would only lead to conditions like those prevailing in Mexico. "Gloire à lui," Schurz wrote to Margarethe. Rejoicing that he was living at a wonderful time, when "the rise of a tyrannical party and the lawless attempts of an anti-social element break down under the honest will power of a simple man," he was looking forward to taking an active part in the coming struggle.[43]

It was his deep commitment as well as his boundless self-confidence that led him to commit a blunder. The border states issued a call for a convention in Washington; perhaps this gathering might still save the Union. Radicals everywhere were afraid that concessions might yet be made to the adamant Southerners and sought to assure the presence of trustworthy delegates at the convention; Schurz, who was in Ohio at the time, had the same idea. "Appoint commissioners—me one—to help our side," he wired to Governor Randall. The governor, who had no special love for his old antagonist, made the telegram public, whereupon a veritable storm of newspaper criticism erupted. At first Schurz's friends tried to deny that he had sent the wire, only to be refuted by the telegraph operator who swore that he had seen him do it. Then Schurz admitted that he had telegraphed the message but denied any impropriety, a point of view shared by the Wisconsin *State Journal*. Professing to be nonplussed by the fuss, he sought to put the onus on the governor. He even came to Madison to appear in person before the Republican caucus. Strongly urging that commissioners be appointed, he declined to be a candidate himself. But the two houses of the legislature were unable to compose their differences, and Wisconsin remained unrepresented.[44]

In his enthusiasm, Schurz wrote again to Lincoln himself. Asserting that the President-elect was the party's best hope for preventing a shameful surrender, he expressed the expectation that no matter what efforts were being made to adopt various compromises, the Crittenden proposal or that put forward by the border state conference, Lincoln would remain firm. What right did Republicans have to ask for votes if they were willing to give away everything for which they had contended? He knew that Lincoln agreed with him.[45]

On February 10, he saw the President-elect in person. Traveling through Springfield, Schurz spent the entire afternoon as well as part of the evening with him. The German-American was in for a surprise. With delight, he revealed to Margarethe that Lincoln told him he would confer a mark of confidence on him that he had shown no other man. Then the President-elect locked the door and showed him his inaugural address. That would prove to his visitor that he was not about to entertain the thought of concessions! It was a most satisfactory meeting.

Schurz was present when Lincoln delivered his first inaugural address. Having come to Washington to bolster the party and incidentally his reputation in it, he heard Abraham Lincoln declare that he would "hold, occupy, and possess the property and places belonging to the government, and to collect the duties and imposts." He observed Douglas holding his former opponent's hat, noted the warlike atmosphere in the city, and began a tour of offices to seek his reward. He had the satisfaction of witnessing an historical event which he believed he had done so much to bring about.[46]

VII

Radical Minister to Spain

SCHURZ'S ADAMANT OPPOSITION to all compromises clearly stamped him a radical Republican, an identification confirmed after the outbreak of the Civil War by his prominent position as an emancipationist. To be effective in the advocacy of advanced policies, however, he needed a prominent office, some post which would enable him to exert influence upon the new administration. He was determined to procure it.

Although Schurz always insisted that he loathed office-seeking and office-seekers, in 1860 he was definitely anxious to be rewarded for his efforts. His great exertions on behalf of the Republican party entitled him to recognition; his standing in the country as the spokesman for the German-Americans gave him the means to press his claims. The radicals would obviously further his quest, and Lincoln was not likely to overlook so important a source of support.

Schurz's pursuit of office began shortly after the end of the campaign. As early as November 10, he boasted to his wife that he was being prominently mentioned for the Sardinian mission. Perhaps the king of Sardinia, who was just about to become king of newly united Italy, would move his court from Turin to Rome. Then the appointment would become even more desirable, with visits to picture galleries and breakfast with the "Pope's family." He was certain that he would receive a substantial offer; his position in the party was already such that he was being consulted about the pending senatorial election.[1]

Shortly afterward, on November 24, as he was traveling through Chicago, he met Lincoln's emissaries, who asked him to make his wishes known. Although he remained noncommittal, a few days later he approached his friend Potter. Making no secret of his desire for the Sardinian mission, he emphasized that he was "generally looked upon as the representative of the German element" and considered it due those he represented that he should not take an inferior place. If he were actually going to be sent abroad, he wanted it understood that he really did not expect to go to either Prussia or France. In Berlin, his past might embarrass the administration, and Paris required an older, more experienced diplomat. But Sardinia, or rather newly unified Italy, if it could be raised to a legation of the first class, would be exactly the place for him. Let Potter confer with Senators Doolittle and Lyman Trumbull and find out what Lincoln really had in mind.[2]

Potter's answer, like other assurances that Sardinia was his, was encouraging. By December 17, however, the secession crisis had become so menacing that the excitement almost pushed the thought of office from his mind. "I must confess that I am so completely preoccupied with the danger threatening our cause, that I cannot think of anything that regards myself," he protested to Potter. "I would willingly sacrifice reputation, prospect and everything if I could but for a few weeks infuse my spirit into the Republican members of Congress." Nevertheless, he kept his lines open to Lincoln and to prominent radicals who might assist him in his quest. Neither Doolittle nor Potter was permitted to forget Schurz's desire to be sent to Turin, despite the known fact that, among others, the Vermont scholar and politician George P. Marsh was also an applicant.[3]

By the end of January, the matter was still unsettled. Schurz had not heard anything, although he had learned that he had been mentioned as a possible member of the cabinet. No doubt mindful of the fact that declination of a higher post might lead to the appointment to a lesser one, he wrote to Lincoln that those who were urging him for a cabinet position were acting without his knowledge. The thought had never entered his mind.[4] He was more than ever determined to obtain a foreign mission.

For a time, his ambitions seemed well on the way to being satisfied. When on February 10 he saw Lincoln in Springfield and asked him for offices for some of his friends, the President-elect replied that he would honor the requests; moreover, he added, he would also look out for his visitor. From other sources, Schurz heard again that Lincoln would offer him the legation at Turin.[5]

When the self-appointed spokesman for the German-Americans went to Washington to attend Lincoln's inauguration, he firmly believed that his trip would result in his securing the mission. Anson Burlingame, who had also been a contender for the post, told him he could not really compete with him. The Wisconsin and New York senators, as well as those from Massachusetts, were about to see the President concerning the matter, and Schurz hoped the appointment would be tendered to him by the end of the week. At any rate, he intended to stay in Washington until he was confirmed.

Confidently expecting news of his nomination, Schurz did not allow Lincoln to forget him. On the day after the inauguration, as one of the spokesmen for the radicals, he came to the White House at seven o'clock in the morning to make sure of Chase's inclusion in the cabinet, a visit unquestionably designed to remind the President of his own claims as much as those of the Ohioan. He received congratulations on the supposed appointment and was confidently looking forward to a trip to Italy. However, on March 6, he heard that Lincoln had told Senators Doolittle and Preston King that one of the contender's own countrymen opposed the nomination. Guessing that Koerner was the culprit, Schurz discovered that his suspicions had been correct. After attempting to silence his adversary in person, he hurried to the White House. Lincoln said he favored the appointment, but that he had to consult with Secretary of State Seward. Schurz could come back later for an answer.

When Schurz saw Lincoln again, he finally learned the unpleasant truth. Seward opposed the appointment. He believed it unwise to send republican refugees to European courts. Let Schurz speak to the secretary himself. The President gave him a note and sent him to the State Department.

The secretary of state proved affable. It would be to Schurz's advantage to stay in the United States or to accept some Latin-American mission, he suggested. Perhaps a territorial governorship would be satisfactory? But it was clear that he was adamantly opposed to sending the former German to Europe. And such influential Republican papers as the *New York Times*, to say nothing of the Democratic opposition, agreed with him.

Schurz immediately returned to the White House. Attempting to exert pressure on Lincoln, he said he had to leave town, only to be gratified by the President's urgent request that he delay his departure. He was ready to give Schurz any job, Lincoln asserted, only he must have the consent of the secretary of state. He too proposed a Latin-American mission, an offer his visitor was half-inclined to accept. But he was still holding out for a better post.

Seward's opposition made it possible for Schurz to obtain additional radical backing. The secretary was then the chief opponent of the proposal to reinforce Fort Sumter, a policy deemed essential by the radicals, who considered Schurz's predicament merely one more count against the conservative New Yorker. His chief antagonist in the cabinet at that time was the postmaster general, Montgomery Blair, who, like his father, Francis P. Blair, Sr., living just outside the capital, was determined to keep the government from compromising. It was to old Blair that his son now took Schurz. Because the former member of Andrew Jackson's kitchen cabinet liked the plucky German-American and had influence with the administration, his visitor had reason to hope for more favorable developments.[6]

During the next few days, rumors about Schurz's predicament kept the capital buzzing. Amid reports that he would be sent to Brazil, the newspapers discussed his fate. Democrats called him a worthless vagabond, an insolent infidel, and even some Republicans voiced grave doubts about the propriety of appointing him to a European court. The very idea disgusted the diplomatic corps, the Sardinian chargé d'affaires flatly refusing to accept the German refugee. But his skill in mobilizing his countrymen could not be overlooked. On March 15, the Germans in Washington tendered him a serenade; it was said that unless Schurz were satisfied, the entire German contingent of the Republican party threatened to resign. Such a development would have deplorable consequences on the spring elections in the Northwest.[7]

The situation became even more menacing when on March 17 the President finally appointed Marsh to the Turin post. The attitude of the Italian envoy could not be disregarded; moreover, the Vermonter was well versed in Italian affairs. But the appointment was considered a grave blow for his competitor, and the newspapers were full of speculations about the consequences. The Germans were reported to be furious, their anger highlighting a problem already very much on Lincoln's mind. "What about Carl Schurz? Or in other words, what about our german [*sic*] friends?" he asked Seward. He would have to do something to assuage their ire. As the hostile New York *Herald* was soon to point out, it was universally conceded that the German vote had turned the scales against the President's competitors, especially in the Northwestern states. And now even Carl Schurz was being cast aside![8]

Schurz himself, in high dudgeon, immediately went to call on Lincoln. It was early in the morning, and the President asked him to come back at night. At the appointed time, Lincoln expressed his regrets about developments. He apologized, offered Brazil, Chile, or Portugal, but received no definitive answer. Then Schurz went to the State Department, where he gave Seward "his mind without reserve," only to obtain the same offers of Latin assignments. On the next day, he accepted Lincoln's tender of Lisbon, provided that the legation there be raised to a first-class mission so that he would earn $12,000 per annum. Because Congress was not in session, this condition was difficult to fulfill, but certain New York bankers offered to pay the difference until the next session. Believing he might enjoy the assignment, Schurz was already thinking of spending some time in Hamburg, Paris, and Italy.[9]

For Lincoln, then fully occupied with the crisis about the Southern forts, Schurz's demands created a grave problem. For even though the New York *Herald* was exaggerating when it wrote that "next to the difficulty about Fort Sumter, the question as to what is to be done about Carl Schurz seems to bother the administration more than anything else," the President was indeed in a quandary about his German friend. Because German-Americans considered the matter a test case, something would have to be done.[10] And Seward proved totally unwilling to raise the status of the Portuguese legation.

On the twentieth of March, Lincoln saw Schurz again. Informing him that Seward refused to comply with the demand about Lisbon, he asked him to come back that night at 8:00 P.M. At that time, Schurz found the secretary of state in the White House, and in the President's presence, he gave Seward a piece of his mind. Lincoln, greatly embarrassed, begged Schurz to get him out of his difficulty, only to be told that he who had got him in ought to get him out. Schurz would settle for nothing but a first-class European mission. The President asked him to return the next morning.

This time the interview was private. Assuring Schurz that he would not permit Seward to disregard him, the President made it clear that he did not want his friend to leave dissatisfied. Schurz saucily replied that the Republicans had elected Lincoln president, not undersecretary of state. The matter was up to him. He, Schurz, would leave Washington the next day. Not even Lincoln's renewed pleas for help in solving the difficulty affected his visitor, who rose and left.

But of course he did not return home the next day. That night the postmaster general came to see him. Lincoln, said Blair, was most anxious to keep Schurz in Washington. Would he be satisfied with Mexico? When the German-American refused, Blair suggested that Cassius M. Clay, the fiery Kentucky antislavery leader, who had been offered the Spanish mission, might be induced to take the Russian legation instead, so that Schurz could go to Madrid. The would-be envoy was intrigued with the idea.[11]

As Schurz correctly surmised, his case had become enmeshed with the cabinet struggle then going on about the fate of the Southern forts. Fort Sumter was about to run out of supplies; whether to sustain it or to abandon it was the main problem confronting the administration and the country. Lincoln polled his cabinet on the issue on March 15; within a day the replies were in. Seward and a number of his conservative colleagues were still adamantly opposed to any action tending to reinforce the fort; Blair, supported to some degree by Chase, was in favor of sending in supplies. The postmaster general's father was so concerned that he bluntly told Lincoln it would be treason to abandon the fort. How much of this he told Schurz is not known, but he did make it clear that he thought Seward's power could be broken. For the radical Schurz, this aim seemed desirable not merely because of his own problems but also because of his conviction that Fort Sumter should not be abandoned. He was already under the impression that he had ''done more than all others to keep Lincoln on the right track.''[12]

He now bided his time. Horace Greeley with his New York *Tribune* was already on his side, while German newspapers pointedly reminded the country that the Germans had turned the tide in the elections. Considering Schurz's predicament a test case, they asserted that the opposition to his appointment signified nothing but greed and nativism.[13] The impatient applicant himself addressed another letter to Lincoln. The postmaster general had informed him the President desired him to remain in Washington a few days longer. If Lincoln wanted to tell him something, he hoped it would be done soon, because he would have to leave Washington on Wednesday, the day before the Senate adjourned.[14]

In the meantime, the Blairs had taken matters in hand. Writing to Clay to explain the situation to him, they urged him to accept St. Petersburg instead of Madrid. This would put the Germans in debt to Clay as well as frustrate Seward. The Kentuckian, who had not been happy about the prospect of going to Spain anyway, agreed. ''Clay, I thank you, for you relieve me of a great embarrassment,'' Lincoln said to him. Now free to offer Spain to Schurz, he did so on March 28.[15]

Schurz was overjoyed. In high spirits, he announced his ''triumph'' to Margarethe. Gloating about his victory over Seward, he wrote that Madrid was even more desirable than Turin. ''Next to Mexico,'' he boasted, ''Spain is the most important diplomatic post—and it is mine.''[16]

The news took the country by surprise. Many Republican journals were satisfied, while the same Democratic newspapers that had earlier attacked the administration for alleged nativism because of its failure to appoint Schurz now declared it an outrage to send this ''foreign adventurer and mercenary soldier'' on an important mission. What Spain's reaction would be remained to be seen.[17]

That Spain would take no less kindly to the appointment of a former revolutionary than Sardinia was to be expected. Indeed, Don Gabriel Garcia y Tassara, the Spanish minister in Washington, had already explained to his government that, because of the debts owed to the Germans who had helped elect Lincoln, Schurz was going to receive a diplomatic post. Characterizing him as a German emigrant deeply compromised by the Revolution of 1848, Garcia y Tassara had minutely explained the offer of Italy, of Brazil, and the tentative plans for Portugal. Then, when he finally learned of the appointment to Madrid, he sent another detailed report to Saturnino Calderon Collantes, the Spanish foreign minister. Repeating his precise description of Schurz's office-seeking and the fact that he had contributed "many thousands of votes" to the election of the President, the Spaniard concluded that it was most unusual for the American government not to have informed him beforehand. It was for Calderon to decide whether or not to acquiesce in the troublesome nomination.

The Spanish government's reaction was not favorable. Insisting that Schurz's revolutionary antecedents were bound to render his European mission fruitless, the foreign minister pointed out that, as a republican in Europe and an abolitionist in America, the prospective envoy was the least appropriate person to reside at the court of the head of an ancient monarchy which tolerated slavery. It was therefore not in Her Most Catholic Majesty's interest to permit him to come to Madrid and become the center of democratic conspiracies.

But the letter from Spain did not arrive in America until early June. By that time, relations between the two countries had already been severely strained because of Spain's reannexation of Santo Domingo, and Schurz was permitted to assume his post.[18] That this development, at least in part, was foreseen by Lincoln is wholly within the realm of possibility.

While no direct evidence about the President's foresight exists, it is certain that he was aware of European opposition to Schurz. He also knew that at a time of threatening civil war he could not risk foreign complications. Anxious to placate his supporter and the German-Americans, he finally sent him to Spain, the one European country which, because of its ever-increasing involvement in the Caribbean, could not afford to create additional complications with the United States. And Seward, who, to reunite the sections, two days later submitted to Lincoln his April Fool's Day proposal advocating war with European powers, and especially with Spain, could not really object too strenuously to an appointment less than welcome in Madrid.[19]

In a state of elation about his success, Schurz, after asking that his partner, Paine, be appointed secretary of the legation, left for home by way of New York. Arriving in Milwaukee, he decided to take advantage of Lincoln's invitation to write to him about the state of public opinion. The local spring elections had not been favorable to the administration; Schurz interpreted the result as a clear indication that "anything"—war, recognition of the Confederacy, any program —would be better than no action. Let the government carry out the policy announced at the inauguration by reinforcing Fort Sumter; the people would sustain the President. Once Sumter was reinforced, Lincoln could call an extra session of Congress, which would give him whatever he wanted.[20] The writer did not know that part of his advice was already being followed. The President, after due warning to the governor of South Carolina, had given orders for sending provisions to Charleston harbor.

At the time war broke out, Schurz was still worrying about the appointment of a secretary for his legation. Seward's choice for the position was Horatio Perry, an American who had long resided in Spain, was fluent in the language, and had married a Spanish lady. Well liked in Spanish circles, his wife a confidante of the queen, he was perfectly suited for the office. But because the new minister was anxious to accommodate his law partner, he protested bitterly.[21]

The first news of the events at Charleston gave him more important matters to think about. Swept up in the general excitement, he rejoiced in the manifestations of national unity in Wisconsin. It was rumored that he would resign to enlist in the militia, and in fact he regretted his inability to join the armed forces. Publicly refusing an invitation to a dinner in his honor on the grounds that in this emergency all good citizens' efforts ought to be channeled toward Washington, he announced his own imminent departure and on April 22 left for the capital.[22]

Schurz's reactions to the outbreak of war were typical of him. Genuinely worried about the national crisis and anxious to serve, he was at the same time fully conscious of the political advantages of a military career. Moreover, he fancied himself an expert in military affairs and was anxious to test his theories in the field.

The trip to Washington was not easy. Because the insurgents had cut the direct rail lines through Baltimore, passengers for the capital had to take a boat from Perryville to Annapolis, where General Benjamin F. Butler was about to reopen communications by way of Annapolis Junction. Greatly encouraged by the patriotic spirit which seemed to prevail everywhere, Schurz finally reached his destination with the first train.[23]

He went to see the President as soon as possible. Making known his own desire to be of service, he even ventured to give strategic advice. All efforts at retaking Charleston ought to be abandoned, he said. Forays into the interior were the answer to the nation's problems! His "wild enthusiasm," "his desire to mingle in this war," his "great confidence in his military powers, and his capacity of arousing the enthusiasm of the young," all seemed appropriate for a leader who was contemplating "the career of a great guerilla chief with ardent longing," as Lincoln's young secretary, John Hay, noted in his diary.[24]

The outcome of this interview was an authorization to raise a cavalry regiment in New York for service with the Federal army. Certain that there were many Germans experienced in cavalry tactics, Schurz was doubtless gratified that in the appropriate orders, the secretary of war referred to him as "Colonel Schurz." Seward gave him a three months' leave of absence, and the proud colonel told Hay he was going home to arm his clansmen. "He will make a wonderful land pirate, bold, quick, brilliant and reckless,'' predicted Lincoln's secretary. Although he correctly foresaw that the German would be hard to control and difficult to direct, he was very favorably impressed, especially as Schurz agreed with him that the Civil War was an excellent opportunity to strike a blow against slavery.[25]

The recruiting mission was beset with difficulties. Winfield Scott, the general-in-chief, opposed the entire enterprise on the grounds that his own strategy—he was then thinking of the Anaconda Plan of blockading the South and starving it into submission—would make the use of volunteer cavalry unnecessary. Simon Cameron, the secretary of war, was also reluctant, and the government refused to pay for the horses and accoutrements. Yet, with the aid of his old friend Schimmelfennig, Schurz did a creditable job. Stopping off at Philadelphia, where despite local resistance he induced at least one unit to make common cause with him, he proceeded to New York, where he found several German regiments in the process of formation. He stayed with his old companion, Dr. Jacobi, went to work organizing the troops, and succeeded in winning their officers' esteem. Favorably disposed toward him because of his reputation and his supposed influence in Washington, they recognized his ability and his capacity for choosing good men. Colonel Louis Blenker especially welcomed him cordially, and even Mrs. Schurz enjoyed meeting his officers at their encampment.[26] By May 13, his preparations had gone far enough for Lincoln to consider the acceptance of a brigade of four regiments for service at Fortress Monroe. If their officers so desired, Schurz would become their brigadier. Even though a problem concerning seniority developed—General Butler was also going to the fort—the President continued to encourage Schurz, who reported that a brigade consisting of the Seventh, Eighth, and Twentieth German regiments, as well as Ellsworth's Zouaves, had been formed by the state. The field officers of the German units had voted for him for brigadier general, and he thought that Butler's recent promotion to higher rank would solve the question of seniority.[27]

Schurz went to Washington in person to speed up matters. He became ever more friendly with Charles Sumner, now the chairman of the Senate's Committee on Foreign Relations, and was a welcome guest at the White House. Sitting with Lincoln on the balcony while the Marine Band was playing on the south lawn, he watched the President kiss numerous babies. After Lincoln retired, he went into the library to play the piano until the President came down and took him to tea. ''Schurz is a wonderful man,'' Hay wrote. ''An orator, a soldier, a philosopher, an exiled patriot, a skilled musician. He has every quality of romance and of dramatic picturesqueness.'' The story of Schurz's playing Beethoven to lull the President to sleep became part of the Lincoln legend; in spite of his close relationship with the White House, however, he never received the appointment to head the German regiments.[28]

The reason he failed in 1861 in his quest for military command was the increased tension between the United States and Spain because of the reannexation of Santo Domingo. For Seward especially, the problem of Spanish-American relations had assumed major proportions. When the President firmly rejected the secretary's original proposal of a European war to reunite the sections, the New Yorker began to take a more reasoned view of the situation and was now attempting to deal with the reannexation of the Caribbean island in a prudent manner. Schurz's predecessor, William Preston, had already lodged a protest with the Madrid government; Seward then instructed Horatio Perry, whom he appointed chargé d'affaires, to make the American objections known once more. But Perry's commission was delayed in transit. Ignorant of his promotion, the new chargé d'affaires signified his intention of returning to the United States, and the secretary of state, not knowing whether Perry was still there or whether he had left, believed that an envoy had to be sent to the Spanish court at once. Accordingly, he instructed Schurz to leave immediately and to protest vigorously against Spain's colonial venture.[29]

After making final arrangements for the disposition of his troops—upon Philip Kearney's advice, he succeeded in securing the appointment of Major Andrew T. McReynolds of Michigan as their commander—the new minister-designate reluctantly complied. On the one hand, it must have been a great feeling to be returning to Europe, which he had left as a refugee only a few years earlier, as envoy extraordinary and minister plenipotentiary of the United States of America, but on the other, he could not rid himself of the thought that it would be much better for him to take an active part in the war. "You are much happier than I am at this moment," he wrote to Paine, to whom he sent his sword upon parting. "You stand at the head of a body of brave men, eager to fight for the greatest of causes . . . and I must leave the country just at a time when it is dearest to me." In a parting letter of gratitude for past favors, he assured Lincoln that he would be happy to come home should the President see fit to call him to a different field of action. "I regret deeply to leave this country just now, in these days of danger and trial," he added, "and I certainly would not, did I not think that in the position you have assigned me I might render the Republic some important service." It was with mixed feelings that on June 8 he left for England on the *New York*. His family accompanied him.[30]

When he arrived in London, he took the first opportunity to pay a visit to Charles Francis Adams, the American minister, who briefed him about the latest developments in European-American relations. "His Excellency, Carl Schurz, the famous German orator recently appointed Minister to Spain by Pres't Lincoln, was here this morning," Benjamin Moran, the secretary of the legation, noted in his diary. "He is a tall, slender, rather thin man, with weak blue eyes, blond hair, a prominent nose, firm expressive mouth, and a highly intellectual face. His manners are courtly, and although he has the bended shoulders of the student, he is a man one would notice instinctively in a crowd. . . . Mr. Schurz is clearly a man of mark, and will represent us both to his own and our credit."[31]

Moran was right. Schurz's mission to Spain was not unsuccessful, despite the original reservations of the Spanish government. Garcia y Tassara had thought better of his objections because of the pending international complications; having just officially informed the United States of Spain's reannexation of Santo Domingo, he was not anxious to cause any more trouble between the two countries by putting obstacles in the way of the minister-designate. Moreover, it was apparent that the North was less inclined to pursue expansionist policies at Spain's expense than the South, and the Spanish government was pleased about Perry's elevation. As J. Kinley Brauer has surmised, it may have considered the simultaneous promotion of Perry as a compensation for Schurz's appointment. At any rate, the chargé d'affaires, who had not left, saw to it that the government in Madrid dropped its objections, so that it proved willing to receive the former revolutionary, republican and abolitionist though he was.[32]

Although Schurz had been looking forward to a long reunion with his family, he was to be disappointed. Because Margarethe had fallen ill again, her husband, worried about the summer climate in Spain, decided to send her and the children to her relatives in Hamburg while he went on to Madrid by himself. After a pleasant time with the Althaus family in London, the Schurzes traveled together to Paris, where Carl had to confer with the American minister, William L. Dayton. Then they separated, Margarethe and the girls turning east toward Germany, Carl south to Marseilles to take a boat to Alicante. From there he continued by train to Madrid, where he arrived alone on July 12.

He reached his post just in time. Perry, whom he found most congenial, informed him that it was essential to be presented at court as soon as possible, as the queen was about to leave for Santander. Schurz agreed, and that very day he saw the foreign minister. Calderon, with whom the new envoy was able to carry on a conversation in French, was extremely courteous. He said that he hoped Schurz bore friendly instructions and that the United States was satisfied with the Neutrality Proclamation the queen had just issued. Equally polite, the American minister replied that this was the case, but that the administration was taking a dim view of Spain's activities in Santo Domingo. The foreign minister then delivered a long disquisition about the desire of the Dominican people to resume their dependence on Spain. He also promised to arrange an interview with the queen.[33]

The audience took place on the following day. Had relations between the two countries not been so delicate, it would have been a comedy from beginning to end. Because his splendidly decorated court uniform had not yet arrived, Schurz, disdainful of monarchies in general and of Queen Isabella II in particular, arrived at the palace in plain evening clothes. This unprecedented costume had occasioned difficult negotiations with the *introductor de los embajadores*, who had finally given his reluctant consent. However, when the medieval guards at the bottom of the stairway saw the inappropriately garbed envoy, they crossed their halberds to block his way to the reception room. Only when the *introductor de los embajadores* in person came down the stairs to settle the matter was the American minister admitted into her Most Catholic Majesty's presence. But another complication had developed. In his hurry to reach the palace, Schurz discovered that he had inadvertently left his letter of accreditation behind. Because he could not go back to retrieve it—it was unthinkable to let a monarch wait—he had recourse to a ruse. Quickly folding a newspaper, he placed it in an envelope addressed to the queen, who was known to hand such documents to her foreign minister without opening them. Perry told Calderon about the embarrassment and promised to give him the genuine document the next day.

Thus Schurz, not properly dressed and equipped with a letter of accreditation which was really a folded newspaper, was introduced to the queen, a fat, squat woman with a reputation for loose living, who did not understand a word of English. Fortunately, the British ambassador preceded him, so that he was able to observe the formalities customary at such occasions. After delivering a brief, formal speech in English, in which, at the foreign minister's request, he did not mention Santo Domingo, and receiving an equally formal reply in Spanish, he managed to converse more naturally with the queen in French. The monarch took the unopened letter he handed her and gave it to the foreign minister. It was not until the next day that Calderon received the actual accreditation.

One last official duty remained. In accordance with an international arrangement, the queen had been married to a Bourbon cousin, Don Francisco de Asís, for whom she had no affection and who was not taken seriously by anybody, but who carried the courtesy title of king. Schurz was led through several corridors to a small room, where the consort was waiting. With a high voice, Don Francisco asked whether his visitor had been seasick during the crossing and was surprised to hear that this was not the case. Otherwise, there was little to say, and Schurz retired.[34]

However, there were diplomatic chores to be performed. Schurz's position was uncomfortable from the beginning, not merely because of the Spanish government's initial opposition to his appointment, but also, as he pointed out to Seward, because of the peculiar circumstances surrounding his arrival. He was presented at court immediately after the United States had lodged a strong protest about the annexation of Santo Domingo, an action which, in the ordinary course of events, was usually followed by the departure of the minister. Now he had come to be introduced to the queen; without specific instructions, he could not immediately leave again, and so he maintained a studied reserve toward the Spanish government. Neither following the court to Santander nor later for a time to San Ildefonso, he stayed in the hot capital and sought to explain the Civil War to the Spaniards. To keep Spain from lending aid to the Confederacy was essential; correctly considering this objective his main task in Madrid, Schurz never failed to present the Union cause in a favorable light, while Perry reminded Calderon that it had been the South, not the North, which had engaged in filibustering expeditions.

Schurz's diplomatic instincts were very sound. Seeing clearly that a foreign war would not be in the interest of the United States, he advised Seward to let the Santo Domingo affair slide. He even discovered that Spain might be inclined to negotiate a new commercial treaty easing some of her ancient colonial trade restrictions and to arrive at some settlement for mutual claims. Considering his lack of experience in foreign affairs, his performance was eminently satisfactory.[35]

Perry had well taken care of his superior's physical needs. Expecting Schurz to arrive with his family, he had engaged rooms at the Hotel de los Embajadores at five dollars per day but made appropriate changes when he heard that the minister was coming alone. The cost was excessive, and so, much to Schurz's delight, Perry then found quarters for him in his own villa, La Quinta, just outside the city gates, which had formerly been the residence of Queen Maria Christina. Sharing the property with the Perrys, he was comfortably housed. Years later, he still remembered La Quinta's peculiar aspect, its wide, wrought-iron gate, its large enclosed courtyard surrounded by a high brick wall, its little dark stone pavillion from which Queen Maria Christina used to watch bull fights, its long, two-story living quarters with heavily barred windows, a winding flight of stone steps leading to a reception room called the *sal de las cabezas* because each of the four corners was ornamented with a huge plaster head of some mythical figure. Fortunately, it had a tree-shaded garden, a rarity in the otherwise bare landscape of Castile.

Spain simply did not appeal to him. The lack of trees as well as the generally low level of education of the kingdom made a poor impression upon Schurz. He could not understand why so much had been said and written about the country's beauty, for he thought that he had never seen a more dreary landscape. Repelled by the political corruption and the widespread superstition even among the middle and upper classes, he considered the crowd's enthusiasm for bull fights a good indication of the general level of culture. Not even Madrid impressed him. Although he admitted that it had some lovely streets and walks, he believed that in magnificence it did not exceed a princely German capital of the second or third rank. And the thought of great events at home made him long for the United States.[36]

News from America, however, was not encouraging. Early in August, he was cast into the deepest gloom. Word of the Confederate victory at Manassas utterly prostrated him. Although he did not know the full details of the battle, the newspapers were full of reports of the Federal defeat. Spaniards jokingly remarked that the engagement ought to be called Patassas (feet) instead of Manassas (hands), because the Union army had run away so ignominiously. For all the embassy knew, Washington was open to the enemy and the next mail might bring news of the Confederate flag flying over the White House.

In his dismay, Schurz unburdened himself to Lincoln. The defeat, he thought, was due to General Scott's mistaken strategy. Instead of exploiting his superiority over the enemy, the general found himself inferior at one point and lost a battle. If the President so desired, the envoy would be glad to come home to assist in the prosecution of the war.

In a covering letter to the secretary of state, Schurz admitted freely that he had no knowledge of the details of the battle. Nevertheless, he was almost certain that his views were correct. Perhaps Seward remembered that shortly before Schurz left, he had tried to point out to the secretary several mistakes which were then being committed, faulty dispositions of the troops which later proved fatal. But Seward had refused to listen.

Schurz's unlimited self-confidence was astonishing. To be sure, during the long leisure hours in Madrid he had augmented his military knowledge by studying military classics. He immersed himself in the campaigns of Frederick the Great, the Archduke Charles, and Napoleon. He attempted to master the works of the Swiss general Antoine Henri Jomini and the Prussian strategist Karl von Clausewitz. He even sought to familiarize himself with the latest works on the French campaign in Italy two years earlier and translated a book on tactics from French into English.[37] But he had never led any troops, and his experience in 1849 was very limited.

Nevertheless, he was so convinced of his military knowledge that on August 13 he sent to the President another letter full of strategic advice. The details of the disaster at Bull Run were clear to him now, he stated. Scott had disregarded his advice about strong artillery support! The trouble was not that the Federal army had moved too early, as conservatives angry at radical demands for speedy action were charging, but that it had moved too late. As Napoleon's campaign in Italy had shown, volunteers needed action. Repeating his desire to return to America, he asserted he would be happy to obtain a command where the fighting was to be done. But he would also be satisfied to help Lincoln grapple with the problems of the war. While the President had many good men in his entourage, there was none upon whose courage and devotion he could more safely rely than Schurz's. The envoy was tired of leading a life of ease and comfort while the country was at war.

What Lincoln thought of his young acquaintance's conceit is not fully known. Although even Perry was induced to write fulsomely on Schurz's behalf, Seward did not answer until September 3. He had conferred with the President about the minister's request, he stated, but Lincoln believed that American interests would be better served by making no changes in the embassy's personnel.[38] The impatient envoy had to content himself with his diplomatic duties.

These he continued to perform very well. Mindful of his main task, the prevention of Spanish aid to the Confederacy, he saw to it that no succor was given to Southern raiders in Cuba or elsewhere in the Spanish empire. He provided material for the liberal press and soon succeeded in influencing its reports about the United States. Because government-supported organs remained hostile, his pointed refusal to follow the court to San Ildefonso was not lost on Calderon. Only after a consultation with Perry and a personal interview did the foreign minister finally induce the envoy to reside near Her Majesty. Calderon assured the American that the government was not responsible for the attacks, which promptly ceased.

Commercial negotiations were less successful. The claims convention failed because of the *Amistad* case. The Spanish slave ship by that name, which in 1839 had been seized by its involuntary passengers, who killed many of their captors, had finally been brought to the United States by the remnant of her crew. Indicted for murder, the slaves were finally freed. Spain claimed damages; however, as Seward correctly pointed out, although some other administrations might have entertained such claims, the present one assuredly was unable to do so. The commercial convention likewise lagged; as Schurz explained to the State Department, in spite of all protestations to the contrary, the Spanish government, like most of its European counterparts, was inherently hostile to the great Republic.

One of the most serious matters with which Schurz had to deal during his stay in Spain was the pending European intervention in Mexico. Long rent by civil war, America's southern neighbor had failed to pay the debts due various European claimants, and British, French, and Spanish efforts to collect these obligations resulted in a planned tripartite intervention. Keeping the State Department fully informed of the developing crisis—he even met with General Juan Prim, the presumptive Spanish commander of the expedition—Schurz pointed out that it was essential to maintain peace with the European powers. America simply could not afford another war.[39]

The longer he stayed in Madrid, however, and the more he associated with his diplomatic colleagues, the more he became convinced that there was only one way to counter the danger of European intervention or recognition of the Confederacy: the announcement of a policy of general emancipation. In the long run, no Western government could withstand the liberal nineteenth-century trend of opposition to slavery; if their governments did not pay heed to this fact, the people would. Accordingly, on September 14, Schurz sent a long dispatch to Seward. Voicing his regret that public opinion in the Old World was not as unconditionally in America's favor as might have been expected, he asserted that only an antislavery policy could remedy the situation. "It is my profound conviction," he continued, "that as soon as the war becomes distinctly one for and against slavery, public opinion will be so strongly, so overwhelmingly, in our favor . . . that no European Government will dare to place itself . . . upon the side of a universally condemned institution."

That Seward, the leader of the conservative faction in the cabinet, could have but little sympathy with such views was evident; however, they were not meant for him, but for the President. In fact, when on October 10 he sent his reply to Madrid, he admitted the propriety of the envoy's reporting on public sentiment in Europe but added that he could not engage in explanations of domestic policy. The administration's policy, he wrote, "must be confined always to the existing condition of political forces and to the political sentiment of the whole country." In addition, he thought that nations could not be saved by outside forces. They must rely upon themselves.

Schurz fumed, especially as at that very time he found out that another dispatch, which Seward had sent somewhat earlier and which had not yet arrived, had already reached Calderon via the Spanish legation in Washington. Interpreting this perfectly natural mishap as a deliberate affront, he became more and more determined to return and to submit his ideas to Lincoln in person. At first he thought of resigning; however, Perry, pointing out that another change in ministers at that time would complicate American relations with Spain, persuaded him to ask for a leave of absence instead. Convinced by these arguments, on November 11 Schurz wrote to Lincoln to request a leave. He had accomplished his mission, he asserted. Newspaper attacks on the United States had stopped, Spain had refrained from intervening in the Civil War, and Perry was so good a diplomat that the legation could easily be entrusted to him. If his request could not be granted, he would have to resign. In a covering letter to Seward, he again expressed his conviction that without emancipation, the war could not be won. Leaving nothing to chance, he also let Sumner know that he wanted to come home to urge emancipation upon the administration. His radical friends would certainly support him.[40]

The impatient envoy now awaited Lincoln's reply. He had already made plans to call for Margarethe in Hamburg and sought permission to travel through Prussian territory. Norman Judd, the American minister in Berlin, and Count Galen, the Prussian ambassador in Madrid, could help him. The latter was especially useful. Finding him congenial, Schurz discovered that he was a distant kinsman of the Wolf-Metternichs and well remembered the Gracht at Liblar. Permission was granted, but communications were slow, so that Schurz had to be patient.[41]

While the legation was awaiting the reply from Washington, new war clouds appeared to disturb American diplomats. On November 8, Commodore Charles Wilkes of the U.S.S. *San Jacinto* stopped the British mail steamer *Trent* on the high seas. After boarding her, he seized two of her passengers, the Confederate commissioners James M. Mason and John Slidell. When news of this violation of international law reached Europe, the British government threatened war unless the two Southerners were returned.

Schurz was worried about this contingency. Excitedly, he wrote to Seward that public opinion universally condemned the action; one week later, with his usual self-confidence, he sought to take a hand in solving the dispute himself. Warning the State Department that war with England would leave the United States without friends, he suggested the king of Italy be asked to mediate. In fact, he took the liberty of inquiring himself of his colleague in Turin whether Italian mediation would not be possible. His recognition of the dangers of foreign war did him credit; his proposal for mediation, however, ran counter to the expressed policy of the administration. The dispute was eventually solved by the timely surrender of the two prisoners.[42]

Seward answered Schurz on December 2. Explaining that the President did not believe Schurz's absence from Madrid was desirable, he nevertheless granted the minister a three months' leave should he still want to come home. Because Margarethe had telegraphed that one of the girls was not well, Schurz did not even wait for the arrival of this dispatch. Hearing from Adams on December 17 that Lincoln had acceded to his request, he took leave from the queen the next day and departed for Hamburg that very night.[43]

As the train approached Germany toward nightfall, Schurz must have experienced ambivalent feelings. Treated with great courtesy at the frontier—the Prussian government had instructed its functionaries accordingly—he listened to the familiar church bells at Cologne as the train stopped briefly at the station. Then he crossed the Rhine. It was a return very different from his hasty departure a dozen years before.

Reunited with his family in Hamburg, he awaited the outcome of the *Trent* affair as well as that of a new difficulty, the landing of the Confederate raider *Sumter* at Cadiz. When both of these crises passed, he decided that the time for his departure had come and during the second week of January 1862 embarked on the *Bavaria* for New York.

It was a terrible trip lasting twenty-two days. Exposing the passengers to extremely rough seas, the ship lost four boats; the bulwarks were crushed, sails were ripped to tatters, yards torn down and broken. Nevertheless, Schurz, a good sailor, managed very well.[44] As soon as he arrived in the United States, he rushed to Washington to report to the administration in person.

Calling on both Seward and Lincoln, he found the President cordial. The real reason for his coming to America, Schurz told Lincoln, was to plead for emancipation. Without it, foreign intervention could not be prevented. The President, who had been thinking along similar lines, seemed pleased; nevertheless, he told his visitor that he could not move too fast ahead of public opinion. The border states had to be considered; the War Democrats could not be offended. Let Schurz look around and within a few weeks submit a report about the state of public opinion.

The radical envoy was pleased with his reception. Even Seward seemed friendly. But of course he had not come home merely to acquaint the administration with his political impressions of Europe. Anxious to be given a command in the army, he tried his best to convince his superiors to accept his resignation. He renewed his acquaintance with Henry Wilson, the chairman of the Senate Committee on Military Affairs, and maintained his friendship with Charles Sumner. Powerful friends in Congress could not do his quest any harm.

Then, for a while, he had to wait. Willie Lincoln, the President's son, was very ill, and when he died, his grief-stricken parents were inconsolable. Temporarily at least, there was little Schurz could do to further his goal. After attending the boy's funeral, he left for New York, where he helped organize an emancipation society, which planned a public meeting for March 6.

After a few days, he returned to Washington to see Lincoln. Informing him of the steps he had taken in New York, he showed him the speech he had prepared for the planned emancipation meeting. The President not only approved but indicated that at the proper time he might have something to add. Greatly encouraged, Schurz made the final preparations for the gathering at Cooper Institute.[45]

On the appointed day, he appeared at the famous New York meeting hall before a distinguished group of antislavery leaders. Confessing that he had been wrong in predicting that the South would not start a war, he reaffirmed his conviction that after the rebellion was put down the Union must be restored. But without the destruction of slavery there could be no restoration; the insurgents could be made loyal only if the peculiar institution was abolished. It must be ended in the District of Columbia; the slaves of rebels must be confiscated. The great American republic must not be afraid of the nineteenth century. When amid great applause he ended his remarks, it was announced that Lincoln had sent a message to Congress advocating gradual emancipation in the border states. The audience was enthusiastic.[46]

Shortly after the antislavery meeting, Schurz fell ill. Headaches and a general malaise kept him confined for several days. When he recovered, his resignation as minister to Spain was finally accepted and he eagerly looked forward to a military career.[47] He had performed his diplomatic duties well. Succeeding in establishing friendly relations with the government to which he was accredited, he had contributed to Spain's neutrality during the Civil War. In addition, his position had given him greater leverage for the advocacy of his radical emancipation policies. It would not be long before Lincoln put into effect many of the steps proposed in the Cooper Institute address. Schurz had every reason to be satisfied with his achievements.

VIII

Radical Brigadier General

EVER SINCE THE ATTACK on Fort Sumter, Schurz had been contemplating a military career. It was because of his firm determination to fight for the cause that he obtained a three months' leave to raise the New York cavalry regiments, and he left for Spain only upon the insistence of the administration. Thus, when he returned to the United States, his principal purpose was to secure a commission in the army. At a time when all kinds of politicians were elevated to high military rank without substantial previous military experience, his request was not unreasonable.

To realize his desire, however, was not so simple. Brigadier generals were not easy to place, and Schurz was wholly unwilling to accept a token command. Moreover, his previous position, to say nothing of his role as spokesman for the German-Americans, required that he be given at least a division. It was therefore not surprising that Lincoln was not as eager to accept his resignation as Schurz was to tender it.

Nevertheless, from the moment of his arrival in Washington, he utilized all the political skills he possessed to secure his nomination. He sought to aid Franz Sigel, one of the leaders of the Baden insurrection and the hero of the Germans because of his success at the battle of Pea Ridge, in his search for promotion. Taking Sigel's friends to the White House and the War Department, now headed by Edward M. Stanton, he stressed the fact that the German element deserved some recognition from the Republican party.[1] That he was referring to himself as well as to the general was obvious. Then, after the emancipation speech at Cooper Union, he returned to the White House to see Lincoln again.

Exactly what transpired at the interview is not certain. In his *Reminiscences* Schurz stated that the President, in high spirits because of the recent victory of the *Monitor* over the *Merrimac*, recounted all the details of the battle and then urged his visitor to reconsider his desire to resign from the diplomatic service. Seward wanted him to go back to Spain, a wish the secretary of state confirmed in person; however, in another interview with Lincoln, Schurz insisted on entering the army, whereupon he was promised a commission. In a somewhat different account in a letter to his parents at the time, he wrote that in his interview with the President (he mentioned only one), Lincoln indicated that in view of the coming political struggles he wanted him to remain in the United States. Of course Schurz readily agreed, only to be told that he could expect a position in America commensurate with the one in Spain. Since there were no civilian jobs available, this commitment meant a commission in the army.[2] Although these two accounts are somewhat contradictory, it is probable that the President would have preferred Schurz to return to Madrid; he had troubles enough without worrying about demands for new jobs. For weeks after he sent the nomination to the Senate, he neither accepted the resignation from the diplomatic service nor assigned the former envoy to a command. In the long run, however, because of Schurz's own persistence, as well as the President's sensitivity to the ethnic issue, he obtained what he wanted.

A propitious development for Schurz took place on March 11, when Lincoln effected a thorough reorganization of the military. General George B. McClellan's Army of the Potomac was divided into corps d'armée; at the same time, General Frémont was given command of the new Mountain Department. As a radical, Schurz must have been glad about McClellan's diminution of power; as a German, he could aspire to assignment with Frémont, who was popular with naturalized citizens. For his part, the Pathfinder, aware of Schurz's political influence, was already in hopes that the new general might not only join him but also obtain for him three additional regiments from the government.[3]

When, on March 25, Lincoln forwarded Schurz's nomination to the War Department, Schurz must have hoped that his troubles were over. Yet he was far from his goal. Not only did he still have to be confirmed by the Senate, but the President also had to give him a fitting assignment. In addition, just at this time he fell ill. Needing care, he left for Philadelphia, where he stayed with the Tiedemanns to await confirmation. In the meantime, he enlisted Sumner and Wilson to secure Senate approval, which finally came on April 15.[4] Whether an appropriate command could be found for the new brigadier remained to be seen.

Somehow or other, the promised troops seemed to elude him. He heard that he would get only a brigade; but, since after a six weeks' march General Blenker's division was demoralized and its commander in trouble, it was possible that Schurz might take it over. To remind Lincoln of her husband's expectations, Margarethe, whom the President liked, went to the White House to plead Carl's cause, and a few days later, Schurz himself wrote again to the President. Perhaps Lincoln did not understand him. He was not seeking a higher office. The legation in Madrid was at least as desirable as any military commission, so that he ought not to be judged by standards applied to the multitude of suitors crowding the White House. He had come to help the President carry out an emancipation policy that was being undermined by so many other generals. This was why he needed an assignment commensurate with his rank, and he was determined to get it.

Fully recovered from his illness, on May 14 he had another personal interview with Lincoln. Unless he could find a suitable command for him, said the President, he would prefer him to return to Spain. He would let him know as soon as something turned up. Schurz, ever more impatient, again enlisted Sumner's help to remind Lincoln of his promise.[5] The would-be general was not dependent on his influence with the Germans alone. His radical credentials were also impeccable. But he still had to wait for more than two weeks.

If Schurz was a radical, he was not an unreasonable one. Fully understanding that Lincoln was moving forward toward emancipation, at a slow pace perhaps, but forward just the same, he sought to cooperate with the President as much as possible in bringing about the desired goal. Thus, when on May 9 General David Hunter proclaimed the freedom of all slaves in his Department of the South, Schurz wrote a cautious letter to the White House. Of course he approved of the proclamation; eventually all slaves would be liberated. But if Lincoln thought the order premature, he hoped that the President would not issue any proclamation for which he would be sorry afterward. In regard to his own affairs, he was confident that Lincoln would soon be able to end "this suspense without much further loss of time." The revocation of Hunter's proclamation did not cause Schurz to write another letter.[6]

Shortly afterward, following Margarethe's solicitation of Chase's assistance, Schurz received his orders. He was to report to Frémont. Hurrying to Washington to pick up his assignment, he was delighted to hear that the President had such confidence in him as to ask him to write directly whenever he thought of something of importance. Then he returned to Philadelphia and, because floods had rendered the normal route via Harper's Ferry impassable, traveled to Cumberland by way of Pittsburgh and Wheeling. From there he rode into the Shenandoah Valley for his rendezvous with Frémont, who was then vainly trying to trap Stonewall Jackson.[7]

Schurz was so conscious of the future importance of the experiences he was likely to have that he began to keep a diary. Day by day, in his cribbed German hand, he recorded his observations—the torrential rains, the beautiful mountain scenery, the excitement of battle, and the boredom of camp life. He also noted his impressions of other generals, of Nathanial P. Banks—"very well behaved" (*sehr artig*), Samuel Wylie Crawford—"elegant and all dressed up"—(*fein geschmiegelt*), Daniel Sickles—"not especially favorable impression of his personality" (*nicht besonders günstiger Eindruck der Persönlichkeit*), and of others. He liked Sigel, managed to get along with Frémont, and established warm relationships with many of the other officers of his command.[8]

To be accepted by his fellow officers was no easy task. Resented as a political upstart with virtually no military experience, in the beginning Schurz was distrusted. Even civilians like Francis Lieber took exception to his rapid rise, to say nothing of Mrs. Anneke, now, possibly because of envy, his implacable enemy. Regular army officers as well as experienced volunteers did not at first take kindly to a politician's assuming command. But by a display of courage in battle, he succeeded in dispelling many of their objections, although his continued political machinations were often taken amiss.[9]

The new general found Frémont in Harrisonburg. It was the day after the repulse at Cross Keys, where the wily Jackson had once more outwitted the Federals; yet in spite of his dimmed reputation the Pathfinder was surrounded by splendidly attired aides-de-camp, many of them Hungarians, who frequently made it difficult to approach their commander. Schurz, however, was immediately admitted. Frémont was affable and promised him two brigades.[10]

General Carl Schurz (Courtesy of Library of Congress)

Within two days, Schurz took advantage of Lincoln's invitation to write to him. Strongly endorsing Frémont, he explained that the Pathfinder had been unable to carry out orders to march from Franklin to Harrisonburg because his troops had been starving and unable to fight. Moreover, the new general did not hesitate to express his opinion that it had been fortunate for Frémont not to have intercepted Stonewall Jackson. The Confederate leader's strength was such as to have made defeat inevitable!

The President answered this strange communication at once. Pointing out Schurz's errors one by one, he nevertheless refrained from crushing his young admirer, whom he assured that his information was valuable. But when he received still another detailed explanation of the Pathfinder's strategy, he did not bother to acknowledge it.[11] It is to be assumed that Frémont appreciated Schurz's efforts.

The new general was given a division consisting of the Fifty-fourth and Fifty-eighth New York, the Seventh and Seventy-fifth Pennsylvania, the Sixty-first Ohio, and the Eighth Virginia (Union). It also contained two artillery batteries and one cavalry troop. Many of his soldiers, though not all, were his countrymen, especially after June 17, when Blenker was removed and Schurz received most of his infantry.

His immediate surroundings were completely German. The chief of staff was a former Prussian engineer officer named Ernest F. Hoffman who had served with Garibaldi. One of his aides-de-camp was Karl Spraul, an ex-infantry officer from Baden who had also campaigned with the Italian patriot; another was Fritz Tiedemann. The engineer was his wife's nephew, Willy Westendarp, and the quartermaster was a German called Wermerskirch. This German character of the command was enhanced when Franz Sigel took Frémont's place, a change which Schurz had favored. He had threatened to resign if anyone else was given the Pathfinder's command. In Sigel's corps, widely though inaccurately known as a German unit, Schurz commanded the Third Division. Robert C. Schenck, after the Second Bull Run to be replaced by Julius Stahel, another German, who had seen action in the Hungarian revolution, led the First, and Adolph von Steinwehr, a graduate of a Prussian military school and an excellent topographer, the Second. General Robert H. Milroy and Colonel John Beardsley were in charge of the two non-German units, one independent and one cavalry brigade. Despite a certain jealousy, especially on von Steinwehr's part, Schurz soon established friendly relations with many of the officers. Stahel became a friend, as did the Polish refugee Wladimir Krzyzanowski, who commanded one of his brigades, and his old mentor Schimmelfennig, who eventually commanded the other.[12]

Schurz loved his new position. Fully convinced of his own abilities, he was pleased with his staff and thought he had never felt better. And he impressed his aide most favorably. "A man in his early thirties, youthful, alert and hardy, a good horseman," he seemed to be "fastening his gaze calmly upon everything new and unexpected, imperturbably judging men and conditions." Whether he was really as unruffled as Captain Spraul remembered is doubtful, but he was certainly extremely self-confident.[13]

At the time Schurz first joined the army, Frémont was in full retreat toward Mount Jackson. Then, after marching via Strasburg to Middletown and bivouacking there, the corps, now part of John Pope's Army of Virginia, was taken over by Sigel. A few days of comparative quiet followed. Margarethe and Mrs. Tiedemann came for a visit; Schurz introduced the ladies to his fellow officers, who extended their hospitality to them. This interlude ended on July 8, when in obedience to Pope's effort to concentrate his scattered forces, Sigel's, Banks's, and McDowell's corps, the command started moving again. Marching through Front Royal and Luray, it crossed the Blue Ridge at Thornton's Gap and halted at Sperryville on the other side, where it stayed for a month. It was so hot that Schurz, who used the time to drill the troops, was finally felled by the weather and his exertions. Sick for several days, he had barely recovered when on August 8 marching orders arrived. His first campaign was about to begin.[14]

For the next three weeks, Schurz participated in Pope's ill-fated Second Bull Run campaign, a Federal effort to protect Washington and to operate on Lee's lines of communication with Gordonsville and Charlottesville while the Army of the Potomac was being withdrawn from the Peninsula. For after McClellan had been unable to capture Richmond, he was recalled to Aquia Creek, while Pope tried to keep Lee busy on the line of the Virginia Central Railroad. But Pope's forces were ill coordinated, distrusted one another, and had no confidence in their commander, who made himself unpopular by boasting of his Western successes as compared with Eastern reverses. His chances of crushing his opponents depended upon close coordination with McClellan, who was neither willing nor able to cooperate, even if he had not been stripped of most of his troops.[15] And since the opposing Confederates were led by some of the greatest captains in military history, Robert E. Lee, Stonewall Jackson, and James Longstreet, the outcome was almost foreordained.

The bickering and mismanagement of the army were apparent from the beginning. Even before the campaign started, Schurz learned that at Pope's headquarters the first corps was considered a "band of wild, untrained, and demoralized marauders." When on August 7 he met Pope, the army commander made no secret of his low opinion of McClellan. Banks, too, became involved in controversy. On the eighth, he engaged Stonewall Jackson's superior forces at Cedar Mountain. Sustaining a repulse, he charged that Sigel had not come to his aid quickly enough. Whether or not the accusation was justified, Schurz arrived in the vicinity only to find the aftermath of a battle—the wounded, the dead—a dreary sight in the rain-soaked countryside. And he knew that the new general-in-chief, Henry Wager Halleck, had long been on bad terms with Sigel as well.[16]

After remaining in the triangle formed by the Rapidan, the Rappahannock, and the Orange & Alexandria Railroad, Pope learned that Lee was planning to pen him in and ordered a withdrawal behind the Rappahannock. On August 20, Schurz crossed the river at Sulphur Springs and then marched down along the left bank to the vicinity of Rappahannock Station. The Confederates occupied the opposite side.[17]

Two days later he saw his first action. Ordered to conduct a reconnaissance in force across the river at Freeman's Ford, he sent Schimmelfennig's Seventy-fourth Pennsylvania to the other bank. It soon had to be reinforced by the Eighth Virginia and later by the Sixty-first Ohio, all part of General Henry Bohlen's brigade. Attacked by Isaac Trimble's Confederates, the Eighth Virginia broke and ran; Schurz and his staff crossed the river and with drawn sabers sought to rally the fleeing troops. Then Longstreet's vanguard harassed the Federal left. Hard pressed, Schurz ordered a bayonet charge to gain enough time for an orderly withdrawal across the river. The maneuver worked, and the general, who lost his hat in the heat of battle, had the satisfaction of completing his mission. Although Bohlen was killed, unfortunately after an argument with his commander, Schurz had demonstrated his willingness to share his troop's dangers. They appreciated it.[18]

The next few days were marked by confusion. Stealing a march on Pope, Jackson, in support of Lee's main army, made plans to cross the Bull Run Mountains to the Union general's rear. Unaware of this threat, Pope was ill prepared to deal with the disaster confronting him. He quarreled with Sigel, whom he deeply distrusted; the troops were disheartened, and the general was wholly in the dark about Jackson's whereabouts. The Confederate leader, finding Thoroughfare Gap unguarded, came out in the open on the Orange & Alexandria Railroad, the main link between Pope and his base, and interrupted telegraph and rail connections with Washington. Then he captured the Federal supply depot at Manassas, which he raided and put to the torch. Thoroughly taken by surprise, Pope nevertheless believed that he might now be able to trap and destroy his opponent before the rest of Lee's army under Longstreet could catch up with its comrades. But he had no idea where Jackson was. Again leaving Thoroughfare Gap insufficiently protected against Longstreet, he established contact with Jackson only after it was too late and Lee's forces were already arriving. On August 28 the two armies clashed near the old Bull Run battlefield, and on the next morning, in an effort to displace the Confederates, Pope finally committed Sigel's corps.[19]

The engagement at Grovetown was Schurz's first major battle. Already wearied after days of continuous marching and countermarching, early in the morning of August 29 the division was awakened in its bivouac near Henry's farm to be unwittingly thrown against the main part of Jackson's corps. At first no enemy was to be seen; the quiet, dense woods seemed eerie, but then a volley broke the calm. Promptly committing his two brigades, Schimmelfennig's on the right and Krzyzanowski's on the left, Schurz pushed forward. He found the woods too dense to see clearly what was going on, although he soon learned from two prisoners what kind of a force he was facing. Asking for reinforcements, he continued to lead the advance, and the Twenty-ninth New York as well as two regiments of Milroy's independent brigade arrived to lend him support. By ten o'clock, General Philip Kearney of Heintzelman's corps, who commanded the unit on Schurz's right, appeared in person and promised to bolster the right flank.

The fighting continued. With their great numerical superiority, the Confederates did not take long to drive back several of Schurz's regiments. But the general, ably rallying them, succeeded in halting the retreat and resumed his forward march. A general attack now seemed in order; when Sigel asked Kearney for assistance, however, he was rebuffed. Kearney wanted no "foreign" interference with his command! Nevertheless, Schurz's men continued their advance. Longstreet had not yet arrived; had an attack supported by greater force been launched, it is conceivable that Jackson might still have been destroyed. Amazingly enough, even Schurz's greatly outnumbered forces managed to reach the uncompleted railroad embankment behind which the enemy had taken a strong position, although of course they were not powerful enough to dislodge him. Finally at 2:00 P.M., after having fought for eight hours, Schurz was relieved by Heintzelman.

The general's respite, such as it was, was made miserable by the sight of the wounded and killed. The division's heavy losses depressed him; he found it difficult to console himself. Only in the evening, when his orderly, a droll Swabian, informed him that he had captured a ham, did he begin to relax a little. The Swabian prepared a splendid meal so that the staff officers were able to feast on the unexpected delicacy.[20]

On the next day, August 30, Schurz, initially in reserve behind Schenck, was reinforced by Johann A. Kiltes's brigade and Hubert Dilger's battery. Dilger was an especially valuable addition; invariably called "Leatherbreeches," he was a fearless young artillery officer whose courage was tested on many a battlefield. The division was facing toward Grovetown; it was easy to see recently arrived elements of the Army of the Potomac on the right, Fitz-John Porter's command in front, and John F. Reynolds with part of McDowell's corps on the left. Early in the afternoon, Porter attacked, only to be repulsed. Then Schurz, supporting Schenck, advanced toward Dongan's farm. But Sigel's corps found itself dangerously exposed. Reynolds was pushed back, Koltes killed, Schenck wounded, and Krzyzanowski had a horse shot from under him. Sigel ordered a withdrawal to a defensive position provided by a low range of hills.

For Schurz, the fighting was by no means over. Finding McDowell in the midst of a confused mass of retreating troops, he sought to rally the dispirited unit. Strenuous combat continued, especially at the left, which he successfully bolstered with one of his brigades, until at dusk the firing stopped. He believed the time was still opportune for a general attack, a possibility he discussed with Sigel. But the corps commander was not known for audacity even in the best of circumstances; he could hardly be expected to push forward at a time when Pope was already in full retreat toward Centreville. All that Schurz could do was to carry out orders to cover the withdrawal, a task he fulfilled with great efficiency. Crossing the stone bridge spanning Bull Run between eleven o'clock and midnight, one of the last to do so, he set fire to its wooden appurtenances and reached Centreville at about seven in the morning. After another confused march during which he ran into the faultlessly attired McClellan, he sought shelter within the entrenchments of Washington. The Second Battle of Bull Run was coming to a close.[21]

Had he not been so downcast because of the disaster that had befallen the army, Schurz might have had every reason to be satisfied with his performance. True, his command had suffered heavy losses, some 20 percent of the total. Nevertheless, he had distinguished himself by daring, skill, and real qualities of leadership. Keeping Jackson's entire corps at bay for a few hours at Grovetown and handling his reserve force so well that he was able to bring it out in good order to cover the general retreat was no mean feat. Lincoln and Stanton recognized his contributions; Pope praised him "in high terms"; Colonel Leopold von Gilsa, a Prussian officer who had originally distrusted him, apologized for having underrated him; the New York *Tribune* praised him for having led "his division in the hottest fight with heroic courage and veteran skill", and even his bitter critic, Mrs. Anneke, felt constrained to give him credit for his "personal bravery." Perhaps the most telling tribute came from his officers and soldiers. As Colonel Stephen J. McGroaty of the Sixty-first Ohio stated in his report, "Through all these trials the regiment behaved with the greatest gallantry, being stimulated thereto by the bearing of Colonel Schimmelfennig and General Schurz, in whom the men learned to repose perfect confidence."[22]

The aftermath of the Second Battle of Bull Run was one of confusion and recrimination. Schurz heard Pope condemn McClellan for "small personal viewpoints"; as a radical, Schurz undoubtedly agreed. But the "Young Napoleon," as McClellan liked to be called, was soon ordered to take command of the eastern army once more, and Sigel's corps, now renamed the Eleventh, became part of the Army of the Potomac. Sigel himself did not escape criticism. Considered incompetent and ill advised in launching piecemeal attacks, he could expect no help from his old adversary, General Halleck. And Schurz, immediately after writing his report of the battle, found himself involved in a controversy with McDowell, who resented the statement that he and his staff had been seen "surrounded by troops in full retreat." Even though Schurz assured him that no offense had been intended, that he had seen the troops and not the general in flight, the touchy officer demanded a written retraction in the New York *Tribune,* a satisfaction he did not obtain. McDowell had already become so unpopular, however, that the controversy did Schurz little harm.[23]

Because Sigel's corps was assigned to the defenses of Washington, Schurz spent the next few months near Fairfax in the vicinity of the capital, within easy access to the White House and War Department. Thus he not only missed the Battle of Antietam but found ample time to see the President, the secretary of war, and other Washington officials, with whom he tried to intercede for Sigel. The corps commander felt himself slighted; he wanted more troops and a more active command, and Schurz indefatigably and loyally supported him. After all, Sigel was the darling of the Germans; to stand by him in the hour of his need could not do his ambitious countryman any harm. And Sigel was indeed in need; engaged in an open row with Halleck, he was actually charged with insubordination. Schurz was so active in his behalf that he even composed drafts of the corps commander's contemplated letter of resignation. That this type of activity annoyed his fellow officers was not surprising.[24]

The proximity to Washington had many compensations. On September 5 Margarethe arrived to stay with her soldier husband. Secretary Stanton was on such good terms with him that he asked Schurz's opinion about McDowell, Pope, Frémont, and Hooker. The secretary of the treasury came to visit the camp, and in October, General James A. Garfield, escorting Chase's daughter Kate, also paid a visit to headquarters. Garfield, who was about to be elected to Congress, was impressed. Prior to 1849, he thought, Americans had hardly ever seen a German of talent. Then the revolution of that year had brought "noble fellows" to the United States. After supper, Schurz and Sigel treated him to piano music. The staff joined in singing German songs, Mrs. Schurz adding her fine voice to the performance. Her husband, who said he could form an entire choir from his command, took his visitor to Bull Run, where he described the battle and "the shameful and unnecessary retreat" which followed.[25] Schurz's enthusiasm for the cause was evident. But then he was known to be a radical, and he had been greatly encouraged by Lincoln's policies.

Schurz had not misjudged his man. Lincoln, following his own sound instincts, had gradually but surely moved forward toward the emancipation policy which Schurz and his fellow radicals had long been advocating. Following Lee's repulse at Antietam, on September 22, 1862, the President published his preliminary Emancipation Proclamation, which promised freedom to all slaves in areas still in rebellion after January 1, 1863. Conservative reaction was very unfavorable; the Republican party lost substantially in the midterm elections, but Lincoln was undeterred. On November 5, tired of McClellan's continued lack of action, he finally removed the controversial commander and appointed Ambrose E. Burnside in his place.[26]

By this time, Schurz and his command had been moved to New Baltimore, a small hamlet near Thoroughfare Gap. The general was kept busy with his command, interrogated prisoners—one of whom, Major Edmund Berkeley, never forgot the chivalrous treatment he received—and energetically carried out his duties as commander of the Third Division. Of course he was terribly excited about the news. An emancipation proclamation! McClellan dismissed! Lincoln evidently was on the right track, but Schurz thought he needed a little prodding. Consequently, with more enthusiasm than discretion, he sat down late at night to write a hectoring letter to the President.[27]

The letter, which Margarethe personally handed to Lincoln, was an amazing example of the general's presumption. Maintaining that the administration's recent reverses were due neither to the proclamation nor to the people's desire for peace at any price, he asserted categorically that the defeat of the administration was its own fault. It had admitted its opponents into its counsels and rewarded its enemies with office, especially in the army. Now a change had been made, but it would remain without effect unless the whole system was changed as well. Let the government appoint generals whose heart was in the cause, who could infuse energy into the army. Only then would success ensue.

This piece of unsolicited, if not impertinent, advice annoyed the President, who sent a stinging reply within two days. Pointing out that the losses in the election were due to the Democrats' taking advantage of the Republicans' presence in the field and the newspaper campaign of villification against the government, he demolished Schurz's every argument. "If you had not made the following statements," he wrote,

I should not have suspected them to be true. "The defeat of the administration is the administration's own fault." (opinion) "It admitted its professed opponents to its counsels" (Asserted as a fact) "It placed the Army, now a great power in this Republic, into the hands of its enemy" (Asserted as a fact) "In all personal questions, to be hostile to the party of the Government, seemed, to be a title to consideration." (Asserted as a fact) "If to forget the great rule, that if you are true to your friends, your friends will be true to you, and that you make your enemies stronger by placing them upon an equality with your friends." "Is it surprising that the opponents of the administration should have got into their hands the government of the principal states, after they have had for a long time the principal management of the war, the great business of the national government."

While he could not dispute the matter of opinion, he would be glad to have Schurz's evidence upon the three matters stated as facts. The plain truth was that the administration had come into power as a minority party. It could not wage war without the help of the Democrats, and not even its friends, "Mr. Schurz (now Gen. Schurz)" included, in 1861 considered all Democrats enemies of the government, unfit for military honors. Consequently, Lincoln had appointed those who came well recommended; he had also appointed many Republicans, but he

could not see that their "superiority of success has been so marked as to throw
great suspicion on the good faith of those who are not Republicans."

As soon as he received this letter, Schurz composed an answer. Again assuring
the President that his motives were only those of a zealous fighter for the cause, he
admitted that not all Democrats were disloyal. But he believed that only those who
thoroughly believed in the war were fit to hold positions of command, a
prerequisite hardly met by McClellan, Buell, or Halleck. He even asserted that
some of Adjutant General Lorenzo B. Thomas's subordinates were furnishing aid
to the enemy and insisted that only relentless determination could turn the tide.
"When a man's whole heart is in a cause like ours," he wrote, "then, I think, he
may be believed not to be governed by small personal pride." Finally, ending on a
note of pathos, he made an appeal on behalf of the soldiers he commanded. As they
might be called upon to die at any moment, he was most perturbed at his lack of
responsibility for seeing to it that they were not sacrificed in vain. "I do not know,
whether you have ever seen a battlefield," he concluded. "I assure you, Mr.
President, it is a terrible sight."

This insolent rejoinder did not go unnoticed. On November 24, Lincoln sent
Schurz another scathing reply. He knew that he would be blamed if the war were
lost, but as he was doing his best, he resented the general's reproaches. And who
was to judge whether men had their hearts in the cause? He could not discard
his own judgment for Schurz's, for, as he put it, "there are men who have 'heart
in it' that think that you are performing your part as poorly as you think I am performing mine." Without disparaging the deeds of heroic Republicans who had
been killed in battle, he could not see how they had done more than their
Democratic fellows. And the accusations against the adjutant general were untrue.
If Schurz had any tangible evidence on the subject, let him come to Washington
and submit it.[28]

That this type of correspondence was tolerated at all was surprising; it proved
Schurz a difficult subordinate, not only for the President but also for his superiors
in the field. Yet Lincoln, unwilling to break with the supposed spokesman for the
Germans, for whom he also had a real affection, soon called a halt to the quarrel.
Schurz came to Washington; upon his arrival at the White House, he was ushered
in to meet the President, who was seated in his armchair before the open-grate fire.
As the general remembered thirty years later, "Mr. Lincoln . . . greeted me
cordially as of old and bade me pull up a chair and sit by his side. Then he brought
his large hand on my knee with a slap and said with a smile: "Now tell me, young
man, whether you really think that I am as poor a fellow as you have made me out
in your letter!" " With a lump in his throat Schurz tried to explain, whereupon the
President put him at his ease, told him he knew he was a warm antislavery man and
a friend, and made some of his own problems clear. Lincoln mentioned his
troubles, his dismissal of McClellan, which he indicated to be final, and the
criticism he had to endure. Then he added, "Didn't I give it to you hard in my
letter? Didn't I? I did not mean to, and therefore I wanted you to come so quickly."

The two men parted good friends, and upon the general's question whether his letters were still welcome, he received a positive answer. His self-esteem had been restored, although the correspondence remained to haunt him for the rest of his life.[29]

In the meantime Sigel, who was still asking for additional troops, had become embroiled in a new row. In his annual report, Halleck included a letter from Pope of August 25 complaining about Sigel's corps. Although he thought it was "composed of some of the best fighting men we have," the general ventured the opinion that it would never do much service under its present commander. In addition, Sigel learned that Halleck had called him a "damned coward." Schurz had written to Lincoln about "the Sigel affair" even before leaving for Washington; now, after remaining in the capital for a few days with his family and visiting various members of the cabinet and Congress, he returned to the field, wholly indignant about the treatment accorded his commander. He even suggested that the officers write to their representatives in Congress about the injustice and that the troops sign a common protest. The matter was finally solved when another corps, the Twelfth, was assigned to the Grand Reserve Division which Burnside had given to Sigel. But the injured commander never succeeded in establishing the same friendly relations with Lincoln as his famous subordinate.[30]

The changes in command of the Army of the Potomac pleased Schurz. Although he accompanied McClellan as the dismissed commander reviewed his troops for the last time, he voiced no regret at Little Mac's departure. True, Burnside said he was not equipped to lead the army; nevertheless, he was an amiable man, generally liked, who would take the offensive where McClellan had refused to do so. Perhaps at last the manpower and material superiority of the Union could be brought into play. And he seemed to make a good beginning by organizing the Army of the Potomac into grand divisions.

Schurz's enthusiasm soon evaporated. On November 15, in Sigel's company, he visited Burnside. The general showed his callers his plan, which envisaged a direct attack on Richmond by way of Fredericksburg. The scheme seemed faulty to Schurz. If Burnside succeeded in crossing the Rappahannock, he would find the enemy at his right flank, with forces threatening his communications as he moved farther south. With a fortified city in front, a large army at his right, and a narrow base of operations, he would face impossible odds. Schurz thought it would be much better if Sigel's corps took the offensive against Jackson and swept the valley clear of Confederates. His reservations were well considered; he even drafted a letter to Chase to warn the secretary.[31] Burnside persisted, however. The disastrous Battle of Fredericksburg was the result.

The Eleventh Corps missed the debacle. When it was finally ordered to Dumfries, some twenty miles north of Fredericksburg, it could hear the noise of the terrible battle that was taking place there. But it was not engaged and escaped the slaughter that marked the destruction of Burnside's hopes.[32]

Although greatly disappointed by the defeat, two weeks later Schurz took heart again, his flagging spirits revived because of the Emancipation Proclamation. On leave to spend New Year's Eve with his family, he was in Washington when Lincoln took the great step Schurz had been urging for so long. That night he went to the White House. The President was worried about the effect of the proclamation; even moderates had told him it might create more trouble than it could solve, and the general thought Lincoln needed the encouragement which he sought to give him.[33]

He himself had no doubts about the new policy. "The development of the great American revolution has recently been especially favorable," he wrote to his sister-in-law in Hamburg. The great disasters of the past had not been able to destroy the country; peace was impossible as long as the South insisted on independence, and with the Emancipation Proclamation, the President had burned all bridges behind him. If the government had displayed weakness in matters of personnel, if it was slow and took half-measures, nevertheless it was "moving in the right direction."[34]

Schurz's leave in Washington, where he found his wife sick again and the children suffering from whooping cough, came to an end on January 13, 1863, when he returned to headquarters at Stafford. But he did not stay long. Sigel's elevation to the command of a grand division had raised the problem of Schurz's own promotion, an objective he had eagerly been pursuing since the beginning of December. In view of his political connections and his popularity with the troops, he should not have had much trouble, but the claims of General Stahel complicated matters. Sigel had asked Lincoln for major general's commissions for both, only to be told that he ought to recommend one, whom the President would appoint. Because the corps commander opted for Stahel, Lincoln agreed, and when at the end of the year Sigel took a temporary leave of absence, Stahel took command of the Eleventh Corps.

But Schurz was not to be superseded that easily. Feverishly active, he succeeded in convincing Burnside, Sigel, and Lincoln of the feasibility of two promotions. He ought to get the corps and Stahel a cavalry command. "Schurz and Stahl [*sic*] should both be Maj. Genls.," the President concluded. "Schurz to take Sigel's old corps, and Stahl to command the Cavalry. They, together with Sigel, are our sincere friends; and while so much may seem rather large, anything less is too small." A few days later, Schurz returned to Washington with a plan of operations for the Eleventh Corps, a scheme for a campaign in North Carolina, which he submitted to Lincoln. On January 19, he rejoined his troops. The War Department was beginning to process an order placing him in command of the corps.[35]

When Schurz came back from the capital, he was just in time for Burnside's disastrous Mud March, an effort to ford the Rappahannock above Fredericksburg. Like the rest of the army, he found himself mired in the deeply rutted roads made impassable by heavy rainstorms. Thoroughly disgusted, he again wrote to the

President. The army was in bad shape, he insisted; officers and generals were critical of Burnside and had no confidence in him. Was not the proper plan of campaign "to spread out our wings," especially the right, bolster the cavalry, and make expeditions with large units around the enemy's flanks? Only in this manner could the army be saved and its morale sustained.

What Lincoln thought of this renewed self-arrogation is unknown; he himself, however, had come to the conclusion that Burnside had to go. He replaced him with Joseph Hooker, who promptly abolished the grand divisions.[36]

Schurz made the most of the new arrangements. Although he had disliked Hooker from the moment he first met him, he gave him credit for enthusiasm and popularity with the troops. Moreover, the change helped to solve a serious problem. Sigel, unwilling to permit Stahel to be superseded without a promotion or new command, had protested to Lincoln about the order appointing Schurz. This infuriated the general. Although he agreed to keep the controversial order in abeyance, he wrote Sigel a strong letter of complaint. Yet, notwithstanding his assurances to the President that he had no wish to be promoted unless his colleague obtained his cavalry units, he continued to lobby for higher rank. Then he asked for permission to go to Washington; he intended to leave Sigel's command altogether. Only when he discovered that the President was wholly unwilling to gratify his wishes did he change his mind. Realizing that the abolition of the grand divisions was making the whole issue academic—Sigel would resume command of his corps in any case—he mended his fences with Sigel and Stahel, enlisted Sumner and Wilson in his quest for promotion, and hoped for the best.[37]

At first, he was greatly disappointed. Early in March, sick with jaundice, he returned to Washington. The list with the new major generals came out, but he had not been promoted. "To-day I saw the list of the President's nominations in the papers, and my name was not among them," he protested to Sumner. "I must confess, I was somewhat painfully surprised at the intelligence. To stand back behind such men as Dan. Sickles and T. Steele, who is more of a secessionist than of a soldier, is a rather severe thing for me. Their military merit is not superior to mine, while my political position is hardly inferior to that of F. P. Blair and C. C. Washburne." He himself might perhaps not care for a promotion were it not for the influence he wanted to possess in the army and for his relations with his "large constituency, with whom a certain kind of success gives prestige and power." But as matters stood, he did care. "This time the jeers of the German pro-slavery papers over the German Republican leader, who was first promoted by the President, when it was not lawful, and then dropped when it was lawful will be disagreeable to my ears." Let the senator visit the President and see what he could do. Margarethe added her appeals; the general sought out Lincoln. Then he left for Philadelphia to recuperate.[38]

Schurz's appeal to radicalism and ethnic politics was successful. On March 14, the Senate finally confirmed his promotion. Stahel also became a major general; Sigel, unwilling to be reduced to corps commander after having been in charge of a grand division, handed in his resignation, and on March 29, Schurz was appointed to temporary command of the Eleventh Corps. He returned to his troops in triumph.[39]

All in all, it had been a most successful year. Securing a command after much difficulty, Schurz, a mere civilian, not only succeeded in winning the respect of his troops but also in establishing a creditable military record. In addition, his cherished goal of emancipation had been endorsed by the President. Finally promoted to major general as a result of his performance, his radical connections, and especially his ethnic appeals, he was looking forward to further glory.

IX

Radical Major General

WHEN SCHURZ WAS APPOINTED to the rank of major general, he reached the pinnacle of his military career. At that time, no higher rank existed in the army, a fact he did not fail to point out in his correspondence with his wife's relatives.[1] He had much reason to be pleased: military affairs had always fascinated him; he was wholly committed to the Union cause and hoped to contribute significantly to the suppression of the rebellion. Moreover, that military laurels won in war would constitute a valuable political asset afterward was obvious.

Nevertheless, Schurz's sudden rise was not good for him. The resentment of professional officers was inevitable; West Pointers, distrusting volunteers in any case, suspected foreign-born outsiders even more. And not only West Pointers were jealous. German officers like General von Steinwehr also took umbrage. Considering himself slighted, von Steinwehr did not wish to serve under Schurz, whose good political connections were giving rise to ugly rumors that he had been scheming for Sigel's removal.[2] As long as success attended his military efforts, these pinpricks were of no account. Should the fortunes of war turn against him, however, the situation would be very different.

How difficult it would be to secure a command commensurate with his rank he found out very quickly. Whatever hopes he had of succeeding Sigel, he was to be sorely disappointed. On April 2, General Oliver Otis Howard, a West Pointer who had lost an arm at Fair Oaks and was known for his extreme piety, was appointed to the command of Eleventh Corps. Schurz returned to the Third Division.

From the very beginning, relations between Howard and his new troops were not happy. Used to the familiar ways of Franz Sigel, the German-Americans in the corps were bound to resent anyone who took his place. Howard's puritanical notions, his belief in temperance and dislike for swearing, deeply offended them. That he was a capable soldier who had rendered valuable service was generally forgotten.[3]

Schurz felt slighted by Howard's arrival. He tried hard to obtain a transfer for himself and his troops by suggesting a swap of two brigades from the Department of Washington. Only when neither Hooker nor Lincoln was willing to oblige him did he bow to the inevitable and establish working relations with his new superior. Yet the shift in command boded ill for the corps' future.

Other changes had taken place as well. Stahel's former division was now commanded by Charles Devens, a Massachusetts lawyer; Schurz's division had been augmented not only by Hecker's Eighty-second Illinois, but also by the Sixty-eighth, 119th, and 157th New York, the Twenty-sixth Wisconsin, and several supporting units.[4] The command was well drilled. When early in April Lincoln came to inspect the army, he was favorably impressed with Howard's troops. And when General Darius Couch pointed out "General Shurs" at the head of the Third Division, the President quickly replied, "Not Shurs, General Couch, but Shoorts."[5]

The Army of the Potomac, now over 112,000 strong, was soon to go over to the offensive. In order to cross the Rappahannock, behind which Lee, with half that force, was strongly entrenched, Hooker decided to send four of his corps some thirty miles upstream, bridge the river there, and after crossing the Rapidan, come back again on the other side. With the troops he left opposite Fredericksburg, he would then be able to crush the numerically inferior enemy, or, by cutting his supply route, force him to withdraw toward Richmond.

Howard's corps was one of those chosen to execute this maneuver. On April 27, in the best of spirits, it marched upstream to Kelly's Ford, which it crossed on the twenty-eighth. Roughly retracing its steps after fording the Rapidan, on the thirtieth it arrived slightly west of Chancellorsville, in a clearing of the Wilderness, as the tangled growth of trees and underbrush in the area was called. Conscious of its advantage in numbers, the army was confident of victory.

But it was to be terribly disappointed. Hooker—Fighting Joe Hooker—suddenly lost his nerve. After ordering a forward movement on May 1 and encountering some resistance, he decided to withdraw to his previous held positions, thus giving up all the advantages he had achieved. Instead of carrying forward a successful offensive, he placed himself in a defensive line.[6]

Hooker's loss of nerve became the cause of Schurz's first and most serious military setback. On May 1 his division was in position in the Wilderness, astride the Old Turnpike between Fredericksburg and Orange Court House, in the midst of a clearing which contained a farm house, Hawkins' farm, the Wilderness Church, and an inn, Dowdall's Tavern, the corps commander's headquarters. The Eleventh Corps formed the Union army's right wing, Devens's division occupying the extreme right, Schurz's the middle, and von Steinwehr's the left. Adequate breastworks protected this position against attacks from the south, but nothing obstructed an approach from the west. Unaccountably, the army's right flank, several miles distant from the river, did not rest on any natural features. It was totally unprotected, a tempting target for an enterprising enemy.

For Lee and Jackson, this opening provided a splendid opportunity. Never collaborating more brilliantly, they took full advantage of Hooker's folly. In the face of an opponent about twice their strength, they split their forces, Lee ordering Jackson to ride through the Wilderness to pounce upon the exposed Federal right flank with superior numbers. Fully convinced that the Confederates were retreating, Hooker was caught completely unawares. Nothing could shake his conviction of the enemy's intention to withdraw, an impression Howard wholly shared.

What happened the next day remains clouded in controversy. After inspecting the Eleventh Corps' position early in the morning, Hooker, in spite of his firm belief in the Confederates' supposed retirement, seemed to sense that something was not quite right. At 9:30 he sent a dispatch to both Howard and Henry W. Slocum of the Twelfth Corps further to the left with a warning to strengthen the right and throw up artificial defenses. Schurz, who had observed suspicious enemy movements along his front, happened to be on duty at corps headquarters and woke Howard to read him the order. Pointing out that von Gilsa's brigade, the corps' extreme right, was in danger of being crushed, he asked his superior to do something about it. But Howard, like Hooker certain that the Confederates were withdrawing, refused. To Schurz's question whether he thought von Gilsa would have any chance of resisting, he merely replied, "Well, he will have to fight." The desperate Schurz, on his own responsibility, then ordered two of his regiments to change front from south to west in von Gilsa's rear, an arrangement to which the corps commander did not object. In addition, the corps was further weakened by the detachment of Barlow's brigade of the Second Division to assist Sickles in a useless attempt to capture some of Jackson's trains.[7]

It is true that the main source for now reconstructing the events at Dowdall's Tavern is Schurz's own recollection. It is also true that Howard later denied ever having received the order. But in view of the fact that in his vague report on the subject, he admitted that "Schurz was anxious," that he was not eager for a court of inquiry, that the printed copy of the order to Howard and Slocum is in the *Official Records,* and that another one to Howard alone was copied two weeks later by one of his clerks, it seems likely that Schurz's recollections, given with a great deal of detail, substantially correspond to the facts. His account of vain efforts to alert Howard to the danger even after the receipt of the order is in accord with Colonel von Gilsa's and Captain Dilger's known attempts to do the same. The recollection of eyewitnesses, as well as the fact that two of Schurz's regiments did indeed change front prior to Jackson's attack, would seem to constitute corroborating evidence.[8] In short, it appears that the general tried his best to alert his superiors. He was not believed, and it was his misfortune to become the scapegoat for the ensuing disaster.

Schurz's fears soon materialized. At about 5:20 p.m., frightened deer and rabbits came running out of the woods—the precursors of the Confederate assault. Falling on von Gilsa's brigade with great numerical superiority, Jackson's foot cavalry, led by Robert E. Rodes's brigade, completely routed Devens's division, which recoiled upon Schurz's. Unfortunately, the general had neglected to alert the troops to their imminent peril, so that they were playing cards and performing household chores when the enemy struck them. Hurrying from headquarters to the junction of the plank road and the turnpike, Schurz tried to pivot Schimmelfennig's brigade to the west and sent orders to Krzyzanowski further to the right to do the same. But the fleeing troops of the First Division, rushing like a torrent upon the troops, made any real stand impossible. Desperately trying to rally his command,

Schurz, ably supported by Captain Dilger's guns, rapidly put together the regiments he had turned around earlier to make a twenty minutes' stand at Wilderness Church. But the enemy, threatening to outflank his left, sent it fleeing down the turnpike. Unable to lend reinforcements to the equally sorely pressed Krzyzanowski, he had to order him to withdraw also, and no matter how hard he tried to rally the troops, the rout soon became complete. Devens and Hecker were wounded, several regimental commanders killed. Whether anyone could have stopped the fleeing soldiers—Jackson had over twenty-five thousand men to Howard's fewer than eleven thousand—is dubious. The confusion was such that not even "Leatherbreeches" Dilger's heroic artillery resistance was of much help. After a temporary stop in the rifle pits near Dowdall's Tavern, where Howard and Schurz, with complete disregard for their own safety, tried to check the rout while Adolph Buschbeck put up a magnificent defense, the corps reeled back toward the plateau near Hooker's headquarters at Chancellorsville, the stampede coming to a halt only as the first shadows began to fall. Although Jackson himself was accidentally killed by his own men that very evening, he had won a brilliant victory. On the following day, the Eleventh Corps, or what was left of it, was ordered to the extreme left of the army and took little part in the subsequent fighting, which ended with Hooker's retreat across the Rappahannock. He never managed to regain the initiative, notwithstanding the availability of reserves which he could have committed to retrieve the disaster.[9]

When Schurz recrossed the river on May 6, his division had sustained a loss of almost one-quarter of its total strength (23 percent). But his losses, the dead and the wounded, were not the only calamity that befell him. Insult was added to injury when on May 5, the *New York Times* correspondent published a story blaming the entire defeat on the Eleventh Corps in general and the Germans in particular. "This corps is composed of the divisions of Schurz, Steinwehr, and Devin [*sic*]," he wrote, "and consists in a great part of German troops. Without waiting for a single volley from the rebels, this corps disgracefully abandoned the position behind their breastworks, and commenced coming, panic stricken, down the road toward headquarters."

And that was not all. To blame everything on the corps was bad enough, but it was especially Schurz who was singled out as a scapegoat. "To the disgrace of the Eleventh be it said," the correspondent continued, "that the division of Gen. Schurz, which was the first assailed, almost instantly gave way . . . . Thousands of those cowards threw down their guns and soon stampeded . . . ." His colleague from the New York *Herald* asserted that "the disastrous and disgraceful giving way of General Schurz's division . . . completely changed the fortunes of the day." The men allegedly fled "like so many sheep before a pack of wolves." Other papers all over the country copied these accounts.[10]

Following immediately upon the great reverse at Chancellorsville, this abuse hit the corps hard. No matter that not even half of its members were Germans, no matter that it was not Schurz's, but Devens's division which was first attacked, no matter that, as General Couch later pointed out, "no corps in the army, surprised as the Eleventh was at this time, could have held its ground under similar circumstances," the "flying Dutchmen" became the butt of the army and the country.

Schurz immediately protested to Howard. By asserting that the Third Division, led by its general, "threw itself flying upon the rest of the corps," the newspapers were unjustly casting reproach on him and his troops; the general had seen Schurz during the battle and must now set the record straight. Howard, who during a staff meeting in the night of May 4–5 had himself condemned his soldiers, now unhesitatingly supported his subordinate. "I am deeply pained to find you subjected to such false and malicious attacks," he replied. "I saw you just as the battle commenced; you hastened from me to your post. I next saw you rallying troops near the rifle pits upon the ground occupied by our corps. After this you were with me, forming a new line of battle near Berry's line. I do not believe that you could have done more than you did on that trying occasion." Correcting the misapprehension concerning the division's position when the attack started, he promised to say more in his official report.

The correspondence was published, as were Schurz's personal protests to the editors.[11] Yet the suspicion that, somehow or other, the "Dutch" and especially Schurz were responsible for the disaster lingered. General Schimmelfennig demanded an official correction; Schurz supported this request in his formal report of the battle; he asked for its publication, a court of inquiry, or a hearing before the Joint Committee on the Conduct of the War, but the War Department refused to do anything. Neither Stanton nor Howard, to say nothing of Hooker, was anxious to initiate an investigation at that time. The fair-minded Chicago *Tribune* might come to the corps' defense; most later historians might absolve it from blame, but the controversy about the Germans at Chancellorsville was never fully laid to rest. "I fights mit Sigel und runs mit Schurz" sneered the army.[12]

For a man as ambitious and confident as Schurz, this unmerited stigma was difficult to bear. For the rest of his life he sought vindication. Ever ready to discuss the subject, he patiently supplied details about the battle to all historians willing to listen. He devoted many pages of his *Reminiscences* to his defense and was delighted with every new account tending to exonerate him. Nonetheless, the episode made him acutely unhappy.[13]

In the last analysis, of course, he had no real reason to feel downcast. His military reputation might have suffered, but he was after all merely a political general who had done his best, which under the circumstances was hardly sufficient to entitle him to military fame. His political influence, however, assuredly had not been diminished. Because the attacks on him were slurs on their honor, the German-Americans, who called a large protest meeting on June 3 in New York, fully supported him. His standing with his fellow countrymen, if anything, was strengthened.[14]

Immediately after the battle, Schurz believed that the disaster was Howard's fault. Repeatedly making it clear to the corps commander that he did not think the corps could continue under his leadership, he tried to induce Sigel to return and besieged the War Department with requests for the changes he desired. But when Howard sought to implement one of Schurz's earlier wishes to be transferred elsewhere, he categorically refused. After the slanderous attacks upon him by the press, he thought that any such move would look like a confession of guilt. He was still convinced that Howard ought to leave to make room for Sigel; Chase agreed with him, but neither Lincoln nor the War Department were willing to oblige.[15]

Disappointed though he was, Schurz found consolation in Margarethe's arrival at headquarters. But his pleasure did not last long. Lee, taking advantage of the victory he had gained, invaded Maryland and Pennsylvania; the Army of the Potomac made ready to pursue him, and Mrs. Schurz had to return home.[16]

The ensuing campaign marked the climax of Schurz's military career. Anxious to retrieve his reputation by excelling in combat, he was looking forward to the next engagement, and, as luck would have it, he was to participate in the Battle of Gettysburg, the greatest contest of the war. Under orders from the new commander of the Army of the Potomac, George G. Meade, to proceed north, on June 30, the Eleventh Corps was encamped at St. Joseph's Seminary in Emmitsburg, Maryland. Schurz's division started its march at seven the next morning. After it had been hurried on by Howard, it began to reach Gettysburg by 12:30. The corps commander, who had ridden ahead with his staff, had received a call for reinforcements from General John F. Reynolds of the First Corps, which, encountering Henry Heth's division north and west of the town, had become seriously engaged. On an eminence later to become famous as Cemetery Hill, Howard gave Schurz command of the Eleventh Corps, he himself taking over all the troops on the field following Reynolds's death at the hands of a sharpshooter. Quickly appreciating the strategic importance of Cemetery Hill, he ordered von Steinwehr's division to remain in reserve there, so that only two divisions were available to Schurz, his own, now commanded by Schimmelfennig, and the First, commanded by Francis Barlow. According to orders, he promptly deployed them north of the town at an obtuse angle to Abner Doubleday's First Corps, with Schimmelfennig at the left between the Mummasburg and Carlisle roads, and Barlow to the right toward the Heidlersburg Road. As at Chancellorsville, the extreme right was again held by von Gilsa's brigade. The entire line was in position by about two o'clock, but since Barlow, apparently with Howard's knowledge, advanced much farther than Schurz had intended, a dangerous gap developed between the two divisions, to say nothing of the one between the two corps.

While A. P. Hill's men were already pressing Howard's left, Richard S. Ewell's corps, with Early in the lead, launched a strong attack upon his right, Schurz's command. Exhausted by their long morning march, the Federals were compelled to yield, their right flank in danger of being outflanked. Schurz had to call for reinforcements, but Coster's brigade of von Steinwehr's division arrived too late to be of much help. In spite of their brave resistance—General Barlow was severely wounded and the Second Brigade of the Third Division lost all its regimental commanders—neither the First Corps, which asked Schurz for reinforcements he did not have, nor the Eleventh was able to stem the tide. Although his horse was shot through the ridge of its neck, Schurz himself escaped injury. But he was severely shaken by the mortal wounds of his friend of Rastatt days, Franz Mahler of the Seventy-fifth Pennsylvania, whose hands he clasped as the fallen colonel was carried to the rear.

By four o'clock, Howard had ordered a general retreat to Cemetery Hill. Streaming pell-mell through the streets of Gettysburg, the two corps became inexorably intermingled until they were re-formed on the hill at the southern end of town. The arrival of General Winfield S. Hancock just at that time caused a dispute with Howard about the overall command but encouraged the troops; later that evening, when Slocum also came up, Howard turned over his authority to him, so that Schurz reverted to the command of his own division. Completely heedless of his own peril, he had energetically rallied his men and sought to spur them on, but the corps had suffered severely. With losses running as high as 45 percent, it was lined up on the hill, the Second Division behind a stone wall on the west side, the Third, immediately opposite the town, and the First on the right. Whether Lee, by pressing an attack on the two badly mauled corps at that time, could have won the battle, and whether Howard should have ordered a retreat earlier, has remained a matter of controversy.[17]

But Gettysburg was not Chancellorsville, and Meade was not Hooker. The new commander, determined to stop the enemy's advance, rushed additional troops to the scene as quickly as possible, and it was with great relief that the nervous Federals on Cemetery Hill watched the approach of the advance elements of the Twelfth and Third Corps. That night some half-dozen generals, some sitting on the floor in a room of the gate house, gathered around a barrel with a candle on top to discuss the events of the day. They expressed the hope that Meade would decide to make a stand on the ground on which they were already drawn up. Then they joined their troops in the cemetery to get some sleep among the tombstones.

On the next day, with Meade directing the battle in person, the Union lines were strengthened by the gradual arrival of the remainder of his army. Howard's men occupied the extreme northern end of the fishhook-like Federal position along Cemetery Ridge, Cemetery Hill, and Culp's Hill, so that during most of the day, July 2, they merely heard but did not see the heavy fighting in the Peach Orchard and the left flank of the line. At dusk, however, Jubal Early launched a strong attack on Cemetery Hill; with great gusto, the Confederates assaulted the batteries on Howard's right. Immediately riding forward, Schurz rallied some of the stragglers. And when the enemy temporarily overran R. B. Ricketts's and Michael Wiedrich's batteries, the infuriated Germans, eager to retrieve the reputation they had lost, drove them back with spirit. "This battery is ours," shouted a triumphant

Southern officer, only to be felled by a sponge-shaft belonging to an artillery man who heatedly replied, "No, dis battery is unser." An offensive against neighboring Culp's Hill was also repulsed.

During the night of July 2–3, a conference of corps commanders at Meade's headquarters decided to make a stand along the existing line, and the army awaited Lee's expected attack in the morning. Schurz and his command were still in position near the gate house of the cemetery, where, after witnessing the recapture of previously lost ground on Culp's Hill, they became spectators to the most dramatic assault of the Civil War, Pickett's charge, the great climax of the battle. After a deafening artillery duel early in the afternoon, during which they were under fire but largely unhurt—Schurz sought to steady them by calmly walking up and down, smoking his cigar—they could see the Confederates coming down from their positions at Seminary Ridge. Bands were playing, flags fluttered in the breeze, until the enemy host was hidden by an intervening line of hills. Intermittently hearing and seeing the great drama as Rebel troops were mowed down by artillery, only to have their places taken by others who kept moving, the Federals were exhilarated by the final repulse of Pickett's men, an event clearly established by the triumphant sounds of "John Brown's Body." The Battle of Gettysburg was over, and although Meade failed to pursue the routed enemy, the turning point of the war had been reached.[18]

On July 4, the survivors of the Eleventh Corps reoccupied Gettysburg. To Schurz's delight, upon entering the town he ran into his friend, General Schimmelfennig, who had been deemed lost on the first day of the battle. Having run into a dead-end alley while hotly pursued by the enemy, the general had found refuge in a pig sty, where he had hidden for more than three days. Emerging none the worse for his ordeal, he was warmly greeted by his comrades, and especially by his commander. But not even Schimmelfennig's fortunate reappearance could help Schurz forget the loss of so many of his soldiers. He was appalled at the terrible sights of the battlefield, arms and legs piled up in heaps as gruesome reminders of the surgeon's grisly work. The hideous recollection of the battle's aftermath always remained vivid in his memory.[19]

Schurz had done his duty at Gettysburg. The Eleventh Corps, however, had again come under suspicion. Did it not flee on the first day as it had fled at Chancellorsville? Those Dutchmen! It was galling to Schurz. His command had dwindled to a mere fifteen hundred men, and the corps' reputation was so bad that officers assigned to it complained to headquarters.

That the Eleventh Corps suffered from various shortcomings cannot be denied. Distrust between its various ethnic constituents, dislike of its commanding general, and bad luck all haunted it. That these difficulties could be ascribed to its Germans, however, was ridiculous. Convenient scapegoats, the much-maligned "Dutch" fought very well on many battlefields, and while Schurz may possibly have held too high a rank for his abilities, he nevertheless was not a poor soldier.

Because of the general situation, Schurz thought he had to do something. So it was that while engaged in the pursuit of Lee's army and after his return to Virginia—a march during which he had a close encounter with Mosby's raiders—the general tried to discover ways of retrieving his and his men's standing in the army. Meade too was contemplating changes in organization; aware of the Eleventh Corps' troubles, he was considering breaking it up, with one division going to the Second, one to the Twelfth, and the Third, Schurz's, to the rear to guard the army's communications. But of course this was not what Schurz wanted; quickly going to see Meade, he forcefully presented his own views. He had no objection to breaking up the corps, he said, only it ought to be done in a manner as little offensive to the feelings of officers and men as possible. His division, possibly reinforced, ought to be sent to the Shenandoah Valley. Neither Meade nor Howard opposed his proposals, the corps commander handsomely praised his past performance, and both generals sent him to Washington to confer with Halleck. His entreaties were in vain, however. The government had other plans. For better or worse, the Eleventh Corps remained intact, and Schurz returned to headquarters at Catlett's Station. His division had been augmented by sufficient troops to enable him to form three brigades, but that was all. Making the best of the situation, he gave one of these to Krzyzanowski, another to Hecker, and the third to a newcomer, Hector Tyndale, a most competent officer who had had three horses shot from under him at Antietam.

The comparative inactivity of the army in Virginia bothered Schurz. The entire Eleventh Corps consisted of only two divisions; whatever action was to take place would obviously take place elsewhere. He used his influence with Lincoln to obtain a commutation of a death sentence for a deserter, he sought to facilitate the promotion of his friend Krzyzanowski, but watching and guarding railroad lines was not an agreeable occupation for him. Falling sick with "camp fever," early in September he went on leave.[20]

Whatever his disease may have been, he quickly shook it off in the peaceful surroundings of Bethlehem, where he joined Margarethe and the children. Reminiscing about the happy days spent there in years gone by, he devoted himself to his small family, his two rapidly growing daughters and his wife. He needed the rest; the two strenuous campaigns which he had just completed had been hard on him.[21]

All Schurz's disappointments did not lessen his enthusiasm for his adopted country. When he came back to his division, he found a letter from his old friend Petrasch, who wanted to come to America. Answering it fully, he bared his thoughts with a frank statement of his purposes in emigrating to the United States and embarking on a public career. His own success had surprised him; although he had not been responsible for the Republican victory as had been asserted, he had nevertheless "contributed something toward raising the breeze which carried Lincoln into the presidential chair and thereby shook slavery to its foundation." He was certain that he would play an important part in the political changes which this revolution was bound to produce. Despite all the jealousies embittering his existence, he had never lost his confidence in people. Perhaps this trait was "artless," but it kept him young and cheerful. And his experiences in America had made him an even better Republican than before.[22]

His subordinates reciprocated his trust in his fellow men. Frederick C. Winkler, the division judge advocate general, presumably spoke for many of his fellows when he wrote, "I like General Schurz, to mental endowments of the first order he adds the kindest disposition, a stern integrity and unquestionable honor." Considering the general a "true friend and genial companion, of a generous and unsuspicious nature," he nevertheless feared that Schurz lacked "the keen eye to policy, the shrewdness without which public men are seldom successful." He thought literature rather than war or politics constituted his superior's proper sphere, and although he was wrong about the general's political skill, his observations were astute.[23] Schurz was rapidly becoming the foremost German in America.

The Eleventh Corps was soon to be tested once more. On September 20, General William S. Rosecrans's Army of the Cumberland was defeated at Chickamauga; retreating to Chattanooga, it was besieged by Braxton Bragg's Army of Tennessee. Anxious to do something to rescue it, the secretary of war prevailed on the administration to send Hooker with the Eleventh and Twelfth Corps to the west by rail as quickly as possible.

So it was that on September 27 Schurz boarded a train bound for the Tennessee Valley by way of Alexandria. Anxious to put himself at the head of the column to straighten out the mixed-up troop trains so that discipline might be maintained, he wired ahead to the station master at Grafton to hold the Third Division there till he arrived. But this ill-considered action threatened to interfere with the entire train movement so meticulously planned by Stanton and his assistants.

The secretary of war was not the type of man to suffer his projects to be torpedoed by his subordinates. Informed of Schurz's action, he unhesitatingly directed the railroad officials to disregard all orders but his own. In addition, he dashed off an order threatening Schurz with immediate arrest and relief from command in case of interference with the trains. Consequently, in spite of his annoyance, the general did not get his way. The railroad officials paid no attention to his request, and when on the next day, he protested to Stanton that he had merely sought to bring order out of chaos, he received a terse reply. Hooker was authorized to arrest any officer who undertook to delay the transportation of the troops, the secretary stated pointedly: "Whether you have done so, and whether he has relieved you from command, ought to be known to yourself." The incident ended with Howard's assurance to the War Department that Schurz had done no harm, an explanation that Hooker weakly endorsed.[24]

After a long trip via Wheeling, Indianapolis, Louisville, and Nashville, Hooker's forces reached Bridgeport, Alabama, just south of the Tennessee line. A few days later, Rosecrans's army passed to General George H. Thomas. Ulysses S. Grant took overall command, with Hooker's two corps destined to play a part in the successful effort to open the "Cracker Line," a thin route of communications to supply Chattanooga directly from the west.

Surrounded by steep mountains, the Tennessee city lay in the narrow valley of the Tennessee River, which looped around Raccoon Mountain before flowing on toward Bridgeport. A railroad connected that place with the town by way of Wauhatchie, but because the Confederates were in position atop Lookout Mountain, directly opposite Moccasin Point, it was not usable. As Generals William "Baldy" Smith and Thomas explained to Grant, a brigade of troops could be floated stealthily down the river past the Confederate positions on Lookout Mountain to Brown's Ferry, on the other side of the loop, a few miles by road from the city. There they would seize the Southern positions on the left bank, while other Union troops would arrive overland on the other side. This brigade would then cross on a pontoon bridge and march across the neck of the second loop to Kelly's Ferry, where it could open communications with Bridgeport downriver. In the meantime, Hooker could use his two corps to connect up with this force via Wauhatchie and clean out the area between Lookout Mountain, Raccoon Mountain, and the river.

The scheme was carried out according to plan. The boats floated down the river, the troops seized the enemy's positions at Brown's Ferry, and Hooker linked up with the Army of the Cumberland. Schurz's division was among those who reached the rendezvous at Brown's Ferry in the afternoon of October 28. But he was ordered to return to Wauhatchie at one o'clock in the morning to relieve John W. Geary, who had suddenly found himself under attack. Promptly complying with Hooker's orders, he marched back toward Wauhatchie in the moonlit night at the head of Tyndale's brigade, which took the lead. Clearing out most of the opposition in the woods toward his left, he expected his other two brigades to follow. However, they were held back by orders from higher headquarters, Hecker by Hooker in person, while Schurz himself was told by one of the commanding general's aides to occupy and take a hill to his left. This he did with dispatch, only to find on his return that Hooker was miffed. Why had he not pushed on to Geary? Schurz, nonplussed, pointed out that he had merely followed orders. His remaining two brigades reverted to him and were sent forward to reach Geary by morning. In spite of the mix-up, the operation had been wholly successful. But Hooker, nervous because of the night march and resentful of Schurz's protests about Chancellorsville, was not satisfied.[25]

The Eleventh Corps had every right to be proud of its part in the opening of the Cracker Line. It needed the boost to its morale, but not even success could stop the slurs to which it was still subjected. On November 3, the Louisville *Journal* printed a letter about Carl Schurz and his "gang of freedom shriekers" fleeing at Chancellorsville, an insult which the general decided not to leave unanswered. In a stinging reply to the editors, he called the author, the Kentucky politician General

Leslie Combs, a liar. Let him spend some time with the corps and accompany its general to battle. Then he might determine whether he would still have the heart to repeat the calumny. It was a telling rejoinder, but the episode served as a reminder that the corps, and especially its most famous German general, would always have to contend with the malice of its detractors.

It was shortly after Wauhatchie that Schurz first met General Grant. He had come to inspect the lines, and in spite of their intervening bitter quarrel, more than thirty years later Schurz still remembered how unassuming the cigar-smoking commander looked. He had no chance to talk with him, but apparently he had full confidence in his abilitites.[26]

The late fall and winter of 1863–64 was not a particularly pleasant period for Schurz. Disliking the routine of camp life, he was appalled by the neighboring countryside. The poverty, the ignorance, and the peculiar habits of the inhabitants astonished him; as he explained to his small daughter, they lived in log houses open to the elements, wore impossibly drab clothing, and were generally unable to read and write. But the tremendous difference between them and the people of the North was easily explained. Slavery had reduced the poor whites to their unenviable position and nothing but emancipation could bring improvements for them.[27]

It must also have been galling to the general that he did not really participate in the great victories at Chattanooga. While Hooker, in the Battle above the Clouds, the mopping up of Lookout Mountain, succeeded in refurbishing his reputation, and Thomas's troops won fame by scaling the heights of Missionary Ridge, Howard's corps had been sent to Thomas's left to lend support to operations in the vicinity of Orchard Knob east of the city. According to Grant's plans, Sherman was to turn Bragg's flank there. But things worked out differently, the main assault, the astonishing ascent to the summit of Missionary Ridge, taking place in the center.

Perhaps it was a sign of Schurz's dissatisfaction about his troubles with his superiors and the press that he was extremely nervous during the fighting near Orchard Knob. Arriving in the vicinity on November 22 and establishing connections with Thomas J. Wood on his right and with von Steinwehr on the left on the next day, he pushed his skirmishers forward to Citigo Creek. But he felt certain that he was going to be killed that very day. No matter that his division was not heavily engaged, no matter that all he had to worry about was intermittent fire from a battery on the slope of Missionary Ridge, he could not rid himself of his apprehension. Only when he remained unhurt as a shell exploded under his horse did he take hold of himself again. He had already been contemplating a farewell letter to his wife and children!

On November 25, Schurz was sent to Sherman's left to support the unsuccesful assault on Tunnel Hill but remained in reserve again. Meeting Sherman, he struck up a conversation and found that he liked the famous general. Yet Schurz's role in the battle of Chattanooga remained peripheral. The glory of the victory was not to be his.

Immediately after the triumph of Chattanooga, the Eleventh Corps was attached to Sherman's expedition for the relief of Burnside, whose forces were under siege at Knoxville. It was a difficult winter march across mountainous terrain with few amenities, an expedition which came to an end when Longstreet broke off the siege. Sherman and the troops had to trudge back again through the rain and cold until they reached the vicinity of Chattanooga. Schurz encamped near Lookout Mountain once more.[28]

He did not like his surroundings any better than before. Utilizing the long winter nights to read Herbert Spencer's *Social Statics*, he could muse about the backward state of the mountaineers and watch his troops dwindle away as their terms of enlistment came to an end. Hecker stayed; the two forty-eighters played cards with one another, but Schurz still thought the old revolutionary's opinions most peculiar. When Major Winkler called on him to tender New Year's congratulations, he found the commanding general, attempting to recover from a fever, hovering over a little fireplace. Winkler quickly lighted a new fire. It was a disagreeable winter.[29]

Worse was to follow. Early in January, Hooker's Wauhatchie report was published. After praising his troops for their victory, he added, "I regret that my duty constrains me to exempt any portion of my command in my commendation of their courage and valor. The brigade dispatched to the relief of General Geary, by orders delivered in person to its division commander, never reached him until long after the fight had ended. It is alleged that it lost its way, when it had a terrific infantry fire to guide it all the way, and also that it became involved in a swamp where there was no swamp or other obstacle between it and Geary which should have delayed it a moment in marching to the relief of its imperiled companions." Immediately protesting this slur on his honor, Hecker demanded a court of inquiry; Schurz not only supported him but joined in the demand. The repeated aspersions upon his military reputation finally became too much; he was determined to justify himself once and for all.

This time his request for a court was granted. Although, contrary to military practice, he outranked all its members, all of whom formed part of Hooker's command, Schurz accepted it. With Major Winkler as his expert counsel, he was able to conduct much of his defense in person. He showed clearly how he had received orders to support Geary; how one of Hooker's staff officers had ordered him to clear Tyndale's Hill; how, even though his Second and Third brigades had been halted by higher authority, he had faithfully and efficiently carried out everything demanded of him, only to be publicly reprimanded. Hooker, mercilessly cross-examined by Schurz, was unable to shake this testimony. Finally, the court, anxious to end the controversy, found that while Hooker had been justified in wishing to relieve Geary as quickly as possible, Schurz had fully explained his actions. He had "exonerated himself from the strictures contained in

General Hooker's official report." He had won his victory. In reality, however, it ended his military career. For it was obvious that he could no longer serve under Hooker.[30]

He himself was fully aware of this fact. Knowing that a reorganization of Hooker's command was in the offing, he sought different employment. Toward the end of February, taken sick with diarrhea, he went to New York on leave and wrote to the President. Lincoln might help him with a new command, he thought; he also felt that his services might be of assistance in the coming presidential campaign.[31]

That Schurz wanted to reenter the political arena was not surprising. Not even in the midst of military activity had he ever given up his interest in public affairs. In the fall of 1863 he complained to Chase about McClellan's activities among the troops. Shortly afterward he sent a strong letter of support for the party to Horace Rublee for publication during the Wisconsin campaign. In January 1864 he suggested to Governor Morgan that the party convention be held in some Southern city. Now he believed that his radical and German connections might be of use to the hard-pressed President, who was even then engaged in a struggle for renomination. But the contentious general's entreaties troubled Lincoln. Not knowing what to do with him, he refused the general permission to come to Washington.

Yet, as usual, Lincoln did not wish to hurt Schurz. Writing him that "on feeling around" he found that he could not invite him to the White House without detriment to the public service, he suggested that it would be foolish to leave the military service even temporarily, because, as he put it, "with a major general once out, it is next to impossible for even the President to get him in again." Naturally he would like to have the active support of a man of Schurz's ability, but he could not properly arrange it without separating the general from the army. When Schurz, forwarding excerpts from the findings of the court of inquiry, persisted, Lincoln merely repeated his previous advice.[32]

The President's unwillingness to extricate the general from his predicament became especially embarrassing in the spring, when the Eleventh and Twelfth corps were consolidated into a new Twentieth, commanded by Hooker. Schurz, who had briefly been in charge during Howard's absence, was clearly a supernumerary, not merely in the corps but in the Army of the Cumberland as well, so that General Thomas was anxious to get rid of him. "If you have sufficient major-generals to dispense with Schurz," he wrote to Sherman, "I would recommend he be relieved from duty with this army. He is neither agreeable to General Hooker nor to General Howard." Sherman, in charge of the Department of the Mississippi now that Grant had become general-in-chief, was willing to oblige. Relieving the German-American from duty with Twentieth Corps on April 12, he finally assigned him to command a camp of instruction near Nashville.[33] It was obvious that Schurz had been shelved.

Unable to do much about his new assignment, Schurz accepted in good grace. He did his best to drill his troops, while keeping his political options open. It was during his stay in Nashville—the camp was at Edgefield, on the other side of the Cumberland River—that he first met Andrew Johnson, then military governor of Tennessee. Apparently Johnson liked him. Seeking to intercede for him with Lincoln, the governor sent a telegram about the general's unhappiness with so inactive a command, only to be told that it was very difficult "to find a place for one of so high rank, when there is no place seeking him." In later years, Schurz in turn professed to have been less favorably impressed with his host; as his memoirs were written long after his quarrel with the Reconstruction President, however, it is likely that his recollections were colored by his unfortunate later experiences. At the time, he thought enough of Johnson to seek his help, just as he asked Sherman to find him a more active assignment and still hoped to confer with the President himself.[34]

Political developments eventually aided his quest. After Lincoln's opponents' failure to supplant him, first by Chase, then by some other more radical candidate, the Union Convention at Baltimore renominated him. Nevertheless Frémont, supported by a number of extremists, allowed himself to be put at the head of a separate ticket, and rumors were rife that Schurz, like other German revolutionaries, would support him. Not even Lincoln's renomination ended the controversy. Angry with the President's veto of the Wade-Davis bill, many radicals still sought to replace him with some other standard-bearer.[35] Needing all the support he could get, on August 9 Lincoln invited Schurz to visit him.

Schurz, who had taken leave and was staying with his family in Bethlehem—he was thinking of settling in Philadelphia after the war—did not have to be asked twice. He rushed to Washington, where the President took him to the Soldiers' Home for a confidential conference. Fully aware that efforts were being made to replace him, Lincoln said he might even step down if he were certain that somebody more qualified would take his place. But so far he had failed to see such a candidate; consequently, he would stay on. Offering to find a command for Schurz in Rosecrans's inactive department, he was not surprised when the general turned it down. The meeting ended with an agreement that Schurz would make a series of campaign speeches for the administration— always with the understanding that after the election he would return to the army[36]

Schurz came back to Bethlehem, full of hope for the cause he considered wholly dependent upon Lincoln's reelection. Like other radicals, he strongly urged that Montgomery Blair, now the conservatives' spokesman in the cabinet, be replaced. But he was absolutely certain about the President. Despite the apparent rift between Lincoln and the advanced elements of the party, the general realized that, in the last analysis, the President was practically a radical himself. "The main thing is that the policy of the government moves in the right direction—that is to say, the slaveholder will be overthrown and slavery abolished," he wrote to

Petrasch. "Whether it moves in that direction prudently or imprudently, slowly or rapidly, is a matter of indifference as against the question of whether a policy should be adopted which would move in another, an opposite and destructive, direction."

Under these circumstances, he had no trouble at all opting for Lincoln. Conceding that the President was a man without higher education whose manners harmonized little with the European conception of the dignity of a ruler, he nevertheless insisted that Lincoln was a "man of profound feeling, just and firm principles, and incorruptible integrity." Schurz had observed the President closely; he understood Lincoln's weaknesses, but they were the weaknesses of a good man. "He is the people personified; that is the secret of his popularity. His government is the most representative that ever existed in world history. . . . In fifty years, perhaps much sooner, Lincoln's name will stand written upon the honor roll of the American Republic next to that of Washington, and there it will remain for all time. The children of those who now disparage him will bless him."[37] In October 1864, not many observers would have agreed with him.

In line with his convictions, Schurz campaigned strenuously for the ticket. The outlook had improved greatly since his visit to Washington. First, the Democrats, asserting that the war was a failure, nominated McClellan on a peace platform; then a series of Federal victories made a mockery of their pessimism. With Mobile Bay taken, Atlanta conquered, and the enemy swept from the Shenandoah Valley, it was obvious that victory was not only possible but not very far off. Feeling certain of success, Schurz sought to impart his optimism to others.[38]

He delivered his first important speech on September 16 at Concert Hall in Philadelphia. Ridiculing the folly of a peace platform, he accused the Democrats of Negrophobia, "that most ridiculous of all mental diseases," which would cause them to send home 200,000 black soldiers. If Europeans accused the United States of seeking an empire, they were right; only the empire America sought was the empire of liberty. "For the great Empire of liberty, forward," he exclaimed in conclusion. The audience responded enthusiastically.

At the Academy of Music in Brooklyn, on October 7, he spoke again. This time his topic was, "The Treason of Slavery." Southern aristocrats had been warring against American democracy; they had insisted upon the perpetuation of slavery; thus the institution itself had become a traitor. For this reason, it must be destroyed once and for all. To be sure, the war had not begun as a struggle against slavery, but revolutions had a way of going forward. Nothing could stop their course. No reunion without emancipation was possible; had not black troops rendered invaluable services? The future was clear; it was "Liberty! Liberty and Union! one and inseparable! now and forever!"

Toward the end of the campaign, he returned to Milwaukee, where on October 28 he delivered another speech at the Academy of Music. He addressed himself to the Democrats. Their leaders were misleading them; peace could not restore the Union. But the war was not a failure, as the victories in the Shenandoah Valley had shown. Since there could be no reunion with slavery, the institution had to go. The successful outcome of the election as well as of the war would vindicate the principles of liberty on which the country was founded. A final tour of the East, where on November 4 he spoke to his fellow Germans at Cooper Union, brought him back to Bethlehem.

Schurz's speeches were well received and widely distributed. As he had predicted, the campaign ended in triumph when, on November 8, Lincoln was reelected. Convinced that the election results were worth more than two successful battles, Schurz was certain that the war would soon be over.[39]

Although the general was still anxious to return to active duty, he could not immediately assume another military assignment. Margarethe, who was expecting a third child, was very ill. Plagued by persistent premonitions of death, she was in need of her husband's care. Thus he stayed in Bethlehem, bound to the house, occupying his time in assembling his speeches for publication, until on December 30 still another daughter was born. He called her Emma Savannah to commemorate the capture of the Georgia city ten days before.[40]

During the first weeks of the new year, while his wife was recuperating, Schurz became impatient again. He wrote to Washington once more to ask for active duty. Receiving no answer, he turned to Congressman Elihu B. Washburne, whose close relations with Grant might be helpful. He even suggested he would accept service under Howard again.

The approach to Washburne proved worthwhile. Obtaining permission to visit Washington, toward the end of the month Schurz hurried to the capital, where he had a long conversation with Stanton and Lincoln. Both were friendly but suggested he await the return of General Grant, who was shortly expected to come back from North Carolina. When the general in chief did not arrive, Schurz went home to Bethlehem without having accomplished anything, except that the President gave him permission to try again as soon as Grant was available.[41]

Nevertheless, the trip did have its compensations. When on January 31 the House of Representatives passed the Thirteenth Amendment abolishing slavery, Schurz was present in the galleries. Pandemonium broke loose as the vote was announced. Members joined in the loud cheering, some embraced one another, and others wept like children. In spite of his disappointments, Schurz felt that he had received his reward for his labors. But he did not join in the general applause. Overwhelmed by emotion, he simply could not speak.[42]

On February 15, he returned to Washington, only to find that Grant had left again, this time for City Point. Because his request had not yet been acted upon, he received permission to go to Virginia himself to find out what his assignment would be. This he did, and when he arrived, Grant, presumably to get rid of him, ordered him to aid Hancock in raising a corps of veteran recruits.

The idea of the corps was a good one. Its object was the reenlistment of veterans whose three-year term of service had come to an end, an enterprise which appealed to Schurz. With his usual energy, he traveled west, to Pittsburgh, Columbus, Cincinnati, Indianapolis, St. Louis, Springfield, Chicago, Madison, Milwaukee, Detroit, and Cleveland. He made every effort to accomplish his mission, but his journey was not very successful. Some of the officers he had come to see were not available, to say nothing of his personal mishaps—no hotel rooms in Columbus, missed connections, and fierce snow storms. Although he managed to take care of some personal business, seeing his father in Milwaukee and discussing his future journalistic career with Judge Stallo in Cincinnati, after a brief stay in Bethlehem he went back to Washington, only to find the corps' prospects dubious. Recruiting had gone so badly in the East that Hancock was ready to rejoin his old command. Conferring with him in Winchester, Schurz decided to look elsewhere for an assignment.[43]

Because Grant had promised him a place in Sherman's army, Schurz set out for City Point to settle his status. Grant was not there when he arrived, but Schurz's orders were ready. He was to report to Sherman, perhaps to get his old division back. And the President was also there, affable as ever. He even invited the general to go back to Washington in the same boat as Mrs. Lincoln, an invitation Schurz accepted with pleasure.

Once aboard, he made himself agreeable to the First Lady, who chided him for not having visited her in the capital. She even arranged for him to be driven to his hotel in her carriage. "I learned more state secrets in a few hours than I could otherwise in a year," he boasted to Margarethe. Then he made ready to leave for North Carolina and Sherman's army.[44]

On April 3, the day he was ready to start for the field, the news of the fall of Richmond reached Washington. The population was delirious; it was obvious that the war would not last much longer. Full of enthusiasm, Schurz went to Norfolk, took a boat to Roanoke Island, and finally reached New Berne, where he sent Sherman a message announcing Richmond's capture as well as his arrival. Then he rode on to Goldsborough to report to the general in person.[45]

Sherman was not too happy to see him. With no troops to spare for a general of such high rank, what could he possibly do with him? Schurz wanted to serve with Twentieth Corps, in Slocum's army, but no division was available for him. At last it was arranged for him to become Slocum's chief of staff. With the war nearing its end, political problems would assume the highest priority. Schurz's political experience might then become very valuable.

So it came about that Major General Schurz ended his war service as chief of staff of Slocum's Army of Georgia. He was not especially pleased with his assignment; his old division, which welcomed him enthusiastically when he came for a visit, would have satisfied him more. In addition, Sherman's style of warfare horrified him. Nothing like it had occurred since the French devastation of the Palatinate in the seventeenth century, he thought. If it kept up, the army would disintegrate to become a mere band of robbers. With the end of hostilities in sight, however, he accepted his position. He was looking forward to the coming of peace.[46]

The remaining weeks of active campaigning would not substantially change the military record Schurz had established, that of a competent officer who had risen too high too fast. Unable to establish satisfactory relations with his superiors, he had often been thwarted. His military instincts had not been faulty, however, even if he had not been the preceptor of the President, as was asserted later.[47] He had succeeded in combining active campaigning with radical politics, and above all, he had been able to strengthen his hold on the German-Americans. He was determined to make the most of it.

X

Reconstruction

WHEN TWO DAYS AFTER the news of Lee's surrender the Army of Georgia entered Raleigh, Schurz was in an exalted mood. The beautiful spring weather, the elation of victory, the hope of a speedy reunion with his family, all served to buoy up his spirits. In company with other generals, he joined Sherman in front of the state capitol to take the salute of the Twenty-fifth Corps marching past in the bright sunshine in seemingly endless columns. "It is all over with us; I see now it is all over," said an attractive young Southern girl as she wiped her eyes with her handkerchief. "A few days ago I saw General Johnston's army, ragged and starved; now when I look at these strong, healthy men and see them coming and coming—it is all over with us!"[1]

Schurz too thought the war had practically ended. Addressing troops from the capitol steps, he urged reconciliation between North and South, an encouraging sentiment for the Confederates who were also listening.[2] It is certain, however, that they would not have approved of his actual thoughts about Reconstruction, for, convinced of the necessity for protecting the rights of the freedmen, he was rapidly coming to favor black suffrage. Only the most advanced radicals endorsed so extreme a step.

Schurz's abiding interest in the success of Reconstruction and emancipation is easy to understand. For years he had given his all to the cause of freedom; now that a bloody civil war had brought the campaign to a successful conclusion, it was time to measure the results. Meticulously keeping himself informed of the difficulties of establishing a free labor system, he had cheered on Sumner in his effort to establish the Freedmen's Bureau. It was certain that blacks could not simply be left at their former owners' mercy; the civil rights of Unionists of both races would have to be protected; the government owed it to them. Moreover, he was too astute a politician not to advocate steps to prevent the return of Southern Democrats to power. He eventually came to the conclusion that to safeguard Southern Unionists, black and white, as well as to keep authority safely in Republican hands, some degree of black participation in politics was essential. President Lincoln in part shared his opinions.[3]

Many of Schurz's fellow radicals quarreled bitterly with the President about the proper way of restoring the South, but the general assessed the Emancipator's aims more accurately than they. Devoting several pages of his *Reminiscences* to the differences between Lincoln and Johnson, he clearly emphasized the distinction between their Reconstruction proposals. Lincoln's plans, ever flexible and designed "as rallying points to the Union men," had been evolved in times of armed conflict. That in a period of peace the President would ever have "sacrificed the rights of the emancipated slaves and the security of the Union men to the metaphysical abstraction of the indestructibility of the States" he could not imagine.[4]

But of course Lincoln did not live to carry out his plans. When the first reports of the tragedy at Ford's Theater reached Raleigh, Schurz was crestfallen. "I should have written to you yesterday if I had been able to shake off the gloom that has settled upon me since the arrival of the news of the murder of Lincoln," he lamented to his wife. "A thunderclap from the blue sky could not have struck us more unexpectedly and frightfully. Our good, good Lincoln!" He thought it was fortunate that the fighting was almost over; otherwise, the conflict would be certain to degenerate into a war of vengeance like the campaigns of Attila. What the new president was going to do was not yet clear.[5]

The news of Lincoln's death coincided with Joseph E. Johnston's request to Sherman for an armistice. When on April 18 the two generals met, they concluded an agreement that not only ended the fighting but also granted the vanquished insurgents several political concessions, including the recall of the Confederate state legislatures. Schurz, who had already asked Sherman to place him in charge of a military district to enable him to assist in the process of Reconstruction, was sitting up late to await General Slocum's return from Sherman's headquarters. It was midnight before he heard the terms, and what he learned deeply troubled him. Openly stating his disapproval of the arrangements, he predicted that the document would not be well received. The mind of the North had been too inflamed by the assassination. That he was right became apparent a few days later, when the President disowned the armistice.

The surrender of Johnston's army, even if not on Sherman's terms, effectively ended the war for Schurz. Relieved from duty with the Army of Georgia, on April 27 he left for Washington to resign his commission.[6] It was time to resume his civilian career.

What that career would be was not at all certain. Schurz's interest in the problems of Reconstruction and the freedmen drew him back toward his earlier journalistic ventures, especially as his law partnership with Paine had lapsed during his military service and he had never been very active in legal affairs. Offers from John W. Forney, the Republican newspaper publisher, to write editorials for his Washington and Philadelphia organs were flattering, but prospects of a full-time newspaper career in Missouri seemed more enticing. The state's large German population would facilitate a new political beginning as well. "I must look about me a little in the political world," he wrote to Margarethe from Washington, and he went to see the President.

Andrew Johnson seemed very cordial to his old acquaintance of Nashville days. Engaging Schurz in a long conversation, he gave him to understand that his objectives were all that "the most progressive friends of human liberty" could desire. But he wanted to achieve his aims without making them the subject of general discussion. In spite of the President's efforts at that time not to alarm his radical acquaintances, Schurz was somewhat uneasy. Unless the right agents were used to carry out federal policy in the South, he warned Sumner, the "mischievous elements" there would regain control. He had already alerted Johnson to this danger; now he thought the senator ought to do the same. One false step in the beginning would cause infinite trouble later.[7]

Immediately after his interview with the President, Schurz went home to his family in Bethlehem. Margarethe, who never seems to have liked the West, was still in Pennsylvania. Plagued by rheumatic attacks since the birth of her last baby, she was looking forward to a possible trip to Europe at the end of the war. But her husband did not feel free to leave; he had to settle his affairs first. Moreover, he did not fully trust the administration.[8]

It was not only Johnson's failure to take decisive action in the South that was unsettling; the proposed secret trial of the Lincoln conspirators was even more so. As the President had told him to write whenever he had something to say, Schurz now took him at his word. In his letter he argued that the government, having accused the leaders of the defunct Confederacy of complicity in the crime, would have to prove its charges in open court. Otherwise, they would not be believed. Fair procedures would go far to determine the opinion of mankind.

Even though Schurz honestly abhorred secret proceedings, what he really wanted was to participate in the prospective trial of Jefferson Davis. Five days after writing his letter to Johnson, he went to Washington in person to see the President. Anxious to be in the capital when the captured Confederate leader arrived, the general pressed his views on the administration. Johnson appeared favorably disposed toward the idea of Schurz's participation, but since it was not at all clear just when and where the trial would be held, nothing definite could be arranged. The proceedings would have to be postponed for at lease three months, the attorney general pointed out. Otherwise the government would be accused of undue haste.

Schurz's failure to accomplish anything definite about the Davis trial did not dampen his optimism concerning his relations with the President. On May 20, he was again at the White House to offer advice about relations with France and Mexico. Someday he might become secretary of state, thought his good friend the Marquis de Chambrun, who was then an attaché at the French legation in Washington. The general himself believed that he was on the way to acquiring a personal influence which might prove of great significance.[9]

It soon turned out, however, that his confidence was not justified. After watching the great victory parade of the Union army on May 23 and 24—the endless columns of blue-clad troops passing in review were an inspiring sight—he saw Johnson again. This time the President seemed perplexed. As a token of his esteem he showed Schurz drafts of the two state papers he was about to issue, a proclamation of amnesty and a call for the white people of North Carolina to reorganize their government. The stunned general made no secret of his reservations. Could not those portions of the proclamation limiting the franchise to whites be modified, he asked. Perhaps the President ought to appoint some reliable person to supervise the political actions of the military commanders in the South. Unwilling to reject this advice completely, Johnson asked Schurz if he would return to Washington to help with this matter, an offer to which his visitor quickly assented. Back in Bethlehem, however, he immediately alerted Sumner. The President was evidently not as firm as had been believed. To counteract the influence of Southern advisers, the senator must come to the capital as soon as feasible.

In spite of Schurz's warnings, on May 29 the President published his proclamations. Unwilling to believe that Johnson was irrevocably committed to the policy he had inaugurated, the general wrote to him again. The reaction of the newspapers made it clear that his reservations about the white suffrage provisions had been justified, he pointed out. The President must reverse himself, especially as an excellent opportunity seemed at hand. South Carolina's constitution limited the franchise to property holders. Why not take advantage of this provision? Let it be discarded when inaugurating the restoration of the Palmetto State by calling on all men, white and black, to write a new basic law. It would be a democratic solution, and since it applied to South Carolina, the cradle of secession, not even the Democrats could object. Thus a change in policy would serve to bring about good relations between the executive and Congress, a development Schurz was anxious to promote in any case. He suggested that he write a series of letters on Reconstruction to the President and hoped Johnson had no objections. In addition, he once again advised that an agent be appointed to supervise the political actions of military commanders in the South.[10]

The answer to this suggestion was an invitation from the White House to return to Washington. Johnson decided to send Schurz on an inspection tour of the South—whether to mollify him or to get rid of him is not certain. The general, who did not know what Johnson wanted when he left Bethlehem, thought that perhaps he himself was to be reconstructed. He was evidently to be called upon to take some part in the reorganization of the South, a prospect that intrigued him. Stopping off at the Tiedemanns' in Philadelphia, he attended a spiritualist séance—he had always been interested in extrasensory phenomena—and asked the medium, one of the daughters of the house, to conjure up the spirit of Lincoln. It not only predicted he would be sent on a mission to the South but also that some day he would be elected senator from Missouri. He wrote about these predictions long after the fact; in view of his political ambitions, his negotiations for a position in St. Louis, and his previous suggestions to Johnson, his allegedly supernatural experiences are not inexplicable.[11]

When he arrived at the White House, Schurz was not disappointed. Johnson, explaining that he wanted him to travel to the Southern states, asked him to inquire into the results of the administration's Reconstruction policy and to make recommendations. Upon Schurz's caution that such a journey would be useless if current policies were already fixed, the President assured him that he had an open mind. Although the general was not entirely convinced and the prospect of a Southern tour during the summer was not inviting, he decided to accept. Stanton urged him to go, Sumner added his encouragement, and in the last analysis, he could hardly say no. Not only was he extremely eager to play a role in the process of Reconstruction, but if he declined, Johnson would always be able to maintain that he had invited a radical to give him his opinions only to meet with a refusal. Moreover, despite all disappointments, there was still a slight chance that the President had not entirely made up his mind. To take care of monetary problems, Sumner agreed to see to it that New England friends would defray the extra premium on Schurz's life insurance, an increase made necessary because of the unhealthy summer climate of the Gulf states. He also promised to arrange for the publication of some of Schurz's letters from the South in some Boston paper, which turned out to be the *Advertiser*.

Evidently still believing that Johnson's opinions were not yet settled, Schurz was clinging to the hope that his trip and the report which he expected to submit to Congress could help arrest the President's Southern policy. As Sumner had expressed it so accurately, Johnson's course was dividing the North; if not reversed, it would only delay the day "of tranquility and reconciliation." Strongly urging Schurz to undertake the journey, the senator emphasized his firm conviction that the President's "shameful policy" must break down. It was encouraging insurgents in the South and Democrats in the North in their resistance to the Declaration of Independence, as he called the opposition to black suffrage. Schurz, who agreed with him, made every effort to convince Johnson of the error of his ways. Seeking to impress upon him the importance of postponing elections in the former insurgent states until after the meeting of Congress, he attempted to counteract the influence of the President's conservative advisers and pleaded with Sumner and his associates to do the same. The general's assessment of the situation as far as Reconstruction was concerned was justified; race relations could never be put on a healthy basis as long as Southern conservatives were in control. But it was wholly mistaken in regard to Johnson. The President was determined to keep the South "a white man's country."[12]

On July 12, Schurz boarded the steamer *Arago* to sail to Hilton Head. If prior to leaving he considered the President's Reconstruction policy mistaken, he became even more convinced of its harmfulness before actually arriving in South Carolina. Aboard ship he engaged in conversation with a planter who told him that there was no way in which the Negro could be made to work except by force; nothing that Schurz could say to the contrary would dissuade him. At Charleston, he found further confirmation of his apprehensions. The war-ravished city with its wharves in disrepair, its streets overgrown with weeds, and horses and cattle grazing among the ruins, was a perfect symbol of the defeated Confederacy. The Southerners he met at the Charleston Hotel, however, while willing to accept the failure of secession, had not changed their minds about the blacks. Totally unprepared to grant anything like equality to their former slaves, they were convinced that Negroes would never work without compulsion, and they felt certain that Johnson, with his Southern background, agreed with them.

Personally assisted by General Quincy Gillmore, the local commander, Schurz pursued his investigations in the interior of the state and on the Sea Islands as well. Watching blacks working on a Yankee lessee's plantation, he found proof that their former masters' prejudices were wholly unjustified. Impressed with this evidence of the freedmen's industry, he was appalled at the whites' refusal to come to terms with emancipation and the frequent accounts of atrocities inflicted upon the blacks. Lest Southerners impose a new labor system differing from slavery only in name, he felt that the continued presence of Federal troops was absolutely essential. "I have come to the conclusion that the policy of the government is the worst that could be hit upon," he complained to his wife. His articles in the Boston *Advertiser* also reflected this opinion, as did his reports to the President, whom he implored again to postpone calling a state convention.[13]

From South Carolina, Schurz traveled to Georgia. The spirit of the people there resembled that of their neighbors; sullen acceptance of Federal military supremacy was combined with an utter refusal to grant any rights to the blacks. The population's bitterness toward Northerners as well was brought home to him at his hotel in Savannah, when a Southern lady indignantly refused a dish of pickles a Federal officer politely sought to offer her. A physician in the southeastern part of the state complained that there was an imminent danger of a black uprising; asked for proof, he cited his Negroes' unwillingness to be ordered to their quarters at 9:00 P.M. and a servant girl's refusal to submit to a flogging! Schurz sent evidence of atrocities against blacks to the White House and recommended that the local Freedmen's Bureau be strengthened. It was obvious that without federal supervision, Georgia was no more prepared than South Carolina to administer her own affairs.

After a time-consuming and uncomfortable voyage up the Savannah River to Augusta, Schurz set out on a tedious overland trip to Atlanta, Milledgeville, and Macon. The slow railroads, the primitive hotels, the horrible food, and the unbearable heat combined to make him uncomfortable, but he moved on to Montgomery, even though he had to cover the last stretch in a hack driven by two young coachmen who constantly got stuck in the mud. In Alabama, too, he collected reports of atrocities against the blacks, in some localities a murder per day. His long list of blacks assassinated, whipped, persecuted for no other reason than their desire to assert their new freedom was designed to impress the President. To stop these outrages, he suggested that troops be deployed in such a way as to be in easy reach of every county. In addition, anxious to demonstrate the effectiveness of the new contract labor system, he advised against the practice of allowing freedmen to work on their former masters' estates. They would do better elsewhere. It was apparent that Johnson's policy was no more effective in Alabama than in other states.[14]

Schurz reached the turning point of his trip in Mississippi. Arriving just after the state convention had adjourned, he was horrified by the conditions he found. Society seemed to be in a state of complete dissolution, with all respect for personal property gone and the blacks' lives in constant danger. Only the freedmen were trying to work, become educated, and make efforts to adjust to their new freedom. Thus, when he found that the commanding general, his old superior, Henry Slocum, had countermanded Governor William Sharkey's attempt to recall the state militia, he promptly wired his approval to the President. The organization of the militia, he stated, would have been a fatal mistake.

But Johnson was in no mood to listen. Fully informed by his supporters of Schurz's total opposition to his policy, he was incensed at the appearance of the general's letters in the newspapers. Expressing the hope that Slocum's order would not be carried out without consultation with the government, he pointed out that to induce the people to come forward in defense of state and federal governments was one of the administration's aims. The organization of the militia in every county would enable the United States to withdraw its forces and curtail expenses. "The main object of Major-General Schurz's mission to the south," he added, "was to aid as far as practicable the policy adopted by the Government. . . . It is hoped that such aid has been given." Sharkey promptly asked for and received permission to publish this reply.

This message reached Schurz on the way to New Orleans, after he had already left Jackson. Responding immediately, he vigorously defended his support of Slocum. No general having the interests of his government at heart could have issued a different order; the recall of the militia would simply put arms into the hands of enemies of the Union. Conditions in the South were not yet ripe for the withdrawal of the army.[15]

Johnson's refusal to sustain Slocum should have squashed any hopes Schurz may still have had of exerting influence on the administration. He could not have been taken wholly unaware; even before receiving the President's answer, he sent an ominous letter describing the militia controversy to Margarethe. "If the President persists in pursuing a false course," he added, "he must not be surprised if, later, I bring into the field against him all the artillery I am assembling now. He will find the armament pretty heavy. . . ." But, although Sumner warned that Johnson was wholly committed to his course, the general still sought to keep the President from acting in haste. The issues at stake in Louisiana were too important.[16]

Louisiana in general and New Orleans in particular furnished ample evidence of the pernicious effects of the administration's policy. Always faction-ridden, local Unionists were rapidly losing power to former secessionists, whom the governor,

J. Madison Wells, was assiduously courting. Appointing them to office, giving them control of the school board, and threatening to scrap the free state constitution of 1864, he enjoyed Johnson's support. No amount of pleading by Schurz could change this state of affairs. In fact, the general's authority was undermined completely when on September 5 a news story about him appeared in the papers. Alleging that because he had written articles for the press he no longer enjoyed the President's confidence, it predicted his speedy recall.

He protested immediately. Emphasizing his surprise at the newspaper clipping which he enclosed, he reminded Johnson that he had not sought his mission. As for his letters, he had to make a living. Had his suggestion of withdrawing his resignation from the army been accepted, he would not have had to look for alternate sources of support. At any rate, he had done no wrong. The material he had submitted to the Boston *Advertiser* was not confidential; moreover, the secretary of war had been fully aware of his commitments. Johnson did not bother to reply.[17]

At this point, Schurz might well have given up and gone home. But from the very beginning he had been anxious to submit a report to Congress as well as the President, and now, convinced of the importance of what he was going to say and implored by Sumner not to cut his trip short, he remained to collect as much evidence as possible. Continuing to send reports to Johnson, he assured his wife that there was no basis for rumors of his recall. At best, the President might still pay some attention to him; at worst, he could furnish valuable information to the opposition.

In New Orleans, he promptly established contact with many Unionists, both radicals and moderates alienated by Wells. Former Governor Michael Hahn, Generals Nathaniel P. Banks and E. R. S. Canby, and others kept him fully informed about the drift of events. So thoroughly did he carry out his inquiries that the conservatives protested to Johnson. In fact, Governor Wells finally sent Mayor Hugh Kennedy and another reactionary, Thomas Cottman, to Washington to counteract the radicals' influence. Since the President's supporters had long been imploring him to pay no attention to Schurz's reports, Kennedy and Cottman's mission was an easy one. Johnson continued to lend his support to the conservative party.

After a trip to Lafourche and up the Bayou Teche, a journey to Mobile, and two reports to the President once more stressing the continued necessity of protecting blacks and Unionists, Schurz returned to Washington. Traveling up the Mississippi to St. Louis, he stopped over at Natchez for another communication to Johnson. His observations had convinced him that nothing could be done in the South unless the ownership of land passed into new hands. This radical notion merely reinforced his conviction that black suffrage was absolutely indispensable. That these views contrasted sharply with Johnson's policies made his homecoming after an absence of three months less than pleasant.[18]

Not even Schurz's worst premonitions could have prepared him for the icy welcome in store for him. After being kept waiting for a long time in the anterooms of the White House, he was finally ushered in to see the President. Receiving him with great coldness and maintaining a sullen reserve, Johnson asked no questions about the results of the Southern trip. In fact, he made it clear that he did not want to hear about them at all. The situation became so embarrassing that at the first opportunity Schurz withdrew. Then he read in the New York *Herald* that he had fallen into disfavor because he had spent most of his time in the South in organizing the Republican party there. Immediately seeking an explanation from the secretary of war, the general received little encouragement, but Sumner offered consolation. He had never believed that Johnson was in earnest when he sent Schurz to the South. Chief Justice Chase, too, had been treated rudely upon his return from the defeated section; it was evident that the only course left was to halt the President's policies in Congress. For this reason, it was essential for Schurz to write a full report.

Schurz needed no urging. Returning to Bethlehem, he began to prepare a detailed account of his experiences. Under no illusions that Johnson would let him publish it, he was nevertheless certain that his friends in Congress would use it to best advantage. For this reason he lavished considerable care on the document.[19]

The result was one of the most interesting publications he ever wrote. Consisting of forty-six pages, not counting some sixty more of finely printed documentation, it constituted a forceful indictment of Johnson's policies. Significantly pointing out that, at the end of the war, Southerners had been ready to accept any conditions a victorious government might have imposed upon them, he emphasized the fact that as soon as Johnson's proclamations appeared to hold out hopes of speedy reconstruction, this attitude changed completely. Southerners remained hostile to the national government; seeking to regain political control of their own affairs as quickly as possible, they merely attempted to reimpose some sort of forced labor upon the freedmen. Thus, if all that were desired was the reestablishment of the forms of civil government in the former Confederacy, then Reconstruction had already been virtually achieved. If, however, the revolution begun in the South was to be completed, if Unionists and blacks were to be protected, it was absolutely necessary to retain the army there, at least for some time to come, to support the Freedmen's Bureau, and to delay the full restoration of the states. He had found so much evidence of hatred for the freedmen and unwillingness to accommodate the new labor system that it was clear that forceful methods were absolutely essential. Southerners must be told that national control of their affairs would not cease until free labor had thoroughly taken root. To protect the blacks, he proposed the introduction of Negro suffrage and, as if this were not radical enough, a redistribution of land. Insisting that in Russia little or no vagrancy had resulted from the emancipation of the serfs because they had been given land, he concluded that a ''similar measure [here] would do more to stop negro vagrancy in the South than the severest penal laws." The appended documents furnished ample proof of his assertions.[20]

As Schurz had expected, he did not receive permission to publish the report, no matter how insistently he applied for the privilege in a personal visit to Washington. The President simply did not answer his request. However, Sumner made plans to call for the paper in Congress.

It must have been clear to Johnson that Schurz's report constituted a powerful argument against his policies. Congress, which would have to recognize the states reconstructed in accordance with his plans, was about to meet, and although the radicals were not in a majority, they were ably led. In view of the passage of a black code virtually reestablishing slavery in Mississippi, they could count on the support of many moderates in their struggle to protect the freedmen. But Johnson could always counter with reports written by conservatives or less perceptive observers, like the pro-Southern journalist Henry Watterson or General Grant. In November, the latter undertook an inspection trip to the South; his political naiveté could be relied upon to produce an innocuous document, which his report proved to be.[21]

Congress met on December 4. Refusing to seat any of the Southern delegates, it set up a Committee of Fifteen on Reconstruction to which all matters pertaining to the South were referred. Then, on December 12, when Johnson's ally, Senator Edgar Cowan of Pennsylvania, moved that the President be requested to furnish information on the suppression of the rebellion, Sumner amended the resolution to require him to transmit copies of reports from officers or agents appointed to visit the South as well. On December 20 the President complied by sending to the Senate an optimistic statement of conditions in the formerly rebellious states. The reports of Generals Grant and Schurz were appended.

Sumner was ready for what followed. Cowan moved the reading of Grant's report; it was a short paper substantially laudatory of the President's measures. Then Sumner asked that Schurz's document also be read. To objections about its length, he replied with a precedent. The long report on the outrages in Kansas had been heard; comparing Johnson's message to Franklin Pierce's "whitewashing" of the atrocities in Kansas, he emphasized the importance of Schurz's findings in reply. After some wrangling, the Senate agreed to have the document printed.[22]

The result was all that Schurz could have hoped for. Over one hundred thousand copies of his indictment of the President's policy were printed and became an important weapon of radical propaganda. If the New York *Herald* sneered at its length by contrasting its author's limited military record with Grant's great successes in the field, Republican papers pointed out that in political affairs Schurz had much more experience than the victor of Appomattox. "General Schurz in a most able and carefully written paper recites the facts of Southern society as he saw them on his official inspection tour," editorialized the Chicago *Tribune*. "It becomes the duty of the President to communicate these documents to Congress

. . . but he writes a note to say that nevertheless his plan is working well, and all is quiet on the Potomac!"[23]

That Schurz's description of Southern affairs was not exaggerated was amply corroborated. The black codes appearing on the statute books of many Southern states shortly after his return bore out his worst fears; the plight of Unionists and freedmen filled pages of testimony in congressional hearings, and the defiant attitudes of Southern conservatives alarmed even travelers friendly to Johnson. Schurz's observations corresponded to the facts. Had the President taken them to heart, much later trouble might have been prevented.[24]

The general himself was delighted with the reception of his report. Gleefully detailing its success to his wife, he fully credited the story that the President said to a senator, "The only great mistake I have made yet was to send Schurz to the South."[25] That the publicity it gave its author would be helpful to his political ambitions was evident.

In the meantime, Schurz had to think of his future. On the way back from New Orleans, he had stopped off at St. Louis to negotiate with local interests about the possibility of his taking up a journalistic career in Missouri. The location pleased him; the numerous Germans in the state promised a good base for future political advancement. Pleased that the Republican politician B. Gratz Brown and Governor Thomas C. Fletcher were trying to make the proper arrangements and that the German journalist George Hillgaertner was available for assistance, Schurz seriously entertained the thought of moving to St. Louis. When he came back, however, he accepted another offer instead. Sidney Howard Gay, the managing editor of the New York *Tribune*, asked him to become chief correspondent of the paper's Washington bureau. It was a tempting invitation; as manager of so influential a journal in the capital just when Congress was about to meet, he might be able to exert some influence on coming events.

Thus he spent part of the winter in Washington. At first, he hoped to find suitable quarters for Margarethe and the children, but Mrs. Schurz, who was ailing again, was reluctant to move. She cautioned him against taking a house; unable to find suitable quarters, he finally left her in Bethlehem and contented himself with the company of his friend, the Marquis de Chambrun. Bethlehem was near enough for a visit at Christmas; afterward, however, he had to go on a lecture tour of New England. He needed the money.[26]

As it turned out, Schurz's efforts to make permanent arrangements in Washington proved premature. Early in 1866, Zachariah Chandler approached him with an invitation to edit a newspaper the radical senator was establishing in Detroit. The general would have preferred St. Louis with its many Germans, but Chandler's proposition was concrete; he had to have an income, and the prospects for the Detroit *Post* seemed favorable. Accordingly, after another lecture tour, this time in the vicinity of New York, he accepted and moved to Detroit.[27]

The Detroit interlude was not a happy one for Schurz. Even before his career in

Michigan had fairly begun, a fire at the railroad station destroyed two large crates with his belongings—books, manuscripts, and highly prized personal letters. The incident depressed him; moreover, his financial situation was not one to cheer him up. The Detroit *Post*, instead of showing a profit, began to lose money, a serious matter for its editor, whose income in part depended on its earnings and who was already being harassed by his creditors in Wisconsin.[28]

In any case, regular daily routines never suited Schurz, who was now tied to his desk from morning to night. Friends who visited him found him on his swivel chair in the office, puffing at his cigar—he loved to smoke. Although he did not complain, he told them he could not say he had too little work. Every morning he collected material for articles that he assembled in the afternoon. Then at night, when he thought he was finished, the foreman and the printers would grumble that half a column was still missing. Even his maid protested about his long hours. And the heat in the summer was not good for Margarethe. To spare her exertion, he sent her to Watertown, where she was able to escape the worst summer weather. But for him, the separation did not make things any easier.[29]

Politically, too, Schurz did not find his stay in Detroit satisfying. His influence in Michigan, a solidly Republican state, could never be as great as in some location where the Germans held the balance of power. Moreover, the rift between Johnson and Congress, which he had seen coming, had become almost irreparable. While rejoicing at the strength of congressional resistance, he nevertheless deplored the harmful effects of the President's policies. Riots in Memphis in the spring of 1866 and at New Orleans in the summer brought this home to him. With several of his acquaintances killed or wounded, he could barely contain his loathing for Johnson. To think that the President himself could have encouraged such misdeeds! Yet there were sycophants seeking "to kiss his hands." Preparing for the midterm campaign, he was determined to see to it that Johnson was defeated.

The midterm elections of 1866 were among the most remarkable ever fought in the United States. After the President had vetoed a bill for the renewal of the Freedmen's Bureau and the Civil Rights Act, which Congress passed over his objections, the rift between Johnson and his party became ever more pronounced. Proposing the Fourteenth Amendment with its comparatively mild disfranchising provisions and its due-process clause, the dominant Republicans in Congress unfolded their Reconstruction plan. The President and his followers, both Democrats and conservatives, adamantly opposed its ratification. The elections would test the popular will.

Although national conventions did not usually meet in nonpresidential years, the administration sought to capture the country's imagination by calling one. The National Union Convention at Philadelphia opened with Northern and Southern delegates entering arm-in-arm. The radicals promptly countered with an assembly of their own, the Southern Loyalists' convention, which Wade and Chandler insisted Schurz attend. Accordingly, he arrived in Philadelphia at the beginning of September. He was welcomed enthusiastically, and at the end of the week he addressed the delegates. Castigating Johnson's policy as reactionary, he protested that, unlike his successor, Lincoln would never have countenanced injustice to the blacks. The Fourteenth Amendment offered the South peace with justice. Let it be accepted and harmony would be restored. The delegates cheered wildly.

During the remainder of the campaign, he lent his aid to various individual congressmen—Schuyler Colfax was one and James M. Ashley another—and delivered speeches in several Northern states. His theme was always the same: Johnson's policy was a great misfortune; Congress must be upheld. Then the President made a series of intemperate remarks in the course of his "swing around the circle" to St. Louis. These furnished Schurz with new ammunition; in fact, at times he doubted Johnson's sanity. Yet the outcome of the election was never in doubt. Completely routed by his Republican opponents, the President was thoroughly repudiated. But he refused to compromise. The struggle between the White House and Congress would have to go on.[30]

Like other radicals, Schurz now believed the time had come to go beyond the Fourteenth Amendment. In an article in the *Atlantic Monthly* he boldly asserted that the proposed addition to the Constitution was not enough. As republican governments had to be based on the consent of the people, universal suffrage was essential. Consequently, he advocated the passage of yet another amendment conferring the franchise on the blacks and requiring every state to establish common schools for all citizens. The article appeared just as Congress was passing the Reconstruction Acts remanding the Southern states to military government until they adopted the Fourteenth Amendment.[31]

While Schurz was satisfied with these public measures, his private affairs were not flourishing. His Watertown creditors brought a successful foreclosure suit, and in January 1867 he lost his farm. His parents had to move to Monee, Illinois, to live with his sister Anna Schiffer; his own financial situation was so bad that he had to go lecturing again. Traveling through the cold in Illinois and Missouri, he had to continue writing his newspaper articles on the train. "This journey is not a pleasure trip," he complained. "The sole delightful moments are those in which I put the money earned into my pocket and think: 'Something more for wife and child.'"

But the trip did have one brighter side. When he arrived at St. Louis, Emil Preetorius, a forty-eighter and the able editor of the *Westliche Post*, sought to interest him in a position with that large German newspaper. One of the owners, Theodore Olshausen, wanted to retire and sell his share; Preetorius believed that Schurz could do wonders for the enterprise. Together with his lawyer, James Taussig, Preetorius decided to invite the general; Taussig undertook to raise $10,000 from twenty wealthy Germans who were each to give $500. The sum was raised within twenty-four hours, and Schurz accepted. Made one of the co-owners of the paper and co-editor, he succeeded in repaying his share within two years and kept his interest in it until the day he died.[32]

Just before completing arrangements in St. Louis, however, he suffered a major blow. In the spring of 1867, while he was away on a campaign trip in Connecticut, he received news that his little daughter Emmy, then three years old, was seriously ill. Hurrying back to Detroit, he found her dying. For the grief-stricken parents, the loss was staggering, and Margarethe's health took a serious turn for the worse. She barely managed to move to St. Louis; her condition was so bad that her husband decided to send her and the two remaining daughters to Europe, the mother for recuperation and the girls for an education. Because of his financial problems, he could not come with them; he accompanied them to New York; then he sadly said goodbye and returned to his newspaper duties in Missouri.[33]

Thus Schurz's stay in St. Louis began under unfavorable circumstances. Disconsolate about the death of his daughter, left alone by his wife, and deeply in debt, he had to establish himself in a new community. That Margarethe may also have felt abandoned probably never occurred to him. And St. Louis lacked the excitement of Washington. Then a city of over 300,000 people, it was the commercial metropolis of the upper Mississippi Valley. Its docks and levies were teeming with steamers, its thirteen trunk lines connected with railroad centers all over the Midwest, and its manufactures were developing at a steady pace. It had theaters and concert halls, but even the tourist guide admitted its lack of great public edifices. Moreover, it was hot, terribly hot—hardly an environment calculated to cure a deep melancholia.

Schurz was depressed and lonely. Living in the Preetorius's apartment, he took his meals at nearby restaurants. The thought of his business failures haunted him. What would Margarethe tell her family? "That I have made poor speculations is true and one can admit it," he wrote her. "But in the end I have worked a lot, and now, after my entry into this venture, chances are good to regain what we lost by and by." He was looking forward to visiting Hamburg, although the thought of facing his brothers-in-law somewhat dampened his anticipation. After all his misfortunes, he did not suppose that his reputation with them was too great. Not even the news of an additional inheritance left by Margarethe's father, which helped solve his most immediate financial problems, really cheered him up. It only made him realize once again how badly he had managed his affairs. "You can imagine how I feel standing before your brothers in this way, especially since I know that my lack of business experience and kindheartedness are to blame for everything," he confessed. "It is a bitter chalice which I have to empty now."

But Schurz was an optimist by nature; if his private affairs were depressing, his political future seemed hopeful. The progress of Reconstruction—the implementation of radical policy in the South, the shackling of Johnson—met with his full approval; the situation was developing so well that he thought both parties would soon have to look for new issues. Whatever these might be, he was certain that he would have a role to play. The German population of Missouri was very large, constituting over one-third of the people of St. Louis alone. They seemed more congenial to him than their compatriots in Wisconsin, presumably because there was a larger proportion of forty-eighters among them, with some of whom he was already on good terms. And he was determined to become their spokesman. To make himself better known to all his countrymen, he undertook a series of trips to their settlements. Early in July he visited a German community at Augusta, an old settlement which received him enthusiastically; a few weeks later he went to Cottlesville near St. Charles, where the Germans were celebrating the anniversary of their defense of the town against the Confederates; in September he traveled to similar settlements at DeSoto and Bonneville. As chairman of the local reception committee, he welcomed General Sheridan to St. Louis. The general had just been dismissed from his post as commander of the Department of the Gulf by Johnson; Schurz delivered an appropriate speech and took him to see *Der Freischütz*. By fall, Schurz had received overtures to run for Congress. But, biding his time, he turned them down.[34]

He could afford to wait, as the party was soon in need of his services again. Johnson's resistance to radical Reconstruction was beginning to have results; the outlook for the elections of 1867 was not favorable. Under the circumstances, the German vote was considered essential, and Schurz was expected to corral it, a task he undertook with his usual aplomb. After writing a public letter warning his countrymen in Wisconsin and elsewhere against the "Copperheads," he campaigned strenuously in Ohio and his former home state. Not even the party's severe losses in the fall dampened his optimism. Adversity would make the organization stronger, he thought. It would clean it of disreputable elements. Moreover, the Republicans carried Wisconsin. He was certain his compatriots had again heeded his appeals.

That his loneliness would be especially hard to bear in Wisconsin was predictable. He looked over the old Watertown house, now owned by a farmer, who, he noted, had planted onions in the flower beds. His uncle still lived in town, but the nephew could not rid himself of the memories of happier days. On the way back, he stopped off at Chicago, where his sister, much given to spiritualism, made him attend a séance where Emmy's ghost seemed to appear. Even if he admitted that it was only a figment of his imagination, he was wholly overcome. More conscious than ever of the absence of his family, he promised Margarethe he would come to Europe to spend Christmas with her.

Before he could leave for a vacation, however, he was determined to go to Washington to mend his political fences. Congress was about to meet, possibly to impeach the President. Moreover, the defeat of Benjamin F. Wade, the president of the Senate and next in line to the presidency, had made the nomination of General Grant a foregone conclusion. Schurz had every intention of playing a part in the campaign and arrived in the capital just as the House was considering an impeachment resolution. Although he had long favored the step, he found that the members were disheartened. The recent election setbacks which had cost the party the legislature of Ohio and serious losses elsewhere had so depressed them that he could only counsel against impeachment. When on December 7 the motion was in fact defeated, Schurz had already boarded the steamer *America* for Germany. But he made arrangements to be back in time for the Republican national convention in 1868.[35]

The general, who had long been planning for his trip, had for years followed the changes in Germany with great interest. When the Austro-Prussian War broke out in 1866, he confessed to his brother-in-law that if he were wealthy, he would be tempted to come back to play a part in the conflict. Then, when Prussia won so quickly, he became convinced that she held the key to Germany's future. A war with France seemed certain; perhaps Bismarck might yet be forced into the right track. But he was still afraid that victorious Prussia would be "too Prussian and too little German." Now he was on his way to Europe to see for himself. Much to his surprise, he received first-hand information—from Bismarck himself.[36]

Schurz arrived in Germany early enough to celebrate Christmas with his family in Wiesbaden. Then he received an inquiry from his old acquaintance, Lothar Bucher, a forty-eighter who had since entered Bismarck's service, whether he would not be able to come to Berlin to meet the great man. Naturally, he accepted with great alacrity.

Bismarck on January 28, 1868, granted Schurz an interview which lasted an hour and a half. After some light banter about the past—the prime minister mistakenly thought he had seen Schurz following Kinkel's escape, Bismarck turned to serious matters. What was America's attitude toward Germany, he wanted to know. Reassured on this point, he was delighted to hear about the German-Americans' favorable reactions toward recent events. They might prove helpful in case of conflict with France. In response to Schurz's question why he had not disposed of Napoleon III right after Austria's defeat at Koeniggraetz, he told him of his difficulties with the South German states and the outbreak of cholera in the army. Had France intervened, he said, he would have had to play his trump card, the raising of Hungarian troops, a course of action which would have made any reconciliation with the Habsburgs impossible. During the conversation, Schurz noticed that it was getting very late. Bismarck, however, did not seem to mind. In fact, he invited his visitor to come back the next day and stay for supper.

Delighted with the second invitation, Schurz appeared once again at the Wilhelmstrasse. This time a commission of jurists then preparing a new legal code for the North German Confederation was present. None of them knew who the stranger in their midst was until Bismarck introduced him. Their surprise and embarrassment at the situation—the revolutionary liberator of Kinkel at the Prussian prime minister's table—knew no bounds, and it took them some time to converse freely with him. As they were preparing to leave, Bismarck asked Schurz to stay a little longer to pump him for some more information. Laughing heartily at the privy counselors' embarrassment, the Prussian relaxed with a bottle of Appolinaris water in the company of his old antagonist, who was still praising the advantages of republicanism. It was then that he explained how Americans would never have become the enterprising people they were had there been a policeman or privy counselor at every mud puddle to keep them from stepping into it.[37]

After a brief sentimental trip to Spandau, a look at Berlin's splendid new synagogue, and visits to the opera and ballet, Schurz returned to Wiesbaden. With understandable pride, he wrote his brother-in-law about his experiences at the Wilhelmstrasse. Making no secret about his admiration for his host, he described the prime minister's amazing lack of restraint in telling anecdotes about all and sundry, including the "old gentleman," as he called the king, and ventured the opinion that Bismarck really sought to lure him back to Germany to enter the Prussian civil service. But, as he put it in a letter to Kinkel, now in Zurich, his roots in the United States were too deep; the work he had begun in America was not yet finished, and so he was going to return. Whether Schurz's impressions were justified is doubtful. While Bismarck was favorably impressed with him, he certainly was not interested in strengthening the liberal opposition.

The newspapers on both sides of the Atlantic made a great deal of fuss about the Bismarck interviews. Rumors were afloat that Schurz had been sent to Europe on a mission from Johnson, and for a while the general contemplated a public denial. But in the long run, he thought better of it. Continuing to write reports for the *Westliche Post*, he simply let the facts speak for themselves. Nevertheless, the reception in Berlin did him no harm. It greatly strengthened his reputation among his compatriots in America.[38]

Schurz spent a few weeks more in Germany. In Frankfurt, he learned about the impeachment of Johnson. Watching the nervous reaction of the stock brokers, he assured them that there would be no trouble in America because of the trial. On the way home, he stopped off to visit his wife's relatives in Hamburg and Kiel, where his brother-in-law owned a beautiful estate. The tall, slender general with his reddish hair and whiskers, his finely chiseled face, and his black-rimmed pince-nez impressed the guests with his simplicity and artlessness. His stories of his flight from Rastatt and Kinkel's liberation were always entertaining. Shortly afterward, he took a steamer for New York. Margarethe, unwell again, stayed behind. Her brother saw to it that she would not have any financial worries.[39]

Depressed though Schurz was about the renewed separation from his family, he was greatly encouraged by his reception in America. In spite of the foul weather—it was snowing and the streets were already white—the customs officers' helpfulness and the waiting carriage to take him to the Fifth Avenue Hotel cheered him. Marshall Jewell, the Republican candidate for governor of Connecticut, was already there and importuned him to deliver some campaign speeches. Anxious to assure the success of radical Reconstruction, the general agreed and left for the Nutmeg State to plunge into politics again. Then he traveled to Washington to hear Ben Butler's opening speech in the impeachment trial.

The impeachment was very much on his mind. Believing that Johnson's conviction, which he confidently expected, would lead to a successful completion of Reconstruction, he was more optimistic than ever about the future. His enthusiasm convinced him once more that the United States was his real home, no matter how much he liked the old country. "How fresh and hearty life is here," he wrote to Margarethe, "and how one feels at every step that one can accomplish something! This is a great cause." He was anxiously waiting for the trial to begin.

On March 30, Butler finally opened the impeachment proceedings with a long speech. Schurz, who heard him, was not impressed. "Had I been able to speak in his place," he mused, "after a few days' preparation, I would have caused the men to gnash their teeth and the women to swoon." As it was, however, he was merely an onlooker, and he had to go back to St. Louis. Still, it was encouraging to hear that Ben Wade, Johnson's legal successor, was allegedly thinking of including him in the cabinet.[40]

In St. Louis, Schurz settled back to resume his newspaper work. The paper was doing so well that he was able to move into a private office, his retreat into which no one was permitted to enter without permission. Nicely wallpapered, a striped runner on the floor, a desk with an upholstered rocking chair and a few caned chairs, it was a comfortable place for work. And the paper, which had just employed the newly arrived immigrant Joseph Pulitzer, offered interesting contacts.[41]

Preetorius had not been inactive during his partner's absence. Making the proper arrangements, he saw to it that Schurz was elected a delegate to the forthcoming Republican national convention, an honor which could only increase his and his paper's national reputation. And although the general became increasingly depressed about the inordinate length of the impeachment trial, he was eagerly looking forward to going to Chicago. When, as de Chambrun had already warned they might, the Republicans failed to convict the "great criminal," the general was ready to believe the worst. Conspiracy, bribery, and treason must have been at work. He was determined to right the great wrong at the national convention.[42]

His experience in Chicago was most agreeable. Elected temporary chairman, he obtained the traditional honor of delivering the keynote address, a task he ably fulfilled. He succeeded in obtaining a plank calling for amnesty for repentent insurgents, although his suggestion of an unqualified endorsement of black suffrage was not accepted. His prominence pleased his German compatriots. That it owed much to this appeal was to be surmised, especially because in recent years the German-Americans had been alienated from the party. Temperance and sabbatarian campaigns had frightened them, to say nothing of their fear of Negro equality. Schurz was determined to educate them, especially on the last point.

It was a foregone conclusion that the convention would nominate General Grant for president. To be sure, he had not been the *Westliche Post*'s favorite, but the paper informed its readers that although Grant was no Napoleon, he was energetic, perspicacious, and honest. Because of its radical slant, it supported Wade for second place—an act of simple justice, it pointed out, as the Senate's failure to convict Johnson had been due to its dislike of the old radical. Accordingly, Schurz seconded Wade's nomination but finally acquiesced in the selection of Colfax, whom he assessed as a man of no great ability. "They do love mediocrities," he commented.[43]

When the delegation returned home, he immediately plunged into the election campaign. The state convention chose him as one of Missouri's presidential electors, and in 1868 as in previous years, he once again put his entire time at the party's disposal. On June 19, he kicked off the contest with a strong plea for the black suffrage amendment then before the voters. The *Westliche Post* sought to popularize the cause among the Germans; its editor traveled through large parts of the country to do the same. Delivering speeches in Chicago and New York as well as in smaller places, he stressed the folly of entrusting the government to unrepentant rebels, called for justice for the blacks, and reminded his countrymen of the glories of the Union cause. As was to be expected, he concentrated on states like Indiana, in which the Germans were presumed to hold the balance of power, and unabashedly reported to Margarethe that members of both parties came to hear his speeches, both in English and German. In New York, several hundred of his old soldiers gave him a triumphant welcome.

The rigors of the campaign were debilitating. By September he had already delivered thirty-three addresses, accommodations were bad and the food worse, and he needed his indomitable spirit to keep going. But he was again engaged in a crusade to which he was fully committed. Convinced that the antislavery work he had begun in the 1850s was nearing completion, he exerted himself to the utmost, especially in Missouri, where he spent the last month of the campaign. Of course he also expected to reap personal benefits for his services. The party would hardly be able to forget so tireless a worker with such a large ethnic constituency.[44]

Nevertheless, his enthusiasm was dampened by his personal problems. The separation from his family was becoming harder and harder to bear. At first, he thought Margarethe might return at the end of November. Full of confidence, he even rented an apartment for her homecoming. But his hopes were dashed again. She did not think her health would permit her to leave Europe; she would have to spend the winter there. Her disappointed husband was more lonely than ever. He toyed with the idea of accepting a diplomatic post; he even thought he might be asked to join the cabinet. All these possibilities were most uncertain, however, and for the time being, he simply knew that he was desperately alone.

And yet, there was hope for the future. Senator John B. Henderson had voted for the acquittal of Johnson; as many former Confederates in the border state were still disfranchised, it was obvious that he could not be reelected. Perhaps Schurz with his appeal to the Germans could become the next senator from Missouri.[45]

It was with a feeling of great satisfaction that in November he was able to announce Grant's victory to his wife.[46] Reconstruction might now be successfully concluded; as for himself, he had done his part in the struggle for the remaking of the South. Now, after all his peregrinations, he had once more found a base for his political advancement. His success was bound to bring her home again.

XI

The Triumph of Ethnic Politics

THE REPUBLICAN VICTORY in 1868 was an event of decisive importance in Schurz's career. Making it possible for him once more to demonstrate his political skill, it opened up great opportunities for him in Missouri. The state legislature would soon have to decide on a successor for Senator Henderson, one of the seven "recusants" who had voted for Johnson's acquittal. And in spite of his assertion that his candidacy for the Senate came to him as a complete surprise, Schurz began to lay the ground for it as soon as the presidential canvass had gotten under way.[1]

The key to his astounding audacity in seeking a Senate seat in a state to which he had only just moved lay in his firm reliance on ethnic politics. The Germans of Missouri, unlike their compatriots in Wisconsin, were almost wholly Republican; their support had been a crucial factor in the party's success. They had played a key role in saving Missouri for the Union, and they retained considerable influence in the postwar years.

In spite of the Germans' prominence in Republican affairs, however, leadership of the party had fallen into the hands of Charles D. Drake, a former Whig, Know-Nothing, and Democrat, who had joined the Union party and become an arch-radical. That the Germans distrusted him was natural, especially since he continued to advocate various measures to which they objected, such as a citizenship requirement for voting and a restriction on church property-holding. In addition, Missouri Republicans were divided about the wisdom of repealing constitutional provisions excluding former rebels from various professions and the franchise. Drake led the radical faction; Senator B. Gratz Brown, whom the Germans had always favored, the more liberal one. When in 1867 Drake became the senator's successor in Washington, the Germans were miffed. They had long trusted Brown, the founder of the Free Soil movement in the state; the arrogant, self-righteous former nativist did not suit them at all, especially as some of them were less than enthusiastic about continued radical demands for black suffrage.

In addition, German-Americans in Missouri as elsewhere had become somewhat disillusioned with the Republican party. Disaffected ever since the Civil War, when they mistakenly believed that Franz Sigel had been treated unfairly, they had been further alienated by the seeming prominence in the party of business interests, often identified with the old Whigs, and by Republican cooperation, at least in some states, with sabbatarian and prohibition forces. Given proper leadership, they might easily be marshaled into a new grouping opposed to radical Reconstruction and the increasingly scandalous patronage system.

That this situation would be exploited by knowledgeable public figures was inevitable. In St. Louis, a group of Drake's opponents led by Colonel William M.

Grosvenor of the *Missouri Democrat*, ex-Senator Brown, and Emil Preetorius were determined to reverse recent trends and seize control of the party. Grosvenor was a gifted newspaperman who believed in free trade. The powerfully built editor, who wore a size 9½ hat on his large head and sported long hair, a magnificent beard, and bristly eyebrows, thought that in Schurz he had the answer to his plans for displacing Drake as Republican leader of Missouri. In this effort he was helped by his employer, William McKee, who was anxious for better access to the federal patronage, as well as by Brown and Preetorius. Schurz was unfettered by past quarrels in Missouri; his Republican credentials were impeccable; and his countrymen, who approved wholeheartedly of his strong endorsement of the impeachment, had long admired him.[2] If some of the St. Louis group's allies were not as firmly committed to black suffrage as Schurz, the newcomer's ambition would make it easy for him to overlook their attitude, no matter how harmful it might be to the progress of radical Reconstruction. By combining the German vote with that of moderate and conservative Republicans, his friends were laying a strong foundation for future political action.

The boom for Schurz began almost at the same time as the national campaign. After the La Grange *American* hoisted his banner on July 30, he made up his mind to spend the last six weeks of the contest in Missouri to further his chances. The only difficulty was that he lived in St. Louis; Drake also came from the city, and traditionally the two United States senators had hailed from differing parts of the state. However, the St. Louis allies furthering his candidacy thought they could overcome this obstacle.[3]

As time went on, Schurz became more and more sanguine about his prospects. While Preetorius kept him informed about the progress of his candidacy, he played a careful game. Refusing to be considered for a House seat from St. Louis, he disclaimed any desire for office. Lest he be accused of working for himself in the forthcoming campaign in Missouri, he asked his associate not to publish any statement from him about the impending vacancy in the Senate. In the meantime, he continued to campaign strenuously for Grant, principally in German. "The German wing of the Rep. party has become so disorganized within the last two years that I am sincerely alarmed . . . ," he wrote to the Massachusetts politician William Clafflin. "An extra effort is therefore required, and I do all I can."[4] His usefulness to the party as spokesman for his countrymen must not be forgotten.

As he had planned, he devoted the last weeks of the campaign to Missouri. Speaking in towns and villages all over the state, he was very satisfied with his reception. Especially the old rebels seemed friendly. Complimenting him on his speeches, they convinced him that they might become amenable to his influence in the future. "My popularity is increasing from day to day and is beginning at times to be terrible," he boasted, more and more certain of his election to the Senate.[5]

Although Schurz based his entire political career on ethnic politics, he always believed in full cooperation of immigrants with native-born Americans. To further this idea, he was instrumental in founding the Twentieth Century Club, a somewhat informal gathering which met every Saturday at the Planters House in St. Louis to unite both Germans and non-Germans in lively political discussions. It was at one of the dinners of this group shortly after the election that Schurz's candidacy was formally launched.[6]

The general now abandoned his public reticence. Having long sought the honor, he no longer hesitated to make every effort to defeat his rivals. Senator Drake, whose leadership was being challenged, became alarmed, not only because of his distrust of Schurz's notions of amnesty but also because of the geographical question. The senator's own reelection in 1874 would be jeopardized if his colleague were also to come from the metropolis. To prevent this contingency, he strongly endorsed Congressman Benjamin F. Loan of St. Joseph, a somewhat lackluster radical upon whom he could fully rely. With the backing of the *Missouri Democrat*, Schurz sought the aid of the incoming administration, made an appearance at the December reunion of the Western armies in Chicago, and actively solicited the support of Eastern papers. In Chicago, he met Grant, Sherman, and others; Grant talked to him about their two reports on the South and conceded that he had been wrong. But he did not impress Schurz as very astute, although the German-American thought that Grant might conceivably make a good president. By the end of the month the entire German press and twenty-nine English newspapers in Missouri favored the newcomer's candidacy.[7]

Yet the campaign was by no means over. Increasingly, protests were heard against Schurz's indifference to religious affiliations, his only too brief residence in Missouri, interrupted by a trip to Europe, and his alleged lack of practical knowledge. The would-be senatorial candidate did not even see fit to have his wife reside in the state! The most serious charge, however, was Schurz's stand on amnesty. If the former Confederates were enfranchised, they would undoubtedly make it difficult for the radicals to retain power. And even should the blacks finally obtain the vote, it would be unlikely that they could restore the balance in the Republicans' favor.[8]

The final decision was to be made in January in Jefferson City, the state capital, where the party caucus would meet prior to the election. Schurz and Loan were to debate each other and, because of the importance of the contest, Senators Drake and Henderson, the latter hopeful of turning the division to his advantage, would be present too. According to Schurz, it was to be "the battle of the giants."

When in the first week of the new year he arrived at Jefferson City, the little town was rapidly filling up with visiting politicians. The contest started on January 7, when he addressed the Republican caucus. He came right to the point. Charges that his Republicanism was unsound were ridiculous, he said. He was friendly with Grant, fully endorsed the Fifteenth Amendment which was about to enfranchise the blacks, and favored the lifting of voting restrictions for former insurgents only after the amendment's passage. Nor would he bear a grudge against Drake, much as he regretted that the senator had seen fit to come in person to oppose him. After the speech, he believed he had made an impression on his audience; as for his opponents, he was convinced that he had dealt them "a terrific blow." On the next day, he and Loan addressed a gathering of delegates from the southwestern counties, normally Drake's strongest supporters. They spoke on the important subject of the state's railroad interests—Schurz was a firm advocate of further construction—and he was again certain that he had completely routed his rival. While excitement in the state capital was mounting, he became ever more confident. The whole country was watching the struggle with deep interest.[9]

The climax came on Monday and Tuesday, January 11 and 12, when Loan, Drake, and Henderson attempted to reply to Schurz. After a brief address by Loan, Drake took the floor. He had not intended to appear at all, he said, but when at Christmas he arrived in St. Louis he learned that Schurz's candidacy was directed against himself. Taking great pride in the radical Missouri constitution he had framed, he pointed out that Schurz, who was attacking it now, had never even been in the state except as a visitor when it was adopted. Exhausted by his effort—Schurz had constantly interrupted him—he retired that night to resume his speech in the morning, a decision he had cause to regret. For, angered by Schurz's assaults, on the next day he allowed himself to be carried away in an attack on the Germans. Charging that the immigrants were being maneuvered by his opponent, he maintained that, in an attempt to dominate the party, for years they had opposed him all along the line. Because it would make it difficult for a few St. Louis Germans to control the organization, he asserted, they had even refused to support the recently defeated black suffrage amendment.

Drake's sally against the Germans gave Schurz his chance. Making the most of his opportunity, he mercilessly flayed the senator. Drake's enmity to the Germans was an old story, he said. Had not the senator denounced the immigrants ever since 1853? Maybe he had not been present at the time, but he was fully familiar with the history of Missouri. As for him, it was not true that he was the candidate of his compatriots. He had been brought forward by his American fellow citizens. But, in a grand play for the German vote, he declared that he was proud to have been born in Germany. It was a great country whose sons had risen to save the Union and to keep the state loyal at a time when Drake was still hesitating and defending the buying and selling of human flesh.

Schurz's clever parrying of the attacks against him was highly effective. Henderson still made a few remarks, but Drake was so disconcerted that, without even waiting for his laundry to dry, he quickly put his wet wash into his bags and left town. "I had one of the greatest triumphs of my life last night," Schurz bragged to Preetorius. "Drake was completely crushed. The party despotism is ended for all time and the liberal element is more powerful than ever." The caucus, mindful of the importance of the German voters and impressed with Schurz's arguments, nominated him on the first ballot by a bare majority. Well-wishers in great numbers converged on his hotel, where they remained till three in the morning. Enthusiastically singing the John Brown song, they insisted on shaking his hand until the right one was so crushed he had to use the left. Serenaders outside contributed to the din, and Schurz got little sleep that night.[10]

The election in the legislature followed in due time; in view of the Republican majority, it was a mere formality. After the vote had been taken, Schurz returned to Jefferson City to deliver the customary acceptance speech. He was exceedingly proud.[11]

Schurz's triumph electrified the German-American community. Whether they liked him or not, whether Democrats or Republicans, his compatriots had been taking a deep interest in the campaign. The *New Yorker Bellatristisches Journal* declared that the question was merely whether a man born in Germany ought to represent Missouri in the Senate, and, when the results were announced, it expressed its heartfelt satisfaction. If Schurz was ambitious, it insisted, he was nevertheless capable. His victory was due to the fact that he was a German, and this was the important truth about the election. Germandom had "found its recognition in a dazzling manner." The Democratic Cincinnati *Volksfreund* agreed. So far only the French had been represented in the government (in the person of Pierre Soulé); now it was the Germans' turn. Torchlight parades, serenades, marching bands honored him; he was overwhelmed with telegrams and well-wishers, and from the very beginning it was clear that he would be known as "the German Senator." Invitations for public dinners came from many quarters, of which the most spectacular was the tender of a banquet at Delmonico's by the New York German community. On the night before the affair, a delegation of the German Republican Committee visited him at Dr. Jacobi's mansion to hail him as "the representative of the German element"; on the following day, the main event took place. Eighty to ninety guests were present, and the proceedings, wholly in German, celebrated the success of the community's foremost public figure. Even his most bitter opponents, critics like Fritz Anneke who had consistently charged him with obtaining office through corrupt means, for the moment were willing to let him prove himself.[12]

In many ways, March 4, 1869, marked a high point in Schurz's career. The day of Grant's inauguration, it was also the occasion of the swearing in of the new senator from Missouri. He was in high spirits as Drake led him down the aisle to take the oath. As it happened, the chapter of his *Reminiscences* devoted to the ceremony proved to be the last one he was able to finish, a fitting end to his memoirs. "Now I had actually reached the most exalted public position to which my boldest dreams of ambition had hardly dared aspire," he wrote. "I was still a young man, just forty. Little more than sixteen years had elapsed since I had landed on these shores, a homeless waif saved from the wreck of a revolutionary movement in Europe. . . . And here I was now, a member of the highest law-making body of the greatest of republics." As he had exulted to Margarethe a few weeks earlier, he was swimming "on the crest of the wave."[13]

The new senator attracted attention. "There is Carl Schurz," wrote the correspondent of the *Missouri Democrat*, "seated not far from poor, old, quaky Brownlow, and daintily clad in the glistening new broadcloth in which he took the oath on inauguration day. Manners are one of Schurz's special qualifications; he possesses them in the highest degree; and graces the Senate chamber admirably. His face, spectacles abolished, would be a little of the old cavalier type; and it is rich in expression and mobile as his mind. He can do more than any other man in our government to rouse the Germans in America from their political apathy, and push them forward to their true place." Only, the clerk had to stop mispronouncing his name as "Shirtz;" it grated badly "on his nice German ear."[14]

His triumph was spoiled by his wife's continued absence. His expectation of her early return had been dashed in the previous fall, although for some time he had still clung to the hope that his impending election might bring her back. "If I am elected," he pleaded in November, "ought you not to be in the gallery when I am sworn in?" The new office would make life more bearable for her; she would be able to live in Washington rather than in St. Louis, which she disliked. But all his entreaties were in vain. Convinced that her health would not permit her to come to the United States that winter, she stayed in Wiesbaden. Complaining to her friends how much she missed him, she was nevertheless unable to make up her mind to be present at his great triumph when he took the oath in the Senate. For Carl, it was a serious blow. He had the reputation of a model husband, he confessed, because he was much too busy for any flirtation. But in view of their long separation, who knew how long his virtue could be preserved?[15]

The senator was in fact very busy. Universally recognized as the representative of the German element in the United States, he was soon called upon to do something for his countrymen. And much though the later president of the National Civil Service Reform League protested against the abuses of the patronage, when he himself first entered the Senate he was a most adept practitioner of the fine art. A German acquaintance from St. Louis, Felix Coste, became surveyor of the port; Schurz's brother-in-law Edmund Jüssen in Chicago was appointed collector of internal revenue, and several other German-American applicants entrusted their fates to the senator, who knew how to look out for liberal native-born supporters as well.[16]

His compatriots from all over the country appreciated his efforts. Considering him not only the senator from Missouri but their special representative, they turned to him with their requests. Veterans wanted favors, office-seekers asked for patronage, prospective immigrants sought his aid, and German-American soldiers asked him to help them out of various scrapes. After all, as everybody was talking about "the Dutch Senator," he ought to be able to assist his countrymen.[17]

His fame reached the farthest portions of the Union. During the adjournment of Congress in the summer of 1869, the Senate Retrenchment Committee, of which he was a member, planned a trip to San Francisco. If he had any qualms about undertaking the journey, they were soon overcome by the news that the Germans of San Francisco, without regard for party, were planning a great reception for him. And it was not only in the bay city that he was feted. Thousands of people were waiting for him as the train pulled into the Sacramento station; three cannon shots announced his arrival. He was taken to the local hotel, introduced to the leading citizens of the city, and delayed so long that the train had to wait for his return. When he finally reached San Francisco, his countrymen turned out in full force. Their enthusiasm about their distinguished compatriot knew no bounds, and he utilized the occasion to tell them that no country on earth was as liberal toward immigrants as the United States. They must show their gratitude by spreading American ideas of liberty. Wild cheers greeted his remarks.[18]

Back in Washington, the German-Americans were not his only well-wishers. The Prussian diplomatic establishment, too, was delighted. Baron von Gerolt, the minister, who knew him well, was happy to entertain him. After all, the famous new senator would be an excellent contact in Congress. During the previous summer he had already helped the envoy frame arguments taking account of the Monroe Doctrine in justification of a possible North German naval station in the Caribbean.[19]

When in December 1869 the new session began, German-Americans had not only the senator to look up to, but also his wife and family. After constant pleadings by her husband, Margarethe, who had still preferred to spend the summer in Switzerland, finally made up her mind to return. Carl had written her about the great social position awaiting her in Washington, and late in October she and the two girls took passage on the *Westphalia*. Her husband called for her in New York; after a slight delay because she was unwell again, the family moved to the capital, at last settling down in a house at 139 F Street between 20th and 21st. Living in comparatively simple style, the Schurzes nevertheless soon became prominent in Washington's social circles. On Saturday evenings, to the delight of the city's musical world, the family gave musicales for Washington society. Handy, as the senator still called his oldest daughter, was a popular belle, and the head of the household took great delight in his newly found domestic life.[20]

His public position too was a source of great satisfaction to him. Convinced that he had something to offer both to his adopted country and to his fellow immigrants, he gladly served as a role model for them. His conception of the importance of immigration in American society embraced both the later idea of the melting pot and the idea of ethnic pluralism. Convinced that German-Americans ought to become good citizens of their new country, he counseled them to learn English and take part in politics. " 'The mission of Germanism' in America . . . ," he believed, "can consist in nothing other than a modification of the American spirit, through the German, while the nationalities melt into one." But while he urged his countrymen to become part of the American mainstream, he adjured them never to give up their own heritage, and he himself set them a good example. As editor of a German-language newspaper, he continued to write, correspond, and speak in German.[21] This concept of dual citizenship was soon to be put to the test, for him as well as for his compatriots, when in 1870 the Franco-Prussian War, the final

Agathe Schurz (Courtesy of the Rutherford B. Hayes Library, Fre-mont, Ohio)

struggle for German unification, entirely altered the fatherland's position in Europe.

The outbreak of war in June 1870 between the German states and France did not come as a surprise for Schurz. His conversations with Bismarck had convinced him that a conflict with Napoleon III was inevitable, and his contempt for the French emperor explains why he was not unhappy about it. His sympathies were so strongly with his compatriots that at times he actually thought of going back to Europe. Speaking in Baltimore and New York, he participated fully in the German-American community's effort to raise money and win sympathy for the German cause, a comparatively easy task because he could always remind his listeners of Louis Napoleon's help to the Confederacy. On the lecturing circuit, too, he had long sought to enlighten American audiences about Germany's justified aims.[22]

News of the great German victories exhilarated Schurz, like most German-Americans. "Today Germany is the world's greatest military power," he wrote to Margarethe. "Long live the old fatherland.[23] He told her how, with his own hands, he raised the new red, white, and black German flag from the windows of the *Westliche Post* editorial rooms and excitedly described the whole building's festive decorations. It was not surprising that at the report of Napoleon III's surrender his enthusiasm knew no bounds. Exulting that the Germans were now the greatest and mightiest nation in the Old World, he was certain that no one could any longer dispute this rank. The tremendous contrast between this new status and the past was almost incomprehensible, yet it was true. The old dream of 1848 had finally been realized, albeit under circumstances very different from those the liberal freedom fighters had imagined.[24]

No matter how great his delight at the triumph of German nationalism, however, he could not forget that the forces of reaction had brought the victory about, a fact that finally somewhat dampened Schurz's enthusiasm. The role of reaction became especially clear after the overthrow of the Second Empire and the proclamation of a republic in France, an event which tended to win many American friends for the new regime. Regretting the fact that King William was still negotiating with the fallen emperor, Schurz gradually regained his composure and finally admitted that German politics looked better from the outside than from within. In the last analysis, he wrote, it was most satisfying to be an American "sovereign" after all.[25]

In spite of Schurz's fervent German nationalism, his compatriots now became critical of him. Some had long resented his positive attitude toward all things American; others had simply been jealous of his success. When American neutrality was seemingly violated by arms sales to French agents, Schurz was severely critized for not speaking out strongly. He did in fact make representations at the State Department, and the practice was ended,[26] but his countrymen had not yet heard the last word from him on the subject. In 1872, when he had broken with the administration, he raised the issue again. A suspicion of large swindles in the War Department in connection with the arms traffic caused Sumner to introduce a resolution of inquiry. Grant's supporters rushed to the administration's defense, and then it fell to Schurz to bear the brunt of the congressional debate. It appeared that government rifles and ammunition specially manufactured for the purpose had been sold to the firm of Remington & Sons, an act of dubious legality because the arms dealers were French agents. Even after this circumstance was discovered and the secretary of war issued orders barring sales to the Remingtons, dealings with their thinly disguised representatives continued until Schurz in January 1871 saw to it that all such transactions stopped. In addition, apparent discrepancies in the moneys paid out and the amounts received by the Treasury Department, which angered the French as much as the sales had affronted the Germans, raised further questions. To what extent the transaction had been the result of bribery became one of the crucial points of the debate.[27]

Because of the reputation of the principal speakers, the galleries were packed, and the duel between Roscoe Conkling and Oliver Morton on one side and Carl Schurz on the other became the event of the day. On February 19, Conkling, the handsome, flamboyant leader of the Stalwarts, in a well-considered address, launched an all-out attack on Schurz, who had spoken four days earlier. The whole object of the controversy was to detach the German-Americans from the Republican party and to deliver them to the Democrats, he said. But the Germans of the country could not be "hoodwinked, or nose led, or handed over, by any man." Quoting the editor of the Chicago *Staats-Zeitung* to prove that Schurz had done nothing for his compatriots while the war was going on, he provoked his antagonist. "The man lies, and he knows it," the Missouri senator interjected, pointing out that the editor in question was the local collector of internal revenue. When Conkling had finished, Margarethe thought it would be impossible to answer him.[28]

On the next day, however, her husband proved her wrong. After making his way through the dense crowds—the galleries were overflowing and the floor was thronged with ladies—he delivered a masterful speech in reply to his challenger. Carefully reiterating the evidence tending to show that the sales had been illegal, he rose to the defense of his friend, the Marquis de Chambrun, who had first alerted the French to the discrepancies between the amounts they had paid and the value they had received. Schurz's tall, erect carriage and his clear, musical voice fully impressed his audience. According to George William Curtis, his listeners "literally hung upon him spell-bound. At the end he played upon them as if he were an organist and they were the living keys which he pressed." But it was his reply to Conkling's references to the Germans' political independence that was most calculated to appeal to his countrymen. "No sir," he declared, "no man owns the German Americans of this country. No politician owns them, no senator does; not even the President of the United States; but least of all are the Germans of this country owned by that class of politicians who desperately cling to the skirt of power through whatever mire that skirt may be trailed."[29] As Conkling was one of the foremost defenders of the spoils system, this sally met its mark.

After Schurz had finished, Senator Morton of Indiana sought to answer him. Accusing him of insolence, he charged him with the desire of merely wanting to make capital against the administration party. Conkling too rejoined the debate and called attention to Schurz's "offensive and unfounded insinuations." But Schurz quickly turned the tables on his opponent again. If he had done or said anything that looked like strutting, he quipped, he begged the Senate's pardon; he certainly did not wish to encroach "upon the exclusive privilege" of the senator from New York. Conkling, who years earlier had been mortally insulted when James G. Blaine had mocked his "turkey-gobbler strut," never spoke to Schurz again.[30]

The debate was not yet over. During the following week, on February 26, Senator Frederick T. Frelinghuysen of New Jersey accused Schurz of trying to incite the Germans against the administration and of trying to help the German Empire rather than his own country. This reproach brought forth a ringing retort. "Let me tell the Senator from New Jersey," the general said,

> that although I am certainly not ashamed of having sprung from that great nation whose monuments stand so proudly upon all the battlefields of thought; that great nation which . . . seems at this moment to hold in her hands the destinies of the Old World; that great nation which for centuries has sent abroad thousands and thousands of her children upon foreign shores with their intelligence, their industry, and their spirit of good citizenship, while I am by no means ashamed of being a son of that great nation, yet I may say I am proud to be an American citizen. This is my country. Here my children were born. Here I have spent the best years of my youth and manhood. All the honors I have gained, all the aims of my endeavors, and whatever of hope and promise the future has for me, it is all encompassed in this my new fatherland. My devotion to this great Republic will not yield . . . to that of any man born in this country."

It was a considered and forceful statement of his philosophy, which he finally summed up by saying, "Those who would meanly and coldly forget their old mother could not be expected to be faithful to their young bride."

In spite of this devastating reply, on February 29 Schurz was again attacked because of his alleged want of patriotism. This time, Senator Matthew Carpenter of Wisconsin took him to task for substantially denigrating the United States in full view of foreign observers, only to be crushed by one of Schurz's most frequently quoted replies. "The Senator from Wisconsin cannot frighten me by exclaiming, 'My country, right or wrong,'" he said. "In one sense, I say so too. 'My country, right or wrong; if right, to be kept right; and if wrong, to be set right.'" The applause in the gallery was deafening.[31]

These speeches and debates, which lasted for several weeks, once more established Schurz as one of the foremost orators of the Senate. The immediate result was disappointing; an investigating committee was set up which carefully excluded most of Schurz's allies from membership. It invited him to question witnesses, but neither his nor the committee's questions brought forth any hard-and-fast evidence of fraud. Schurz called its final report a total whitewash.[32]

Yet his position as the foremost spokesmen for his countrymen, his leadership of the ethnic Americans, had been immeasurably strengthened. The German-American press readily acknowledged his skill; the attacks of hostile journals were so violent as to become counterproductive. Sumner was so delighted with his colleague that when he met Margarethe after the reply to Conkling he gave her his hand and said, "Madam, I congratulate you. Your husband has just made the greatest speech that has been made in the Senate for twenty years." Garfield too was impressed with Schurz's "brilliant" address, and national periodicals wrote admiring reviews of the debate.[33] The German-Americans had found a capable spokesman for their causes.

It was precisely Schurz's ability to speak on behalf of his compatriots that gave him so much influence in the Senate during his one term. Had he merely represented Missouri, his appeal would have been limited, but as he was presumed to speak for millions of German-Americans all over the land, he exerted an influence far greater than that of an ordinary one-term senator. It was this power base that made it possible for him to take a lead in the Liberal Republican movement which was to do so much to shape his career for years to come.

XII

The Break with Grant

WHEN SCHURZ TOOK HIS OATH in Congress, he considered himself a good Republican, an administration senator. Yet, the manner of his election and the exigencies of politics were soon to drive a wedge between the President and himself, a split that grew and grew until he came to be considered the leader of the Liberal Republican opposition to Grant and his Stalwart supporters.

The senator's rupture with the administration was the start of his deliberate course of independence in politics, a pattern of behavior which in the long run kept him outside of the major party organizations and the mainstream of American political action. Together with other liberal reformers who liked to consider themselves "the best men" in public life regardless of political affiliation, he consistently sought to further his ideas of nineteenth-century liberalism, its insistence on clean government, low tariffs, and hard money, as well as its traditional commitment to personal freedom.[1] In view of his great talents and his evident pleasure in public life, his decision to break with his organization must be viewed as one of his cardinal mistakes, although he never admitted it. In effect, in the long run it condemned him to political oblivion. And it seriously compromised his otherwise remarkably advanced record on race relations.

That Carl Schurz, the committed revolutionary of 1848, should abandon his radical outlook to become identified with the decidedly unrevolutionary liberal movement requires some explanation. In his own mind, of course, he never changed his principles. But for him as for others like him, the success of emancipation, the protection of civil rights in the Fourteenth Amendment, and the guarantees of black suffrage in the Fifteenth must have seemed to indicate the fulfillment of all that he had worked for. The fact that he could now consider the civil service crusade as important as the struggle for freedom indicates the shifting of his priorities. A nineteenth-century liberal in the original sense of that term, he was unable fully to grasp the implications of the changing industrial order, particularly the shortcomings of laissez-faire. But he was not the only one; what happened to him befell many of his associates as well.

In view of the manner of Schurz's election to the Senate—his challenge of the Missouri radical machine and his opposition to Drake—his estrangement from Grant was probably unavoidable. The President did not relish party irregularity. In the inevitable contest for patronage between the Missouri factions, he was unlikely to desert his friend Charles D. Drake. Schurz was bound to be disappointed.

The first problem beclouding his relations with the administration was civil service reform, a movement Schurz considered particularly important. In later years, he asserted that he had always been wholly committed to the cause. He seemed to remember that as early as 1854 when he visited Washington he had been repelled by the spoils system. Yet at the time he never mentioned the matter, and his avid search for office during the Lincoln administration tends to shed some doubt on his devotion to civil service reform at that time. In fact, when he arrived in Washington in 1869, he immediately went to see Grant and members of the cabinet for his share of the patronage. And his brother-in-law Edmund Jüssen anxiously sought and procured the position of collector of internal revenue at Chicago. Even though Schurz always maintained that Jüssen obtained his post without his aid, the fact that the applicant was so closely related to the senator did not do him any harm.[2]

Schurz's experiences with the distribution of the patronage were not pleasant for him. Hating the siege of office-seekers who harassed him day and night, he roundly cursed the existing system. When he asked for an appointment for one of his friends to the St. Louis post office only to find that the position had already been given to someone else, the President told him, "Why, Mr. Schurz, I know Missouri a great deal better than you do." He was able to secure a few appointments, but he was not really satisfied. Grant's preferences seemed strange; the Germans, for whom the senator considered himself especially responsible, did not fare as well as he thought they should have. Sigel, for example, was left out entirely, and only repeated calls on the President and his advisers resulted in some successes. "Nothing can be more physically and mentally exhausting than this constant running around and scrambling for what is called by the very descriptive name of 'the public plunder,'" the senator complained. "Never has the absolute absurdity of the present system of filling offices appeared in a more glaring light . . . ; but at the same time the conviction that a reform *must* come has never been so marked and so general." Those who would successfully bring about this reform were bound to be hailed as public benefactors. Disgusted as he was, however, he did not yet blame the administration. In fact, he enjoyed a number of pleasant evenings at the White House, where Mrs. Grant especially received him with great friendliness, introducing him to her father and family as "our new Senator from Missouri." As for the trouble with the appointments, he thought Grant was innocent. It was simply impossible to avoid mistakes under the existing system.[3]

Having convinced himself of the necessity of civil service reform, Schurz determined to make the issue particularly his own. The subject could be expected to appeal to the Germans, whose respect for the Prussian civil service was axiomatic. As the Senate was then debating the proposed repeal of the Tenure of Office Act, originally passed to shackle Johnson, he was able to utilize the opportunity to deliver his first address and to emphasize the necessity of civil service reform at the same time.

His maiden speech on March 19, 1869, was not his best. Pleading for the suspension rather than for an outright appeal of the law, he argued that the real problem was not removal from but appointment to office. Simple repeal would make further debate on the subject difficult, while suspension would provide an opportunity to debate the issue fully at the next session. Although it had considerable merit, this argument did not impress his friends favorably. As the *Missouri Democrat* pointed out, usually Schurz was not on two sides of a question. However, he was confident of having done the right thing. On the day after the speech, he was put on the Joint Committee on Retrenchment, an agency established to effect savings in government expenditures. Although he would have preferred the Committee on Foreign Relations, from this vantage point it was easy to pursue his newly found goal. In fact, together with Representative Thomas A. Jenckes of Rhode Island, the main advocate of civil service reform, he became a member of a subcommittee dealing exclusively with the subject.[4] When at the end of the session, after staying in Washington for another week to take care of some remaining patronage problems, he returned to St. Louis, the *Missouri Democrat* expressed its satisfaction with his performance. Had he not secured important positions for his friends and thus rendered good service to the state? He himself was less certain.[5]

During his stay in St. Louis that spring and summer, Schurz thoroughly prepared for the task he had set himself, the destruction of the patronage system. In the fall, the undertaking seemed more urgent than ever because he learned that Grant intended to name General John A. McDonald, later the principal figure in the Whiskey Ring, supervisor of internal revenue in the district of which Missouri was a part. Although he joined with others to protest against the appointment, he failed to prevent it. But when Congress met for the short session, he was ready with a bill to reform the civil service completely.[6]

In December of 1869 some change in the existing method of filling offices seemed to be in the offing. Several years earlier Congressman Jenckes had introduced a measure calling for competitive civil service examinations administered by a commission of four members to hold office for five years; shortly after the beginning of the session Senator Lyman Trumbull proposed legislation which would make it a misdemeanor for any congressman to advise the President on appointments. Then, on December 20, Schurz introduced his bill. In a brief speech on December 29, he outlined a measure similar to Jenckes's, but at the same time more comprehensive. Unlike its earlier model, it would cover all federal officers except the cabinet, the foreign service, and a few judicial positions. Moreover, the commission, consisting of nine members, one-third of whom would be appointed for four, eight, and twelve years, respectively, would be stronger than that envisioned by Jenckes. Fully aware of the fact that at first the measure would not have much of a chance, the senator nevertheless believed that he had made some impression on his colleagues. Many of his fellow reformers were delighted. The President's principal supporters, however, became the chief opponents of the proposed change. And in October 1870, Schurz's friend, Secretary of the Interior Jacob D. Cox, resigned, in part at least in an apparent struggle over the patronage question.[7]

Civil service reform was only one of the issues that drove the Missouri senator into opposition to the President. From the very first, Schurz had been anxious to play a role in foreign affairs, and ignoring the fact that in the spring of 1869 there was no vacancy on the Senate Committee on Foreign Relations, he took the trouble to establish friendly relations with Secretary of State Hamilton Fish. A conservative former Whig, Fish was a patrician New Yorker who sought to maintain peace with Great Britain and Spain while keeping on tolerable terms with the President. When Schurz first met him, the secretary impressed him favorably; unlike Seward, he appeared to be "honest and a gentleman." Moreover, the senator thought Fish was anxious to seek his advice because of his knowledge of European affairs.

The secretary tried hard to humor the ambitious German-American. In an effort to keep Schurz satisfied, he invited him to make suggestions concerning the instructions to be given to John Lothrop Motley, the new envoy to Great Britain, and received a lengthy letter in reply. He also allowed Schurz to keep open certain channels of communication in Germany; the senator had been corresponding with an important person in Berlin, probably Bismarck himself, and had offered his contacts as a channel to the British in the matter of the *Alabama* claims. But Fish knew how to keep Schurz at arm's length and did not always answer his communications.[8]

The *Alabama* claims had disturbed Anglo-American relations ever since the Civil War. The losses inflicted upon Union shipping by Confederate raiders had been considerable; Great Britain had violated international law by allowing such vessels as the *Alabama* to escape after having been fitted out in British shipyards, and Americans believed she ought to pay for the damages. After reporting unfavorably upon the Johnson-Clarendon Convention negotiated in Andrew Johnson's days to settle the matter, Sumner, the chairman of the Senate's Committee on Foreign Relations, delivered an intemperate speech asking for restitution. He demanded payment not only of the direct losses suffered by the United States but also of the indirect ones arising from England's alleged prolongation of the Civil War for two years. The sum involved would exceed $2 billion, an unheard-of amount at the time. It was widely assumed that the only way in which Great Britain could satisfy these demands was by the cession of Canada.[9]

Schurz fully agreed with Sumner. While not in total accord either with the Massachusetts senator's heavy-handed style or with all his friend's views on international law, he too thought that Canada ought to be American. That an anti-British policy might be popular with the Germans must have occurred to him; moreover, he was certain that conditions in Europe were propitious for some pressure on England. Sumner's speech would alert Great Britain to the seriousness of the situation, he pointed out to Fish. The momentum gained should not be lost, especially since Napoleon III's evident weakness was creating a dangerous situation in Europe. Now was the time to utilize Schurz's private channels. "We ought to have all hands on deck," he wrote. "If things shape themselves in Europe as they now promise, we ought, under pressure of an impending crisis and such diplomatic influences as we may command, to carry any demand we can reasonably make."

The senator's proposition did not impress the secretary. Motley too had reported that Bismarck was ready to act as an intermediary; Schurz, once more offering himself as a go-between, on June 22 wrote again that his contact in Berlin was ready to cooperate and thought the cession of Canada the proper payment for the claims. But he received no reply. The last thing the United States needed was Prussian interference, and although Schurz, indicating that the Prussians had already sounded out the British, tried to renew his proposition, Fish refused to make use of his services.[10]

In the meantime, the senator had laid out a busy schedule for himself in St. Louis. He studied until eleven in the morning; then he worked in the newspaper office till six and after supper returned to his preparation for the coming session. Still determined to specialize in foreign affairs, he asked his brother-in-law in Germany for out-of-print books on economics and international relations. His chief recreation was an occasional game of billiards, and he sometimes unwound by playing with Preetorius's young son. Thus, as he complained to Margarethe, one day passed much like another.[11]

By the time Schurz's efforts on behalf of Canadian annexation seemed to have reached a dead end, he was finally invited to take a place on the Senate Committee on Foreign Relations. Senator Fessenden's death had created a vacancy; Sumner did not forget his friend, and Schurz gladly accepted. He remained on the committee for the remainder of his senatorial career.[12]

At the very time Schurz joined the committee, it was about to become involved in a major controversy with the President. Grant wanted the United States to annex the Republic of Santo Domingo, and his aide, General Orville E. Babcock, had negotiated a treaty for that purpose. In this endeavor, he had been assisted by two American speculators, Joseph W. Fabens and William L. Cazneau. Instrumental in advising the Dominican dictator Buenaventura Baez, who was already in grave difficulty with the domestic opposition as well as with neighboring Haiti, they had also carefully worked for the treaty's acceptance in Washington. Grant himself was so anxious to annex the island that around New Year's he personally sought out Charles Sumner at his home on Lafayette Square to urge him to support the scheme. According to Schurz, to whom he told it the next day, the Massachusetts senator replied, "Mr. President, I am an Administration man, and whatever you will do will always find in me the most careful and candid consideration." Exactly what he said is not clear; Grant, however, was sure that he had promised his full cooperation.[13]

For Schurz as for Sumner, the Santo Domingo imbroglio became a major point of departure that led to their final break with the administration. Never a racist in modern terms, Schurz had nevertheless long believed that climate and conditions had an important effect upon people and that the tropics tended to be debilitating. Santo Domingo was a tropical island; its long history of political disorder seemed to him to demonstrate the inhabitants' unsuitability for democratic government. He thought they could never become good Americans, and he always opposed annexations of populations presumably incapable of assimilation.[14]

Thus, he distrusted the annexation scheme from the very beginning. When late in November Fish informed him privately that two protocols were already in existence, he immediately alerted Preetorius, although the matter was still confidential. He did not like the proposition at all. "I believe I shall oppose it," he wrote to his partner. Preetorius then printed some factual articles on the subject until January 18, 1870, when the treaty was formally submitted to the committee. Schurz, who moved to reject it, instructed his partner to "open up strongly against the proposal." Conscious as he was of his dependence on the German-American vote, he doubtless took seriously a warning against any involvement with the Dominican Republic which Gustave Koerner sent him. But his own convictions as well as Sumner's strong antiannexationist feelings were probably the determining factor in his bitter opposition to the proposed expansion into the Caribbean.[15]

It was not until March, after the Senate had received a special message from the President on the subject, Grant personally appearing at the President's Room to convince senators of the advantages of annexation, that the committee took up the pending treaty. The long delay had given the members an opportunity to find out more about the unsavory background of the transaction. Babcock had conducted unauthorized negotiations with the financially embarrassed Dominican president; American speculators were vitally interested in the scheme; and Grant had employed naval units to prop up Baez. Influenced by these revelations, on March 15 the committee, by a vote of 5 to 2, rendered an adverse report to the Senate.

The Senate took up the subject in executive session during the following week. On March 24, Sumner delivered a great oration against annexation which he did not complete until the following day; then Morton spoke for the treaty; and on the 28th, Schurz attacked the proposition for more than an hour. The country already had enough trouble with its own South, he said, without seeking further tropical or subtropical possessions. Emphasizing his climatic theories, he insisted that a tropical population could not and would not assimilate with the majority of the continental United States. On the contrary, if permitted to participate in politics, it would become a dangerous element of corruption and demoralization, if not an invitation to military despotism. Avowing his opposition to southward expansion, he called for the annexation of Canada as the proper fulfillment of manifest destiny. In spite of the administration's intense lobbying and such stunts as the display in the Senate of a piece of Dominican salt and hemp to give the lawmakers a chance to sample these products, the treaty did not come to a vote. It was obvious that the two-thirds necessary for ratification were lacking.[16]

Grant reacted angrily to this crossing of his desires. The matter had become a personal issue with him, and he held Schurz and Sumner especially responsible for his troubles. When on May 14 Schurz showed Fish a list of senators opposed—enough to block the treaty—the secretary of state decided to recommend a modification by an amendment giving Santo Domingo an option for future independence. But he failed. Even though the senator from Missouri thought that no real breach between himself and the administration had taken place—had he not frankly told Grant his opinion about the treaty weeks ago, while others had deceived the President?—Grant was unforgiving. Believing the amendment to have been Schurz's suggestion, he refused even to consider Fish's idea. That the senator played the principal role in the investigation of the claims of Davis Hatch, an American who had been jailed and maltreated by Baez allegedly with Babcock's connivance, only made matters worse. Then, when on June 30 the treaty was finally defeated by a vote of 28–28, the President was so angry that he recalled Sumner's friend Motley from London. As for Schurz, he called him an infidel and atheist who had been a rebel in his own country, as much a rebel as Jefferson Davis.[17]

Schurz's final break with the administration—his abandonment of the radicals on the question of Reconstruction—followed in short order. Of all his many switches in politics, his desertion of the blacks—for that is what it was, whether he recognized it or not—was the most difficult to explain. That he genuinely believed in racial justice is certain; he had advocated equal rights for years prior to his election, and in the late 1890s and early 1900s he was to endorse it again.[18] But the circumstances of his election in Missouri, and presumably the Germans' lukewarm attitude toward the freedmen, soon made him invent all kinds of excuses for his course of apparently caring more for the restoration of the political rights of former Confederates than the protection of those of the blacks.

When Schurz first entered the Senate, he was still fully committed to radical Reconstruction. Having insisted during the campaign that Negro suffrage must precede the lifting of voting restrictions for former rebels, when he reached Washington he voted for a bill to require the ratification of the Fifteenth Amendment by the still unreconstructed states of Virginia, Texas, and Mississippi. The *Westliche Post*, praising the constitutional change, insisted that test oaths for prospective voters in Virginia then advocated by the radicals were wholly justified; Schurz warned Boutwell not to end military government in Texas too soon, and when he came back to the Senate for the long session, he again supported a stringent measure for the reconstruction of recalcitrant Georgia, where blacks had been excluded from the state legislature.[19] But then a change set in.

Schurz was not a vindictive man. His treatment of prisoners during the war and his insistence on an amnesty plank in 1868 had proven his compassion, and when the former insurgents responded favorably to his overtures, he was highly flattered. Soon he went further. With a state election in Missouri in the offing that fall, battle lines were being drawn between the followers of incumbent Governor Joseph W. McClurg and the Liberals, as Schurz's friends were beginning to call themselves, mainly on the question of the enfranchisement of former insurgents. As Drake supported McClurg, an advocate of temperance whom the Germans disliked (he refused to serve hard liquor in the governor's mansion), the general naturally became one of the leaders of the governor's opponents.[20]

The first sign of the senator's change of sentiment was his attitude on the question of the admission of Virginia. After complying with all the conditions laid down in the various Reconstruction acts, the state asked for readmission. Sumner strongly argued for a bill making her restoration dependent on certain further requirements, test oaths for voters and a perpetual guarantee of the blacks' political rights. Schurz voted for it, but he made it clear that he thought Virginia ought to be admitted even without it. Some two months later, in March 1870, when Congress was once again dealing with the reconstruction of Georgia, he went further. In that state, after the legislature's exclusion of blacks following readmission, Congress demanded new conditions, including the ratification of the Fifteenth Amendment, before it would seat the Georgia congressional delegation. Although the state complied, the radical governor, Rufus Bullock, now wanted to postpone new elections for two years. Notwithstanding his friend Sumner's determined advocacy of the measure, Schurz, attacking it as unsound, voted with moderate Republicans and Democrats to defeat it. Although still ridiculing Democratic assertions that radical Reconstruction in the South was comparable to the horrors of counterrevolution in Poland and Hungary, during the course of the debates he consistently sided with the moderates. And while he spoke in favor of the first force bill to protect black voters, he criticized some of its more far-reaching provisions and warned against excessive federal interference in local affairs. It was symptomatic of his changing attitude that he did not think it necessary to be present when the final vote on the measure was taken.[21]

When Congress adjourned and Schurz was preparing to leave Washington, he realized that his relations with the White House had suffered severely. Taking advantage of the excitement engendered by the Franco-Prussian War, he addressed the President directly. Matters of importance to the administration and the party had made it desirable for him to see Grant, he wrote. Recent events which could not fail to excite strong feelings among the German population of the country had devolved upon him an influence and responsibilities "more comprehensive than any that had formerly fallen" to his lot. And although he was "painfully sensible of the change" which their mutual relations had suffered in consequence of their differences on the Santo Domingo treaty, he was anxious to dispel any false notions brought to the President by tale-bearers. It was absolutely untrue that he had attacked Grant in the secret sessions of the Senate; hoping that the annexation question had been laid to rest, he was eager to continue to lend his support to the administration in the future. Grant invited him to come the next day, but evidently there was no meeting of the minds. The two men had become irreconcilable enemies.[22]

After addressing German meetings in Baltimore and New York in support of the fatherland's cause against France, Schurz returned to St. Louis. He left his family in the East, for Margarethe was unwilling to accompany him to the city she had loathed ever since Emma died,[23] and immediately upon his arrival he plunged into the gubernatorial campaign.

The split between the Drake radicals and the liberal faction in Missouri had greatly widened since Schurz's election to the Senate. Demanding the immediate passage and implementation of amendments ending the former insurgents' disabilities, the Liberals were impatient with radical delaying tactics. Moreover, Grosvenor had become ever more insistent on tariff reform; Drake and McClurg were protectionists, and the Liberals, including Schurz, tended to favor free trade. For this and other reasons, they advocated the nomination of B. Gratz Brown for governor. As the former senator's candidacy would strongly appeal to the Germans, Schurz in the *Westliche Post* had made sure to undermine whatever appeal the governor still had by pointing out that McClurg was not friendly to his countrymen. Grant, on the other hand, anxious to uphold the regulars, on February 14 ordered McDonald to establish his headquarters in St. Louis. He was to use his office to counteract any possible split in the party.

The Democrats took full advantage of the developing rift among their opponents. Refraining from putting up a gubernatorial ticket of their own, they adopted a "possum policy" of entering merely local and congressional contests. Even as they were bound to benefit by the expected Liberal victory, the blacks, whose newly won rights they sought to diminish, were bound to suffer.

When on August 31 the Republican convention met at Jefferson City, Schurz was confident of victory. He still hoped to prevail in a united party, but he was prepared to bolt if necessary. His majority faction—he was the chairman of the resolutions committee—reported a platform pledging support for the pending constitutional amendments and their immediate implementation. His opponents also endorsed the amendments but wanted to await the proper time to put them into effect. When the convention, reflecting undue radical strength because of the arbitrary assignment of additional delegates for newly enfranchised blacks, adopted the minority report, the Liberals led by General John McNeil bolted, soon to be followed by Lieutenant Governor Edwin O. Stanard and his group of moderates, who had tried to bring about a reconciliation. Schurz became the presiding officer of the new convention, which promptly nominated Brown and adopted the Liberal platform, including a civil service reform plank. The regulars nominated McClurg, but with the aid of the German vote, the seceders' chances of beating him were excellent. "Bolting is fun when the bolters take the principles and ideas of the party with them, and leave only a dismal chance for office to those who stay behind," wrote the *Missouri Democrat*. Black voters, however, did not agree with this interpretation. Correctly judging that their interests were endangered by the split, they generally remained in the radical camp.[24]

Schurz honestly sought to stay within the Republican party. In his remarks to a ratification meeting at St. Louis, he spoke highly of Grant; in the *Address to the People of Missouri* justifying the split, he again emphasized his loyalty to the party. He sent the document to Fish, whom he also warned against interference in Europe now that Napoleon III had surrendered, and declared that the bolt had been an absolute necessity. He even tried to warn his associates against attacks upon the President.[25] But his efforts were of no avail. Considering the Liberal movement a deliberate effort to break up the party and to carry a portion of it over to the Democrats, Grant began a purge of Schurz's appointees. Even the senator's brother-in-law eventually lost his Chicago collectorship, and Collector McDonald in St. Louis used his dubious sources of revenue to counteract the bolters. Nevertheless, Schurz, appealing as usual to his compatriots, campaigned confidently throughout the state. He challenged Drake to a debate; the *Westliche Post* charged that the radical leaders and McClurg had become regular nativists and called for a reform of existing abuses. Schurz gloried in his clashes with his rivals. Engaging in many debates with his opponents, he boasted to Margarethe that he was routing his adversaries in the manner of Blücher.[26]

Nevertheless, the canvass was not easy for him. Absolutely refusing to come to Missouri, his wife constantly asked him to join her in the East. Of course she was in frail health; pregnant again, she did not relish travel, but it would have been perfectly feasible for her to stay in St. Louis. He tried to explain to her that he could not abandon the field; his entire public position depended on victory. But Margarethe remained dissatisfied. Her stubborn nature had never been more evident.[27]

In the November 8 election the Liberals won a complete victory. Whether Schurz admitted it or not, however, the result was really a triumph for the Democrats, who succeeded in capturing the legislature and several congressional seats.[28] In effect, he had contributed to his own ultimate political downfall. The Democratic legislature would never reelect him.

Such defeat, however, lay in the future, and for the time being, Schurz was optimistic. He rushed to Washington by way of New York to call for Margarethe, whose pregnancy caused her to feel unwell. Considering himself the sole representative of the new movement in the Senate, he was determined to beat the administration, especially as he thought he had to reflect honor on the German name as well as on his own.[29]

Whether, in view of the damage he was doing to racial adjustment, he really brought honor to the German-Americans remained a matter of dispute, but that his position as their spokesman was an element of great strength for him was beyond question. When Congress met in December, it was widely rumored that the Republican caucus would reorganize the Foreign Relations Committee, possibly excluding Schurz. Nothing came of this gossip, however. "Schurz's removal from the Committee of Foreign Relations, just at the time of the German-French War and in view of the administration's and the entire American establishment's inclination toward France, would be a deliberate, irresponsible, and unforgivable insult of the entire German element in America," complained the Missouri *Washingtoner Post*, undoubtedly reflecting German sentiment elsewhere. Although charges of Grant's pro-French sympathies were untrue, the administration was careful not to alienate so important a portion of the electorate as the German-Americans.[30]

Yet the President himself did not forgive Schurz. When shortly after his arrival in the capital the senator sought to make the customary courtesy call at the White House, he found that Grant would not receive him; he was busy interviewing Indian agents. In fact, he never saw the senator again. Not until Grant was close to death was a reconciliation effected.[31]

Schurz refused to take the rebuff lying down. Anxious to justify his course before the whole country, on December 12 he introduced a resolution to remove all disqualifications and disabilities of former insurgents as soon as practicable. Three days later, he delivered a forceful speech on the subject. Standing behind his chair with the manuscript before him, he read successive sheets and then laid them aside, keeping the Senate spellbound with his elegant language. He pleaded strongly for national reconciliation, an end to formerly necessary restrictions, and went into some detail about the split in the Missouri party. It was the Liberals' insistence upon the immediate removal of disabilities that caused the bolt, he asserted, severely ridiculing Drake's charges that he had always intended to desert the party that elected him. Although he had been in close contact with revenue reformers since the election, he sought to emphasize not the differences between himself and his opponents about the tariff, but the question of amnesty. Branding the senior senator's assertion that he was less interested in protection for American than for German industry a species of demogoguery of the lowest order, he charged that it amounted to a questioning of the patriotism of all German-Americans, "and this in the face of that spirit of self-sacrificing devotion which but yesterday led far more than a hundred thousand German-born citizens upon all the battlefields of the Republic." If the Missouri election resulted in a defeat of the administration, the President and his advisers were responsible. "We did not attack him; he attacked us," Schurz insisted. He had merely sought to carry out the amnesty plank of the 1868 Republican platform upon which Grant had been elected. Finally, he turned to the accusation that he had given aid to the Democrats. Maintaining that every campaigner sought to win over the opposition, he made a forceful statement of his views of the current situation. He believed that the Republican party had virtually completed its mission; unless it found new issues, unless it became the party of reform—something the Democrats with their machines and reactionary views were unlikely to do—it was finished.[32]

Although his remarks were widely praised,[33] he had actually totally misread

American political developments. The type of issue-oriented party that he considered necessary for a healthy polity did not emerge in the United States after the Civil War. His faulty interpretation of the prevailing trends was to cost him dearly. And how far his new stance had carried him from his former commitment to equal rights was revealed by his attitude toward further efforts to safeguard equal rights in the South. He actually opposed them.[34]

Schurz's break with the administration soon lessened his political effectiveness. That very winter he suffered disappointment in his struggle for civil service reform, the one subject closest to his heart. Although in the previous session none of the proposed reform bills had been adopted, Grant felt that he had to react in some positive way. Accordingly, in his annual message in December 1870, he also called for "a reform in the civil service of the country." Congress debated both Jenckes's and Trumbull's proposals, and on January 27, 1871, Schurz delivered a major speech in favor of substituting his own bill. Dramatically picturing the abuses of the spoils system by citing the damaging evidence the Committee on Retrenchment had uncovered, he pleaded for a new version of the measure he had introduced thirteen months earlier. But Congress was not receptive. The only provision which the friends of reform were able to secure was a rider to an appropriation bill in March empowering the President to appoint a civil service commission. In accordance with this mandate, Grant set up the new agency. Its head was Schurz's friend, George William Curtis.[35]

Curtis did not have an easy job. Grant's principal supporters, the powerful Stalwart members of Congress directing great political machines in their states—Oliver Morton of Indiana, Roscoe Conkling of New York, and Ben Butler of Massachusetts, to mention only a few—hated civil service reform. Grant himself was subject to various pressures he was unable or unwilling to resist, and corruption, to say nothing of the spoils system, flourished under his administration as never before. It soon became evident that his Civil Service Commission could not accomplish much, so that Schurz, like other ardent civil service reformers, was deeply dissatisfied.[36]

In the meantime, the controversy about Santo Domingo had not ended. Unwilling to give up his scheme of annexation, the President, after first trying to bring about by joint resolution what he could not accomplish by treaty, sought to revive the issue by calling for an investigation commission. In the subsequent debates about this proposal, Sumner and Schurz, anxious to defeat it, favored its referral to the Committee on Foreign Relations; their opponents resisted this demand. Thoroughly aroused, in the night of December 21, Sumner delivered his acerbic Naboth's Vineyard speech, in which he charged that the proposition committed Congress to a "dance of blood." Castigating the President, Baez, and the whole idea of annexation, he was especially solicitous about the implied threat to the black Republic of Haiti. But notwithstanding his dramatic appeal and

Schurz's support in the debates that followed, the resolution was not referred to the Foreign Relations Committee. Late that night, it passed. And although this did not really mean that opposition to annexation had been overcome, it was obvious that Congress did not relish Sumner's virulence.[37]

Early in the new year, when both houses were considering an amendment disclaiming any intention of taking over the island, Schurz too obtained a chance to voice his sentiments in public. Still on tolerable terms with Fish, whose opposition to intervention in Cuba he supported and with whom he was then negotiating about the arms sales to France, he did not indulge in personalities. Nevertheless, he forcefully restated all his arguments against the acquisition of tropical territories. Their inhabitants sapped the vitality of Anglo-Saxons; they were unsuited for free government; if the country was to follow its manifest destiny, let it expand northward to acquire Canada, where there were people with similar customs, language, and origin. Ridiculing objections that other powers might take Santo Domingo if the United States refused it, he replied that England, Spain, and France had already realized the folly of tropical acquisitions, and although it was charged that Germany was anxious to expand, he assured his colleagues that no country desired friendly relations with America more avidly than the North German Confederation. It was led by enlightened statesmen; moreover, it already had colonies—commercial settlements of its nationals in the major ports of the world—and would need no others. Engaging in continual repartee with other senators throughout the speech, he thought he had been wholly successful. But although the resolution was adopted by an overwhelming majority and he received many compliments on his speech, the commission to sail to the island was appointed. Among its unofficial observers was Franz Sigel, apparently named to propitiate the Germans for whom Schurz was presuming to speak.[38]

Sumner's bitter attack on the administration and his subsequent break in relations with Fish led to further complications. Grant, who took Sumner's opinions as a personal affront, was determined to get rid of him once and for all; the secretary of state, equally offended and anxious to have the obstreperous senator out of the way pending renewed negotiations with Great Britain concerning the *Alabama* claims, fully concurred. Consequently, when in March the new Congress assembled, the Republican caucus failed to reappoint the senator chairman of the Committee on Foreign Relations.

Schurz did not permit this act of revenge to go unchallenged. Protesting vigorously, he charged executive interference and dramatically asked for the reasons for the change, seeking thus to avert the final decision on the Senate floor. But it was of no avail. The administration prevailed. It maintained that it could not conduct business with a chairman of the Foreign Relations Committee who refused to have social intercourse with the President and the secretary of state.[39]

Until that time Schurz had refrained from attacking Grant personally, but now he threw all inhibitions to the wind. After the Santo Domingo commission returned, on March 27 he fully supported Sumner in the course of a long speech castigating the administration for violations of international law and the usurpation of war powers. Sitting behind the aggrieved man, Schurz handed him books and documents as needed. Then, on the following two days, he himself spoke on the same subject. At issue were a series of resolutions condemning the administration and calling for the withdrawal of American naval forces from the island, and Schurz took the opportunity to reply to criticism of Sumner's philippic.

Schurz's thorough command of his subject impressed his audience. Referring to the threat to Haiti, he categorically accused the administration of wrongdoing. "In ordering the naval commanders of the United States to capture and destroy by force of arms the vessels of a nation with whom the United States was at peace," he declared, the President "did usurp the warmaking power of Congress." Skillfully refuting the precedents cited by Senators Morton and Frelinghuysen in defense of executive use of the armed forces without prior congressional authorization, Schurz defined the issue as one of constitutional law, the maintenance of the rights of the legislative branch in a constitutional government. "Let this first precedent of acquiescence in an act of usurpation by a successful soldier pass into our history," he warned, "and you will have struck a blow at the cause of free government that will resound throughout the earth." Even the *Missouri Democrat,* then switching to the President's support, admitted that the speech constituted an effort "which, for eloquence, clearness of statement, wit, sarcasm, and readiness of repartee," had perhaps never been surpassed in any assembly of the world.[40]

Schurz's attacks on the President's foreign policy did not fully extend to the Treaty of Washington, which was about to be submitted to the committee. A comprehensive settlement of the outstanding issues between the United States and Great Britain, including the *Alabama* claims, it constituted a triumph for Secretary Fish. Schurz himself had been urging Fish to take advantage of the disturbed conditions in Europe to press for the cession of Canada; the secretary, willing to settle for less, made good use of the Franco-Prussian War to bring the negotiations to a successful conclusion. And although the senator was accused of obstructing ratification of the treaty, in reality he did not oppose it and voted for its acceptance. However, his support of this settlement with Great Britain could not bring about a rapprochement with the administration.[41]

In the meantime, the senator had become a father again. On February 28, Margarethe gave birth to a son, whom the proud parents called Carl Lincoln. Schurz was delighted. For years he had been longing for a male heir, a *Stammhalter.* And if the boy at first had some difficulty with his eyes—one was a bit smaller than the other—the trouble turned out to be temporary.[42]

Schurz's relations with his former political associates did not improve. How final his break was, not only with Grant but also with his own past, became clear with his renewed opposition to further Reconstruction legislation. Not even the unwelcome news that the Democrats organized the new Missouri legislature and elected Frank Blair to the United States Senate—Drake had resigned following his appointment to the Court of Claims—made Schurz take stock and reconsider his advocacy of the enfranchisement of former insurgents. Thus, it was not surprising that he showed no interest in the second Force bill of February 1871, a measure designed to strengthen federal supervision of elections. It is true that at the time it was being debated he was rarely present in the chamber—his wife's approaching confinement had rendered her so ill that he was forced to stay away from his official duties—but had he been in his seat, he probably would have voted against it, just as he finally opposed the third Force Act a few weeks later.[43]

Schurz's speech against the Ku Klux Act, as the measure was called, did not do him much credit. Although Horace White, who sympathized with him, called it a "masterpiece of political philosophy" and compared it to the orations of Edmund Burke, in reality it was an attempt to overlook the admitted atrocities of the secret society in the pious hope that moderates in the South might themselves prevent the disorders. Deploring the outrages that had given rise to the call for federal intervention and holding the old proslavery spirit rather than Reconstruction responsible for them, Schurz nevertheless argued that to pass laws against the Klan would constitute an interference with states' rights and thus undermine American liberties. Conciliation, not repression, was the answer to the attacks on blacks and Republicans, an argument of little help to the victims of the terror.[44] Schurz was so anxious to win Southern support for his campaign against Grant that he was oblivious of the fact that he was in effect betraying his lifelong advocacy of human equality.

Thus the senator from Missouri, after breaking with the President on patronage, foreign affairs, and Reconstruction, became one of the founders of the Liberal Republican movement. Because he had played so prominent a role in the revolt against the administration, it was clear that the dissidents would look to him for guidance. He was not at all loath to provide it.

XIII

The Liberal Republican Debacle

AT THE TIME of the first difficulties between Schurz and the administration, the senator was not at all committed to the formation of a new party. On the contrary, again and again he emphasized his desire to reform the Republican organization, cleanse it from within, and see to it that it chose a worthy candidate as its next standard-bearer. Even after the break with Grant had become irrevocable, Schurz persisted in these efforts. He could not support any Liberal mass convention, he warned Preetorius. The Republican party must be captured from within; nothing could be done from outside.[1]

Convinced of the accuracy of his analysis, he sought to discourage others from going too far. Much though he approved of revenue reform, for example, he cautioned E. L. Godkin, the opinionated, influential liberal editor of the *Nation*, that he did not think it too wise to make too much of the issue at the beginning. Trumbull agreed with him, he insisted. The party was presently controlled by "office mongers" who supported the administration. To save "the vitality of the Republican party," that leadership must be broken up and the public at large convinced of the impracticability of Grant's renomination. Once this was done, "the liberal and vigorous elements of the Republican party," who alone could save its future usefulness, would have a chance "to assume control of the organization and shape its future policy." In the same vein, he reassured Jacob D. Cox, whose associates had formed a Republican reform organization in Ohio, "If we only succeed in rallying those who think alike, the Republican organization will in truth be the *new party* of the future." His purpose was Grant's replacement by some other Republican nominee.[2]

His desire to save the Republican party was closely connected with his continued dislike for the Democrats. The owners of the *Westliche Post*, troubled about his frequent absences, suggested that he give up his Senate seat and devote more time to the paper. Aside from his great pride in his distinguished office, he believed such a course of action to be completely impossible. It would result in the election of a Democrat. Accordingly, he made a new arrangement with the paper that allowed him to keep his seat.[3]

When after the end of the congressional session the senator returned to St. Louis, his friends organized a grand reception for him at the Southern Hotel. Many of his former Democratic opponents joined with Liberal Republicans to express their appreciation for his course. In a brief address he outlined his policies, stressing the reunion of all citizens, civil service and revenue reform, as well as the importance of the separation of powers. Pointedly referring to the Santo Domingo controversy, he insisted the President must not presume to exercise the war-making power.[4]

In the meantime, Liberal movements were springing up in various parts of the country. The Central Republican Association of Hamilton County formed the nucleus of the Ohio revolt; in New Hampshire reformers were beginning to organize; and in New York the dominant Conkling faction had a complete falling-out with its rivals, led by Reuben Fenton. "My trials have been considerable," Grant complained to his friend Washburne. "Sumner and Schurz have acted worse than any other two men." The Democrats, delighted at these signs of disarray among their rivals, embarked on new experiments of their own. On May 18, the most notorious Peace Democrat in the country, Clement L. Vallandigham, announcing a "new departure," endorsed the Reconstruction amendments.[5] The material for a new combination was at hand—perhaps even an entirely new party.

Schurz believed the time for action had come. Explaining to Margarethe that the German element was more than ever in a fluid condition, he was determined to mold it in such a way as to enhance its influence as an independent force, although he had not entirely abandoned the idea of marshaling the reform forces within the Republican party.[6] An invitation to address the Germans of Chicago gave him an opportunity to launch his campaign.

He was well prepared when he arrived in the Windy City. Wearing a grey summer suit and a light hat, he greeted the formally attired welcoming committee of his countrymen, who nevertheless approvingly noted the changes in his appearance. Instead of his reddish brown mustache, he now sported a slightly darker full beard, which, in view of his sharply delineated eyebrows, they thought, gave his face a remarkably attractive character. His speech was not too different from those he had been delivering all along. He reaffirmed his belief in the necessity of the Reconstruction amendments, stressed his opposition to the Santo Domingo scheme, and again emphasized his support for civil service reform. Appealing to his audience's pride in the recently completed unification of Germany, he used for the first time the metaphor of his loyalty to his old mother and his new bride. On this occasion Schurz went further than before; in view of the President's unconstitutional assumption of the war-making power in ordering the navy to interfere in Santo Domingo, he announced that he would not be able to support Grant for a second term.[7]

This open avowal of party disloyalty furnished the administration press with powerful arguments against him. Calling his declaration an "ultimatum," the *Missouri Democrat* insisted that his whole course in Missouri had tended in the direction of a bolt. Other papers followed suit. As Schurz explained to Margarethe, his daring stand had turned all the Grant organs against him, and although the Liberal journals approved, he regretted the fact that his fellow Liberals were not courageous enough to assume his advanced position.[8]

In the meantime, after a stay at Bethlehem with his family, where he suffered a slight injury when the baby poked its finger into his eye, he received a bid to deliver a major address in Nashville. The offer came from Henry S. Foote, the well-known Southern statesman who had long played an important role in national politics. In spite of warning that there were few if any Republicans among those who had tendered the invitation, Schurz accepted. The resulting speech has been called the beginning of the national Liberal Republican movement.[9]

The senator did not hesitate to explain his stand. Appearing on September 20 before a large audience, he started out by expressing his appreciation for the invitation. It was an honor to have been asked by former Confederates and Unionists alike. Although again maintaining the importance of the postwar amendments, he flattered his listeners by stressing the theme of national reconciliation. Demanding an end to carpetbag rule in the South, he called once more for civil service and revenue reform, advocated the resumption of specie payments, and reaffirmed his unwillingness to support Grant because of the President's unconstitutional use of the navy in Santo Domingo. Then came the climax. Because the Democrats were too reactionary and many Republicans were not ready for progressive measures, he advocated the formation of a new party. Such an organization, unencumbered by the traditions of the past, would be able to face the future with confidence.

His audience liked his arguments. Congratulatory letters, especially from the South, poured in, Schurz taking special pride in a communication from some two hundred former Confederate soldiers who pledged their support. Sumner, though troubled about Reconstruction, announced his agreement, and a Wisconsin correspondent expressed hope that the constitutional restriction of the presidency to native-born citizens might be lifted. Pleased with himself, Schurz kept busy forming new Liberal groupings, especially a Tennessee Reunion and Reform Association, which became the model for similar organizations elsewhere.[10]

In a highly optimistic mood, the senator was certain that he had made a real beginning in winning over former Confederates. "Three months of agitation in the South in the way that I am conducting it could do more to restore quiet than all Ku Klux laws," he wrote to Margarethe. "It would destroy the Democratic party there and open up the way for the election of a good man to the presidency." He even thought that his approach was resulting in the destruction of the terrorist organization, probably because Foote assured him that he was doing everything in his power to stop outrages.[11] That at the same time his movement seriously undermined the Reconstruction process did not occur to him.

Still, he needed more support from his Republican associates. Finally certain that the time had come for the formation of a new party, he sought to persuade Sumner to join him. "*You* ought to be the great leader of this movement which will create the party of the future," he wrote to the senator from Massachusetts, whom he tried to win over to the theory that the new organization would be a much better means of controlling the South than all force acts. To Cox, whom he had only recently written of his hopes for Democratic defeats in the fall elections, he now suggested that the Central Republican Association open its ranks to the opposition. The progressive elements of both parties must be united.[12]

The Democrats were not displeased with his activities. The rift in the Republican organization augured well for them, and when in November Schurz, lecturing on civil service reform in various Eastern cities, arrived in New York, the newspapers devoted considerable space to reports of his meetings with the leaders of the opposition. "He is the great political missionary, laboring for the organization of a fusion party, for the defeat of General Grant next year. He came here, no doubt, upon that mission, and he has evidently been doing something too," wrote the New York *Herald*. When in June 1872 Zachariah Chandler charged that "a distinguished Senator who had formerly been a Republican" made an arrangement with Samuel J. Tilden and other Democrats to launch a new party while the Democrats promised to remain on the sidelines to facilitate the nomination of an independent candidate, he was not far from wrong.[13] What the exact terms were is unknown; in effect, however, the Democrats did encourage the formation of the new political organization, which they eventually endorsed.

After finishing his lecture tour in December of 1871, Schurz arrived in Washington and immediately resumed his attacks on the administration. At issue was Trumbull's proposal to reactivate the Retrenchment Committee, an attempt to investigate the scandals of the New York customs house. One of Grant's wartime associates, George W. Leet, making use of a letter of introduction from the President, had succeeded in cornering the entire general order business in New York—a system of provisionally storing imports in private warehouses—and the scandal directly affected Conkling's henchman, Collector Thomas Murphy. The Stalwart defenders of the administration referred the matter to a committee from which all the President's opponents had been carefully excluded, but in the debates that preceded this decision, Schurz unmercifully castigated the perpetrators and their protectors in Washington.[14] Considering this a direct attack on the President's probity, the administration press once more launched an assault upon him.

The general lent himself easily to attack. Cartoonists had a great time caricaturing his lanky features, and before long, Thomas Nast, the gifted artist of *Harper's Weekly*, would delight the country with a flood of increasingly bitter cartoons of the bespectacled senator. For the time being, regular Republican newspapers, led by the *New York Times*, opened up on the one statesman who was increasingly considered the leader of the insurgent movement. Accusing him of insinuating that the President himself was corrupt and had been keeping up the general order system in New York for his own personal profit, it scathingly reviewed Schurz's career. In 1859 had he not refused to support the ticket after spurning second place because of his failure to win the gubernatorial nomination in Wisconsin? Then, in 1860, had he not been amply compensated for his campaign speeches? And after his appointment as minister to Spain, did he not use the supposed power of the German-Americans to force Lincoln to give him a general's commission, "without manifesting any striking evidences of military genius?" After the war, again relying on the influence of his compatriots, he allegedly sought other advantages, "by no means favorably distinguished himself" as editor of the Detroit *Post*, and moved to Missouri. There he repaid his election to the Senate with treason to the party. The general picture was that of a self-seeking, self-appointed spokesman for the German-Americans, a disappointed office-seeker who broke with the administration because the President refused his patronage requests.

As soon as the Christmas recess was over, Schurz took the first opportunity to reply. Denying that he had called the President corrupt, he explained to the Senate that the payments for his speeches had merely covered expenses. He pointed out that, contrary to the accusations of the *New York Times*, in 1859 he had supported the Republican ticket, and if in 1869 he had recommended some unworthy candidates for office, he regretted it. As he had already stated repeatedly, his brother-in-law had been appointed without his help. The only reason the *Times* was attacking him was that he had been pointing a finger at corrupt practices in the New York customs house.

Of course his enemies did not let up. On the next day, the *Times* renewed its attacks. Charging that the German element was his stock in trade, it ridiculed the notion that he had it in his pocket. Then it published a story about the arrest of General Krzyzanowski, Schurz's friend and supervisor of internal revenue in Georgia, incessantly reiterated the shortcomings of the senator's appointees, and stressed his alleged nepotism in connection with his brother-in-law. As time went on, these barbs became more and more pointed, with emphasis on the tangled problem of his Wisconsin debts, which became a subject of national dispute.[15]

By and large, these assaults were wholly unjustified. But when Nast castigated the opposition for attacking Grant in a cartoon entitled, "Why They Don't Like Him," with a subsection explaining, "He Won't Allow the South to Hang Niggers," he had a point.[16] Exaggerated as the accusation was, the Liberal movement was no boon for the blacks. Schurz's position on the pending amnesty bill made this abundantly clear.

The consideration of amnesty legislation was important for the senator, who was anxious to strengthen the Liberal movement in the South. A political football rather than a meaningful reform, it merely offered relief to the handful of former Confederates still barred from office-holding by the Fourteenth Amendment. But Charles Sumner, determined to crown his antislavery crusade with a civil rights measure, offered an amendment calling for desegregation of inns, schools, and other public facilities. When the proposal came up for a vote, Schurz repeatedly voted nay. His desire to woo the South was stronger than his friendship for Sumner or his concern for the freedmen.[17]

A few weeks later, on January 30, while the amnesty bill was once more under discussion, Schurz attempted to explain his position. Asserting that both expediency and justice required amnesty, he questioned the wisdom of making ignorant former slaves eligible for office while excluding experienced Southern leaders. Not that he begrudged the blacks privileges; it was not their fault that they were inexperienced, and, by and large, he believed they had behaved much better than any other people recently emancipated. But the misgovernment which had sprung up in the South was not beneficial for the blacks; possibly the restoration of full rights to Southern whites might improve conditions. In a special plea to Sumner, he asked him not to complicate matters by attaching conditions that he knew could not pass. While he honored his friend for his solicitude for the "welfare of the lowly," while he maintained that his own desire "to see their wrongs righted" was "no less sincere and no less unhampered by any traditional prejudice than his," he could not agree to endanger the prospects of the amnesty bill. Southerners congratulated him on his speech; most likely, blacks were less convinced of his sincerity.[18]

By this time, Schurz was wholly committed to the third-party idea. Contemplating the holding of a national convention and the nomination of a complete ticket, he thought the Democrats would then have to follow suit. Brown, Adams, and Trumbull might all be suitable candidates. To initiate the movement, cooperating with Grosvenor and others, he planned to induce the Liberal state convention in Missouri to adopt a platform and issue a call for the national meeting.

He fully carried out his plan. On January 24 the convention assembled at Jefferson City and acted. Espousing a program of reconciliation, tariff and civil service reform, as well as local self-government, it extended an invitation to like-minded patriots to meet at Cincinnati in May. The endorsement by the convention of civil rights and the Reconstruction amendments could not alter the fact that its devotion to black rights was suspect at best.[19]

During the two months that followed, Schurz was busy preparing for the Cincinnati convention. Although his time in the Senate was taken up with the French arms sale debates—Sumner raised the issue in February to embarrass the administration further—the Missouri senator kept in touch with all the various factions likely to oppose the President. This was no easy matter. He himself might sympathize with colleagues like Lyman Trumbull and with editors like Samuel Bowles of the Springfield *Republican*, Horace White of the Chicago *Tribune*, Murat Halstead of the Cincinnati *Commercial*, and Henry Watterson of the Louisville *Courier-Journal*, who favored low tariffs, civil service reform, hard money, and an end to Reconstruction, but the anti-Grant movement also attracted other elements with different ideas. Senator Reuben Fenton of New York bitterly resented his colleague, Roscoe Conkling, yet he was hardly interested in reform; Horace Greeley of the New York *Tribune*, a long-time advocate of all kinds of progressive causes, was unalterably opposed to Grant's reliance on spoilsmen although he was a firm protectionist; and the regular Democratic party was hoping to benefit from the now irreversible Republican split. Moreover, Charles Sumner, as firmly opposed to the administration as Schurz, distrusted any movement that might undermine the crusade for justice for the blacks.[20]

Schurz sought to bring all these factions together. As he explained the situation to his brother-in-law Adolph Meyer, a few months earlier he had been all alone, but now he could count on a regular group of followers in the Senate—"a small phalanx," as he put it—and the movement was rapidly growing in the lower house as well. He was fully confident of the success of his program of opposition to corruption, protection, and the patronage system. "Although I cannot become President," he added, "nevertheless, between ourselves, I will have to make the next one and can do it."[21]

Yet who would be a suitable candidate? Lyman Trumbull had a considerable following but was considered somewhat colorless; B. Gratz Brown had ambitions but was personally offensive to Schurz; Judge David Davis was very willing but had little appeal for most Republicans; Horace Greeley was the choice of many but was obnoxious to the Germans because of his views on temperance, to say nothing of his known advocacy of high tariffs. Schurz finally concluded that Charles Francis Adams, the wartime minister to Great Britain, would be the best choice. But Adams too had shortcomings; totally aloof, he refused to make any concessions to popular feeling, was on bad terms with Sumner, and wrote a haughty letter to David A. Wells, thus offending the Cincinnati convention.[22]

Schurz's prominence in the new movement did not make life easy for him. The attacks on him became more and more frequent, Thomas Nast especially now opening up in earnest. His cartoons in *Harper's Weekly*, so acerbic that George William Curtis, the editor, apologized, appeared week after week. On February 3, in a cartoon entitled "Children Cry for It," Nast drew a triumphant Grant ladling out a brew called civil service reform to reluctant Liberals, easily recognizable as Schurz, Trumbull, and Sumner, with the words, "If you can stand it, I can." On March 9, he showed Schurz as "Mephistopheles at Work for Destruction," deviously suggesting the French arms-sale resolutions to Sumner in a shameless bid for German votes. The *New York Times* endlessly discussed the shortcomings of some of Schurz's appointees, until finally the administration press charged that the senator was in league with the Jesuits. At times, Schurz asked Preetorius to print denials and replies in the *Westliche Post*; when he met Nast in Washington, he unsuccessfully tried to stop the artist; in general, however, he confined himself to continuing his own offensive against the administration.[23]

It was Schurz's considered opinion that the selection of a candidate at Cincinnati was to be the precursor of the dissolution of the old party system. As it appeared more and more likely that Grant would once more head the Republican ticket, the senator hoped that the Democrats would postpone their convention until after the President's renomination. Then they might be induced to endorse the Liberals' choice and merge with the new party.[24] Because of this conviction, he entered into negotiations with August Belmont, the New York banker and Democratic leader, who appeared to favor some of his plans.[25] But presumably the Democratic bigwigs had no notion of dissolving their party; if Schurz hoped to be able to absorb it, they could be equally sanguine of a repetition of their experience in Missouri. There they had been the principal beneficiaries of the Liberal revolt.

In preparation for the 1872 campaign, on April 12 Schurz and Trumbull appeared at a Liberal mass meeting at Cooper Union in New York. Enthusiastic crowds cheered as Schurz addressed them; his persuasive speech was a clarion call for action. It was not the first time that he had been in the hall, he recalled. He had campaigned there for Lincoln in 1860, for emancipation in 1862, for Lincoln's reelection in 1864, for Grant in 1868, and more recently for civil service reform. And he had not changed his opinions. Tariff and civil service reform were absolutely necessary, amnesty must be granted without further delay, and the Cincinnati Convention would see to it that partisanship became a thing of the past. The meeting was highly successful.[26]

As in previous years, Schurz was counting on the full support of his fellow countrymen. Generally favorably disposed toward civil service reform, hard money, and low tariffs, the German-Americans had been deeply offended by the revelations of the arms sales to France. Whether they would easily break their party bonds, however, remained to be seen. To be sure, they were proud of the prominence achieved by their famous compatriot, but considerable segments of the German press remained faithful to the administration. Moreover, as Franz Sigel pointed out to Friedrich Hecker, Schurz was courting serious trouble. "Only the Germans have given him the importance and power which he has," he explained. "Americans don't like to be dominated by another nationality . . . ." Marshaling the German vote to break with its accustomed party ties would be difficult.[27]

In spite of portents of trouble, Schurz arrived in Cincinnati with high hopes. Addressing a Kentucky Liberal Republican meeting in Covington on the day before the official opening of the Liberal gathering, he vowed that no deals were to be made in the convention. The fact that he was seeing so many old faces of the 1860 campaign reassured him, and the welcome his countrymen in Cincinnati gave him was all that he could desire.[28]

The wheeling and dealing had already started, however. Schurz met his fellow editors at the St. Nicholas Hotel, where he was staying. Gathering in a drawing room between his and Watterson's bedrooms, Bowles, Watterson, Halstead, and White, dubbed the Quadrilateral after the four strong Austrian fortresses in northern Italy, decided to scotch Davis's candidacy once and for all. Their newspapers simply printed simultaneous attacks on the jurist, and the field of available candidates was narrowed principally to Adams and Trumbull. But their plans went awry because, believing they could not leave out the powerful New

York *Tribune*, they admitted Whitelaw Reid to their counsels. Reid, Greeley's managing editor, expertly looked after his principal's interests.[29]

The convention assembled on May 1 in a huge hall. The crowds were tremendous, the excitement infectious. According to the Cincinnati *Enquirer*, Schurz was "a tower of strength" who was enthusiastically welcomed. He was wildly cheered when he appeared on the platform. "This convention means business," he said, promising to deliver a speech at the proper time.

On the next day, he was elected permanent president. Advancing to the platform to the strains of "Hail to the Chief," he began to deliver his long-awaited address. "The question might well have been asked," he said, "have the American people become so utterly indifferent to their own interests . . . that they should permit themselves to be driven like a flock of sheep by those who assume to lord it over them?" The great assembly he was addressing was the answer to this question. Its platform must be one of reform, its candidate not simply anybody to beat Grant but a statesman able to carry out a thorough reform—"the overthrow of a pernicious system." Above all, he warned against underhanded political deals. "We stand on the threshhold of a great victory," he concluded, "and victory will surely be ours if we truly deserve it." The speech galvanized the crowd; according to the *Enquirer*, it was itself "a platform for every friend of honest government to stand on."[30]

Later that day, the platform committee met. Encountering little difficulty with most Liberal demands, it speedily endorsed civil service reform, local self-government, the postwar amendments, the resumption of specie payments, and, among other improvements, a one-term amendment for the presidency. The tariff plank, however, caused great difficulty. Confronted with the necessity of pleasing both free traders and the protectionist followers of Horace Greeley, the delegates wrangled all evening about its wording. It was again Schurz, with his consuming desire to lead the movement to victory, who brought about a compromise. The issue would be left to local congressional committees. Many of his revenue reform associates were very unhappy about his giving way on so important a question.[31]

Balloting took place on the following day. Schurz's favorite, Adams, at first commanded a comfortable lead, followed by Trumbull, Greeley, Brown, Davis, and a few others. Then disaster struck. Brown and Blair, informed that Schurz might be successful in foisting Adams on the convention, had rushed to Cincinnati to prevent such accretion of power to the man the governor now considered his principal rival in Missouri. Ostentatiously stepping forward, Brown withdrew in favor of Greeley, whose nomination was brought about by a stampede on the sixth ballot.[32]

As presiding officer, Schurz had felt constrained not to interfere. But considering the nomination of the protectionist Greeley with Brown as a running mate an utter disaster, he was heartbroken. At a dinner Reid gave for his crestfallen fellow editors that night, Schurz was "as a death's head at the board." Visiting his friend

Judge Stallo, he found Koerner, Hecker, and other Germans drowning their sorrows in wine. He said nothing as he came in, but walked to the piano and played Chopin's Funeral March. Then he joined the company in drinking Marcobrunner.[33]

It was asserted then and afterward that a nefarious bargain had been struck between Greeley's supporters and Brown, the governor in effect selling himself to the New Yorker in order to ruin his rival. The senator never believed Greeley to have been a party to such a deal, nor is there any real evidence for it. As Brown's biographer has pointed out, the governor had been deeply hurt by Schurz's opposition to his collaboration with the Democrats. Consequently, he was ready to oppose his rival no matter what the cost, even the nomination of Greeley, the candidate whose nomination was most disagreeable to the general. It was also charged that had Schurz been more forceful, he could have averted the disaster that befell the Liberal Republicans with the selection of so unlikely a candidate. Had he only called for a vote immediately after his speech, his critics have maintained, he could have nominated Adams. But, acutely conscious of the antagonism aroused by his foreign birth, he feared that any interference on his part might have done more harm than good.[34] The outcome of the convention was not his fault; it was the natural result of the incongruous coalition which he had done so much to bring together. His plans for dislodging Grant and ending the Stalwart's control of the Republican party were simply unworkable.

Schurz was utterly downcast in the days following the debacle. "The result of the Cincinnati Convention has been a severe blow for me," he complained to his parents. "When somebody with so much effort and under such difficult circumstances has succeeded in building up a great enterprise, and then all of a sudden sees it collapse, it is a very hard trial of patience." To Bowles he admitted that his situation was "surrounded by unusual perplexities."

> Everything seemed to promise so well. And then to see a movement which had apparently been so successful, beyond all reasonable anticipations, at the decisive moment taken possession of by a combination of politicians striking and executing a bargain in the open light of day—and politicians, too, belonging to just that tribe we thought we were fighting against—and the whole movement stripped of its higher moral character and dragged down to the level of an ordinary political operation; this, let me confess it, was a hard blow, and if I appear in the light of a defeated party, I do under such circumstances not object.

Bowles understood. He thought Schurz's stature had been greatly enhanced as a result of the events at Cincinnati.[35]

As for Greeley, although he had once employed Schurz, he had never been very close to him. The senator in turn had differed with the editor about protection and abstinence. Now he had to make up his mind whether he would endorse him. In a long letter to the candidate on May 6, while expressing his personal regard, he made no secret of his dismay. "On Friday morning," he explained, "the Cincinnati *Commercial* informed the public that Frank Blair and Gratz Brown had arrived the night before and effected an arrangement between your and Brown's friends, by which Brown should withdraw as a candidate for the Presidency in your favor and then take the second place. I did not at first believe the story. But in the Convention the piece was enacted in literal accordance with the program announced; trade and delivery appeared in the open light of day. I am very far from suspecting you of having been a party to this arrangement. I believe in you as a pure and honest man. But the managers of this case did not act as you would have acted."

It was not merely the appearance of a bargain and the routing of the revenue reformers that upset the senator. His most pressing concern was once more for the German vote. His countrymen, or rather the influence that he might exert over them, had given him whatever political strength he possessed; Greeley's nomination would severely test their loyalty to their supposed leader. As he pointed out to the editor, "when the convention opened, we had nearly the whole German vote with us. . . . When we came out of that Convention, that force was almost entirely lost to us." At that time, his was the only German paper in the country to have come out for the ticket; in view of Greeley's past as a protectionist and prohibitionist, it was doubtful whether this trend could be reversed.[36]

The events of the next few weeks were hardly calculated to cheer up Schurz. The German community received the Cincinnati nominations with scorn; correspondents in various parts of the country warned the senator that the German vote could not be held for Greeley, and despite occasional dissenters like Koerner, he had a hard time keeping even his own newspaper in line. Advising Preetorious to stress the fact that Greeley was better than Grant, he nevertheless cautioned him not to engage in polemics with those of different opinion.[37]

The nominee himself sincerely sought to secure his critic's support. In a prompt answer to Schurz's letter, Greely pointed out that he had expected to back Adams or Davis "under circumstances scarcely dissimilar from yours." Admitting that the Germans disliked him, he attributed their opposition not to his stand on protection but to his endorsement of total abstinence and expressed the conviction that sober second thought would bring about good relations. Schurz petulantly replied that it was not primarily abstinence, nor even the tariff, that annoyed the Germans, but the appearance of a political deal. Correcting this impression would help materially. Greeley continued to plead for understanding and, after some further correspondence, in which Schurz hinted strongly that the nominee ought to decline but also suggested renewed emphasis on civil service reform, the New Yorker finally wrote an acceptance letter generally in accord with Schurz's wishes.[38]

Nevertheless, many of the leading Liberals in the country did not abandon hope that Greeley's decision might yet be reversed. Godkin was so incensed about the editor's nomination that he proposed a meeting of reformers in his New York home immediately after the Republican convention in Philadelphia to consult about further action. Sumner's friend Edward Atkinson, the liberal economist, also thought that another candidate might yet shunt the protectionist aside, and Schurz seemed to agree. Refusing to endorse Greeley in public, the general began to prepare for another meeting.[39]

Their opponents' discomfiture delighted the regular Republicans. "There is nothing more agreeable than to find reason to believe that our estimate of a public man has been less favorable than his merits deserve," gloated the *New York Times*. Conceding that Schurz's speech at the convention had been "worthy of the extraordinary enthusiasm with which he is regarded by men of unquestionable ability," it admitted that his behavior at Cincinnati seemed to have been "reasonably free from those base influences which cast suspicion on the whole movement." The *Missouri Democrat* quoted articles written by Bowles about Schurz's grief and his doleful piano playing on the night of the nomination, and the *Bellatristisches Journal* pointedly remarked that if he had been honored with the chairmanship of the convention because he was a German, his subsequent fate was typical of the treatment intended for his countrymen. The President, certain that the Greeley candidacy would fail, predicted that the Democrats would refuse to endorse the ticket.[40]

Grant proved a bad prophet. After he himself was triumphantly renominated on June 5, the Democrats, meeting in Baltimore five weeks later, swallowed their distaste. Despite some opposition, they accepted the Liberal ticket. Only a few die-hards refused to go along and organized a separate slate. It was said that in far-off Africa, Dr. Livingstone refused to believe the news when Stanley told him.[41]

In the meantime, the dissatisfied Liberals had sought in earnest to replace their nominee with somebody else. Inviting their sympathizers to a conference at the Fifth Avenue Hotel in New York, Schurz, Cox, Bryant, David A. Wells, Oswald Ottendorfer of the New York *Staats-Zeitung*, and Jacob Brinckerhoff asked them to "take such action as the situation of things may require." Some one hundred participants from twenty states attended. Nevertheless, despite considerable sentiment for a new nomination, late at night Schurz squelched this movement. Believing that Greeley, of whose acceptance by the Democrats he was certain, was the only candidate able to beat Grant at this stage, he delivered a rousing speech in favor of the editor, who was promptly endorsed. Godkin refused to follow suit and finally campaigned for Grant; Sumner, after some initial hesitation, promised his support but left for Europe shortly afterward.[42]

The 1872 campaign was not a happy period for Schurz. Shortly before the Fifth Avenue Hotel conference, he had been invited to attend the German Sängerfest in St. Louis. Because of the artistic nature of the occasion, he had hopes that Margarethe, always interested in music, might come with him. But, stubborn as ever, she refused to go to the city she disliked so much. Her husband mildly chided her for missing an event she might have enjoyed; then he accompanied her to the steamer that was to take her and the children once more to Europe. She certainly was not a dependable helpmate.[43]

Then there was the problem of Greeley. The "White Hat," as he was called, was opinionated, quixotic, and erratic. Given to impulsive campaigns, he had joined the Liberal crusade because of his loathing for corruption, his enmity for Conkling, and his strong interest in amnesty. However, his book on the Civil War had been severely critical of Schurz and the Eleventh Corps at Chancellorsville; he had long been known for his passionate advocacy of protection and had never been a prominent supporter of civil service reform. It was therefore necessary for the senator to have a personal interview with him, and in the second week of July, Schurz came to New York to iron things out. In a confidential chat, he managed to reach an agreement of sorts with the editor, who had already written him a letter promising to implement civil service legislation by insisting on the one-term principle for the presidency. Schurz was beginning to feel a bit more optimistic about the ticket's chances.[44]

He started the campaign on July 22 at Temple Hall in St. Louis. Stressing the alleged corruption of the Grant regime, he now came out in public for Greeley and the Liberal Republican party. The President's policy would never close "the bloody chasm" between North and South; carpetbag rule was utterly corrupt, and no Ku Klux laws would ever lead to reconciliation. Pronouncing Grant's civil service commission and policies a sham, he contrasted them with Greeley's letter to him. He even accused the President of having tried to win him over to the projected annexation of Santo Domingo with offers of patronage, and while admitting that he would have preferred a revenue reformer to a protectionist, Schurz asserted that once in power, Greeley would be constrained to act in accordance with the platform. Reminding his listeners that he had been a faithful Republican since the beginning of his public life, he declared that the present regular organization was not the Republican party to which he had given his allegiance. Because he had come to this country to enjoy the blessings of republican government and to live in the moral pride of a free man, he could not sacrifice both to a party which had been false to itself. Moreover, the Liberal platform proved that the new party had supplanted the old organizations. A program endorsing the Reconstruction amendments and civil liberties was hardly that of the old proslavery Democracy! Even the critical *Harper's Weekly* characterized the speech as an address possessing "the independence, sincerity, and ability" which distinguished all his discourses. But in keeping with the prevailing trends, it ridiculed his attempt to make Horace Greeley palatable to the electorate.[45]

From St. Louis, Schurz traveled to North Carolina to preach his doctrine of reconciliation. Greatly encouraged by his welcome, he noted that old rebels were singing Union songs. Then he began reminiscing. How much time had passed since the war! He continued his efforts in the Midwest, and wherever he went, in Illinois, in Indiana, in Ohio, he faced the same grueling schedule. Rising early to reach the towns in which he was billed to speak, he was welcomed by brass bands, greeted with shouts for addresses both in English and German, and hardly given time to eat. But the good reception the Germans gave him reassured him. Perhaps their distaste for voting for Greeley might yet be overcome.[46]

Because of the senator's prominence in the Liberal movement, the attacks on him were becoming more and more virulent. Incensed about his remarks concerning the President's offers of patronage, the *Missouri Democrat* professed to be surprised that he had not mentioned the incident earlier and in reply reprinted Conkling's sarcastic remark that Schurz must have been considered approachable. The *New York Times*, outraged at his castigation of the carpetbaggers, held his own frequent changes of residence up to scorn, and the Chicago *Inter-Ocean* rehashed the tale of his difficulties in connection with real estate deals in Watertown. "A Story of Overweening and Baffled Ambition," it entitled its revelations, charging that the senator had in effect cheated unsuspecting buyers of his town lots because he did not have a clear title to them. "He settled in Watertown, and has since settled in so many other promising towns that he may be said to have acquired the habit of settling—everything but accounts," it punned. The old accusation that he had spoken during political campaigns for large sums of money was endlessly repeated, and there was little he could do to refute it.

It was again Thomas Nast, however, who delivered the most effective blows. Now picturing Schurz as Richard III, now as a played-out piano player, now as a rider on a Trojan horse in company with Democrats, Klansmen, and Boss Tweed—"Anything to Get In" was the caption of the cartoon—in time he went so far as to show the senator in a coffin in a caricature labeled "A Dead Issue." Shortly afterward, making the most of an article in the *Frankfurter Zeitung* about Schurz's criticism of certain features of American politics, Nast drew the dejected senator at the piano playing "Mein Herz ist am Rhein," with a stern Uncle Sam telling him, "Look here, stranger, there is no law in this country to compel you to stay." Finally, on September 7, under the heading "Carl Schurz and His Victims," the artist showed the senator haunted by Negroes and whites killed and whipped by the Klan.

The *Westliche Post* reprinted some of these criticisms and attempted to answer them. Because it was asserted that Schurz did not dare show himself in Watertown, he made a point of visiting his old home, where he spoke in the public square. According to one of Grant's supporters, who wrote many years later, the crowd was largely apathetic. Nevertheless, he admitted that while he was listening to the senator's speech, "he nearly took me off my feet." Schurz did not say much about Greeley until the end; he concentrated on a general arraignment of the adminis-tration instead.[47]

One of the most difficult problems of the campaign was the reaction of the

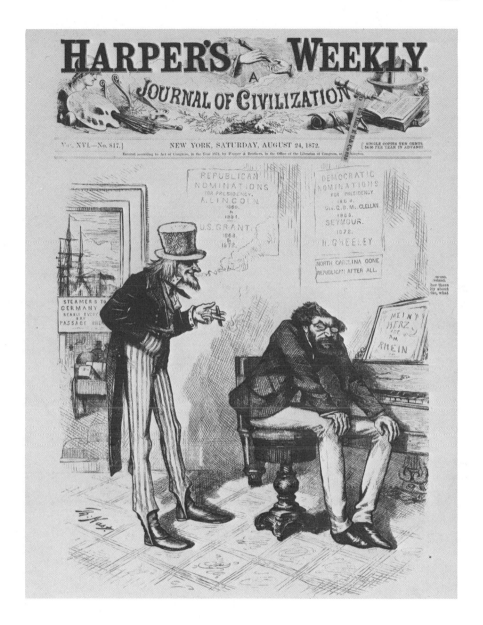

"Carl Is Disgusted With American Politics," Harper's Weekly,
August 24, 1872

"Mr. Carl Schurz and His Victims," Harper's Weekly, *September 7, 1872*

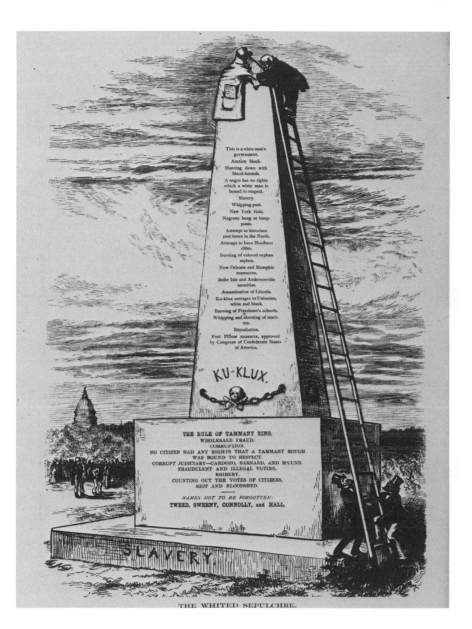

"The Whited Sepulchre," Harper's Weekly, *September 7, 1872*

214

"The Man with the Carpet Bags," Harper's Weekly, *November 9, 1872*

German-Americans. As usual, Schurz was anxious to be considered their spokesman, and administration leaders were afraid of his influence. Was it not conceivable that just as he had once led many of his countrymen into the Republican party, he might now lead them out again? In order to counteract these efforts, the regulars started a newspaper, the *Östliche Post*, in New York, held a convention of German-American United Associations of the United States to endorse Grant, and relied on Franz Sigel to make appeals to his compatriots' loyalty to the Republican party. How successful these measures were is difficult to say; the German press was finally almost evenly divided between Grant and Greeley, and in the end the President's victory was so overwhelming that it is clear the German vote could not have made any difference.[48]

As the campaign went on, not even Schurz's innate optimism could make him believe in ultimate victory. Joseph Pulitzer warned that the outlook in Missouri was terrible. Everything depended on Ohio, where the October elections were usually considered a bellwether for the national contest. But, as General Cox warned, things were not going well in the Buckeye State, and when the returns were in, it was obvious that Greeley would not win. Schurz, who had gone to New York to address his countrymen at Cooper Union, admitted as much to his wife. Nevertheless, he thought he would have to go on to finish up the campaign in Missouri. Thus he came back to his home state, spoke frequently in English and German, and finally had the satisfaction of at least having kept Missouri in the Greeley column. Elsewhere, however, the defeat was so complete that little was left of the Liberal movement. With the exception of Texas and Georgia, the new party carried only a few border states—Missouri, Kentucky, Maryland, and Tennessee. The unfortunate Greeley, whose wife died shortly before the election, was disconsolate. But in a magnanimous note a few weeks before he also passed away, he gratefully acknowledged Schurz's help. "My dear Sir," he wrote in a letter marked "Private forever," "I wish I could say with what an agony of emotion I subscribe myself Gratefully yours, HORACE GREELEY."

Hardly surprised at the outcome, Schurz sought to defend himself for his role in the debacle. Taunted by Godkin for his part at Cincinnati, he explained his reasons for not having taken a stronger stand there. He had been overconfident and did not wish to appear too prominent in the choice of a candidate. Later on in June, a new nominee would only have split the ticket. To Horace White, however, who also felt the sting of defeat, he was more plainspoken. The result "could not have been more unfortunate," he admitted. Nevertheless, he felt it was necessary to continue the fight for civil service and revenue reform, honesty in government, and an end to Reconstruction. He was sure the Democratic party could not be reconstituted; the amendments had finally been generally accepted.[49]

Thus ended the Liberal crusade of 1872. For Schurz it had been a time of supreme effort and of abject defeat. Whether he would ever be able to regain the influence he had lost remained to be seen.

XIV

Independent Liberal Leader

WHEN SCHURZ RETURNED TO WASHINGTON for the 1872–73 session of Congress, he was not in an enviable position. A bolter whose old party had won, an ex-Republican who had not become a Democrat, the organizer of a movement that had been disastrously defeated, he had no idea what to expect. The fact that his wife had again stayed behind in Europe did not make things any easier for him, nor would his sad duty as one of Horace Greeley's pallbearers make his outlook less gloomy.[1]

Yet his career as a liberal leader was by no means over. After all, he was still the most prominent German-American in the country, and sooner or later, his vaunted influence with his countrymen would once again make him politically useful. In addition, he had retained the goodwill and esteem of the Liberal Republicans, many of whom considered him their real head.[2] New opportunities to marshal this host once more might soon arise, for if nineteenth-century American liberalism had any meaning at all, Schurz was its perfect representative. He believed that government interference was generally bad, abandoning this position only to secure for the blacks those fundamental rights deemed essential in liberal society, personal freedom and political liberty. As soon as these aims had seemingly been accomplished, he again opposed all public intermeddling, whether in support of the blacks through civil rights acts, of industry through protective legislation, or of debtors through inflation. His devotion to civil service reform merely spelled out these convictions in an attempt to root out corruption. Devoting all his efforts to the realization of liberal ideals, he could count on influential support far beyond the ethnic community he served.

In view of the troubles affecting the administration, liberal ideals still had considerable appeal. The scandal linking many regular Republicans with the Crédit Mobilier, a scheme of insiders to corner the construction contracts for the Union Pacific Railroad, was a case in point. Many members of Congress had readily accepted stocks of the company at favorable prices; as Schurz wrote to Margarethe, Grant's followers seemed to have dealt themselves more severe blows than the Liberals had ever been able to give them. An independent comeback was certain.

Then came the salary grab, a measure raising not only the President's compensation, but also that of members of Congress. Many of its beneficiaries ostentatiously refused to accept the increase; the senator, who had voted against the bill, at first wanted to let matters be, lest he embarrass colleagues whom he respected. But then the outcry in the country was so great that like many others he had to return the extra money to the treasury at once. The Grant regime seemed to be collapsing of its own weight; anything the Liberals might say would only slow things down.[3]

To reassert leadership in the Liberal cause was simple. Many of his fellow independents had never been as committed to radical Reconstruction as Schurz, so that they could appreciate his renewed opposition to further Reconstruction measures. If this attitude merely highlighted his practical abandonment of the ideal of racial harmony he had once championed, it was nevertheless fully in keeping with the opinions of most Liberals. He forcefully denounced federal efforts to uphold the radical regime in Louisiana. At the same time, he attacked corruption by speaking effectively in favor of ousting Senator Alexander Caldwell of Kansas, whose election had been secured by bribery.[4]

So weakened did the administration appear that in the spring Charles Francis Adams, Jr., the civic-minded scion of the famous family, as active in public affairs as in business, thought the time had come for the Liberals to issue a manifesto of their faith. Schurz, who had plans to spend the summer in Europe, was not ready for such a move, but Adams was willing to wait for the senator's return in the fall.[5] The Liberal movement was still very much alive.

Schurz had successfully spoken for his Liberal followers, but he did not neglect to mend his fences with the German-Americans. Although his financial problems were once again unsettled and affairs of the *Westliche Post* somewhat tangled, he explained to Preetorius that his wife's inheritance in Germany required his attention. A trip to the old country would not only be pleasant but also would give him much favorable publicity in the German-American press, and late in April, he sailed for Europe.[6]

It had been a long time since he had last seen the fatherland, and much had happened since his previous visit. The country was now unified; business was booming. After rejoining his wife and children in Wiesbaden, where they maintained an apartment, Schurz traveled to the newly annexed provinces of Alsace and Lorraine to see for himself what was going on there; then he took a nostalgic trip to Liblar, and on July 4 he responded handsomely to toasts at a celebration in Munich, which he left to be received by the Austrian foreign minister in Vienna shortly afterward. Full details of his activities in American newspapers were bound to impress his countrymen back home.

However, his lengthy vacation troubled the senator. He was restless; he did not feel well and was anxious to return to his active life in America. In October, he took passage for New York; only this time, he did not sail alone. Except for his younger daughter Marianne, who remained behind to go to school in Germany, his family came with him, and when he arrived in Washington for the new session of Congress, for once he was able to enjoy domestic bliss.[7]

It was good for Schurz to have a normal home life again. His elder daughter, Agathe, had become a sought-after belle, and the baby was a source of never-ending pleasure for him. As for Margarethe, she was a complete success in the

Marianne Schurz (Courtesy of the Rutherford B. Hayes Library)

capital. "Missouri is still well represented socially," wrote the St. Louis *Republican*, "for the cheer of Carl Schurz's home, with its unaffected German hospitality, could well represent the hearthstone of a nation, and Miss Schurz, with her modest, unassuming beauty, and her charming unhackneyed culture, could well represent the young ladyhood of the continent. And for the part of Madame Schurz, there is no computing the scope of matronly grace, dignity, and attractiveness that would find in her an inadequate exponent." The senator read his speeches to her; she was well liked by the secretary of state and his family; and as long as her husband was in Washington, she was satisfied.[8]

Politically, too, Schurz's position had improved. Even more than other Liberals, many of whom considered him their leader, he had every reason to be content. Grant was in such difficulty that, in retrospect, the Liberal Republican revolt seemed fully justified. "Isn't the administration very feeble?" asked Sumner. His friend agreed. "The hand of the Lord is upon the unrighteous," he wrote, adding that he believed the Liberals would be able "to render the country some service this winter." And although he did not want to rush matters—he rebuffed Adams, who was still planning a Liberal meeting, perhaps to mark Schurz's return—he soon became wholly absorbed in one of the independents' favorite causes, the struggle against inflation. His unwavering advocacy of hard money was bound to reaffirm his leadership in the movement.[9]

Financial questions had long interested Schurz, and like most of his fellow Liberals, he had always believed that inflation was one of the worst evils that could befall a nation. That America's money supply was grossly inadequate for an expanding industrial society and that deflationary pressures were placing heavy burdens on the indebted farmers did not faze him. "Honest money" became one of his most frequently expressed prescriptions for national health. If later generations might find this position somewhat inflexible, it nevertheless appealed to his strongly anti-inflationist fellow Germans as well as to the Liberals.

It was almost inevitable that the Forty-third Congress should become deeply involved in controversy about the currency. The Panic of 1873 had caused great suffering in the country, and people were looking to Congress for relief. The result was a series of extended debates on financial policy taking up much time and accomplishing very little. On the one hand, greenbackers wanted to issue greater amounts of paper currency; on the other, inflexible financial conservatives—the "liberal" economists—denounced all departures from a strict hard-money course. The question of national banking policy also figured strongly in the congressional arguments, the advocates of free banking frequently clashing with their opponents. Schurz could see only one side of the question: The nation's plighted troth must be preserved; free banking would result in inflation, and inflation was always a delusion. Prosperity would return only when the country pursued a strictly conservative financial policy in accordance with the canons of the liberal economists.

In view of the general interest in the monetary question, the senator's speeches on the subject were widely reported. On January 14, Schurz, attacking the policies of former Secretary of the Treasury George S. Boutwell, made a strong case for the resumption of specie payments. During the following month, he engaged in debate with Indiana inflationist Oliver Morton as well as with Senators Thomas W. Ferry and Logan, and on February 25, he delivered a long speech once more setting forth what he considered the evils of paper money. Quoting copiously from the travels of Marco Polo, he sought to use medieval Chinese precedents to demonstrate the folly of printing paper money; then, citing the experiences of an illiterate Southerner, Old Tatum, who had told him that he did not trust the printed word but was certain that the sun moved about the earth, he attempted to illustrate the importance of relying on standard economic texts. But in spite of applause from the galleries in his debates with Simon Cameron, in spite of his quick replies to Morton, his efforts were unavailing, and the soft-money forces succeeded in passing an inflation bill. Then, when Grant vetoed it, the country was treated to a rare spectacle, as the senator from Missouri supported the administration. The independents fully approved.[10]

His prominence in liberal circles was again highlighted when early in 1874 his friend and fellow liberal Charles Sumner, with whom he had remained close despite his lapse on civil rights, fell seriously ill. The Massachusetts senator had long been suffering from angina pectoris. In the midst of the debates on the inflation bill, to which he was as opposed as his German-American friend, his condition became critical. Telling Schurz that he was afraid he might not be able to support him with a speech on the subject, he left the capitol to go home. Then he suffered a heart attack. Schurz and Judge E.R. Hoar came quickly to his house, only to find him semiconscious. His friends Pierce, Congressman Samuel Hooper, and the journalist Ben:Pearly Poore were already present. Trying hard to make himself understood, the dying senator begged Hoar to take care of his civil rights bill. Shortly after noon, Schurz asked him, "Do you know me?" Sumner opened his eyes and replied, "Yes, but I do not see you." Schurz left the room for a short time; when he returned, his friend was dead.

The Senate immediately adjourned; the House followed suit. Elaborate ceremonies, never before rendered a senator, were arranged. Sumner's body lay in state in the rotunda; bells tolled as the funeral train brought the coffin back to Boston. Schurz became a prominent member of the committee on arrangements; he also served as one of the pallbearers who accompanied his friend's remains to their final resting place.

He sincerely mourned Sumner's passing. "Nobody knows what I have lost," he wrote to Preetorius. "He was my only friend here and a real friend. In him I have lost a piece of my existence which cannot be replaced." It was therefore only natural that the city government and citizens of Boston, in arranging for a great memorial meeting, should invite Schurz to deliver the eulogy. The entire liberal establishment was certain to be present.

It was a distinguished audience that assembled on April 29 to hear Schurz pay his last tribute to Sumner at Boston's Music Hall. Henry Wadsworth Longfellow, the mayor, the city council, members of the state legislature and of Congress, the judges of the Massachusetts courts—all were there to show their respect for the departed statesman. One of Oliver Wendell Holmes's poems was read, Wendell Phillips spoke, and then it was Schurz's turn. Carefully reviewing Sumner's life and contributions, he praised him for his fearless stand against slavery, for his masterful handling of foreign affairs, and for his unwavering commitment to moral causes. But unlike others, who probably would have used the occasion to plead for the enactment of the civil rights bill, Sumner's last wish, Schurz, who opposed the measure, emphasized the fallen senator's independence—his refusal to be bound by party ties. It was good liberal doctrine and, according to the Boston *Advertiser*, the speech was "universally accepted as a just, noble and eloquent tribute." *Harper's Weekly* commented that it proved its author had earned another term in the Senate. His independence and eloquence were needed in Washington.[11]

The Missouri legislature, however, was not convinced. In appealing to his liberal and German supporters throughout the country, Schurz had not always pleased the voters of his home state. His financial arguments, for example, may have delighted his liberal friends in the East, but his constituents in the West thoroughly disapproved of them. The elections of 1874 would decide the composition of the legislature that would have to reelect him, and as time went on the chances of his success, never too good after the Missouri Democrats' return to power, dwindled even further. Many a former supporter who liked his independent stand now repudiated his hard-money approach. After all, the West with its many debt-ridden farmers was the citadel of inflation sentiment, so that his debates with Western senators like Morton, Ferry, and Logan did not increase his popularity in Missouri. Moreover, although it had been Schurz himself who had made possible the return of the Bourbons to active politics, the arch-conservatives, demanding full allegiance to the Democratic party, could never forgive his refusal to abandon his insistence on independent Liberal Republicanism.[12]

Although Schurz, thoroughly disillusioned, professed not to care, his friends were unwilling to give up without a fight. The political situation in the state that year was peculiar; an independent ticket was being formed, and, just as the Democrats had done in 1870, the Republicans were preparing to give it their tacit support. Missouri independents differed from those in the East, especially on financial questions; if successful, however, they might reelect the senator after all. That he would accept the honor was considered certain, and on May 7, the St. Louis *Republican* in effect launched his campaign in a two-and-a-half-column article. Arguing that he would be in a good position to serve the people because of his lack of ties to either party machine, it insisted that the issue was popular government and the fight against monopoly, a struggle for which the senator was particularly well suited.

Schurz immediately disavowed the article—it was unauthorized, he said—yet he was not at all averse to making an attempt to retain his seat. Cooperation with the Republicans and local independents was his only hope, and although his influence with the latter had dwindled because of his monetary views, he could still appeal to the German vote. As the *Republican* pointedly emphasized, the Republicans ought to make common cause with the senator. Without the Germans, they would never have been able to organize a Republican party in Missouri in the first place.[13]

Unfortunately, just at this time Schurz came down with a fever. Plagued by intermittent headaches, he could not even attend the daily Senate sessions, much less devote time to his reelection. And although Grosvenor warned him that unless he wanted to make a political hermit, a "Simeon Styletes" of himself, his presence in Missouri was essential, he decided to take a few weeks off and seek to regain his health at the beach. He had always enjoyed sea bathing. Consequently, after the adjournment of Congress, he did not go home but took a vacation at Narragansett instead.[14]

Late in July, when he finally returned to St. Louis, he still seemed to have some chance. Some Republicans were wooing him; the local independents were preparing a state convention; and the Democrats adopted a platform of repudiation and protection. Perhaps he might yet recoup his political fortunes. But somehow or other not even his habitual optimism was of much help. Because of the currency issue his Liberal connections were no longer of much use in Missouri, not even with the state's independents. Moreover, he lacked his customary energy. That Margarethe, who as usual had remained in the East, was again giving him trouble with her jealousy did not make things any easier for him.[15]

Finally, in September 1874 a group of local independents supported by the Republicans launched the Missouri People's party. Calling for control of the railroads, an end to corruption, and strict economy in government, it nominated a well-known former Liberal, William Gentry, for governor. Many of the Grangers endorsed the ticket, and despite the party's demand for an end to contraction of the currency, Schurz began to campaign for it. The move was his only hope for success.

As usual, he sought support from liberals and Germans. Notwithstanding the currency issue, the liberal independents' dislike of radical Reconstruction still had a great appeal in the former slave state. Accordingly, when on September 2 the senator started campaigning at the Temple in St. Louis, he emphasized the evils of Grant's Southern policy. The recent attempt of Louisiana White Leagues to displace the Republican government of William P. Kellogg by force, with its sequel of federal intervention, furnished him with a pretext. Calling for an end to such tactics, he charged that the New Orleans carpetbag government had been installed by fraud. But that was not all. Totally oblivious of the real plight of the blacks, all his assertions to the contrary notwithstanding, he tried to make capital out of his refusal to support the civil rights bill. The measure had been brought forward "by the dearest friend I ever had . . . a man whose memory I shall never cease to cherish and revere," he said; nevertheless, he felt compelled to oppose it. Integration in the public schools would only harm the blacks because prevailing prejudice would lead to the closing of public schools in the South; if the freedmen wanted to assert their political clout, let them follow the example of the foreign born and distribute their votes among the two parties. Yet although he succeeded in drawing large crowds in the ensuing campaign, his task was hopeless. The Democrats won the legislature by a substantial majority, and his days in the Senate were numbered.[16]

The question of what to do after his retirement would now have to be faced. Mindful of Margarethe's dislike of St. Louis, he was looking for employment elsewhere. Toying with the idea of writing a history of the United States, he briefly considered selling his shares in the *Westliche Post* and turning to his Massachusetts acquaintances for help in establishing himself in New England. Nothing came of the idea; for the time being he simply resumed his lecturing on a trip to the Midwest and the Northeast. If Margarethe was jealous again, he was unable to humor her.[17]

His last months in the Senate showed that despite his defeat he was still an important spokesman for the liberals. When General de Trobriand in full uniform led a unit of soldiers into the Louisiana state house to restore order by ejecting Democratic claimants who had previously helped to throw out their Republican opponents, Schurz seized the opportunity to denounce military interference with the legislature as a portent of the death of democratic government. And his vote against the civil rights bill again highlighted his total abandonment of his former radical views in favor of his present insistence on noninterference.[18]

His liberal admirers appreciated his services, and notwithstanding the hopelessness of the cause, several newspapers and periodicals throughout the country were still calling for his reelection. "Our candidate for the Senate" was the headline of an article in the St. Louis *Republican* emphasizing that Schurz had occupied his seat with credit "to his State, the German element and to himself." Pointing out that the Democrats' sincerity could be tested by their magnanimity in reelecting the famous senator, the liberal New York *Evening Post* was one with the *Nation*, which said, "If the Missouri legislature substitutes for him one of the ignorant and obscure or ignoble busybodies or intriguers who now so often play the game called 'a senate election,' it will not only be a serious injury to the country, but as serious a disaster as could befall the party. . . ." The New York *Staats-Zeitung* agreed, but of course the Bourbons who controlled the state legislature could not be swayed. Without any hesitation, they repudiated the Liberal who had done so much to restore their political rights and elected Francis M. Cockrell, a former Confederate general, to his seat. Much as Schurz's defeat dismayed his supporters—the St. Louis *Republican* wrote that he had held the attention of the country as no man had done since the days of Webster, Clay, Benton, and Calhoun—his senatorial career was over. But his reputation as a liberal leader remained, strengthened if anything by his acrid remarks in the closing days of the session about the evils of the protective tariff.[19]

Although no longer a senator, Schurz was no more disheartened than after the 1872 debacle. He could still rely on his tested sources of strength, the liberals and the Germans, and when after another lecture tour to the Northeast he returned to St. Louis, a splendid reception tendered to him by his friends reminded him of his continued political influence. It was obvious that the independent movement could easily be reactivated.

The occasion for this revival arose in New York, where Schurz had traveled to accompany Margarethe to Europe—she had stayed in the East because she could not be persuaded to overcome her dislike for St. Louis.[20] Just before he sailed, his old Liberal associates, long anxious to use the opportunity to revive the party for the following year's campaign, gave him a lavish dinner. Former Attorney General William M. Evarts, who had been one of Johnson's counsel in the impeachment trial, introduced the guest of honor. Then Schurz spoke. Choosing his words carefully to fit the purpose, he said now that the antislavery struggle was over, new issues had arisen, but neither of the old parties was equipped to deal with them. Problems of the currency, the tariff, and reconciliation of the South required an independent movement. Repeating his call for nonpartisan action on the next day, when the the Germans gave him another dinner at Delmonico's and topped it off with a torchlight parade, he called for close cooperation between immigrants and natives. That his political career was not ended was so obvious that he was already entertaining visions of nominating a presidential candidate to his liking and entering the cabinet.[21]

The honors and attention paid to him in Europe further increased his political availability. Embarking for Germany with his wife and children, he met Margarethe's family in Hamburg and visited its splendid estate, Forsteck, near Kiel. Then he received an invitation from the presiding officers of the Reichstag and the Prussian Landtag to come to Berlin, where he was feted at the Hotel St. Petersbourg at a banquet attended by many of Germany's leading parliamentary and scientific figures, including the pathologist Rudolph Virchow and the historian Theodor Mommsen. And these honors assured him of a good reception elsewhere. Traveling to London in June to meet John Bright, Sir Charles Dilke, and other prominent Britons, he went to the House of Commons and heard Disraeli speak. He received considerable publicity, and the whole experience—the majesty of the mother of parliaments, the magnificent vista from the terrace of the House—made a deep impression on him. Then he returned to the Continent to take Margarethe to Switzerland for a rest cure. Americans could not fail to notice how prominent the former senator was.[22]

He did not have to wait long for proof of this fact. The liberal independents, anxious to secure his help with the Germans, believed that he ought to return. A crucial campaign was to be waged in Ohio, where the Democrats had nominated a greenbacker, William Allen, for governor. His opponent was the Republican reformer Rutherford B. Hayes, whose ideas in some respects were not too different from Schurz's, although of course he was much more conventional, had been a Whig, and had never left the Republican party. And the German-Americans allegedly once again held the key to the election.

Under these circumstances, several Liberals—Halstead, Adams, Charles Nordhoff, and young Henry Cabot Lodge—decided to call Schurz back. "Enclosed is a note from Halstead of some interest," Adams wrote him. "Its views seem to me crisp and sound. Allen's election will be our destruction; his renomination on the ragmoney issue was a defiance and insult to us, and his success would render us contemptible. . . . The weapon with which to kill him is the German vote . . . , and you are its holder. You must come back in time to strike in just at the close with all the freshness and prestige of your recent German reception." Although at first inclined to reject this invitation, Schurz finally accepted it. The pull of ambition was too strong. Breaking off his vacation, he sailed on the *Pomerania* in September.[23]

His return heartened both Republicans and Liberals. Delighted at the news, Hayes suggested that he speak in a number of crucial cities. Henry Adams, Charles Francis's famous literary brother, thought that if Schurz succeeded in beating the inflationists in Ohio, the independents would be able to control the next presidential election. And the general did not disappoint his backers. Delivering pointed speeches in several cities against a weakening of the currency, he was well received, especially by the Germans. "The coming of Mr. Schurz is an event of prime importance," commented the *New York Times*. "He reaches the one doubtful element—the German Liberals—who need some good strong excuse for abandoning their Democratic allies and returning to the Republican camp. Wherever Mr. Schurz is heard in Ohio he is making votes for Hayes." That this assessment was not exaggerated was shown in October, when Allen was beaten by a narrow margin. Schurz, "that crout-eating Greeleyite," was widely credited with his defeat. "I got home this morning, serene in the knowledge that 'old Bill Allen's grey and gory scalp was safely dangling at your girdle," exulted Adams. Schurz modestly acknowledged the fact.[24]

After the close of the Ohio campaign, Schurz rented an apartment at 40 West 72d Street in New York. Margarethe was pregnant again and not feeling well; he wanted to be with her, but she could not be induced to come to Missouri. He was delighted that she had made up her mind to follow him across the ocean; at first, she had been looking for an apartment in Hamburg, while he had sadly been contemplating a lonely life in St. Louis. He kept busy writing articles for his newspaper and going on speaking tours, but he did not for a moment abandon his

ultimate purpose of leading and directing the independents in 1876. The victory in
Ohio had established his primacy among those Liberals planning to make a
comeback in the presidential year. Perhaps they might yet witness the realization
of their hopes of 1872; only, he did not plan to summon another mass convention.
The disaster of Cincinnati must not be repeated.

Together with other independents—Henry and Charles Francis Adams, Jr.,
Henry Cabot Lodge, Samuel Bowles, and Horace White, to mention but a
few—Schurz was making preparations for the calling of a conference "to devise
means to prevent the campaign of the Centennial Year from becoming a mere
scramble of the politicians for the spoils." The political situation in 1876 seemed
ripe for renewed reform action. Seriously weakened by the scandals of the Grant
administration, the Republicans were divided between the badly compromised
Stalwart backers of the President, their equally tarnished Half-Breed opponents
favoring James G. Blaine, and the reform element. The Democrats, certain to
make the most of these difficulties, had troubles of their own because of the
greenback issue.

Schurz sought to take avantage of this situation by persuading both parties to
endorse a reformer, preferably the elder Charles Francis Adams. A meeting of
independents might issue a call to demonstrate their strength and influence the two
major parties. In the beginning of the new year, however, Secretary of the
Treasury Benjamin H. Bristow, the one reformer still in the administration,
seemed to be a stronger candidate. After conferring with Bristow's emissaries in
New York, Schurz consulted with Lodge, who went to Washington to sound out
the secretary. Henry Adams, too, wrote the general a long letter in support of
Bristow, and Schurz addressed Bristow directly, strongly pleading with him
not to resign; Schurz assured him that the people needed a representative in the
administration. But although he stayed in the cabinet, the secretary remained
noncommittal.[25]

The active candidacy of James G. Blaine, the speaker of the House, complicated the situation. A magnetic leader who had a devoted following, the speaker
was a formidable challenger. Yet Schurz thoroughly distrusted him. Believing him
to be totally unreliable, he exercised all his influence to counteract Blaine's gains.
And when the independents discovered that the speaker had been involved in
dubious transactions concerning Little Rock & Fort Smith Railroad bonds, they
spared no effort in torpedoing his candidacy.[26]

Late in February, still another hopeful submitted his claims. In a seventeen-
page letter from Alfred E. Lee, his private secretary, Rutherford B. Hayes, the
governor of Ohio for whom Schurz had campaigned in the fall, set forth his
qualifications. Lee pointed out that it was a pity that Hayes and Schurz had never
met; sharing a common outlook, they both deplored corruption, believed in hard
money, and sought fair treatment for the South. While Hayes was not seeking the
presidency, he was nevertheless precisely the man for whom the liberals were

looking. At first Schurz did not respond favorably; nevertheless, the letter evidently made an impression on him.[27]

Shortly afterward, the reform cause received a new boost by the discovery that the secretary of war, William W. Belknap, had accepted bribes in the assignment of Indian agency concessions. Only his hasty resignation saved him from impeachment. Bowles urged Schurz to issue the call for the planned independent conference at once.[28]

At this point personal tragedy interfered with Schurz's political activities. While lecturing in upstate New York, he was called to Monee because his father was desperately ill. Hurrying to Illinois, he comforted the old man and was assured that his father was better. As soon as he came home, however, he received the sad news of Christian Schurz's death. With Margarethe's confinement imminent—she had been unable to walk the stairs for months—he could not leave her to attend the funeral. Then, on March 5, his second son, Herbert, was born. It was a difficult delivery; Margarethe never recovered, and on March 15 she too died.

Her husband was heartbroken. "For grief like this there is no real consolation," he wrote to F. W. Bird. "It must be lived out. The loss of the wife of one's youth is unlike any other bereavement. It is the loss of the best part of one's life." Although his marriage with its frequent separations had been a stormy one, it had been reasonably successful. As Margarethe's sister pointed out, in spite of all difficulties, Mrs. Schurz had devoted herself wholly to her husband and he had always understood and supported her.[29] Left widowed with four children at the age of forty-seven, he felt terribly lonely. He would never marry again.

In spite of his bereavement, Schurz continued to take part, indeed a leading part, in the presidential campaign. As Bowles wrote him, the best service his friends could render him at this time was to involve him in public affairs. Pulling himself together, the general responded favorably, and with the help of Lodge and Brooks Adams, drew up a draft of an invitation to a conference of independents. Eventually the call, signed by himself, William Cullen Bryant, President Theodore D. Woolsey of Yale, Governor Alexander H. Bullock of Massachusetts, and Horace White, asked selected liberals to meet on May 15 in New York in order to "secure the election of men . . . whose character and ability will satisfy the exigencies of our present situation and protect the honor of the American name."

Schurz spelled out his purposes in a letter to Bristow. Certain that spoilsmen would dominate the forthcoming conventions, he wanted to make it clear to them that unless they nominated a reformer they would be defeated. Though he remained noncommittal until after the conventions, he indicated that he would be happy to cooperate with his old Republican friends.[30]

The conference finally met on May 15 at the Fifth Avenue Hotel in New York. Attended by some two hundred leading reformers, it was an impressive assembly.

President Woolsey was in the chair; Lodge called the meeting to order; Mark Hopkins, David A. Wells, Dorman Eaton, William G. Sumner, Peter Cooper, Francis A. Walker, Godkin, Bryant, and the Adams brothers were all present. Schurz, whom the independents called "the master spirit of the occasion," wrote an "Address to the People" deploring corruption and calling for civil service reform, hard money, and reconciliation with the South, which was adopted on May 16. Instead of endorsing any one candidate, the conference, in the words of Schurz's address, pledged itself to support only such nominees as "deserved not only the confidence of honest men, but also the fear and hatred of the thieves."[31]

The Fifth Avenue Hotel meeting has been criticized for its failure to take decisive action, but it materially furthered Schurz's career. Again occupying the limelight, he was ready to be courted by the leading presidential contenders. The hopes of James G. Blaine dwindled, and both major parties nominated candidates not uncongenial to the reformers. The Republicans at Cincinnati chose Hayes, and the Democrats at St. Louis, Samuel J. Tilden, famed for his exposure of the Tweed Ring. Although the reformers subsequently divided, some endorsing the Ohioan and others the New Yorker, Schurz did not find it difficult to make up his mind.[32]

The general was strongly attracted to Hayes. While it was later charged that he had made some derogatory remarks about the governor in New York, his correspondence with the nominee's secretary and his dislike for the Democratic vice presidential candidate, the inflationist Thomas A. Hendricks, probably predisposed him toward the Republican from the outset. At any rate, while he convened the executive committee appointed by the Fifth Avenue Hotel conference for consultation, he personally addressed a letter to Hayes in which he urged him in his acceptance letter to come out strongly for civil service reform and hard money. And just to make sure that Hayes would respond favorably, a few days later he reminded him that the Germans would particularly welcome such a declaration. Already fully cognizant of the importance of the German-American vote, the Hayes forces were sure to listen.[33]

It was not long before Schurz came out publicly for the Republican nominee. In order to escape the heat in New York, he had taken his children with him to spend a few weeks with the Tiedemanns at Fort Washington, Pennsylvania. On July 1, however, he had to travel to St. Louis. Passing through Columbus, he met Hayes for the first time. The governor had come to the station, and apparently the interview was reassuring to Schurz. When the general reached Missouri, he wrote a stong condemnation of the Democratic platform in the *Westliche Post*. Then, much to the Republicans' satisfaction, he spoke in the same vein. "Senator Schurz delivered a very firm address last evening—" one of Hayes's St. Louis friends wrote to him on July 4. "His sympathies are with us—his positive cooperation absolutely necessary. Reform is a political bonanza to the German element of our

The Fifth Avenue Hotel Conference, May 16, 1876 (Courtesy of Library of Congress)

great city as well as of the whole country. We must oblige it to the fullest extent.''[34]

Hayes took this advice to heart. Inviting the general to help him draft his letter of acceptance—a bid that was quickly accepted—he followed most of Schurz's suggestions, especially in strongly emphasizing civil service reform. Independent and German support was essential for victory.

The general was delighted. ''Unless I am very much mistaken the Cincinnati Convention has nominated our man without knowing it,'' he explained to Charles Francis Adams, Jr. The letter was all the reformers could desire, and while he did not think it necessary for the independents as a group to endorse either one candidate or the other, he himself was perfectly satisfied with Hayes. Many of his friends disagreed. Adams remained unconvinced and his brother Henry vowed that he would never follow Schurz's lead again.[35]

That the German vote would be as important as that of the liberals was clear to both parties. In June when they nominated Tilden at St. Louis, the Democrats made a major effort to secure it; naturally Schurz, then still uncommitted, refused to cooperate. When he endorsed Hayes, his former friend Ottendorfer in the New York *Staats-Zeitung* accused him of having turned his back on his past and of having betrayed his convictions. Of course, the general did not permit this attack to go unanswered. In a public letter to the paper he struck back by stressing Ottendorfer's own inconsistencies. Had not Hayes come out strongly for civil service reform and would not a Democratic victory after so many years of Republican rule merely result in a scramble for offices? Hayes and the Republican platform offered guarantees for a conservative financial policy; the Democrats, on the other hand, proposed to repeal the Resumption Act, a measure both Schurz and Ottendorfer, in spite of initial reservations, had always supported.[36] As both hard money and civil service reform appealed to the Germans, the letter was an effective defense.

For the remainder of the campaign, the German vote was rarely forgotten. In August, the Republicans received urgent calls from Wisconsin that German support must be secured; a visit from Carl Schurz ''would do more than anything else to this end.'' The warning was repeated in October, when a wartime companion wrote to Hayes that the Germans were lukewarm. For the good of the cause, ''Generals *Schurze* and *Bristow* ought to be sent to the German districts without delay. They could do the most good there.''[37]

The general made the most of this situation. Just as in 1860 when he had capitalized on his appeal to his countrymen, so in 1876 he again stressed his usefulness in cornering the ethnic vote. Campaigning energetically in the Midwest, he advised Hayes that the German vote was crucial and that his own influence with his compatriots could be increased if the candidate followed his advice. According to Schurz, the Germans were not particularly interested in the Southern question; what they wanted was reform, so that the civil service aspects of the campaign ought to be stressed. Hayes generally agreed; frequently corresponding with Schurz and seeking his advice, he met him several times and established a close working relationship with him.

Nevertheless, there was trouble. Zachariah Chandler was the chairman of the Republican National Committee; a loyal member of the administration, he was naturally hostile to the leader of the independents. Moreover, he persisted in the custom of levying assessments on Republican office-holders, a practice Schurz never failed to denounce. At one time he threatened to quit unless the tactic were repudiated; he never ceased to protest against it, but Hayes was unable to satisfy him. It was difficult for the governor to keep both Schurz and Chandler contented, yet he desperately needed both.[38]

In his campaign speeches, Schurz stressed the same points he had made in his letter to Ottendorfer. Opening the canvass on August 26 at Cleveland, he spoke for two hours at the Globe Theater, largely on civil service reform and financial rectitude, and on the 31st, he repeated his call for reform in Cincinnati. Alleging that Lincoln, seeing a crowd of office-seekers, had predicted that the spoilsmen would endanger the republic more than the rebels, he asserted that Hayes would be able to carry out reforms that Tilden would be unable to accomplish. He boasted of his reputation for having done something to awaken the popular conscience against the prevailing demoralization and insisted that the time for fulfillment of the promises for civil service reform had come. Continuing in similar fashion elsewhere in Ohio and Indiana, he hoped to win over these October states, but when election day arrived, the results were inconclusive. The Republicans carried Ohio and the Indiana legislature by a small margin; the Democrats, the governorship in Indiana. Nevertheless, he immediately took credit for the success, however small. "I am glad to hear that the Germans did well in Ohio," he wrote to Hayes, expressing the hope that they would respond as well in New York, where he went next. After speaking repeatedly in the metropolitan area, both in English and in German, at the end of October he left for Missouri. The Germans would be as "sound as ever," he assured Hayes.[39]

In spite of his seeming optimism, ever since the summer he had not been certain about the outcome of the campaign. In view of German defections—Judge Stallo, Gustave Koerner, Friedrich Hassaurek, and several important German papers supported Tilden—to say nothing of the Republicans' general weakness, his caution was not surprising, and he shared his fears with Hayes. But not even he anticipated the actual results.[40]

When on November 7 the election was held, it appeared at first that Tilden had won. Carrying the solid South as well as a number of Northern states, including New York, Indiana and New Jersey, he seemed to have a safe majority of the popular as well as of the electoral vote. But on the next day, doubts about the outcome began to arise. Because the results in the three Southern states still under Republican rule, South Carolina, Louisiana, and Florida, were being contested by local returning boards, Zachariah Chandler, as Republican chairman, boldly claimed that Hayes had 185 electoral votes and was the victor. In effect, the

Ohioan had 165 uncontested votes to the New Yorker's 184. If he could secure all twenty disputed ones, he would obtain the necessary majority; if Tilden could secure but one, the victory would be his.

Like others, Schurz was at first quite certain that the cause was lost, but while he was looking for a house in St. Louis, where he had moved his children into a hotel, he had second thoughts. He immediately wrote to Hayes. Since it looked as if the three doubtful Southern states had voted Republican, he suggested that reputable observers be sent to Louisiana to check on the returning board and the outcome there. "I am sure you are as anxious as I am," he pontificated, "that such a result should not be tainted by any suspicion of unfair dealing."

Hayes replied at once. Could not Schurz himself go to Louisiana? The general, still tied down because of his house hunting, declined, but in an increasingly frequent correspondence with the governor he continued to urge great care lest the title to the presidency be besmirched. Then, after he had found a furnished apartment for his children and his widowed mother, he collaborated with Senator John B. Henderson to suggest a settlement of the dispute by constitutional amendment. There was enough time to pass and rush through the state legislatures an amendment to enable the Supreme Court to settle the matter, he editorialized in the *Westliche Post*. But Hayes, to whom he gave the same advice, was only mildly interested. Although the governor thought the idea was a good one, he had already convinced himself that he was "justly and legally entitled to the Presidency."[41]

Schurz's proposal for a settlement was only one of many. Stalwart Republicans wanted the president of the Senate, a Republican, to count the votes; loyal Democrats insisted that the Democratic House decide. It was not until the end of January that a compromise was arranged that provided for an electoral commission of fifteen, taken equally from the House, Senate, and Supreme Court. Although Schurz did not think the proposal was as good as his, while it was still pending he urged the reluctant Hayes to accept it as one legal way out of the difficulty. With many of his friends demanding that he advise the governor to yield peacefully— the inauguration of a Democrat would be better than securing the presidency by dubious means, they said—he considered the compromise a good way out. Constantly calling for an untainted result, he was very anxious, as one of the probable members of the new cabinet, for Hayes's victory. His endorsement of the electoral commission was easy to understand.[42]

Even before the commission had been set up, Hayes's supporters had made certain arrangements with Southern industrial and railroad interests anxious to secure some federal support. Generally former Whigs, they distrusted the Northern Democrats, and with their help and a series of bargains involving Republican promises to withdraw the remaining federal troops from the South, a final compromise was arranged. The verdict of the electoral commission was strictly partisan. The eight Republicans favored Hayes and the seven Democrats Tilden, but the latter, more particularly those from the South, anxious to prevent violence and encouraged by Hayes's independent backers, refrained from filibustering in the House, and Hayes was at last seated. Yet the result was not the untainted solution Schurz had considered essential. The action of the Southern returning boards especially looked highly suspicious.[43]

Nevertheless, the general accepted the result. Convinced that had there been a fair election free from intimidation, not only the disputed states but Mississippi as well would have been in the Republican column because of their large black populations, he considered the outcome just. It was the one favorable development in an otherwise bleak period for him, for he suffered still another personal tragedy when in February his mother also died. "This was the third time that the hand of death knocked at my door during the last twelve months," he wrote to Hayes.[44]

Then the general turned to the consideration of the cabinet, a question which had been on Hayes's mind for several weeks. On January 17, before the electoral commission had even been established, the governor had begun to solicit his friends' views about his inaugural address and his advisers. Schurz did not hesitate to respond. Hard money, civil service reform, reconciliation of the South, and the advocacy of a one-term amendment for the presidency he considered necessary to win the independents' confidence; as for the cabinet, he suggested Evarts for secretary of state, Bristow for the treasury, and several others. But in fact, Hayes really wanted to include the famous German-American in his official family. In February, Murat Halstead launched a campaign on his fellow editor's behalf, Medill and Cox joined in endorsing him, and Grosvenor sought to dispel fears that his friend was impractical. "Circumstances, faults of manner, and the ingenuity of foes, have combined to make Mr. Schurz less truly known than almost any other man in public life," Grosvenor wrote to Cox for transmittal to Hayes. "But it would be a real misfortune . . . if these should deprive Governor Hayes of his practical assistance at Washington. . . ." Praising him as a practical man who knew how to conciliate opponents, he emphasized Schurz's capacity for hard work and close application. The President-elect, favorably impressed with Schurz's stand on civil service reform and finance and undoubtedly mindful of his independent and German-American backing, finally offered him a choice of the Department of the Interior or the Post Office.[45]

The former senator accepted the Interior Department. True, shortly before, he had indicated a preference for secretary of state or treasury and expressed the opinion that the Department of the Interior was not as interesting to one who had never paid much attention to the Indian problem, patents, pensions, and public lands. But now he felt great pride in the appointment. While he thought the postmaster general had to have more familiarity with business details than he had, he hoped to master satisfactorily the affairs of the Interior Department.[46] It was the highest honor that had come to a foreign-born citizen since the days of Albert Gallatin.

Thus Schurz, hard hit by defeat and the death of three of the closest members of his family, by relying on the independents and the German-Americans, succeeded in making a splendid political comeback. If his commitment to human rights had been gravely compromised by his virtual abandonment of the blacks, he had nevertheless survived the political annihilation both friends and foes had expected. He had every reason to be satisfied.

XV

Secretary of the Interior

SCHURZ'S TENURE as Hayes's secretary of the interior unquestionably constituted the pinnacle of his political career. First as senator and then as the first foreign-born cabinet member in seventy years, he had reached the two highest offices open to naturalized citizens. Yet the problems he faced as a member of the new administration were staggering. The attempt to introduce civil service reform was bound to excite hostility. The withdrawal of the troops from Southern state houses would jeopardize the safety of Republicans and blacks. A more enlightened approach to the Indian question was likely to encounter insoluble difficulties, and efforts to conserve the nation's resources were so much ahead of their time that they too would meet with insurmountable obstacles. In addition, the labor unrest engendered by the depression and the country's rapid industrialization would confront the administration with an issue which, with its laissez-faire orientation, it was ill-equipped to understand. Schurz, however, was determined to try.

The new secretary entered upon his duties with high hopes. Delighted with the honor that had come to him, he believed that it afforded him an opportunity finally to apply the principles of the Fifth Avenue Hotel conference.[1] Moreover, he had arrived; his relatives in Hamburg could not fail to be impressed. That his compatriots would welcome his new prominence was self-evident; his position would help him win back his influence with those who had refused to support his return to the Republican party. And although he missed Margarethe, who would have enjoyed the position of a cabinet minister's wife,[2] it was during his stay in Washington that he met a new helpmeet, who, if she did not marry him, nevertheless played an important role in his life for the rest of his days.

Schurz's tenure of office was made more pleasant because of his increasing intimacy with the President. Aside from fundamentally agreeing with Hayes on such issues as civil service reform, Southern policy, and opposition to inflation, the widowed secretary greatly appreciated the President's domestic life, his close relations with his wife and children. Admiring Hayes's even-tempered approach to matters, he believed him to be patriotic and unselfish as well as intelligent. The President in turn considered his secretary of the interior "a gentleman of the purest character . . . an able, patriotic and scholarly statesman," and the two saw a great deal of each other during their four years' association in Washington. Together with William M. Evarts and John Sherman, Schurz was part of an inner circle credited with much more influence than the rest of the cabinet. Hayes so respected his literary skill and political acumen that prior to preparing his veto of the military appropriations bill of 1879, he read it to the secretary for comment and advice; Schurz was a frequent dinner guest at the White House and, to the great

Carl Schurz Playing the Piano for the Hayes Family (Courtesy of National Carl Schurz Association)

amusement of scoffers, often played religious hymns on the President's piano. The first family and Vice President William Wheeler, an enthusiastic hymn singer, did the vocalizing. The real friendship which developed between the two men lasted to the end of Hayes's life.[3]

This close bond grew despite the incessant opposition to Schurz's inclusion in the cabinet. Politically speaking, the appointment caused the President endless trouble. Stalwart senators were outraged when the famous bolter's name was presented to them for ratification; Cameron, Logan, Conkling, and their followers sought to defeat the nomination, and many Half-Breeds were equally unhappy. To be sure, they also criticized the selection of Evarts for secretary of state, to say nothing of the elevation of David M. Key, a Democrat and former Confederate officer, for postmaster general; Schurz, however, incurred their special venom. Pilloried as a visionary with no administrative ability or practical business sense, he was derided as a godless German philosopher, as mercenary as he was fickle. It was even said that as early as 1872 he had bargained for a cabinet position with Horace Greeley. But in spite of these calumnies, he finally won confirmation. That his recent opponent Oswald Ottendorfer of the New York *Staats-Zeitung* interceded with some of his Democratic friends did no harm.[4]

The new cabinet member lost little time preparing for his job. Stopping off in New York on his way to the capital, he received a telegram to come as soon as possible. Enthusiastically complying with the President's request, he took the first available train and arrived in Washington before breakfast on March 4.[5]

He soon met his new colleagues. Most of them were old acquaintances. Secretary Evarts was not really his type—he found him much too dilatory—but the secretary of state shared many of Schurz's political opinions. John Sherman, the new secretary of the treasury, had served in the Senate with Schurz; a foe of soft money, he enjoyed Schurz's trust, which not even controversies about Indian policy with his brother, William, the general, were able to disturb. Charles Devens, the attorney general, was an old fellow soldier who had commanded the extreme right at Chancellorsville. George W. McCrary of Iowa, the secretary of war, Richard Thompson of Indiana, the secretary of the navy, and Postmaster General David M. Key, the Southerner, were less well known to Schurz, but he found it easy to get along with them. In the surviving pictures of the cabinet in session, the stern general with his pince nez, light trousers, dark coat, vest, and bow tie, prominently occupies a chair at the far end of the table opposite the President, with his colleagues sitting in between. After three weeks of close association with them, he was able to write to his children that his relations with the administration could not be better.[6]

Once his appointment had been confirmed, he promptly took up his duties. Early in the afternoon on March 12, after taking the oath of office and attending the first meeting of the cabinet, he arrived at the Interior Department. His predecessor, Zachariah Chandler, introduced him to the heads of the bureaus—

Cabinet of Rutherford B. Hayes (Courtesy of National Carl Schurz Association)

Indian, patent, land, and pensions—as well as to the miscellaneous collection of other officers, and after making some complimentary remarks, the new secretary set to work. Henceforth he could be seen laboring regularly at his desk from nine to five, an hour longer than had been customary, often staying over late at night to catch up with the accumulation of business. He set out to prove that he was no mere visionary, but rather an adept administrator who knew how to direct a complicated organization. Eventually, the *New York Times* admitted that he succeeded in demonstrating that a scholar could be practical.[7]

That Schurz's appointment, though widely criticized, pleased his fellow Germans was not surprising. Their congratulations filled his mail; as one army officer wrote in 1879, "Every real German is proud that in you we have the first representative of our people who has held and is still holding the two highest positions attainable by a naturalized citizen in our country." But not only Schurz received these congratulations; the President, though incessantly criticized for including so notorious a bolter in his cabinet, also heard from many a correspondent praising his choice of the German-American. As Joseph Medill assured him, the appointment had done much to strengthen the administration by reconciling those Germans who had remained hostile during the campaign.[8]

Schurz's independent friends were also pleased. "I am just tickled clear through that you have gone to the head at last," wrote Samuel Bowles. Although he considered the "Louisiana steal" "dreadful," he expressed the opinion that if the Republican party could follow Andrew Jackson's example and "get religion," it might yet cheat the devil. Pierce, Bristow, Lodge, and others made known their delight, and even the Adams family, despite its support for Tilden, was reconciled. As one admirer wrote to the secretary, "What 1872 failed to accomplish, 1876 has realized; as witness your being at the head of the Department of the Interior."[9]

The first problem confronting the President and his cabinet was the Southern question. Having come into office largely as a result of various deals with Southern whites, Hayes did not wait long before withdrawing support from the remaining Republican regimes, which promptly collapsed. His policy was to build up party strength in the South by attempting to win over the dominant race; although this approach was disastrous for the blacks, he convinced himself that they too would benefit by the more relaxed atmosphere he was hoping to create.

Schurz fully supported his chief's Southern policy. Like Hayes, he had long since come to the conclusion that the answer to the race problem in the South was an end to party divisions along the color line; once blacks were found in both political organizations, they would no longer be taken for granted and might use their voting strength for their own benefit. If this analysis overlooked the obvious difficulties confronting the freedmen in an area where one of the two parties was determined to eliminate their political rights altogether, it was nevertheless an idea he tenaciously held and propagated. For this reason, he had long advised Hayes to reiterate in his inaugural address the sentiments for sectional peace included in his letter of acceptance. Although as a good liberal he was not particularly interested in federal help for domestic improvements in the South, one of the terms of the preinaugural bargaining, he continued to plead for the other, an end to government by force. He was even willing to settle the Louisiana problem in the way Vice President Wheeler had arranged matters two years earlier—permitting the radical governor to remain but turning over the legislature to the Democrats. Consequently, when Hayes finally carried out his peaceful policies by withdrawing the troops from the remaining Southern Republican-controlled statehouses—in Louisiana after sending a commission of inquiry to New Orleans—his secretary of the interior was in perfect accord with him. "The Louisiana Commission has vindicated itself," he explained to Pierce. "We acted carefully to avoid ulterior difficulties, and I think the result has justified the means." To his brother-in-law, he boasted that the pacification of the South had been a complete success. That it also meant the end of any real protection for black rights did not seem to occur to him. In view of the fact that the President had received pledges for the fair treatment of the freedmen from the conservative beneficiaries of his measures and that he appointed Frederick Douglass marshal of the District of Columbia, this blindness was understandable.[10]

"Now for civil service reform," Hayes wrote in his diary after he had settled the Southern problem. His secretary of the interior not only shared this interest but became its chief advocate. On March 12, the first full meeting of the cabinet, he was appointed one of the members of a committee—Evarts was the other—to draft a set of civil service rules that were eventually promulgated. Only applicants for the lowest grade who passed a standard examination were to be hired; promotions were to be from within. However, the application of these regulations was left to the individual secretaries.[11]

Schurz, who since slavery had ended considered the reform the remaining great issue of his life, introduced it fully in his department. In effect an unmanageable collection of bureaus, Interior had long been one of the most graft-ridden agencies of the government. Now the secretary, hoping civil service reform and businesslike methods would provide the means, sought to clean it up. Seeking information about possible increased efficiency from his subordinates shortly after he assumed control, he prepared himself carefully. Then, within a few weeks he promulgated rules setting up procedures for enforcing civil service regulations for hiring, firing, and competitive bidding. The President supported him with an order prohibiting the active participation of government employees in political campaigns.[12]

That the heads of the political machines would not take a favorable view of these changes was to be expected. Ben Butler considered civil service reform a political trick; he had long since announced that when George William Curtis and Carl

Schurz were speaking for the Republican party, he would remain in the rear. Roscoe Conkling broke completely with the administration in a fierce struggle for control of the New York Customs House. "When Dr. Johnson defined patriotism as the last refuge of a scoundrel, he was unconscious of the then undeveloped capabilities and uses of the word, 'Reform,'" he declared at the 1877 New York State Republican convention. His opponent, James G. Blaine, no less opposed to any interference with his political organization, for once fully agreed, and Blaine's niece Abigail Dodge, writing in the New York *Tribune* under the pen name of Gail Hamilton, launched a series of bitter attacks on the administration's civil service policy in general and on the secretary of the interior in particular. Schurz became so incensed about her revival of the old accusations of his having been paid excessive amounts for his political speeches that he asked Preetorius to challenge her by offering to pay her ten dollars for every dollar he had received above and beyond the fees due him for expenses. Preetorius complied, but Miss Hamilton did not take up the offer, and unfounded rumors of the secretary's impending resignation frequently appeared in the press.[13]

While Schurz's department unquestionably continued to carry out policies based on the merit principle, the Hayes administration as a whole was unable to do so. Often forced to make political appointments distasteful to reformers, the President even named Schurz's enemy Chauncey I. Filley postmaster of St. Louis. Nevertheless, he regained the reformers' confidence by engaging in his mammoth contest with Conkling about the patronage in New York. Twice thwarted by the Senate, he finally succeeded in replacing Collector Chester A. Arthur and Surveyor Alonzo B. Cornell, under whose management corruption had been flourishing. Yet in view of Secretary Evarts's desire to build up a rival machine in the Empire State, these efforts to end the Conkling organization's grip on the port were not entirely unselfish. Moreover, in the end Cornell was elected governor, while Arthur became president. Thus Schurz's example of civil service reform in the Interior Department was limited. It even laid him open to the charge that he terrorized his employees by constantly inspecting their efficiency reports.[14]

Perhaps the most useful innovation the secretary introduced during his tenure of office was the effort to preserve the national forests. Timber thieves had been playing havoc with the national domain; Schurz instituted measures to control and stop their depredations. Like all his other efforts, however, his policies provoked his opponents to furious attacks. Accused of trying to introduce German methods into free America in total disregard of the needs of frontiersmen for firewood, he was mercilessly castigated in the Senate. "The Secretary of the Interior does not happen to be a native of this country . . . ," said his old enemy Blaine. "He is a native of the Kingdom of Prussia. The Kingdom of Prussia is 15,000 square miles less in extent than the Territory of Montana, and it has a population of 25 million people. Montana with this vast area of mountain gorges and mountain tops has a sparse and adventurous population of 25,000 people . . . and now the Secretary of the Interior, perhaps with the traditions of his young manhood and boyhood, applies to that country the land laws of Prussia, not the land laws of the settled Territories of the United States." Because of the unwillingness of Congress to support him properly—the legislation it finally passed was an open invitation for special interests—it was not until many years later that the secretary finally saw his point of view vindicated by a national conservation policy. [15]

It was in connection with his responsibilities for the Indian Bureau, however, that Schurz experienced his greatest problems. His tenure of office coincided with the last outbreaks of the Indian wars on the frontier; bringing to the perennial Indian question little first-hand knowledge, he was nevertheless willing to learn. But he committed many blunders in the process.

American policy toward the aborigines had long been a scandal. Often nomadic, the native Americans found themselves overrun by increasing numbers of settlers who took their land, destroyed their means of livelihood, and had no understanding for their ways. Prior to 1849, Indian affairs had been managed by the War Department; then the Department of the Interior became responsible for the administration of the Indian laws. A commissioner was in charge of its Indian Bureau, although of course the army's cooperation was still needed to deal with "refractory" tribes. In addition, there was a civilian board of Indian commissioners to make recommendations. This system was cumbersome and invited large-scale corruption; the agents on the various reservations were located far from headquarters and had many opportunities for personal enrichment. Moreover, the War Department, charged with pacifying the Indians, was anxious to resume control, an effort that reached a climax during the late seventies.

When Schurz first took over the Interior Department, the practice of resettling various tribes on large compact reservations, especially the Indian Territory (modern Oklahoma), was still the policy of the land. Whether because of ignorance or sheer bureaucratic inertia, in the beginning he supported this practice and sought to carry it out, so that he became tragically involved with the cruel transfer to the Southern plains of various Northern tribes. The Nez Percés under their brilliant chief, Joseph, were apprehended after a thousand-mile chase and transported from their northwestern homes to the far different climate of the Indian territory, and many died. A portion of the Northern Cheyennes, who sought to escape from their new and unsuitable homes by returning to their old hunting grounds, were overwhelmed and decimated, and other tribes suffered a similar fate. His complicity in these ill-conceived policies did not enhance Schurz's reputation. [16]

As time went on, however, he began to reconsider. As a good liberal and humanitarian, he was open to the arguments of philanthropists such as William Welsh of Philadelphia and experienced army officers like General Pope, who held that the Indians ought to be treated decently and an effort made to assimilate them. That this would mean the breakup of the tribal system through the introduction of landholding in severalty did not seem incongruous to nineteenth-century reformers, who believed that they were protecting the native Americans against the War Department's policy of virtual extermination. Schurz was eventually so thoroughly convinced by reformers' arguments that he wholeheartedly sought to further the concept of integration. Realizing that his goal of assimilation could be better furthered by leaving the tribes where they were, he attempted to encourage them to support themselves by the white man's methods. Consequently, he gave his full support to the establishment of Indian schools at Hampton Institute, Virginia, Carlisle Barracks, Pennsylvania, and Forest Grove, Oregon, where he hoped modern methods could be taught to impressionable young minds who would bring back their experiences to their reservations. He also established an Indian police force and by all the means at his command sought to induce Indians to take up a white lifestyle.[17]

Before anything positive could be accomplished, however, Schurz believed that the entire Indian service would have to be cleansed of corruption. For this purpose, he sent the Indian commissioner, John Q. Smith, on an inspection tour to investigate the various agents' methods of business. Instructing him that it was of the highest importance to adopt a well-defined policy toward peaceable tribes "so that the efforts made towards introducing among them habits and occupations of civilized life be systematized," he sought specific information. Which tribes were suited for agriculture? Which ones were better prepared for pasturage? What kind of schools existed for the children, and how might an Indian policy best be introduced?[18]

Smith, however, was not the right man for an inquest. A holdover from the previous administration, he was not in sympathy with his chief and could not procure the required information. Accordingly, in June 1877 Schurz issued an order creating a board to examine the methods used in the finance and accounting divisions, with special emphasis on the property accounts of Indian agents. In the fall, Smith resigned. Schurz replaced him with a former member of the Board of Indian Commissioners, Ezra A. Hayt, who appealed to him especially because he had not been able to get along with Zachariah Chandler. When in January 1878 the board rendered its report showing widespread corruption and want of central control, its secret proceedings had already resulted in the dismissal of several officials; its findings seemed to indict Chief Clerk S. A. Galpin, whom Schurz also discharged. He hoped to be able to carry on with a thoroughly reformed agency.[19]

The secretary's energetic steps pleased the reformers, but a large segment of the public was highly critical of his methods. The secrecy of the investigation gave rise to charges that he was conducting star chamber proceedings, and even a philanthropist like President Julius H. Seelye of Amherst, known for his solicitude for the Indians, came to Galpin's defense by questioning Schurz's conduct of the investigation. Nevertheless, the secretary remained firm. "The members of the Board have rendered so great a public service, and they have shown so grea courage in exposing themselves to the hostility of powerful and unscrupulous combinations, that if they are permitted in any way to suffer . . . for the good work they have done the moral effect cannot but be disastrous," he wrote to the President. Hayes upheld him, although he found new jobs for some of the displaced officials. Not even Senator Howe's sarcastic attacks in Congress—he accused his old antagonist of having failed in everything he had ever undertaken—shook the President's confidence in the secretary, who received another bill of good health when in 1880 the Board of Indian Commissioners conducted a final inquiry into the methods of the Indian Bureau.[20]

Schurz's attempt to cleanse the Indian service coincided with renewed attempts of the War Department to take it over. William T. Sherman, then the commanding general of the army, came to Commissioner Smith's defense, and a pending bill to transfer the bureau to the War Department received new impetus. Even though in the spring the measure did not come to a vote, Congress established a committee to look into the problem. General Sheridan attacked Interior's handling of the bureau; Schurz, who sent him a stinging reply, on December 6, 1878 personally testified before the committee. Clearly demonstrating the danger of entrusting the Indians to their military antagonists, he materially contributed to the ultimate failure of the War Department's designs and thus retained the most troublesome of his responsibilities.[21]

Schurz's humanitarian attitude toward the Indians brought him unavoidably into conflict with the army. Charged with the responsibility of enforcing government policy, the officers and men on the ground could hardly be expected to take an enlightened view of their opponents. At first, when Schurz still approved of congregating the Indians on large reservations, the incipient conflict was muted. He fully cooperated with the military in the conflict with the Nez Percés, the Paiutes, the Northern Cheyennes, the Apaches, and the Bannocks.[22] In the fall of 1879, however, he actively interfered with the army's handling of the Indians. Surprised by an uprising in western Colorado, where the Utes killed the local agent, Nathan C. Meeker, and took his wife and daughters prisoners, both the army and local whites could barely be restrained. The secretary stepped in just in time to prevent bloody retribution. Aided by the fact that concern for the women prisoners made caution obligatory, he began a lengthy course of negotiations. His skillful dealings with Chief Ouray, for whom he had great respect, and his prompt dispatch of Charles Adams, an agent of marked ability, to settle the difficulty, contributed to the comparatively peaceful solution of the crisis. In the end, despite the clamor of settlers and speculators led by the governor of Colorado, a solution was worked out. Permitting the Utes to receive compensation and to retain at least a small reservation in the southwest corner of the state, it facilitated their acquisition of land in severalty where they were and removed the remainder to Utah. Schurz's success in preventing a general war and his fair treatment of the Utes gained general approbation. Chief Ouray, who died during the negotiations, appreciated "Four Eyes" so much that he left him his deerskin jacket and pants as well as his powderhorn and tobacco pouch. The secretary could always treasure the gift as a memento of this crowning triumph of his new policies.[23]

If Schurz's responsibility for the Indians proved troublesome, it also had its compensations. In 1879 and 1880 he undertook two lengthy trips to the West to inspect Indian agencies and reservations. Accompanied by the President's son Webb and other friends, he utilized the time not only to transact business but to go hunting and to enjoy the wilderness. In 1879, traveling partially by private car and partially by horse and wagon, he met various Indian tribes, at powwows which convinced him that his policy of assimilation and pacification had been successful. Even the once warlike Ogalalla Sioux were working peacefully and gave him a colorful ceremonial welcome, Chief Crazy Horse presenting him with a to-mahawk and war shirt which he put over the visitor's head, saying, "He Ogalalla."[24]

The next year he went west again. First going to San Francisco—Agathe and Marianne came along—he visited Yosemite before returning to Salt Lake City, where his daughters left the party to go home. Then, accompanied by General George Crook and an immense retinue, he went north to Yellowstone Park to hunt for elk, moose, and, as he put it, grizzly bears. Even Crook's aide, who had referred to him as "the spindleshanked Mephistopheles at present presiding over the Department of the Interior," was forced to admit that he was "a congenial companion, a good shot, and an excellent linguist." As he boasted to Webb Hayes, his party bagged numerous antelopes, deer, and elk. His large wagon train furnished excellent meals, which he liked to wash down with champagne, and for supper on one occasion he downed some prairie hens while some of the party supplied fresh mountain trout. The magnificent views, the geysers, the wilderness—he could hardly stop raving about his experiences. And again, the Indian tribes he visited seemed to confirm his conviction that his policy had been correct. Only Sitting Bull in Canada still refused to surrender.[25]

But in spite of his enthusiasm—he proudly declared that he had changed his formerly mistaken policies so as to "respect such rights as the Indians have in the land they occupy"—he was unable to induce Congress to pass the severalties bill he was advocating,[26] and his efforts remained merely the precursor to later successes. Moreover, because of his earlier insistence on removing unwilling tribes, he ran into severe trouble with one of them.

The Poncas on the Dakota-Nebraska line were a small, peaceful group that had never had any trouble with the whites. In 1868 in a treaty with the Sioux the government inadvertently ceded their lands to their hereditary enemies. The result of this oversight was that the Poncas had to be relocated, and shortly after Schurz took office, they were conveyed to the Indian Territory, in total disregard of their protests. This removal, sometimes called the Ponca Trail of Tears, proved disastrous; many died, and the new lands given to them were found unsuitable for their needs. Accordingly, some of the Ponca chiefs visited the Department of the Interior to protest; Schurz, deeply impressed, in his first annual report pleaded for compensation for their wrongs. But he was unwilling to let them return.[27]

This refusal soon caused more trouble. Although in 1878 a better location was found for the tribe, early the following year a desperate group of Poncas led by Chief Standing Bear, who carried with him a bag containing the pitiful remains of his grandchild, attempted to return to their ancestral home. The army apprehended them, but outraged reformers in Omaha, led by a former abolitionist newspaperman and cleric, Thomas H. Tibbles, came to their rescue. Unable to obtain relief from the Interior Department, they succeeded in securing the Indians' release on a writ of habeas corpus, when federal Judge Elmer S. Dundy in Omaha ruled that tribesmen were persons covered by the due-process clause of the Fourteenth Amendment. Yet Schurz was unwilling to lessen the native American population of the Indian Territory, which he was trying to protect from the onrush of white settlers, to say nothing of his fear of a new Sioux war. Declining to carry the suit to the Supreme Court, he refused to be swayed by the Poncas' friends, who now considered him the chief obstacle to the Indians' return.[28]

His negative attitude caused an outcry among the very groups in the East that might ordinarily be expected to sympathize with his efforts to inaugurate a new Indian policy. In part, the excitement may have been due to the clergy's anger at his success in lessening the influence of the various denominations on the reservations; in part, he had only himself to blame. In Boston, New York, and other cities, protest meetings were held; Wendell Phillips, who had already feuded with Schurz because of his financial views, entered the fray; and Helen Hunt Jackson, novelist, author, and poet, became so impressed with Standing Bear's cause that she began the researches which led to her famous book, A *Century of Dishonor*, a passionate defense of the Indians. Tibbles, lecturing on the chief's woes, traveled through the country accompanied by an attractive Indian girl, Bright Eyes, and Senator Henry L. Dawes of Massachusetts introduced a bill for the Poncas' relief. This resulted in the establishment of a committee which recommended the tribe's return.[29]

The secretary had a difficult time defending himself. No matter how vigorously he replied to all attacks, no matter how often he pointed out that it had been he who had originally called the attention of Congress to the Poncas' plight, the impression lingered that he was a heartless official persecuting an unoffending nation for bureaucratic reasons. After a mammoth protest meeting in December 1880 in Boston, Governor John D. Long wrote him an open letter to which he returned a stinging reply. The cabinet met to discuss the question, and Hayes, who believed his secretary of the interior had been "most shamefully treated," finally appointed a commission to settle the matter. After a number of Ponca chiefs had come to Washington to declare themselves satisfied with their new location and the commission had reported accordingly, the President in a special message to

Congress recommended ample restitution to the tribe, thus in effect upholding the secretary.[30]

In the congressional investigation attending this last flareup of the controversy, Schurz again figured as a scapegoat. Accused by Senator Dawes of complicity in the assassination of Standing Bear's brother and of suppressing evidence of the Poncas' desire to return, he singled out renewed references to his foreign birth in replying to his tormentor. Reviewing the evidence Dawes had disputed, he proved beyond doubt that a majority of the chiefs had indeed expressed a desire to remain, indignantly showed that the Indian's death had been an accident, and ridiculed the aspersions concerning his foreign birth. "From the Pequot War to our days there never was an Indian unjustly killed in this country until a German-born American citizen became Secretary of the Interior," he wrote. Public opinion began to turn. As the President's commission had recommended that the Poncas be compensated, that those willing to remain in the Indian Territory be allowed to do so, and that the small band desirous of going back also be granted its wish, Congress finally authorized the payment of $165,000 to the tribe. Yet, when Mrs. Jackson's book appeared, Schurz received no credit for his efforts on behalf of the Indians. He was pictured as a heartless bureaucrat who had unjustly persecuted the Poncas.[31]

That his actions in the Ponca affair were inept is beyond question. To be sure, as he pointed out to Governor Long, he had obligations to all Indians, not merely to one tribe, and could not countenance the danger of another uprising. It was also true that he had to protect the Indian territory against white settlers. Nevertheless, his initial failure to be fully cognizant of the Poncas' sufferings, his adherence to the ill-advised policy of forced repatriation, and his clumsy handling of Sitting Bear and Tibbles's relief committee did not show great adminsitrative or political finesse. It was a performance not in keeping with his usual acumen. Standing Bear never forgave him, and the controversy did much to render his well-meant Indian policies somewhat less than a complete success.[32]

This setback could not be entirely overcome by the secretary's obvious efficiency in the conduct of the decennial census of 1880, a task for which he appointed one of the country's foremost economists and statisticians, General Francis A. Walker. Aided by new legislation setting up greatly improved machinery, Walker carried out the most extensive enumeration of the American people ever attempted, for the first time counting religious groups and furnishing other vital information. The resulting report in twenty-two quarto volumes was widely recognized as a model of its type.[33]

Because of his close relations with the President, Schurz was deeply involved even in those administration policies for which he did not bear direct responsibility. Although he cautioned that he himself had need of soldiers in connection with Indian difficulties, he firmly supported the dispatch of troops to break the railroad strikes of 1877. Convinced that the disorders were caused by communist agitators, he thought they had to be stopped; yet he also admitted that the strikers themselves were decent people who did not wish to be associated with the mob. While he realized that economic problems had assumed major proportions now that the United States had become an industrial nation, his nineteenth-century liberal outlook had poorly prepared him for dealing with labor unrest.[34]

In view of his unwavering hard-money theories, it was not surprising that he was one of the President's firmest supporters of the veto of the Bland-Allison Act. Providing for monthly coinage of two to four million ounces of silver bullion, the measure represented a compromise version of a much more extreme bill for the free coinage of silver. Other members of the cabinet warned Hayes, but Schurz thought that a veto would save the country from an "immoral and dangerous measure." The President followed his advice, only to find that Congress would not sustain him.[35]

Because of his influence with the Germans, during the 1878 elections the secretary was in great demand as a campaign speaker. He again made hard money his principal theme. Attempting to explain at Cincinnati that contraction of the currency had nothing to do with the origins of the Panic of 1873, he praised the national banking system and made much of the signs of returning prosperity. In Boston, he used similar arguments to help hard-money Republicans turn back Ben Butler's defiance of the Brahmins in a bid for the governorship. The results were satisfactory in Ohio; in Massachusetts, Butler suffered defeat, and the Republicans were grateful. But no matter how often Schurz sought to explain that the Republicans had done better than expected and saved the policy of specie resumption about to go into effect, the Democrats captured both houses of Congress.[36]

The secretary's successes were limited, but he nevertheless enjoyed himself in Washington. Comfortably installed in a large house at 1719 H Street, he delighted his visitors with his performances on the piano. Commenting favorably on the pleasant atmosphere in his home, they remarked on the warmth of his family life, his daughters' skill as housekeepers and linguists—they spoke English, French, and German—and on his ability to combine serious work with domestic comfort. During the hot summer months, he sent the children to the country, while he and Postmaster General Key shared quarters at a nearby establishment at Edgewood.[37]

Schurz's social life was very active. As he explained to Althaus, society in the capital was distinguished by the fact that money meant nothing, and education, good manners, and industry, everything. While this was an exaggeration, it was true that many interesting people came to the city for the winter. The Henry Adamses were frequent guests and invited the secretary in turn; the diplomatic community conferred distinction on local parties, and journalists and members of Congress made life agreeable. The wife of the Danish minister organized an eating society called the National Rational International Dining Club, of which Schurz, the German minister, and his popular Turkish colleague, Aristarchi Bey, were enthusiastic members.[38] The President himself sometimes dropped in at 1719 H Street and often asked the Schurzes to the White House—on one occasion, with Mrs. Hayes out of town, Agathe served as hostess. Hayes, who must have enjoyed the powwows arranged by the secretary with visiting Indian chiefs in full regalia, also liked to take him along on his tours to various parts of the country; in May of 1877 Schurz accompanied him to New York and Harvard, in the fall to the South, and in October 1878 to Montpelier, James Madison's Virginia home.[39]

Because the secretary of the interior was a widower, and a very eligible one at that, gossip about his marital plans never ceased. Now he was linked with Evarts's daughter, now with one of the President's friends—the papers constantly speculated about his alleged remarriage. But the rumors were all false.[40]

That Schurz was lonely was true, but eventually he managed to fill the void in his life caused by Margarethe's death. The object of his new affections was Fanny Chapman, the thirty-three-year-old daughter of a wealthy Doylestown, Pennsylvania judge, whom he probably met through Henry Adams, a Massachusetts neighbor of Fanny's sister. Pretty, intelligent, and vivacious, she became the prototype for Sybil in Adams's novel *Democracy*, where she appears as the heroine's attractive lively sister. Apparently she and Schurz met in the winter of 1879–80; Schurz was so smitten that he was very dejected when because of his Western trip he had to part from her. ''You ask me whether I am happier now than I was a year ago this time,'' he chided her. ''What a superfluous question! Was it not answered before it was written down? That solitude of the heart has disappeared which then made my life lonesome and dreary. I was poor and I am rich again, rich in the noblest sense, rich by the love of a human being I love. And what a store of happiness is there in the assurance you have given me, that my love makes you happy! Is that answering the question?''[41]

The correspondence started at that time was to last for the rest of Schurz's life, and although he never married Fanny, apparently because of Agathe, who never permitted any reference to Fanny in published materials over which she had control, he met the Doylestown heiress as frequently as possible. She even learned German and began to correspond with him in his native tongue. Though he encouraged her linguistic endeavors, nineteenth-century German scholar that he was, he could not forbear lecturing to her. She had made great progress in the language, but as her lover pointed out, there were a few errors in the letter she had sent him. A lengthy correction followed. Apparently Fanny was not discouraged; his subsequent letters to her were in German, and expressions of love once more took the place of learned exhortations.[42]

Eighteen-eighty was a presidential year, and because Hayes had announced his opposition to a second term, a fierce struggle for the Republican nomination developed. Unavoidably, Schurz played a role in it. In part, his efforts were not

Fanny Chapman (Courtesy of National Carl Schurz Association)

fruitless, yet the subsequent elections only revealed the total failure of the administration's Southern policy.

To the secretary's great dismay, Conkling and his followers were hopeful of nominating Grant for a third term, and Blaine, who had so narrowly missed the prize four years earlier, was also in the running. Both of these candidates were wholly unacceptable to Schurz, yet Blaine was anxious to win him over. In February he met the secretary at a Massachusetts congressman's home. Seated next to him at the dinner table, Mrs. Blaine asked him for a card and he signed it. "Take it, Abby," she said to her niece Gail Hamilton, "and keep it as a memento of this most delightful evening," much to the amusement of her dinner companion, who could hardly keep from laughing. Later, in an obvious bid for support, in connection with the pending Ute treaty, Blaine made some complimentary remarks about the secretary on the Senate floor. But of course all these efforts were in vain.[43]

To defeat these two unwelcome candidates, Schurz sought to further the chances of Secretary Sherman. At times he also considered the possibility of backing Senator George Edmunds. As he explained to Preetorius, the *Westliche Post* must do everything possible to prevent Grant's renomination. No other Republican candidate must be attacked and even Blaine must be treated gingerly. He sought to stress the fact that the Germans would never vote for Grant, and it was an open secret that he was ready to resign rather than support the former President.[44]

In spite of his opponents' efforts, when the convention met, Grant was clearly the front runner. It was obvious that only a combination of all the other candidates could prevent his nomination. To contribute to this goal, Schurz sought an interview with Blaine at the apartment of Charles Nordhoff, the Washington correspondent of the New York *Herald*. Telling Blaine that he could perform a great service for his country if he instructed his delegates to unite on a third candidate, he was not surprised to hear Blaine retort that he himself was a candidate and still expected to win. Without hesitation, Schurz said that he would not be nominated, and if he were, he could not be elected. "What, are there Republicans who would note vote for me?" asked the Plumed Knight. "Yes," said the secretary, "I know, I am one of them." Jumping up and walking excitedly up and down, Blaine exclaimed, "You wouldn't? If I were nominated? And brought me here to tell me?" His antagonist reaffirmed his statement and repeated that he could render a service by instructing his friends. On the next day, when Blaine's supporters went over to Garfield, Schurz was convinced that they had received the appropriate telegrams during the night and that in this way he had helped bring about the nomination of Garfield, who had for some time been mentioned as an alternative to Grant.[45]

The Ohioan's success was a relief for Schurz; the third-term danger and with it his contemplated resignation had been squelched; Blaine had been sidetracked, and although the nominee was not one of the secretary's intimates and had frequently criticized his inclusion in the cabinet, he had nevertheless maintained friendly relations with him since the visit after Bull Run. "Schurz and your mother are the happiest people you ever saw," Hayes wrote to his son after the convention, and the secretary promptly sent Garfield his heartiest felicitations. "The country is to be congratulated as well as yourself" he wired.[46]

As was his habit, he immediately began to give advice to the nominee. When the candidate visited him in Washington, he discussed policy with him, much to the disgust of Roscoe Conkling, who called on Garfield at the same time only to find him out in conference with the hated secretary of the interior. Shortly afterward, when the Democrats nominated General Hancock, Schurz wrote to Garfield that he might now safely ignore the Southern question. Let him stress the accomplishments of the administration, especially its concern for business. A few weeks later, he urged him to emphasize civil service reform in his letter of acceptance, only to be very much disappointed when his advice was disregarded. Notwithstanding this setback, for which he promptly chided Garfield, he began to campaign for the ticket in July on his way to the West, when he delivered a speech in Indianapolis. He followed it up with two addresses in San Francisco, and in spite of his outspoken criticism and unsolicited advice, the nominee was happy with his support. The German vote was important, and although there was some question about Schurz's ability to deliver it, Garfield apparently considered the secretary's help vital. Accordingly, he was grateful when in the fall Schurz came to Ohio, Indiana, and metropolitan New York for additional speeches, and the orator did not hesitate to emphasize how enthusiastically the Germans were receiving him. When in November the Republicans won by a narrow margin, Schurz was completely satisfied. That the party failed to carry a single Southern state despite the administration's Southern policy did not seem to bother him unduly.[47]

Talk of Schurz's remaining in the cabinet or obtaining some diplomatic mission had been current for some time; whether he believed it or not, he professed that he had made up his mind not to accept an appointment even if it were tendered. Late in November he saw Garfield in Washington, where he informed him that a "talk with the 'freest man in the world,'" as the President-elect had called him because of his refusal to seek further office, might be a "grand thing" for Garfield. Presumably he was again very liberal with his advice, and during the following months he continued to offer his counsel to the President-elect. In spite of fresh rumors of a new position, probably because he did not believe them, he was determined to leave public service, and although his last months in office were spoiled by the continuing Ponca controversy, he was gratified to receive a number of invitations for dinners in his honor after his retirement. They showed that many reformers still supported him.[48]

Thus at the end of his four years' service as secretary of the interior, Schurz left Washington convinced that he had done a creditable job. That his performance was marred by many setbacks did not seem to bother him. He was looking forward to a renewed writing career. Only, this time it would be in the East.

XVI

Mugwump

AFTER 1881, Schurz never held public office again, but he still had considerable prestige, not merely as a former senator and member of the cabinet, but as the uncontested leader of the German-Americans. It was this fact that continued to give him importance, importance far beyond that of most independents, who after 1881 became known as Mugwumps. And although his lack of firm party ties stood in the way of new personal preferment, he continued to wield strong influence as a journalist, writer, and orator.

Given his financial needs at the end of his term of office, his return to journalism was natural. Never an astute businessman, in 1881 he was in a difficult position. The *Westliche Post* had not done as well as he had hoped, and although even without direct participation he could still realize between $7,000 and $8,000 per annum from his shares, the only way he could meet his expenses was by continued reliance on his wife's legacy in Germany. This state of affairs was so irksome that he was seriously thinking of resuming his lectures to supplement his income. However, journalistic activity was much more to his taste.[1]

Of course he had the option of returning to St. Louis and resuming active direction of his paper. There was even talk of his joining an English-language journal in Missouri. But he had always liked the Atlantic seaboard—Boston, where in March his Massachusetts friends gave him a dinner and he renewed contacts with Longfellow, F. W. Bird, Edward Atkinson, Francis Parkman, and others; New York, where Abraham Jacobi, still his best friend, had established a flourishing pediatric practice and maintained a beautiful residence on West 34th Street, and Washington, where he had become so comfortably settled. In addition ever since 1874 he had been contemplating a history of the United States, and almost all the sources for such a work were in the East. This consideration became pressing when in 1881 he was asked to prepare a biography of Henry Clay for the American Statesmen Series. But above all, there was Fanny. As long as Schurz stayed in the East, he could see her frequently, arranging for reunions that would have been very difficult in the Middle West. He could no longer live without her.[2]

At just about that time, a real opportunity was opening up to solve his financial and personal problems while at the same time providing him with a new forum for propagating his ideas. Henry Villard, the famous German immigrant entrepreneur who was as interested in journalism as he was adept at organizing railroads, was anxious to acquire a newspaper in New York. Parke Godwin, William Cullen Bryant's son-in-law, was eager to sell some of his shares of the *Evening Post*. Negotiating with him, Villard brought together E. L. Godkin of the *Nation*,

Horace White, formerly of the Chicago *Tribune*, and Schurz. The financier agreed to remain in the background; the active management of the newspaper was to be in the hands of the triumvirate of editors, with Schurz assuming the duties of editor-in-chief.[3] Embarking on the new venture with some trepidation, Schurz nevertheless considered it a promising proposition. He told Fanny he felt a bit uneasy about it, just as he had always done when he was to speak in the Senate, but as he had usually managed to get over his apprehensions about his speeches after the first sentences, he was certain he would also be able to do justice to his new duties.[4]

Under the new direction, the *Evening Post* developed into an effective advocate of the editors' ideology. Civil service reform, tariff revision, independent political action—these pillars of Mugwumpery became the mainstay of the editorial page, where they shared space with other liberal causes. Schurz took responsibility for politics and foreign relations, Godkin for social and political affairs, and White for economics. The editor-in-chief wrote well and succinctly; yet even his admirer Oswald Garrison Villard, Henry's journalist son, thought his editorials read more like speeches than articles. Sometimes a bit ponderous, he fell short of becoming a really great newspaperman. His forte, as always, was in polemics, in the same way in which he had long known how to rally his compatriots. While his positions were more enlightened and more attuned to the changing industrial conditions of the country than Godkin's, his associate knew how to write much livelier editorials, which he laced with biting sarcasm.[5]

Schurz's chief interest—it was almost becoming an obsession—was civil service reform. Devoting his very first editorial to it, he never permitted his readers to forget his total devotion to the cause, especially after he became a member of the newly organized National Civil Service Reform League under the presidency of George William Curtis. He enjoyed its conventions at Newport, particularly when he was able to see some forward movement.[6] And the assassination of President Garfield made his crusade a topic of vital national concern.

Garfield's administration had not gotten off to a good start. Beset by patronage problems, hampered by Conkling's enmity, and troubled by clashing factions pulling him in different directions, the new President, who had appointed the Half-Breed Blaine secretary of state, barely had sufficient time to chart his course. On July 2, 1881, at the Baltimore & Potomac Station in Washington he was struck by the bullets of a self-proclaimed Stalwart. "Arthur is now President of the United States," boasted the mentally deranged assassin, Charles J. Giteau, thus proclaiming his disappointment with the patronage system as the chief motive for his crime. It was obvious that civil service reform could not be put off much longer.[7]

The deed horrified Schurz. In frequent telegraphic communication with the reform-minded postmaster general, Thomas L. James, he expressed his satisfaction at the President's apparent escape. As time went on, however, it became evident that optimism was ill founded; Garfield's wounds were serious, and the likelihood of Arthur's elevation to the presidency was a prospect Schurz did not relish. In fact, he was so upset that he felt he could write but not talk about it, although he published tactful editorials and tried to reassure his Hamburg relatives. In spite of the vice president's limited abilities and dubious political connections, he asserted, the country was healthy enough to withstand the shock.[8]

In September, Garfield finally succumbed, and Schurz wrote a carefully worded editorial wishing the new president well. While the *Evening Post* tried to be fair to the new administration, it could never wholly overcome its prejudice against Conkling's former lieutenant. It gave him credit for his endorsement of civil service reform in his first annual message; it praised him for vetoing the particularly offensive River and Harbor bill of 1882; and it was delighted when in January 1883 the long-awaited civil service reform measure written by the New York lawyer Dorman B. Eaton in consultation with Schurz and others and sponsored by Senator George H. Pendleton finally became law. Firmly convinced of the injustice of the anti-Chinese madness then sweeping the West, Schurz editorially lauded Arthur's veto of a Chinese Exclusion bill, just as he naturally approved of the appointment of a new secretary of state to take Blaine's place. This was true even though the new officer was Senator Frelinghuysen, with whom he had so passionately argued while in Congress. But the old suspicions were inflamed anew when the President offered Conkling a seat on the Supreme Court and appointed the spoilsman William E. Chandler secretary of the navy.[9]

While the *Evening Post* published editorials on the tariff and consistently emphasized the importance of independent political action, the editors strongly endorsed other causes as well.[10] One of these was its crusade against anti-Semitism. Schurz himself had always detested religious bigotry; his personal relations with Jews went back to his experience with his father's friend Aaron in Liblar. Since that time, he had formed many close relationships with them. Dr. Jacobi was his most intimate friend; Simon Wolf, the registrar of deeds of the District of Columbia and a prominent member of the Board of Delegates of American Israelites, was a frequent companion in Washington; and he enjoyed the company of Jewish bankers and businessmen. Once, on a lecture tour in upstate New York, his audience wanted to take him to church on Sunday. As he explained to his wife, however, he much preferred to stay with one of his Jewish banker friends in Buffalo, who would serve him an excellent dinner with good wine. Isaac Seligman, the Straus brothers, and Jacob Schiff were among his acquaintances, so that it was hardly surprising that the revival of anti-Semitism in the 1880s struck him as a reversion to medieval barbarism.[11]

It was in Russia that the most sensational excesses against the Jews were taking place. Widespread pogroms following the assassination of Alexander II in 1881 were so ferocious that they caused a feeling of revulsion in liberal circles all over the world. Asked by prominent American Jews to take an interest in their coreligionists' plight, Schurz responded handsomely. Publishing article after article in the *Evening Post* deploring anti-Semitic excesses, he featured sympathetic discussions of the problems of the victims. The paper even criticized a local Sunday closing law because of its unfairness to non-Christians who kept their holy day on Saturdays.[12]

While the Russian outbursts against the Jews were sensational, German anti-Semitism was also on the rise again. "Conditions over there make me feel quite uncomfortable, so uncomfortable in fact that I don't like to think about them," Schurz complained to his brother-in-law, "What we have seen in the papers here about [your] Jew-baiting we Germans could not read without being ashamed."[13] In the *Evening Post* he deplored Bismarck's reactionary tendencies and, before long, spoke out publicly against the revival of German bigotry. The occasion was a eulogy on the German statesman Eduard Lasker, who had died suddenly in New York while on a visit to the United States. A progressive, a foe of protectionism, and an eminent member of the Reichstag, Lasker had become Bismarck's bitter opponent. In his eulogy, Schurz praised him as a great fellow countryman and legal scholar. Then he launched his all-out attack against anti-Semitism. "It sounds like a slander of human nature when we hear from over there how the fanatics of renewed persecution of the Jews, that vile insult to the 19th century's famous enlightenment and humanitarianism, are even now trying to besmirch the deceased's good name . . . because he was a Jew," he said. "Let us pity those who do not realize their own shame and disgrace, for evidently they know not what they do." The *Evening Post* had naturally given full coverage to Lasker's visit.[14]

The newspaper's forthright stand often made trouble for its editor. The financier Jay Gould, angry at the *Evening Post*'s attacks on his manipulations in connection with the New York Elevated Railroad, reciprocated by seeking to blacken Schurz's character. Using the New York *World*, which he controlled, he charged that a land-grant decision rendered by the secretary of the interior in favor of the Northern Pacific Railroad in the case of Nelson Dudymott had been dictated by a desire to aid Villard's interests. Schurz replied with an angry editorial stressing the fact that the decision was made two years before Villard acquired an interest in the road. He even demanded a congressional investigation, a course of action hardly warranted by mere newspaper talk, as Senator Edmunds pointed out. When in 1883 George W. Julian, who would have been secretary of the interior had Tilden become president, repeated similar allegations in a detailed article in the *North American Review* about railroad influence in the Land Office, Schurz again reacted furiously. Justifying his decisions in a long public letter, he reminded his accuser that he had acted wholly in accordance with the law as construed by the attorney general, at times contrary to his own original opinions. Moreover, in the Dudymott decision, he had tried to confer great benefits upon actual settlers. Julian's rejoinder merely reiterated the charges in a more personal form, so that

Schurz felt constrained to publish another reply. Although he had the last word and the press generally sided with him, the incident took its toll.[15]

But his job had its compensations. He became one of New York's more prominent citizens, with apartments in Washington Heights and later in East 68th Street. Sought out by visitors of all kinds, he met writers, statesmen, and foreign dignitaries. Lord Bryce, Matthew Arnold, Henry James, ex-President Hayes, George William Curtis, Theodore Roosevelt, and young Frederick Bancroft all associated with him, Hayes taking great pleasure in riding with him to the end of the elevated line. And when Herbert Spencer was honored at a public dinner, Carl Schurz was one of the featured speakers, a fitting assignment for a general whose commitment to social Darwinism went back to his studies in the field of *Social Statics*. Andrew Carnegie appreciated him. The Seligmans invited him to spend some time with them at the Jersey shore. The Jacobis, at whose house he was always a welcome guest, prevailed on him to join them in the summer at Bolton Landing on Lake George, where he eventually built a summer house right next to the doctor's cottage, and Villard took him along on a long trip to the Northwest to celebrate the completion of the Northern Pacific Railroad.[16]

What made life really worthwhile in New York, however, was the knowledge that he could frequently see Fanny Chapman. When he first came to the city, she was in Europe, where she undertook a sentimental pilgrimage to the Quai St. Michel in Paris to look at the house where Schurz had once stayed. Her eyes filled with tears as she saw it, she wrote. In the middle of the night she had been standing at the window to look down upon the moonlit gardens and to think of him. When he read this confession of love, he thought he was close to tears himself. ''I wanted to leave everything to rush to you, take you into my arms and put your head on that spot which you know so well,'' he wrote. ''What a rare good fortune it is to be loved so well by a noble human soul.'' After she came home, the two lovers met whenever possible. They took a trip to Baltimore together, spent as much time in each other's company as feasible, and supported each other in all their trials.[17]

He needed her support, for he was soon in difficulty again. The partnership at the *Evening Post* had shown strains from the very beginning, Godkin especially resenting Schurz's management and position. The prissy editor of the *Nation* (which for a time in effect became the *Post*'s weekly) was much more conservative than his German-American associate. An excellent writer, often more attuned to the readers' interests than his partner, he considered Schurz too much given to sentiment. Henry Adams thought this was useful. ''You relieve me greatly by telling me Schurz is sentimental,'' he wrote. ''If you dry one of his tears I will denounce you at a stock holders' meeting. Every tear he drops is worth at least an extra dollar on the dividends. Cultivate them! collect them! point to them! You are no good yourself in the sobbing business.''[18] It was good advice, but Godkin could not adjust to his loss of independence. He differed with Schurz on general policy as well as on specific questions—for example, the relations between capital and labor—and in the summer of 1883 he sought to assume sole control. Convinced that under Schurz's management the *Evening Post* had lost circulation and that a radical change was required, he persuaded White and Villard that he ought to take over.

A complete break occurred soon afterward. A telegrapher's strike inconvenienced the press, and the two men wrote conflicting editorials. Schurz tried to maintain his perspective, while Godkin unconditionally condemned the strikers. As it had been arranged that Godkin would take charge when at the beginning of August Schurz went on vacation, the general left for the Catskills as he had intended. On August 8, however, he was startled when he read in the *Evening Post* that Godkin had referred to the strikers as soldiers who ought to be under military discipline. "I dissent emphatically from the assertion that the 10,000 or 40,000 men whom some of our modern corporations employ in telegraphic or railroad service have to be governed on the same principle as an army," he protested. No man who had not voluntarily enlisted in the military could be held to such a discipline, and the idea that laboring men should be treated in that way seemed to him "monstrous."[19]

Godkin wrote an angry reply, which, however, he never mailed. Completely disagreeing with his associate, he pointed out that although he was sorry Schurz did not like his editorial stance, during the past two years he had been equally troubled by his partner's articles. Moreover, he had made it clear to Villard and White that under no circumstances would he remain connected with the *Post* under Schurz's editorship. The two men agreed to the change.

Schurz, realizing that he could not continue his association with the haughty Godkin, hurried to see Villard at Dobbs Ferry, where he stayed overnight. He let it be understood that he was willing to leave but demanded that his departure be dignified. He could quit only under decent conditions.

What these were to be caused more contention. Insisting on a public statement of the reasons for his severing of relations with the *Evening Post*, Schurz at first could not secure Godkin's consent. Thus matters dragged along until December, when he told White in no uncertain terms what he thought of his antagonist. He demanded the right to be heard. After a final contretemps over Godkin's giving a story to the Springfield *Republican* that his former associate disliked, over the daily chores connected with the job, and Schurz's protest about certain disparaging remarks about his writing ability, an interview appeared in the *New York Times* which gave Schurz's side of the story. Leaving the *Evening Post*, he had the last word with an explanation for his disagreement with Godkin in an article in the *North American Review*.[20]

But what was he to do next? He had lost $20,000 in the newspaper venture, and his financial condition was deplorable. A number of friends attempted to raise a fund of $100,000 for him, which, much to their dismay, he felt constrained to reject. To his brother-in-law, who also wanted to help, he wrote that he intended to make his living by literary work. He hoped that the contract for Henry Clay would see him through for a while, and he had an offer from a German firm to write a history of the United States. As he freely admitted to Fanny, however, he was worried. Financial stability seemed to elude him.[21]

But then, before fully coming to grips with the important question of his future, he became once again involved in a national election, this time in an effort to keep James G. Blaine from becoming president. He had long distrusted the Plumed Knight; after he had opposed him in 1876, the antagonism between the two men had grown apace. Gail Hamilton's articles, the senator's attack on the Interior Department, Schurz's rejections of his overtures in 1880—all these heightened the estrangement. The fact was, Blaine was the incarnation of the type of politician that Schurz disliked. Flamboyant, charming, idolized by his followers, he had risen rapidly since his election to Congress in 1862. Speaker of the House in 1869, in 1876 he became an active candidate for the presidency. But his connection with the Little Rock & Fort Smith Railroad became a stumbling block to his ambitions. It appeared that when speaker he had rendered a ruling in favor of the company, an action which began to look suspicious because he later became its agent in various land transactions and retained much of the proceeds, sums that were customarily given to the purchasers. Then, when the railroad became insolvent, he obtained funds from other railroads at advantageous rates so that he was enabled to reimburse the purchasers and save his political career. All these transactions came to light because of the so-called Mulligan letters, mailed by Blaine to a Boston promoter named Warren Fisher, Jr., and held by his bookkeeper, James Mulligan. After seizing them by a ruse, Blaine read portions of them to a fascinated House of Representatives. But he failed to be convincing enough to obtain the coveted presidential nomination, although Garfield appointed him secretary of state. In 1884 he hoped to capture the prize that had eluded him so long.[22]

In spite of Blaine's occasional efforts to effect a reconciliation, when Schurz became associated with the *Evening Post*, he frequently attacked the Plumed Knight and the machine politicians he accused him of representing. When in the late summer of 1882 the presidential hopeful seemed to endorse civil service reform, the paper published a devastating critique. Charging that Blaine had been guilty of civil service abuses and profited by them all his life, it asserted that "as a member of the administration, far from giving his mind to reform, he plunged into spoils and wallowed in them for three months, like a rhinoceros in an African pool."

This was too much for the aspiring statesman. Not realizing that the article in question had been written by Godkin rather than Schurz, in an interview with the Chicago *Tribune* he sought to turn the tables on his old enemy. Blaine maintained that he had accomplished more in his ten months in office than Schurz in his four years, accused him of violating his own rules by swamping the Census Bureau with his appointees, and ridiculed him for committing an egregious blunder in dismissing Commissioner Smith only to replace him with Hayt. "No more persistent office seeker than Mr. Schurz ever landed on these shores or was born on this soil," he insisted. "He has tried it in three states and is now settled in the fourth."

Schurz immediately replied. He had not been the author of the article in question, he stated, since he was on vacation two hundred miles away at the time, but he did indeed believe that "the author of the Mulligan letters can never be, and ought not to be, President of the United States." This conviction became more and more firmly rooted, until it finally drove him to break completely with the Republican party.[23]

During the gubernatorial elections that fall, the Democrats in New York elected Grover Cleveland, who as mayor of Buffalo had established a record for independence that naturally appealed to Schurz. Stolid, unexciting, and unmovable, the forty-five-year-old Cleveland was anathema to Tammany Hall, believed in hard money, and was not beholden to any well-known machine. Schurz thought their defeat was a good lesson for the Republicans; they would either have to mend their ways or lose the next presidency.[24]

The test would come in 1884. Determined to prevent the nomination of Blaine, whom he now identified with the worst excesses of the spoils system and considered personally dishonest, Schurz relied on all the influence he possessed. He might no longer be in charge of the *Evening Post*, he might no longer be a public official, but he could still speak for the German-Americans. Combined with his continued popularity with the independents, his political power could not safely be disregarded. And he never hesitated to fight for what he considered right.

He started the campaign in February. In a speech on Washington's Birthday to independent Republicans at the Brooklyn Academy of Music, he linked the need for party idealism with the principles of the Father of the Country. Pleading for a moral uplift in politics, he warned his audience that it must not be said, "The party might have done a great deal worse," but that the motto must be, "No party could have done better."[25]

During the following months, independents cautioned party leaders not to disregard their wishes. No unwavering organization candidate, and especially not Blaine, could obtain their votes. Because New York, where they had considerable strength, was doubtful, it was necessary to humor them. They were willing to endorse Senator Edmunds, they would accept Gresham, Hawley, or Robert Todd Lincoln, but they would never support Blaine. To make sure that their views were taken into account, Schurz, who had sent his children to Europe so that he could devote his whole time to the campaign, attended the Chicago Republican National Convention in person.[26]

Yet Blaine could not be stopped. His magnetism, his devoted organization, his undoubted popularity were too much for his opponents, Mugwumps as well as Arthur's supporters. When on the fourth ballot the favorite from Maine obtained the nomination, Schurz, who was sitting on the platform, took out his watch. Calling the minute and the hour of the day, he said, "From this hour dates the death of the Republican party." General Logan, whom he had specifically warned not to run because he could not be elected, accepted second place on the ticket.[27]

The nominations caused independents everywhere to take counsel. At a meeting in New York on June 17, presided over by Curtis, Schurz took the lead in advocating negotiations with the Democrats. He entered into communication with his old friend, Thomas F. Bayard, the Democratic senator from Delaware, and urged him to see to it that the party nominate either Cleveland or himself. Many influential newspapers, including the *New York Times, Herald*, and *Evening Post*, the Springfield *Republican* and Boston *Transcript*, as well as *Harper's Weekly* and the *Nation*, refused to support Blaine, and the Republicans had real cause for worry.[28]

To add to Blaine's troubles, it was obvious that the Germans were seriously disaffected. His manager learned that there was a formidable effort to organize an anti-Blaine movement among them; he himself received confirmation from Medill, who pointed out that one of the reasons for the immigrants' unhappiness was Blaine's quarrel with Schurz, whom he had repeatedly slandered as a representative "Teuton." It was essential that he try to repair this damage.[29]

Blaine took these warnings at face value. Especially worried about Schurz's attitude, he made one last effort to win him over by asking former Senator Henderson of Missouri to intercede for him. Henderson tried to see the general in New York; not finding him at home, he left a note expressing his conviction that if Blaine, to whom Schurz's opposition was giving "more concern than that of any and all others," had in the past behaved like Prince Hal, he would be a Henry V when assuming real responsibility. But Schurz was not convinced. Unable to look upon Blaine as "a mere jolly Prince Hal," he insisted that he could not support a man "who had sold his public trust for personal profit and thus set an example of large scale corruption."[30]

When on July 11 the Democrats nominated Cleveland, the Mugwumps found it easy to endorse him. The issue seemed clear-cut: Although not brilliant, Cleveland had given his city and state a clean administration. Blaine's elevation, on the other hand, would mean that a brazen corruptionist could become president of the United States. That the governor was an unwavering supporter of laissez-faire who had gone so far as to veto a bill mandating a five-cent fare on the New York Elevated Railroad did not bother them. They believed in laissez-faire themselves.

Yet the Mugwumps' initial enthusiasm received a damper. On July 21, the Buffalo *Evening Telegraph* revealed that many years earlier Cleveland had fathered an illegitimate child. To be sure, he had never shirked responsibility, but the religious press was upset. Stories of continuing debauchery reached the public, and soon Republican crowds were shouting, "Ma! Ma! Where's my pa? Gone to the White House, Ha! Ha! Ha!"[31] Henry Ward Beecher, himself not above suspicion in his relations with women, warned Schurz to put off his endorsement of the Democrat.

The general, however, refused to pause. Although he was troubled by Cleveland's indiscretion, his civil service reform associate in Rochester, Henry Richmond, assured him that the stories of Cleveland's continued debaucheries were false. Unless he heard further damaging evidence, he replied to Beecher, he was going ahead and deliver his long-planned speech on August 5 at the Grand Opera House in Brooklyn in support of the Democratic candidate.[32]

And deliver it he did. Addressing himself to follow Republicans who could not support their party's nominee, he slashed into Blaine's record by quoting from the senator's own letters. A man who had used his position as speaker of the House to peddle his influence to railroad companies, a man who had deceitfully taken away from Mulligan the letters that might impugn him—such a man was not fit to be president of the United States. All other issues faded in comparison. The charge that the Mugwumps were merely free-traders disliking Blaine's protectionism could be disproven by the fact that Schurz had favored the nomination of Edmunds, a high-tariff senator; the accusation that it was unsafe to entrust the country to the Democrats could be refuted by the fact that Cleveland had given New York a good administration. Moreover, it was absurd to suppose that in a free country only one party could be trusted with its administration. The duty of patriotic citizens was plain. It was to see "that the honor of the American people be preserved intact, and that all political parties . . . become forever impressed with the utter helplessness of any attempt to win success without respecting the vital condition of our greatness and glory, which is honest government."

The speech was an immediate success. Widely praised by contemporaries as well as later historians, it contributed greatly to the impetus of the anti-Blaine campaign.[33] The Republicans were so disturbed that they felt it necessary to publish a reply, and because of Schurz's standing in the German-American community, Senator Hoar, who took charge of the answer, sought to put it in the form of a letter to a young German. In Milwaukee, the German-American Republicans published an open challenge to their bolting countryman; he wrote scathing rejoinders to them as well as to Hoar and made sure to campaign in Wisconsin as well as in other states with large German populations.[34] Crowds in Indiana, Illinois, Michigan, Ohio, New York, New Jersey, and New England all heard the famous orator, and the more he spoke, the more the Republicans became worried. German defections must be stopped, advisers warned Blaine, only it must be done in such a way as not to attack Schurz. His compatriots were too proud of him.[35]

But Schurz soon struck another blow. Together with other Mugwumps, he sent a New York lawyer, Horace Deming, to Boston for additional Mulligan letters, and what turned up was most helpful. One of the letters, a communication from Blaine to Fisher, instructed the promoter to send him a statement which he enclosed for use in the congressional investigation of his railroad deals. For greater security, he added, "Burn this letter." As he had always maintained that he had nothing to hide about his relations with the railroads, the postscript had a damning effect. "Blaine, Blaine, James G. Blaine, the continental liar from the State of Maine, Burn this letter!" Democrats could now hoot in reply to Republican taunts about Cleveland's dubious past.[36] Their adversaries tried to subsidize German newspapers; they sought to lessen Cleveland's New York vote by secretly contributing to the independent candidacy of Ben Butler; but all their efforts were in vain. After the election, it became apparent that Blaine had lost by a hair. A few votes in New York would have changed the picture; to guard against fraud, a committee of eminent lawyers and citizens, including Schurz, carefully scrutinized the returns, and the Republicans were unable to change the verdict.[37]

To what extent Schurz was responsible for Blaine's defeat is difficult to say. Often credited with a major role in the Mugwump assault on the Plumed Knight, he certainly contributed to the latter's downfall. Nevertheless, such circumstances as the Reverend Dr. Samuel D. Burchard's characterization of the Democratic party as the party of "Rum, Romanism, and Rebellion," a banquet of multimillionaires in his honor at Delmonico's, and the defection of Roscoe Conkling in New York, were equally important.[38] As in 1860, however, the perception of Schurz's role in the outcome was decisive. Blaine never forgave him. Devastatingly flailing him as an inconstant wanderer in his *Twenty Years in Congress*, he charged him with want of patriotism and failure to appreciate the greatness of the Republic. Cleveland was sure that he owed a great deal to the famous German-American, but unlike Lincoln, he did not reward him.[39] Yet even without office, Schurz retained his reputation as a fearless reformer and his position as the best-known spokesman for the German-Americans.

XVII

Independent

THE CAMPAIGN OF 1884 had shown that Schurz, though no longer in office, still possessed considerable influence. Rapidly becoming the country's best-known independent, he was going to exert that influence for the remainder of his life. His German-American and Mugwump constituency furnished a secure base; his oratorical talents won him ample opportunity to voice his opinions; and his increasing literary output enabled him to reach more and more followers. However, his position outside of the main political parties kept him from ever holding important office again.

In spite of his prominence, Schurz's financial problems continued to cause him trouble. In 1884 and 1885 he was in such dire financial straits that he dissolved his household, sent his children to his in-laws in Germany, and stayed with the Jacobis. In 1885 he was contemplating the acquisition of either the Boston *Post* or the *Advertiser*, but financial difficulties as well as Godkin's interference thwarted this opportunity.[1] For a brief period he edited an export almanac; he also served as a representative of European bondholders of two American railroads, until in 1888 he accepted the position of American manager of the Hamburg-American Packet Company, a job he kept for four years. Thus, as time went on his situation improved. His lectures, his publications, his investments, and various positions provided him with sufficient income to pursue his scholarly career. And after Curtis's death in 1892, he became one of the editorial contributors to *Harper's Weekly*, for which he wrote the weekly lead articles.[2]

During this entire period, Schurz remained most passionately committed to civil service reform. Failing to grasp the strength of the steady nonideological development of the two-party system, he naturally came to believe in impartial competitive examinations as a cure for all the ills that faced the country.[3] That civil service tests would hardly remedy the industrial evils from which America was suffering did not occur to him; as a nineteenth-century liberal, he never did comprehend the complexity of the relations between labor and management, much less understand the necessity for state intervention. He even disapproved of women's suffrage—why should anyone wish to enfranchise prostitutes, of whom there were thousands in New York alone, he queried.[4] But he always remained loyal to his own revolutionary past. Opposing monopolies, cheap money, high tariffs, and unjust immigration restrictions, he continued to fight for freedom as he understood it. No form of bigotry, religious or otherwise, failed to arouse him to attack, even though in the case of the blacks his remedies were amazingly naive. And the welfare of his German-American fellow citizens, their Americanization combined with their continued loyalty to their origins, remained his special concern.

That such a maverick would constitute a problem for the incoming administration was natural. Although Schurz did not ask for an office for himself—he explained that he could not afford it—from the very beginning he and his associates pressured Cleveland to make civil service reform the cornerstone of his administration. The National Civil Service Reform League, in which Schurz was increasingly active, in December addressed a letter to the President-elect reminding him that the new administration had an excellent opportunity to prove its commitment to the cause, and it received an encouraging reply. Schurz was delighted. Whether words would be followed by deeds, however, remained to be seen.[5]

Although Cleveland urged Schurz to come to Albany to discuss problems of mutual interest, the general hesitated. Taking off for a lecture trip to the South, he said he did not want the papers to speculate about his availability for office. Only late in February, when he returned, did he finally visit the governor. Talking about the importance of remaining on good terms with independent supporters, he emphasized the necessity of strong leadership and a firm program. "I fear you think I am much better equipped for this business than I am," protested Cleveland. "You have these things at your fingers' reach, but I do not know them yet." Encouraged by his host's determined opposition to an inflationary silver policy, the general, who stayed for four hours interrupted only by lunch, also discussed cabinet prospects. Doubtless praising his friend Senator Thomas F. Bayard, whom Cleveland chose for secretary of state, he was worried and expressed his reservations about the likelihood of the appointment of Daniel Manning. Long the governor's mentor, Manning was Tilden's lieutenant in New York; though an opponent of Tammany, he was a machine politician and therefore anathema to the reformers. The same was true of William C. Whitney, the financier and traction magnate equally close to the President-elect, against whom Schurz also cautioned. But Cleveland did not mention Whitney, so that the general left fully satisfied.

A few days later the governor announced his nomination of Whitney for secretary of the navy, and Schurz was deeply offended. In an angry letter to Senator Lucius Q. C. Lamar, the incoming secretary of the interior, he protested that Manning's selection for the treasury was bad enough, but Whitney's elevation would simply belie the independents' assertion that they had been working for a reform administration. His cooperation with the Democrats for good ends always left him with "strange experiences." He had helped them to power in Missouri only to be driven out of the Senate, and now they made him look ridiculous by appointing people whom the Mugwumps detested. As far as he was concerned, he was simply going to lapse into silence.[6]

It is unlikely that Lamar believed Schurz would remain quiet. Because it was impossible for the new Democratic administration not to recognize all the factions of the party that had so long been in opposition, a certain degree of dissatisfaction on the part of the reformers was to be expected. But at times they could also be gratified. Schurz and his fellow Mugwumps took especial pains to procure the retention of Henry G. Pearson, the efficient Republican postmaster of New York. To the general's great satisfaction, Cleveland listened to their entreaties. And when Schurz met the President for an hour one evening at Whitney's house in New York, he was delighted to hear Cleveland talk "as if he were a Mugwump." That he was also pleased by his brother-in-law Jüssen's appointment as consul in Vienna was evident, although he denied that he had anything to do with it.[7]

In the long run, however, Schurz and his fellow independents were bound to be disappointed. With the best of intentions, as the leader of the Democratic party Cleveland could not disregard the demands of his associates, and as time went on there were many appointments which made the reformers unhappy. The new collector of internal revenue in Cleveland, John Farley, proclaimed civil service reform to be nonsense; the collector of the port of New York, E. L. Hedden, was closely connected with Hubert O. Thompson, a machine politician who had been indicted after serving as commissioner of public works; Eugene Higgins, the new chief of appointments at the Treasury Department, was a notorious Maryland spoilsman, and Aquia Jones, the postmaster of Indianapolis, categorically announced that he would hire no Republicans. Although the President displaced fewer of his political opponents than his predecessors, he tended to replace them as their terms expired, so that as time went on, fewer and fewer Republicans were left in office.[8]

This tendency greatly upset the general. Writing letter after letter to the President, he admonished him to remain true to his promises, but his very repetitiousness irritated Cleveland, who called his critics "those fool friends of civil service reform." Then, when in early 1886 Schurz, seeking to inject himself into a controversy between the President and Senate about the Tenure of Office Law, advised Cleveland to make public his reasons for suspending officers, the President took offense. Complaining to Silas Burt, the famous civil service reformer whom he had reappointed naval officer of the port of New York, he insisted the Mugwumps criticized him unfairly. Had he not resisted the demands of his own party? But Schurz only wrote again. He had the strongest confidence in Cleveland's sincerity, he assured him, yet there was danger that the administration might "sit down between two chairs," going far enough to exasperate the opponents of reform and not far enough to satisfy its friends. He felt that it was his duty to caution the President.[9]

Schurz's constant admonitions were in fact most irksome. Cleveland finally decided not to answer them, and his critic complained to Bayard. But the general refused to join the opposition. As he explained to his fellow reformer Wayne McVeagh, while he did not think the President had fully kept his word, he did not undervalue "the good things Cleveland had done." "The only kind of power we

Independents have springs from the popular belief that we speak the truth without fear or favor," he wrote. He was merely seeking to live up to that expectation.

As time went on, Schurz became more and more disappointed with the administration. Cleveland's yielding to pressure, his appointment of Democrats as deserving Republicans' terms expired, and his annoyance at the constant letters of admonition, all depressed the general. "I undertook the ungrateful role of the friend who utters disagreeable truths . . . ," he protested. "If for this [Cleveland] 'thinks hardly' of me, I am sorry." He was ruffled at the President's failure to answer him. How differently Lincoln had acted! If Cleveland maintained he could not find three or four hours to reply to his letters, might not Schurz say that he "found three or four months to advocate his election?" By August of 1887, when in his presidential address to the National Civil Service Reform League Curtis complained sharply about the administration's lax policies, Schurz decided that the reformers would have to make up their minds not to communicate with the President any more. Cleveland had apparently decided to get along without them.[10]

This totally pessimistic assessment did not last. In December, when the President sent Congress a message entirely devoted to tariff reform, the general took heart again. Cleveland's courageous stand certainly merited support, he thought, even though he doubted whether the Democratic party would follow suit. He had always considered tariff reform of great importance.[11]

By this time, the general's complete political independence had become proverbial. In 1885 he supported the Republican candidate for governor of New York against the successful Democratic machine politician David B. Hill; in 1886 he came to the aid of the Democrat Abram Hewitt, who was running for mayor of New York City in a three-way campaign against Theodore Roosevelt and Henry George, only to turn against the victorious Hewitt in 1887 when the mayor made some appointments not to the reformers' liking. His enemies severely castigated him for his repeated party switches, but he always maintained that while they were constantly changing principles, he was the one who remained true to his convictions.[12]

Considering his frequent disappointments with the administration, Schurz was not anxious to take part in the 1888 campaign. He spent the summer and most of the fall in Germany, on a trip combining business with pleasure. He had to go to Frankfurt to confer with the bondholders he had been representing, and he wanted to visit some European archives in connection with his historical projects. In addition, he was anxious to see his wife's relatives in Hamburg and Forsteck again.

He had certainly picked an interesting time for his visit. Early in March, Emperor William I died, succeeded by his son Frederick III, who was so ill with cancer that he reigned for only 99 days. His untimely death disturbed liberals everywhere, because they believed his ideas to be similar to theirs. What the new Kaiser, William II, would do was not yet clear.

Schurz assured himself of an exceptionally good reception because of a eulogy in praise of the old emperor he had delivered before leaving. Briefly touching on the fact that the departed monarch had once been his bitter enemy, he rendered tribute to his old persecutor's grand achievement in presiding over the unification of Germany. Widely reprinted in Europe as well as in America, the speech reaffirmed his position as the undoubted leader of the German-American community.[13]

He reaped the rewards of his magnanimity when he arrived in Berlin. Feted, banqueted, and welcomed by Germany's political and academic establishment, he was again received by the chancellor. Bismarck had aged considerably; to Schurz's remarks about his health, he replied, "Believe me, the first 70 years of life are still the best." In a lengthy conversation over a bottle of Rhine wine, followed by a walk in the chancellery garden, he told Schurz all kinds of anecdotes about European politics: How he had supposedly started the war with France by doctoring up the Ems dispatch, how all Hohenzollerns had allegedly been under the influence of their wives (an obvious allusion to his hostility to Empress Victoria), how he had induced the king to accept the imperial title—he was so voluble that he kept his visitor for two and one-half hours, a fact that caused much comment. In later years Bismarck's aide remembered that not even the arrival of papers in a red brief case, the usual sign that a guest's time was up, distracted the chancellor from his talk with the famous German-American. In fact, he enjoyed his conversation so much that he asked Schurz to come back for supper.

After meeting with the crown prince, the later William II, the general eagerly accepted Bismarck's informal invitation. Seated at the table with his family and a few guests and periodically feeding scraps to his two huge dogs, the chancellor listened avidly to everything Schurz had to say about the United States. After the meal, his children and grandchildren kissed him; then he stretched out on a couch in the parlor and continued the conversation. His visitor returned to Forsteck in high spirits.

Schurz's reception in his old fatherland was exhilarating, even though his enjoyment was somewhat dampened by the fact that his older son, Carli, as he called him, was gravely ill and needed several operations. Schurz traveled to Frankfurt, planned a trip up the Rhine, and finally attended a naval display in Hamburg, which had just joined the German Customs Union. William II, now emperor, invited him aboard his ship. Expressing himself favorably about his guest's furthering of German institutions in America, he impressed Schurz as an intelligent though not very robust ruler.

In November the general, dressed in a long chinchilla overcoat and blue felt hat and wearing black-rimmed glasses, arrived in Hoboken; reporters commented favorably upon once more seeing the familiar figure.[14] He was glad to have missed the presidential campaign; his only part, after refusing to back the successful Republican nominee, Benjamin Harrison, whom he considered a mere front for Blaine, had been to write a public letter in support of Cleveland's reelection.[15]

The trip to Europe had been profitable, not only personally but also financially. Schurz had successfully completed his mission for the German bondholders, and before he returned, he accepted the position of American representative of the Hamburg-American steamship company at $18,000 a year. Although he had no experience in the shipping business, he took the post because it gave him steady employment and provided him with much-needed income. The company profited by his name and the prestige he would bring with him. It was a mutually satisfactory arrangement that necessitated two more trips to Germany, one in 1889 and another in 1891, when he again visited the familiar places. He especially enjoyed the long Wagnerian performances at Bayreuth, at which meals were served between the acts and the guests summoned back to the theater by trumpets.[16]

Schurz's new employment kept him busy, but it did not really interfere with his principal activity during these years—the writing of biography, history, essays, articles, and speeches. When he went south in 1885, he delivered a carefully planned lecture on Benjamin Franklin, whom he praised for his pragmatism, tolerance, and diplomatic skill.[17] Then, after he suffered many setbacks and obtained his editor's reluctant permission to publish two volumes rather than just one, his *Henry Clay* was finally completed in 1887. Based on extensive research, the end product was a well-balanced, favorable biography, so readable and elegantly written that it has been called the only one of the American Statesmen Series that has retained its value to the present day.[18]

As soon as *Henry Clay* was finished, Schurz seriously contemplated undertaking a history of the United States leading up to and possibly including the Civil War, a book on which he was working when he went to Germany. But for some reason, he never went ahead with the project. The historian James Ford Rhodes, with whom he became very friendly, had already preempted the field, and it is likely that the task of preparing his own memoirs, eagerly solicited by publishers at home and abroad, made writing any other volumes impossible. In 1888 Schurz was approaching his sixtieth birthday; uncertain of how much time would be left to him, he was anxious to devote it to his *Reminiscences*.[19] Yet he always found enough leisure to write articles and essays for various publications, an activity for which he was increasingly well paid.[20]

Perhaps the most memorable essay he wrote in the early nineties was his brief article on Lincoln. Published in the form of a review of John G. Nicolay and John Hay's multivolume biography, it was really his own assessment of the Civil War president. In his view, Lincoln's most remarkable characteristics were his qualities of leadership, "leadership which does not dash ahead with brilliant daring, no matter who follows, but which is intent upon rallying all the available forces, gathering in all the stragglers, and closing up the column, so that the front may advance well supported." This ability and Lincoln's marvelous sense of timing accounted for his success. The assassination was therefore an especially deplorable catastrophe, for the Great Emancipator might well have rendered great services during Reconstruction. Retaining the confidence of the vanquished Southerners, he could still have safeguarded the interests of the Union and protected the rights of the freedmen.[21]

Schurz's most ambitious literary task was the preparation of his *Reminiscences*. Long pressed by publishers for his memoirs, he was anxious to commit something to paper as long as he still had the opportunity. Indeed, he was haunted by the thought that he might not have enough time to finish and, meticulous historian that he was, refused to rely on his memory alone. By checking and counterchecking, he hoped to avoid the factual errors of so many writers of autobiographies, but this method was time consuming. In the summer of 1887, plagued by rheumatism and kept at home by Carli's illness, he finally started the enterprise. He hoped to make considerable progress by the end of the summer, but in fact he never succeeded in completing the three volumes that eventually appeared. They were not published until some time after his death twenty years later with an essay by Frederick Bancroft and William A. Dunning to cover the period he had been unable to reach.[22]

The general's literary work was most successful. Dictating nearly everything, he habitually wrote down things as they occurred to him. Then he went over the material, adding, deleting, and checking, until the final product emerged.[23] His style was lively, his language clear, and the result was eminently readable. After praising his *Henry Clay* as "one of the ablest and most important of recent political writings," the *New York Times* pointed out that it was a work that belonged "to good literature, being pervaded by literary and artistic sense, written in elegant language, charming for its lucidity." The *Atlantic Monthly* praised the book as the best of the American Statesman Series, "if . . . not the best work of this nature which has ever been produced in this country."[24] Eminent public figures were lavish in their compliments, President Cleveland, ex-President Hayes, and George William Curtis sending their congratulations. Fellow writers like Moses Coit Tyler remarked on its excellent literary style; Horace White thought the chapter on party chiefs to be the best he had ever read; and George Bancroft, the dean of American historians, admired it so much that he took the time to make marginal annotations on his copy. Even such former antagonists as Charles D. Drake and Henry L. Dawes wrote him how much they enjoyed the book, and Gustave Koerner characterized it as a "literary gem."[25]

The Lincoln essay, too, was a triumph. Theodore Roosevelt, then a rising politician and fellow contributor to the American Statesmen Series who had deeply resented the fact that two volumes had been allotted to Schurz for *Clay* while others had only one, liked it and wanted the author to prepare a full-sized biography of the Civil War president. Hayes thought nothing better would ever be written about the man he called "the greatest, most wonderful character who has appeared in public affairs in any age," and Herbert Spencer added his heartfelt congratulations. Schurz had every reason to be proud of his reviews.[26]

Neither Schurz's literary activities nor his duties as manager of the German steamship company kept him from continuing his active interest in politics. The advent of the Harrison administration after a campaign marked by huge expenditures confirmed his conviction that civil service reform remained a problem of the first importance. Although he was not directly connected with any member of the new regime in which Blaine served as secretary of state, he retained considerable influence because of his acquaintance with Republican reformers. One of these was Roosevelt, whom Harrison appointed civil service commissioner. Chagrined at Schurz's failure to support him for mayor in 1886, he had nevertheless continued to maintain reasonable relations with him. Others, like William Dudley Foulke and Lucius B. Swift, the Indiana Republican reformers, also remained friendly, as did Charles J. Bonaparte, the Baltimore Republican who was one of the mainstays of the National Civil Service Reform League. Suggesting to Roosevelt that the House inquire into Postmaster General John Wanamaker's failure to investigate election frauds and their connection with the Baltimore post office, he was able to assist the commissioner in making a success of the probe. He had long since castigated Wanamaker for his lavish expenditures during the 1888 campaign and earned the millionaire's intense dislike.[27]

Schurz's membership in various prestigious societies also provided him with a continuing forum for influencing public affairs. One of these was the Commonwealth Club, which on January 12, 1889 honored him with a dinner at the Westminster Hotel. Pointing out that the political parties' failure to stand for principles had created an incontestable need for independent politics, he utilized the occasion to warn the incoming Harrison administration that civil service reform was the issue upon which it would stand or fall. In October 1889, in a speech before the Forestry Association at Philadelphia, he made a strong plea for conservation, and in the fall of 1890, at the Massachusetts Reform Club in Boston, he excoriated the recently passed McKinley tariff, while at the same time condemning the new Force bill Henry Cabot Lodge was proposing for the protection of the increasingly harassed Southern blacks.[28]

The general's attitude toward the race question was still marred by his break with the Grant administration. Blinded as he was by his conviction that blacks could solve many of their problems by joining both parties, he actually believed during his 1885 visit to the South that he was seeing some progress. He summed up his findings in an article, "The New South," an essay which merely repeated his often-stated opinions. Not even the mounting evidence of steadily worsening race relations caused him to change his mind until his involvement in the anti-imperialist crusade at the end of the century led him to rethink his premises.[29]

Because of his distaste for the Harrison administration, Schurz was anxious to bring about in 1892 the renomination of Cleveland as the strongest Democratic candidate. Afraid that the machine elements and silverites backing the New York politician David B. Hill might be successful, he conferred with fellow reformers and with Whitney, the ex-President's manager. In an interview with the New York *World* on June 15, Schurz strongly advocated Cleveland's renomination as the party's best hope, and at Whitney's request he even wrote some resolutions for use at the Democratic national convention. As Cleveland was nominated without much trouble, however, they were not needed.[30]

The general had every intention of taking an active part in the campaign. "I am like an old cavalry horse hearing the bugle again," he wrote to his friend, the author and translator Frances Hellman. "Then it stretches the stiff legs and snorts as if it were still young. But perhaps the fighting spirit is no longer as mirthful as formerly. Nevertheless, some of it is still there." However, in the summer he had a serious recurrence of his gall bladder disorder, so that all strenuous activity was out of the question.[31] Although his help seemed crucial to the Democrats, especially after Curtis died in August and Schurz assumed his editorial duties at *Harper's Weekly*, all he could do was to write a public letter to a meeting in Brooklyn reiterating his reasons for supporting Cleveland.

The last weeks of the campaign were troublesome. Before sending his letter, Schurz, hearing that the candidate was negotiating with the machine politicians in New York, demanded that Cleveland endorse the general's line of thinking before Schurz made the document public. Only after he was satisfied by other civil service reformers' repeated assurances about the candidate's intentions did he finally publish the letter. Emphasizing the importance of curbing the expenditure of huge sums of money by political parties, he asserted that the Republicans were totally beholden to the money power and responsible for ruinous high tariffs. The election of Cleveland, a man of proven conscience, would restore faith in the system and augur well for sound financial policies and civil service reform. As Schurz's recovery progressed, he was able to deliver a speech in German at Cooper Union. When Cleveland won, the general again had a claim on the new administration. It is true that the labor unrest of 1892—especially the Homestead riot in Pennsylvania which Whitelaw Reid, Harrison's running mate, unsuccessfully tried to settle, and the President's dispatch of Federal troops to crush a silver miner's strike in Idaho—to say nothing of the administration's unpopularity, probably had more to do with the victory than the support of the Mugwumps. For Schurz, however, Cleveland's return to power represented a vindication of independent politics.[32]

But active campaigning was no longer one of Schurz's main interests. He spent his time writing and editing, turning out articles on all manner of subjects. After his acceptance of the editorial position at *Harper's*, he could not write as often for others, although his weekly editorials (signed, beginning in 1897) made up for the limitation. European affairs, "the Decay of Political Parties," Indian problems, immigration questions, the evils of the annexation of tropical islands, and, of course, civil service reform were among the topics he discussed.[33] Crisply written, lucidly presented, and always interesting, his articles kept alive his reputation as an excellent writer and a fearless fighter against corruption.

Although never rich, Schurz managed to live comfortably in New York. After he had overcome his financial stringency, late in 1885 his family rejoined him, and thereafter his daughters managed his household for him. During the summer months, he went to the Jersey shore, to Westchester, or further into the country. Later in the decade, he lived in the so-called Spanish flats, an apartment complex at 175 West 58th Street; in 1892 he bought a country home, "Solitude," at Pocantico Hills near Tarrytown.[34] The old farm house with its many additions, surrounded by a park with a small pond and a beautiful view of the Hudson River, enchanted him, and he told his friends how easy it was to reach it by connecting with the railroad at the 155th Street "El" station. On Sundays, friends would come out to visit. Animatedly entertaining them, he liked to take them hiking, always ending up at a hill beyond the orchard to look out over the broad valley, until the supper bell called him back. "How beautiful is the world," he said. "I hope it won't be necessary to depart from it for a long, long time to come." He stayed at "Solitude" until 1896, when he sold it to move back into the city, into a house on East 68th Street.[35]

It was also during this period that Schurz built his home at Bolton Landing on Lake George. His friend the doctor owned the neighboring cottage and the property; Schurz had spent several summers in the vicinity until in 1892 he acquired his summer house. Located two hundred feet above the lake, it contained a small porch with a magnificent view of the water, a hall with a high ceiling and galleries upon which Agathe put her easels, a dining room, kitchen, and bedroom, with additional bedrooms upstairs. In the morning before breakfast, the owner, rising early, took long walks in the woods, accompanied by two old St. Bernards, the poodle Gyp, and later by two dachshunds belonging to his daughters. Back in time for breakfast on the porch, he would join his family, and generally the Jacobis came to take their meals with him also. Then he would go to his room to write, an opera glass always beside him so that he might watch the boat traffic on the lake. At night the family often enjoyed reading the latest books aloud together. Schurz loved Bolton Landing; he felt comfortable with his family, the doctor, and the many visitors who came to see him in unceasing numbers.[36]

These domestic arrangements did not interfere with his continuing relationship with Fanny Chapman. Meeting her frequently at various places, he wrote her long letters about virtually everything that concerned him or her—his political forays, his brother-in-law Adolph's death in 1889, his son's enrollment at Harvard. "How I love you, my dear *Herzensfanny*," he assured her, "and how I am longing for you." Bemoaning the fate that had made it impossible for him to make her truly happy, he nevertheless refused to let it interfere with their lasting intimacy.[37]

For a man getting on in years, Schurz enjoyed fairly good health. Recurrent bouts with his gall bladder gave him some trouble—at times, Jacobi forbade him his favorite Rhine wines—and in 1885 he sprained both feet while stumbling over a rock in the street. Two years later, at the corner of 42nd Street and 6th Avenue, he fell again, this time breaking his thigh, but his recovery was so complete that eventually he even managed to go horseback riding again.[38] He was able to continue his active life, attending innumerable dinners and receiving visitors from near and far—Paderewski, Hayes, Cleveland, Lilli Lehmann, and various traveling German dignitaries, among others. He took great satisfaction in his position as a writer and elder statesman, and if he missed public office, he always denied it.[39]

The general's relations with the President during Cleveland's second administration were less disappointing than those during the first. In December, the two men appeared together at a Reform Club dinner, where Schurz publicly offered Cleveland his congratulations and praised him for having appealed to the moral force of the American people.[40] Nevertheless, the German-American, about to assume the presidency of the National Civil Service Reform League, again kept pressing the administration for civil service reform. Denying that he had any interest in any office for himself—he much preferred his scholarly life to public service, he assured his sister-in-law—he constantly offered advice to the President. Cleveland must send him advance copies of the inaugural address so that he could treat it properly in *Harper's Weekly*; he must not sign an extradition treaty with Russia that might jeopardize the right of asylum; good men must be appointed to represent the United States in Berlin; a special session of Congress must be called to repeal the Sherman Silver Purchase Act; and Theodore Roosevelt must be reappointed civil service commissioner. Because Schurz was now an influential editor and president of the National Civil Service League, his letters could not simply be disregarded, and the President sent him polite replies. And when in May 1893 he came to Washington to urge extension of the civil service lists, Cleveland asked him to have dinner with him and his wife privately before the public interview. Receiving his visitor most cordially, he managed to retain good relations with the intransigent reformer.[41]

This was true in spite of the fact that at the beginning the administration's performance was spotty, at least from Schurz's point of view. Although he retained Roosevelt, Cleveland made a number of objectionable appointments. The new secretary of the treasury, John G. Carlisle, was not particularly friendly to civil service reform, and even Postmaster General Wilson S. Bissell, fundamentally in sympathy with the reformers, came in for his share of criticism in connection with employment procedures in the post offices. Through constant admonitions, both personal and editorial, Schurz continued to press for his objectives, until in the end the President gratified him by substantial extensions of the civil service lists.[42]

In other ways, too, the President lived up to Schurz's expectations. In spite of the severe depression which set in in 1893 and the immense pressures to which he was subjected, Cleveland refused to compromise with the silverites. The Sherman Silver Purchase Act was repealed, the gold standard maintained, and if the effort substantially to reduce the tariff was not entirely successful, it was not the President's fault. In addition, he vetoed an immigration restriction bill. To be sure, the end result was a serious split in the Democratic party, but Schurz, independent as ever, could not have cared less. Cleveland's conventional philosophy was much to his liking.[43]

In New York, too, Schurz participated actively in independent politics. Fully supporting the effort to end Tammany's misrule of the city, in 1894 he was enthusiastically engaged in rallying reformers and his fellow countrymen to the Republican-reform ticket of William L. Strong for mayor and to an independent Democratic candidate for governor to defeat David B. Hill. The reformers were successful; the Republicans won in the city and state, and in the following spring, Theodore Roosevelt became police commissioner of New York.[44] This appointment led to a break in reform ranks, because the new commissioner soon aroused the German-Americans when he began a policy of strict enforcement of the Sunday liquor laws. The general tried to defend him in a letter to the *Staats-Zeitung*, but his efforts to convince his fellow Germans that clean government was more important than beer were fruitless. Roundly abused by the German press, he was unable to maintain his compatriots' commitment to reform in the November elections. In the long run, however, the incident did not affect his standing in the German-American community. Moreover, the Republican governor, Levi P. Morton, proved friendly to civil service reform and carried through a satisfactory program in the state.[45]

As time went on, Schurz's countrymen took increasing pride in his prominence. No major German Day was complete without him. He spoke at German-American affairs whenever the sponsors were able to secure him, and on both sides of the Atlantic he was considered *the* representative of the German-American community.[46] "As a German, I am proud of Carl Schurz," Bismarck told Andrew D. White; William II said to Poultney Bigelow that he was gratified at Schurz's making travel on German steamships popular; the New York educational authorities asked his opinion of applicants for professorships of German at City College; he delivered the principal German Day address at the Chicago International Exhibition; and he was active in the struggle to erect a monument to Heinrich Heine.[47] He played his role as a mediator between the two countries very well.

His prominence in German-American affairs soon involved him in delicate diplomatic negotiations. Always a good American patriot—he abhorred the nationalistic excesses of Bismarckian and Wilhelmine Germany—he was very disturbed about the worsening relations between his old and his new country.[48] Clashes between German and American interests in Samoa had led to a dangerous situation. German traders had long established their supremacy in the western part of the archipelago; American treaty rights gave the United States special privileges at Pago Pago, and Great Britain likewise had a stake in Samoa. By January 1889, the conflict became more intense because local German authorities made war against one of the native factions; German marines were landed and private property destroyed.

Because of the danger of a rupture between Germany and the United States, Count Arco-Valley, the German minister in Washington, sought out Schurz in a New York hotel. The general told him he thought the Germans had behaved badly and advised a speedy settlement with the United States, preferably by negotiations restoring the rights of all three powers. In a subsequent letter which Arco-Valley forwarded to Bismarck, Schurz graphically outlined the dangers of a German-American war. He warned that the conflict would take a long time, lead to the destruction of German commerce on the high seas, and eventually redound to the benefit of third parties. Reporting his conversations to Secretary Bayard, he offered himself as an intermediary. Fortunately, his services were not needed. On March 16, a hurricane destroyed almost all of the warships of the contending powers, and a few months later, after he had seen Acro-Valley again, a Tripartite Agreement for the common administration of Samoa was successfully completed.[49]

When in 1893 the Democrats returned to power, Schurz was delighted with their apparent opposition to imperialistic adventures. Fully approving of Cleveland's withdrawal of the treaty of annexation with Hawaii that the Harrison administration had negotiated, he thundered against Manifest Destiny in *Harper's*.[50] Toward the end of Cleveland's second term, however, Schurz was greatly disappointed by the President's warlike message demanding that Great Britain submit to one-sided settlement of her dispute with Venezuela concerning the boundary with British Guyana. Vitally interested in the passage by the New York Chamber of Commerce of resolutions calling upon Britain to accept impartial arbitration, he seized the opportunity of Abram Hewitt's absence because of illness to take his place and deliver an emotional speech. He ridiculed the idea of the usefulness of wars, pointed out the horrors of armed conflict to which his generation had been subjected, and strongly urged the adoption of the resolutions. They were carried, although Great Britain's pacific attitude made them unnecessary. Thereafter, in collaboration with Andrew Carnegie, he devoted his energies to work for an arbitration treaty with the British.[51] His countrymen had every reason to be proud of him.

Thus, the loss of important public office did not end Schurz's role as America's foremost ethnic politician. Writer, speaker, and publicist, he continued to exert his influence. However, his lack of a political base would soon become painfully obvious. His last fight—the struggle against imperialism—lay ahead.

XVIII

Anti-Imperialist: The Last Years

In 1896, Schurz was approaching seventy and deserved some respite from strife. He was content to live the life of an elder statesman and publicist, writing, lecturing, and occasionally giving advice to presidents. But the last years of his life were not to be peaceful. First the fight against free silver and then a constant struggle against imperialism kept him almost incessantly involved in public controversy. The success of the first was gratifying; the apparent failure of the second, most disturbing. Personal tragedy also embittered this period, so that the old general might well have despaired. But he never fully lost his optimism.

Because of the ever-deepening depression, during the 1890s inflationist forces had been gaining steadily. Debt-ridden farmers on the Great Plains demanded relief from their onerous mortgages; the unemployed threatened the established order; and the People's party frightened conservatives with its program of reform and the restoration of the old standard of 16:1 as a rate of exchange between silver and gold. Although Cleveland remained firm against the increasing pressure for the remonetization of silver, insurgents in his own party were becoming more and more powerful.

Like most Mugwumps, Schurz loathed inflationary schemes. Convinced of the standard maxims of orthodox finance, he not only refused to admit that there was any justification for cheapening the currency but considered the countrywide agitation an open invitation for social revolution. That the unusual deflationary trends of the past thirty-five years had given some substance to the farmers' complaints did not faze him. "Call fifty cents a dollar and you'll have more dollars, but not more wealth," he insisted, and most of his independent associates agreed. Consequently, he watched the political developments of 1896 with great misgivings. Appalled at the success of the silver Democrats, he believed that the Democratic party would split, indeed, that it had already thrown away its chance of emerging as the better of the two major political organizations. And the Republicans were about to rally behind William McKinley, the author of the highest tariff within memory. It was a distressing prospect.[1]

In June, the Republicans duly nominated McKinley on a platform promising to settle the financial question by international agreement. A few weeks later, the Democrats in Chicago, captivated by the rousing appeal of the young Nebraskan, William Jennings Bryan, "not to press down upon the brow of labor this crown of thorns, . . . not [to] crucify makind upon a cross of gold," nominated the orator on a silver platform. A few break-away Republicans also endorsed Bryan, as did the Populists, while Cleveland and a small remnant of the old organization supported an independent gold Democrat. Schurz was certain of the course he had to take. Much though he might disagree with McKinley's tariff views, he would have to defeat the silver heresy.

The fact that most German-Americans tended to oppose inflation gave Schurz considerable leverage. A German Sound Money League, with which he cooperated, approached the Republican National Committee and found its chairman, Marcus A. Hanna, most anxious to obtain his support. Although refusing his suggestion that McKinley pledge himself to veto any tariff bill with a silver rider attached, Hanna finally came to an understanding with the general, who insisted throughout the campaign on stressing the financial question. Schurz would maintain his independence and speak under the auspices of such organizations as the National Sound Money League, managed by his friend, the Chicago reformer Edwin Burritt Smith.[2]

Schurz was wholly convinced that the country was in serious danger. Believing that the Democratic party had "thrown itself into the arms of the silver fraud and nominated for President a young man who has a gift for oratory and is clearly seeking to incite the have-nots against the haves," he was determined to work hard for a victory of law and order which would make future assaults on society impossible.[3] Exaggerated as these notions were, they were by no means uncommon.

Schurz was as good as his word. Setting out to lecture to his countrymen, he concentrated on Illinois, where another leader of German birth, John Peter Altgeld, was trying to win them for the other side. After delivering a long address on sound money in Chicago, he sought to demolish Altgeld's theories in Peoria, and his speeches were persuasive. "The effect of your Chicago speech has been wonderful," exulted Marcus Hanna, asking him to continue the good work. When McKinley won by an overwhelming majority, Schurz expressed his relief at "the great deliverance." That the general had closely collaborated with many of the country's leading bankers did not bother him. Hanna himself credited him with a major part in the outcome.[4]

As he had always done, Schurz immediately attempted to make use of the victory to exert influence on the incoming administration. Assuring Hanna that he did not want to be included in the cabinet—an unlikely event in any case, considering his former strained relations with the President-elect—he strongly urged that Cleveland's capable appointees be retained in office and that civil service lists be extended. The National Civil Service Reform League sent a committee to Washington to propagate its point of view, and when in April the new President came to New York for the dedication of Grant's tomb, Schurz spent an hour and a half with him at the Windsor Hotel. Comfortably puffing away at his cigar, McKinley assured his guest that he was a civil service reformer himself. And, when on July 1 the general visited the White House and had supper with the President, he was again cordially received.

At first, McKinley seemed to be true to his word. He issued a number of orders strengthening the civil service, but this behavior did not last long. Although the civil service reformers praised him at their 1897 convention, they would soon become his determined opponents.[5]

The first jolt to the reformers came in New York, where in 1897 the Republican governor, Frank S. Black, signed a civil service law which in effect constituted a step backward by setting up two categories for examinees, merit and fitness, the latter to be decided by the appointing officers. Traveling to Albany to testify against the pending bill, Schurz engaged in bitter controversy with the governor but could do little except to excoriate the change in his annual presidential address to the National Civil Service Reform League.[6] Then one of the leading Republicans in the Senate, Jacob S. Gallinger of New Hampshire, launched a slashing attack on civil service reform and on Schurz. After first allowing his friend, the league's secretary George McAneny, to answer Gallinger, Schurz himself sent him one of his acerbic letters, which was widely reprinted together with the ensuing correspondence. In the winter an equally prominent Republican in the House, Charles H. Grosvenor, reopened the assault only to receive another devastating letter from the general.[7] Finally, on May 29, 1899, McKinley ordered the exemption of over thirty-six hundred positions from the civil service rules. Schurz and his collaborators were appalled,[8] but by that time they had already been so disillusioned by the President's conversion to imperialism that his abandonment of their cause was merely an anticlimax.

In the late 1890s the search for colonies was popular in America as well as in Europe. Supposed economic necessity, theories of the importance of sea power first popularized by Alfred Thayer Mahan, racial absurdities emphasizing the special mission of the white race, to say nothing of ever-increasing nationalist sentiments, led all major powers to undertake colonial adventures. The United States was no exception; in fact, Schurz's former friends, Roosevelt and Lodge, were in the forefront of those preaching a "large policy."

That Schurz would deplore this development was not surprising. Most of his Mugwump associates hated imperialism also, but for the general, who had long opposed the acquisition of tropical islands, the issue finally became a matter threatening to undermine those beliefs which he valued most. Because he had come to America in order to find what he considered the model republic, he looked upon the trend toward the acquisition of empire as an unmitigated disaster that would eventually undermine the very foundations of democracy. Imperialism would lead to the annexation of foreign populations against their will, people totally unable to participate in the American experiment in self-government. Above all, the incorporation of distant peoples in the fabric of the great republic would render it faithless to the ideals of the Declaration of Independence and oblivious to the Constitution. It might even destroy it altogether. Dejected about the outbreak of the Spanish-American War, which he saw as a threat to everything he held dear, Schurz unburdened himself to his sister-in-law. "It is hard to see the results of the labors of a lifetime endangered in this way," he wrote her, and the more the administration committed itself to imperialism, the more depressed he became.[9]

There was also another consideration which made the anti-imperialist crusade so important for Schurz. Foreign adventures inevitably associated with the "large policy" were leading the United States into clashes with other powers, and in view of the developing rapprochement with Great Britain, it was especially Germany that seemed to stand in America's way. To so fervent a German-American patriot as Schurz, nothing could be more ominous than a possible rupture between the two countries he loved, and it is no coincidence that the last letter included in the printed version of his writings is a paean to the friendship between Germany and America. "There is between the two nations not the slightest occasion for discord," he insisted. "To provoke such a discord without the most imperative cause would be a crime as well as an absurdity—a criminal absurdity as well as a foolish crime."[10]

From the very beginning Schurz had made his opposition to imperialism clear. Delighted with Cleveland's withdrawal of the Hawaiian annexation treaty, he set forth his objections to expansion in his October 1893 article in *Harper's Monthly*. In effect, he merely repeated the arguments he had used twenty years earlier against the acquisition of Santo Domingo. Democratic government could not flourish in a hot climate; tropical countries were not congenial to men of "Germanic blood"; and the mixed populations of such areas were so unlike the people of the United States as to make their equal participation in the government problematical. But unless new acquisitions could eventually become states, they would have to be held as dependencies, an idea totally at variance with the Constitution. Making light of arguments for the necessity of overseas naval bases, he pointed out that the United States was so powerful and so well located as to be fully protected against foreign attack. And while he did not reject the idea of commercial expansion, he denied that American exports needed any colonial underpinning.[11] These tenets became his standard theme in the years to come.

Prior to his election, McKinley had said little about expansion. Meeting him in New York shortly after the inauguration, Schurz complimented him on his foreign appointments. There was one exception: The minister to Hawaii, Harold M. Sewall, had long sympathized with the imperialist aims of the local sugar planters. Assuring him that the envoy had been given firm instructions against annexation, the President promised that if the minister went beyond his guidelines, he would be instantly recalled. "Permit me to take your hand on this," said Schurz, reaching out to the President. "This is the best thing you have told me yet—that your administration will not countenance anything of that kind." Vigorously shaking the general's hand, McKinley replied, "Ah, you may be sure there will be no jingo nonsense under my administration." At least that was what Schurz remembered a few years later.

But soon it became apparent that the President had changed his mind. He negotiated a treaty with Hawaii, and the general rushed to Washington to question him. McKinley received him cordially, although he insisted Schurz's anti-imperialist point of view was entirely new to him. Explaining that he had acted because Japan was "stretching out its hand to Hawaii," he invited his critic to send him everything he wrote about the problem. The treaty would lie over until the winter in any case.[12]

The general did not have to be asked twice. Forwarding a long exposition of his views to the White House, he predicted that the incorporation of tropical islands would lead to the end of "the Republic of Washington and Lincoln." To make certain the President understood the depth of his feeling, he added, "I am so firmly convinced of this that, cordial advocate of civil service reform and of a sound currency as you certainly believe me to be, I would rather see . . . the whole civil service law repealed and a free silver coinage law enacted than Hawaii annexed."[13]

But of course the President refused to listen. When the treaty of annexation could not command the necessary two-thirds majority in the Senate, he accomplished his object by a joint resolution. By that time, however, Hawaii was no longer the imperialists' main concern. Their attentions had shifted to Cuba, where as a result of a rebellion against the motherland, the Spanish-American War had broken out.

For Schurz, the war with Spain was an utter calamity. Not that he did not sympathize with the sufferings of the Cubans—he was revolted by Spanish "tyranny" in the island and assured his sister-in-law that American impulses to free the oppressed were rooted in genuine idealism. But he loathed war; he had seen too much of it at Chancellorsville, Gettysburg, and Chattanooga, and he correctly foresaw the lift the outbreak of hostilities would give to the imperialists.[14]

For these reasons, he was at first delighted with the President's apparent failure to yield to the pressure of the jingoes. Not reacting forcefully to the clamor set up by newspaper kings like William Randolph Hearst and Schurz's former assistant, Joseph Pulitzer, nor willing to go along with members of his own administration urging prompt interference to end the Cuban war, McKinley initially kept the country at peace. Not even provocations like the sinking of the *Maine* and the inflammatory Dupuy de Lôme letter, in which the Spanish envoy insulted him, seemed to shake his pacific disposition. Schurz published editorials in *Harper's Weekly* deprecating the need to vindicate national honor—the United States was so much stronger than Spain, he argued, that no glory was to be gained from any conflict with her—and praised the President's forbearance. "The conservative and unselfishly patriotic sentiment of the country stands behind your peace policy with confidence, gratitude, and admiration," he wrote to McKinley on April 1, 1898. Inducing the New York Chamber of Commerce to adopt peace resolutions, he assured the President that if he succeeded in maintaining the peace the American people would never cease to be grateful to him. Even when McKinley finally sent Congress a message which, though couched in ambiguous terms, led directly to a declaration of war, Schurz overlooked the main point and was still hopeful. "Permit me to offer you my personal thanks for your excellent message . . . ," he wrote on April 12. "I have no doubt that the people will sustain you in your efforts for peace." War broke out a few days later, and he was utterly downcast. "I must confess to you that I am profoundly distressed by the present unhappy state of affairs," he complained to Bayard. "The impulses of the great mass of our people are no doubt generous and noble. But the reckless passions of unruly spirits have acquired a sway which bodes ill to the country."[15]

Notwithstanding his fears, as a good American he wholeheartedly backed the war effort. Although his initial opposition to war had already cost him his editorship at *Harper's,* he never faltered in the support of the national cause. He even wrote a defense of American policy for publication in Germany, but his efforts were not appreciated. McKinley did not always bother to answer Schurz's frequent letters of warning against annexations; welcoming the incorporation of Hawaii, the President was already looking beyond this new possession, to the Philippines, Puerto Rico, and possibly even Cuba.[16]

Schurz was so unhappy about these developments that he began to devote all his energies to the battle against imperialism. Writing, lecturing, cajoling, he sought to popularize the idea of a speedy peace without annexations. But like many of his coworkers in the anti-imperialist crusade, he was too old and too far out of the mainstream to be effective. At a conference at Saratoga under the auspices of the Civic Federation, he ably presented his point of view, only to fail in swaying the delegates. The administration became more and more committed to a peace treaty including the cession of Puerto Rico and one of the Ladrone Islands, and McKinley gradually became converted to the idea of taking the entire Philippine archipelago as well. Schurz concluded that the only way to prevent the conclusion and ratification of an annexationist peace was to defeat the Republican party in the November elections.[17] The result was a head-on clash with his old friend, Theodore Roosevelt.

Schurz had long been uneasy about his fellow civil service reformer's increasingly bellicose attitude. "He gives too much rein to his restless and combative temperament," he remarked three years earlier. In 1896, during the drive for an arbitration treaty with Great Britain, Roosevelt added a handwritten postscript to a long typewritten letter about civil service reform. "Some time I wish another chance to discuss war & peace with you, oh Major General, Cabinet Minister, Senator & Historian! I only hope all of you international arbitration people don't finally bring us literally to the Chinese level." Then, when Roosevelt joined the McKinley administration as assistant secretary of the navy and resigned to become lieutenant colonel of the Rough Riders, a break with Schurz became inevitable. Delivering an address at the Newport Naval War College in June 1897, he called for a stronger fleet, glorified the triumphs of armed struggle, and used the word "war" sixty-two times. Schurz immediately attacked these ideas in *Harper's Weekly,* and when the Rough Rider, fresh from the triumphs of San Juan Hill, became the Republican nominee for governor of New York, the general refused to support him. No matter that he stood for civil service reform, no matter that his Democratic opponent, Augustus van Wyck, had close ties to Tammany—Roosevelt was one of the principal advocates of expansion, as he reemphasized on October 5 at Carnegie Hall. For Schurz, the struggle against imperialism overrode all other considerations.[18]

Roosevelt was still anxious to obtain the general's backing. "I don't know whether you are with me in this fight or not," he wrote, "but I hope you are, for on State issues we are as one, and the war is over now, and I am as anxious for peace and quiet as you possibly can be." Schurz immediately rebuffed him. He had long been hoping to be able to offer his support, he replied, but after the Carnegie Hall address, he could not possibly do so. In a public letter to the *Evening Post,* he explained that the governorship of New York was often a stepping-stone to the presidency, so that state issues alone were not at stake. He was going to vote for Theodore Bacon and his independent ticket.[19]

The split between the two former allies was never healed. As time went on, Roosevelt became more and more contemptuous of Schurz and the "goo goos," as he called the good government anti-imperialists. "I didn't read what Schurz said," he boasted in 1899. "I don't care what that prattling foreigner shrieks or prattles. . . ." By 1904, he denied that he had ever been friendly with the general. Calling him "insincere and hypocritical," he rarely missed an opportunity to ridicule him. And Schurz, though still conceding the colonel's good qualities—his popular appeal, his devotion to civil service reform—no longer trusted him. He thought Roosevelt would have cut a splendid figure at the time of the Crusades or the Wars of the Roses. "But," he warned, "the Lord protect the country if he ever should become President."[20]

The New York election and Roosevelt's victory only spurred Schurz on to greater efforts in the fight against the proposed peace treaty. Together with other Mugwumps, men like Charles Francis Adams, Erving Winslow, and Edward Atkinson, he started a movement that led to the organization of an anti-imperialist league in Boston headed by former Secretary of the Treasury George S. Boutwell. Senators George F. Hoar, George Edmunds, and John B. Henderson, reformers like Edwin Burritt Smith, Edward M. Shepard, and Moorfield Storey, and intellectuals like Charles E. Norton and William James also cooperated with the anti-imperialists, and Carnegie supplied funds. "You have brains and I have dollars," the multimillionaire wrote to the general. "I can devote some of my dollars to spreading your brains." Schurz proposed a plebiscite on imperialism—a totally impractical idea—and when the Treaty of Paris was signed, he redoubled his attacks on its annexationist provisions to prevent ratification. On January 4, 1899, in the midst of that "hot-bed of jingoism," as he called the Windy City, he delivered a convocation address at the University of Chicago entitled "The Issue of Imperialism." Repeating his arguments against the acquisition of tropical areas and appealing to the spirit of the Declaration of Independence, he also warned of the danger of armed insurrection in the Philippines, which in the end the United States would have to put down by force. Let the Republic return to the faith of the fathers, neutralize the Philippines, and carry out the pledge of freedom given to Cuba at the beginning of the war.[21]

It was a powerful speech—"about the best missionary work that can be done," Carnegie called it—but the general pleaded in vain. Despite Senator Hoar's assurances that there were enough votes to defeat the treaty, despite a memorial of protest drawn up by Schurz, Charles Francis Adams and others, on February 6, 1899 the Senate ratified the treaty by a narrow margin.[22] And just as Schurz had predicted, a rebellion broke out in the Philippines.

The ratification of the treaty was a hard blow, but the general refused to lose hope. "Well, we now have a long campaign before us, the conduct of which, under changed circumstances, will require calm judgment and tough perseverance," he wrote to Adams. And persevere he did. He saw to it that with Carnegie's help his Chicago speech was widely distributed, and in April, at the third annual conference of the American Academy of Political Science in Philadelphia, he delivered another onslaught against expansionism. "Militarism and Democracy" was the title of his address. Military glory was the most "unwholesome food" for democracies, he explained. The two Napoleons and the Dreyfus affair in France, to say nothing of Oliver Cromwell in England, showed how destructive large armies were to republics. Fortunately, until recently the United States had stood clear of this danger, but its involvement in colonial wars was threatening to undermine this tradition, a change which in the course of time would make the American people "ruefully remember how free and great and happy they once were with less military glory and with no outlying dominions and subject populations."[23]

The bloody progress of the war against the Philippine insurrectionists infuriated Schurz. "President McKinley has proved himself to be in almost every way a real miserable customer, who never has the courage of his own convictions, most generally listens to the worst advisers, and then thinks he can make everything well again with unctious phrases," he wrote to Emilie Meyer. Afraid that the more firmly the President committed the country to the Phillipine war, the more difficult it would be to get out again, the general nevertheless believed the people were beginning to tire of imperialist excesses like the unjust expedition against the rebels.[24] In fact, he was looking forward with great confidence to a national gathering of anti-imperialists at Chicago.

The meeting, which drew a total of 160 delegates from all over the country, featured Schurz as the main speaker. This time he concentrated upon the injustice of the military action in the islands. Emilio Aguinaldo, the leader of the insurrectionists, had been America's friend, a friend who had been cruelly betrayed. If Great Britain had ceded the American colonies to France, would not the patriots have been justified in taking up arms against the French? Demanding that the United States negotiate an armistice based on independence for the archipelago, he ended with his old slogan, "Our country—when right to be kept right; when wrong to be put right." The league adopted a platform embracing most of Schurz's demands, though it omitted his proposal of neutralizing the Philippines and said nothing about his warning about wars started by the President without congressional sanction.[25]

He continued the struggle when he returned to New York. When his hopes for some expression of disapproval of the administration in the 1899 elections were not entirely disappointed—he called the results a "drawn battle"—he joined other anti-imperialists to plan for political action in 1900. At a conference in the New York Plaza Hotel in January, they decided to launch a third party. Firmly believing in this tactic, the general compared the proposed organization to the Gold Democrats in 1896. He was confident of contributing to McKinley's defeat.[26]

Schurz spent the following months in pursuit of this quest. At a Washington's Birthday anti-imperialist conference in Philadelphia, he made an impassioned appeal for the return to the principles of the Founding Fathers. McKinley was to blame for the disgraceful conflict in the Philippines, he said. And he went further. Scathingly describing the administration's betrayal of Aguinaldo's trust, he declared, "I challenge any one of the President's defenders to point out in the whole history of the world a single act of perfidy committed by a republican government more infamous than that which has been committed by this administration against our confiding Filipino allies." His audience and friends, among them William James, liked his sally, but many Republicans were outraged. Even his sister Toni was worried. "Do you really intend to go for Bryan," she asked. "Can't you find anybody else?"[27]

Bryan's unpopularity was indeed a problem. That the Commoner would again be the Democratic candidate was a foregone conclusion, and if the third-party project did not materialize, he would be the only alternative to McKinley. But the general was so convinced that anti-imperialism was more important than anything else that he reluctantly contemplated the possibility of supporting the man he loathed. Edwin B. Smith tried to convince him that the Democrats offered the only hope of defeating McKinley; Erving Winslow also tried to win him over; yet he sought to stay true to the third-party movement as long as possible. The German-

Americans, who opposed imperialism, so detested Bryan that it would be difficult to retain their loyalty. Thus Schurz continued to work for a third party long after the Republicans renominated the President with Theodore Roosevelt as his running mate, and the Democrats, Bryan, on a platform condemning imperialism but otherwise similar to that of 1896.[28]

Schurz was wholly committed to the cause. Delivering a forceful speech at Cooper Union in May, he engaged in recurrent controversy with the newspapers and planned for a Liberty Congress at Indianapolis in August. In an interview in the New York *Herald*, he called the campaign against imperialism "the greatest crisis since the Civil War."[29] But the third-party project fell through. Carnegie, who would have to put up the money, was negotiating the sale of his steel works to the Morgan interests and eventually supported McKinley; no viable candidate could be found and finally Schurz was reluctantly forced to give in. He decided to support Bryan, or rather the Democratic ticket, in order to defeat imperialism, but it was a decision that was made with a heavy heart. His friends Jacobi and Oswald Garrison Villard warned him; Henry Villard, too, begged him not to back the "Commoner." He even felt constrained to resign the presidency of the National Civil Service Reform League, but he could not go along with Charles Francis Adams's plan to elect McKinley and checkmate him with a Democratic Congress.[30]

To vote for Bryan, Schurz later recalled, was the "most distasteful thing" he ever did. Nevertheless, convinced that his "entire moral existence" was at stake, he sadly began the campaign. Speaking in September at a large rally at Cooper Union, he sought to justify his course, although he knew very well that his exertions would be in vain. In some respects, his position was similar to his course in 1872. Unlike Greeley, however, Bryan stubbornly refused to make any concessions to his Mugwump supporters. After first declaring that the issue of imperialism was paramount, in the latter phases of the campaign he reverted to the Populist phrases that only upset his independent supporters. In November the Republicans, relying on their slogan of "the full dinner pail" and widespread fears of the "Commoner," defeated him completely. The anti-imperialists had little to comfort them.[31]

The year 1900 would have been tragic for Schurz even without its political disappointments. It was not merely that he was getting old and that so many of his friends were passing away—his brothers-in-law, Henry Villard, Frank Bird, William Steinway—but his children caused him grief as well. The older son, Carl Lincoln, had become a lawyer in the firm of Schurz's friend, Edward M. Shepard and married Fritz Tiedemann's daughter. But the unfortunate bride lost her infant son soon after birth and suffered a nervous breakdown.[32] Handy, as he still called Agathe, his chief housekeeper and companion, was getting on in years. When in 1897, presumably at Schurz's urging, she refused a proposal of marriage, she too was unhappy. Her sister Marianne also remained unmarried, but it was his

The Old Carl Schurz

younger son who was to cause him the greatest grief. After studying law at Columbia, he showed great histrionic abilities and in 1900 went to Europe to take acting lessons with Henry Irving. His father was at Bolton Landing when he received a telegram that Herbert had died. He had been found dead in his bed in a London hotel room, apparently after suffering a cerebral hemorrhage. Disconsolate and distraught, Schurz hardly knew what to do. His situation was not made easier by the fact that he continued to receive letters from Herbert after he already knew of his son's death. His sister Toni came to Lake George to console him; he took long walks in the woods, but the personal tragedy he had suffered left its mark. At the funeral of still another old companion, General Sigel, he broke down and wept in the middle of his eulogy.[33]

And yet life had to go on. The anti-imperialists, though seriously hampered by McKinley's reelection, were by no means ready to give up. Because of the outcome of the campaign, they hoped that they were finally rid of Bryan, whom Schurz considered a major liability—"the evil genius of the anti-imperialistic cause." Ex-President Harrison had spoken out against colonial expansion; Grover Cleveland's detestation of the "large policy" was well known, and soon there were new issues to take up. When in 1901 the United States forced the Cubans to agree to the Platt Amendment turning the island into a virtual protectorate, the league vigorously denounced it. Reports of atrocities in the Philippines also gave the cause renewed urgency. On July 4, 1901, the anti-imperialists, declaring that "those who deny liberty to others deserve it not themselves," issued an address strongly condemning the Platt Amendment and the methods used to quell the insurrection in the Philippines. Together with such prominent opponents of expansion as William Dean Howells and Mark Twain, among others, Schurz signed it. He was still hoping to arouse the country.[34]

Two months later President McKinley was shot, a crime which horrified Schurz. "Yes, there is no doubt," he wrote, "the assassination of McKinley, in itself a nefarious crime and a peculiar symptom of the moral brutalization of our period, is at the same time the hardest blow which until now the anti-imperialist cause has sustained." The opponents of colonialism would have to wait until the popular hysteria engendered by the murder had spent itself. At the same time, he doubted rumors that Theodore Roosevelt, the new president, was more likely to withdraw from the Philippines than his predecessor. "It is a little much to suppose that the whole impetuousness and pugnacity of his temperament has suddenly disappeared," he commented, and of course he was right.[35] Far from retreating, Roosevelt upset the antiexpansionists even more by seizing the isthmus of Panama and announcing the Roosevelt Corollary of the Monroe Doctrine.

For a short time after the assassination, Schurz was kept busy with the campaign to elect Seth Low mayor of New York. Deeply mortified that his friend Edward

M. Shepard was the opposing candidate, he nevertheless energetically supported the reformer, whose previous try in 1897 he had also backed. He was delighted when the fight was won, made up with Shepard, to whom he had already written a letter of apology, and resumed his anti-imperialist activities.[36] Newly revealed atrocities such as the indiscriminate shooting of women and children on Samar and a drastic treason law called for a vigorous response. Drawing up a petition to the Senate to investigate, Moorfield Storey strongly argued that the time to act had come. Reconcentration camps like those General Weyler had established in Cuba were being set up and the American people ought to be informed. Schurz agreed. "I don't think anything more despotic [than the treason law] has ever been enacted by any despotic government in the old world," he replied to Storey. "And this in the name of the United States!" The petition, which Edwin Burritt Smith finally forwarded from Chicago, contained more than five hundred signatures and was not without effect. The Senate started its investigation on February 1.[37]

The hearing, buttressed by General Nelson A. Miles's assertion that cruelties were indeed being committed, gave the anti-imperialists renewed hope. At a meeting in New York's Plaza Hotel with Schurz in the chair, they appointed a committee to assist the investigators. Schurz was one of the members, although he complained that the work was exceedingly unwelcome to him. "I am old and sometimes feel tired . . . ," he wrote to President Jacob G. Schurman of Cornell.

> But this is a great and solemn crisis. . . . Recent events have touched me perhaps more keenly than they have touched others. Can you imagine the feelings of a man who all his life has struggled for human liberty and popular government, who for that reason had to flee from his native country, who believed he had found what he sought in this Republic, and thus came to love this Republic even more than the land of his birth, and who at last, at the close of his life, sees that beloved Republic in the clutches of sinister powers which seduce and betray it into an abandonment of its most sacred principles and traditions and push it into policies and practicies even worse than those which once he had to flee from?

The committee, especially Schurz, Adams, Smith, and Herbert Welsh, the Philadelphia Indian reformer who had already been cooperating with the Senate investigation, took its task seriously. It sent a memorial to Congress; Welsh supplied witnesses to the Democratic senators; and further gruesome details about atrocities in the islands—the so-called water cure to extract information, for example—came to light.[38]

Schurz was once more deeply distressed by these revelations. Privately he heard that Roosevelt might at last tire of the Philippine affair. The insurrection was virtually over; Congress was preparing an organic act for the government of the islands; and Senator Hoar, who always managed to speak for the anti-imperialists while keeping on good terms with the administration, assured the general that the President was really sympathetic. Schurz was not convinced. In a twelve-page letter to Hoar, he assured him of his good will toward his former friend, whom he would much rather support than oppose. But why did not Roosevelt publicly state that he was prepared to pull out of the archipelago? In spite of previous rebuffs, however, the general joined Adams and Welsh in a memorial asking the President to investigate the atrocities further. Roosevelt, who considered the petition "an unpardonable bit of folly and impertinence," merely gave a perfunctory reply, thus confirming Schurz's misgivings. "Oh, how does this Republic now appear in the eyes of the civilized world," he complained to Fanny Chapman. "It breaks my heart when I think of it." To Carnegie, he wrote that atrocities reminiscent of Genghis Khan and Tamerlane had been committed in the name of the Republic of Lincoln and Washington; whenever the Turkish sultan again indulged himself in "Armenian atrocities," or the czar of Russia again established "order in Warsaw," they could fall back upon the precedents set by "this great Republic."[39]

In the years that followed, Schurz continued his fight for Philippine independence. Further petitions, efforts to interest Congress and the public, and a final attempt to take the issue to the polls kept him busy. Although he enjoyed the support of many Germans, however, his success was minimal, because anti-imperialism did not appeal to a large middle-class constituency.[40] In 1904 the Democrats, who jettisoned Bryan, nominated the ultraconservative Judge Alton B. Parker on a platform not questioning the gold standard and promising to treat the Philippines like Cuba. Schurz, considering this pledge sufficient—he had long toyed with the idea of a protectorate—threw his support to Parker. Castigating Roosevelt, who was seeking a term in his own right, for his bellicose attitude, for his action in Panama, and for other imperialist excesses, including the atrocities in the Philippines, he used such severe language in a public letter that many old friends were outraged. A committee of German-Americans, endorsing the President in turn, not only took issue with the general but accused him of changing his politics as often as his residences and always collecting his rewards. Deeply offended, he nevertheless continued the campaign and sought to rally his countrymen against the popular "T.R."[41]

As he had predicted, however, Roosevelt was easily reelected. Nevertheless, Schurz held fast to his beliefs in the final triumph of anti-imperialism. He might congratulate the President on his success in ending the Russo-Japanese War, yet he still considered the impetuous Rough Rider a danger for the country. Hoping conservative Republicans would exert their influence, he never lost faith that the country would finally return to its traditions.[42] Inasmuch as no further territory was annexed to the United States at the time and the country eventually committed itself to Philippine independence, he was not entirely mistaken.

The anti-imperialist struggle also caused Schurz to reexamine his attitude toward the blacks. His optimism that they would join both parties and thus become able to take care of themselves had proven to be unwarranted; the increasing racial violence in the South and the passage of laws virtually disfranchising them could no longer be disregarded. Moreover, racists justified the campaign in the Philippines on the grounds of the alleged superiority of the white race. Although many anti-imperialists shared these prejudices—Schurz himself held peculiar notions about tropical nations—the logic of events did not escape him. As early as 1897 he wrote an article in *Harper's Weekly* deprecating Southern bigotry and advocating education for the blacks. Booker T. Washington, then the leader of his race, was so impressed that he asked the general to speak on behalf of Tuskegee Institute and became one of his great admirers. In 1903, Moorfield Storey suggested that anti-imperialists ought to rekindle the antislavery spirit of the Republican party; their opponents could not be pro-Negro. Schurz agreed fully. "Unless the reaction now going on can be stayed," he predicted, "we shall have to fight the old anti-slavery battle over again."[43]

He did his part in the struggle. In a widely publicized article in *McClure's Magazine* in January 1904, "Can the South Solve the Negro Problem?" he deplored the current effort of Southern "reactionists" to circumvent the Civil War amendments. "There will be a movement either in the direction of reducing the negro to a permanent condition of serfdom . . . or a movement recognizing him as a citizen in the true sense of the term," he argued. Showing that educational advances for blacks were imperative, he insisted that Southerners themselves held the key to the problem. Let them emphasize education against prejudice to counteract the folly of rabble-rousers' advocating the restoration of quasi-slavery. Education would uplift the South, the Negro, and the nation.[44]

The reaction to the article was predictable. Many Northerners endorsed it; most white Southerners condemned it.[45] Washington characterized the essay as the "strongest and most statesmanlike word that has been said on the subject of the South and the Negro for a long number of years." Other black leaders were equally enthusiastic; George H. White, one of the last Negroes to serve in Congress for years to come, expressed their appreciation: "I feel that every American Negro owes you a debt of gratitude for your out-spoken, manly statement at this critical moment when public sentiment is being welded so strongly against our race," he wrote. "I wish the article could be read by every American citizen."[46]

Even Theodore Roosevelt temporarily overcame his aversion. Alerted to the article by J. S. Clarkson, one of his less fortuitous appointments against whom Schurz as head of the New York Civil Service Reform League had to protest strenuously, he quickly congratulated the author. He fully agreed with Schurz, he wrote. The two most serious problems facing the country were the labor and Southern race questions. He knew how to handle the first; the second, however, baffled him.

Schurz answered politely. The way to fight Southern prejudice, he thought, was to let Southerners lead the way. "In memory of old times," he added, "it does me good to speak to you on things on which we substantially agree, while it makes me feel more keenly the sorrowful regret [that] there are other things of fundamental importance on which we differ." A second letter from the President followed, but when in 1904 Schurz supported Parker, Roosevelt was furious. "If Mr. Schurz was sincere when he wrote that article," he declared, "he cannot be sincere now." Did not the racist John Sharp Williams preside over the Democratic nominating convention? The blacks did not seem to agree, however. They continued to consider him a good friend.[47]

The article on the blacks was only one of Schurz's many literary productions during this time. Constantly busy, he turned out essay after essay, article after article. "Grover Cleveland's Second Administration" appeared in *McClure's Magazine*, a biographical sketch of Daniel Webster in *The World's Best Literature*, a piece on the Indians in *The Youth's Companion*, an account of Rutherford B. Hayes in the *Encyclopaedia Britannica*, and a condemnation of anti-Semitism for use at a protest meeting in New York against the Kishinev massacre. In addition, he was working on an essay on Sumner and was constantly called upon to deliver speeches—"the bane of my life," as he called them.[48]

His principal literary energy during his last years was devoted to his memoirs. After weighing the increasingly profitable offers of various publishers, he decided to sign a contract with the McClure Company. The famous muckraker, Ida Tarbell, was one of the firm's editors and collaborated most effectively with him. At first uncertain about publishing his *Reminiscences* while he was still alive, as time went on he became so worried about completing them that he was anxious to devote every free moment to the work. Certain that he had but little time left, he finally decided to allow the publisher to bring out excerpts in serial form.[49] They began to appear in the fall of 1905 and were exceedingly well received. William Dean Howells found them "utterly charming and touchingly beautiful," and a Congregational minister was so affected by Schurz's description of his mother that he used it in a sermon. Some Catholics objected to the passages about his loss of faith in the church's doctrines of salvation, but he defended himself by explaining that he did not intend to offend anyone and was glad to be corrected about current doctrine. Yet as he had feared, he never lived to finish the third volume. When the completed *Reminiscences* finally appeared in book form, they not only found wide acceptance but became a testimony to his life's work of combining German and American culture. He had written the first volume, dealing with European events, in German, and the other two in English.[50]

However marked the decline of Schurz's political influence might have been toward the end of his life, his position as the leading German-American had never been stronger. On both sides of the ocean, he was considered the foremost representative of his compatriots, and he used this position to propagate his ideology among them. In 1897, for example, when on the fiftieth anniversary of the New York Deutsche Liederkranz Society he was asked to deliver a speech, he called it "The German Mothertongue." A paean to the beauties of his native language, it reemphasized his long-held belief in the necessity of combining American citizenship with the retention of German culture. "Nobody will dispute that the German-American in America must learn English," he said. "He owes it to his new country and he owes it to himself. But it is more than folly to say that he ought, therefore, to give up the German language. I have always been in favor of sensible Americanization, but this need not mean a complete abandonment of all that is German. It means that we should adopt the best traits of American character and join them to the best traits of German character. By so doing we shall make the most valuable contribution to the American nation, to American civilization." A large sign at the door in his house read "Hier wird deutsch gesprochen"; he spoke German with his family and corresponded in it with all who could respond in it. And his German was never contaminated by English terms; it retained its purity and force to the end.[51]

The German community showed its pride in its foremost citizen on the occasion of his seventieth birthday. The festivities began in Germany in February 1899 with a well-attended celebration in Berlin. Ambassador Andrew White, Theodor Mommsen, distinguished members of the Reichstag, and others assembled to listen to Schurz's friend, the liberal editor Theodor Barth, who called his speech "Schurz as the Meditator Between Two Nations." Then a great celebration took place at Delmonico's in New York, and in the following week, the German Social Scientific Society of New York tendered him still another banquet at Liederkranz Hall, richly decorated with German and American flags. Six hundred German-Americans were present for what the papers called a "thoroughly Teuton affair." The general, who professed not to like such testimonials, enjoyed the publicity. At Delmonico's, he responded with a brief review of his career in America, his reaffirmation of the necessity of joining American citizenship with the German heritage, and a hymn of praise for American democracy. He was not a man who had lost faith in the American institutions, he said in closing. "The truth is . . . that you will look in vain for a people that have achieved as much of freedom, of progress, of well-being and happiness, as, in spite of their occasional failures, the American people have under their democratic institutions of government."[52]

Because of his prominence as a German-American leader, it was natural that he was called upon to represent the community as often as possible. One of the board of visitors of the German department at Harvard, he was routinely questioned about the fitness of German professors at other universities; he still addressed German Day meetings; and when Harvard began to think of establishing a Germanic Museum, he became the project's presiding officer.[53] In addition, he was devoted to the furtherance of good relations between Germany and the United States. Worried about the disturbances between the two countries' fleets in Manila Bay, he offered his services to President McKinley; outraged about the anti-

American tone of the German press, he wrote a vigorous defense of America's position in the Spanish-American War, which was widely reprinted in German publications. No matter how much he disapproved of the war and its imperialist aims, his duties as an American citizen came first.[54] And when in 1902 Prince Henry of Prussia, the Kaiser's brother, came to the United States, Schurz attended the White House banquet in the prince's honor and delivered the farewell speech in New York. Its theme was "The Old Friendship Between Germany and America."[55]

The German community had every reason to be proud of him, for his astonishing career had brought him recognition from far and wide. Still active as president of the New York Civil Service Reform League even after his resignation as president of the national organization, he was a prominent citizen of the metropolis, often taking part in its political campaigns. Columbia University conferred an LL.D. on him in 1899; George Washington University in St. Louis followed suit five years later; and the University of Wisconsin, where he first established contact with American academic life, similarly honored him in 1905. Attending the ceremonies connected with these degrees, he spoke at innumerable gatherings despite his disinclination to do so, and he was a member of many prestigious societies.[56] In addition, he was so friendly with Andrew Carnegie that in 1902 the millionaire sold him a house near his own on East 91st Street. Always ready to receive him, the steelmaker invited him to take an automobile ride with him, a very novel experience at the time.[57] Visitors from two continents still came to visit. His acquaintances included Franz Boas, Hermann Eduard von Holst, and Frederick Bancroft as well as eminent statesmen and public figures. From his house at 24 East 91st, he could easily take walks in nearby Central Park, where he loved to walk around the reservoir.[58] If it had not been for his political and personal misfortunes, he might have been able to enjoy a most rewarding old age.

Schurz was getting on in years. The reddish beard had turned to grey, and although he still astounded visitors with his youthful manner, especially his undiminished sense of humor, his health was deteriorating. In 1899, when returning from Lake George on a Hudson River steamer, he ate some bass and contracted ptomaine poisoning. With Dr. Jacobi's help, he recovered; in the years that followed, however, he was frequently plagued by his old gallstone problems and bronchial infections. He had to refuse more and more invitations; in the winter, he finally sought to escape from his respiratory problems by going south, first to Virginia and then to Georgia.[59] In November 1905 he slipped and fell getting off a trolley car, an accident which caused a concussion with attendant severe headaches. After his return from Augusta early in 1906, he thought he had escaped his usual bronchial troubles, only to fall seriously ill shortly afterward.[60] In the second week of May the newspapers reported that the old statesman was sinking fast. His family and Dr. Jacobi were at his home on 91st Street; Mark Twain, William D. Howells, and other distinguished visitors called, but they found there was no hope. "How easy it is to die," he said to the doctor, whom he finally, after all these years, addressed with the familiar "du." A priest attempted to offer the last rites of the Catholic church only to be denied admission by the family—Schurz had long since been friendly with Dr. Felix Adler of the Ethical Culture Society. Early in the morning of May 14, 1906, he died, one of the last of the surviving major generals of the Civil War.[61] His work as an anti-imperialist was unfulfilled, but his mission as "the main intermediary between German and American culture" was completed.

Epilogue

SCHURZ'S DEATH was a major news item on two continents. "Carl Schurz Is Dead After a Week's Serious Illness. Statesman and Soldier Expired Yesterday," headlined the *New York Times*. Editorials commented on his achievements, heads of state sent their condolences, and so numerous were the obituaries that the family collected them in a huge scrapbook.[1] "No native born citizen was ever a better American than Carl Schurz, and no foreign born citizen placed the Republic more deeply in his debt," wrote the Cleveland *Plain Dealer*. The St. Louis *Post Dispatch* stressed Schurz's fidelity to his convictions, regardless of consequences, and the *Kölnische Zeitung* called him the "greatest citizen of North America of German heritage."[2] Theodore Roosevelt was equally laudatory. "The country has lost a statesman of Lincoln's generation, whose services both in peace and war at the great crisis in the Republic's history, will not be forgotten while that history lasts," he wired. The Kaiser extended his sympathy to the family, and friends and acquaintances everywhere added their encomiums. If the hostile Chicago *Inter-Ocean* commented on the military shortcomings and alleged lack of "constructive ability" of the deceased, even it could not deny that he had left his mark. In the words of the *Frankfurter Zeitung*, the German-American community had lost its recognized intellectual leader and its most prominent representative.[3] It was never to see so skillful a spokesman again.

The funeral took place on Thursday, May 17. For three hours mourners waited in line outside Schurz's house at 24 East 91st Street to pay their respects. The family was in the rear room with the bier; the pallbearers, the McAneny family, William Dean Howells, and other intimate friends were in the two front parlors. Felix Adler of the Ethical Culture Society spoke in English, Dr. Jacobi in German, and a quartet from the Arion Society furnished the music. Then the mourners went to the Harlem Station to meet the funeral train that had left Grand Central Terminal at 3:42 P.M., its first section carrying the body, family, and pallbearers, the second, friends and acquaintances. The pallbearers included old intimates and friends like Dr. Jacobi, Charles Francis Adams, and Horace White, representatives of the business and banking world like Andrew Carnegie and Isaac N. Seligman, public figures like Joseph H. Choate, Oscar S. Straus, and former Senator Henderson, civil service reformers like Silas W. Burt and Edward M. Shepard, General Stahel, and leading members of the German-American community as well as the German consul. The rain was falling when they reached Sleepy Hollow Cemetery not far from Pocantico Hills; Dr. H. P. Frissell, the president of Hampton Institute, delivered a brief address lauding Schurz's work for blacks and Indians. Then the general was laid to rest next to his son Herbert.[4]

Shortly after the funeral, McAneny, Choate, Straus, Shepard, and others took the initiative in founding a committee of one hundred to honor the memory of the great German-American. Planning to cooperate with similar organizations in other cities, they hoped to establish a permanent memorial and to prepare for a great commemorative convocation in New York in the fall.[5]

Other admirers also held memorial meetings. On June 3, Wilhelm Vocke, the president of the newly founded Carl Schurz Memorial Association in Chicago, chaired an assembly in that city, at which Harry Rubens, Schurz's former secretary, General Winkler, and various academic notables eulogized the dead statesman. Two days later, the German community of New York honored its departed leader at Carnegie Hall. His bust draped with banners, appropriate funeral marches by Wagner and Chopin, and a large audience of mourners gave the proper solemnity to the occasion.[6]

The long-advertised general memorial, also at Carnegie Hall, finally took place on November 21, 1906. Choate presided; Frank Damrosch led the orchestra in the funeral march from *Götterdämmerung* and the prelude to the *Meistersinger*, two of Schurz's favorites; and speaker after speaker extolled the achievements of the deceased. President Cleveland praised his moral courage, Ambassador Choate his patriotism, President Eliot of Harvard his literary and oratorical accomplishments, Secretary of the Navy Charles J. Bonaparte his civil service reform contributions, Professor Hermann Schumacher of the University of Bonn his idealism, and Booker T. Washington his work for the blacks. Professor Eugene Kühnemann of the University of Breslau, fittingly speaking in German, stressed his bridging the civilizations of Germany and America, and R. W. Gilder of the Century Company read an original poem. The presence of the ex-President, the secretary of the navy, and of Booker T. Washington guaranteed nationwide publicity.[7]

The memorial committee did not disband following these obsequies. Collecting funds for the erection of a monument and for the perpetuation of Schurz's ideas, it commissioned Carl Bitter, a well-known German-American sculptor who had cast the general's death mask, to execute the statue. He completed the work in 1913, when in the presence of George McAneny, now borough president of Manhattan, and Count Johann von Bernstorff, the German ambassador, the monument was dedicated at Morningside Heights. The city provided the platform; Bitter's statue, a standing likeness of the general, faces Columbia University.

CARL SCHURZ
MDCCCIXXX–MCMVI
A DEFENDER OF LIBERTY
AND A FRIEND OF HUMAN RIGHTS

reads the inscription on the pedestal.[8] A park fronting the East River on the other side of the city, where Gracie Mansion, later the residence of the mayors of New

York, was located, had already been named for Schurz, and similar honors were conferred on him in cities and towns in Europe and America.[9] The committee also contributed to the furtherance of civil service reform, the extension of "Germanistic culture" in the United States, and the advancement of blacks and Indians. In addition, after Frederick Bancroft and William A. Dunning completed the unfinished third volume of the *Reminiscences*, it financed the collection and publication of the papers of Carl Schurz under the editorship of Bancroft. With Agathe's help, he finally brought out the completed work in six volumes, and additional papers were published in the third volume of the German edition of the *Lebenserinnerungen*.[10]

The establishment of the Weimar Republic in Germany gave renewed impetus to the commemoration of Carl Schurz in his homeland. In 1927 a Carl Schurz Vereinigung was founded in Berlin, and in 1929, on the occasion of the one-hundredth anniversary of his birth, the Reichstag specially paid tribute to the great liberal and democrat with speeches by Gustav Stresemann and Ambassador Jacob Schurman, among others, while the appearance of books and articles attested to Germany's pride in her great interpreter in America.[11]

In the United States the immigrant leader's memory was also honored. Although all of Schurz's children had died—Agathe in 1915, Carl Lincoln in 1924, and Marianne in 1929[12]—collateral descendants and friends continued to do their part in keeping his legacy alive. In 1928, in preparation for his one-hundredth anniversary, Joseph Schafer of the Wisconsin Historical Society published the *Intimate Letters of Carl Schurz*; the centennial was widely observed, and articles and books made their appearance.[13] In 1930 the Pennsylvania manufacturer Ferdinand Thun and his partners Henry Janssen and Gustav Oberlaender took the initiative in founding the Carl Schurz Memorial Foundation, for which they enlisted the cooperation of the Warburg brothers and Lessing Rosenwald. By 1931, the organization was able to begin operations with an endowment of $1 million, the Oberlaender Trust. It was especially interested in student exchanges with Germany.[14]

The rise of Hitler soon caused trouble for the German-American community in general and the various Carl Schurz societies in particular. The Berlin Vereinigung fell completely under Nazi domination. The American foundation, which had nothing at all to do with its German counterpart, attempted to steer a middle course by helping refugee scholars but still maintaining contacts with the Reich. This decision did not satisfy James Speyer, its Jewish treasurer, who resigned after first trying to induce it to make a public declaration of opposition to Naziism.[15] In 1935 Oswald Garrison Villard, incensed about the cruelties of the Hitler state, wrote a letter to the German ambassador protesting against the appropriation of Schurz's name by Nazi organizations. "Nothing could be in worse taste," he insisted, "than the use of Carl Schurz's name by the Hitler Government, for Carl Schurz stood at the opposite pole of thought and philosophy." At the same time, he collected the signatures of as many surviving friends and relatives as he could and published a strong appeal in the *New York Times*. Decrying the identification of Schurz with the German Vereinigung, which had been taken over by the Hitler state, and the American foundation, which continued "to aid German universities and otherwise deal with the despotism that has succeeded the Republic of Weimar," the signers recalled Schurz's long struggle for liberty. "No more eloquent defender of democracy ever came to our shores," they wrote.

> He served our Republic on the battlefield, in the diplomatic service, and a thousand platforms and in the Senate of the United States, without once ever failing to make clear his belief, his complete and absolute faith in what he called the great colony of free humanity. . . . No American was a more ardent champion of freedom for the Negro, justice and freedom for the Indian, and tolerance and freedom . . . for every sect and every group in our democracy. A friend to many Jews, he never failed to denounce anti-Semitism. A distinguished veteran of many battlefields, he abhorred from the depth of his soul every manifestation of militarism. . . . Justice to this man, to his life and his noble teachings, makes it imperative for us to . . . protest against the use of his name in connection with the societies we have cited. We earnestly ask that it be immediately discontinued.[16]

If the appeal did some injustice to the American foundation, it nevertheless set the record straight.

Carl Schurz was indeed the representative of the very antithesis of the Germany made notorious by Hitler and his cohorts. His life, his work, his teachings so clearly reflected an older and more humane German tradition that it is not surprising if comparatively little was said about him in the Third Reich.[17] Only after World War II, when the western part of Germany again sought its democratic moorings, did he really become popular once more, so that he again symbolizes the unity of democratic traditions in two worlds.

In the course of his long career, Schurz truly captured his contemporaries' imagination. His foes might have thought him overbearing, overambitious, a scold. He might have been faulted for always attempting to justify himself—to his parents, to his fellow students at the university, to his in-laws in Hamburg, and to his constituents. He always remained touchy about attacks on his foreign origins. Yet, uncompromisingly honest, little given to the usual prejudices of the time, and always in the forefront of the fight for political and social justice, he remained true to the liberal and democratic ideals of his youth. In time, as industrial problems loomed larger than purely political ones, his philosophy was no longer very revolutionary. As an ex-revolutionary who was a member of an administration using federal troops to disperse strikers, he must have jarred radicals of a later age. But Schurz the independent was really no different from Schurz the forty-eighter. He continued faithful to his convictions even though times were changing. An effective leader of his countrymen, he deserved their general esteem. In fact, his chief contribution remains his use of ethnic politics, his effort to lead the German-Americans to a realization of their role in a new country while yet retaining their old identity. If at the same time he lessened their influence by his insistence on independent politics, he nevertheless gave them and their descendants something to cherish and to remember with pride.

Abbreviations

AHR	*American Historical Review*
CU	Columbia University
CHiS	Chicago Historical Society
DAB	*Dictionary of American Biography*
HC	Hogue Collection; papers in possession of Arthur R. Hogue, Bloomington, Indiana
HU	Harvard University
IL	*Intimate Letters of Carl Schurz, 1841–1869*, ed. Joseph Schafer, ed. (Madison: State Hist. Soc. of Wisconsin, 1928)
JAH	*Journal of American History*
JMH	*Journal of Modern History*
JSH	*Journal of Southern History*
LC	Library of Congress
MC	Morlang Collection; papers in possession of Mrs. Cissa Morlang, Hamburg, Germany
MHiS	Massachusetts Historical Society
MVHR	*Mississippi Valley Historical Review*
MoHiS	State Historical Society of Missouri
NA	National Archives
NYHiS	New-York Historical Society
NYPL	New York Public Library
OHiS	Ohio Historical Society
OR	*The War of the Rebellion . . . Official Records of the Union and Confederate Armies* (Washington: Government Printing Office, 1880-1901)
PaHiS	Historical Society of Pennsylvania
PU	Princeton University
SC	*Speeches, Correspondence and Political Papers of Carl Schurz*, Frederick Bancroft, ed. (New York: Putnam's 1913)
SP	Schurz Papers, Library of Congress (arranged chronologically unless otherwise noted)
SR	Carl Schurz, *The Reminiscences of Carl Schurz*, 3 vols. (New York: McClure, 1907-8)
WiHiS	State Historical Society of Wisconsin, Madison
WRHS	Western Reserve Historical Society
YU	Yale University

Translations of German quotes are the author's, except where printed English versions are available.

Notes

NOTES TO CHAPTER 1

1. *SR*, I, 5, 7–8; Dr. Graf Metternich, "Carl Schurz und seine deutsche Heimat," in Anton Erkelenz and Fritz Mittelmann, eds., *Carl Schurz, der Deutsche und Amerikaner* (Berlin: Sieben Stäbe, 1929), 11, 12, 19 (including facsimile of birth certificate); Karl Stommel, *Das Kurkölnische Amt Lechenich: Seine Entstehung und seine Organisation* (Euskirchen: Veröffentlichungen der Geschichts-und Heimatsfreunde des Kreises Euskirchen, Series A, Pamphlet 7, 1961), 65.

2. Metternich, "Schurz," in Erkelenz and Mittelmann, *Schurz*, 11–14; Reiner Keller, *Eifel-Börde-Ville: Landschaftskunde des Kreises Euskirchen* (Euskirchen: Veröffentlichungen des Vereins der Geschichts-und Heimatsfreunde des Kreises Euskirchen, Series A, Pamphlet 9, 1964), 59; *SR*, I, 26.

3. *SR*, I, 37–38.

4. Hans Kisky, *Burgen, Schlösser und Hofesfesten im Kreise Euskirchen* (Euskirchen: Verein der Geschichts-und Heimatsfreunde des Kreises Euskirchen, Series A, Pamphlet 6, 1960), 93; Metternich, "Schurz," 13–14, 16ff.; Wilhelm Prasuhn, *Rund um Schloss Brühl* (Brühl: Volkmann, 1956), 37; *SR*, I, 7–8, 14–15, 22.

5. *SR*, I, 5–53; *IL*, 1–2; Antonie Schurz Jüssen, Lebenserinnerungen, HC.

6. F. J. Kiefer, *Description Nouvelle et Complète de la Ville de Cologne* (Cologne: F. C. Eisen, 1842), 9–66; Richard, *Manuel du Voyager sur les Bords du Rhin* (Paris: Audin, 1836), 18–31; Frederick Knight Hunt, *The Rhine: Its Scenery and Historical and Legendary Associations* (London: Jeremiah How, 1845), 97; Victor Hugo, *The Rhine* (London: D. Aird, 1843), 78–79, 84–85.

7. *SR*, I, 53–72; *IL*, 2–42. A few of Schurz's gymnasium compositions have been preserved. SP, ctr. 207.

8. *IL*, 1–2; *SR*, I, 72–85; Jüssen, Lebenserinnerungen, 1–18, in HC; Marie Jüssen, "Carl Schurz," *Deutsche Rundschau* 98 (1899), 389–90; W. D. Robson Scott, *The Literary Background of the Gothic Revival in Germany* (Oxford: Oxford Univ. Press, Clarendon, 1965), 287ff.

9. Jüssen, Lebenserinnerungen, 18ff., in HC; *SR*, I, 83–87; Schurz to Georg Jüssen, Sept. 3, Oct. 28, Dec. 16, 1847, Carl Schurz Papers, Watertown Historical Society, Watertown, Wis.

10. *IL*, 3, 6, 7; C. Hölscher to Schurz, Mar. 30, 1880, SP; Jüssen, Lebenserinnerungen, 18–29; in HC.

11. Richard, *Manuel*, 45ff.; Hunt, *The Rhine*, 132–40; Max Braubach, *Bonner Professoren und Studenten in den Revolutionsjahren 1848/49* (Cologne: Westdeutscher, 1967), 11–12; Renate Kaiser, *Die politischen Strömungen in den Kreisen Bonn und Rheinbach, 1848–1849* (Bonn: Ludwig Röhr, 1963), 18; *SR*, I, 92, 98ff.; Richard Sander, ed., *Gottfried Kinkels Selbstbiographie, 1838–1848* (Bonn: Friedrich Cohen, 1931), 30, 48–60, 96.

12. Friedrich Schulze and Paul Ssymank, *Das deutsche Studententum von den ältesten Zeiten bis zur Gegenwart* (Leipzig: R. Voigtlander, 1910), 236–58; Friedrich Spielhagen, *Finder und Erfinder: Erinnerungen aus meinem Leben* (Leipzig: L. Staakmann, 1890), I, 267ff.; *SR*, I, 89, 97–98.

13. *SR*, I, 93–98; Max Braubach, "Carl Schurz als Bonner Student," in Erkelenz and Mittelmann, *Schurz*, 25–37; Spielhagen, *Finder und Erfinder*, I, 255; Otto Dannehl, *Carl Schurz: Ein deutscher Kämpfer* (Berlin: Walter deGruyter, 1929), 127–32, 136.

14. *SR*, I, 92–93; *IL*, 37–39; Richard Wanderer MS, ctr. 196, SP; Zeugnis der Reife, Carl Schurz, 28 Aug. 1847, Friedrich Wilhelm Universität Archives, Bonn.

15. *SR*, I, 93ff.; Braubach, "Carl Schurz als Bonner Student," in Erkelenz and Mittelmann, *Schurz*, 28–37; Dannehl, *Schurz*, 128–30; *IL*, 21, 25–26.

16. Spielhagen, *Finder und Erfinder*, I, 282–85.

NOTES TO CHAPTER II

1. *SR*, I, 112. He told George Haven Putnam that the loss of his manuscripts was one of the tragedies of the failure of the revolution! George Haven Putnam, *Memoirs of a Publisher, 1865–1915* (New York: Putnam's, 1916), 29.

2. Adolph Strodtmann, *Gottfried Kinkel: Wahrheit ohne Dichtung* . . . (Hamburg: Hoffmann & Campe, 1851), II, 63–70; A. Ernst von Ernsthausen, *Erinnerungen eines preussischen Beamten* (Bielefeld: Velhagen & Klassing, 1894), 62; *SR*, I, 112ff.; Friedrich von Bezold, *Geschichte der Rheinischen Friedrich-Wilhelms-Universität von der Gründung bis zum Jahre 1870* (Bonn: A. Marcus & E. Webers, 1920), 427–30; Dannehl, *Schurz*, 182–84. The exact dates for the celebration are not entirely clear.

3. Braubach, *Bonner Professoren*, 34–37; Dannehl, *Schurz*, 193ff.; Strodtmann, *Kinkel*, II, 71ff.; *SR*, I, 125–27; *Bonner Zeitung*, May 29, 1848.

4. Senatsprotokol, Universität Bonn, May 25, 1848, Friedrich Wilhelm Universität, Archives, Bonn; Bezold, *Geschichte*, 430–33; Dannehl, *Schurz*, 150, 182–84, 193ff.; Strodtmann, *Kinkel*, II, 153–54; Braubach, *Bonner Professoren*, 35ff.

5. Braubach, *Bonner Professoren*, 40–43, 52; *IL*, 44–49; Dannehl, *Schurz*, 145, 202–3; *SR*, I, 127–29; *Bonner Zeitung*, July 15, 1848.

6. *IL*, 42–49; Dannehl, *Schurz*, 204; Engelbrecht Scheiffarth, *Das Amt Menden* (Siegburg: F. Schmidt, 1964), 238ff.; Bezold, *Geschichte*, 442; Strodtmann, *Kinkel*, II, 83.

7. *SR*, I, 140; Strodtmann, *Kinkel*, II, 70; Veit Valentin, *1848: Chapters of German History* (London: Allen & Unwin, 1940), 419; *Der Zug der Freischärler unter Kinkel, Schurz und Anneke behufs Plünderung des Zeughauses in Siegburg* (Bonn: P. Hanstein, 1886), 4; Friedrich Althaus, "Erinnerungen an Gottfried Kinkel," *Nord und Süd* 24 (Feb. 1883), 236–37.

8. Strodtmann, *Kinkel*, II, 153–54; Ernst von Ernsthausen, *Erinnerungen*, 66–68.

9. Spielhagen, *Finder und Erfinder*, 285–89.

10. Dannehl, *Schurz*, 210–11, 219ff., 135–36; *IL*, 49–50. In November, he wrote a new constitution for the fraternity.

11. Veit Valentin, *Geschichte der deutschen Revolution von 1848–49* (Berlin: Ullstein, 1930), II, 139–69.

12. *Bonner Zeitung*, Sept. 23, 24, 26, 1848, in Braubach, *Bonner Professoren*, 148–51; *SR*, I, 143–45; Strodtmann, *Kinkel*, II, 127–35.

13. Karl Schurz, *Der Studentenkongress zu Eisenach am 25. September 1848, seine Bedeutung und Resultate* (Bonn: W. Salzbach, 1848), copy in ctr. 188, SP; Georg Heer, *Geschichte der deutschen Burschenschaft* (Heidelberg: Carl Winters, 1929), III, 139–45; *SR*, I, 145–54; *Bonner Zeitung*, Oct. 5, 12, 1848, in Braubach, *Bonner Professoren*, 152–56; Vienna *Wartburg*, IV (March 1903, ctr. 208, SP. The appeal is in ctr. 179, SP.

14. Valentin, *Geschichte der deutschen Revolution*, II, 173–275.

15. *SR*, I, 157–59; Bezold, *Geschichte*, 445–46; Dannehl, *Schurz*, 249–50; *Bonner Zeitung*, Nov. 15, 17, 23, 25, 1848; Heer, *Geschichte*, III, 171; Braubach, *Bonner*

Professoren, 63–68, 70ff., 131–34; Proceedings of the Bonn University Senate, Nov. 23, 1848, Friedrich Wilhelm Univeristät Archives, Bonn; Kaiser, *Strömungen,* 43–44.

16. *SR*, I, 160–61.

17. Ibid.; *IL*, 50–52; Strodtmann, *Kinkel,* II, 172–73; *Bonner Zeitung,* Dec. 21, 1848; *Neue Bonner Zeitung,* Jan. 2, 1849; Braubach, *Bonner Professoren,* 77, 160ff., 225ff.

18. Braubach, *Bonner Professoren,* 83ff.; *SR*, I, 159; Peter Wioharz to Schurz, Apr. 13, 1894, SP; Eberhard Kessel, ed., *Die Briefe von Carl Schurz an Gottfried Kinkel,* Beihefte zum Jahrbuch für Amerikastudien, pt. 12 (Heidelberg: Carl Winter, 1965), 49; *IL*, 52–56; *Neue Bonner Zeitung,* Feb. 28, Mar. 14, 15, 22, 1849.

19. Heer, *Geschichte,* III, 172; Hans Kaiser, "Carl Schurz," in Hermann Haupt and Paul Wentzcke, eds., *Hundert Jahre Deutscher Burschenschaft* (Heidelberg: Carl Winters, 1921), 181; *SC*, V, 417ff.

20. *IL*, 52–58; Kessel, *Briefe,* 52–53.

21. Frank Eyck, *The Frankfurt Parliament, 1848–1849* (London: Macmillan, 1968), 384–85; Valentin, *1848,* 373.

22. *Neue Bonner Zeitung,* Mar. 21, May 2, 1849, in Braubach, *Bonner Professoren,* 179–82, 188.

23. Ibid., 105–13; *Neue Bonner Zeitung,* May 10, 1849; Dannehl, *Schurz,* 343–50; Strodtmann, *Kinkel,* II, 254–57; *SR*, I, 170–78; *Zug der Freischärler,* 11ff.; Spielhagen, *Finder und Erfinder,* 292ff.; Schurz to Mrs. Schurz, June 28, 1868, HC.

24. *SR*, I, 179–200; Strodtmann, *Kinkel,* II, 259–62; Ferdinand Fenner von Fenneberg, *Zur Geschichte der rheinpfälzischen Revolution* (Zurich: E. Kiesling, 1849), 27ff.; *Neue Bonner Zeitung,* May 22, 23, 1849, in Braubach, *Bonner Professoren,* 196, 197.

25. Strodtmann, *Kinkel,* II, 261–63; *SR*, I, 196, 198–99.

26. *SR*, I, 200–3; *IL*, 60–61, 72–73.

27. *Berliner Börsen Courier,* July 31, 1892, SP. The order was dated June 14, 1849.

28. *SR*, I, 203–15; Carl Schurz, "The Surrender of Rastatt," trans. Joseph Schafer, *Wis. Mag. of Hist.* 12 (Mar. 1929), 239–57; Albert Förderer, *Erinerungen aus Rastatt 1849* (Lahr: Schömperlen, 1899), 10, 46–72.

29. Otto Corvin, *A Life of Adventure* (London: Richard Bentley, 1871), III, 258–86; Schurz, "The Surrender of Rastatt," 251–70.

30. *IL*, 58–67. The letter to his parents and sisters is dated July 31, 1849; that to his friends, "on the day of the capitulation July 23, 1849."

31. Schurz, "The Surrender of Rastatt," 267–70.

32. *SR*, I, 216–36. According to Carl Schurz, *Lebenserinnerungen* (Berlin: Georg Reimer, 1906), I, 223, the sewer was about 4–4½ ft. high and 3–3½ ft. wide. For a description of the escape route, cf. A. E. Zucker, "Carl Schurz's Escape Route from Rastatt," *American-German Review* 14 (April 1948), 3–6.

NOTES TO CHAPTER III

1. *SR*, I, 237–40; *IL*, 67. Although Schurz maintained that he wrote home immediately after leaving Germany, the letter from Dornachbruck clearly states that it was the first.

2. *SR*, I, 235–36; Jüssen, Lebenserinnerungen, 29–37, HC.

3. *IL*, 67–71. Most of the diary has been lost.

4. *IL*, 71–74; *SR*, I, 241–46; *Neue Bonner Zeitung,* Nov. 15, 25, 28, 1849; Feb. 8, 15, 16, 22, 24, Mar. 1, 1850, in Braubach, *Bonner Professoren,* 215–25; Dannehl, *Schurz,* 367–76.

5. *IL*, 75–80.

6. Johanna Kinkel, "Erinnerungsblätter aus dem Jahr 1849," *Deutsche Monatsschrift*

für Politik, Wissenschaft, Kunst und Leben 2 (1851), 39–108; *SR*, I, 246–50, 264–74; Martin Bollert, "Kinkel vor dem Kriegsgericht," *Preussische Jahrbücher* 155 (1914), 488–512. The public was confused about the sentence; Kinkel had been condemned, not to arrest in a fortress, but to penal imprisonment in a fortress, a more onerous sentence than civil imprisonment. Cf. Franz Mehring, *Karl Marx* (London: Allen & Unwin, 1936), 196–97, The Cologne trial involved Schurz as well, as he was one of the defendents in absentia. All defendents were acquitted. *Zug der Freischärler*, 4.

7. *SR*, I, 250–58; Jüssen, *Lebenserinnerungen*, 37–43, HC; Rhoda Truax, *The Doctors Jacobi* (Boston: Little, Brown, 1952), 137–8.

8. Johanna Kinkel to Margarethe Blessing, May 8, 1850, in Gertrud Ferber, "Carl Schurz und Gottfried Kinkel nach der März-Revolution," in Erkelenz and Mittelmann, *Schurz*, 47–48.

9. *SR*, I, 257–64; Schurz, *Lebenserinnerungen*, I, 281–83.

10. Moritz Wiggers, "Gottfried Kinkel's Befreiung," *Die Gartenlaube* (1863), 122–24; *SR*, I, 275, 285–89. At the time, despite his acquittal in the Siegburg case, Schurz was still liable to be punished for his participation in the Baden rebellion. Chester V. Easum, *The Americanization of Carl Schurz* (Chicago: Univ. of Chicago Press, 1929), 39–40.

11. Friedrich Althaus, "Erinnerungen an Gottfried Kinkel," *Nord und Süd* 25 (April 1883), 55–75; *IL*, 86–90.

12. *SR*, I, 275–90; K. A. Varnhagen von Ense, *Aus dem Nachlass Varnhagen's von Enses Tagebücher*, ed. Ludmilla Assing (Leipzig: F. A. Brockhaus, 1861–70), XIII, 241–42; Bettina von Arnim, *Sämtliche Werke*, ed. Waldemar Oehlke (Berlin: Propyläen, 1922), VII, 470–82, 487–97; Althaus, "Kinkel," 56; Wiggers, "Kinkel's Befreiung," 122–24. According to the *Reminiscences*, Schurz met the spy at the theater, but Althaus based his account of the meeting in the back room on Schurz's own story in 1856 and was probably correct. On Malwida von Meysenbug, cf. Malwida von Meysenbug, *Memoiren einer Idealistin* (Berlin: Schuster & Loeffler, 1905), II, 70–71.

13. Wiggers, "Kinkel's Befreiung," 122–24; Althaus, "Kinkel," 57; *SR*, I, 290–94; Walter Heynen, "Kinkels Flucht," *Preussische Jahrbücher* 236 (Apr.–June 1934), 162–76; Georg von Rauh, "Eine baltische Frau im Wirbel des Jahres 1848," *Jahrbuch des baltischen Deutschtums* 10 (1963), 29–36; Hermann Baron Bruiningk, *Das Geschlecht von Bruiningk in Livland* (Riga: N. Kymmels, 1913), 261.

14. Wiggers, "Kinkel's Befreiung," 104–7, 120–22, 134–38, 152–55; Althaus, "Kinkel," 59–63; *SR*, I, 294–323.

15. *SR*, I, 325–36; *IL*, 96.

16. Althaus, "Kinkel," 62; *IL*, 93–95; Marie Goslich, "Briefe von Johanna Kinkel," *Preussische Jahrbücher* 97 (July–Sept., 1899), 430.

17. *IL*, 96–97; Claude Fuess, *Carl Schurz, Reformer (1829–1906)* (New York: Dodd, Mead, 1932), 32, 35; Easum, *Americanization*, 42–43; Albert Bernhardt Faust, *The German Element in the United States* (Boston: Houghton Mifflin, 1909), II, 156; Walter Heynen, "Kinkels Flucht: Eine Schurz Nachlese auf Grund der Akten," *Preussische, Jahrbücher* 236 (Apr.–June 1934), 109, contains a comparison of Wiggers's and Schurz's accounts and concludes that they were based on an early version by Schurz. For an example of the embellishments, cf. Milwaukee *Daily Sentinel*, Sept. 7, 1860. The other participants in the rescue did not fare as well as Schurz. Brune was convicted of complicity and served three years in the penitentiary; Krüger, who said he took in all well-behaved guests, including the prince of Prussia when he was fleeing during the troubles of 1848, was acquitted but lost his innkeeper's license and his position as town councilor; Dr. Falkenthal also received a jail sentence when Kinkel's clothes were found at his home, although Schurz tried to shield him as he could swear the doctor had not been present at the actual rescue, as had been asserted. *National Zeitung*, Oct. 22, 1851; *New Yorker Volkszeitung*, June 22,

1890, ctrs. 202, 208, SP; *Vossische Zeitung,* Feb. 4, 1932, Schurz Papers, WiHiS; Kessel, *Briefe,* 117–18, 91–92. For an early American account, cf. New York *Herald,* Feb. 6, 1851.

18. *SR*, I, 337, 342–54; *IL*, 96–103; Kessel, *Briefe,* 55–73, 146–47; Kinkel to Christian Schurz, Mar. 2, 1851; Schurz to Parents, Apr. 4, 1851, ctr. 180, SP.

19. *SR*, I, 353–66; Ferber, "Carl Schurz und Gottfried Kinkel," in Erkelenz and Mittelmann, *Schurz,* 60, 61–63, 66, 70–75; *IL*, 103–4; Schurz to parents, May 3, 1851, SP; Kessel, *Briefe,* 77. On July 31, Otto von Bismarck, then at Frankfurt, informed the Berlin police president that Schurz had been sighted in the vicinity of Bonn, allegedly traveling in the guise of a salesman with a British passport. Erkelenz and Mittelmann, *Schurz,* 67.

20. *SR*, I, 368ff. It is hard to believe that Schurz knew no English while living in London. One of the reasons he went there was to learn the language, and although he later asserted that he learned more on his trip to the United States than during his entire stay in England, he did not say he was entirely ignorant of the language. Schurz to parents, Apr. 4, 1851, SP; Kessel, *Briefe, 107–10.*

21. Friedrich Althaus, "Beiträge zur Geschichte der deutschen Colonie in England," *Unsere Zeit* 9 (1873), 224–45; Malwilda von Meysenbug, *Memoiren einer Idealistin* (Berlin: Schuster & Loeffler, 1905), II, 63–70; Kessel, *Briefe,* 29–34, 78–81, 83–86. Mehring, *Marx,* 212; *SR*, I, 368–78ff., 389ff.; *IL*, 104–7; Gustave Koerner, *Memoirs of Gustave Koerner,* ed. Thomas J. McCormack (Cedar Rapids, Iowa: Torch Press, 1909), I, 575–79; Carl Wittke, *Refugees of Revolution: The German Forty-Eighters in America* (Philadelphia: Univ. of Pennsylvania Press, 1952), 99–104; Heinrich Börnstein, *Fünfundzwanzig Jahre in der alten und der neuen Welt* (Leipzig: O. Weigand, 1884), II, 124–36; Arthur Hogue, "An Unpublished Mazzini Letter," *JMH* 38 (Sept. 1956), 266–69; Hermann Baron Bruiningk, *Das Geschlecht von Bruiningk in Livland* (Riga: N. Kymmels, 1913), 264ff.

22. *SR*, I, 391–402; Kessel, *Briefe,* 38, 91–95, 101–4; Schurz to Parents, Feb. 14, 1852, HC.

23. Ibid., Schurz to Adolph Meyer, May 31, 1852, HC; Fuess, *Schurz,* 38; Easum, *Americanization,* 50–55.

24. Fragment, ctr. 202, SP; Heinrich Ad. Meyer, *Erinnerungen an Heinrich Christian Meyer—Stockmeyer* (Hamburg: Lütcke & Wulff, 1900), 38ff., 86ff., and passim; *Independent,* Mar. 30, 1876. The biography by Hannah Werwarth Swart, *Margarethe Meyer Schurz* (Watertown: Watertown Historical Society, 1967), is unreliable. Although Mrs. Schurz came from a family which had befriended Jews, she was not Jewish, as has been asserted. Meyer, *Erinnerungen,* 82, 107; Mrs. E. L. Follen, *The Peddler of Dust Sticks* (Boston: Whittemore, Niles & Hall, 1856), 19.

25. Fragment, ctr. 202, SP.

26. Gabriel Monod, "Briefe von Malwida von Meysenbug an ihre Mutter," *Deutsche Revue* 31 (1906), 363; Charlotte Voss to Adolph Meyer, Apr. 14, 1852, HC.

27. Fragment, ctr. 202, SP; Charlotte Voss to Adolph Meyer, Apr. 14, 1852; Schurz to parents, Apr. 21, 1852, HC; *IL*, 107–11.

28. Fragment, ctr. 202, SP; *IL*, 107–11.

29. Schurz to Adolph Meyer, May 31, 1852; Schurz to Margarethe Meyer, June 3, 1852, HC.

30. Schurz to Parents, n.d., but evidently late June 1852, HC.

31. Fragment, ctr. 202, SP; Marie Kortmann, *Emilie Wüstenfeld, Eine Hamburger Bürgerin* (Hamburg: Georg Westermann, 1927), 55. According to Schurz's fragment, only Bertha Ronge, Toni Schurz, Kinkel, Mrs. Bruiningk, and Löwe were present at the actual wedding. Emilie Wüstenfeld described the larger affair at home.

32. *IL*, 115–16; Kessel, *Briefe*, 105–6; Joseph Schafer, *Carl Schurz, Militant Liberal* (Evansville, Wis.: Center Press, 1930), 76.

33. *SR*, I, 380, 402–6, II, 3. On the inheritance, cf. Dr. von Lehe to Walter Stahl, May 25, 1955, HC.

34. The Prussian police were still pursuing him; in the spring he was reported to have been sent to various German cities and to be traveling with a false passport and beard, no glasses, a grey cap, black jacket, and a short coat. The Prussian envoy in London reported that "the notorious Carl Schurz" was said to have been in Germany prior to June 26, dressed as a woman. Ferber, "Kinkel and Schurz," in Erkelenz and Mittelman, *Schurz*, 70ff., 73–75.

NOTES TO CHAPTER IV

1. Kessel, *Briefe*, 109; *SC*, I, 1–2; *SR*, II, 34.

2. *SR*, II, 5–7; *SC*, I, 2–4; *New-York in a Nutshell, or Visitor's Handbook to the City* (New York: T. W. Strong, 1853), 9ff.

3. *SC*, I, 1.

4. Kessel, *Briefe*, 107; *SR*, II, 8–9.

5. *SR*, II, 9; Schurz to Adolph Meyer, Sept. 29, 1852, HC; Fritz Anneke to Mrs. Anneke, Oct. 10, 1852, F. A. Anneke Papers, WiHiS.

6. *SR*, I, 337; II, 9–11; Kessel, *Briefe*, 107.

7. Horace White to Carl Schurz Memorial Committee, Jan. 31, 1910, George McAneny Papers, PU; Alexander K. McClure, *Colonel Alexander K. McClure's Recollections of Half a Century* (Salem, Mass.: Salem Press, 1902), 200; *Diary and Letters of Rutherford Birchard Hayes*, ed. Charles Richard Williams (Columbus: Ohio State Archaeological and Historical Society, 1924), III, 141; *Addresses in Memory of Carl Schurz* (New York: Committee of the Carl Schurz Memorial, 1906); Toledo *Express*, Mar. 29, 1892, in Martin Freidber to Schurz, Mar. 30, 1892, SP; William Dudley Foulke, *Fighting the Spoilsmen: Reminiscences of the Civil Service Reform Movement* (New York: Putnam's, 1919), 205–6; James G. Blaine, *Twenty Years of Congress* (Norwich, Conn.: Henry Bill, 1884), II, 438; Rockford, Ill., *Gazette*, May 16, 1906, in Scrapbook, Schurz Papers, WiHiS.

8. Walter Vulpius, "Carl Schurz, The Man and Friend: Personal Reminiscences," *American-German Review* 7 (Dec. 1940), 21.

9. Schurz to Adolph Meyer, Sept. 29, 1852, HC: *SC*, I, 1–8; Kessel, *Briefe*, 109.

10. Kessel, *Briefe*, 107–13; John A. Hawgood, *The Tragedy of German-America* (New York: Putnam's, 1940), 231; Wittke, *Refugees*, 99ff.; A. E. Zucker, ed., *The Forty-Eighters: Political Refugees of the German Revolution of 1848* (New York: Columbia Univ. Press, 1950), 161–67. Schurz also sought to assist Georg Brune and Dr. Falkenthal among the participants in the rescue of Kinkel. Kessel, *Briefe*, 117–22.

11. Kessel, *Briefe*, 115; Adolf Busse, "Briefe Gottfried Kinkels an Karl Schurz," in Paul Wantzke, ed., *Quellen und Darstellungen zur Geschichte der Deutschen Burschenschaft und der deutschen Einheitsbewegung*, XIV (Berlin: Verlag der Deutschen Burschenschaft, 1934), 249–50; Margarethe Schurz to Adolph Meyer, Feb. 15, 1853; Margarethe Schurz to Amalie [Meyer], Apr. 7, 1853; Schurz to Adolph Meyer, Mar. 26, 1853; Margarethe Schurz to Family, Apr. 10, 1853, HC.

12. Kessel, *Briefe*, 113–16.

13. Schurz to Adolph Meyer, July 27, Aug. 12, Nov. 20, 1853; Aug. 27, Oct. 25, 1854, HC.

14. *SR*, II, 14–15; Margarethe Schurz to Family, June 10, 1853; Schurz to Mrs. Schurz, July 25, 1853, HC; *IL*, 222–23; Ellis Paxson Oberholtzer, *Jay Cooke: Financier of the*

Civil War (New York: Burt Franklin, 1970), II, 468. Agathe at times spelled her name Agatha.

15. Schurz to Adolph Meyer, Nov. 20, 1853, HC.

16. Schurz to Adolph Meyer, Dec. 20, 1853, Feb. 20, 1854, HC.

17. Schurz to Mrs. Schurz, Mar. 13, 23, 1853, HC; Schurz to Mrs. Schurz, Mar. 15, 1854, SP; *SR*, II, 19ff.; Sarah T. Bolton, *The Life and Poems of Sarah T. Bolton* (Indianapolis: Fred A. Horton, 1880), xl–xli.

18. *SC*, I, 12; Schurz to Mrs. Schurz, Mar. 23, 1854, HC.

19. Schurz to Mrs. Schurz, Mar. 23, 1854, HC; *SR*, II, 30–37. As Michael Burlingame has pointed out, Schurz described his trip "disingenuously" without going into details about his real purposes. Michael Burlingame, "The Early Life of Carl Schurz, 1829–1865" (Ph.D. diss., Johns Hopkins, 1971), 143ff.

20. Schurz to Adolph Meyer, Aug. 22, 27, 1854; Schurz to Mrs. Schurz, Sept. 1, 1854, HC: *IL*, 125–26.

21. Schurz to Mrs. Schurz, Sept. 30, 1854, HC; Easum, *Americanization,* 89–90.

22. *IL*, 132–40; Schurz to Mrs. Schurz, Oct. 9, 1854, HC.

23. William F. Whyte, "Chronicles of Early Watertown," *Wis. Mag. of Hist.* 4 (Mar. 1921), 288ff.; Chester V. Easum, "Carl Schurz at Watertown," *American-German Review* 14 (June 1948), 34–35, 44.

24. Schurz to Adolph Meyer, Oct. 25, Dec. 27, 1854, HC; Kessel, *Briefe,* 117–21.

25. Kessel, *Briefe,* 121, 122–24; *IL*, 142–44.

26. Kessel, *Briefe*, 122; Whyte, "Chronicles of Early Watertown," 288ff., 314; Jüssen, "Carl Schurz," 393; Wilhelm Spael, *Karl Schurz* (Essen: Fredebeul & Koenen, 1948, 1949), II, 73–74; Easum, "Carl Schurz at Watertown"; Edwin B. Quiner, *City of Watertown, Wisconsin: Its Manufacturing & Railroad Advantages, and Business Statistics* (Watertown: City Council, 1858), esp. 3; Milwaukee *Daily Sentinel,* July 30, 1855; Schafer, *Schurz*, 92–93; *Watertown, Wisconsin Centennial, 1854–1954* (n. d., n. p.), 33ff.

27. Schurz to Adolph Meyer, Mar. 21, 1855, HC.

28. Kessel, *Briefe,* 122–24; *SC*, I, 19.

29. Schurz to Adolph Meyer, Mar. 21, 1855, Apr. 1, 1855, HC.

30. *SC,* I, 18–20.

31. *SR*, II, 49–61; Schurz to Ronge, July 3, 1855; Schurz to Adolph Meyer, May 29, 1855, HC. On Ronge, cf. Meysenbug, *Memoiren,* II, 72; Eyck, *The Frankfurt Parliament,* 21.

32. Schurz to Parents, June 7, 1855; Schurz to Adolph Meyer, June 9, 1855, HC.

33. Schurz to Mrs. Schurz, July 6, 23, 27, Aug. 2, 6, 8, 12, 27, Sept. 3, 1855, HC; Milwaukee *Daily Sentinel,* July 30, 1855; *IL*, 147–54.

34. Schurz to Mrs. Schurz, Sept. 25, 1855; Schurz to Adolph Meyer, Apr. 4, 1856, HC. The exact arrangements about the farm and lots are unclear. Schurz wrote to his wife that the total sum was $15,700; to his brother-in-law, he put the amount at $10,000. It appears that he took a mortgage for $8,500 for the farm and paid $1,500, a total of $10,000. Possibly the other $5,700 was for the adjacent lots. Cf. pamphlet, *The Charges of 1872 Against Carl Schurz* (n.p., n.d.), NYPL; also undated clipping, Washington *Post,* ctr. 211, SP; Schafer, *Schurz*, 94–95.

35. *SC,* I, 21–23; *IL*, 153–58.

36. *IL*, 156–59; Schurz to Mrs. Schurz, Sept. 18, Oct. 15, 28, Nov. 21, 1855, HC.

37. Schurz to Family, Jan. 18, Feb. 6, 1856; Schurz to Hans (Heinrich) Meyer, Jan. 21, Feb. 6, 1856, HC.

38. Mrs. Schurz to H. Meyer, Jan. 21, 1856; Schurz to Family, Feb. 6, 1856, HC; Alexander Herzen, *My Past and Thoughts* (New York: Knopf, 1968), III, 1065. Althaus then married Margarethe's friend, Charlotte Voss.

39. Mrs. Schurz to H. Meyer, Feb. 15, 1856, HC; *IL*, 166–69, 159–66.

40. Schurz to Family, Apr. 29, 1856, May 4, 1856; Schurz to Heinrich Meyer, June 12, 30, 1856, HC.

NOTES TO CHAPTER V

1. *IL*, 159–61.

2. Ibid., 171–73; Schurz to Heinrich Meyer, Nov. 15, 1856, ctr. 181, SP; *SC*, I, 23–27; Schurz to Heinrich Meyer, Jan. 10, 1857, HC. He established a partnership with C. D. Palme as a notary public and public land agent. Watertown *Democrat*, Feb. 26, 1857.

3. *SC*, I, 19; *SR*, II, 65–66; La Vern J. Rippley, *The German-Americans* (Boston: Twayne, 1976), 52ff.; Ernest Bruncken, "The Political Activity of Wisconsin Germans, 1854–1860," *Proceedings of the State Historical Society of Wisconsin . . .* (Madison: Democrat Printing, 1902), 190ff.

4. *SC*, I, 23.

5. Strodtmann, *Kinkel*, II, 167; Hans Zeek, ed., "Kinkels Briefe aus Amerika 1851/2," *Die Neue Rundschau* 49 (1938), Pt. I, 600–14, Pt. II, 27–47; Kessel, *Briefe*, 104.

6. *SC*, I, 5, 16.

7. Schurz to Heinrich Meyer, May 1, 1858, HC. In 1857, Schurz campaigned on a platform including black suffrage. Milwaukee *Daily Sentinel*, Sept. 19, 1857.

8. *SR*, II, 19, 14; Easum, *Americanization*, 94; Rudolf Baumgardt, *Carl Schurz: Ein Leben zwischen Zeiten und Kontinenten* (Berlin: Wilhelm Andermann, 1940), 250–51; *IL*, 135–73.

9. Kessel, *Briefe*, 119, 114; *SC*, I, 15.

10. Easum, *Americanization*, 135; Schafer, *Schurz*, 104; Bruncken, "Wisconsin Germans," 202; Ernest Bruncken, "German Political Refugees in the United States During the Period from 1815–1860," *Deutsch-Amerikanische Geschichtsblätter* 4 (1904), 53; Richard O'Connor, *The German-Americans* (Boston: Little, Brown, 1968), 132. Cf. Kathleen Neils Conzen, *Immigrant Milwaukee, 1836–1860: Accommodation and Community in a Frontier City* (Cambridge: Harvard Univ. Press, 1976), 227. On the persistence of ethnicity in politics, cf. Michael Parenti, "Ethnic Politics and the Persistence of Ethnic Identification," *American Political Science Review* 61 (Sept. 1967), 717–26, and on the difference between Germans and other groups, Nathan Glazer and Daniel P. Moynihan, *Beyond the Melting Pot: The Negroes, Jews, Italians and Irish of New York City* (Cambridge: M.I.T. Press, 1963), 312.

11. Schurz to Fritz [Tiedemann], n.d., ctr. 179, SP.

12. *SR*, II, 66–70; Milwaukee *Daily Sentinel*, Sept. 15, Oct. 3, 1856; Bruncken, "Wisconsin Germans," 190ff.; William Francis Raney, *Wisconsin: A Story of Progress* (New York: Prentice-Hall, 1940), 153–54; Koerner, *Memoirs*, II, 21–22.

13. Watertown *Democrat*, Nov. 6, 1856; A. M. Thomson, *A Political History of Wisconsin* (Milwaukee: E. C. Williams, 1900), 132–35; Whyte, "Chronicles of Early Watertown," 289.

14. *IL*, 173–75.

15. *SC*, I, 23–26; original in Kessel, *Briefe*, 129–34.

16. *IL*, 173; *SC*, I, 26. Although baptized "Carl," Schurz used the German form, "Karl," for many years until he gradually reverted to the original.

17. Fuess, *Schurz*, 50; *IL*, 171–72, 175–76.

18. *SR*, II, 72–75; Marie Jussen Monroe, "Biographical Sketch of Edmund Jussen," *Wis. Mag. of Hist.* 12 (Dec. 1928), 146ff., 162; Easum, *Americanization*, 105–6; Swart, *Margarethe Meyer Schurz*, 37, 41; C. Wiggenhorn to Schurz, July 23, 1904, SP; Schurz to

Mrs. Schurz, Sept. 8, 1855, HC; Whyte, "Chronicles of Early Watertown" 314; Ralph D. Blumenfeld, *Home Town* (London: Hutchinson, 1944), 14; Wilhelm Hense-Jensen, *Wisconsin's Deutsch-Amerikaner bis zum Schluss des neunzehnten Jahrhunderts* (Milwaukee: Verlag der Deutschen Gesellschaft, 1900), I, 138.

19. Kessel, *Briefe,* 134; Schurz to Heinrich Meyer, Apr. 29, 1857, HC. For the nickname, cf. Schurz to Handy, Apr. 14, 1878, HC.

20. *IL*, 176–78; Schurz to Mrs. Schurz, Mar. 20, 21, 27, 1857; Schurz to Heinrich Meyer, Apr. 29, 1857, HC; Schurz to F. C. Winkler, Mar. 9, 1899, Frederick C. Winkler Papers, Univ. of Wisconsin, Milwaukee; Watertown *Democrat,* Apr. 9, 1857.

21. Schurz to Mrs. Schurz, Mar. 28, 1857, HC. On the citizenship question, cf. *SR*, II, 81. The rest of the account of the 1857 campaign is unreliable.

22. Watertown *Democrat,* Apr. 23, May 7, Aug. 13, 20, 1857; L. P. Harvey to Schurz, July 20, 1857, SP; Schurz to Squire Hustis, Aug. 13, 1857, Schurz Papers, WiHiS; O. B. Quinn to H. A. Tenney, Sept. 22, 1857, Tenney Papers, WiHiS; Carl Wittke, *The German Language Press in America* (Lexington: Univ. of Kentucky Press, 1957), 98. Schurz resigned as improvement commissioner on May 4.

23. Thomson, *Wisconsin,* 139–42; Harvey to Schurz, July 20, 1857, SP.

24. Clipping from unknown paper, HC.

25. Milwaukee *Daily Sentinel,* Sept. 4, 9, 1857; Milwaukee *Atlas,* Sept. 5, 1857; Watertown *Democrat,* Sept. 10, 1857. The *Sentinel* pointed out that he obtained 145 of 185 votes on the first ballot.

26. Watertown *Democrat,* Sept. 17, 24, 1857; Milwaukee *Sentinel,* Oct. 3, 6, 7, 8, 12, 22, 1857.

27. Milwaukee *Sentinel,* Oct. 8, 9, 23, 24, 28, Nov. 2, 1857; *IL*, 178–79; Edward M. MacGrow to H. A. Tenney, Sept. 23, 1857, Tenney Papers, WiHiS; Milwaukee *Atlas,* Aug. 1, 1857.

28. Milwaukee *Daily Sentinel,* Nov. 6, 16, 19, 30, Dec. 8, 15–19, 1857; *IL*, 179–81; Erkelenz and Mittelmann, *Schurz,* 202–5; Harvey to Schurz, Dec. 20, 1857; W. S. [Winfield Smith] to Schurz, Dec. 10, 1857, SP; J. N. Dantt to Tenney, Jan. 3, 1858, Tenney Papers, WiHiS; Richard N. Current, *The History of Wisconsin,* II, *The Civil War Era, 1848–1873* (Madison: State Historical Society of Wisconsin, 1976), 263ff. Schurz carried Watertown, 501 to 484. Watertown *Democrat,* Nov. 5, 1857. According to the Milwaukee *Sentinel,* the results were: Randall (R), 44,693; Cross (D), 44,239; Schurz (R), 44,844; Campbell (D), 45,013. After a recount, Schurz maintained he lost by only 48 votes.

29. Kessel, *Briefe,* 136–37; Watertown *Democrat,* Jan. 21, 1858; Appointment to Board of Regents, Sept. 1, 1858, Schurz Papers, WiHiS; Thomson, *Wisconsin,* 140.

30. Schurz to Heinrich Meyer, Nov. 25, 1857, HC; Winfield Smith to Schurz, Dec. 10, 1857; Smith & Salomon to Schurz, Dec. 18, 1857, SP; Schafer, *Schurz,* 84–85, 172–73; *IL*, 413–14n.; Whyte, "Chronicles of Early Watertown," 297–98. Schurz's postwar troubles are described in Schurz to Mrs. Schurz, Aug. 20, 1866, Sept. 22, 1872, HC. For a hostile account, cf. *The Charges of 1872 Against Carl Schurz* and a clipping from the Washington *Post* in ctr. 211, SP.

31. Watertown *Democrat,* Jan. 14, 20, 1858; Milwaukee *Daily Sentinel,* Feb. 1, 1858; Schurz to Tenney, July 24, 1858, Tenney Papers, WiHiS.

32. Kessel, *Briefe,* 134–40; *SC*, I, 32–33; Swart, *Margarethe Meyer Schurz,* 40.

33. Schurz to Mrs. Schurz, Mar. 12, 1858; Schurz to Heinrich Meyer, May 5, 1858, HC.

34. Carl Schurz, *An Address, Delivered Before the Archean Society of Beloit College, At Its Anniversary, July 13, 1858* (Beloit: E. B. Hale, 1858); Robert K. Richardson, "A Beloit Episode in the Life of Carl Schurz," *Transactions of the Wisconsin Academy of Sciences, Arts, and Letters* 41 (1952), 5ff.; *SC*, I, 35–36. Two weeks later, he repeated the

same speech before the Literary Society of the University of Wisconsin. Madison *Wisconsin Daily State Journal*, Sept. 23, 1858; Easum, *Americanization*, 204.

35. Watertown *Democrat*, Apr. 15, June 2, 1858; Schurz to M. M. Davis, Apr. 29, Aug. 24, 1858, Moses M. Davis Papers, WiHiS.

36. Milwaukee *Daily Sentinel*, Aug. 30, Oct. 14, 30, Nov. 1, 1858; Madison *Wisconsin Daily State Journal*, Oct. 5, 1858; Easum, *Americanization*, 204.

37. *SR*, II, 88ff.; Carl Schurz, *Speeches of Carl Schurz* (Philadelphia: Lippincott, 1865), 9ff.; Roy P. Basler, ed., *The Collected Works of Abraham Lincoln* (New Brunswick, N.J.: Rutgers Univ. Press, 1953–55), II, 524; Milwaukee *Daily Sentinel*, Oct. 2, 8, 1858; *SC*, I, 37.

38. Milwaukee *Sentinel*, Oct. 21, 1858; Lincoln Lecture, ctr. 195, SP.

39. John W. Burgess, "Carl Schurz und Abraham Lincoln," in Erkelenz and Mittelmann, *Schurz*, 137–83.

40. Milwaukee *Sentinel*, Oct. 30, Nov. 1, 2, 20, 1858; Madison *Wisconsin Daily State Journal*, Nov. 5, 1858.

41. *IL*, 186–87.

42. *SR*, II, 104–5; Partnership Agreement, Jan. 1, 1859, SP; Milwaukee *Sentinel*, Jan. 13, 1859; Schafer, *Schurz*, 96. Schafer believes he never actually practiced, but he seems to have been involved in the Booth case and saw other clients as well. Schurz to Mrs. Schurz, July 14, 1859, HC; *SC*, I, 109.

43. Milwaukee *Atlas*, Nov. 29, 1858; Schurz to Mrs. Schurz, Jan. 7, 1859, HC.

44. Schurz to Mrs. Schurz, Jan. 7, 1859, HC; *IL*, 188–89; Kessel, *Briefe*, 140–41.

45. Schurz to J. F. Potter, Dec. 24, 1858, James F. Potter Papers, WiHiS; *SC*, I, 38–41; Milwaukee *Atlas*, Dec. 23, 28, 1858; Mar. 1, 1859; Watertown *Democrat*, Jan. 12, 1859.

46. Boston *Post*, Feb. 19, 1859; Newbury *Daily Herald*, Feb. 21, 1859; *SC*, I, 41–45; *SR*, II, 116ff.; Schurz to E. L. Pierce, Apr. 7, 1859, SP; Wittke, *Refugees*, 210–12.

47. *SC*, I, 48–77; *IL*, 190–92; Pierce to Schurz, Apr. 28, May 5, 1859, SP; New York *Tribune*, Apr. 22, 30, 1859; Milwaukee *Daily Sentinel*, Apr. 19–May 5, 1859; Richardson, "A Beloit Episode," 7–9. As quoted in the *Sentinel*, Apr. 27, 1859, William Lloyd Garrison's *Liberator* called it "the most eloquent speech" made in Faneuil Hall in fifty years.

48. Charles Warren, *The Supreme Court in United States History* (Boston: Little, Brown, 1926), II, 258–66, 332–34, 357; Milo Milton Quaife, *Wisconsin: Its History and Its People, 1634–1924* (Chicago: J. S. Clarke, 1924), I, 544–47; Milwaukee *Daily Sentinel*, Mar. 22, 1859.

49. Milwaukee *Daily Sentinel*, Mar. 24, 1859; Current, *Wisconsin*, 270–73; Burlingame, "Schurz," 200–9; T. O. Howe to Schurz, Dec. 29, 1858; Schurz to Howe, Apr. 2, 1859; Howe to Horace Rublee, Mar. 27, 1859, Timothy O. Howe Papers, WiHiS. When shortly afterward Booth was indicted for the seduction of a 14-year-old girl, Schurz was thoroughly disgusted with him.

50. Milwaukee *Daily Sentinel*, Apr. 25, May 12, 16, 1859; Watertown *Democrat*, May 5, 1859; Milwaukee *Atlas*, Apr. 30, May 4, 9, 14, 1859; *Pionier* (Boston), May 14, 1859; W. H. Watson to Schurz, May 14, 1859; James Sutherland to Schurz, June 2, 1859; H. L. Rann to Schurz, June 19, 1859, SP.

51. Wisconsin Assembly *Journal*, 1859, 198; L. P. Harvey to Schurz, June 21, 1859; Karl Stöser to Schurz, June 29, 1859; Carl Schäfer to Schurz, June 29, 1859; C. Röser to Schurz, Aug. 7, 1859, SP; C. C. Washburn to Potter, July 10, 1859, Potter Papers, WiHiS; M. M. Davis to Potter, Aug. 4, 1859, Davis Papers, WiHiS; Schurz to Potter, Aug. 12, 1859, Potter Papers; Hense-Jensen, *Wisconsin's Deutsch-Amerikaner*, I, 176–78; Thomson, *Wisconsin*, 142; Bruncken, "Wisconsin Germans," 205–6. His opponent for regent was his enemy, Leonard Mertz of Beaver Dam.

52. Schurz to Mrs. Schurz, Apr. 13, 1859, July 14, Aug. 21, 1859, HC.

53. Schurz to Mrs. Schurz, Aug. 17, 1859, HC; C. W. Cork to Tenney, Aug. 13, 1859, Tenney Papers, WiHiS; J. W. Hoyt to Schurz, Aug. 19, 1859; Henry Cordier to Schurz, Aug. 22, 1859; John Ericson to Schurz, Aug. 22, 1859; N. H. Sorgenson to Schurz, Aug. 23, 1859, SP; Milwaukee *Atlas*, Aug. 13, 29, 1859; Duane Mowry, "Letters of Carl Schurz, B. Gratz Brown, James S. Rollins, G. G. Vest et al., Missourians, From the Private Papers and Correspondence of James Rood Doolittle of Wisconsin," *Missouri Historical Review* 11 (1916), 1–7.

54. Milwaukee *Daily Sentinel*, Sept. 1–3, 1859; Madison *Wisconsin Daily State Journal*, Sept. 1, 2, 1849; Bruncken, "Wisconsin Germans," 205–6; F. C. Winkler to Schurz, Aug. 28, 1902 (with enclosure), SP.

55. *Der Pionier* (Boston), Sept. 24, 1859; Watertown *Democrat*, Sept. 8, 14, 1859; Doolittle to Potter, Sept. 16, 1859, Potter Papers, WiHiS. Mrs. Anneke, the wife of Schurz's former commander, had taken a violent dislike to him and did not agree with her countrymen. She boasted that she had contributed to his defeat by delaying Sherman M. Booth so that he could not go to Madison where he might have used his influence in Schurz's favor. Mrs. Anneke to Fritz Anneke, Sept. 26, 1859, Anneke Papers, WiHiS.

56. Milwaukee *Daily Sentinel*, Sept. 6, 7, 1859; Schurz to Potter, Apr. 30, Aug. 12, 1859; Doolittle to Potter, Sept. 10, 1859, Potter Papers, WiHiS; Schurz to Chase, Sept. 3, 1859, Samuel P. Chase Papers, PaHiS.

57. Daniel Rohrer to Schurz, July 26, 1859, SP; *IL*, 192–202; Hildegarde Binder Johnson, "The Election of 1860 and the Germans in Minnesota," *Minnesota History* 28 (Mar. 1947), 28–30; *SR*, II, 143–57.

58. Watertown *Democrat*, Oct. 27, 20, 1859; Watertown *Weltbürger*, Oct. 15, 1859; Milwaukee *Daily Sentinel*, Oct. 27, 28, 1859; Milwaukee *Atlas*, Oct. 4, 6, 11, 21, Nov. 2, 1859; M. K. Young to Schurz, Sept. 20, 1859; F. J. Tschudi to Schurz, Sept. 15, 1859; Tschudi to Lindemann, Sept. 17, 1859, SP; *IL*, 202–4; Ralph G. Plumb, *Badger Politics, 1836–1930* (Manitowoc: Brandt Printing, 1930), 37–38; Madison *Wisconsin Daily State Journal*, Oct. 24, 28, 29, 1859.

NOTES TO CHAPTER VI

1. *SR*, II, 157ff.; Milwaukee *Daily Sentinel*, Dec. 7, 1859; E. L. Pierce to C. F. Adams, Dec. 1, 1859, SP.

2. Schurz to Doolittle, Jan. 31, 1860, James Wright Brown Collection, NYHiS; Pierce to Adams, Dec. 1, 1859, SP; New York *Tribune*, Dec. 2, 1859; *IL*, 204–5. On January 17, 1860 he took part again in matters affecting the National Committee by suggesting that for strategic reasons, the time for the national convention be moved forward from June to May. Schurz to E. D. Morgan, Jan. 17, 1860, E. D. Morgan Papers, New York State Library, Albany, N.Y.

3. *SC*, I, 79–107; Madison *Wisconsin Daily State Journal*, June 25, Feb. 29, 1860.

4. Schurz to Lincoln, Feb. 23, 1860, Abraham Lincoln Papers, LC. For Douglas's proposal, cf. Robert W. Johannsen, *Stephen A. Douglas* (New York: Oxford Univ. Press, 1973), 723.

5. *IL*, 204–5; Schurz to Mrs. Schurz, Jan. 12, 1860, HC.

6. *SR*, II, 163–65; *Cong. Globe*, 36 Cong., 1 Sess., App., 95 (Jan. 25, 1860); Schurz to Doolittle, Jan. 31, 1860, Brown Collection, NYHiS; Schurz to Mrs. Schurz, Feb. 17, 1860, HC.

7. Schurz to Mrs. Schurz, Feb. 20, 1860, HC; *IL*, 205–8; T. O. Howe to Grace Howe, Feb. 23, 1860, Howe Papers, WiHiS; Madison *Wisconsin Daily State Journal*, Feb. 29–Mar. 2, 1860; Schafer, *Schurz*, 129–32; Easum, *Americanization*, 254–55; *SC*, I, 108–9.

8. *SC*, I, 109–10; Don E. Fehrenbacher, *Chicago Giant: A Biography of "Long John" Wentworth* (Madison: American Historical Research Center, 1957), 174; J. G. Randall, *Lincoln the President* (New York: Dodd, Mead, 1945), I, 131.

9. *SC*, I, 107, 110–11; Schurz to Mrs. Schurz, Feb. 20, Mar. 14, Apr. 12, 26, 27, 1860, HC; *IL*, 208–9. The account of the meeting with Schurz in *SR*, II, 169–72, is not dated accurately.

10. Schurz to Chase, Feb. 2, July 30, Dec. 5, 1859, Chase Papers, PaHiS; W. H. Brisbane to Schurz, Feb. 7, Apr. 4, July 14, 1859; Brisbane to Chase, Mar. 14, July 13, June 22, 1859, William H. Brisbane Papers, WiHiS; James M. Ashley to Chase, July 29, 1859; Amos Tuck to Chase, Mar. 14, 1860, Samuel P. Chase Papers, LC; Donnal V. Smith, *Chase and Civil War Politics* (Columbus: K. J. Heer, 1931), 64.

11. Max Eberhardt, "Schurz Erinnerungen," in Erkelenz and Mittelmann, *Schurz*, 211–13; *SC*, I, 110.

12. *IL*, 209–11; Schurz to Mrs. Schurz, Mar. 31, 1860, HC; Milwaukee *Daily Sentinel*, Apr. 1, 2, 5, 31, 1860; Madison *Wisconsin Daily State Journal*, Mar. 24–Apr. 10, 1860; *SC*, I, 111–15; Schurz to Potter, Apr. 20, 1860, Potter Papers, WiHiS.

13. Schurz to Mrs. Schurz, Apr. 12, 1860, HC; New York *Tribune*, May 12, 14, 15, 1860; F. I. Herriott, "The Conference at the Deutsches Haus, Chicago, May 14–15, 1860," *Transactions of the Illinois State Historical Society for the Year 1928* (Springfield: Phillips Bros., 1928), 147–56; Zucker, *Forty-Eighters*, 134, 137ff.

14. *Proceedings of the First Three Republican National Conventions of 1856, 1860, and 1864 . . .* (Minneapolis: Charles W. Johnson, 1893), 105, 133–43, 152–57; Murat Halstead, *National Political Conventions of the Current Presidential Campaign* (Columbus, Ohio: Follett, Foster, 1860), 136–37, 144–50, 128, 130; *SR*, II, 173–85; Koerner, *Memoirs*, II, 86–87.

15. Lincoln, *Works*, III, 380–81, 383, 391; Schurz to Sumner, June 8, 1860, SP.

16. *SR*, II, 187–88; Schurz, Lincoln Lecture, ctr. 195, 6–7, SP.

17. *SC*, I, 116–18.

18. Schurz, *Speeches*, 105–20; Albany *Evening Journal*, June 4, 1860.

19. Lincoln, *Works*, IV, 78–79

20. *SC*, I, 170–72; Max Hoffmann to Schurz, June 21, 1860; C. Schmidt to Schurz, June 21, 1860; M. S. Feldheimer to Schurz, June 22, 1860; F. W. Jansen to Schurz, June 27, 1860; H. H. Stumm to Schurz, Aug. 12, 1860; T. H. Dudley to Schurz, Aug. 24, 1860; James L. Green to Schurz, Aug. 25, 1860, SP; Andrew Dickinson White, *Autobiography of Andrew Dickinson White* (New York: Century, 1905), I, 86; Ella Lonn, *Foreigners in the Union Army and Navy* (Baton Rouge: Louisiana State Univ. Press, 1951), 45–46.

21. For the charges, cf. St. Louis *Missouri Democrat*, Aug. 26, 27, 1872. Cf. Norman Judd to Schurz, Aug. 15, 1860, Schurz to Sumner, June 8, 1860, SP; Schurz to Mrs. Schurz, Aug. 15, 1860, HC; *SC*, I, 163–64, 170–72; Reinhard H. Luthin, *The First Lincoln Campaign* (Cambridge, Mass.: Univ. Press Harvard, 1944), 168; Schurz to E. D. Morgan, July 4, Aug. 7, 1860, Morgan Papers, New York State Library. In addition, he received funds for the Milwaukee *Atlas* and the Watertown *Volkszeitung*. Schurz to Morgan, July 1, Aug. 7, 1860, ibid.

22. Schurz to parents, June 25, 1860; Schurz to Mrs. Schurz, June 26, July 1, 1860, HC; Milwaukee *Atlas*, July 14, 1860; Cleveland *Plain Dealer* in Watertown *Democrat*, July 26, 1860.

23. Madison *Wisconsin Daily State Journal*, Mar. 1, 1860. Cf. Allan Nevins, *The Emergence of Lincoln* (New York: Scribner's 1950), II, 306.

24. *IL*, 213–17; Koerner, *Memoirs*, II, 98–99.

25. Schurz, *Lebenserinnerungen*, III, 179–80; *SR*, II, 196–97. Shortly afterward, Lincoln sent Schurz a scrapbook of his speeches as requested. Lincoln, *Works*, IV, 88.

26. *SC*, I, 122–60; Madison *Wisconsin Daily State Journal*, Aug. 13, 1860; Börnstein,

Fünfundzwanzig Jahre, II, 251–52; *IL,* 217; William Ernest Smith, *The Francis Preston Blair Family in Politics* (New York: Macmillan, 1933), I, 493–94.

27. *IL,* 217–19; Schurz to Mrs. Schurz, Aug. 15, 1860, HC; Schurz to Lincoln, Aug. 22, 1860, Lincoln Papers, LC.

28. Schurz to Mrs. Schurz, Aug. 15, 17, 18, 22, Nov. 14, 18, 1860; Schurz to Parents, June 25, 1860, HC.

29. Schurz to Mrs. Schurz, Sept. 8, 17, 21, 24, 26, 1860, HC; *IL,* 219–27; Schurz, *Speeches,* 162–221; *SC,* I, 160–63; Schurz to Mrs. Schurz, Sept. 28, 1860; Horace Rublee to Schurz, Sept. 28, 1860, SP (Rublee letter in ctr. 181); *SR,* II, 204–7. He had originally asked Governor Morgan to get the New York Academy of Music for his speech. Then, when he was invited to Cooper Union, he accepted on condition he be alloted two hours, though the governor felt no audience could listen for so long a time. Schurz to Morgan, Sept. 2, 5, 6, 1860, Morgan Papers, New York State Library.

30. Schurz to Lincoln, Oct. 10, 1860, Lincoln Papers, LC.

31. Milwaukee *Atlas,* Sept. 29, 1860; J. H. Howe to Schurz, Oct. 11, 1860, SP; *IL,* 227.

32. *IL,* 227–32; Milwaukee *Daily Sentinel,* Oct. 17, 20, 23–25, 31, 1860; Milwaukee *Atlas,* Oct. 24, 1860; *New-Yorker Demokrat,* Oct.–Nov. 1860, esp. Oct. 23; Whyte, "Chronicles of Early Watertown," 298.

33. Schurz to Lincoln, Nov. 9, 1860, Lincoln Papers, LC.

34. Milwaukee *Sentinel,* Nov. 19, 20, 1860.

35. Herriot, "The Conference at the Deutsches Haus," 105–6; William E. Dodd, "The Fight for the Northwest, 1860," *AHR* 16 (1911), 774–88; Donnal V. Smith, "The Influence of the Foreign-Born in the Northwest in the Election of 1860," *MVHR* 19 (Sept. 1932) 192–204; Schafer, *Schurz,* 134–45; Hense-Jensen, *Wisconsin's Deutsch-Amerikaner,* 181; Rudolf Cronau, *Drei Jahrhunderte deutschen Lebens in Amerika* (Berlin: Dietrich Reimer, 1909), 334; *Die Glocke* (Chicago) I (1906), 164–66; Bruncken, "Political Refugees," 4 (1904), 49. Cf. Frederick C. Luebke, ed., *Ethnic Voters and the Election of Lincoln* (Lincoln: Univ. of Nebraska Press, 1971). Lincoln's and Schurz's beliefs are borne out by their actions. As Schurz wrote to his wife in September from Ft. Wayne, his importance in the campaign was greater than he knew at the beginning. Schurz to Mrs. Schurz, Sept. 28, 1860, SP. For Lincoln, cf. n. 38, below.

36. Joseph Schafer, "Who Elected Lincoln?" *AHR* 47 (1941), 51–63; Andreas Dorpalen, "The German Element and the Issues of the Civil War," *MVHR* 29 (1942), 55–76; articles by Hildegard Binder Johnson on Minnesota, George H. Daniels on Iowa, Ronald P. Formisano on Michigan, Jay Monaghan and James M. Bergquist on Illinois in Luebke, *Ethnic Voters.* Illinois forms an exception and the Germans apparently did contribute greatly to Lincoln's victory there.

37. Schurz to Mrs. Schurz, Feb. 13, 1861, HC.

38. William Vocke, "Our German Soldiers," *Paper Read . . . Before the Commandery of the State of Illinois Military Order of the Loyal Legion* (Chicago: Dial, 1899), 349; Milwaukee *Daily Sentinel,* Oct. 19, 24, 1860; New York *Weekly Tribune,* Sept. 29, 1860; Columbus *Westbote,* Nov. 1, 1860, quoted in Lonn, *Foreigners,* 54, n. 37.

39. *SC,* I, 170–72; Israel Jackson to Schurz, July 19, Sept. 8, 19, 1860; Hervey, Anthony & Galt to Schurz, Oct. 11, 1860, SP; Lincoln, *Works,* IV, 144; *IL,* 233–49; *SR,* II, 159–61 (where the Mississippi crossing is not properly dated); Schurz, *Speeches,* 222–41; Schurz to Parents, Dec. 28, 1860, HC.

40. *SC,* I, 165–68.

41. Ibid., 168–70; Schurz to Lincoln, Dec. 18, 1860, Lincoln Papers, LC.

42. Schurz to Mrs. Schurz, Dec. 20, 1860, HC; *IL,* 235–41; *SC,* I, 172–79; Schurz to Lincoln, Dec. 28, 1860, Lincoln Papers, LC; Schurz to Morgan, Dec. 21, 1860, Morgan Papers, New York State Library.

43. *IL*, 237–41; *SR*, II, 213–16; Schurz, *Lebenserinnerungen*, III, 191–93. Schurz wrote several letters to his wife in French. For Corwin's speech, which dates Schurz's visit to Washington, cf. *Cong. Globe*, 36 Cong., 2 sess., 72ff. (Jan. 21, 1861).

44. *IL*, 244–47; Robert Grey Gunderson, *Old Gentlemen's Convention: The Washington Peace Conference of 1861* (Madison: Univ. of Wisconsin Press, 1961), 77–78; Milwaukee *Daily Sentinel*, Feb. 7, 9, 16, 17, 1861; Wisconsin Assembly, *Journal*, 1861, 183–84; Madison *Wisconsin Daily State Journal*, Jan. 31–Feb. 20, 1861.

45. Schurz to Lincoln, Jan. 31, 1861, Lincoln Papers, LC.

46. *IL*, 179–80; *SR*, II, 218–20.

NOTES TO CHAPTER VII

1. Schurz to Mrs. Schurz, Nov. 10, 1860, HC. For a detailed account of Schurz's office-seeking, cf. Barbara Donner, "Carl Schurz as Office Seeker," *Wis. Mag. of Hist.* 20 (Dec. 1936), 127–43.

2. Schurz to Potter, Nov. 30, 1860, Potter Papers, WiHiS; Lincoln, *Works*, IV, 144.

3. Lincoln, *Works*, IV, 168–70, 172–76; Schurz to Lincoln, Dec. 18, 1860, Lincoln Papers, LC.

4. Schurz to Lincoln, Jan. 31, 1861, Lincoln Papers, LC.

5. *SC*, I, 179–80; Schurz to Mrs. Schurz, Feb. 13, 1861, HC.

6. Schurz to Mrs. Schurz, Mar. 4, 9, 10, 1861, *IL*, 249–50; *New York Times*, Mar. 9, 18, 1861; New York *Herald*, March 7, 13, 14, 1861; Lincoln, *Works*, IV, 280; Gideon Welles, *The Diary of Gideon Welles*, ed. Howard K. Beale (New York: Norton, 1960), II, 391. He also sought a post office for his uncle and a Swiss consulate for his former Watertown partner in journalism, Hermann Lindemann.

7. Milwaukee *Daily Sentinel* with quotes, Mar. 13, 14, 20, 1861; Donner, "Carl Schurz as Office Seeker," 131; *New York Times*, Mar. 9, 18, 1861; New York *Tribune*, Mar. 11, 16, 1861; New York *Herald*, Mar. 15, 17, 1861; Schurz to Mrs. Schurz, Mar. 15, 1861, HC; Charles Francis Adams, *Charles Francis Adams, 1835–1915: An Autobiography* (Boston: Houghton Mifflin, 1916), 103; David Lowenthal, *George Perkins Marsh: Versatile Vermonter* (New York: Columbia Univ. Press, 1958), 208; *IL*, 250–52. The Italian chargé d'affaires said he would have to refer the matter to his government, which had the right to declare Schurz persona non grata. Sexson E. Humphreys, "United States Recognition of the Kingdom of Italy," *Historian* 21 (May 1959), 304.

8. Lincoln, *Works*, IV, 292–93; New York *Tribune*, Mar. 19, 1861; New York *Herald*, Mar. 19, 28, 1861.

9. Schurz to Mrs. Schurz, Mar. 17–19, 1861, HC.

10. New York *Herald*, Mar. 19, 1861; Harry J. Carman and Reinhard H. Luthin, *Lincoln and the Patronage* (New York: Columbia Univ. Press, 1943), 82–85.

11. Schurz to Mrs. Schurz, Mar. 22, 26, 1861, HC.

12. Richard N. Current, *Lincoln and the First Shot* (Philadelphia: Lippincott, 1963), 66–68; Schurz to Mrs. Schurz, Mar. 22, 1861, HC.

13. New York *Tribune*, Mar. 16, 19, 1861; *Anzeiger des Westens*, quoted in Chicago *Evening Post*, Mar. 24, 1861, cited by Donner, "Carl Schurz as Office Seeker," 135.

14. Schurz to Lincoln, Mar. 26, 1861, Lincoln Papers, LC.

15. Cassius Marcellus Clay, *The Life of Cassius Marcellus Clay: Memoirs, Writings and Speeches* (New York: Negro Universities Press, 1969), 255ff., 278.

16. *IL*, 252–53.

17. New York *Herald*, Mar. 29, 1861; Milwaukee *Daily Sentinel*, Apr. 1. 1861.

18. Garcia to Foreign Minister, Mar. 12, 15, 29, 1861; Foreign Minister to Garcia, Apr. 29, 1861, Ministerio de Asuntos Exteriores, Madrid, Archives; Kinley J. Brauer,

"The Appointment of Carl Schurz as Minister to Spain," *Mid-America* 56 (Apr. 1974), 75–84.

19. For Seward's anti-Spanish motivation of the April 1 Memorandum, cf. Allan Nevins, *The War for the Union* (New York: Scribner's 1959), I, 61–63.

20. Schurz to Seward, Mar. 29, 1861; Schurz to Lincoln, Apr. 5, 1861, Lincoln Papers, LC; *IL*, 252–53. On the election, cf. Baird Still, *Milwaukee: The History of a City* (Madison: State Hist. Soc. of Wis., 1948), 155–56.

21. Schurz to Secretary of State, Apr. 4, 1861, Department of State, Diplomatic Despatches, Despatches From United States Ministers to Spain, 43, National Archives (hereafter cited as NA, DS, Spain, 43); draft, Schurz to Lincoln, Apr. 13, 1861, SP.

22. Schurz to Mrs. Schurz, Apr. 16, 1861, HC; *IL*, 253–54; Milwaukee *Daily Sentinel*, Apr. 22, 1861.

23. *SR*, II, 223–27.

24. Tyler Dennet, ed., *Lincoln and the Civil War in the Diaries and Letters of John Hay* (New York: Dodd, Mead, 1939), 12 (hereafter cited as Hay, *Diaries*).

25. Schurz to Lincoln, Apr. 27, 1861 (misdated Apr. 11), Lincoln Papers, LC; Recruiting Authority from Cameron, Apr. 27, 1861, SP; *OR*, Ser. I, III, Pt. I, 140–41; Hay, *Diaries,* 13, 22; *SR*, II, 229–30; *IL*, 254–55.

26. *SR*, II, 230–37; *OR*, Ser. I, III, Pt. I, 140–41; James H. Stevenson, *"Boots and Saddles:"* A History of the First Volunteer Cavalry of the War Known as the First New York (Lincoln) Cavalry (Harrisburg, Pa: Patriot Publishing, 1879), 13–24; Lehigh Valley Railroad, *Personally Conducted Tour of the 20th (Turners) Regiment of the City of New York, September 9–15, 1906, to Gettysburg, Antietam, Harpers Ferry and Washington* (pamphlet, n.d., n.p.), 8; Seward to Schurz, May 8, 1861, SP. Although Schurz wrote in his memoirs that Cameron favored the project, Stevenson's assertion of the opposite reaction is more creditable because the secretary of war refused to accommodate his chief by appointing Schurz. Cf. p. 105 and n. 27, below.

27. Lincoln, *Works*, IV, 367–68, 371–72; Schurz to Lincoln, May 19, 1861, Lincoln Papers, LC.

28. *SR*, II, 240–44; Hay, *Diaries,* 23; Schafer, *Schurz*, xi–xii. Schurz greatly impressed his visiting brother-in-law Heinrich Meyer when he took him to the White House for lunch.

29. Secretary of State to Perry, May 9, 21, June 1, 3, 1861, Department of State, Diplomatic Instructions, Spain, National Archives, 15 (hereafter cited as NA, Spain, 15); Perry to Secretary of State, May 27, 1861, NA, DS, Spain, 43; Secretary of State to Schurz, May 29, 1861, NA, Spain, 15.

30. Schurz to E. D. Morgan, May 30, 1861, Chase Papers, PaHiS; Stevenson, *"Boots and Saddles,"* 23; Schurz to Lincoln, June 6, 1861, Carl Schurz Papers, Boston Public Library; Milwaukee *Daily Sentinel*, June 29, 1861; Schurz to Lincoln, June 5, 1861, Lincoln Papers, LC; Schurz to Secretary of State, June 5, 1861, NA, DS, Spain, 43; Schurz to Parents, June 20, 1861, HC; *IL*, 255–56. Paine had been appointed colonel of the Fourth Wisconsin. Paine to Schurz, May 27, 1861, SP.

31. Sarah Agnes Wallace and Frances Elma Gillespie, eds., *The Journal of Benjamin Moran* (Chicago: Univ. of Chicago Press, 1949), II, 833; *SR*, II, 245–46.

32. Garcia y Tassara to Secretary of State, Apr. 4, June 30, 1861, Department of State, Notes from the Spanish Legation in the United States to the Department of State, 1790–1906, 16A, National Archives; Garcia y Tassara to Foreign Minister, June 4, 1861, Ministerio de Asuntos Exteriores, Madrid, Archives; also cited in Brauer, "The Appointment of Carl Schurz as Minister to Spain," 78–80; Horatio Perry to Schurz, July 8, 1861, SP.

33. *SR*, II, 247; Adolph Meyer to Schurz, June 27, 1861; William Dayton to Schurz,

July 4, 1861; Perry to Schurz, July 9, 1861, SP; Schurz to Secretary of State, July 15, 1861, NA, DS, Spain, 43.

34. Schurz to Secretary of State, July 15, 1861, NA, DS, Spain, 43; *SR*, II, 248–53.

35. Schurz to Secretary of State, July 15, 18, 22, Aug. 5, 19, 26, Sept. 2, 1861, NA, DS, Spain, 43. Schurz's efficient diplomatic performance has been generally recognized. Cf. Barbara Donner, "Carl Schurz, the Diplomat," *Wis. Mag. of Hist.* 20 (Mar. 1937), 291–309; Burlingame, "Schurz," 409.

36. Perry to Schurz, July 8, 9, 1861, SP; *SR*, II, 256–59; *IL*, 258–66.

37. *SR*, II, 270–74; Schurz to Lincoln, Aug. 6, 1861, Lincoln Papers, LC; Schurz to Secretary of State, Aug. 6, 8, 1861, NA, DS, Spain, 43.

38. Schurz to Lincoln, Aug. 13, 1861, Lincoln Papers, LC; Perry to Secretary of State, Aug. 19, 1861, NA, DS, Spain, 43; Secretary of State to Schurz, Sept. 3, 1861, NA, Spain, 15.

39. Schurz to Secretary of State, July 22, Aug. 5, 8, 19, 26, Sept. 2, 5, 7, 11, 19, 20, 21, 27, Oct. 1, 4, 9, 14, 15, 17, 21, 26, Nov. 3, 7, 9, 16, 17, 1861, NA, DS, Spain, 43; Secretary of State to Schurz, Aug. 15, 1861, NA, Spain, 15.

40. *SC*, I, 185–200; Schurz to Secretary of State, Oct. 9, 17, 26, Nov. 11, 1861, NA, DS, Spain, 43; *SR*, II, 287–305.

41. *SR*, II, 265, 306; *SC*, I, 183–84; Schurz to Judd, Sept. 21, 1861; Judd to Schurz, Sept. 23, 1861, SP.

42. Schurz to Secretary of State, Nov. 30, Dec. 7, 1861; Schurz to Marsh, Dec. 3, 1861, NA, DS, Spain, 43; Secretary of State to Schurz, Dec. 31, 1861, NA, Spain, 15.

43. Secretary of State to Schurz, Dec. 2, 1861, NA, Spain, 15; Perry to Secretary of State, Dec. 21, 1861, NA, DS, Spain, 43; Schurz to Lincoln, Dec. 23, 1861, Lincoln Papers, LC.

44. *SR*, II, 306–9; Schurz to Secretary of State, Jan. 8, 1862 (draft), SP; *IL*, 267–69.

45. *SR*, II, 309–30; Schurz to Parents, Feb. 26, 1862; Mrs. Schurz to Parents-in-law, Feb. 26, 1862, HC; Charles A. Knoderer to Franz Sigel, Feb. 18, 1862, Franz Sigel Papers, NYHiS; Lincoln Lecture, ctr. 195, 38–39, SP.

46. New York *Tribune,* Mar. 7, 1862; Schurz, *Speeches,* 240–68; Schurz to C. A. Dana, Mar. 8, 1862, James W. Eldridge Papers, Huntington Library.

47. *IL*, 269–72; Perry to Schurz, May 8, 1862; Seward to Schurz, June 21, 1862, SP. Koerner became his successor in Madrid. Koerner, *Memoirs,* II, 211–13.

NOTES TO CHAPTER VIII

1. C. A. Knoderer to Sigel, Feb. 18 and Feb. n.d., 1862, Sigel Papers, NYHiS; J. G. Nicolay to Schurz, Feb. 9, 1862, Lincoln Papers, LC.

2. *SR*, II, 327–30; *IL*, 269–70.

3. Frémont to Schurz, Mar. 29, 1862, SP.

4. Lincoln, *Works,* Suppl., 292; *IL*, 270–72; Schurz to Sumner, Apr. 6, 1862, Charles Sumner Papers, Harvard.

5. Schimmelfennig to Schurz, Apr. 24, 30, 1862; Schimmelfenning to Gritzner, Apr. 28, 1862; Gustave Paul Cluseret to Schurz, Apr. 27, 1862; John Hayt to Mrs. Lincoln, Apr. 20, 1862, SP; Schurz to Lincoln, May 5, 1862, Lincoln Papers, LC; *IL*, 270; *SC*, I, 208.

6. *SC*, I, 206–7.

7. Mrs. Schurz to Chase, May 29, 1862, Chase Papers, LC; *SR*, II, 341; *IL*, 272; *OR*, Ser. I, XII, Pt. III, 307.

8. Schurz, Diary, ctr. 175, SP, esp. June 7, 14, 21, 22, 28, 29, Nov. 19, 1862.

9. Frank Freidel, *Francis Lieber: 19th Century Liberal* (Baton Rouge: Louisiana State

Univ. Press, 1947), 319; Mrs. Anneke to M, Apr. 20, 1862, Anneke Papers, WiHiS; Wilhelm Kaufmann, *Die Deutschen im amerikanischen Bürgerkriege* (Munich: R. Oldenbourg, 1911), 467.

10. Schurz, Diary, June 10, 1862; Schimmelfenning to Schurz, Apr. 24, 1862, SP; *IL*, 272–74.

11. Schurz to Lincoln, June 12, 1862, Lincoln Papers, LC; Lincoln, *Works*, V, 274–75.

12. *SR*, II, 345–51; *IL*, 272–74; Hermann Nachtigall, *Geschichte des 75sten Regiments, Pa. Volunteers* (Philadelphia: C. B. Kretschman, 1886), 5–6; Schurz, Diary, June 27, 24, 28, 29, July 4, 1862, SP; Kaufmann, *Die Deutschen*, 42–72, 523, 575; *OR*, Ser. I, LI, Pt. I, 709; Schurz's Eulogy of Krzyzanowski, Feb. 2, 1887, ctr. 190, SP. Schurz enlisted Sumner's aid in favor of Sigel but was accused of plotting against Blenker. Schurz to Sumner, July 2, 1862, Sumner to Schurz, July 5, 1862, SP; Gustav Struve, *Diesseits und Jehnseits des Oceans* (Coburg: F. Streit, 1863), 53–54. For Krzyzanowski, cf. James S. Pula, *For Liberty and Justice: The Life and Times of Wladimir Krzyzanowski* (Chicago: Polish American Congress Charitable Foundation, 1978).

13. Schurz, Diary, June 14–July 28, 1862, SP; *IL*, 272–74; Karl Spraul to Editor, *New-Yorker Bellatristisches Journal*, Mar. 9, 1877, SP. His social intercourse with his fellow officers was most agreeable, and one of his friends was the French military adventurer Col. Gustave Paul Cluseret.

14. Schurz, Diary, June 9–Aug. 10, 1862, SP; *IL*, 274–78.

15. Bruce Catton, *The Centennial History of the Civil War*, II, *Terrible Swift Sword* (Garden City, N.Y.: Doubleday, 1963), 282–91; Shelby Foote, *The Civil War* (New York: Random, 1958), I, 527ff.; James Ford Rhodes, *History of the United States from the Compromise of 1850* (New York: Macmillan, 1902), IV, 97, 114ff.; *OR*, Ser. I, XI, Pt. II, 3; Clarence Buel and Robert Johnson, eds., *Battles and Leaders of the Civil War* (New York: Yoseloff, 1956), II, 257ff.

16. Schurz, Diary, Aug. 4, 7–11, 17, 1862, SP; Kaufman, *Die Deutschen*, 149ff., 316–19; *SR*, II, 404.

17. Catton, *Terrible Swift Sword*, 417–18; Foote, *Civil War*, I, 605ff.; Schurz, Diary, Aug. 20, 21, 1861, SP; *SR*, II, 356.

18. *SR*, II, 356–59; Schurz, Diary, Aug. 22, 1862, SP; Schopps, Gefecht bei Freeman's Ford, Franz Sigel Papers, WRHS. Bohlen, annoyed at Schurz's countermanding his orders to the Virginia troops to withdraw, challenged him to come to his beleaguered brigade if he wanted to give orders to it. Schurz wisely paid no attention to this unexpected insubordination.

19. Nevins, *War for the Union*, II, 175–79; Schurz, Diary, Aug. 24–28, 1862, SP.

20. Schurz, Diary, Aug. 29, 1862, SP; *SR*, II, 362–71; Sigel Memoirs, Aug. 28, 29, 1862, Sigel Papers, WRHS; E. W. Sheppard, *The Campaign in Virginia and Maryland, June 26 to September 20, 1862* . . . (New York: Greene, Allen, 1911), 123ff.; A. R. Barlow, *Company G: A Record of the Services of One Company of the 157th New York Vols. in the War of the Rebellion* . . . (Syracuse: A. W. Hall, 1899), 6; Kaufmann, *Die Deutschen*, 322–26, 456; Charles A. Page, *Letters of a War Correspondent*, ed. James R. Gilmore (Boston: L. C. Page, 1899), 24ff.; Oliver Otis Howard, *Autobiography of Oliver Otis Howard* (New York: Baker & Taylor, 1907), I, 264; Lenoir Chambers, *Stonewall Jackson* (New York: Morrow, 1959), II, 160; *OR*, Ser. I, XII, Pt. II, 296–303, 265.

21. *OR*, Ser. I, XII, Pt. II, 296–303; Schurz, Diary, Aug. 30, 31, Sept. 1, 2, 1862, SP; *SR*, II, 371–79; Edward J. Stackpole, *From Cedar Mountain to Antietam* (Harrisburg, Pa.: Stackpole, 1959), 182; Kaufmann, *Die Deutschen*, 329–31.

22. *OR*, Ser. I, XII, Pt. II, 296–303, 48; *SR*, II, 380–81; Mrs. Anneke to Mother, Sept. 25, 1862, Anneke Papers, WiHiS; New York *Tribune*, Sept. 5, 1862.

23. Schurz, Diary, Aug. 31, Sept. 9, 1862, SP; Sheppard, *Campaign,* 144; *OR*, Ser. I, XII, Pt. II, 355–57, 342; XIX, Pt. I, 1.

24. Schurz, Diary, Sept. 4–9, 1862, SP; Sigel to Halleck, Sept. 16, 1862; Halleck to Sigel, Sept. 16, 1862; n.d., Sigel to Lincoln (in Schurz's hand); Adolph Roland to Sigel, Oct. 31, 1862, Sigel Papers, NYHiS; David Donald, ed., *Inside Lincoln's Cabinet: The Civil War Diaries of Salmon P. Chase* (New York: Longmans, Green, 1954), 147.

25. Donald, *Lincoln's Cabinet,* 147; Schurz, Diary, Sept. 4, 5, 8, 9, 1862, SP; Hay, *Diaries,* 48; Theodore Clarke Smith, *The Life and Letters of James Abram Garfield* (New Haven: Yale Univ. Press, 1925), I, 242–43.

26. John Hope Franklin, *The Emancipation Proclamation* (Garden City: Doubleday, 1963), 46ff.; Hans L. Trefousse, *Lincoln's Decision for Emancipation* (Philadelphia: Lippincott, 1975), 43–47; T. Harry Williams, *Lincoln and His Generals* (New York: Grosset & Dunlap, 1952), 179ff.

27. Schurz, Diary, Nov. 2–9, 1862; Edmund Berkeley to Schurz, Dec. 17, 1895, SP; *OR*, Ser. I, XIX, Pt. II, 525, 534, 541; *SR*, II, 389–93.

28. *SC*, I, 209–21; Lincoln, *Works,* V, 493–95, 509–11.

29. *SR*, II, 393–96; Schurz, Diary, Dec. 2, 1862; Emil von Schleinitz to Schurz, Oct. 6, 1899, SP; Schurz to Frederick Bancroft, Apr. 1, 1905, Frederick Bancroft Papers, CU. Theodore Roosevelt was one of those who cited the correspondence to Schurz's detriment. Elting E. Morison *et. al.,* eds., *The Letters of Theodore Roosevelt* (Cambridge: Harvard Univ. Press, 1954), IV, 819 (hereafter cited as Roosevelt, *Letters*).

30. *OR*, Ser. I, XII, Pt. II, 13; Sigel to Lincoln, Oct. 9, 1862; Sigel to Burnside, n.d.; Burnside to Sigel, Dec. 5, 1862; Sigel to Hooker, Dec. 1862; Halleck to Sigel, Dec. 4, 1862; G. L. Lyon to Sigel, Dec. 10, 1862, Sigel Papers, NYHiS; Schurz, Diary, Nov. 29–Dec. 4, 1862, SP; Charles Eliot Slocum, *The Life and Public Services of Major-General Henry Warner Slocum* (Toledo: Slocum Publishing, 1913), 60.

31. Schurz, Diary, Nov. 8–10, 15, 16, 1862; draft, Schurz to Chase, Nov. 22, 1862, Schurz Papers; *SR*, II, 397–98; *OR*, Ser. I, XIX, Pt. I, 3; Pt. II, 583.

32. Schurz, Diary, Dec. 12–14, 1862, SP. The corps finally moved to Stafford to establish headquarters.

33. Schurz, Diary, Jan. 1, 1863. Schurz's entry was: "Leute, die in jeder Beziehung gemässigte Ansichten haben, haben ihm gesagt, dass die Proklamation möglicher Weise mehr Schwierigkeiten als Erleichterungen hervorbringen würde."

34. Schurz to Mrs. Adolph Meyer, Jan. 2, 1863, SP.

35. Ibid.; Schurz, Diary, Jan. 13, 18, 19, 1863; George G. Lyon to Schurz, Dec. 10, 1862, Sigel to Lincoln, Jan. 17, 1863, SP; John G. Parke to Sigel, Dec. 16, 1862; Sigel to Mrs. Sigel, Dec. 18, 1862, Sigel papers, NYHiS; Lincoln, *Works,* VI, 5–6, 43, 55; *OR*, Ser. I, LI, Pt. I, 960; XXXI, 925; XXI, 181. Friedrich Hecker, who now commanded the Eighty-second Illinois Regiment, which had just been assigned to Schurz's division, approached Trumbull in Schurz's behalf. Hecker to Trumbull, Dec. 18, 1862, SP.

36. Schurz, Diary, Jan. 22, 1863, SP; *SC*, I, 221–22; *SR*, II, 400–3.

37. Schurz, Diary, Nov. 19, 1862, Jan. 24–Feb. 1, 1863; Schurz to Lincoln, Jan. 20, 1863; Schurz to Stahel, Feb. 5, 1863; Schurz to Sumner, Feb. 13, 1863, SP; *SR*, II, 403; Lincoln, *Works,* VI, 79–80, 93; Schurz to Sigel, Jan. 28, 1863; Schurz to Stahel, Jan. 30, 1863, enclosing Schurz to Sigel, Jan. 30, 1863, Sigel Papers, WRHS; Schurz to Washburne, Jan. 29, 1863, Elihu Washburne Papers, LC. On January 26, von Steinwehr, who was jealous of Schurz, asked Sigel for a transfer because he considered it humiliating to serve under him. Carl Wittke, *Refugees,* 235.

38. *IL*, 280–81; Schurz to Sumner, Mar. 8, 12, 1863; Mrs. Schurz to Sumner, Mar. 10, 1863, Sumner Papers, HU.

39. *OR*, Ser. I, XXV, Pt. II, 146; XXX, Pt. I, 2; Lincoln, *Works, VI,* 93.

NOTES TO CHAPTER IX

1. *IL*, 285.

2. Augustus Choate Hamlin, *The Battle of Chancellorsville* (Bangor, Me.: privately printed, 1896), 222–25, 156–58; Lincoln, *Works,* VI, 168; Schurz to von Steinwehr, June 16, 1863; von Steinwehr to Schurz, June 16, 1863, SP; Schurz to Sigel, Mar. 19, 1863; Sigel to Schurz, Mar. 21, 1863 and fragment, Sigel Papers, WRHS; Wittke, *Refugees,* 235.

3. John A. Carpenter, *Sword and Olive Branch: Oliver Otis Howard* (Pittsburgh: Univ. of Pittsburgh Press, 1964), 43; Bruce Catton, *Never Call Retreat* (Garden City, N.Y.: Doubleday, 1965), 152–53. It is possible that one of the reasons for the appointment of Howard was Hooker's desire to supersede Schurz. Cf. Hamlin, *Chancellorsville,* 158.

4. Schurz to Hooker, Apr. 9, 1868, War Department, RG 94, NA; Lincoln, *Works,* VI, 168; Oliver Otis Howard, *Autobiography,* I, 348; *SR*, II, 404–7.

5. *Die Glocke* (Chicago), I (1906), 190; Carpenter, *Howard,* 43.

6. Foote, *The Civil War,* II, 266ff.; 277ff.; *SR*, II, 411–14.

7. *SR*, II, 414–21; Owen Rice, "Afield with the Eleventh Army Corps at Chancellorsville," *Papers Read before the Ohio Commandery of the Military Order of the Loyal Legion of the United States* (Cincinnati: Robert Clarke, 1888), I, 371–79; *OR*, Ser. I, XXV, I, 647ff.; Hamlin, *Chancellorsville,* 20–21; Abner Doubleday, *Chancellorsville and Gettysburg* (New York: Scribner's, 1882), 25–27; Lenoir Chambers, *Stonewall Jackson* (New York: Morrow, 1959), II, 403–4.

8. Howard, *Autobiography,* I, 363–75; Oliver O. Howard, "The Eleventh Corps at Chancellorsville," in Buel and Johnson, *Battles and Leaders,* III, 189–202, 196; *OR*, Ser. I, XV, I, 658–59, II, 660–61; John Bigelow, *The Campaign of Chancellorsville* (New Haven: Yale Univ. Press, 1910), 276–77; Hartwell Osborn, *Trials and Triumphs: The Record of the Fifty-fifth Ohio Volunteer Infantry* (Chicago: McClurg, 1904), 69–74; Barlow, *Company G,* 99–100; Rice, "Chancellorsville," 374–80; Hamlin, *Chancellorsville,* 69; *SR*, II, 414–21.

9. *SR*, II, 421–31; *OR*, Ser. I, XV, I, 647ff., 627–30; John Bigelow, *The Campaign of Chancellorsville* (New Haven: Yale Univ. Press, 1910), 301–14, 405; Theodore R. Dodge, *The Campaign of Chancellorsville* (Boston: Osgood, 1881), 100–5; William Swinton, *Campaigns of the Army of the Potomac* (New York: Charles P. Richardson, 1866), 286; Johns S. Applegate, *Reminiscences and Letters of George Arrowsmith of New Jersey . . .* (Red Bank, N.J.: John H. Cooke, 1893), 199; Kaufmann, *Die Deutschen,* 351–65; Pula, *Krzyzanowski,* 77–87.

10. *OR*, Ser. I, XXV, I, 647ff.; *New York Times,* May 5, 1863; New York *Herald,* May 6, 1863; Philadelphia *Ledger,* May 6, 1863; J. Cutler Andrews, *The North Reports the Civil War* (Pittsburgh: Univ. of Pittsburgh Press, 1955), 371.

11. Hamlin, *Chancellorsville,* 26–33; Darius N. Couch, "The Chancellorsville Campaign," in Buel and Johnson, *Battles and Leaders,* II, 163; *New York Times,* May 11, 1863; New York *Herald,* May 11, 1863; *Report of the Joint Committee on the Conduct of the War* (Sen. Rep. No. 142, 38th Cong., 2d sess., (Washington, D.C., 1865), I, 135.

12. *SR*, II, 433–36; Chicago *Tribune,* May 7, 12, 1863. In addition to the sources already cited, the following also absolve the Eleventh Corps: Fletcher Pratt, *Ordeal by Fire* (New York: Pocket Books, 1952), 180–81; Catton, *Never Call Retreat,* 152–54; Edwin B. Coddington, *The Gettysburg Campaign* (New York: Scribner's, 1968), 608–9. For the quotation, cf. Pula, *Krzyzanowski,* 92.

13. Greeley to Schurz, Mar. 4, 1867, July 4, 1868; Schurz to Greeley, Nov. 28, 1867; Hooker to Schurz, Apr. 8, July 17, 1876; William Barlow to Schurz, Nov. 24, 1879; T. A. Dodge to Schurz, June 13, 1881; C. H. Howard to Schurz, Feb. 11, 1886; C. C. Buel to

Schurz, Aug. 7, July 8, 1886; A. Hamlin to Schurz, Nov. 20, 1890, Mar. 23, 1896; J. F. Rhodes to Schurz, June 1, 1897; J. C. Ropes to Schurz, Feb. 24, 1899; Schurz to Sister-in-Law, Sept. 10, 1863, SP; Schurz to Frank Moore, June 6, 1865, André de Coppet Collection, PU; *SR*, II, 407–43. The Joint Committee on the Conduct of the War in 1865 rendered an unfavorable report. Sen. Report No. 142, 38th Cong., 2d sess., I, xlix.

14. *New York Times,* June 3, 1863; Wittke, *German Language Press,* 151–52.

15. Schurz to Sigel, May 8, 19, 27, 29, June 16, 1863, Sigel Papers, WRHS; Schurz to Howard, May 26, 1863; Howard to Schurz, May 26, 1863, SP; Howard to Schurz, May 27, 1863, RG 393, Pt. I, War Department, Records of the U.S. Army Continental Command, 1821–1920, NA; *OR,* Ser. I, XV, I, 659–60; Carpenter, *Howard,* 49.

16. Frederick C. Winkler, *Letters of Frederick C. Winkler, 1862–1865* (Milwaukee: privately printed, 1963), 62.

17. *SR,* III, 3–18; *OR,* Ser. I, XXVII, I, 727–32, 701–7; Winkler, *Letters,* 68–72; Osborn, *Trials and Triumphs,* 95–98; Doubleday, *Chancellorsville and Gettysburg,* 150; Arrowsmith, *Reminiscences,* 213; Jesse Bowman Young, *The Battle of Gettysburg* (New York: Harper, 1913), 192; Coddington, *Gettysburg Campaign,* 282–306; W. R. Kiefer, *History of the 153d Regiment Pennsylvania Volunteers, Infantry, 1862–1863* (Easton: Chemical Publishing, 1909), 63ff., 73–78. Coddington states authoritatively that the usually accepted stories that overwhelming numbers routed the Eleventh Corps are false.

18. *SR,* III, 19–34; Kaufmann, *Die Deutschen,* 375–80; Coddington, *Gettysburg Campaign,* 432–37; *OR,* Ser. I, XXVII, I, 704–6; Henry J. Hunt, "The Second Day at Gettysburg," in Buel and Johnson, *Battles and Leaders,* III, 312–13; John Gibbon, "The Council of War at Gettysburg," in ibid., 313–14; Winkler, *Letters,* 72.

19. *SR,* III, 34–41; Barlow, *Company G,* 13–32; Alfred C. Raphaelson, "Alexander Schimmelfennig: A German-American Campaigner in the Civil War," *Pennsylvania Magazine of History and Biography* 87 (Apr. 1963), 156–81.

20. *New Yorker Staats-Zeitung,* July 20, 1863; *SR,* III, 42–54; Fairfax Downey, *The Guns at Gettysburg* (New York: David McKay, 1958), 46ff.; Coddington, *Gettysburg Campaign,* 305–6, 407; Howard to F. Irsch, Oct. 10, 1890, SP; Frederick Winkler's Reminiscences of Frank Haskell, Winkler Papers, Univ. of Wisconsin; *OR,* Ser. I, XVII, I, 105; III, 650, 778–79, 784–85, 792–93; Schurz to Lincoln, Aug. 7, 1863, de Coppet Collection, PU; Schurz to Sigel, Aug. 17, 1863, Sigel Papers, WRHS; Schurz to Williams, Sept. 2, 1863, War Department, RG 94, NA; *IL,* 281–82.

21. Schurz to Sister-in-law, Sept. 10, 1863, SP; *IL,* 281–82.

22. *IL,* 282–89; Hans Höwing, *Carl Schurz, Rebell—Kämpfer—Staatsmann* (Wiesbaden: Limes, 1948), 484.

23. Winkler, *Letters,* 86–87.

24. *OR,* Ser. I, XXIX, I, 151, 167, 169, 170, 172, 181–82; Schurz to Stanton, Oct. 3, 1863, SP; Benjamin Thomas and Harold M. Hyman, *Stanton: The Life and Times of Lincoln's Secretary of War* (New York: Knopf, 1862), 285–89.

25. Catton, *Never Call Retreat,* 256–60; Foote, *The Civil War,* II, 804–11; *SR,* III, 55–67; *OR,* Ser. I, XXI, I, 110–11, 62–63, 96–97; Osborn, *Trials and Triumphs,* 120–23; Michael Hendrick Fitch, *The Chattanooga Campaign . . .* (Madison: Wisconsin Historical Commission, 1911), 177ff.; Pula, *Krzyzanowski,* 122–29.

26. *SC,* I, 223–24; *SR,* III, 68–69.

27. *SR,* III, 56–58, 67; *IL,* 289–93.

28. *OR,* Ser. I, XXXI, II, 346ff., 381–83; Catton, *Never Call Retreat,* 261–65; *SR,* III, 71–85. After the Knoxville expedition, Sherman sent Howard a warm letter of appreciation of the Eleventh Corps and its generals. *OR,* Ser. I, XI, III, 439.

29. Clipping, Nov. 9, 1873, ctr. 184; Schurz to Tiedemann, Jan. 5, 1864, SP; Winkler, *Letters,* 111.

30. *SR*, III, 85–94; *OR*, Ser. I, XXXI, I, 137–215; Pula, *Krzyzanowski,* 137–56; Walter H. Hebert, *Fighting Joe Hooker* (Indianapolis: Bobbs-Merrill, 1944), 348; Henry Villard, *Memoirs of Henry Villard* (Boston: Houghton Mifflin, 1904), II, 228.

31. Schurz to Brig. Gen. W. D. Whipple, Feb. 22, 1864; Schurz to Lt. Col. Meysenburg, Mar. 14, 1864, War Department, RG 94, Generals' Papers, NA; Lincoln, *Works,* VII, 244–45.

32. Donald, *Lincoln's Cabinet,* 201; Chicago *Tribune,* Oct. 29, 1863; Schurz to Morgan, Jan. 6, 1864, Morgan Papers, New York State Library; Lincoln, *Works,* VII, 244–45, 262–63. Concerning his request for a transfer, Assistant Secretary of War Charles A. Dana promised Schurz to submit it to Stanton but advised him to stay with his command. Dana to Schurz, Mar. 24, 26, 1864, SP.

33. *OR,* Ser. I, XXXII, III, 292, 306, 397, 436, 505; Hooker to Brig. Gen. Whipple, Apr. 10, 1864; Thomas to Sherman, Apr. 11, 1864, Special Field Order, Apr. 17, 1864, War Department, RG 94, NA; General Order No. 10, Mil. Div. of the Mississippi, Apr. 25, 1864, SP. Schurz presumably caused further trouble with his superiors by demanding that the court of inquiry findings be published and that justice be done to Col. Krzyzanowski, who had been unjustly slighted by the court. Schurz to Secretary of War, Apr. 7, 1864, Schurz to Whipple, Apr. 7, 1864, SP.

34. *SR,* III, 95–97; Lincoln, *Works,* VII, 466; Schurz to Sherman, May 19, 1864; Schurz to Col. Sawyer, June 1, 1864, War Department, RG 94, NA.

35. Hans L. Trefousse, *The Radical Republicans: Lincoln's Vanguard for Racial Justice* (New York: Knopf, 1969), 289–95; *IL,* 303; Sigel to Mrs. Sigel, June 1, 1864, Sigel Papers, NYHiS.

36. Schurz to Tiedemann, Aug. 24, 1864; Hay to Schurz, Aug. 11, 1864, SP; *IL,* 304; Schurz to Washburne, Jan. 18, 1865, Washburne Papers, LC. Hay's August 11 telegram shows that the date in *SR,* III, 103–5, is wrong (late July), although the rest of the account appears to be correct.

37. *IL,* 303–11; Hay, *Diary,* 222.

38. Schurz to Parents, Sept. 4, 1864, HC.

39. *"For the Great Empire of Liberty, Forward!", Speech of Maj.-Gen. Carl Schurz, of Wisconsin, Delivered at Concert Hall, Philadelphia . . .* (New York: Gray & Green, 1864); *SC,* I, 225–48; Schurz, *Speeches,* 359–92; Schurz to Rublee, Oct. 11, 1864, SP; Henry H. Wright, *A History of the Sixth Iowa Infantry* (Iowa City: State Historical Society of Iowa, 1923), 348; *New York Times,* Oct. 11, Nov. 5, 1864; Schurz to Parents, Nov. 10, 1864, HC.

40. Schurz to Washburne, Jan. 18, 1865, Washburne Papers, LC; Schurz to Heinrich and Emmy Meyer, Jan. 6, 1865, HC; *IL,* 314; Schurz, *Speeches,* i–ix.

41. Schurz to Washburne, Jan. 18, 1865, Washburne Papers, LC; Schurz to Mrs. Schurz, Jan. 29–Feb. 1, 1865, HC; Lincoln, *Works,* VIII, 257.

42. *IL,* 314–15; Trefousse, *Radical Republicans,* 299–300.

43. Schurz to Mrs. Schurz, Feb. 15, 1865, HC; *OR,* Ser. I, XLVI, 573, 592; Schurz to Mrs. Schurz, Mar. 4, 7, 11, 1865; Schurz to H. H. Crapo, Mar. 17, 1865, SP; *IL,* 315–25; *SR,* III, 108.

44. *SR,* III, 109–11; *OR,* Ser. I, XLVII, II, 712; XLVI, III, 395; *IL,* 326–27.

45. *IL,* 327–29; *OR,* Ser. I, XLVII, III, 110, 113.

46. *IL,* 320–31, *OR,* Ser. I, XLVII, III, 112, 121, 213, 222; Slocum, *Slocum,* 307; Schurz to Mrs. Schurz, Apr. 9, 1865, HC.

47. Arguing that there was no English translation of Clausewitz until 1873 and that there was a remarkable similarity between Lincoln's strategic views and those of the German writer, John M. Palmer advanced a theory that the President must have obtained his ideas from Schurz, who had read Clausewitz. John McAuly Palmer, *Washington, Lincoln, Wilson: Three War Statesmen* (Garden City, N.Y.: Doubleday, 1930), 233, 238, 247.

NOTES TO CHAPTER X

1. *IL*, 331–52.
2. Wright, *History of the Sixth Iowa Infantry,* 451–52.
3. For Schurz's views on Reconstruction, cf. *SR*, III, 221ff. His close friendship with Sumner and the opinions of his *Report on the South* show his attitude toward black enfranchisement. For his interest in the new labor system and the Freedmen's Bureau bill, cf. copies of T. J. Henderson to Louis B. Collins, Nov. 16, 1864; J. M. Forbes to E. B. Ward, Dec. 29, 1864; B. F. Flanders to W. P. Fessenden, Dec. 8, 1864; Schurz to Sumner, Feb. 8, 1865, SP.
4. *SR*, III, 221–25.
5. *SC*, I, 252–53.
6. *OR,* Ser. I, XLVII, Pt. III, 323.
7. George H. Boker to Schurz, Mar. 30, 1865; Forney to Schurz, May 21, 1865; Stallo to Schurz, May 16, 1865, SP; Schurz to Mrs. Schurz, May 21, 1865, HC; *IL*, 335; *SC*, I, 254–55.
8. Schurz to Heinrich and Emmy Meyer, May 25, 1865, HC; *IL*, 324.
9. *SC*, I, 256–58; Schurz to Mrs. Schurz, May 19, 21, 1865, HC; *IL*, 335–37; Marquis Adolphe de Chambrun, *Impressions of Lincoln and the Civil War: A Foreigner's Account (New York: Random, 1952), 156–57.*
10. *SC*, I, 258–63; *SR*, III, 137.
11. *SR*, III, 153–57; Schurz to Tiedemann, June 11, 1865, SP.
12. *SC*, I, 265–67; Sumner to Schurz, June 29, July 8, 1865; Schurz to Sumner, June 22, July 3, 1865; Stanton to Schurz, July 7, 11, 1865, SP; Schurz to G. L. Stearns, June 20, 1865, George L. Stearns Papers, MHiS.
13. Memorandum of Southern tour with dates, July 12 to Oct. 12, 1865; Letter for Boston *Advertiser,* July 17, 21, 25, SP; *SR*, III, 159–80; Schurz to Johnson, July 28, 1865, Andrew Johnson Papers, LC; Schurz to Mrs. Schurz, July 18, 1865, HC; *IL*, 343–44.
14. Letter for Boston *Advertiser,* July 31, Aug. 8, 15, 1865; communication to Brig. Gen. Swayne from Freedmen's Bureau, July 29, 1865, Affidavit of B. Taylor, July 26, 1865, SP; Schurz to Johnson with enclosures, Aug. 18, 21, 1865, Johnson Papers, LC; *IL*, 344–48; Chicago *Tribune*, Aug. 11, 30, 1865; Joseph F. Mahaffey, "Carl Schurz's Letters from the South," *Georgia Historical Quarterly* 25 (Sept. 1951), 222–57.
15. *SC*, I, 268–72; Schurz to Mrs. Schurz, Aug. 27, 1865, HC; Schurz to Johnson, Aug. 29, Sept. 2, 4, 1865; Sharkey to Johnson, Aug. 30, Sept. 2, 1865; Steedman to Johnson, Aug. 15, 1865, Johnson Papers, LC; Johnson to Schurz, Aug. 30, 1865, SP; William C. Harris, *Presidential Reconstruction in Mississippi* (Baton Rouge: Louisiana State Univ. Press, 1967), 72ff.
16. *IL*, 348–50; Sumner to Schurz, Aug. 28, 1865, SP; Schurz to Johnson (telegrams), Sept. 3, 8, 1865, Johnson Papers, 2nd Ser., LC.
17. Schurz to Johnson, Sept. 4, 15, 22, 1865, with enclosures, Johnson Papers, LC; *SC*, I, 270–72.
18. *IL*, 341, 348–52; Schurz to Johnson, Sept. 4, 5, 15, 23, 26, 1865, with enclosures; Hugh Kennedy to Johnson, Sept. 7, 10, 12, 1865; Banks to Johnson, Sept. 8, 1865; Cottman to Johnson, Sept. 9, 1865; S. P. Sullivan to Johnson, Sept. 14, 1865; Wells to Johnson, Sept. 23, 1865, Johnson Papers, LC; Schurz to Mrs. Schurz, Sept. 28, 1865, HC.
19. *SC*, I, 272–78; Sumner to Schurz, Oct. 20, Nov. 15, 1865; Schurz to Sumner, Oct. 17, 1865, SP; New York *Herald,* Oct. 14–16, 1865.
20. Carl Schurz, *Report on the Condition of the South*, H. Report, No. 11, 39th Cong., 1st sess., Dec. 18, 1865 (Reprint: New York: Arno, 1969).
21. Schurz to Johnson, Nov. 22, 25, 1865; Schurz to Col. Johnson, Nov. 25, 1865, Johnson Papers, LC; Sumner to Schurz, Nov. 15, 1865, SP; Eric L. McKitrick, *Andrew*

Johnson and Reconstruction (Chicago: Univ. of Chicago Press, 1960), 164; La Wanda and John H. Cox, *Politics, Principle, and Prejudice, 1865–66* (New York: Free Press of Glencoe, 1963), 139–42; Trefousse, *Radical Republicans,* 324ff.

22. Trefousse, *Radical Republicans,* 324ff.; Kenneth M. Stampp, *The Era of Reconstruction, 1865–1877* (New York: Knopf, 1965), 83ff.; *Cong. Globe,* 39th Cong., 1st sess, 17 (Dec. 11, 1865), 30 (Dec. 12, 1865), 78 (Dec. 19, 1865), 129 (Jan. 5, 1866), 265 (Jan. 17, 1866).

23. Hans L. Trefousse, "Carl Schurz's 1865 Southern Tour: A Reassessment," *Prospects* 2 (1976), 293–308; New York *Herald,* Dec. 24, 1865; Chicago *Tribune,* Dec. 21, 1865, Jan. 6, 1866.

24. W. R. Brock, *An American Crisis: Congress and Reconstruction, 1865–1867* (New York: Harper, 1966), 36–37; U.S. Congress, *Report of the Joint Committee on Reconstruction,* 39th Cong., 1st sess. (Washington, D.C., 1866); Benjamin Truman to W. A. Browning, Nov. 9, 1865, Johnson Papers, LC.

25. *IL,* 357–59.

26. Schurz to Mrs. Schurz, Sept. 28, 1865; Schurz to Parents, Nov. 1, Dec. 27, 1865; Schurz to Mrs. Schurz, Dec. 8, 9, 13, 1865, Jan. 17, 29, 1866, HC; Schurz to Preetorius, Oct. 31, 1865, SP; *SC,* I, 260, 276; *IL,* 353–58; Schurz to Sidney Howard Gay, Nov. 24, 30, 1865, Sidney Howard Gay Papers, CU.

27. Schurz to Parents, Feb. 9, 1866; Schurz to Mrs. Schurz, Jan. 29, 31, Feb. 2, 1866, HC; Schurz to S. H. Gay, Feb. 18, 1866, Gay Papers, CU; *IL,* 358–61; Mary Karl George, *Zachariah Chandler* (East Lansing: Michigan State Univ. Press, 1969), 141–42.

28. *SC,* I, 375–76; John A. Russell, *The Germanic Influence in the Making of Michigan* (Detroit: Univ. of Detroit, 1927), 292; Schafer, *Schurz,* 170–73; *Detroit Post,* Apr. 28, 1866.

29. *Detroit Post,* Apr. 28, 1866; Karl Knortz, "Mein Erster Besuch bei Carl Schurz," *Die Glocke* (Chicago) I (1906), 179–80; Schurz to Mrs. Schurz, June 25, 28, Aug. 17, 1866; Lise to Mrs. Schurz, June 22, 1866, HC.

30. *IL,* 365–70; Schurz to Mrs. Schurz, Aug. 19, 1866; Schurz to Heinrich Meyer, June 10, 1866, HC; *SC,* I, 377–418; New York *Tribune,* Oct. 24, 1866; Schurz to Preetorius, Sept. 21, 1866, SP.

31. *Atlantic Monthly* 19 (March 1867), 371–78.

32. Schafer, *Schurz,* 170–73; Schurz to Mrs. Schurz, Aug. 14, 17, 1866, Feb. 7, 20, Apr. 18, 19, 21, 1867; Schurz to Parents, Mar. 10, 1867, HC; *IL,* 371–74; Schurz to Mrs. Schurz, Apr. 17, 1867, SP; J. Thomas Scharf, *History of St. Louis and County* (Philadelphia: Louis H. Everts, 1883), I, 941; William Taussig, "Erinnerungen an Carl Schurz," *Die Glocke* (Chicago) 1 (1906), 167–69. He also lost some $5,000 in railroad speculations.

33. Schurz to Petrasch, Apr. 4, 1867, SP; Schurz to Fritz [Tiedemann], May 7, 1867; Schurz to Mrs. Schurz, Apr. 17, 1867; Schurz to Adolph Meyer, June 2, 1867, HC; *IL,* 374–77; Schafer, *Schurz,* 174.

34. J. L. Tracy, *Tracy's Guide to Missouri and St. Louis* (St. Louis: R. P. Studly, 1871); Schurz to Mrs. Schurz, June 23, July 16, Aug. 4, Sept. 4, 1867; Schurz to Mother, July 23, 1867, HC; *IL,* 377–404; St. Louis, Missouri, *Westliche Post,* Sept. 10, 1867.

35. *IL,* 398–418; Schurz to Fritz [Tiedemann], Oct. 11, 1867; Schurz to Preetorius, Dec. 5, 1867, SP; *New York Times,* Sept. 20, 1867; Schurz to Mrs. Schurz, Sept. 28, Oct. 4, 12, 1867, HC; Hans L. Trefousse, *Impeachment of a President: Andrew Johnson, the Blacks, and Reconstruction* (Knoxville: Univ. of Tennessee Press, 1975), 85ff., 110.

36. *IL,* 363–65, 410–17; Schurz to Heinrich Meyer, June 10, 1866, HC. Schurz solicited the help of the American minister in Berlin, George Bancroft, to ascertain whether he would be welcome in Prussia. The answer was positive. Schurz to Bancroft, Nov. 26, 1867; Bancroft to Schurz, Dec. 12, 1867, SP; Schurz to Bancroft, Dec. 23, 1867, George Bancroft Papers, MHiS.

37. *SR*, III, 263–80; Otto von Bismarck, *Die Gesammelten Werke* (Berlin: Otto Stolberg, 1924–35), VII, 240–42; Richard Fester, "Bismarck's Gespräch mit Karl Schurz am 28. Januar 1868," *Süddeutsche Monatschefte* 11, no. 1 (1913/14), 363–68; Dr. R. Koch, "Eine Erinnerung an Fürst Bismarck," *Deutsche Revue* 33 (1908), 162–65.

38. *IL*, 418–28; Busse, "Briefe Gottfried Kinkels an Carl Schurz," 265–67; *New York Times*, Mar. 22, 29, 1868; St. Louis, Missouri, *Westliche Post*, Mar. 25, 29, 30, 31, 1868; Schurz to Preetorius, Feb. 19, 1868; Schurz to Bancroft, Feb. 15, 1868, Bancroft to Schurz, Feb. 17, 1868, SP; *New-Yorker Bellatristisches Journal*, Feb. 14, 1868. In 1877, Bismarck, learning of an alleged possibility of Schurz's appointment as minister to Germany, expressed his disapproval to prevent the American's collaboration with the liberal opposition. Otto Graf zu Stolberg-Wernigerode, *Deutschland und die Vereinigten Staaten im Zeitalter Bismarcks* (Berlin: Walter de Gruyter, 1933), 176–77.

39. *SR*, III, 281–82; Schurz to Adolph Meyer, Feb. 3, 16, 1868, HC; Charitas Bischoff, *Amalie Dietrich* (Berlin: G. Grote, 1911), 334–35; Schurz to Bancroft, Feb. 16, 1868, SP.

40. Schurz to Mrs. Schurz, Mar. 20, 29, Apr. 5, 18, 26, 1868, HC, *IL*, 427–33; *SR*, III, 306–7.

41. Schurz to Mrs. Schurz, June 8, 1868, HC. *Die Glocke*, I (1906), 167–69.

42. Schurz to Mrs. Schurz, Apr. 4, 18, May 11, 18, 1868, HC; Chambrun to Schurz, May 12, 13, 14, 1868, SP.

43. Henry H. Smith, ed., *All the Republican National Conventions . . . Proceedings, Platforms, and Candidates* (Washington, D.C.: Robert Beall, 1896), 31–32; *Proceedings of the National Union Republican Convention Held at Chicago, May 20 and 21, 1868* (Chicago: Evening Journal, 1868), 8–10, 86, 89–90, 104; St. Louis *Westliche Post*, May 20–27, 1868; *New-Yorker Bellatristisches Journal*, May 29, 1868; Stewart Woodford to Schurz, Apr. 13, 1868, SP; *IL*, 399, 433–38.

44. *IL*, 438–47; Schurz to Mrs. Schurz, June 8, July 5, 19, 27, Aug. 16, 23, 24, Sept. 7, 14, 30, 1868, HC; Schurz to William Clafflin, Aug. 2, 1868, R. B. Hayes Papers, Hayes Library; Speech at Young Men's Republican Club, St. Louis, June 19, 1868, ctr. 184; Schurz to Preetorius, Sept. 5, 9, 1868, SP; *SC*, I, 419–72; *New York Times*, Sept. 6, 1868; Leon Burr Richardson, *William E. Chandler, Republican* (New York: Dodd, Mead, 1940), 107; St. Louis *Westliche Post*, July 16, 21, Sept. 17, 20, Oct. 1, 15, 17, 25, 1868; William E. Parrish, *Missouri Under Radical Rule, 1865–1870* (Columbia: Univ. of Missouri Press, 1965), 250.

45. Schurz to Mrs. Schurz, June 15, July 19, 27, Sept. 21, 30, Oct. 9, 11, 15, 17, 25, Nov. 2, 9, 15, 1868, HC.

46. *IL*, 449–51. The Negro suffrage amendment was defeated, but the Fifteenth Amendment soon took its place.

NOTES TO CHAPTER XI

1. *SR*, III, 292; *IL*, 441–43; Parrish, *Missouri Under Radical Rule*, 259.

2. Parrish, *Missouri Under Radical Rule*, 20, 228–60, 329, n. 15; Norma Peterson, *Freedom and Franchise: The Political Career of B. Gratz Brown* (Columbia: Univ. of Missouri Press, 1965), 169; John Gerow Gazley, *American Opinion of German Unification* (New York: Columbia Univ. Press, 1926), 448–50; Thomas S. Barclay, *The Liberal Republican Movement in Missouri, 1865–1871* (Columbia, Mo.: State Hist. Soc. of Missouri, 1926), 219; *DAB*, VIII, 126; *IL*, 435.

3. *IL*, 442–43; Barclay, *Liberal Republican Movement*, 152.

4. Schurz to Preetorius, Aug. 15, 16, 1868, SP; St. Louis *Westliche Post*, Aug. 18, Oct. 15, 28, 1868; Schurz to William Clafflin, Aug. 2, 1868, William Clafflin Papers, Hayes Library; Richardson, *Chandler*, 107.

5. Schurz to Mrs. Schurz, Sept. 30, Oct. 9, 11, Nov. 2, 1868; Schurz to Parents, Nov. 17, 1868, HC; Schurz to Preetorius, Sept. 30, Oct. 4, 1868, SP; St. Louis *Westliche Post*, Sept. 17, Oct. 25, 1868.

6. Barclay, *Liberal Republican Movement*, 153–56; *SR*, III, 294–95. On Schurz's views on ethnicity, see below, pp. 264–65, 292–93.

7. Parrish, *Missouri Under Radical Rule*, 259–62; *IL*, 449–59; Schurz to Mrs. Schurz, Dec. 6, 13, 20, 1868, HC; Schurz to Washburne, Dec. 10, 1868, Washburne Papers, LC; Schurz to Fritz [Tiedemann], Dec. 20, 1868, SP; Chicago *Tribune*, Dec. 14–16, 1868. Washburne sent a somewhat noncommittal reply, although he assured Schurz that the new administration fully valued his services and would recognize them, "a recognition . . . demanded by what we owe to the German element of the country." Washburne to Schurz, Dec. 29, 1868, SP.

8. C. H. Howland to W. H. McLane, Dec. 8, 1868, McLane Papers, MoHiS; George L. Orne to "Dear Colonel" [Grosvenor], Dec. 16, 1868, SP; St. Louis *Westliche Post*, Dec. 28, 1868; *IL*, 459–62.

9. *IL*, 459–63; St. Louis *Missouri Democrat*, Jan. 8, 10, 1869; *New York Times*, Jan. 9, 1869.

10. St. Louis *Missouri Democrat*, Jan. 13, 14, 20, 1869; *IL*, 464–67.

11. *IL*, 467–69; *SC*, I, 474–80; Parrish, *Missouri Under Radical Rule*, 264–67.

12. *New-Yorker Bellatristisches Journal*, Jan. 22, 29, 1869; Cincinnati *Volksfreund*, Jan. 13, 1869; St. Louis *Missouri Democrat*, Mar. 3, 1869; *New York Times*, Feb. 28, 1869; Schurz to Mrs. Schurz, Mar. 3, 1869, HC; Anneke to Mrs. Anneke, Dec. 27, 1868, Jan. 24, 1869, Anneke Papers, WiHiS; *IL*, 465–69.

13. *IL*, 467; *SR*, III, 302.

14. St. Louis *Missouri Democrat*, Apr. 15, 1869.

15. Schurz to Mrs. Schurz, Sept. 24, Oct. 11, 25, 1868, Feb. 8, Mar. 20, 31, Apr. 3, 12, May 16, 1869, HC; *IL* 451, 453; Erkelenz and Mittelmann, *Schurz*, 223–24.

16. Schurz to Preetorius, Mar. 4, 12, 13, Apr. 15, 25, 1869; Schurz to Mrs. Schurz, Mar. 26, Apr. 12, 18, May 2, 1869; Schurz to Mother, Apr. 14, 1869, Schurz to Grant, Apr. 14, 1869, HC; Schurz to Sigel, Apr. 11, 1869, Sigel Papers, NYHiS; Schurz to Hamilton Fish, May 3, 17, 1869, Fish Papers, LC; St. Louis *Missouri Democrat*, Mar. 3, 1869, Apr. 22, 1870.

17. Max Weber to Schurz, Jan. 18, 1870; Frederick Meier to Schurz, Mar. 20, 1870; S. H. Brockman to Schurz, Apr. 15, 1870; Adolph Becker to Schurz, Dec. 17, 1870; Gustav Heinrich to Schurz, Dec. 26, 1870; Emil Brendel to Schurz, Apr. 3, 1871; Nicholas Bertram to Schurz, Apr. 27, 1871; Joseph Strauss to Schurz, May 5, 1871; Fred Brunner to Schurz, July 4, 1871, are only a few of the examples in SP.

18. Schurz to Mrs. Schurz, Aug. 15, 28, Sept. 13, 1869, HC; St. Louis *Missouri Democrat*, July 1, Sept. 8, 1869; St. Louis *Westliche Post*, Sept. 5, 8, 22, 29, 1869.

19. Gerolt to Schurz, June 29, 1868, SP; Schurz to Mrs. Schurz, Jan. 11, Mar. 20, 1869, HC.

20. Schurz to Mrs. Schurz, Mar. 20, 31, Apr. 3, 12, May 16, 23, Aug. 8, 1869; Schurz to Parents, Oct. 23, Nov. 14, Dec. 2, 1869; Schurz to Preetorius, Nov. 23, 1869; Schurz to Grosvenor, Nov. 30, 1869, HC; *Independent*, Mar. 30, 1876.

21. *IL*, 383; *SC*, V, 334–38; Cronau, *Drei Jahrhunderte*, 345–47; Ernest Tonnelat, "Les Allemands aux États-Unis," *Revue de Paris* 13 (1906), 224; Schurz to Mrs. Schurz, July 28, 1871, HC. Almost all of Schurz's letters to his family and to Germans are in German.

22. *SR*, III, 272–73; *IL*, 364–65; Schurz to Mrs. Schurz, Sept. 6, 1870; Schurz to Emilie [Meyer], Dec. 26, 1870, HC; Baltimore *Der Deutsche Correspondent*, July 21, 22, 1870; St. Louis *Missouri Democrat*, July 24, 1870; Schurz to Preetorius, Aug. 1, 2, 5, 1870, ctr. 176; lecture on Germany, ctr. 194, SP.

23. Schurz to Mrs. Schurz, Aug. 9, 1870, HC.

24. Schurz to Mrs. Schurz, Aug. 14, 17, 27, 29, Sept. 3, 6, 1870, HC.

25. Schurz to Mrs. Schurz, Sept. 10, 1870, HC. American public opinion during the war tended to be pro-German, with some change after the establishment of the French Republic. Henry Blumenthal, *France and the United States: Their Diplomatic Relations, 1789–1914* (Chapel Hill: Univ. of North Carolina Press, 1970), 116–27; Clara Eva Schieber, *The Transformation of American Sentiment Toward Germany, 1870–1914* (New York: Russell & Russell, 1973), 14–37.

26. Kaufmann, *Die Deutschen,* 466–67; *New-Yorker Bellatristisches Journal,* Feb. 23, Mar. 1, 1872; Fish to Schurz, Jan. 23, 1871; Belknap to Schurz, Jan. 24, 1871; Schurz to Preetorius, ctr. 176, Jan. 16, 29, 1871, SP.

27. *Cong. Globe,* 42d Cong., 2d sess., 1008–11 (Feb. 13, 1872), 1041–48 (Feb. 15, 1872); Allan Nevins, *Hamilton Fish: The Inner History of the Grant Administration* (New York: Dodd, Mead, 1936), 403–4; *Frank Leslie's Illustrated Newspaper,* Mar. 9, 1872; Pierce, *Sumner,* IV, 504–14.

28. *Cong. Globe,* 42d Cong., 2d sess., App. 58–67 (Feb. 19, 1872); *SC,* V, 33–37.

29. *SC,* V, 33–37; *Cong. Globe,* 42d Cong., 2d sess., App., 67–74 (Feb. 20, 1872); Curtis to Effie, Feb. 21, 1872, SP.

30. *Cong. Globe,* 42d Cong., 2d sess., 1131–34 (Feb. 20, 1872), 1115–58 (Feb. 21, 1872); App., 74–82 (Feb. 19, 1872); David Jordan, *Roscoe Conkling of New York: Voice in the Senate* (Ithaca: Cornell Univ. Press, 1971), 175–78, 80–81; Donald Barr Chidsey, *The Gentleman from New York: A Life of Roscoe Conkling* (New Haven: Yale Univ. Press, 1935), 159–61.

31. *Cong. Globe,* 42d Cong., 2d sess., App., 106–17 (Feb. 26, 27, 1872), 120–27 (Feb. 29, 1872); 42d Cong., 2d sess., 1286 (Feb. 28, 1872).

32. St. Louis *Missouri Democrat,* June 4, 1872; *Sale of Arms by Ordnance Department,* Sen. Report No. 183, 42d Cong. 2d sess.; *Cong. Globe,* 42d Cong., 2d sess., App. 531–40 (May 31, 1872); *The Nation,* Mar. 7, 1872, 145.

33. Cincinnati *Volksfreund,* Feb. 17, 19, 1872; *New York Times,* Feb. 24, 1872; St. Louis *Missouri Democrat,* Feb. 17, 1872; *SC,* V, 36; Harry James Brown and Frederick D. Williams, eds., *The Diary of James A. Garfield* (Ann Arbor: Michigan State Univ. Press), II, 21, 59–60; *Nation,* Feb. 29, 1872, 129; Mar. 14, 1872, 162; *Frank Leslie's Illustrated Newspaper,* Mar. 9, 1872; Curtis to Effie, Feb. 21, 1872, SP.

NOTES TO CHAPTER XII

1. John G. Sproat, *"The Best Men": Liberal Reformers in the Gilded Age* (New York: Oxford Univ. Press, 1968), 7, passim.

2. *SR,* II, 25–28; Schurz to Preetorius, Mar. 4, 12, 1869; Schurz to Mrs. Schurz, Apr. 12, 1869; Schurz to Grant, Apr. 14, 1869; Schurz to Mother, Apr. 14, 1869, HC; Schurz to Fish, Apr. 16, 1869, Fish Papers.

3. *IL,* 470–78; Ari Hoogenboom, *Outlawing the Spoils: A History of the Civil Service Reform Movement, 1865–1883* (Urbana: Univ. of Illinois Press, 1968), 60; Schurz to Mrs. Schurz, Mar. 26, Apr. 12, 18, 1869; Schurz to Preetorius, Mar. 12, 13, 1869, HC; Schurz to James Taussig, Apr. 18, 1869, SP.

4. *Cong. Globe,* 41st Cong., 1st sess., 155–56 (Mar. 19, 1869); St. Louis *Missouri Democrat,* Mar. 21, 24, 25, 1869; Schurz to Grosvenor, Mar. 28, 29, 1869, William Grosvenor Papers, CU; Schurz to Preetorius, Mar. 29, 1869, HC; Herbert Sonthoff, *Revolutionär—Soldat—Staatsmann: Carl Schurz* (Leipzig: Reklam, 1936), 55; *IL,* 476–77.

5. Schurz to Preetorius, Apr. 25, 1869; Schurz to Mrs. Schurz, May 2, 1869, Apr. 12, 1869, HC; St. Louis *Missouri Democrat,* May 8, 1869.

6. *IL*, 477–78; John McDonald, *Secrets of the Great Whiskey Ring and Eighteen Months in the Penitentiary* (St. Louis: W. S. Bryan, 1880), 25.

7. Hoogenboom, *Outlawing the Spoils,* 13–15, 71–74; *Cong. Globe*, 41st Cong., 2d sess., 236–38 (Dec. 29, 1869); Schurz to Preetorius, Dec. 27, 1869, HC; *Harper's Weekly,* Jan. 15, 1870; *The Nation,* Jan. 13, 1870; William B. Hesseltine, *Ulysses S. Grant: Politician* (New York: Dodd, Mead, 1935), 217–19.

8. *IL*, 473–76; Schurz to Mrs. Schurz, Apr. 25, 1869, HC: Schurz to Fish, May 9, 1869, Fish Papers, CU; Fish to Schurz, May 8, 1869, SP; Schurz to Fish, June 13, 22, July 11, 1869, Fish Papers, LC; Nevins, *Fish,* 223–24.

9. David Donald, *Charles Sumner and the Rights of Man* (New York: Knopf, 1970), 358–78; Carl Schurz, *Charles Sumner,* ed. Arthur Reed Hogue (Urbana: Illinois Univ. Press, 1951), 116–17.

10. Schurz to Mrs. Schurz, June 20, 1869, HC; Schurz to Fish, June 13, 22, July 13, 1869, Fish Papers, LC; Nevins, *Fish,* 223–24.

11. Schurz to Mrs. Schurz, June 5, 13, 20, 1869, HC; *IL*, 478–80.

12. Schurz to Sumner, Sept. 25, 1869, Sumner Papers, HU; Pierce, *Sumner,* IV, 417. The other members were Simon Cameron, Oliver Morton, James Harlan, James W. Patterson, and Eugene Casserley. Sumner was the chairman.

13. Nevins, *Fish,* 250–78, 309–12; Schurz, *Sumner,* 117–19.

14. Schurz to Heinrich Meyer, May 1, 1858, HC; *IL*, 289–93; Chicago *Tribune,* Mar. 29, 1870.

15. Schurz to Preetorius, Nov. 28, 1869, HC; St. Louis *Westliche Post*, Nov. 23, Dec. 9, 31, 1869; Schurz to Preetorius, Jan. 19, 1870, ctr. 176; Koerner to Schurz, Jan. 17, 1870, SP.

16. Nevins, *Fish,* 316–28; Donald, *Sumner,* 439–44; Pierce, *Sumner,* IV, 436–40; Schurz, *Sumner,* 118–19; Chicago *Tribune*, Mar. 25, 29, 1870; J. C. B. Davis to Fish, Mar. 27, May 15, 16, 1870, Fish Papers, LC.

17. Fish, Diary, I, 474–76 (May 14, 21, 1870), Fish Papers, LC; Schurz, *Sumner,* 118–19; Schurz to Grosvenor, Mar. 31, 1870, Grosvenor Papers, CU; *Davis Hatch Claim,* Sen. Report No. 234, 41st Cong., 2d sess., esp. xxvi–xlvii; Pierce, *Sumner,* IV, 444; Hayes, *Diary,* III, 110–12.

18. For the best examples of his wartime views, cf. *New York Times,* Oct. 11, 1864; Schurz, *Speeches,* 282; for his postwar sentiments, his *Report on the Condition of the South,* and for his ideas after the 1890s, *Harper's Weekly,* Sept. 4, 1897; Schurz to Storey, June 26, 1903, SP; and Carl Schurz, "Can the South Solve the Negro Problem?" *McClure's Magazine* 22 (Jan. 1904), 258–75. Cf. L. Moody Simms, Jr., "Carl Schurz and the Negro," *The Bulletin, Missouri Historical Society* 25 (Apr. 1969), 236–38.

19. *New York Times,* Jan. 9, 1869; Edward McPherson, *The Political History of the United States of America During the Period of Reconstruction* (New York: Da Capo Press, 1972), 409, 410, 610, 611; Schurz to Boutwell, Aug. 14, 1869, SP; St. Louis *Westliche Post,* July 19, Sept. 2, 8, 1869.

20. Schurz to Mrs. Schurz, July 18, 1869, HC; Parrish, *Missouri Under Radical Rule,* 277–90.

21. *Cong. Globe*, 41st Cong., 2d sess., 473–75 (Jan. 14, 1870), 2022–23 (Mar. 17, 1870), 2061–65 (Mar. 18, 1870), 2814–16 (Apr. 19, 1870), 2829 (Apr. 19, 1870), 3607 (May 19, 1870), 3690 (May 21, 1870); Donald, *Sumner,* 447–48, 424ff.

22. *SC*, I, 509–10; Grant to Schurz, July 18, 1870, Ser. II, U.S. Grant Papers, LC.

23. St. Louis *Missouri Democrat,* July 24, 1870; Baltimore *Der Deutsche Correspondent,* July 21, 22, 1870; Schurz to Mrs. Schurz, Aug. 9, 1870, HC. For Mrs. Schurz's dislike of St. Louis, cf. Schurz to Agathe, Aug, 24, 1867, HC. It was probably induced by her grief during her first visit following Emmy's death.

24. Parrish, *Missouri Under Radical Rule*, 268–99, 302–3; Peterson, *Brown*, 178–84; Barclay, *Liberal Republican Movement*, 238–47; St. Louis *Westliche Post*, Aug. 23, 24, 1870; St. Louis *Missouri Democrat*, Aug. 31–Sept. 4, 1870; McDonald, *Secrets*, 28–29.

25. St. Louis *Missouri Democrat*, Sept. 10, 1870; *SC*, I, 510–20; Schurz to Preetorius, Oct. 11, 1870, ctr. 176, SP.

26. *Cong. Globe*, 41st Cong., 3d sess., App. 6 (Dec. 16, 1870); Hesseltine, *Grant*, 207–8, 220, 380; Schurz to Mrs. Schurz, Sept. 1, 10, 15, 19, 28, Oct. 9, 13, 1870, HC; St. Louis *Westliche Post*, Sept. 22, Oct. 1, 14, 29, 30, Nov. 5, 8, 1870; Edmund Jüssen to Schurz, April 16, 1871, ctr. 176, SP.

27. Schurz to Mrs. Schurz, Oct. 17, 19, 22, HC.

28. Parrish, *Missouri Under Radical Rule*, 309–14. Much to Schurz's annoyance, in his Serenade Speech on November 14, Brown recognized his debt to the Democrats.

29. Schurz to Rollins, Nov. 8, 1870, SP; Schurz to Parents, Nov. 25, 1870; Schurz to Adolph Meyer, Dec. 11, 1870, HC. During the second half of November, he also went on another lecture tour in New England. J. L. Haynes to Schurz, Nov. 14, 1870, SP.

30. Horace White, *The Life of Lyman Trumbull* (Boston: Houghton Mifflin, 1913), 343; Washington, Missouri, *Washingtoner Post*, Dec. 1, 1870.

31. St. Louis *Missouri Democrat*, Dec. 2, 1870. Trumbull had been urging Schurz to call on Grant. William S. McFeely, *Grant: A Biography* (New York: Norton, 1981), 351. For the deathbed reconciliation, cf. Schurz to his Children, Apr. 27, July 28, Aug. 10, 1885, HC. Schurz sent his card to the dying general, whose son told him he was especially pleased with it.

32. *Cong. Globe*, 41st Cong., 3d sess., 53 (Dec. 12, 1870), 118–28 (Dec. 15, 1870); St. Louis *Missouri Democrat*, Dec. 17, 22, 1870. Drake replied the next day. In spite of Schurz's insistence that the tariff was not the main issue, he was in close contact with the American Free Trade League, which held a meeting in New York on November 17. Mahlon Sands to Schurz, Nov. 10, 1870, SP; Sproat, *"The Best Men,"* 78.

33. Benjamin Loan to Schurz, Dec. 20, 1870; Charles Nordhoff to Schurz, Dec. 21, 1870; Daniel R. Goodloe to Schurz, Dec. 23, 1870; Rollins to Schurz, Dec. 25, 1870; Horace White to Schurz, Dec. 25, 1870; J. D. Cox to Schurz, Dec. 27, 1870, SP; St. Louis *Missouri Democrat*, Dec. 22, 1870, with excerpts from the Cincinnati *Commercial*.

34. *Cong. Globe*, 42d Cong., 1st sess., 686–93 (Apr. 14, 1871).

35. Edward McPherson, *Handbook of Politics, 1872–1876* (New York: Da Capo, 1972), 21; *Cong. Globe*, 41st Cong., 3d sess., 779–80 (Jan. 27, 1871), App. 68–77 (Jan. 27, 1871); St. Louis *Missouri Democrat*, Jan. 28, 1871; Hoogenboom, *Outlawing the Spoils*, 86–87, 90. Henry Wilson also introduced a bill.

36. Hoogenboom, *Outlawing the Spoils*, 90ff.; Rhodes, *History of the United States*, VI, 386–90; Hans L. Trefousse, *Ben Butler: The South Called Him Beast* (New York: Twayne, 1957), 220, 313 n. 16.

37. *Cong. Globe*, 41st Cong., 3d sess., 191ff., 252ff., 254, 260–64 (Dec. 21, 1870); Donald, *Sumner*, 468–75.

38. *Cong. Globe*, 41st Cong., 3d sess., App. 25–34 (Jan. 11, 1871); Schurz to Tiedemann, Apr. 6, 1869, SP; Schurz to Fish, June 13, 1869, Fish to Schurz, Jan. 23, 1871, Fish Papers, LC (last in letterbooks, 2, 871–72); *Chicago Tribune*, Jan. 12, 13, 28, 1871; Schurz to Mrs. Schurz, Nov. 17, 1873, HC; Schurz to Preetorius, Jan. 16, 1871, ctr. 176, SP; Hesseltine, *Grant*, 227–28.

39. Hesseltine, *Grant*, 232–37; Donald, *Sumner*, 475–97; *Cong. Globe*, 42d Cong. 1st sess., 34, 35–39, 52 (Mar. 10, 1871).

40. Donald, *Sumner*, 511ff.; *Cong. Globe*, 42d Cong., 1st sess., 51–62 (Mar. 28, 29, 1971), App., 51–65 (Mar. 28, 29, 1871); Chicago *Tribune*, Mar. 28, 1871; St. Louis *Missouri Democrat*, Mar. 29, 30, 1871. For the *Missouri Democrat*'s switch, cf. Peterson, *Brown*, 197.

41. Schurz, *Sumner,* 121–22; Fish to Schurz, May 8, 1871; Schurz to Preetorius, May 13, 1871, ctr. 176, SP; St. Louis *Westliche Post,* May 28, 1871. According to an unsubstantiated account by Samuel F. Barr, the clerk of the committee, Schurz introduced amendments in the hope of killing the treaty but was outmaneuvered by Hannibal Hamlin. Charles Eugene Hamlin, *The Life and Times of Hannibal Hamlin* (Cambridge, Mass.: Riverside Press, 1899), 531–32. Whatever his original attitude, Schurz in his instructions to Preetorius cited above asked him to criticize the treaty but not to come out against it because he had decided to accept it.

42. Schurz to Adolph Meyer, Mar. 1, 1871; Schurz to Parents, Mar. 30, 1871; Schurz to Heinrich Meyer, Apr. 16, 1871, May 26, 1873, HC.

43. McPherson, *Handbook of Politics,* I, 87–91; Schurz to Preetorius, Dec. 19, 1870, Jan. 16, Feb. 25, 1871, ctr. 176, Schurz to Rollins, Jan. 7, 1871, SP; St. Louis *Westliche Post,* Nov. 24, 1870.

44. *Cong. Globe,* 42d Cong., 1st sess., 686–93 (Apr. 14, 1871); White, *Trumbull,* 358.

NOTES TO CHAPTER XIII

1. Schurz to Preetorius, Mar. 18, 1871, ctr. 176, SP.

2. *SC,* II, 252–54. For a time, Schurz served as the *Nation's* weekly secret unpaid Washington correspondent. William M. Armstrong, *E. L. Godkin: A Biography* (Albany: State Univ. of New York Press, 1978), 103.

3. Theodore Plate to Schurz, Apr. 16, 1870, SP; Schurz to Mrs. Schurz, May 26, 1870, Apr. 29, May 5, 1871, HC.

4. Schurz to Mrs. Schurz, May 3, 1871, HC; St. Louis *Republican,* May 2, 1871; St. Louis *Missouri Democrat,* May 3, 1871; St. Louis *Westliche Post,* Apr. 30–May 3, 1871.

5. Earle Dudley Ross, *The Liberal Republican Movement* (New York: Holt, 1919), 17ff., 47ff., 68ff., John H. Goddall to Schurz, Apr. 12, 1871, SP; Grant to Washburne, May 17, 1871, Grant Papers, CHiS.

6. Schurz to Mrs. Schurz, July 28, 1871, HC; *SC,* II, 256–57. When the Illinois *Staats-Zeitung* charged that only Democrats had invited him, he quickly secured a second invitation signed only by prominent Republicans. St. Louis *Westliche Post,* July 20, 1871. Frederick C. Luebke believes that the Germans' reliance on independent politics greatly lessened their effectiveness. Letter to author, Jan. 7, 1980; cf. Frederick C. Luebke, "The Germans," in John Higham, ed., *Ethnic Leadership in America* (Baltimore: Johns Hopkins Univ. Press, 1978), 64–79.

7. Max Eberhardt, "Schurz Erinnerungen," Erkelenz and Mittelmann, *Schurz,* 213–17; St. Louis *Westliche Post,* Aug. 13–16, 1871.

8. St. Louis *Missouri Democrat,* Aug. 13, 22, 25, 1871; Schurz to Mrs. Schurz, Aug. 21, 1871, HC.

9. Schurz to Preetorius, Sept. 4, 1871, ctr. 176; Henry Foote to Schurz, Aug. 10, 1871; John Ruhm to Schurz, Sept. 3, 15, 1871, SP; Patrick W. Riddleberger, "The Radicals' Abandonment of the Negro During Reconstruction," *Journal of Negro History* 45 (Apr. 1960), 88–102, esp. 92–93.

10. *SC,* II, 257–315; G. E. Purvis to Schurz, Sept. 28, Oct. 3, 7, 1871; H. S. Foote to Schurz, Sept. 29, 1871; M. H. Bruce to Schurz, Sept. 30, 1871; N. S. Brown to Schurz, Oct. 1, 1871; J. B. Bolens to Schurz, Oct. 2, 1871; Sumner to Schurz, Sept. 25, 1871, SP; Ross, *Liberal Republican Movement,* 75; Schurz to Mrs. Schurz, Sept. 23, 29, 1871, HC.

11. Schurz to Mrs. Schurz, Sept. 29, 1871, HC; Foote to Schurz, Oct. 5, 1871, SP.

12. *SC,* II, 310–15.

13. New York *Herald,* Nov. 15, 16, 19, 21, 1871; *Cong. Globe,* 42d Cong., 2d sess., 4473 (June 10, 1872); Ross, *The Liberal Republican Movement,* 72–75.

14. Schurz to Mrs. Schurz, Nov. 26, 1871, HC; Hesseltine, *Grant,* 264–65; White, *Trumbull,* 362–68; *Cong. Globe,* 42d Cong., 2d sess., 86ff., 94–95 (Dec. 13, 1871), 208 (Dec. 19, 1871).

15. *New York Times,* Dec. 28, 1871, Jan. 9, 10, 11, 15, 1872; St. Louis *Missouri Democrat,* Jan. 3, 10, 11, 14, 1872; *Cong. Globe,* 42d Cong., 2d sess., 291–93 (Dec. 21, 1871). On Nast, cf. Albert Bigelow Paine, *Th. Nast: His Period and His Pictures* (Gloucester: Peter Smith, 1967).

16. *Harper's Weekly,* Sept. 16, 1871.

17. James A. Rawley, "The General Amnesty Act of 1872," *MVHR* 47 (1960), 480–84; Donald, *Sumner,* 529–36; *Cong. Globe,* 42d Cong., 2d sess., 263, 274, 277 (Dec. 21, 1871), 818 (Feb. 5, 1872), 871 (Feb. 7, 1871).

18. *SC,* II, 320–53; J. A. Nisbets to Schurz, Feb. 2, 1872, SP. Frederick Douglass had long since condemned the Liberal movement. Philip S. Foner, *The Life and Writings of Frederick Douglass* (New York: International, 1955), IV, 254–55.

19. Rollins to Schurz, Dec. 3, 1871, SP; Schurz to Trumbull, Jan. 21, 1872, Lyman Trumbull Papers, LC; *SC,* II, 315–20; Roeliff Brinkerhoff, *Recollections of a Lifetime* (Cincinnati: Robert Clarke, 1900), 214f.

20. Brinkerhoff to Schurz, Feb. 1, 1872; Glancey Jones to Schurz, Feb. 3, 15, 1872; Rollins to Schurz, Feb. 4, Apr. 14, 1872; A. L. Anderson to Schurz, Feb. 11, 1872; J. D. Cox to Schurz, Feb. 14, Apr. 5, 1872; Thomas Gantt to Schurz, Mar. 17, 1872; Bowles to Schurz, Mar. 18, 1872; Michael Boland to Schurz, Apr. 4, 1872; M. B. Brown to Schurz, Apr. 15, 1872; R. Strickland to Schurz, Apr. 18, 1872; J. W. Smith to Schurz, Apr. 20, 1872, SP; Horace White to Trumbull, Mar. 9, 1872; Trumbull to Koerner, Mar. 9, 1872; Trumbull to Brinkerhoff, Mar. 20, 1872, Trumbull Papers, LC; Greeley to Brockway, Mar. 5, 13, 1872; T. W. Conway to Greeley, Apr. 11, 1872, Greeley Papers, LC; J. D. Cox to Grosvenor, Mar. 23, 1872, Grosvenor Papers, CU; Ross, *Liberal Republican Movement,* 64ff., 87–88; Sproat, *"Best Men,"* 79–81, Donald, *Sumner,* 540ff.

21. Schurz to Adolph Meyer, Feb. 3, 1872, HC.

22. Koerner to Schurz, Apr. 16, 1872; Edward Eggleston to Schurz, Mar. 27, 1872; L. Ritter to Schurz, Apr. 22, 1872; J. W. Smith to Schurz, Apr. 20, 1872, SP; Grosvenor to Smith, n.d., Grosvenor Papers, CU; Peterson, *Brown,* 211–14; Martin B. Duberman, *Charles Francis Adams, 1807–1886* (Boston: Houghton Mifflin, 1961), 354–58; *SR,* III, 350–51.

23. Curtis to Schurz, Jan. 25, 1872, Schurz to Preetorius, Apr. 20, 1872, ctr. 176; SP; *Harper's Weekly,* Feb. 3, 10, Mar. 9, 16, 23, 30, Apr. 6, 13, 20, 1872; *New York Times,* Jan. 10, 11, Apr. 18, 20, 1872; St. Louis *Westliche Post,* Apr. 17, 1872.

24. Rollins to Schurz, Dec. 31, 1871, SP; Schurz to Adolph Meyer, Feb. 3, 1872, HC.

25. Belmont to Schurz, Apr. 1, 1872, SP; Irving Katz, *August Belmont: A Political Biography* (New York: Columbia Univ. Press, 1968), 197.

26. New York *Tribune* (semi-weekly), Apr. 16, 1872; Koerner, *Memoirs,* II, 543; Ross, *Liberal Republican Movement,* 59–60; Chicago *Tribune,* Apr. 16, 1872.

27. O'Connor, *German-Americans,* 174–75; Ross, *Liberal Republican Movement,* 166; *SC,* II, 371–72; Washington, Missouri, *Washingtoner Post,* Jan. 26, 1871, Mar. 7, 1872; P. A. Grossmann to Schurz, Mar. 15, 1872; G. A. Balzer to Schurz, Mar. 18, 1872; F. Ternow to Schurz, Mar. 9, 1872, SP; St. Louis *Missouri Democrat,* Aug. 12, 1872; Sigel to Hecker, Apr. 27, 1872, Sigel Papers, NYHiS; Faust, *German Element,* II, 138–39.

28. St. Louis *Westliche Post* (weekly), May 8, 1872; Cincinnati *Enquirer,* May 1, 1872; Fuess, *Schurz,* 186. How mistaken he was about the attitude of the old antislavery forces is

shown in James M. McPherson, "Grant or Greeley? The Abolitionist Dilemma in the Election of 1872," *AHR* 71 (Oct. 1965), 43–61.

29. Henry Watterson, *"Marse Henry": An Autobiography* (New York: Doran, 1919), I, 242–46; Brinkerhoff, *Recollections,* 217.

30. Cincinnati *Enquirer*, May 2, 3, 1872; *Proceedings of the Liberal Republican Convention in Cincinnati, May 1st, 2d, and 3d, 1872* (New York: Baker & Godwin, 1872), 3–12.

31. *Proceedings of the Liberal Republican Convention,* 12–18; F. W. Bird to Sumner, May 7, 1872, Sumner Papers, HU; Mahlon Sands to Schurz, May 14, 1872, SP.

32. *Proceedings of the Liberal Republican Convention,* 18–32; Watterson, *"Marse Henry,"* 255–56; Koerner, *Memoirs,* II, 554–56; Horace White to David Davis, May 4, 1872, David Davis Papers, CHiS; White, *Trumbull,* 385–86; Clay, *Clay,* 504–5.

33. *SC*, II, 447, 369–70; Watterson, *"Marse Henry,"* 255–57; White, *Trumbull*, 257, 385–86; Koerner, *Memoirs,* II, 557; Schurz to Preetorius, May 7, 1872, ctr. 176, SP. Members of Blair's family doubted that he really favored Greeley. Elbert B. Smith, *Francis Preston Blair* (New York: Free Press, 1980), 430.

34. Matthew T. Downey, "Horace Greeley and the Politicians: The Liberal Republican Convention of 1872," *JAH* 53 (Mar. 1967), 727–50; Peterson, *Brown,* 211–20; White to Davis, May 4, 1872, Davis Papers, CHiS; Bird to Sumner, May 7, 1872, Sumner Papers, HU; White to Trumbull, May 4, 1872, Trumbull Papers, LC; White, *Trumbull*, 385–89; Daniel Reed to Schurz, May 16, 1872, SP; *SC*, II, 447.

35. *SC*, II, 368–70; Schurz to Parents, May 26, 1872, HC; George S. Merriam, *The Life and Times of Samuel Bowles* (New York: Century, 1885), II, 210.

36. *SC*, II, 361–68.

37. Louis Lowenthal to Schurz, May 7, 1872; L. C. Wagner to Schurz, June 1, 1872; Koerner to Schurz, May 9, 1872, Schurz to Preetorius, May 7, 20, 31, 1872, ctr. 176, SP; St. Louis *Westliche Post*, May 8, 22, 1872; *New-Yorker Bellatristisches Journal,* May 10, 1872; *Die Neue Zeit,* May 11, 1872; Cincinnati *Enquirer,* May 6, 1872; Horace White to Trumbull, May 13, 1872, Trumbull Papers, LC.

38. Greeley to Schurz, May 6, 10, 12, 17, 20, 1872, SP; *SC*, II, 370–77; Glyndon Van Deusen, *Horace Greeley: Nineteenth Century Crusader* (New York: Hill & Wang, 1964), 407–8.

39. Godkin to Trumbull, May 29, 1872, Trumbull Papers, LC; Godkin to Schurz, May 29, 1872; Atkinson to Sumner, May 23, 1872; Atkinson to Schurz, June 1, 1872, SP; Schurz to Park Godwin, May 28, 1872, Bryant-Godwin Collection, NYPL; *SC*, II, 376, 379–81; Koerner, *Memoirs,* II, 559.

40. *New York Times,* May 9, 1872; St. Louis *Missouri Democrat,* May 11, 1872; *New-Yorker Bellatristisches Journal,* May 10, 1872; Grant to Washburne, May 24, 1872, Davis Papers, CHiS.

41. William Gillette, *Election of 1872,* in Arthur M. Schlesinger, Jr., and Fred L. Israel, eds., *History of American Presidential Elections, 1789–1968* (New York: Chelsea House, 1971), II, 1303–30, esp. 1318, 1320–21; Richard Allan Gerber, "The Liberal Republicans of 1872 in Historical Perspective," *JAH* 67 (June, 1975), 40. The dissidents nominated Charles O'Connor and John Quincy Adams, both of whom declined. Ross, *Liberal Republican Movement,* 146–47.

42. Call for Fifth Avenue Hotel Conference, June 6, 1872, SP; Brinkerhoff, *Recollections,* 220; Chicago *Tribune,* June 22, 1872; *New York Times,* June 14, 1872; Koerner, *Memoirs,* II, 559; *SC*, II, 384–88; Armstrong, *Godkin,* 133–34; Donald, *Sumner,* 551–55. A dissident faction nominated William S. Groesbeck and F. L. Olmsted, who declined. Ross, *Liberal Republican Movement,* 124–25.

43. Schurz to Parents, May 26, 1872; Schurz to Mrs. Schurz, June 13, 1872, HC; St.

Louis *Missouri Democrat*, June 13, 15, 1872. Mrs. Schurz arrived in Hamburg in July. Edward Robinson to Schurz, July 6, 1872, SP.

44. Van Deusen, *Greeley*, 382–97; Greeley to Schurz, Mar. 4, Nov. 28, 1867, SP; Schurz to Mrs. Schurz, July 12, 1872, HC; *SC*, II, 390–92.

45. *SC*, II, 392–443; *Harper's Weekly*, Aug. 10, 1872.

46. Schurz to Mrs. Schurz, Aug. 3, 11, Sept. 1, 1872, HC; Greeley to Schurz, Aug. 20, 1872; Schurz to Grosvenor, Sept. 11, 1872, SP; St. Louis *Westliche Post*, Aug. 14, 1872.

47. St. Louis *Missouri Democrat*, Aug. 13, 26, 27, 1872; *New York Times*, July 29, 1872; Chicago *Inter-Ocean*, Sept. 2, 7, 11, 1872, in *The Charges of 1872 Against Carl Schurz; Harper's Weekly*, May 4, June 15, Aug. 10, 24, Sept. 7, 1872; St. Louis *Westliche Post* (weekly), Aug. 5, Sept. 4, 9, 11, 12, 1872; Whyte, "Chronicles of Early Watertown," 300; Schurz to Mrs. Schurz, Sept. 22, 1872, HC.

48. Freidel, *Lieber*, 411; St. Louis *Westliche Post* (weekly), Sept. 4, 1872; *Report of the Proceedings of the Grand German National Convention Held on Thursday, October 24, 1872, at Teutonia Assembly Rooms . . . in the City of New York Under the Auspices of the German-American United Associations . . .* (n.p., n.d.); Richardson, *Chandler*, 149, 154; *New York Times*, July 2, 1872; Hesseltine, *Grant*, 287; St. Louis *Missouri Democrat*, Aug. 12, 1872. The paper reported that 119 German journals supported Grant to 105 for Greeley. In Wisconsin, the majority seems to have remained committed to the Liberal Republican ticket. Hense-Jensen, *Wisconsin's Deutsch-Amerikaner*, I, 237–39.

49. Pulitzer to Schurz, Sept. 24, 1872; Cox to Schurz, Oct. 7, 1872, SP; Schurz to Mrs. Schurz, Oct. 9, 16, 24, Nov. 2, 9, 1872, HC; St. Louis *Westliche Post* (weekly), Oct. 7, 1872; Greeley to Margaret Allen, Nov. 4, 1872, Greeley Papers, LC; *SC*, II, 443–48; Van Deusen, *Greeley*, 418–24. For Pulitzer, cf. George S. Johns, "Joseph Pulitzer," *Missouri Hist. Review* 26 (1931), 201–18.

NOTES TO CHAPTER XIV

1. Schurz to Mrs. Schurz, Dec. 2, 10, 1872, HC. When the committee assignments were announced, he was surprised to find that he was permitted to remain on the Committee on Foreign Relations. Although he had not attended the Republican caucus, he informed the Democrats that he did not wish to take the place of a member of the minority party. He was not a Democrat. Ibid.; St. Louis *Westliche Post*, Dec. 8, 10, 1872.

2. Sproat, *"Best Men,"* 90.

3. Schurz to Mrs. Schurz, Jan. 14, 24, Feb. 1, Mar. 5, 12, 18, 1873, HC; Godkin to Schurz, Mar. 21, 1873; Schurz to Secretary of Senate, Mar. 28, 1873; Schurz to Preetorius, ctr. 176, Feb. 5, 1873, SP.

4. *Cong. Globe*, 42d Cong., 3d sess., 1873–76 (Feb. 27, 1873); *Cong. Record*, 43d Cong., Special sess., 30–38 (Mar. 10, 1873), 85–89 (Mar. 14, 1873), 132–34 (Mar. 20, 1873). Although Caldwell's defenders maintained that the number of bribed votes would not have made any difference in his election and that the Senate had no right to go behind the returns, Schurz curtly dismissed these arguments. In a two-hour speech, during which the galleries rapidly filled, he characterized the prevailing corruption as a danger to the safety of the Republic. A renewed debate with Conkling heightened interest in the case, and in the end, Caldwell resigned. Cf. St. Louis *Missouri Republican*, Mar. 15, 1873; T. A. Bayard to T. F. Bayard, Mar. 16, 1873, Thomas F. Bayard Papers, LC.

5. Adams to Schurz, Mar. 17, 25, 1873; Schurz to Adams, Mar. 23, 27, 1873, SP.

6. Schurz to Mrs. Schurz, Feb. 1, Mar. 25, Apr. 8, 14, 1873, HC; Schurz to Preetorius, Dec. 20, 1872, Feb. 5, 1873, ctr. 176, SP; James Wyman Barrett, *Joseph Pulitzer and His World* (New York: Vanguard, 1941), 41.

7. Schurz to Adolph Meyer, May 12, 26, July 25, 1873, HC; Count Andrassy to Schurz, July 21, 1873; Schurz to Preetorius, ctr. 176, June 14, Sept. 18, 1873; Schurz to Pussy, Oct. 16, 1873, ctr. 176, SP. The business boom ended while he was in Germany, and a depression, the Panic of 1873, set in.

8. Schurz to "Liebe Freundin," Dec. 1, 1873; Charlotte Althaus to Margot, May 16, 1874; ctr. 176, Schurz to Pussy, Feb. 15, 1875, ctr. 176, SP.

9. Donald, *Sumner,* 579; Adams to Schurz, Nov. 13, 1873; Schurz to Adams, Nov. 24, 1873, SP.

10. Irwin Unger, *The Greenback Era* (Princeton: Princeton Univ. Press, 1964), 233ff.; *Cong. Record,* 43d Cong., 1st sess., 634–45 (Jan. 14, 1874), 1590–95 (Feb. 18, 1874), 1626–28 (Feb. 19, 1874), 1717–27 (Feb. 24, 1874), 1771–75 (Feb. 25, 1874), 2648–52 (Mar. 31, 1874), 2827–34 (Apr. 6, 1874), 3436 (Apr. 28, 1874); Koerner, *Memoirs,* II, 583–84; Grosvenor to Schurz, Apr. 25, 1874; Koerner to Schurz, Apr. 25, 1874, SP.

11. St. Louis *Republican,* Mar. 12, 1874; Pierce, *Sumner,* IV, 595ff.; *Cong. Record,* 43d Cong., 1st sess., 2142–43 (Mar. 12, 1874). *New York Times,* Apr. 30, 1874; Boston *Daily Advertiser,* June 10, 1874; Donald, *Sumner,* 1–6; *SC,* III, 2–72; Schurz to Preetorius, Mar. 18, 1874, ctr. 176, SP; *Harper's Weekly,* May 16, 1874.

12. F. P. Blair to Schurz, Feb. 13, 1874; A. L. Gilstrap to Schurz, Jan. 26, May 5, 1874; J. F. Hawkins to Schurz, Jan. 25, 1874, A. V. M. Gindley to Schurz, Feb. 20, 1874, SP; Parrish, *Missouri Under Radical Rule,* 324ff.; St. Louis *Westliche Post,* May 9, 1874.

13. St. Louis *Republican,* May 7, 12, 13, 1874; Schurz to Rollins, Jan. 6, May 16, 1874, James S. Rollins Papers, MoHiS; Schurz to Preetorius, Apr. 2, 13, May 9, 11, 16, 17, 1874, ctr. 176; Grosvenor to Schurz, May 9, 16, 19, 1874, ctr. 176, SP.

14. Schurz to Preetorius, May 21, June 3, 15, July 2, 1874 ctr. 176,; Grosvenor to Schurz, June 21, 1874, SP; Schurz to Grosvenor, June 19, July 5, 1874, Grosvenor Papers, CU; Schurz to F. W. Bird, June 25, 1874, Francis W. Bird Papers, HU.

15. Schurz to Mrs. Schurz, Aug, 5, 17, 28, Sept. 1, 8, 12, 1874, HC; Rollins to Schurz, July 31, 1874, SP; *New York Times,* Sept. 3, 1874; St. Louis *Republican,* Aug. 13, 1874; Edwin C. McReynolds, *Missouri: A History of the Crossroads State* (Norman: Univ. of Oklahoma Press, 1962), 287–88; Eugene Morrow Violette, *A History of Missouri* (Cape Girardeau: Ramfre Press, 1960), 427.

16. Violette, *History of Missouri;* Schurz to Mrs. Schurz, Sept. 25, 27, Oct. 16, 27, 1874, HC; *SC,* III, 74–113; St. Louis *Republican,* Sept. 25–30, Oct. 1, 3, 7, Nov. 4, 6, 9, 1874. The Whiskey Ring actively opposed his reelection. McDonald, *Secrets,* 47.

17. *SC,* III, 114–15; Schurz to Mrs. Schurz, Nov. 6, 12, 17, 26, 29, 1874, HC; Schurz to Bird, Nov. 27, 1874, Bird Papers, HU.

18. *Cong. Record,* 43d Cong., 2d sess., 365–71 (Jan. 11, 1875), 391–97 (Jan. 12, 1875), 654–63 (Jan. 22, 1875), 853 (Jan. 29, 1875), 1870 (Feb. 27, 1875). On Louisiana, cf. Joe Gray Taylor, *Louisiana Reconstructed, 1863–1877* (Baton Rouge: Louisiana State Univ. Press, 1974), 305–7.

19. St. Louis *Republican,* Nov. 14, Dec. 2, 1874, Jan. 17, 21, Apr. 17, 1875; New York *Evening Post,* Dec. 31, 1874; *The Nation,* Dec. 31, 1874; *New-Yorker Staats-Zeitung,* Jan. 13, 1875; *Cong. Record,* 43rd Cong., 2d sess., 1971–73 (Mar. 1, 1875).

20. St. Louis *Republican,* Apr. 17, 1875; Schurz to Mrs. Schurz, Mar. 12, Apr. 17, 18, 19, 20, 1875; Schurz to Emilie Meyer, Mar. 7, 1875, HC.

21. *New York Times,* Apr. 28, 29, 1875; St. Louis *Westliche Post,* May 1, 1875.

22. Schurz to Emilie Meyer, June 5, 1875; Schurz to Mrs. Schurz, June 9, 11, 12, 16, 21, 23, 1875, HC; Schurz to Lodge, July 9, 1875; Henry Rose to Schurz, May, 1875; London *Daily News,* June 10, 1875; Berlin *International Gazette,* June 12, 1875, ctr. 184, SP; St. Louis *Westliche Post,* June 25, 29, July 2, 13, 18, 1875; *New York Times,* June 9, 10, 1875.

23. *SC*, III, 156–61; Schurz to Mrs. Schurz, Aug. 21, Sept. 3, 1875, HC; T. Harry Williams, ed., *Hayes: The Diary of a President, 1875–1881* (New York: McKay, 1964), xiv–xviii; Keith Ian Polakoff, *The Politics of Inertia* (Baton Rouge: Louisiana State Univ. Press, 1973), 33–36. Schurz had already made arrangements to have Cyrus Field contribute to a renewed liberal campaign chest. Schurz to Grosvenor, July 16, 1875, Grosvenor Papers, CU.

24. Hayes to A. T. Wickoff, Sept. 20, 1875, Hayes Papers, Hayes Library; Hayes, *Diary*, III, 293; Worthington Chauncey Ford, ed., *Letters of Henry Adams* (London: Constable, 1930), I, 272; *New York Times*, Sept. 20, 22, 28, Oct. 7, 1875; Royal Cortissoz, *The Life of Whitelaw Reid* (New York: Scribner's 1921), I, 321–22; Unger, *Greenback Era*, 279–80, 282–83; *SC*, III, 161–216; Carl Wittke, "Carl Schurz and Rutherford B. Hayes," *The Ohio Historical Quarterly* 65 (1956), 340.

25. Schurz to Mrs. Schurz, Sept. 3, 16, 1875; Schurz to Adolph Meyer, Nov. 8, 1875; Schurz to C. F. May, Mar. 21, 1876, HC; Schurz to Fritz Tiedemann, Oct. 27, 1875, ctr. 176, SP; St. Louis *Westliche Post*, Nov. 9, 13, 20, Dec. 6, 19, 31, 1875; *SC*, III, 229, 217–22; Schurz to Grosvenor, July 16, 1875, Grosvenor Papers, CU; Schurz to Bowles, Nov. 23, 1875, Samuel Bowles Papers, YU; Lodge to Schurz, Dec. 13, 23, 1875, Feb. 15, 1876; Schurz to Lodge, Dec. 25, 1875, Jan. 7, 16, 1876, SP; John A. Garraty, *Henry Cabot Lodge* (New York: Knopf, 1953), 43–45; Ross A. Webb, *Benjamin Helm Bristow* (Lexington: Univ. Press of Kentucky, 1969), 220–21; Ford, *Letters of Henry Adams*, I, 273–77, 79; J. H. Wilson to Bristow, Feb. 15, 1876, Benjamin Helm Bristow Papers, LC; John M. Dobson, *Politics in the Gilded Age* (New York: Praeger, 1972), 46–48; Polakoff, *Politics of Inertia*, 78.

26. Polakoff, *Politics of Inertia, 47*–48; Horace White to Schurz, Feb. 22, 25, 1876; Schurz to Lodge, Jan. 7, 16, 1876; W. Gilbert to Schurz, Mar. 1, 1876, SP; *SC*, III, 219–20.

27. Alfred E. Lee to Schurz, Feb. 28, 1876, SP. No reply has been found.

28. Hesseltine, *Grant*, 395–86; Bowles to Schurz, Mar. 14, 1876, ctr. 176, SP; Schurz to Bowles, Mar. 7, 1876, Bowles Papers, YU.

29. Schurz to E. D. Morgan, Jan. 27, 1876, Morgan Papers, New York State Library; Schurz to Mrs. Schurz, Jan. 27, 29, 1876; Schurz to Adolph Meyer, Mar. 6, 7, 1876; Schurz to "Familie," Mar. 28, Apr. 7, 1876, HC; Schurz to Lodge, Feb. 18, 1876; Amalie Westendorp to Schurz, ctr. 176, Nov. 14, 1876, SP; Schurz to F. W. Bird, Apr. 17, 1876, Bird Papers, HU.

30. *SC*, III, 224–25, 226–29; Bowles to Schurz, Mar. 25, 1876, SP.

31. *New York Times*, May 16, 17, 1876; *Independent*, May 25, 1876; *SC*, III, 240–48; Garraty, *Lodge*, 46.

32. Polakoff, *Politics of Inertia*, 42–44; Sproat, *"The Best Men*," 91–94.

33. Koerner, *Memoirs*, II, 599–602; Schurz to Parke Godwin, June 20, 1876, Bryant-Godwin Collection, NYPL; *SC*, III, 248–53; A. E. Lee to Schurz, May 8, 1876, SP; W. H. Mason to Hayes, June 21, 1876, Hayes Papers, Hayes Library.

34. Schurz to A. E. Lee, June 27, 1876, SP; Wittke, "Carl Schurz and Rutherford B. Hayes," 340; *New York Times*, July 7, 1876; W. H. Powell to Hayes, July 4, 1876, Hayes Papers, Hayes Library.

35. *SC*, III, 253–61; C. F. Adams, Jr., to Schurz, July 11, 1876, SP; Ford, *Letters of Henry Adams*, I, 293, 298–99; Wittke, "Carl Schurz and Rutherford B. Hayes," 343; Hayes, *Diary*, III, 331; Polakoff, *Politics of Inertia*, 102–3.

36. Charles Reemelin, *Life of Charles Reemelin* (Cincinnati: Weier & Daiker, 1892), 218–19; *New-Yorker Staats-Zeitung*, July 7, 15, 26, 1876; *SC*, III, 261–80; Koerner, *Memoirs*, II, 610. The Resumption Act of 1875 was really a compromise, which, by authorizing an increase in national bank notes and permitting more subsidiary silver

coinage, made concessions to the soft money and silver elements of the Republican party. Because of its provisions for the reduction of the total amount of greenbacks in circulation as well as for the resumption of specie payments in 1879, however, it had considerable appeal to the financial conservatives. Cf. Walter T. K. Nugent, *The Money Question During Reconstruction* (New York: Norton, 1967), 94.

37. A. C. Botkin to William Henry Smith, Aug. 1876; F. B. Schmelby to Hayes, Oct. 23, 1876, Hayes Papers, Hayes Library.

38. Schurz to Hayes, Sept. 12, 1876; Hayes to Schurz, Aug. 14, 17, Sept. 6, Oct. 12, 1876, SP; *SC*, III, 280–90, 338–39; Hayes to Schurz, July 24, Aug. 18, Oct. 19, 1876; Schurz to Hayes, Aug. 22, 31, Sept. 3, 5, 12, 13, 23, 25, Oct. 6, 15, 21, 22, 31, 1876; W. H. Smith to Hayes, Sept. 13, 1876; R. C. McCormick to Hayes, Sept. 14, 1876, Hayes Papers, Hayes Library; Schurz to Children, Oct. 18, 1876; Schurz to Adolph Meyer, Oct. 9, 1876, *HC; New York Times,* Sept. 14, 1876; Brown and Williams, *Garfield Diary,* III, 353.

39. *New York Times,* Aug. 27, Sept. 1, 13, Oct. 6, 9, 15, 21, 22, Nov. 2, 1876; Cincinnati *Commercial,* Sept. 28, 1876; Schurz to Hayes, Aug. 22, Sept. 3, 5, 13, Oct. 15, 30, 1876, Hayes Papers, Hayes Library; Polakoff, *Politics of Inertia,* 157.

40. Schurz to Hayes, Aug. 7, 1876; Hayes to Schurz, Aug. 25, 1876, SP; Wittke, "Carl Schurz and Rutherford B. Hayes," 343.

41. Harry Barnard, *Rutherford B. Hayes and His America* (Indianapolis: Bobbs-Merrill, 1954), 315–17; Schurz to Family, Nov. 9, 13, 1876, HC; Schurz to Hayes, Nov. 10, 18, Dec. 4, 5, 1876, Hayes Papers, Hayes Library; Hayes, *Diary,* III, 378–79; *SC*, III, 339–46.

42. *SC*, III, 354–66; Horace White to Schurz, Dec. 21, 1876; Lodge to Schurz, Dec. 22, 1876; C. A. Adams to Schurz, Dec. 26, 1876, SP; Schurz to Adolph Meyer, Dec. 15, 1876, HC; Rhodes, *History of the United States,* VII, 239–61.

43. C. Vann Woodward, *Reunion and Reaction: The Compromise of 1877 and the End of Reconstruction* (Boston: Little, Brown, 1951). Cf. J. F. Wilson to Schurz, Feb. 18, 1877, SP; Barnard, *Hayes,* 331; Michael Les Benedict, "Southern Democrats and the Crisis of 1876–1877: A Reconsideration of *Reunion and Reaction, JSH* 46 (Nov. 1980), 489–524.

44. Schurz to J. D. Cox, Dec. 28, 1876, SP; *SC*, III, 352, 389–97.

45. *SC*, III, 361–62, 366–83, 388, 403; Wittke, "Carl Schurz and Rutherford B. Hayes," 347; Halstead to Hayes, Feb. 13, 22, 1877; W. H. Smith to Richard Smith, Feb. 18, 1877; J. D. Cox to Hayes, Feb. 17, 24, 1877; Medill to Richard Smith, Feb. 17, 1877; William Grosvenor to Cox, Feb. 19, 1877, Hayes Papers, Hayes Library; Cox to Schurz, Jan. 26, 1877; Halstead to Schurz, Feb. 16, 20, 21, 24, 1877, SP.

46. *SC*, III, 403–4, 397–99.

NOTES TO CHAPTER XV

1. *SC*, III, 405; Schurz to Higginson, Mar. 24, 1877, Thomas Wentworth Higginson Papers, HU.

2. Schurz to his Children, Mar. 4, 1877, HC.

3. William Henry Smith Memorandum, Apr. 4, 1883, Hayes Papers, Hayes Library; Hayes, *Diary,* III, 548–49, IV, 610; Marguerita Spalding Gerry, ed., *Through Five Administrations: Reminiscences of Colonel William H. Crook* (New York: Harper, 1910), 224; *New York Times,* Mar. 13, 1878; Wittke, "Carl Schurz and Rutherford B. Hayes," 337–55; Kenneth E. Davison, *The Presidency of Rutherford B. Hayes* (Westport, Conn.: Greenwood, 1972), 85, 96–97.

4. Schurz to Children, Mar. 7, 9, 1877, HC; Montgomery Blair to Schurz, Mar. 8, 1877; C. Goepf to Schurz, Mar. 11, 1877, SP; O. Benson to W. K. Rogers, Mar. 8, 1877; S. S. Gould to Hayes, Mar. 1877, Hayes Papers, Hayes Library; Fish to J. B. C. Davis, Letterbooks, XVII, 295–97, Mar. 22, 1877, Fish Papers, LC; Hayes, *Diary,* III, 126–27; *New York Times,* Mar. 5, 10, 12, 1877.

5. Schurz to Children, Mar. 4, 1877, HC.

6. Henry Cabot Lodge, *Early Memories* (New York: Arno, 1975), 257; William H. Smith, Private Memorandum, Nov. 22, 1879, Hayes Papers, Hayes Library; Schurz to Children, Mar. 18, 1877, HC; Davison, *Hayes,* 95–117. Alexander Ramsey of Minnesota replaced McCrary in 1879, Horace Maynard took Key's portfolio in 1880, and Nathan Goff of West Virginia replaced Thompson during the last few months of the administration.

7. Webb C. Hayes I and Watt P. Marchman, comps., "The First Days of the Hayes Administration: Inauguration to Easter Sunday, 1877," *Hayes Historical Journal* 1 (Fall 1977), 248; Detroit Post Tribune, *Zachariah Chandler: An Outline Sketch of His Life and Public Services* (Detroit: Detroit Post Tribune, 1880), 354–55; *New York Times,* Mar. 13, 1877, Nov. 28, 1879; Cincinnati *Commercial,* Feb. 4, 1878, ctr. 211; Schurz to Bowles, Aug. 29, 1877, ctr. 182, SP; Henry L. Nelson, "Schurz's Administration of the Interior Department," *International Review* 10 (1881), 380–96, esp. 380–81. For the organization of the Interior Department, cf. Leonard D. White, *The Republican Era: A Study in Administrative History, 1869–1901* (New York: Free Press, 1965), 175–231.

8. The Schurz Papers for March 1877, are full of such letters. A. H. von Luettwitz to Schurz, May 10, 1879, SP; Dee Brown, *The Year of the Century: 1876* (New York: Scribner's, 1966), 343; E. C. Hamburgher to Hayes, Mar. 8, 1877; Robert Johnstone to Hayes, Mar. 8, 1877; Medill to Hayes, Apr. 4, 1877, Hayes Papers, Hayes Library.

9. Pierce to W. K. Rogers, Mar. 10, 1877, Hayes Papers, Hayes Library; Lodge to Schurz, Mar. 8, 1877; C. F. Adams to Schurz, Mar. 10, 1877; T. J. Wood to Schurz, Mar. 16, 1877, SP; *SC,* III, 408–10; Ford, *Letters of Henry Adams,* I, 303.

10. Vincent P. De Santis, *Republicans Face the Southern Question: The New Departure Years, 1877–1897* (Baltimore: Johns Hopkins Univ. Press, 1959), 70ff.; Barnard, *Hayes,* 420–32; *SC,* III, 94, 139–40, 374–75, 382–83, 384–87, 389–90, 400–1; Schurz to Pierce, May 4, 1877, SP; Schurz to Adolph Meyer, July 17, 1877, HC.

11. T. H. Williams, *Hayes Diary,* 87; Gerry, *Through Five Administrations,* 233–34; Hayes and Marchmann, "The First Days of the Hayes Administration," 249; *New York Times,* Mar. 21, 1877.

12. "Schurz's Testimony on Civil Service Reform," Box 5, McAneny Papers, PU; Zucker, *Forty-Eighters,* 245; White, *Republican Era,* 175ff., 187–89, 205–8, 215–20; *New York Times,* Mar. 24, 27, Apr. 6, 12, 1877; Hoogenboom, *Outlawing the Spoils,* 147–52; Hayes's Civil Service Order, June 22, 1877, SP; Department of the Interior, Proposals for Stationery, Apr. 24, 1877, Schurz Papers, NYPL.

13. Trefousse, *Butler,* 220, 234; Hoogenboom, *Outlawing the Spoils,* 159–60, 163; New York *Tribune,* July 21, 28, Aug. 4, 11, 23, 1877; Schurz to Preetorius, Aug. 27, 1877, ctr. 176, SP; St. Louis *Westliche Post,* Aug. 30, 1877; Philadelphia *Evening Telegraph,* Jan. 8, 1878; Philadelphia *Public Ledger,* Jan. 9, 1878; *New York Times,* Jan. 12, 16, 1878; San Francisco *Chronicle,* Oct. 26, 1878.

14. Detroit *Post and Tribune,* Nov. 16, 1877; Reid to Schurz, June 10, 1877; Bowles to Schurz, June 13, 1877, SP; *SC,* III, 490–91; Hoogenboom, *Outlawing the Spoils,* 151–78. At the *Westliche Post,* he also had the reputation of being a driving employer. Schurz to Mrs. Schurz, July 16, 1867, HC.

15. *New York Times,* Aug. 22, Sept. 4, 1877, Mar. 2, 13, 14, 25, 1878; *Cong. Record,* 45th Cong., 2d sess., 1721 (Mar. 13, 1878); Fred A. Shannon, *The Farmer's Last Frontier* (New York: Farrar & Rinehart, 1945), 61–62. It was also during Schurz's

administration that the Geological Survey was established. Nelson, "Schurz's Administration," 392.

16. Loring Benson Priest, *Uncle Sam's Stepchildren: The Reformation of United States Indian Policy, 1865–1887* (New Brunswick: Rutgers Univ. Press, 1942), 13, 68–69; White, *The Republican Era,* 181–95; Dee Brown, *Bury My Heart at Wounded Knee: An Indian History of the American West* (New York: Holt, Rinehart & Winston, 1970), 334–49; John G. Bourke, *On the Border With Crook* (New York: Scribner's, 1891), 425–26; Robert M. Utley, *Frontier Regulars: The United States Army and the Indian, 1866–1890* (New York: Macmillan, 1973), 296ff.

17. R. W. Milroy to Schurz, May 25, 1877; Pope to Schurz, June 11, 1877; Welch to Schurz, Sept. 21, 1877, SP; John B. Wolff to Schurz, Aug. 6, 1877, Hayes Papers, Hayes Library; Philadelphia *Public Ledger,* Sept. 20, 1877; U.S. Interior Department, *Annual Report of the Secretary of the Interior, 1877–1880* (Washington, D.C.: Government Printing Office, 1877–80); Francis Paul Prucha, *American Indian Policy in Crisis: Christian Reformers and the Indian, 1865–1900* (Norman: Univ. of Oklahoma Press, 1976), 271–73; Davison, *Hayes,* 187.

18. Draft of Instructions, May 25, 1877; Schurz to J. Q. Smith, May 25, 1877, Letterbooks, ctr. 166, SP; Robert Winston Mardock, *The Reformers and the American Indian* (Columbia, Mo., Univ. of Missouri Press, 1977), 156–57.

19. Nelson, "Schurz's Administration," 383–85; *New York Times*, June 8, 30, July 15, Aug. 11, 14, 24, 1877; Jan. 8, 16, 1878; Schurz to Fritz Tiedemann, Sept. 26, 1877, ctr. 176, SP; J. Q. Smith to Hayes, Jan. 9, 1878, Hayes Papers, Hayes Library; Youngstown *Register & Tribune,* Jan. 10, 1878, ctr. 211, SP. Hayt was also finally dismissed under a cloud. Priest, *Uncle Sam's Stepchildren,* 69–71.

20. *New York Times,* Aug. 14, 1877; Jan. 16–18, 22, 1878; *Harper's Weekly,* Feb. 2, 1878; Smith, *Garfield,* 665; Schurz to Hayes, Feb. 11, 1878, Hayes Papers, Hayes Library; Schurz to Committee of Board of Indian Commissioners, Feb. 12, 1880, Letterbooks, V, SP; Albert H. Smiley to Schurz, Mar. 8, 1880, SP; *Cong. Record,* 43d Cong., 2d sess., 2001 (Mar. 25, 1878).

21. *New York Times*, Jan. 26, Mar. 29, Nov. 15, 22, 24, Dec. 1, 2, 1878; Jan. 2, 10, 1879; *Report of the Joint Committee Appointed to Consider the Expediency of the Transfer of the Indian Bureau to the War Department,* H. Report No. 93, 45th Cong., 3d sess., 11–12 (1879); Richard O'Connor, *Sheridan, The Inevitable* (Indianapolis: Bobbs-Merrill, 1953), 345; Prucha, *American Indian Policy in Crisis,* 96–98, 102; Priest, *Uncle Sam's Stepchildren,* 22.

22. Utley, *Frontier Regulars,* 299, 323; Department of the Interior, *Annual Report of the Secretary of the Interior* (1878), 6–10.

23. *Letter from the Secretary of the Interior, Communicating . . . Information in Relation to the Number of Mining Camps Located on the Ute Indian Reservation in Colorado,* Sen. Ex. Doc. 29, 46th Cong., 2d sess., Feb. 28, 1881; *Letter from the Secretary of the Interior Transmitting . . . Correspondence Concerning the Ute Indians in Colorado,* Sen. Ex. Doc. 31, 46th Cong., 2d sess., Jan. 6, 1880; Department of the Interior, *Annual Report of the Secretary of the Interior* (1879), 16–19, and ibid. (1880), 20–22; Robert G. Athearn, ed., "Major Hough's March into Southern Ute Country, 1879," *Colorado Magazine* 25 (1948), 97–109; Schurz to Hayes, Oct. 13, 1879, Hayes Papers, Hayes Library; Mrs. C. W. Wiegel, "The Death of Ouray, Chief of the Utes," *Colorado Magazine* 7 (Sept. 1930), 187–91; Priest, *Uncle Sam's Stepchildren,* 225; David B. Parker, *A Chautauqua Boy in '61 and Afterward* (Boston: Small, Maynard, 1912), 258–62; W. H. Berry to Schurz, Jan. 28, 1881; clipping, ctr. 77, SP.

24. Schurz to Children, Aug. 29, Sept. 7, 1879; Schurz to Adolph Meyer, Oct. 6, 1879, HC; Schurz to Hayes, Aug. 31, 1879, Hayes Papers, Hayes Library; H. Gaullieur to Schurz, Aug. 6, 1879; Schurz to J. W. Hoyt, Aug. 18, 1879; Memo, Feb. 7, 1907, ctr.

205, SP; Schurz to William H. Smith, Aug. 9, 1879, William Henry Smith Papers, OHiS.

25. Schurz to Adolph Meyer, July 1, Sept. 22, 1880, HC; Schurz to Children, Aug. 14, 19, Sept. 4, 14, 1880, ctr. 176, SP; Schurz to Webb Hayes, July 20, 24, Sept. 23, 1880, Hayes Papers, Hayes Library; Bourke, *On the Border with Crook,* 429; Martin F. Schmitt, ed., *General Crook: His Autobiography* (Norman: Univ. of Oklahoma Press, 1946), 235–37.

26. Department of the Interior, *Annual Report of the Secretary,* (1880), 1ff.; Prucha, *American Indian Policy in Crisis,* 242.

27. James H. Howard, *The Ponca Tribe,* Bureau of American Ethnology Bulletin 195, Smithsonian Institution, (Washington, D.C.: Government Printing Office, 1965), 21–22, 31–39; *Annual Report of the Secretary of the Interior, 1877,* 8.

28. Mardock, *The Reformers and the American Indian,* 186–77; Thomas Henry Tibbles, *Buckskin and Blanket Days* (New York: Doubleday, 1957), 198ff.; Bourke, *On the Border with Crook,* 427ff.; 25 *Fed. Cases* 695; *SC,* III, 497, IV, 57; Sen. Report 670, 46th Cong., 2d sess., 358ff. (1880).

29. Mardock, *The Reformers and the American Indian,* 157–59, 177–91; Priest, *Uncle Sam's Stepchildren,* 76–80; Evelyn I. Banning, *Helen Hunt Jackson* (New York: Vanguard, 1973), 144–52; Tibbles, *Buckskin,* 205–24; Oscar Sherwin, *Prophet of Liberty: The Life and Times of Wendell Phillips* (New York: Bookman, 1958), 628–29; *Cong. Record,* 46th Cong., 2d sess., 912 (Feb. 16, 1880), and Sen. Report 670 (1880). Tibbles finally married Bright Eyes.

30. "Removal of the Poncas," Memo, Nov. 29, 1880; A. C. Barstow to Schurz, Dec. 2, 6, 24, 1879; Walter Allen to Schurz, Dec. 5, 1879; Hayes to Schurz, Dec. 3, 1880, SP; Schurz to John D. Long, Dec. 11, 1880, John D. Long Papers, MHiS; *SC,* III, 481–89, 496–506; IV, 50–78; Hayes, *Diary,* III, 626, 629; George F. Hoar, *Autobiography of Seventy Years* (New York: Scribner's, 1903), II, 29–30; *Independent,* Dec. 18, 1879, Jan. 1, 1880; Sen. Ex. Doc. 30, 46th Cong., 3d sess (1881).

31. Sen. Ex. Doc. 30, 46th Cong., 3d sess. (1881); Prucha, *American Indian Policy in Crisis,* 116–18; *Cong. Record,* 46th Cong., 3d sess., 1056ff. (Jan. 31, 1881); *SC,* IV, 91–114; New York *Evening Post,* Jan. 31, 1881; *Nation,* Feb. 3, 1881; Ward Thoron, ed., *The Letters of Mrs. Henry Adams* (Boston: Little Brown, 1936), 489f., 265, 270, 271, 491ff., 503; Helen Hunt Jackson, *A Century of Dishonor* (New York: Harper, 1881), 186–217, 369–74; Philadelphia *Bulletin,* Feb. 12, 1881; *Removal and Situation of the Ponca Indians,* Sen. Misc. Doc. 49, 46th Cong., 3d sess. (1881). Schurz vigorously cross-examined witnesses in Dawes's Select Committee.

32. When the chief was informed that Schurz had died, he said, "Good." *New York Times,* May 27, 1906. For the threats to the Indian Territory, cf. ibid., Apr. 26, 1879; N. W. Harris to Schurz, May 8, 1879, SP. Schurz published an article in the July 1881 issue of the *North American Review* in which he set forth his humane Indian policy in detail. *SC,* IV, 116–46.

33. Schurz to Walker, Feb. 12, 1879, SP; James Phinney Munroe, *A Life of Francis Amasa Walker* (New York: Holt, 1923), 194–95, 197–99; Ann Herbert Scott, *Census, U.S.A.: Fact Finding for the American People, 1790–1970* (New York: Seabury, 1968), 33; W. Stull Holt, *The Bureau of the Census: Its History, Activities and Organization* (Washington, D.C.: Brookings Institution, 1929), 20–27. In connection with his responsibilities for the Bureau of Railroad Accounts, Schurz demonstrated the ability of the railroads to establish a sinking fund for the payment of their indebtedness to the United States. In the Nelson Dudymott case, he rendered a decision to the effect that settlers might claim railroad lands not disposed of within three years. It was later overturned. *New York Times,* July 24, 26, Sept. 4, 1878; *SC,* IV, 179–80; Nelson, "Schurz's Administration," 393.

34. T. H. Williams, *Hayes Diary,* 91; Schurz to Adolph Meyer, Aug. 25, 1877, HC.

35. Hayes, *Diary,* III, 46–62; Barnard, *Hayes,* 461–63.

36. J. M. Millikan to Hayes, Sept. 20, 1878; McKinley to Hayes, Sept. 23, 1878, Hayes Papers, Hayes Library; Schurz to G. F. Hoar, Oct. 12, 1878, G. F. Hoar Papers, MHiS; E. R. Hoar to Schurz, Oct. 29, 1878; Richard Smith to Schurz, Oct. 11, 1878, SP; Boston *Journal*, Oct. 29, 1878; *SC*, III, 422–80; Schurz to Emilie Meyer, Oct. 19, 1878; Schurz to Adolph Meyer, Nov. 9, 1878, HC; Eugene H. Roseboom and Francis P. Weisenburger, *A History of Ohio,* ed. James H. Rodabaugh (Columbus: Ohio State Archaeological and Historical Society, 1953), 236–37. In 1879, he again helped the party by campaigning on the hard money issue. *New York Times*, Aug. 21, 1879.

37. E. P. Hammond to Schurz, Mar. 1, 1906; Schurz to Children, Aug. 15, 1877, ctr. 176; clipping, Cincinnati *Commercial,* Feb. 4, 1878, ctr. 211, SP; *Die Glocke* (Chicago) 1 (1906), 168.

38. Schurz to Althaus, Oct. 10, 1879; Schurz to Bayard, Mar. 29, 1879, SP; Wittke, "Carl Schurz and Rutherford B. Hayes," 350; Ford, *Letters of Henry Adams,* I, 303; Helen H. Gemill, "Elizabeth Lawrence: Dr. Mercer's 'Auntie Mame!'" *Bucks County Historical Journal* 2 (Spring 1978), 78–79.

39. T. H. Williams, *Hayes Diary,* 136, 145, 165, 299, 172; Schurz to Hayes, Dec. 26, 1877; Agathe Schurz to Hayes, Nov. 6, 1878, Hayes Papers, Hayes Library; *New York Times*, May 15, 16, June 28, 1877. At Harvard, he walked in the commencement procession, proud of the LLD he had received the year before and was elected an honorary member of the local Phi Beta Kappa chapter. Schurz to Lodge, July 7, 1876; C. L. Smith to Schurz, July 2, 1877, SP.

40. C. H. Mohun to Schurz, n.d. (Baltimore *Post & Sun*), item 12320; *Tägliche Abendpost,* Mar. 3, 1879; Schurz to Tiedemann, Mar. 9, 1879, Schurz to Preetorius, ctr. 176, Mar. 29, 1879, SP.

41. *Bucks County Daily News,* May 16, 1924; identification in memo. H. C. Lodge, n.d., Adams Family Papers, MHiS; Gemill, "Elizabeth Lawrence," 80–81; Schurz to Fanny [Chapman], July 14, [1880], Schurz-Chapman Correspondence, University of Münster (hereafter cited as Chapman Cor.).

42. Schurz to Fanny, Nov. 20, 1883, Chapman Cor. The remainder of the letters show how frequently the two met.

43. Schurz to "Meine liebe Freundin," Jan. 29, 1893, ctr. 176, SP; *Cong. Record,* 46th Cong., 2d sess., 2251 (Apr. 9, 1880); Allan Peskin, *Garfield* (Kent, Ohio: Kent State Univ. Press, 1978), 452ff.

44. Private Memo, W. H. Smith, Nov. 22, 1879, Hayes Papers, Hayes Library; Schurz to Adolph Meyer, Mar. 9, 1880, HC; Schurz to J. H. Wilson, Mar. 23, 1880; John Sherman to Schurz, May 30, 1880; Schurz to Preetorius, ctr. 176, Feb. 16, May 16, 1880, SP; Chauncey I. Filley to D. K. Abeel, Feb. 20, 1880, Filley Papers, MoHiS; *SC*, III, 494–96, 506–7; Philadelphia *Record,* Dec. 26, 1879; Schurz to Rollins, May 29, 1880, Rollins Papers, MoHiS.

45. Peskin, *Garfield,* 460–80; E. E. Lockwood to Schurz, Apr. 21, 29, 1880; Schurz to "Meine liebe Freundin," ctr. 178, Jan. 29, 1893, SP.

46. Hayes to Webb Hayes, June 9, 1880, Hayes Papers, Hayes Library; Brown and Williams, *Garfield Diary,* III, 455; Peskin, *Garfield,* 422–23; Schurz to Garfield, June 8, 1880, James A. Garfield Papers, LC.

47. Schurz to Garfield, June 24, July 9, Aug. 11, Sept. 22, 23, 27, Oct. 1, 21, 1880; Garfield to Schurz, July 6, 1880, Garfield Papers, LC; Garfield to Schurz, July 22, Sept. 24, 1880, SP; Chester Arthur to Schurz, Oct. 5, 12, 1880, Arthur Papers, LC; Wade Hampton to Hayes, with clipping of July 3, 1880, Hayes Papers, Hayes Library; *SC*, III, 507–8, IV, 1–50; *New York Times*, Aug. 9, Oct. 19, 20, 31, 1880; Smith, *Garfield,* 997; Cortissoz, *Reid,* II, 36; Thomas C. Reeves, *Gentlemen Boss: The Life of Chester Alan Arthur* (New York: Knopf, 1975), 188–89; Cleveland *Leader,* Oct. 2, 1880; DeSantis,

Republicans Face the Southern Question, 101–2; Schurz to Rollins, Nov. 3, 1880, Rollins Papers, MoHiS.

48. Schurz to Emilie Meyer, June 18, 1880; Schurz to Adolph Meyer, Jan. 2, 1881, HC; B. Koch to Schurz, Nov. 27, 1880; Garfield to Schurz, Nov. 26, 28, 1880; Atkinson to Schurz, Feb. 10, 1881; Francis Parkman to Schurz, Feb. 12, 1881; Horace White to Schurz, Feb. 17, 1881, SP; Schurz to Garfield, n.d. [Nov. 28, 1880], Garfield Papers, LC; *SC*, IV, 78–91, 115. Garfield assured Reid that despite all rumors he would not take Schurz into the cabinet. Cortissoz, *Reid,* II, 43.

NOTES TO CHAPTER XVI

1. Schurz to Adolph Meyer, Sept. 22, 1880, Jan. 2, June 22, 1881, Oct. 6, 1882; M. J. Bode to Schurz, Aug. 21, 1884, HC; Redpath Lyceum Bureau to Schurz, Jan. 22, Feb. 2, 1881; Schurz to Redpath Lyceum Bureau, Feb. 2, 1881; E. F. Shepard to Schurz, Nov. 18, 30, 1880, SP. A lecture program for the fall of 1881 was finally arranged. B. W. Williams to Schurz, Sept. 30, Oct. 18, 1881, SP. The term "Mugwumps" was commonly applied to the independents who refused to support Blaine in 1884, but it had been used as early as 1872 to designate independents. David Saville Muzzey, *James G. Blaine: A Political Idol of Other Days* (New York: Dodd, Mead, 1934), 293.

2. G. B. Hunter to William Laurence, Feb. 14, 1881; Parkman to Schurz, Feb. 12, 1881; Schurz to Bowles, Nov. 27, 1874; J. T. Morse to Schurz, Apr. 3, 1881, SP; Schurz to Fanny Chapman, May 22, 1881, Chapman Cor.; Schurz to Adolph Meyer, Jan. 2, Apr. 3, 1881, HC; Thoron, *Letters of Mrs. Henry Adams,* 273–74; Hayes, *Diary,* IV, 179; Truax, *The Doctors Jacobi,* 147–60, 184.

3. Villard, *Memoirs,* II, 338–39; Allan Nevins, *The Evening Post: A Century of Journalism* (New York: Boni & Liveright, 1922), 438; William M. Armstrong, "The Godkin-Schurz Feud, 1881–83, Over Policy Control of the *Evening Post*," *New-York Historical Society Quarterly* 48 (Jan. 1964), 5–29, esp. 10–13.

4. Schurz to Fanny Chapman, May 22, 23, 1881, Chapman Cor.

5. Nevins, *Evening Post,* 444–54; Oswald Garrison Villard, "Carl Schurz als Journalist," in Erkelenz and Mittelmann, *Schurz,* 196–97; Armstrong, *Godkin,* 140–45.

6. New York *Evening Post,* May 26, 1881 and frequent following editorials, esp. July 21, Aug. 12, Dec. 14, 1881, Aug. 3, Nov. 2, 1882; Frank Mann Stewart, *The National Civil Service Reform League* (Austin: Univ. of Texas Press, 1929), 23–38; Everett P. Wheeler, *Sixty Years of American Life: Taylor to Roosevelt, 1850–1910* (New York: Dutton, 1917), 277–79.

7. Peskin, *Garfield,* 543–96; Hoogenboom, *Outlawing the Spoils,* 207–10.

8. Schurz to T. L. James, July 3, 4, 1881; James to Schurz, July 3, 4, 1881, SP; Schurz to Emilie [Meyer], July 5, 1881; Schurz to Adolph Meyer, Aug. 26, 1881, HC; New York *Evening Post,* July 5, 6, 8, 1881.

9. New York *Evening Post,* Sept. 10, Dec. 7, 12, 21, 1881, Mar. 4, 27, Apr. 5, May 29, Aug. 3, Dec. 5, 13, 1882, Jan. 12, 1883; Wheeler, *Sixty Years,* 277; Nevins, *Evening Post,* 450–51. When Arthur signed a different version of the Chinese Exclusion Bill, the paper criticized him for it. New York *Evening Post,* Apr. 29, May 9, 1882.

10. New York *Evening Post,* Sept. 5, 1882, Apr. 4, Oct. 4, Nov. 21, 1882.

11. Putnam, *Memoirs,* 28–29; Simon Wolf, *The Presidents I Have Known From 1860 to 1910* (Washington: Byron & Adams, 1918), 83, 101, 105; Schurz to Mrs. Schurz, Nov. 29, 1874; Jacob Schiff to Schurz, Oct. 31, 1881; Jesse Seligman Eulogy, Scrapbook 2, 100ff., ctr. 185, SP; Oscar S. Straus, *Under Four Administrations: From Cleveland to Taft* (Boston: Houghton Mifflin, 1922), 44.

12. M. S. Isaacs to Schurz, Sept. 27, 1881, Jan. 1, 9, 23, 1882; Jacob Schiff to Schurz,

Oct. 31, 1881, SP; New York *Evening Post*, Aug. 22, Oct. 25, Nov. 2, 1881, Jan. 23, Feb. 1, 2, 6, Apr. 25, Dec. 26, 1882.

13. Schurz to Adolph Meyer, Jan. 2, 1881, HC.

14. New York *Evening Post*, June 15, Dec. 1, 1882, June 23, 1883; St. Louis *Westliche Post*, May 9, 1884. When the House of Representatives passed resolutions of sympathy for transmittal to the Reichstag, Bismarck refused to forward them and considerable acrimony resulted. Schurz considered Bismarck's action an outrage and suggested to Senator Edmunds that the American minister in Berlin be recalled. Schurz to Edmunds, Mar. 9, 12, 1884, SP. For the Lasker affair, cf. Louis L. Snyder, *Roots of German Nationalism* (Bloomington: Indiana Univ. Press, 1978), 134–56.

15. New York *World*, Jan. 12–17, 1882, Apr. 12, 1883; New York *Evening Post*, Jan. 14, 1882; *North American Review* 116 (Mar. 1883), 237–56; *SC*, IV, 150–54, 168–81, 183–94; Schurz to W. H. Smith, Jan. 25, 1882, Smith Papers, OHiS; Cincinnati *Commercial Gazette*, Mar. 19, 1883; Schurz to Fanny Chapman, Mar. 22, 1883, Chapman Cor.; Patrick W. Riddleberger, *George Washington Julian: Radical Republican* (Indianapolis: Indiana Historical Bureau, 1966), 292, 302ff. Ctr. 205, SP, contains clippings from various newspapers concerning the incident.

16. Schurz to Emilie Meyer, Aug. 5, 1882; Schurz to Children, Sept. 2, 13, 1883, July 23, 1884, HC; Schurz to S. M. Howe, June 1, 1881; Curtis to Schurz, June 10, 1881; Randall to Schurz, Dec. 13, 1881; Carnegie to Schurz, Feb. 2, 1884; Elliot Roosevelt to Schurz, Nov. 6, 1882; Dr. Jacobi to Schurz, ctr. 176, July 26, 1882, SP; Schurz to Fanny Chapman, Feb. 27, 1883, Chapman Cor.; Schurz to Frederick Bancroft, Aug. 30, 1884, Bancroft Papers, CU; Hayes, *Diary*, IV, 44–45, 76–77, 179; Thoron, *Letters of Mrs. Henry Adams*, 440; Joseph Frazier Wall, *Andrew Carnegie* (New York: Oxford Univ. Press, 1970), 388.

17. Schurz to Fanny Chapman, May 22, 1881, Nov. 21, 1882, Apr. 3, 26, 29, Dec. 9, Apr. 17, Oct. 26, 1884, Chapman Cor.

18. Harold Dean Cater, comp., *Henry Adams and His Friends: A Collection of His Unpublished Letters* (Boston: Houghton Mifflin, 1947), 112; Armstrong, "The Godkin-Schurz Feud."

19. Armstrong, "The Godkin-Schurz Feud"; Schurz to Godkin, June 17, 1883; Godkin to Schurz, June 18, 1883, SP; New York *Evening Post*, July 17–19, Aug. 8, 1883; Schurz to Godkin, Aug. 9, 1883; Godkin to Schurz, Aug. 11, 1883 (unsent), Godkin Papers, HU.

20. Schurz to Godkin, Oct. 3, Dec. 10, 11, 14, 15, 1883; Godkin to Schurz, Dec. 7, 1883, Godkin Papers, HU; Schurz to Children, Aug. 14, 1883, HC; *New York Times*, Dec. 11, 12, 1883; Springfield *Republican*, Dec. 11, 12, 1883; *North American Review* 138 (Feb. 1884), 101–19; Armstrong, *Godkin*, 144–58; Schurz to Fanny Chapman, Nov. 11, Dec. 9, 1883, Chapman Cor.

21. Schurz to Fanny Chapman, Nov. 27, 1883, Mar. 27?, 1884, Chapman Cor.; Schurz to Adolph Meyer, Jan. 1, 24, Apr. 26, 1884, HC; G. Schwab to Schurz, Mar. 22, 24, 1884, SP; *SC*, IV, 197–98.

22. Louis Filler, ed., *Democrats and Republicans,* by Harry Thurston Peck (New York: Capricorn, 1964), 17; Rhodes, *History of the United States,* VII, 194ff.; Dobson, *Politics in the Gilded Age,* 93ff.

23. Blaine to Schurz, May 26, 1881, Oct. 9, 1881; S. H. Boyd to Schurz, Aug. 5, 1881, SP; New York *Evening Post*, Feb. 3, 7, 11, Mar. 24, Sept. 11, 1882; Chicago *Tribune*, Sept. 19, 26, 1882; Muzzey, *Blaine*, 269–71.

24. Filler, *Democrats and Republicans*, 29–32; Schurz to Adolph Meyer, Nov. 12, 1882, HC.

25. Brooklyn *Eagle*, Feb. 23, 1884.

26. Schurz to Adolph Meyer, Mar. 18, 1884, HC; Schurz to Edmunds, Mar. 9, 12,

1884; F. C. Barlow to Schurz, May 21, 1884; J. H. Wilson to Schurz, May 28, 1884, SP; *SC*, IV, 200–4.

27. John W. Foster, *Diplomatic Memoirs* (Boston: Houghton Mifflin, 1909), II, 267; *SC*, IV, 194–95; Robert D. Marcus, *Grand Old Party: Political Structure in the Gilded Age, 1880–96* (New York: Oxford Univ. Press, 1971), 80–85.

28. Muzzey, *Blaine,* 290; *SC*, IV, 205–8; Dobson, *Politics in the Gilded Age,* 110–12; Schurz to T. F. Bayard, July 10, 1884, Bayard Papers, LC.

29. Alexander Sullivan to S.B. Elkins, June 12, 1884; J. Medill to Blaine, June 13, 1884, James G. Blaine Papers, LC.

30. Preetorius to Schurz, July 1, 1884; Schurz to Fritz Tiedemann, June 27, 1884, ctr. 177, SP; *SC*, IV, 212–13, 214–15.

31. Schurz to Children, June 19, 1884, HC; New York *Evening Post*, Feb. 1, Mar. 2, 1883; Allan Nevins, *Grover Cleveland: A Study in Courage* (New York: Dodd, Mead, 1932), 4–5, 157f., 162ff., 177.

32. Schurz to H. W. Beecher, July 29, 30, 1884, Beecher Family Papers, YU. At the same time, he was seriously embarrassed by the refusal of the *Westliche Post* to follow him into Cleveland's camp. He unsuccessfully tried to divest himself of his shares. Schurz to Children, July 14, 23, Sept. 20, 1884, HC.

33. *SC*, IV, 224–72; *New York Times*, Aug. 6, 7, 9, 1884; Muzzey, *Blaine,* 300–1; Nevins, *Cleveland,* 162.

34. *Senator Hoar's Answer to Carl Schurz's Brooklyn Address of August 5, 1884,* Document 5, Republican National Committee, Campaign of 1884, pamphlet in English and German in Blaine Papers, LC; Richard E. Welch, Jr., *George Frisbie Hoar and the Half-Breed Republicans* (Cambridge: Harvard Univ. Press, 1971), 130–31; G. W. Hazleton to Blaine, Aug. 16, 1884, Blaine Papers, LC; *SC*, IV, 275–84; *New York Times*, Sept. 7–11, 1884.

35. *New York Times*, Sept. 16, 19, Oct. 1, 14, 23, 24, 28, 1884; Schurz to Children, Sept. 30, 1884, HC; J. F. C. Beyland to W. E. Chandler, Aug. 19, 1884, William E. Chandler Papers, LC; Thomas Ewing to Blaine, Aug. 23, 1884, Blaine Papers, LC.

36. Sohier and Welch to Schurz, Sept. 3, 1884; P. A. Cullins to Schurz, Sept. 4, 1884; Horace Deming to Schurz, Sept. 20, 1884, SP; Muzzey, *Blaine,* 300–301, Nevins, *Cleveland,* 160–62, 177.

37. J. F. C. Beyland to W. E. Chandler, May 12, 27, Aug. 19, 30, Oct. 23, 1884, Chandler Papers, LC; Trefousse, *Butler,* 252–53; Cleveland, *Nevins, 185ff.*

38. Fuess, *Schurz,* 299; Schafer, *Schurz,* 239; Carl Russell Fish, "Carl Schurz—the American," *Wis. Mag. of Hist.* 12 (June 1929), 356; Muzzey, *Blaine,* 271, 296ff.; Nevins, *Cleveland,* 1881 ff.; Jordan, *Conkling,* 420–21.

39. Blaine, *Twenty Years of Congress*, II, 438–40; *SC*, IV, 297.

NOTES TO CHAPTER XVII

1. Curtis to Schurz, July 15, 1885; George F. Williams to Schurz, Aug. 28, Sept. 5, 11, 13, 14, Oct. 28, 30, Nov. 3, 5, 7, 1885, and Schurz's replies; Storey to Schurz, Nov. 20, 24, 1885, SP; G. F. Williams to W. C. Endicott, Nov. 12, 1885, William C. Endicott Papers, MHiS; Hayes, *Diary*, IV, 179; Schurz to Children, Jan. 6, 18, Mar. 30, 1885, HC.

2. J. H. Senner to Schurz, Aug. 31, Oct. 17, 1887; Schurz to Atkinson, Nov. 26, 1887; Nissen to Schurz, Dec. 1, 1888; Harper & Bros. to Schurz, July 12, 1892, SP; Schurz to Children, Apr. 7, May 11, 1885, HC.

3. New York *Evening Post*, Jan. 14, 1889; Schurz to E. P. Wheeler, Mar. 27, 1885, Carl Schurz Papers, NYPL; *SC*, V, 143–76.

4. Schurz to Mary Jacobi, July 26, 1894, Putnam Family Papers, Radcliffe College.

5. *SC*, IV, 288–90, 294–95, 305–8; Stewart, *National Civil Service Reform League,* 12–14, 48.

6. Schurz to Children, Dec. 1, 9, 23, 1884; Jan. 6, 18, Mar. 2, HC; Schurz to Silas Burt, Feb. 16, 1885, Silas W. Burt Papers, NYHS; *SC*, IV, 355–60.

7. *SC*, IV, 360–67; Schurz to Children, May 27, 1885, HC; clipping, unknown German paper, with quote of Mar. 3, 1885, ctr. 204, SP.

8. *SC*, IV, 401–4; Nevins, *Cleveland,* 240, 248, 236.

9. *SC*, IV, 288–90, 297–305, 360–63, 401–6, 408–9, 414–20, 421–24; George F. Parker, *Recollections of Grover Cleveland,* (New York: Century, 1909), 251.

10. *SC*, IV, 437–46, 435–36, 463–77; Schurz to G. F. Williams, Apr. 8, 1886; Curtis to Schurz, Aug. 2, 1887, SP; Schurz to Burt, Aug. 15, 1887, Burt Papers, NYHS.

11. Schurz to Atkinson, Dec. 7, 1887, SP; Schurz to Adolph Meyer, Dec. 25, 1887, HC; fragment, No. 21, Chapman Cor.

12. *SC*, IV, 409–14, 461–62, 482–90, V, 403–11, 417–29; "Brown" to Schurz, Sept. 19, 1892; Exeter, N.H., Newsletter, July 9, 23, 1897, ctr. 185, SP; Fuess, *Schurz,* 213.

13. Schurz to Henry Villard, Apr. 22, 1888, Villard Papers, HU; *SC*, IV, 493–507; Schurz to Adolph Meyer, Mar. 24, 1888, HC; Munich *Allgemeine Zeitung,* Apr. 14, 1888, SP, ctr. 187.

14. Schurz to Adolph Meyer, Apr. 28, Oct. 31, 1888, HC; Schurz, Diary, May 1, 7, 11, 16, 18, June 10, Oct. 29, 1888, ctr. 175, SP; Schurz to Fanny Chapman, May 22, 24, 1888, in author's possession through the courtesy of the owner, Baron Bernard Friesen, Pembroke, Wales; Schurz to Henry Villard, July 12, 1888, Villard Papers, HU; Ernst Feder, ed., *Bismarcks grosses Spiel: Die geheimen Tagebücher Ludwig Bambergers* (Frankfurt: Societätsverlag, 1932), 535, 555; *New York Times*, May 1, Nov. 14, 15, 1888; Schurz to Oscar Strauss, July 3, 1888, SP; *Leipziger Neuste Nachrichten,* Nov. 5, 1905.

15. *SC*, IV, 509–28.

16. Schurz to Adolph Meyer, Apr. 28, 1888, HC; Schurz to Henry Villard, July 6, 1888, Villard Papers, HU; Contract, Hamburg-American Paketfahrt A. G., Aug. 6, 1888; Schurz, Diary, Aug. 19, 22, 1889, SP; Schurz to Mrs. Hellman, July 27, Aug. 11, 22, 1891, Schurz Papers, WiHiS. He stayed with the steamship company until July 1892, remaining the last few months at the special urging of the management. He felt he needed more time for literary work. Schurz to Emilie Meyer, Oct. 7, 1891, MC; Schurz to "Dear Friend," Jan. 13, 1892, ctr. 183, SP.

17. *SC*, IV, 309–48.

18. J. T. Morse to Schurz, Jan. 7, 1883, Jan. 19, 1884, Jan. 6, Apr. 22, Sept. 10, 25, 1885, June 28, 1886, SP; Carl Schurz, *Henry Clay* (Boston: Houghton Mifflin, 1887); Garraty, *Lodge,* 65–57. The Schurz Papers for the 1880s contain substantial evidence of the author's research.

19. *SC*, IV, 491–93; Schurz to Frederick Bancroft, Jan. 13, 1889, Bancroft Papers, CU; Pierce to Schurz, ctr. 183, Nov. 27, 1892; Schurz to Morse, Mar. 18, 1891; G. H. Putnam to Schurz, Oct. 27, 1887; R. W. Gilder to Schurz, Jan. 22, 1892; E. L. Burlingame to Schurz, Mar. 3, 1893; Deutsche Verlagsbuchhandlung to Schurz, June 10, 1892, SP; Schurz to Fanny Chapman, Mar. 2, 1892, Chapman Cor.

20. *Bradstreet's,* Mar. 22, 1890; *Atlantic Monthly,* June 1891; *McClure's Magazine,* May 1897; H. D. Scudder to Schurz, Mar. 27, 1891; Theodore Dodge to Schurz, Dec. 20, 1891; C. D. Warner to Schurz, June 5, 1897, SP; Schurz to Mrs. Hellman, Aug. 5, 1897, Schurz Papers, WiHiS.

21. *Atlantic Monthly,* June 1891, 721–50.

22. Schurz to Emilie Meyer, June 1, 1887; Schurz to Herman Rose, Apr. 9, 1902, HC; Schurz to C. F. Adams, Aug. 23, 1901; Minna Kinkel to Schurz, Nov. 7, 1901, SP; *SR*, III, 311–455, esp, 450–52; Schurz to Fanny Chapman, Mar. 2, 1892, Chapman Cor.

23. Schurz to Dr. E. R. A. Seligman, Feb. 28, 1888, E. R. A. Seligman Papers, CU; The Reminiscences of George McAneny (1905), in the Oral History Collection of Columbia University, 19ff.

24. *New York Times*, July 10, 1887; *Atlantic Monthly,* Oct. 1887, 556–66.

25. *SC*, IV, 479–80, 481–82; Horace White to Schurz, May 26, 1887; George William Curtis to Schurz, Aug. 2, 1887; George Bancroft to Schurz, Oct. 18, 1887; Drake to Schurz, Nov. 18, 1887; Koerner to Schurz, Oct. 11, 1887; Dawes to Schurz, Dec. 11, 1887, SP; Schurz to George Bancroft, Oct. 6, 1887, George Bancroft Papers, MHiS.

26. Spencer to Schurz, May 3, 1892, SP; *SC*, V, 82; Roosevelt, *Letters,* 1, 109, 305.

27. Charles Bonaparte to Schurz, Feb. 10, 1889; Roosevelt to Schurz, May 2, 1891, Schurz to Foulke, Mar. 9, 1889; Foulke to Schurz, Feb. 23, 1890; Schurz to Foulke, Feb. 25, 1890; Henry Richmond to Schurz, Dec. 23, 1890, SP; Schurz to Henry Richmond, Jan. 2, 1891, Frederick M. Dearborn Collection, HU; Curtis to Burt, Mar. 20, 1889, Dec. 19, 1890, Burt Papers, NYHiS; *SC*, V, 13–15; Roosevelt, *Letters,* I, 281; Stewart, *National Civil Service Reform League,* 52–53; William Dudley Foulke, *A Hoosier Autobiography* (New York: Oxford Univ. Press, 1922), 92, 104–5; Edmund Morris, *The Rise of Theodore Roosevelt* (New York: Coward, McCann & Geoghegan, 1979), 447ff.

28. New York *Evening Post*, June 14, 1889; *SC*, V, 22–33, 40–80.

29. *SC*, IV, 368–400; Schurz to Children, Jan. 25, Feb. 6, 12, 22, 1885, HC; *Harper's Weekly,* Sept. 4, 1897. Schurz believed that he was being boycotted on Northern lecture circuits because of his support of Cleveland.

30. M. Stevens to Schurz, Oct. 29, 1891; David Gray to Schurz, Jan. 4, 1892; W. C. Whitney to Schurz, Feb. 2, June 15, July 8, 1892, SP; *SC*, V, 82–84; *New York Times*, June 16, 1892.

31. Schurz to Mrs. Hellman, June 25, [1892], Schurz Papers, WiHiS; Schurz to Henry Richmond, July 18, 1892, Bernard K. Schaefer Collection, PU; Schurz to Emilie Meyer, June 20, Aug. 26, MC; Schurz to Edward M. Shepard, Aug. 9, 16, 24, Sept. 4, 1892, Edward M. Shepard Papers, CU.

32. *SC*, V, 87–121, 124; Schurz to Shepard, Sept. 11, 14, 1892; Shepard to Schurz, Sept. 13, 1892, Shepard Papers, CU, Villard to Schurz, Sept. 13, 1892, Villard Papers, HU; *New York Times*, Oct. 28, 1892; Nevins, *Cleveland,* 501–2; Harold U. Faulkner, *Politics, Reform and Expansion, 1890–1910* (New York: Harper, 1959), 131–34.

33. J. H. Harper to Schurz, Dec. 24, 1896, SP; *Harper's Weekly,* editorials from June 1892 to April 1898. He also wrote the obituaries of George William Curtis, Rutherford B. Hayes, and Louis Kossuth. Ibid., Sept. 10, 1892, Jan. 28, 1893, Mar. 31, 1894.

34. Schurz to Preetorius, Oct. 12, 1885; Schurz to W. H. Page, Oct. 9, 1885; H. Gaullieur to Schurz, Aug. 25, 1885; Horace White to Schurz, Sept. 3, 1885; Schurz to Norton, July 8, 1886; G. P. Lowry to Schurz, July 10, 1892, SP; Schurz to Hayes, Aug. 12, 1885, Jan. 17, 1886, Hayes Papers, Hayes Library.

35. Schurz to Emilie Meyer, May 10, Sept. 9, Nov. 20, 1892, MC; Marie Jüssen, "Wie Carl Schurz lebte und wirkte," *Die Glocke,* (Chicago) 1 (1906), 177–78; Schurz to E. L. Pierce, Oct. 7, 1892; Schurz to C. F. Adams, Dec. 16, 1896, SP.

36. George McAneny to O. G. Villard, Sept. 23, 1925, McAneny Papers, PU; Jüssen, "Carl Schurz," 398–99; Schurz to Henry Richmond, July 18, 1892, Schaefer Collection, PU; Schurz to Emilie Meyer, July 18, 1892, MC; Vulpius, "Carl Schurz," 22; Reminiscences of Franziska Boas (1972) in the Oral History Collection of Columbia University, 50; Frederick Bancroft's Notes of Interviews with Carl Schurz, 1884–1906, Bancroft Papers, 50 (hereafter cited as Bancroft, Notes).

37. Schurz to Fanny Chapman, June 6, 1887, Friday [1889], July 10, 1889, Tuesday [1889], July 7, 30, 1889, Tuesday [Sept. 1889], Nov. 20, 1889, Dec. 7, 1890, Mar. 2, May 31, 1892, Chapman Cor.; Schurz to Fanny Chapman, Aug. 19, 1889, HC.

38. Schurz to Emilie Meyer, Oct. 29, Nov. 27, 1891, Aug. 26, 1892, MC; Schurz to J.

Taussig, Nov. 14, 1885, Mar. 12, 1887, SP; *New York Times*, Feb. 27, 1887; Schurz to Mrs. Hellman, July 15, 1890, Schurz Papers, WiHiS.

39. Schurz to Fanny Chapman, Nos. 50, 58, Chapman Cor.; Hayes, *Diary,* IV, 84, 345, V, 76; *New York Times*, Mar. 20, 1927; Schurz to Emilie Meyer, Feb. 17, Apr. 17, 1893, MC; Schurz to E. L. Pierce, Nov. 28, 1892; T. Barth to Schurz, Oct. 16, 1893; Schurz to Carnegie, Nov. 24, 1896, SP; Schurz to Cleveland, Dec. 1, 1885, Dec. 6, 1886, Grover Cleveland Papers, LC; Bancroft, Notes, 45.

40. New York *Evening Post*, Dec. 12, 1892.

41. Schurz to Emilie Meyer, Nov. 20, 1892, May 17, 1893, MC; Burt to Schurz, Nov. 2, 1892; Cleveland to Schurz, Feb. 28, 1893; Schurz to L. B. Swift, May 2, 1893; Schurz to A. M. Howe, May 16, 1893, SP; Schurz to Shepard, Feb. 24, 1893, Shepard Papers, CU; *SC*, V, 124–42, 177–81.

42. *SC*, V, 143–81, 226–31, 249; Roosevelt, *Letters,* I, 322, 327–30, 334–40, 342, 387–91; *Harper's Weekly,* July 22, Aug. 5, 1893, May 23, June 6, 1896; Nevins, *Cleveland,* 516–18; Foulke, *Fighting the Spoilsmen,* 99–103; Straus, *Under Four Administrations,* 113; Stewart, *National Civil Service Reform League,* 99.

43. Carl Schurz, "Grover Cleveland's Second Administration," *McClure's Magazine* 10 (May 1897), 633–44.

44. Schurz to Fanny Chapman, Oct. 11, 1894, Chapman Cor.; *SC*, V, 231–48; *New-Yorker Staats-Zeitung,* Oct. 31, 1894; Morris, *Roosevelt,* 475–79.

45. Morris, *Roosevelt,* 596–13; Schurz to G. Schwab, Aug. 1, 5, 1895; James Speyer to Schurz, Nov. 6, 1895, SP; Schurz to John Jay Chapman, Oct. 13, 24, Nov. 7, 1895, John Jay Chapman Papers, HU; *New York Times*, July 13, Oct. 15, 16, 27, 1895; Robert McElroy, *Levi Parsons Morton* (New York: Putnam's, 1930), 249.

46. Schurz to Adolph Meyer, Feb. 19, 1889, HC; C. Hauselt to Schurz, Oct. 21, 1884; E. Karpowsky to Schurz, Oct. 8, 1892; Fred Harr to Schurz, Dec. 12, 1892; J.J. Sontheimer to Schurz, Nov. 27, Dec. 4, Mar. 8, 1893, SP; H. Villard to Schurz, Aug. 11, 1892, Villard Papers, HU; *New-Yorker Staats-Zeitung,* Oct. 29, 1890, Oct. 5, 1891; *New York Times*, May 1, 1888, Dec. 2, 1888.

47. Poultney Bigelow to Schurz, Oct. 3, Nov. 8, 1891; New York City Board of Education to Schurz, May 14, 1892; Gallus Thomann to Schurz, Nov. 27, Dec. 4, 1895, SP; *Illinois Staats-Zeitung,* June 16, 1893; White, *Autobiography,* I, 585–86.

48. Schurz to Adolph Meyer, Jan. 2, 1881, Jan. 2, 1883, Feb. 10, 1887, Feb. 1, 1889, HC; Schurz to Emilie Meyer, July 14, 1895, Dec. 8, 1896, MC.

49. Schurz to Count Arco-Valley, Feb. 3, 1889; Memo on Conversation with Count Arco-Valley, Mar. 17, 1889, SP; Bayard to Schurz, Feb. 6, 1889, Letterbook No. 203, Bayard Papers, LC; *SC*, V, 1–10, 15–17; Schurz to Fanny Chapman, No. 30, Chapman Cor.; Charles Callan Tansill, *The Foreign Policy of Thomas F. Bayard, 1885–1897* (New York: Fordham Univ. Press, 1940), 22ff., 103ff., 111–12; Stollberg-Wernigerode, *Deutschland,* 279–98.

50. *Harper's Weekly,* Feb. 25, Mar. 18, 1893; *Harper's New Monthly Magazine* (Oct. 1893), 736–46.

51. *SC*, V, 249–59; Allan Nevins, *Abram Hewitt with Some Account of Peter Cooper* (New York: Harper, 1935), 580; Schurz to Andrew Carnegie, Apr. 26, 1896, Carnegie Papers, LC.

NOTES TO CHAPTER XVIII

1. Notes, ctr. 118, item 26071–72, SP; Sproat, *"The Best Men,"* 170ff.; Schurz to Henry Richmond, May 28, 1896, HC.

2. Gustav Schwab to Schurz, June 17, 1896, Emil Dorn to Schurz, June 3, 1896; Powell Clayton to Schurz, Aug. 6, 1896; E.B. Smith to Schurz, Aug. 25, 1896, SP; Joseph Benson Foraker, *Notes of a Busy Life* (Cincinnati: Stewart & Kidd, 1917), I, 474; Henry Villard to Schurz, July 29, 1896, Villard Papers, HU; Schurz to Shepard, Aug. 21, 1896, Shepard Papers, CU; *New York Times*, Sept. 6, 1896.

3. Schurz to Emilie Meyer, Aug. 10, 1896, MC.

4. *SC*, V, 276–328, VI, 268; *New York Times*, Sept. 6, 20, 1896; Chicago *Tribune*, Oct. 25, 1896; Hanna to Schurz, Sept. 30, Nov. 30, 1896; E.B. Smith to Schurz, Oct. 31, Nov. 10, 1896; Jacob Schiff to Schurz, Sept. 6, 1896; Isaac Seligman to Schurz, Sept. 8, 1896, SP; Schurz to F. Bancroft, Nov. 5, 1896, Bancroft Papers, CU.

5. Schurz to McKinley, Nov. 7, 1896, Mar. 4, 10, July 5, 1897, SP; *SC*, V, 328–29, VI, 269–70; Foulke, *Fighting the Spoilsmen*, 113ff., 122; *New York Times*, July 11, Dec. 17, 1897.

6. Schurz to Henry Richmond, May 27, 1897, HC; *New York Times*, May 7, Dec. 17, 1897; *SC*, V, 373–96; *Annual Report of the New York Civil Service Reform Association* (New York: Civil Service Reform Association, 1898).

7. Exeter, N.H., *Newsletter,* July 9, 23, Sept. 4, Nov. 12, 1897; *SC*, V, 403–11, 417–29; *Life* 30 (Sept. 16, 1897), 796; draft, Schurz to Grosvenor, Jan. 1898, SP.

8. Stewart, *National Civil Service Reform League,* 62; *SC*, VI, 122–50.

9. Schurz to Emilie Meyer, June 15, 1898, MC; *SC*, V, 191–214, VI, 288–91; Robert L. Beisner, *Twelve Against Empire: The Anti-Imperialists, 1898–1900* (New York: McGraw Hill, 1968), 18–34.

10. Schurz to R.W. Gilder, Aug. 8, 1898, SP; Goldwin Smith to Schurz, July 6, 1899, Goldwin Smith Papers, Cornell University; *SC*, VI, 444–45.

11. *Harper's New Monthly Magazine* 87 (Oct. 1893), 736–46.

12. *SC*, VI, 266–73; Schurz to Handy, July 4, 1897, HC.

13. Schurz to McKinley, July 16, 1897 (draft), SP.

14. Schurz to Emilie Meyer, June 15, 1898, MC; *SC*, V, 250–51; *New York Times,* Apr. 8, 1898.

15. *Harper's Weekly,* Mar. 19, Apr. 16, 1898; Schurz to McKinley, Apr. 1, 12, 1898, SP; *SC*, V, 457–58, 464–65.

16. Bancroft, Notes, 116; Schurz to McKinley, May 10, 1898, SP; *SC*, V, 465–66, 475–76, 515–20; Margaret Leech, *In the Days of McKinley* (New York: Harper, 1959), 213, 326ff.; Beisner, *Twelve Against Empire,* 94–95.

17. Beisner, *Twelve Against Empire,* 9ff., 230ff.; Schurz to Mrs. Hellman, July 21, Aug. 7, 22, Sept. 7, 1898, Schurz Papers, WiHiS; *Independent,* July 14, 1898; Chicago *Record,* Aug. 9, 1898; *Century Magazine* 56 (Sept. 1898), 781–88; *SC*, V, 477–94, 528–29; *New York Times*, Aug. 20, 1898; Foulke, *Autobiography,* 106–7; New York *Evening Post*, Aug. 19, 1898.

18. Schurz to Storey, Nov. 12, 1895, ctr. 183; Roosevelt to Schurz, Apr. 30, 1896, SP; Morris, *Roosevelt,* 569–71, 680–81; *Harper's Weekly,* June 19, 1897; *SC*, V, 520–121.

19. Roosevelt, *Letters,* II, 884; *SC*, V, 521–27.

20. Roosevelt, *Letters,* II, 889, 1086, IV, 1037–38, 1071, VI, 1540; Philip C. Jessup, *Elihu Root* (New York: Archon, 1964), II, 68; Kessel, *Briefe,* 154–56; Schurz to Emilie Meyer, Feb. 25, 105, MC.

21. Schurz to C.F. Adams, Nov. 10, 15, 17, 1898; Adams to Schurz, Nov. 14, 16, 28, 1898; Schurz to Erving Winslow, Nov. 23, 1898; Winslow to Schurz, Nov. 22, 1898; D.G. Haskins to Schurz, Nov. 23, Dec. 10, 1898; Winslow Warren to Schurz, Dec. 16, 1898, SP; Daniel B. Schirmer, *Republic or Empire: American Resistance to the Philippine War* (Cambridge, Mass.: Schenkman, 1972), 95ff., 176; New York *Evening Post*, Nov. 21, 23, 1898; Schurz to Shepard, Nov. 24, 1898, Shepard Papers, CU; Schurz to Carnegie,

Nov. 27, 30, Dec. 24, 1898, Carnegie Papers, LC; Beisner, *Twelve Against Empire,* iv–vi, 98–99; *SC*, V, 530–31, VI, 1–36; Richard E. Welch, Jr., *Response to Imperialism: The United States and the Philippine-American War, 1899–1902* (Chapel Hill: Univ. of North Carolina Press, 1979), 43ff.; E. Berkeley Tompkins, *Anti-Imperialism in the United States: The Great Debate, 1890–1920* (Philadelphia: Univ. of Pennsylvania Press, 1976).

22. Carnegie to Schurz, Feb. 10, 1899; Hoar to Schurz, Jan. 28, 1899; Memorial in the United States Senate with Respect to the Spanish Treaty, ctr. 204, Jan. 30, 1899; Schurz to C. F. Adams, Jan. 19, 20, 29, 1899; Hoar to Schurz, Feb. 9, 1899, SP; Schurz to Shepard, Feb. 3, 4, 1899, Shepard Papers, CU.

23. Schurz to C. F. Adams, Feb. 10, 1899; Carnegie to Schurz, Feb. 10, 1899, SP; Schurz to Carnegie, Feb. 9, 1899, Carnegie Papers, LC; *SC*, VI, 48–77.

24. Schurz to Emilie Meyer, June 11, 1899, MC.

25. New York *Evening Post*, Oct. 17–21, 1899; *SC*, VI, 77–120.

26. C. B. Wilby to Schurz, Nov. 8, 1899; Storey to Schurz, Nov. 9, 1899; Schurz to E. B. Smith, Dec. 10, 1899, Mar. 19, 1900; Smith to Schurz, Dec. 16, 1899, SP; Schurz to Goldwin Smith, Nov. 22, 1899, Smith Papers, Cornell; Cincinnati *Enquirer,* Oct. 29, 1899; R. F. Pettigrew, *Triumphant Plutocracy: The Story of American Public Life from 1870 to 1920* (New York: Academy Press, 1921), 323–28; Schirmer, *Republic or Empire,* 180–82. The Republicans suffered some setbacks, especially in Ohio, where Schurz had appealed to the Germans. Yet he expressed disappointment with the outcome.

27. *SC*, VI, 150–90; New York *Evening Post*, Feb. 23, 1900; William James to Schurz, Mar. 16, 1900; Toni (Jüssen) to Schurz, ctr. 178, Feb. 26, 1900, SP; Foulke, *Fighting the Spoilsmen,* 206; *New York Times*, July 17, 1900.

28. *SC*, VI, 121–22, 199–204; E. B. Smith to Schurz, Mar. 17, July 20, 1900; Winslow to Schurz, June 26, 1900; Schurz to E. B. Smith, Mar. 28, 1900, SP; Schurz to Shepard, July 13, 1900, Shepard Papers, CU; Henry Villard to Schurz, July 19, 1900; Schurz to Oswald G. Villard, July 17, 21, 1900, Villard Papers, HU; Schurz to J. B. Henderson, July 31, Aug. 12, 1900, F. Bancroft Papers, CU.

29. "For American Principles and American Honor," May 24, 1900, ctr. 186, SP; *New York Times*, May 25, July 17, 25, 30, Aug. 4, 5, 1900; New York *Herald,* June 29, 1900; John R. Dos Passos, *A Defense of the McKinley Administration from Attacks of Mr. Carl Schurz and Other Anti-Imperialists* (pamphlet, n.p., n.d.); *SC*, VI, 199–202.

30. *SC*, VI, 257–64; Schirmer, *Republic or Empire,* 189; E. V. Abbott to Schurz, Aug. 20, 1900; Storey to Schurz, Aug. 21, 23, 27, 28, 1900; Schurz to Storey, Aug. 25, Sept. 1, 1900; O. E. Villard to Schurz, Aug. 30, 1900, SP; Schurz to Oswald G. Villard, Sept. 1, 1900; Henry Villard to Schurz, July 14, 1900, Villard Papers, HU; Foulke, *Fighting the Spoilsmen,* 125.

31. Schurz to Emilie Meyer, Nov. 15, 1900, MC; *Die Glocke* (Chicago) 1 (1906), 168; Leech, *In the Days of McKinley,* 558–59; Paolo Coletta, *William Jennings Bryan* (Lincoln: Univ. of Nebraska Press, 1964), I, 272ff.; *SC*, VI, 215–57, 264–66, 276. He even wrote two public letters to Secretary of the Treasury Lyman J. Gage to disprove Gage's charges that Bryan's election would result in widespread debt payments in silver. Ibid., 204–15.

32. Schurz to Shepard, June 16, 25, 1895, Shepard Papers, CU; Schurz to Emilie Meyer, Dec. 8, 1896, Dec. 13, 1897, Dec. 31, 1899, Mar. 5, May 18, 1901, MC; Fritz Kessler, "Carl Schurz—Zur Familien und Sippengeschichte," *Heimatskalender des Kreises Euskirchen* (1972), 64–74. Carl Lincoln Schurz later married Marie Hart, but left no children.

33. Schurz to Agathe Schurz, Feb. 19, Mar. 11, 1897, HC; Schurz to Emilie Meyer, Jan. 29, 1894, Feb. (n.d.) 1897, Dec. 13, 1897, Aug. 13, 1900, MC; Bancroft, Notes, 151; McAneny to Claude Fuess, Dec. 1, 1931, McAneny Papers, PU; Vulpius, "Carl

Schurz," 23; Schurz to Henderson, July 31, 1900; Mimi to Schurz, ctr. 178, SP; New York *Northside News,* Aug. 28, 1902; Schafer, *Schurz,* 253; Fuess, *Schurz,* 376.

34. *SC,* VI, 275–76; *New York Times,* July 4, 1901; Schirmer, *Republic or Empire,* 225–30, 132.

35. Schurz to "Geehrtes Fräulein," ctr. 178, Sept. 22, 1901; O. G. Villard to Schurz, Sept. 23, 1901, SP; Schurz to Villard, Sept. 25, 1901, Villard Papers, HU.

36. *New-Yorker Staats-Zeitung,* Oct. 23, 30, 1897, Oct. 25, Nov. 2, 1901; *SC,* VI, 277–78; Schurz to Emilie Meyer, Nov. 28, 1901, MC. Schurz cooperated with the newly formed Citizens Union in both campaigns. Gerald W. McFarland, *Mugwumps, Morals, and Politics* (Amherst: Univ. of Mass. Press, 1975) 100; Gerald Kurland, *Seth Low: The Reformer in an Urban and Industrial Age* (New York: Twayne, 1971), 83ff., 106–7.

37. Storey to Schurz, Dec. 21, 1901; Schurz to Storey, Dec. 24, 1901, Jan. 1, 1902, SP; Storey to Edward Ordway, Jan. 4, 1902; Schurz to Ordway, Jan. 2, 20, 25, 28, 1902, Edward Ordway Papers, NYPL; Schirmer, *Republic or Empire,* 232–36.

38. Schirmer, *Republic or Empire,* 237 38; Schurz to J. G. Schurman, Apr. 28, 1902; Herbert Welsh to Schurz, Feb. 10, Apr. 30, 1902; Schurz to Welsh, Feb. 11, 1902; Schurz to Welsh, ctr. 183, May 7, 30, 1902; C. F. Adams to Schurz, Apr. 30, May 6, 1902; C. F. Adams to Schurz, ctr. 183, May 19, 29, June 15, 1902; Schurz to Adams, June 6, 1902; Schurz to Adams, ctr. 183, May 25, 1902; Memorial, June 1902, ctr. 143, SP; *SC,* VI, 288–91.

39. Hoar to Schurz, June 3, 19, 1902; Schurz to Shepard, June 7, 1902; Schurz to Hoar, June 17, 1902; Schurz, et al. to Roosevelt, July 22, 1902; C. F. Adams to Carnegie, July 25, 1902, SP; *Selections From the Correspondence of Theodore Roosevelt and Henry Cabot Lodge* (New York: Scribner's, 1929), I, 521; Schurz to Fanny Chapman, June 21, 1902, Chapman Cor.; Schurz to Carnegie, Aug. 2, 1902, Carnegie Papers, LC. Cf. Welch, *Response to Imperialism,* 142–43.

40. Schurz to C. F. Adams, Dec. 17, 24, 1902; Schurz to Winslow, Jan. 11, Aug. 26, Sept. 11, 1902; Schurz to Storey, Feb. 1, 1903; C. F. Adams to E. W. Camack, Feb. 13, 1903; J. L. Smith to Schurz, May 2, 1903, SP; Schurz to Ordway, Feb. 12, Dec. 13, 1903, Ordway Papers, NYPL; *SC,* VI, 301, 302 3, 306 7; Schirmer, *Republic or Empire,* 241ff.; Hense-Jensen, *Wisconsin's Deutsch-Amerikaner,* II, 242.

41. *SC,* VI, 351–52, 353–56, 358–403, 105–6; Foulke, *Autobiography,* 144–45; New York *Evening Post,* Nov. 4, 1904; Jacob Schiff to Schurz, Nov. 11, 21, 1904, Jan. 24, 31, 1905; Schurz to Schiff, Nov. 9, 1904, Jan. 30, 1905, SP; *New York Times,* Nov. 3, 1904.

42. Schurz to Emilie Meyer, Feb. 25, 1905, MC; *SC,* VI, 431–41; Schurz to Ordway, Mar. 2, 1906, SP.

43. Beisner, *Twelve Against Empire,* 26, 160, 232–33; *Harper's Weekly,* Sept. 4, 1897; Washington to Schurz, Nov. 6, 1897; Storey to Schurz, June 10, 1903; Schurz to Storey, June 26, 1903, SP; *Addresses in Memory of Carl Schurz,* 38–41.

44. *McClure's Magazine* 22 (Jan. 1904), 258–75.

45. William Dean Howells to Schurz, Dec. 26, 1903, Storey to Schurz, Dec. 31, 1903; Joseph Shippen to Schurz, Jan. 25, 1904; Frank Johnson to Editor, *McClure's Magazine,* Dec. 24, 1903; David T. Duncan to Editor, *McClure's Magazine,* Jan. 21, 1904; H. C. Watson to Schurz, Jan. 10, 1904, SP. There were a number of exceptions.

46. Washington to Schurz, Dec. 28, 1903, Jan. 18, 1904; J. G. Merrell to Schurz, Jan. 8, 1904; P. W. Frisbie to Schurz, Jan. 14, 1904; H. M. Browne to Schurz, Jan. 18, 1904; G. H. White to Schurz, Jan. 2, 1904, SP.

47. J. S. Clarkson to Roosevelt, Dec. 23, 1903; Roosevelt to Schurz, Jan. 2, 1904, SP; Roosevelt, *Letters,* III, 679–82, IV, 875; *SC,* VI, 309–11; *Addresses in Memory of Carl Schurz,* 38–41.

48. *SC,* V, 343–72, 431–47, VI, 303–5; *The Youth's Companion* 71 (Sept. 3, 1897),

441; Schurz to J.B. Gilder, Apr. 29, 1896, Schurz Papers, NYPL; Schurz to Mrs. Hellman, Aug. 5, 1897, Schurz Papers, WiHiS; Editors, *Encyclopaedia Britannica,* to Schurz, May 22, 1900; Schurz to C. F. Adams, Nov. 3, 1903, SP.

49. Schurz to Mrs. Hellman, June 22, 1902, Schurz Papers, WiHiS; Schurz to Emilie Meyer, June 8, Dec. 15, Dec. 20, 1903, June 22, 1904, Feb. 25, Dec. 11, 1905, MC; Schurz to F. Bancroft, Aug. 3, 28, 1903, June 20, 1904, Apr. 1, 1905, and Carl Lincoln Schurz to Bancroft, Sept. 6, Oct. 6, 1904, and Bancroft, Notes, 185–87, Bancroft Papers, CU; Schurz to Fanny Chapman, Jan. 7, Apr. 11, 1903, Chapman Cor.; Schurz to Hermann Rose, Apr. 9, 1902, HC; Schurz to Page, May 12, 1896; Ida Tarbell to Schurz, July 12, 1901, Oct. 28, Nov. 12, 1903; R. W. Gilder to Schurz, Oct. 29, Nov. 12, 1902; G. H. Putnam to Schurz, Apr. 6, 1903; Carl L. Schurz to Schurz, Sept. 14, 22, Oct. 1, 1904; Schurz to Wilfred Holt, Sept. 11, 1905, SP.

50. William Dean Howells to Schurz, Oct. 29, 1905; W. A. Aikens to Schurz, Jan. 21, 1906; J. J. Walsh to Schurz, Nov. (n.d.) 1905; Mary Monagan to Schurz, Dec. 1, 1905; Schurz to Mary Monagan, Dec. 3, 1905, SP; *SR*, I, 3–5; *New York Times*, Dec. 14, 1907; *Literary Digest,* Dec. 7, 14, 1907; *Dial,* Dec. 16, 1907, Dec. 12, 1908; *Review of Reviews* 36 (Dec. 1907); *Independent,* Mar. 11, 1909. Mrs. Francis P. Kinnicutt translated the first volume.

51. J. A. Schnalke to Schurz, Feb. 15, 1897; W. H. Carpenter to Schurz, Jan. 18, 1898; Leopold Sonnemann to Schurz, Mar. 5, 1898; Siegfried Gurthe to Schurz, Nov. 15, 1898; Karl Lohmann to Schurz, Aug. 22, 1904, SP; New York *Weltblatt,* Feb. 15, 1899; *SC*, V, 334–38; *Frankfurter Zeitung,* May 31, 1906; Julius Goebel, "Karl Schurz als Deutsch-Amerikaner," *Deutsch-Amerikanische Geschichtsblätter* 29 (1929), 102–32, esp. 108; *Berliner Illustrierte Zeitung,* Mar. 9, 1902.

52. *New York Times*, Feb. 26, Mar. 5, 9, 1899; Kuno Francke, "Carl Schurz und das Germanische Museum der Harvard Universität," Erkelenz and Mittlemann, *Schurz*, 244; Schurz to Emilie Meyer, Mar. 21, 1899, MC; *SC*, VI, 39–46. Roosevelt refused to attend the dinner because of Schurz's position in the 1898 gubernatorial election. Roosevelt, *Letters,* II, 927–28.

53. Low to Schurz, Nov. 29, 1895; Francke to Schurz, Jan. 14, 1897, May 24, 1901, SP; Cincinnati *Commercial Tribune,* Sept. 6, 1897; Milwaukee *Sentinel,* May 3, 1900; St. Louis *Westliche Post*, Oct. 7, 1904.

54. Schurz to McKinley, Sept. 22, 1898, McKinley Papers, LC; Schurz to Henry Villard, Aug. 6, 1898, Villard Papers, HU; Theodor Barth to Schurz, June 20, July 15, 1898, SP; *Kieler Zeitung,* June 26, 1898, SP, ctr. 187.

55. Bancroft, Notes, 165; *New-Yorker Staats-Zeitung,* May 9, 1902.

56. Schurz to Low, Nov. 13, 1901, Seth Low Papers, CU; Schurz to Ordway, July 21, 1902, Ordway Papers, NYPL; Schurz to Emilie Meyer, June 11, 1899, MC; C. R. Van Hise to Schurz, Jan. 20, Feb. 2, 1904; W. S. Chaplin to Schurz, Apr. 27, 1904, SP.

57. H. R. Butler to Schurz, May 15, 1901; Schurz to Howe, Apr. 28, 1902; Carnegie to Schurz, n.d., 35762, SP.

58. Franz Boas to Schurz, Feb. 21, 1900; E. E. Prussing to Schurz, Dec. 24, 1895; F. W. Holls to Schurz, May 29, 1896, SP; Bancroft, Notes, 36, 136–37; Schurz to Cleveland, Feb. 22, 1899, Cleveland Papers, LC; G. C. Riggs to Schurz, Mar. 16, 1903, HC; Bancroft, Notes, 166, 179.

59. *The New Voice,* Apr. 8, 1899; Bancroft, Notes, 36; Agathe Schurz to Bancroft, Aug. 1, 1899, May 16, 1908, Bancroft Papers, CU; Schurz to Emilie Meyer, May 18, 1901, Dec. 15, 20, 1902, June 22, 1904, Feb. 25, 1905, MC; Schurz to Winslow, June 7, 1901, SP; personal statement of Mrs. Cissa Morlang.

60. Schurz to Emilie Meyer, Dec. 11, 1905, MC; Schurz to Storey, Apr. 18, 1906, SP.

61. *New York Times*, May 11, 14, 15, 1906; Bancroft, Notes, 221–23; Joachim Maass,

Der unermüdliche Rebell: Leben, Taten und Vermächtnis des Carl Schurz (Hamburg: Claasen & Gowerts, 1949), 115–16; R. W. DeForest to Schurz, Dec. 15, 1904, SP.

NOTES TO EPILOGUE

1. *New York Times*, May 15, 18, 1906; scrapbook of obituaries, Schurz Papers, WiHiS; London *Times,* May 15, 1906.

2. Cleveland *Plain Dealer,* May 15, 1906; St. Louis *Post Dispatch,* May 14, 1906; *Kölnische Zeitung,* May 14, 1906.

3. *New York Times*, May 15, 1906; Speck von Sternburg to C. L. Schurz, n.d., with translation of Kaiser's note, HC; Chicago *Inter-Ocean,* May 15, 1906; *Frankfurter Zeitung,* May 14, 1906.

4. *New York Times*, May 17, 18, 1906; New York *Sun,* May 18, 1906.

5. McAneny, et al. to Carnegie, May 26, 1906, McAneny Papers, PU; *New York Times*, May 26, 1906.

6. *New York Times*, June 4, 7, 1906; *Die Glocke* (Chicago) 1 (1906), 146–48.

7. *Addresses in Memory of Carl Schurz,* passim.

8. Memorandum for Mr. Choate re Nov. 21, 1906; M. R. Corwine to McAneny, Feb. 2, 1909, McAneny Papers, PU; *New York Times*, Mar. 4, 1907; *The Carl Schurz Memorial,* HC; New York *Evening Post*, May 12, 1913.

9. McAneny to George D. Crimmins, Sept. 30, 1910, McAneny Papers, PU.

10. M. R. Corwine to McAneny, Feb. 2, 1909; McAneny to Isaac Seligman, April 1, 1912, Sept. 15, 1917; S. Ranger to McAneny, Mar. 25, 1914, McAneny Papers, PU; Postscript to Bancroft, Notes. Agathe Schurz approached many of her father's acquaintances for documents.

11. *New-Yorker Staats-Zeitung,* Mar. 30, 1927; George McAneny's Address, Carnegie Hall, Mar. 21, 1929, McAneny Papers, PU. The Dannehl and the Erkelenz and Mittelmann volumes are examples.

12. Fuess, *Schurz*, 38.

13. Schafer, *Schurz*, ix, 4; E. Hall to McAneny, June 8, 1929; Victor Ridder to McAneny, Nov. 27, 1929, McAneny Papers, PU. The Schafer biography is an example.

14. Eugene E. Doll, *Twenty-five Years of Service, 1930–1955* (Philadelphia: Carl Schurz Memorial Foundation, 1955); History of the Carl Schurz Memorial Foundation, Inc., documents in McAneny Papes, PU.

15. James Speyer to Wilbur K. Thomas, Sept. 9, Oct. 20, 30, 1933; Thomas to Speyer, Oct. 11, 1933; Speyer to Ferdinand Thun, Dec. 13, 1933, McAneny Papers, PU.

16. O. G. Villard to Hans Luther, Jan. 18, 1935, Villard Papers, HU; *New York Times*, Jan. 21, 1935.

17. At a celebration of the 10th anniversary of the founding of the Carl Schurz Vereinigung, the Nazi representatives assembled at Liblar said little about the man they were supposed to honor. *The Nation,* June 17, 1936.

Bibliography

MANUSCRIPT COLLECTIONS

Boston Public Library, Boston.
  Carl Schurz Papers.
Chicago Historical Society, Chicago.
  David Davis Papers.
  U.S. Grant Papers.
Columbia University, New York, N.Y.
  Frederick Bancroft Papers.
  Franziska Boas, Reminiscences, Oral History Collection.
  William H. Carpenter Papers.
  Hamilton Fish Papers.
  Sidney Howard Gay Papers.
  William Grosvenor Papers.
  Frederick William Hollis Papers.
  Seth Low Papers.
  George McAneny, Reminiscences, Oral History Collection.
  E.R.A. Seligman Papers.
  Edward M. Shepard Papers.
Library of Congress, Washington, D.C.
  Chester A. Arthur Papers.
  Thomas F. Bayard Papers.
  James G. Blaine Papers.
  Benjamin Helm Bristow Papers.
  Andrew Carnegie Papers.
  William E. Chandler Papers.
  Samuel P. Chase Papers.
  Grover Cleveland Papers.
  John Chandler Bancroft Davis Papers.
  Hamilton Fish Papers.
  James A. Garfield Papers.
  U.S. Grant Papers.
  Horace Greeley Papers.
  Walter A. Gresham Papers.
  Andrew Johnson Papers.
  Friedrich Lieber Papers.
  Abraham Lincoln Papers.
  William McKinley Papers.
  Carl Schurz Papers.
  Lyman Trumbull Papers.
  Elihu Washburne Papers.
Cornell University, Ithaca, N.Y.
  Goldwin Smith Papers.
Friedrich Wilhelm Universität Archives, Bonn, Germany.

Baron Bernard Friesen Papers (private), Pembroke, Wales.
Houghton Library, Harvard University, Cambridge.
    Francis W. Bird Papers.
    John Jay Chapman Papers.
    William Warland Clapp Papers.
    Frederick M. Dearborn Collection.
    E. L. Godkin Papers.
    Thomas Wentworth Higginson Papers.
    William Dean Howells Papers.
    Charles Sumner Papers.
Rutherford B. Hayes Library, Fremont, Ohio.
    William Clafflin Papers.
    Rutherford B. Hayes Papers.
Arthur Reed Hogue Collection (private), Bloomington, Ind.
Henry E. Huntington Library, San Marino, Cal.
    James W. Eldridge Papers.
    Friedrich Lieber Papers.
Massachusetts Historical Society, Boston.
    Adams Family Papers.
    George Bancroft Papers.
    William C. Endicott Papers.
    G. F. Hoar Papers.
    John D. Long Papers.
    George L. Stearns Papers.
Ministerio de Asuntos Exteriores, Madrid, Spain.
    Archives
State Historical Society of Missouri, Columbia.
    W. H. McLane Papers.
    James S. Rollins Papers.
    Chauncey I. Filley Papers.
    Carl Schurz Papers.
Cissa Morlang Collection (private), Hamburg, Germany.
University of Münster.
    Schurz-Chapman Correspondence.
National Archives, Washington, D.C.
    Department of State, Diplomatic Despatches, Despatches from United States Ministers
        to Spain, 43.
    Department of State, Diplomatic Instructions, Spain, 15.
    Department of State, Notes from the Spanish Legation in the United States to the
        Department of State, 1790–1906, 16A.
    War Department, Record Group 54, Generals' Papers.
    War Department, Record Group 94, Records of the Adjutant General's Office.
    War Department, Record Group 393. Records of the United States Army Continental
        Command.
Newberry Library, Chicago.
    Hermann Raster Papers.
New Hampshire Historical Society, Concord, N.H.
    Jacob Gallinger Papers.
New-York Historical Society, New York.
    James Wright Brown Collection.
    Silas W. Burt Papers.

Franz Sigel Papers.
New York Public Library, New York.
  Bryant-Godwin Collection.
  Horace Greeley Papers.
  Edward Ordway Papers.
  Carl Schurz Papers.
New York State Library, Albany.
  E. D. Morgan Papers.
Ohio Historical Society, Columbus.
  William Henry Smith Papers.
Historical Society of Pennsylvania.
  Samuel P. Chase Papers.
Princeton University, Princeton, N.J.
  André de Coppet Collection.
  George McAneny Papers, Seeley G. Mudd Manuscript Library.
  Bernard K. Schaefer Civil War Collection.
Radcliffe College, Cambridge, Mass.
  Putnam Family Papers.
Watertown Historical Society, Watertown, Wis.
  Carl Schurz Papers.
Western Reserve Historical Society, Cleveland, Ohio.
  Franz Sigel Papers.
State Historical Society of Wisconsin, Madison.
  F. A. Anneke Papers.
  William H. Brisbane Papers.
  Moses M. Davis Papers.
  Timothy O. Howe Papers.
  James F. Potter Papers.
  Carl Schurz Papers.
  Horace A. Tenney Papers.
University of Wisconsin, Milwaukee.
  Frederick C. Winkler Papers.
Yale University, New Haven, Conn.
  Samuel Bowles Papers.
  Richard Henry Pratt Papers.

PUBLISHED WRITINGS BY CARL SCHURZ CITED IN THIS BOOK

Mowry, Duane. "Letters of Carl Schurz, B. Gratz Brown, James S. Rollins, G. G. West et
  al., Missourians, from the Private Papers and Correspondence of Senator James Rood
  Doolittle of Wisconsin." *Missouri Historical Review* 11 (1916), 1–20.
Schurz, Carl. "Abraham Lincoln." *Atlantic Monthly* 67 (June 1891), 721–50.
———. *An Address, Delivered Before the Archean Society of Beloit College, At Its
  Anniversary, July 13, 1858.* Beloit: E. B. Hale, 1858.
———. "Can the South Solve the Negro Problem?" *McClure's Magazine* 22 (Jan. 1904),
  258–75.
———. *Charles Sumner,* ed. Arthur R. Hogue. Urbana: Univ. of Illinois Press, 1951.
———. *"For the Great Empire of Liberty, Forward!", Speech of Maj.-Gen. Carl
  Schurz, of Wisconsin, Delivered at Concert Hall, Philadelphia . . . .* New York: Gray
  & Green, 1864.

————. "Grover Cleveland's Second Administration." *McClure's Magazine* 10 (May 1897), 633–44.

————. *Henry Clay.* 2 vols. Boston: Houghton Mifflin, 1887.

————. *Intimate Letters of Carl Schurz, 1841–1869,* ed. and trans. Joseph Schafer. Madison: State Historical Society of Wisconsin, 1928.

————. *Lebenserinnerungen.* 3 vols. Berlin: Georg Reimer, 1906–12.

————. "Party Schisms and Future Problems." *North American Review* 306 (May 1882), 431–55.

————. *The Reminiscences of Carl Schurz.* 3 vols. New York: McClure, 1907–8. Vol. III includes *With A Sketch of His Life and Public Services* by Frederic Bancroft and William A. Dunning.

————. *Report on the Condition of the South.* H. Report No. 11, 39th Cong. 1st sess., Dec. 18, 1865. Reprint: New York: Arno, 1969.

————. *Speeches, Correspondence and Political Papers of Carl Schurz,* ed. Frederic Bancroft. 3 vols. New York: Putnam, 1913.

————. *Speeches of Carl Schurz.* Philadelphia: Lippincott, 1865.

————. *Der Studenkenkongress zu Eisenach am 25. September 1848, seine Bedeutung und Resultate.* Bonn: W. Salzbach, 1848.

————. "The Surrender of Rastatt," trans. Joseph Schafer. *Wisconsin Magazine of History* 12 (March 1929), 239–70.

NEWSPAPERS AND PERIODICALS

Baltimore *Der Deutsche Correspondent.*
Bonner Zeitung and *Neue Bonner Zeitung.*
Boston *Journal.*
Brooklyn *Eagle.*
Chicago *Inter-Ocean.*
Chicago *Record.*
Chicago *Tribune.*
Cincinnati *Commercial.*
Cincinnati *Gazette.*
Cincinnati *Volksfreund.*
Detroit Post.
Frank Leslie's Illustrated Newspaper.
Die Glocke (Chicago).
Harper's Weekly.
The Independent (New York).
Madison *Wisconsin Daily State Journal.*
Milwaukee *Atlas.*
Milwaukee *Banner & Volksfreund.*
Milwaukee *Daily Sentinel.*
The Nation (New York).
Die Neue Zeit (New York).
New York *Herald.*
New York Times.
New York *Tribune.*
New York *Evening Post.*
New York *World.*
New-Yorker Bellatristisches Journal.

New-Yorker Demokrat.
New-Yorker Staats-Zeitung.
Philadelphia Daily Ledger.
Der Pionier (Boston).
St. Louis Missouri Democrat.
St. Louis, Missouri, Republican.
St. Louis, Missouri, Westliche Post.
Springfield Republican.
Washington, Missouri, Washingtoner Post.
Watertown Democrat.
Watertown Weltbürger.

GOVERNMENT DOCUMENTS

Congressional Globe.
Congressional Record.
Davis Hatch Claim. Sen. Reports No. 234, 41st Cong., 2 sess.
Department of the Interior. Annual Report of the Secretary of the Interior. 1877–1881.
Department of the Interior. Report of the Board of Inquiry to Investigate Certain Charges
    Against S.A. Gilpin. Washington, D.C.: Government Printing Office, 1878.
Letter from the Secretary of the Interior, Communicating in compliance with a resolution of
    the Senate of December 8, 1879, information in relation to the number of mining camps
    located on the Ute Indian Reservation in Colorado. Sen. Ex. Doc. No. 29, 46th Cong.,
    2d sess., Feb. 28, 1881.
Letter from the Secretary of the Interior Transmitting in Compliance with a resolution of the
    Senate of December 8, 1879, correspondence concerning the Ute Indians in Colorado.
    Sen. Ex. Doc. No. 31, 46th Cong., 2d sess., Jan. 6, 1880.
Report of the Joint Committee Appointed to Consider the Expediency of the Transfer of
    Indian Bureau to the War Department. H. Report No. 93, 45th Cong., 3d sess., Jan. 31,
    1879.
Report of the Joint Committee on the Conduct of the War. S. Report No. 142, 38th Cong.,
    2d sess. 3 vols.
Report of the Joint Committee on Reconstruction. H. Report No. 30, 39th Cong., 1st sess.,
    1866.
Sale of Arms By Ordnance Department. S. Report No. 183, 42d Cong., 2d sess., May 11,
    1872.
Testimony Before the Select Committee on Removal of Northern Cheyennes as to the
    Removal and Situation of the Ponca Indians. Sen. Misc. Doc. No. 49, 46th Cong., 3d
    sess., Feb. 28, 1881.
The War of the Rebellion: . . . Official Records of the Union and Confederate Armies.
    Washington: Government Printing Office, 1880–1901. 128 vols.
Wisconsin. Journal of the Assembly of Wisconsin, 1861. Madison: E. A. Calkins, 1861.

OTHER WORKS

Adams, Charles Francis. Charles Francis Adams, 1835–1915: An Autobiography. Bos-
    ton: Houghton Mifflin, 1916.
Adams, Henry. See Ford, Worthington Chauncey.
Adams, Mrs. Henry. See Thoron, Ward.

Addresses in Memory of Carl Schurz, Carnegie Hall, New York, November 21, 1906. New York: Committee of the Carl Schurz Memorial, 1906.

Alterman, Hyman. *Counting People: The Census in History.* New York: Harcourt, Brace, 1969.

Althaus, Friedrich. "Beiträge zur Geschichte der deutschen Colonie in England." *Unsere Zeit* 9 (1873), 225–45.

———. "Erinnerungen an Gottfried Kinkel." *Nord und Süd* 24 (Feb. 1883), 227–356; 25 (Apr. 1883), 55–204.

Ames, Blanche Butler, ed. *Chronicles from the Nineteenth Century: Family Letters of Blanche Butler and Adelbert Ames.* Clinton, Mass.: Colonial Press, 1957.

Andrews, J. Cutler. *The North Reports the Civil War.* Pittsburgh: Pittsburgh Univ. Press, 1955.

Applegate, John S. ed. *Reminiscences and Letters of George Arrowsmith of New Jersey, Late Lt. Col. of the 157 Regiment, New York State Volunteers.* Red Bank, N.J.: John H. Cooke, 1893.

Armstrong, William M. *E. L. Godkin: A Biography.* Albany: State Univ. of New York Press, 1978.

———. "The Godkin-Schurz Feud, 1881–83, Over Policy Control of the *Evening Post.*" *New-York Historical Society Quarterly* 48 (Jan. 1964), 5–30.

Arnim, Bettina von. *See* Oehlke, Waldemar.

Arrowsmith, George. *See* Applegate, John S.

Assing, Ludmilla, ed. *Aus dem Nachlass Varnhagen's von Enses Tagebücher.* 14 vols. Leipzig: F. A. Brockhaus, 1861–70.

Athearn, Robert G., ed. "Major Hough's March into Southern Ute Country, 1879." *Colorado Magazine* 25 (May 1948), 97–109.

Bancroft, Frederic, and Dunning, William A. *See* Schurz, Carl, *Reminiscences.*

Banning, Evelyn I. *Helen Hunt Jackson.* New York: Vanguard, 1973.

Barclay, Thomas S. *The Liberal Republican Movement in Missouri, 1865–1871.* Columbia, Mo.: State Historical Society of Missouri, 1926.

Barlow, A. R. *Company G: A Record of the Services of One Company of the 157th New York Vols. in the War of the Rebellion . . . .* Syracuse: A. W. Hall, 1899.

Barnard, Harry. *Rutherford B. Hayes and His America.* Indianapolis: Bobbs-Merrill, 1954.

Barrett, James Wyman. *Joseph Pulitzer and his World.* New York: Vanguard, 1941.

Barrows, Chester Leonard. *William M. Evarts: Lawyer, Diplomat, Statesman.* Chapel Hill: Univ. of North Carolina Press, 1941.

Basler, Roy P., ed. *The Collected Works of Abraham Lincoln.* 9 vols. New Brunswick, N.J.: Rutgers Univ. Press, 1953.

Bates, Samuel P. *The Battle of Chancellorsville.* Meadville, Pa.: E. T. Bates, 1882.

Bauchle, Mary L. "The Shopiere Shrine." *Wisconsin Magazine of History* 10 (Sept. 1926), 29–34.

Baumgardt, Rudolf. *Carl Schurz: Ein Leben zwischen Zeiten und Kontinenten.* Berlin: Wilhelm Andermann, 1940.

Beale, Howard K., ed. *Diary of Gideon Welles.* 3 vols. New York: Norton, 1960.

Beisner, Robert L. *Twelve Against Empire: The Anti-Imperialists, 1898–1900.* New York: McGraw-Hill, 1968.

Benedict, Michael Les. "Southern Democrats and the Crisis of 1876–1877: A Reconsideration of *Reunion and Reaction.*" *JSH* 46 (Nov. 1980), 489–524.

Bezold, Friedrich von. *Geschichte der Rheinischen Friedrich-Wilhelms Universität von der Gründung bis zum Jahr 1870.* Bonn: A. Marcus & E. Webers, 1920.

Bigelow, John. *The Campaign of Chancellorsville.* New Haven: Yale Univ. Press, 1910.

————, ed. *Letters and Literary Memorials of Samuel J. Tilden*. 2 vols. New York: Harper, 1908.

Bischoff, Charitas. *Amalie Dietrich: Ein Leben erzählt von Charitas Bischoff*. Berlin: G. Grote, 1911.

Bismarck, Otto von. *Die Gesammelten Werke*. 19 vols. Berlin: Otto Stolberg, 1925–35.

Blaine, James G. *Twenty Years of Congress*. 2 vols. Norwich, Conn.: Henry Bill, 1884.

Blumenfeld, Ralph D. *Home Town*. London: Hutchinson, 1944.

Blumenthal, Henry. *France and the United States: Their Diplomatic Relations, 1789–1914*. Chapel Hill: Univ. of North Carolina Press, 1970.

Bollert, M. "Ein Brief von Karl Schurz aus dem Jahre 1850." *Preussische Jahrbücher* 151 (Jan.–Mar. 1913), 33–42.

Bollert, Martin. *Gottfried Kinkels Kämpfe um Beruf und Weltanschauung bis zur Revolution. Studien zur Rheinischen Geschichte*, pt. 10. Bonn, 1913.

————. "Kinkel vor dem Kriegsgericht." *Preussische Jahrbücher* 155 (1914), 488–512.

Bolton, Sarah T. *The Life and Poems of Sarah T. Bolton*. Indianapolis: Fred A. Horton, 1880.

Börnstein, Hermann. *Fünfundzwanzig Jahre in der alten und der neuen Welt*. Leipzig: O. Wiegand, 1884.

Bose, Georg von. *Karl Schurz: Deutschlands beste Gabe an Amerika*. Vol. 33, pt. 1, *Zeitfragen des christlichen Volkslebens*. Stuttgart: Christian Belser, 1908.

Bourke, John G. *On the Border with Crook*. New York: Scribner's 1891.

Braubach, Max. *Bonner Professoren und Studenten in den Revolutionsjahren 1848/49*. Wissenschaftliche Abhandlungen der Arbeitsgemeinschaft für Forschung des Landes Nordrhein-Westfalen, vol. 38. Cologne: Westdeutscher Verlag, 1967.

Brauer, Kinley J. "The Appointment of Carl Schurz as Minister to Spain." *Mid-America* 56 (Apr. 1974), 75–84.

Brinkerhoff, Roeliff. *Recollections of a Lifetime*. Cincinnati: Robert Clarke, 1900.

Brock, W. R. *An American Crisis: Congress and Reconstruction, 1865–1867*. New York: Harper, 1966.

Brown, Dee. *Bury My Heart at Wounded Knee: An Indian History of the American West*. New York: Holt, Rinehart & Winston, 1970.

————. *The Year of the Century: 1876*. New York: Scribner's, 1966.

Brown, Harry James, and Williams, Frederick D., eds. *The Diary of James A. Garfield*. 3 vols. Ann Arbor: Michigan State Univ. Press, 1967–73.

Bruiningk, Hermann Baron. *Das Geschlecht von Bruiningk in Livland*. Riga: N. Kymmels, 1913.

Bruncken, Ernest. "German Political Refugees in the United States During the Period from 1815–1860." *Deutsch-Amerikanische Geschichtsblätter* 3 (1903), 33–48; 4 (1904), 33–59.

————. "The Political Activity of Wisconsin Germans, 1854–1860." *Proceedings of the State Historical Society of Wisconsin . . . December 12, 1901 . . . .* Madison: Democrat Printing Co., 1902.

Buel, Clarence, and Johnson, Robert, eds. *Battles and Leaders of the Civil War. 4 vols*. New York: Yoseloff, 1956.

Burlingame, Michael Ashton. "The Early Life of Carl Schurz." Ph.D. diss. Johns Hopkins Univ., 1971.

Busse, Adolf. "Briefe Gottfried Kinkels an Karl Schurz," in Paul Wantzke, ed., *Quellen und Darstellungen zur Geschichte der Burschenschaft und der deutschen Einheitsbewegung*, XIV, 247–67. Berlin: Verlag der deutschen Burschenschaft, 1934.

Carman, Harry J., and Luthin, Reinhard H. *Lincoln and the Patronage*. New York: Columbia Univ. Press, 1943.

Carpenter, John A. *Sword and Olive Branch: Oliver Otis Howard*. Pittsburgh: Univ. of Pittsburgh Press, 1964.

Cater, Harold Dean, comp. *Henry Adams and His Friends: A Collection of His Unpublished Letters*. Boston: Houghton Mifflin, 1947.

Catton, Bruce. *Centennial History of the Civil War*. 3 vols. Garden City, N.Y.: Doubleday, 1961–65.

Chambers, Lenoir. *Stonewall Jackson*. 2 vols. New York: Morrow, 1959.

Chambrun, Marquis Adolphe de. *Impressions of Lincoln and the Civil War: A Foreigner's Account*. New York: Random, 1952.

Chapman, Daniel T. "The Great White Father's Little Red Indian School." *American Heritage* 22 (Dec. 1970), 48–53, 103.

The Charges of 1872 Against Carl Schurz. Pamphlet, n.d., n.p. (copy in NYPL).

Chase, Salmon P. *See* Donald, David.

Chidsey, Donald Barr. *The Gentleman from New York: A Life of Roscoe Conkling*. New Haven: Yale Univ. Press, 1935.

Clay, Casiuss Marcellus. *The Life of Cassius Marcellus Clay: Memoirs, Writings and Speeches*. New York: Negro Universities Press, 1969.

Cochran, William C. "'Dear Mother . . .' An Eyewitness Report on the National Republican Convention of 1876." *Hayes Historical Journal* 1 (Fall, 1976), 89-97.

Cochran, William Cox. "Political Experiences of Major General Jacob Dolson Cox" (privately distributed typescript). Cincinnati, 1940.

Coddington, Edwin B. *The Gettysburg Campaign: A Study in Command*. New York: Scribner's, 1968.

Coletta, Paolo. *William Jennings Bryan*. 3 vols. Lincoln: Univ. of Nebraska, Press, 1964–69.

Conzen, Kathleen Neils. *Immigrant Milwaukee, 1836–1860: Accommodation and Community in a Frontier City*. Cambridge, Mass.: Harvard Univ. Press, 1976.

Cooke, Sidney J. "The First Day of Gettysburg." *War Talks in Kansas: Military Order of the Loyal Legion of the United States*. Kansas Commandery. Kansas City: Franklin Hudson, 1906.

Cortissoz, Royal. *The Life of Whitelaw Reid*. 2 vols. New York: Scribner's, 1921.

Corvin, Otto. *A Life of Adventure*. 3 vols. London: Richard Bentley, 1871.

Cox, Jacob Dolson. *Military Reminiscences of the Civil War*. 2 vols. New York: Scribner's, 1900.

Cox, LaWanda, and John H. *Politics, Principle, and Prejudice, 1865–1866: Dilemma of Reconstruction America*. New York: Free Press of Glencoe, 1963.

Cox, Samuel S. *Three Decades of Federal Legislation, 1855 to 1885*. Providence, R.I.: Reid, 1885.

Cronau, Rudolf. *Drei Jahrhunderte deutschen Lebens in Amerika: Eine Geschichte der Deutschen in den Vereinigten Staaten*. Berlin: Dietrich Reimer, 1909.

Crook, William H. *See* Gerry, Marguerita Spalding.

Current, Richard N. *The History of Wisconsin: Vol. II: The Civil War Era, 1848–1873*. Madison: State Historical Society of Wisconsin, 1976.

———. *Lincoln and the First Shot*. Philadelphia: Lippincott, 1963.

Curry, Richard O., ed. *Radicalism, Racism, and Party Alignment: The Border States during Reconstruction*. Baltimore: Johns Hopkins Univ. Press, 1969.

Dahlinger, Charles W. *The German Revolution of 1849*. New York: Putnam's, 1903.

Dannehl, Otto. *Carl Schurz: Ein deutscher Kämpfer*. Berlin: Walter de Gruyter, 1929.

Davis, Allen F. *American Heroine: The Life and Legend of Jane Addams*. New York: Oxford Univ. Press, 1977.

Davison, Kenneth. *The Presidency of Rutherford B. Hayes*. Westport, Conn.: Greenwood, 1972.

Dennett, Tyler, ed. *Lincoln and the Civil War in the Diaries and Letters of John Hay*. New York: Dodd, Mead, 1939.

De Santis, Vincent P. "President Hayes' Southern Policy." *Journal of Southern History* 21 (Nov. 1955), 476–94.

————. *Republicans Face the Southern Question: The New Departure Years, 1877–1897*. Baltimore: Johns Hopkins Univ. Press, 1959.

Detroit Post Tribune. *Zachariah Chandler: An Outline Sketch of His Life and Public Services*. Detroit: Detroit Post Tribune, 1880.

Dobson, John M. *Politics in the Gilded Age: A New Perspective on Reform*. New York: Praeger, 1972.

Dodge, Theodore A. *The Campaign of Chancellorsville*. Boston: Osgood, 1881.

Dodd, William E. "The Fight for the Northwest, 1860." *AHR* 16 (1911), 774–88.

Doll, Eugene E. *Twenty-five Years of Service, 1930–1955*. Philadelphia: Carl Schurz Memorial Foundation, 1955.

Donald, David. *Charles Sumner and the Rights of Man*. New York: Knopf, 1970.

————, ed. *Inside Lincoln's Cabinet: The Civil War Diaries of Salmon P. Chase*. New York: Longmans, Green, 1954.

Donner, Barbara. "Carl Schurz as Office Speeker." *Wisconsin Magazine of History* 20 (Dec. 1936), 127–43.

————. "Carl Schurz, the Diplomat." *Wisconsin Magazine of History* 20 (March 1937), 291–309.

Dorpalen, Andreas. "The German Element and the Issues of the Civil War." *MVHR*, 29 (June 1942), 55–76.

Dos Passos, John R. *A Defence of the McKinley Administration From Attacks of Mr. Carl Schurz and Other Anti-Imperialists*. Pamphlet, n.d., n.p. (copy in NYPL).

Doubleday, Abner. *Chancellorsville and Gettysburg*. New York: Scribner's, 1882.

Downey, Fairfax. *The Guns at Gettysburg*. New York: McKay, 1958.

Downey, Matthew T. "Horace Greeley and the Politicians: The Liberal Republican Convention in 1872." *JAH* 53 (Mar. 1867), 727–50.

Duberman, Martin B. *Charles Francis Adams, 1807–1886*. Boston: Houghton Mifflin, 1961.

Dunbar, Willis Frederick. *Michigan: A History of the Wolverine State*. Grand Rapids, Mich.: Ardmans, 1965.

Duncan, Bingham. *Whitelaw Reid: Journalist, Politician, Diplomat*. Athens: Univ. of Georgia Press, 1975.

DuPont, Samuel Francis. *See* Hayes, John D.

Easum, Chester V. *The Americanization of Carl Schurz*. Chicago: Univ. of Chicago Press, 1929.

————. "Carl Schurz at Watertown." *American-German Review* 14 (June 1948), 34–35, 44.

Emery, Charles Wilson. "The Iowa Germans in the Election of 1860." *Annals of Iowa* 22 (Oct. 1940), 421–54.

Enders, Carl. *Gottfried Kinkel im Kreise seiner Kölner Jugendfreunde*. Studien zur Rheinischen Geschichte, vol. 9. Bonn: A. Marcus & E. Weber, 1913.

Erkelenz, Anton, and Mittelmann, Fritz, eds. *Carl Schurz, der Deutsche und Amerikaner*. Berlin: Sieben Stäbe, 1929.

Ernst von Ernsthausen, A. *Erinnerungen eines preussischen Beamten*. Bielefeld: Velhagen & Klassing, 1894.

Eyck, Frank. *The Frankfurt Parliament, 1848–1849*. London: Macmillan, 1968.

Faulkner, Harold U. *Politics, Reform and Expansion, 1890–1910*. New York: Harper, 1959.

Faust, Albert Bernhardt. *The German Element in the United States*. 2 vols. Boston: Houghton Mifflin, 1909.

Feder, Ernst, ed. *Bismarcks grosses Spiel: Die geheimen Tagebücher Ludwig Bambergers*. Frankfurt: Societätsverlag, 1932.

Fehrenbacher, Don E. *Chicago Giant: A Biography of Long John Wentworth*. Madison, Wis.: American History Research Center, 1957.

Fenner von Fenneberg, Ferdinand. *Zur Geschichte der rheinpfälzischen Revolution*. Zurich: Kiesling, 1849.

Fester, Richard. "Bismarcks Gespräch mit Karl Schurz am 28. Januar 1868." *Süddeutsche Monatschefte* 11, no. I, 363–68.

Filler, Louis, ed. *Democrats and Republicans*, by Thurston Peck. New York: Capricorn, 1964.

Fish, Carl Russell. "Carl Schurz—the American." *Wisconsin Magazine of History* 12 (June 1929), 345–58.

Fitch, Michael Hendrick. *The Chattanooga Campaign . . . .* Madison: Wisconsin Historical Commission, 1911.

Follen, Mrs. E. L. *The Peddler of Dust Sticks*. Boston: Whittemore, Niles & Hall, 1856.

Foner, Philip S. *The Life and Writings of Frederick Douglass*. 4 vols. New York: International, 1955.

Foote, Shelby. *The Civil War: A Narrative*. 3 vols. New York: Random, 1958–74.

Foraker, Joseph Benson. *Notes of a Busy Life*. 2 vols. Cincinnati: Stewart & Kidd, 1917.

Ford, Worthington Chauncey, ed. *Letters of Henry Adams*. London: Constable, 1930.

Förderer, Albert. *Erinnerungen an Rastatt 1849*. Lahr: Chr. Schömperlen, 1899.

Foster, John W. *Diplomatic Memoirs*. 2 vols. Boston: Houghton Mifflin, 1909.

Foulke, William Dudley. *A Hoosier Autobiography*. New York: Oxford Univ. Press, 1922.

———. *Fighting the Spoilsmen: Reminiscences of the Civil Service Reform Movement*. New York: Putnam's, 1919.

Frank, Louis F., and Anderson, Harry H. *German-American Pioneers in Wisconsin and Michigan: The Frank-Kerler Letters, 1849–64*. Milwaukee: Milwaukee City Historical Society, 1971.

Franklin, John Hope. *The Emancipation Proclamation*. Garden City, N.Y.: Doubleday, 1963.

Friedel, Frank. *Francis Lieber: 19th Century Liberal*. Baton Rouge: Louisiana State Univ. Press, 1947.

Fritz, Henry E. *The Movement for Indian Assimilation, 1860–1890*. Philadelphia: Univ. of Pennsylvania Press, 1963.

Fuess, Claude Moore. "Carl Schurz, Henry Cabot Lodge, and the Campaign of 1884: A Study in Temperament and Political Philosophy." *New England Quarterly* 5 (July 1932), 453–82.

———. *Carl Schurz, Reformer (1829–1906)*. New York: Dodd, Mead, 1932.

Garfield, James A. *See* Brown, Harry James.

Garraty, John A. *Henry Cabot Lodge: A Biography*. New York: Knopf, 1953.

Gazley, John Gerow. *American Opinion of German Unification*. New York: Columbia Univ. Press, 1926.

Gemmil, Helen H. "Elizabeth Lawrence: Dr. Mercer's 'Auntie Mame'". *Bucks County Historical Journal* 2 (Spring 1978), 63–89.

George, Mary Karl. *Zachariah Chandler: A Political Biography*. East Lansing: Michigan State Univ. Press, 1969.

Gerber, Richard Allen. "The Liberal Republicans of 1872 in Historiographical Perspective." *JAH* 62 (June 1975), 40–73.

Gerry, Marguerita Spalding, ed. *Through Five Administrations: Reminiscences of Colonel William H. Crook, Body-Guard to President Lincoln.* New York: Harper, 1910.

Gillette, William. *The Election of 1872,* in Arthur M. Schlesinger, Jr., and Fred L. Israel, eds., *History of American Presidential Elections, 1789–1968.* New York: Chelsea House, 1971. Vol. II, 1303–30.

Glazer, Nathan, and Moynihan, Daniel Patrick. *Beyond the Melting Pot: The Negroes, Puerto Ricans, Jews, Italians, and Irish of New York City.* Cambridge, Mass.: MIT Press, 1963.

Goebel, Julius. "Karl Schurz als Deutsch-Amerikaner. Auf Grund Persönlicher Erinnerungen." *Deutsch-Amerikanische Geschichtsblätter* 29 (1929), 102–32.

Goslich, Marie. "Briefe an Johanna Kinkel." *Preussische Jahrbücher* 97 (July–Sept. 1899), 430.

Greeley, Horace. *The American Conflict . . . .* 2 vols. Hartford: O. D. Case, 1866.

Gresham, Mathilda. *Life of Walter Quintin Gresham, 1832–1895.* Chicago: Rand-McNally, 1919.

Gunderson, Robert Grey. *Old Gentlemen's Convention: The Washington Peace Conference of 1861.* Madison: Univ. of Wisconsin Press, 1961.

Halstead, Murat. *National Political Conventions of the Current Presidential Campaign.* Columbus, Ohio: Follett, Foster, 1860.

Hamlin, Augustus Choate. *The Battle of Chancellorsville . . . .* Bangor, Me: privately printed, 1896.

Hamlin, Charles Eugene. *The Life and Times of Hannibal Hamlin.* Cambridge, Mass: Riverside Press, 1899.

Harlan, Louis, et al., eds. *The Booker T. Washington Papers.* Urbana: Univ. of Illinois Press, 1972–.

Harris, William C. *Presidential Reconstruction in Mississippi.* Baton Rouge: Louisiana State Univ. Press, 1967.

Hartman, William. "Pioneer in Civil Service Reform: Silas W. Burt and the New York Custom House." *New-York Historical Society Quarterly* 39 (Oct. 1955), 369–79.

Hawgood, John A. *The Tragedy of German-America: The Germans in the United States of America during the Nineteenth Century—and After.* New York: Putnam's, 1940.

Hawkins, Brett W., and Lorinskas, Robert A., eds. *The Ethnic Factor in American Politics.* Columbus, Ohio: Merrill, 1970.

Hayes, John D., ed. *Samuel Francis DuPont: A Selection From His Civil War Letters.* 3 vols. Ithaca, N.Y.: Cornell Univ. Press, 1969.

Hayes, Rutherford B. *See* Williams, Charles Richard.

Hayes, Webb C., and Marchman, Watt P., eds. "The First Days of the Hayes Administration: Inauguration to Easter Sunday, 1877." *Hayes Historical Journal* 1 (1977), 231–62.

Hay, John. *See* Dennett, Tyler.

Hayter, Earl W. "The Ponca Removal." *North Dakota Historical Quarterly* 6 (July 1932), 262–75.

Hebert, Walter H. *Fighting Joe Hooker.* Indianapolis: Bobbs-Merrill, 1944.

Heer, Georg. *Geschichte der deutschen Burschenschaft.* Vol. III of *Quellen und Dokumente zur Geschichte der Burschenschaft und der deutschen Einheitsbewegung.* 11 vols. Heidelberg: Carl Winters, 1929.

Heinzen, Karl. *Der teutsche Editoren-Kongress zu Cincinnati, oder das gebrochene Herz.* Boston: privately printed, 1872.

Hense-Jensen, Wilhelm. *Wisconsin's Deutsch-Amerikaner bis zum Schluss des neunzehnten Jahrhunderts.* 2 vols. Milwaukee: Verlag der Deutschen Gesellschaft, 1900–1902.

Herriott, F.I. "The Conference at the Deutsches Haus, Chicago, May 14–15, 1860." *Transactions of the Illinois State Historical Society for the Year 1928*. Springfield, Ill.: Phillips Bros., 1928.

Herzen, Alexander. *My Past and Thoughts: The Memoirs of Alexander Herzen*. New York: Knopf, 1968.

Hesseltine, William B. *Ulysses S. Grant, Politician*. New York: Dodd, Mead, 1935.

Heynen, Walter. "Kinkels Flucht: Eine Schurz Nachlese auf Grund der Akten." *Preussische Jahrbücher* 236 (Apr.–June 1934), 162–76.

Higham, John, ed. *Ethnic Leadership in America*. Baltimore: Johns Hopkins Univ. Press, 1978.

———. *Send These To Me: Jews and Other Immigrants in Urban America*. New York: Atheneum, 1975.

Hinsdale, Mary L., ed. *Garfield-Hinsdale Letters: Correspondence Between James Abram Garfield and Burke Aaron Hinsdale*. Ann Arbor: Univ. of Michigan Press, 1949.

Hoar, George F. *Autobiography of Seventy Years*. 2 vols. New York: Scribner's, 1903.

Hogue, Arthur R. "An Unpublished Mazzini Letter." *JMH* 38 (Sept. 1956), 266–69.

———. "Carl Schurz in the Light of New-Found Papers." Paper Read at the April 1949 meeting of the Mississippi Valley Historical Association at Madison, Wisc.

———. "Civil Service Reform, 1869." *American-German Review* 18 (June 1952), 5–8, 39.

Holt, W. Stull. *The Bureau of the Census: Its History, Activities and Organization*. Washington, D.C. Brookings Institution, 1929.

Hoogenboom, Ari. *Outlawing the Spoils: A History of the Civil Service Reform Movement, 1865–1883*. Urbana: Univ. of Illinois Press, 1968.

Horner, Harlan Hoyt. "Lincoln Scolds a General." *Wisconsin Magazine of History* 36 (Winter 1952–53), 90–96, 143–46.

Höroldt, Dietrich. *Stadt und Universität: Rückblick aus Anlass der 150-Jahr-Feier der Universität Bonn*. Bonn: Ludwig Röhrscheid, 1969.

Howard, James H. *The Ponca Tribe*. Bureau of American Ethnology Bulletin No. 195, Smithsonian Institution. Washington, D.C.: Government Printing Office, 1965.

Howard, Oliver Otis. *Autobiography of Oliver Otis Howard*. 2 vols. New York. Baker & Taylor, 1907.

Howe, George Frederick. "President Hayes's Notes of Four Cabinet Meetings." *American Historical Review* 37 (Jan. 1932), 286–89.

Howe, M.A. DeWolfe. *The Life and Letters of George Bancroft*. 3 vols. New York: Scribner's, 1908.

———. *Moorfield Storey: Portrait of an Independent, 1845–1929*. Boston: Houghton Mifflin, 1932.

Höwing, Hanns. *Carl Schurz: Rebell—Kämpfer—Staatsmann: Nach seinen Briefen, Erinnerungen und Veröffentlichungen*. Wiesbaden: Limes, 1948.

Hüffer, Hermann. *Lebenserinnerungen*. Berlin: Georg Reimer, 1912.

Hugo, Victor. *The Rhine*. London: Aird, 1843.

Humphreys, Sexson E. "United States Recognition of the Kingdom of Italy." *Historian* 21 (May 1959), 296–312.

Hunt, Frederick Knight. *The Rhine: Its Scenery and Historical & Legendary Associations*. London: Jeremiah How, 1845.

Jackson, Helen Hunt. *A Century of Dishonor: A Sketch of the United States Government's Dealings with Some of the Indian Tribes*. New York: Harper, 1881.

Jessup, Philip C. *Elihu Root*. 2 vols. New York: Archon, 1964.

Johannsen, Robert W. *Stephen A. Douglas*. New York: Oxford Univ. Press, 1973.

Johns, George S. "Joseph Pulitzer." *Missouri Historical Review* 26 (Jan. 1931), 200–18.

Johnson, Hildegard Binder. "Carl Schurz and Conservation." *American-German Review* 23 (Feb.–Mar. 1957), 4–8.

———. "The Election of 1860 and the Germans in Minnesota." *Minnesota History* 28 (Mar. 1947), 20–36.

Jordan, David. *Roscoe Conkling of New York: Voice in the Senate*. Ithaca, N.Y.: Cornell Univ. Press, 1971.

Julian, George W. *Political Recollections*. Chicago: Jansen, McClurg, 1884.

Jüssen, Marie. "Carl Schurz." *Deutsche Rundschau* 98 (1899), 386–99.

Kaiser, Hans. *Carl Schurz*, in Hermann Haupt and Paul Wentzke, eds. *Hundert Jahre Deutscher Burschenschaft*, vol. VII, 180–91 of *Quellen und Darstellungen zur Geschichte der Burschenschaft und der deutschen Einheitsbewegung*. Heidelberg: Carl Winters, 1921.

Kaiser, Renate. *Die politischen Strömungen in den Kreisen Bonn und Rheinbach, 1848–1849*. Bonn: Ludwig Röhr, 1963.

Katz, Irving. *August Belmont: A Political Biography*. New York: Columbia Univ. Press, 1968.

Kaufmann, Paul. "Johanna Kinkel: Neue Beiträge zu ihrem Lebensbild." *Preussische Jahrbücher* 221 (Sept. 1930), 290–304.

Kaufmann, Wilhelm. *Die Deutschen im amerkanischen Bürgerkriege (Sezessionskrieg 1861–1865)*. Munich: Oldenbourg, 1911.

Keller, Morton. *The Art and Politics of Thomas Nast*. New York: Oxford Univ. Press, 1968.

Keller, Reiner. *Eifel-Börde-Ville: Landschaftskunde des Kreises Euskirchen*. Veröffentlichungen des Vereins der Geschichts-und Heimatsfrende des Kreises Euskirchen, Series A, Pamphlet 9. Euskirchen, 1964.

Kessel, Eberhard ed. *Die Briefe von Carl Schurz an Gottfried Kinkel. Beihefte zum Jahrbuch für Amerikastudien*, pt. 12. Heidelberg: Carl Winter, 1965.

———. "Carl Schurz und Gottfried Kinkel," in Otto Brunner and Dietrich Gerhard, eds., *Festschrift für Egmont Zechlin*, 109–34. Hamburg: Hans Bredow Institut, 1961.

Kessler, Fritz. "Carl Schurz—Zur Familen und Sippengeschichte." *Heimatkalender des Kreises Euskirchen* (1972), 64–74.

Kiefer, F.J. *Description Nouvelle et Complète de la Ville de Cologne*. Cologne: F.C. Eisen, 1842.

Kiefer, W.R. *History of the 153d Regiment Pennsylvania Volunteers, Infantry, 1862–1863*. Easton, Pa.: Chemical Publishing, 1909.

King, Willard. *Lincoln's Manager, David Davis*. Cambridge, Mass: Harvard Univ. Press, 1960.

Kinkel, Gottfried. *See* Sander, Richard.

Kinkel, Johanna. "Erinnerungsblätter aus dem Jahr 1849." *Deutsche Monatsschrift für Politik, Wissenschaft, Kunst und Leben* 2 (1851), 39–108.

Kirkland, Edward Chase. *Charles Francis Adams, Jr., 1835–1915: The Patrician at Bay*. Cambridge, Mass.: Harvard Univ. Press, 1965.

Kisky, Hans. *Burgen, Schlösser und Hofesfesten im Kreise Euskirchen*. Verein der Geschichts-und Heimatsfreunde des Kreises Euskirchen, Series A, Pamphlet 6. Euskirchen, 1960.

Koch, Dr. R. "Eine Erinnerung an Fürst Bismarck." *Deutsche Revue* 33 (1908), 162–64.

Koerner, Gustave. *See* McCormack, Thomas J.

Kortmann, Marie. *Emilie Wüstenfeld: Eine Hamburger Bürgerin*. Hamburg: Westermann, 1927.

Koss, Rudolf A. *Milwaukee*. Milwaukee: Milwaukee Herald, 1871.

Kruger, S.K. "Schurz-Kinkel Correspondence with Friedrich Krüger." *American-German Review* 14 (June 1948), 32–33.

Kurland, Gerald. *Seth Low: The Reformer in an Urban and Industrial Age.* New York: Twayne, 1971.

Leech, Margaret. *In the Days of McKinley.* New York: Harper, 1959.

Lincoln, Abraham. *See* Basler, Roy P.

Lindsay, David. *"Sunset" Cox: Irrepressible Democrat.* Detroit: Wayne State Univ. Press, 1959.

Lodge, Henry Cabot. *Early Memories.* New York, Scribner's, 1913. Reprint: New York: Arno, 1975.

———. *Selections from the Correspondence of Theodore Roosevelt and Henry Cabot Lodge, 1884–1919.* New York: Scribner's, 1924.

Logsdon, Joseph. *Horace White: Nineteenth Century Liberal.* Westport, Conn.: Greenwood, 1971.

Lonn, Ella. *Foreigners in the Union Army and Navy.* Baton Rouge: Louisiana State Univ. Press, 1951.

Lowenthal, David. *George Perkins Marsh: Versatile Vermonter.* New York: Columbia Univ. Press, 1958.

Luebke, Frederick C., ed. *Ethnic Voters and the Election of Lincoln.* Lincoln: Univ. of Nebraska Press, 1971.

———. *The Germans,* in John Higham, ed., *Ethnic Leadership in America,* 64–90. Baltimore: Johns Hopkins Univ. Press, 1978.

Luthin, Reinhard H. *The First Lincoln Campaign.* Cambridge, Mass.: Harvard Univ. Press, 1944.

———. "Lincoln Appeals to German-American Voters." *American-German Review* 25 (July 1959), 4–6, 15.

Lynch, Dennis Tilden. *The Wild Seventies.* New York: Appleton-Century, 1941.

Maass, Joachim. *Der unermüdliche Rebell: Leben, Taten und Vermächtnis des Carl Schurz.* Hamburg: Claasen & Goverts, 1949.

McCabe, Raphaella Catherine. "The Department of the Interior, 1877–81 under Carl Schurz." B.A. thesis, Univ. of Wisconsin, 1916.

McClure, Alexander K. *Colonel Alexander K. McClure's Recollections of Half a Century.* Salem, Mass.: Salem Press, 1902.

McCormack, Thomas J., ed. *Memoirs of Gustave Koerner, 1809–1896: Life Sketches Written at the Suggestion of His Children.* 2 vols. Cedar Rapids, Ia.: Torch Press, 1909.

McDonald, John. *Secrets of the Great Whiskey Ring and Eighteen Months in the Penitentiary.* St. Louis: W.S. Bryan, 1880.

McElroy, Robert. *Levi Parsons Morton: Banker, Diplomat and Statesman.* New York: Putnam's, 1930.

McFarland, Gerald W. *Mugwumps, Morals, and Politics, 1884–1920.* Amherst: Univ. of Massachusetts Press, 1975.

McFeely, James M. *Grant: A Biography.* New York: Norton, 1981.

McKitrick, Eric L. *Andrew Johnson and Reconstruction.* Chicago: Univ. of Chicago Press, 1960.

McPherson, Edward. *The Political History of the United States of America During the Period of Reconstruction, 1865–1870.* Washington: Philip & Solomons, 1871. Reprint: Harold M. Hyman and Hans L. Trefousse, eds., New York: Da Capo Press, 1972.

———. *Handbook of Politics, 1871–1876.* New York: Da Capo, 1972.

McPherson, James M. "Grant or Greeley? The Abolitionist Dilemma in the Election of 1872." *American Historical Review* 71 (Oct. 1963), 43–61.

McReynolds, Edwin C. *Missouri: A History of the Crossroads State.* Norman: Univ. of Oklahoma Press, 1962.

Mahaffey, Joseph H. "Carl Schurz's Letters From the South." *Georgia Historical Quarterly* 25 (Sept. 1951), 222–57.

Marcosson, Isaac F. "Marse Henry:" A Biography of Henry Watterson. Westport, Conn.: Greenwood, 1951.

Marcus, Robert D. *Grand Old Party: Political Structure in the Gilded Age, 1880–1896.* New York: Oxford Univ. Press, 1971.

Mardock, Robert Winston. *The Reformers and the American Indian.* Columbus: Univ. of Missouri Press, 1977.

Mehring, Franz. *Karl Marx.* London: Allen & Unwin, 1936.

Merriam, George S. *The Life and Times of Samuel Bowles.* 2 vols. New York: Century, 1885.

Meyer, Heinrich Adolf. *Erinnerungen an Heinrich Christian Meyer—Stockmeyer.* Hamburg: Lütcke & Wulff, 1900.

Meysenbug, Malwida von. *Memoiren einer Idealistin.* 3 vols. 9th ed. Berlin: Schuster & Loeffler, 1905.

Milne, Gordon. *George William Curtis and the Genteel Tradition.* Bloomington, Ind.: Indiana Univ. Press, 1956.

Monaghan, Jay. "Did Abraham Lincoln Receive the Illinois German Vote?" *Journal of the Illinois State Historical Society* 35 (Mar. 1942), 131–39.

Monod, Gabriel. "Briefe von Malwida von Meysenbug an ihre Mutter." *Deutsche Revue* 30 (1905), 229–41; 31 (1906), 359–70.

Monroe, Marie Jussen. "Biographical Sketch of Edmund Jussen." *Wisconsin Magazine of History* 12 (Dec. 1928), 146–75.

Moran, Benjamin. *See* Wallace, Sarah Agnes.

Morgan, H. Wayne. *From Hayes to McKinley: National Party Politics, 1877–1896.* Syracuse: Syracuse Univ. Press, 1969.

Morison, Elting E. *et al,* eds. *The Letters of Theodore Roosevelt.* 8 vols. Cambridge, Mass.: Harvard Univ. Press, 1951–54.

Morris, Edmund. *The Rise of Theodore Roosevelt.* New York: Coward, McCann & Geoghegan, 1979.

Munroe, James Phinney. *A Life of Francis Amasa Walker.* New York: Holt, 1923.

Murphy, James B. *L.Q.C. Lamar: Pragmatic Patriot.* Baton Rouge: Louisiana State Univ. Press, 1973.

Muzzey, David Saville. *James G. Blaine: A Political Idol of Other Days.* New York: Dodd, Mead, 1934.

Nachtigall, Hermann. *Geschichte des 75sten Regiments, Pa. Volunteers.* Philadelphia: C.B. Kretschman, 1886.

Nelson, Henry L. "Schurz's Administration of the Interior Department." *International Review* 10 (1881), 380–96.

Nerrlich, Paul, ed. *Ruges Briefwechsel und Tagebuchblätter aus den Jahren 1825–1880.* 2 vols. Berlin: Weidmann, 1886.

Nevins, Allan. *Abram Hewitt with Some Account of Peter Cooper.* New York: Harper, 1935.

———, ed. *A Diary of Battle: The Personal Journals of Colonel Charles S. Wainwright.* New York: Harcourt, Brace, 1962.

———. *The Emergence of Lincoln.* 2 vols. New York: Scribner's, 1950.

———. *The* Evening Post: *A Century of Journalism.* New York: Boni & Liveright, 1922.

———. *Fremont—Pathmarker of the West.* New York: Appleton-Century, 1939.

———. *Grover Cleveland: A Study in Courage.* New York: Dodd, Mead, 1933.

———. *Hamilton Fish: The Inner History of the Grant Administration.* New York: Dodd, Mead, 1936.

———, ed. *Letters of Grover Cleveland, 1850–1908.* Boston: Houghton Mifflin, 1933.

———. *The War for the Union.* 2 vols. New York: Scribner's, 1959, 1960.

New York Civil Service Reform Association, *Annual Reports*.

New-York in a Nutshell, or Visitor's Handbook to the City. New York: T. W. Strong, 1853.

Nugent, Walter T. K. *The Money Question During Reconstruction*. New York: Norton, 1967.

Oberholtzer, Ellis Paxson. *Jay Cooke: Financier of the Civil War*. 2 vols. New York: Burt Franklin, 1970.

O'Connor, Richard. *The German-Americans: An Informal History*. Boston: Little, Brown, 1968.

————. Sheridan: The Inevitable. Indianapolis: Bobbs-Merrill, 1953.

Oehlke, Waldemar, ed. *Bettina von Arnim, Sämtliche Werke*. Berlin: Propyläen, 1922.

Ogden, Rollo. *Life and Letters of Edwin Lawrence Godkin*. 2 vols. New York: Macmillan, 1907.

Osborn, Hartwell, et al. *Trials and Triumphs: The Record of the Fifty-fifth Ohio Volunteer Infantry*. Chicago: McClurg, 1904.

Page, Charles A. *Letters of a War Correspondent* ed. James R. Gilmore. Boston: L. C. Page, 1899.

Paine, Albert Bigelow. *Th. Nast: His Period and Pictures*. New York: Pearson, 1904. Reprint: Gloucester, Mass.: Peter Smith, 1967.

Palmer, John McAuly. *Washington, Lincoln, Wilson: Three War Statesmen*. Garden City, N.Y.: Doubleday, 1930.

Parenti, Michael. "Ethnic Politics and the Persistence of Ethnic Identification." *American Political Science Review* 61 (Sept. 1967), 717–26.

Parker, David B. *A Chautauqua Boy in '61 and Afterward*. Boston: Small, Maynard, 1912.

Parker, George F. *Recollections of Grover Cleveland*. New York: Century, 1909.

Parrish, William E. *Missouri Under Radical Rule, 1865–1870*. Columbia: Univ. of Missouri Press, 1965.

Peck, Thurston. *See* Filler, Louis.

Peskin, Allan. *Garfield*. Kent, Ohio: Kent State Univ. Press, 1978.

Peterson, Norma L. *Freedom and Franchise: The Political Career of B. Gratz Brown*. Columbia: Univ. of Missouri Press, 165.

Pettigrew, R. F. *Triumphant Plutocracy: The Story of American Public Life from 1870 to 1920*. New York: Academy Press, 1921.

Pierce, Edward L. *Memoir and Letters of Charles Sumner*. 4 vols. Boston: Roberts, 1893.

Pitollet, Camille. "Sur un Prétendu Roman à Clef de Johanna Kinkel 'Hans Ibeles in London.'" *Revue Germanique* 3 (1907), 361–407.

Plumb, Ralph. "The Schurz-Hobart Joint Debate—1859." *Wisconsin Magazine of History* 49 (1955–56), 40–43.

Plumb, Ralph G. *Badger Politics, 1836–1930*. Manitowoc, Wis.: Brandt Printing, 1930.

Polakoff, Keith Ian. *The Politics of Inertia: The Election of 1876 and the End of Reconstruction*. Baton Rouge: Louisiana State Univ. Press, 1973.

Pratt, Fletcher. *Ordeal by Fire*. New York: Pocket Books, 1952.

Prasuhn, Wilhelm. *Rund um Schloss Brühl*. Brühl: Volkmann, 1956.

Priest, Loring Benson. *Uncle Sam's Stepchildren: The Reformation of United States Indian Policy, 1865–1887*. New Brunswick, N.J.: Rutgers Univ. Press, 1942.

Proceedings at the Annual Meeting of the National Civil Service Reform League. (Annual).

Proceedings of the First Three Republican National Conventions of 1856, 1860 and 1864. . . . Minneapolis: Charles W. Johnson, 1893.

Proceedings of the Liberal Republican Convention in Cincinnati, May 1st, 2d, and 3d, 1872. New York: Baker & Godwin, 1872.

Proceedings of the National Union Republican Convention Held at Chicago, May 20 and 21, 1868. Chicago: Evening Journal, 1868.

Prucha, Francis Paul. *American Indian Policy in Crisis: Christian Reformers and the Indian, 1865–1900.* Norman: Univ. of Oklahoma Press, 1976.

Pula, James S. *For Liberty and Justice: The Life and Times of Wladimir Krzyzanowski.* Chicago: Polish American Congress Charitable Foundation, 1978.

Putnam, George Haven. *Memoirs of a Publisher, 1865–1915.* New York: Putnam's 1916.

Quaife, Milo Milton. *Wisconsin: Its History and Its People, 1634–1924.* 4 vols. Chicago: J. S. Clarke, 1924.

Quiner, Edwin B. *City of Watertown, Wisconsin. Its Manufactures & Railroad Advantages, and Business Statistics.* Watertown: City Council, 1858.

Randall, J. G. *Lincoln the President.* 4 vols. Vol. IV coauthored by Richard N. Current. New York: Dodd, Mead, 1945–55.

Raney, William Francis. *Wisconsin: A Story of Progress.* New York: Prentice-Hall, 1940.

Raphaelson, Alfred C. "Alexander Schimmelfenning, A German-American Campaigner in the Civil War." *Pennsylvania Magazine of History and Biography* 87 (Apr. 1963), 156–81.

Rauh, Georg von. "Der Widerhall der Revolution von 1848 im baltischen Deutschtum." *Hamburger mittel-und ostdeutsche Forschungen* 4 (1963), 9–29.

———. "Eine baltische Frau im Wirbel des Jahres 1848." *Jahrbuch des baltischen Deutschtums* 10 (1963), 29–36.

Rawley, James A. "The General Amnesty Act of 1872." *MVHR* 47 (1960), 480–84.

Reemelin, Charles. *Life of Charles Reemelin.* Cincinnati: Weier & Daiker, 1892.

Reeves, Thomas C. *Gentleman Boss: The Life of Chester Alan Arthur.* New York: Knopf, 1975.

Rhodes, James Ford. *History of the United States from the Compromise of 1850.* 7 vols. New York: Macmillan, 1900–1910.

Rice, Owen. "Afield with the Eleventh Army Corps at Chancellorsville . . . ." *Papers Read before the Ohio Commandery of the Military Order of the Loyal Legion of the United States,* I, 358–91. Cincinnati: Robert Clarke, 1888.

Richard. *Manuel du Voyager sur les Bords du Rhin.* Paris: Audin, 1863.

Richardson, Leon Burr. *William E. Chandler, Republican.* New York: Dodd, Mead, 1940.

Richardson, Robert K. "A Beloit Episode in the Life of Carl Schurz." *Transactions of the Wisconsin Academy of Sciences, Arts and Letters* 41 (1952).

Riddleberger, Patrick W. "The Break in Radical Ranks: Liberals *vs.* Stalwarts in the Election of 1872." *Journal of Negro History* 44 (Apr. 1959), 136–37.

———. *George Washington Julian, Radical Republican: A Study in Nineteenth Century Politics and Reform.* Indianapolis: Indiana Historical Bureau, 1966.

———. "The Radicals' Abandonment of the Negro During Reconstruction." *Journal of Negro History* 45 (Apr. 1960), 88–102.

Rippley, La Vern J. *The German-Americans.* Boston: Twayne, 1976.

Roosevelt, Theodore. *See* Morison, Elting.

Ross, Earle Dudley. *The Liberal Republican Movement.* New York: Holt, 1919.

Roseboom, Eugene H., and Weisenburger, Francis P. *A History of Ohio,* ed. James H. Rodabaugh. Columbus: Ohio State Archaeological and Historical Society, 1953.

Ross, Joel H. *What I Saw in New-York, or a Bird's Eye View of City Life.* Auburn, N.Y.: Derby & Miller, 1851.

Ruge, Arnold. *See* Nerrlich, Paul.

Russell, Charles Edward. *Blaine of Maine: His Life and Times*. New York: Cosmopolitan, 1931.

Russell, John Andrew. *The Germanic Influence in the Making of Michigan*. Detroit. Univ. of Detroit, 1927.

Samuels, Ernest. *Henry Adams, The Middle Years*. Cambridge, Mass.: Harvard Univ. Press, 1958.

Sander, Richard, ed. *Gottfried Kinkel's Selbstbiographie, 1838–1848*. Bonn: Friedrich Cohen, 1931.

Schafer, Joseph. *Carl Schurz, Militant Liberal*. Evansville, Wis.: Center Press, 1930.

———. "Carl Schurz's Historical Output." *Wisconsin Magazine of History* 12 (June 1929), 424–32.

———. "Who Elected Lincoln?" *AHR* 47 (Oct. 1941), 51–63.

Scharf, Thomas J. *History of St. Louis and County*. 2 vols. Philadelphia: Louis H. Evarts, 1883.

Scheiffarth, Engelbrecht. *Das Amt Menden*. Siegburg: F. Schmidt, 1964.

Schieber, Clara Eve. *The Transformation of American Sentiment Toward Germany, 1870–1914*. New York: Russell & Russell, 1973.

Schirmer, Daniel B. *Republic or Empire: American Resistance to the Philippine War*. Cambridge, Mass.: Schenkman, 1972.

Schmeckebier, Laurence P. *The Office of Indian Affairs: Its History, Activities and Organization*. Baltimore: Johns Hopkins Univ. Press, 1927.

Schmitt, Martin F., ed. *General Crook: His Autobiography*. Norman: Univ. of Oklahoma Press, 1946.

Schulze, Friedrich, and Ssymank, Paul. *Das deutsche Studententum von den ältesten Zeiten bis zur Gegenwart*. Leipzig: R. Voigtländer, 1910.

Schwarz, Mia. *Malwida von Meysenbug*. Lübeck: Charles Coleman, 1933.

Scott, Ann Herbert. *Census, U.S.A.: Fact Finding for the American People, 1790–1970*. New York: Seabury, 1968.

Scott, W. D. Robson. *The Literary Background of the Gothic Revival in Germany*. Oxford. Oxford Univ. Press, Clarendon, 1965.

Selections from the Correspondence of Theodore Roosevelt and Henry Cabot Lodge. New York: Scribner's, 1925.

Seward, Frederick W. *Reminiscences of a War-Time Statesman and Diplomat, 1830–1915*. New York: Putnam's, 1916.

Shannon, Fred A. *The Farmer's Last Frontier*. New York: Farrar & Rinehart, 1945.

Sheppard, E. W. *The Campaign in Virginia and Maryland, June 26 to September 20, 1862*. . . . New York: Greene, Allen, 1911.

Sherwin, Oscar. *Prophet of Liberty: The Life and Times of Wendell Phillips*. New York: Bookman, 1958.

Simmers, William, and Brachschmid, Paul. *The Volunteer's Manuel [sic], or Ten Months With the 153d Penna. Volunteers*. Easton, Pa.: Free Press, 1907.

Simms, L. Moody, Jr. "Carl Schurz and the Negro." *Bulletin, Missouri Historical Society* 25 (Apr. 1969), 236–38.

Slocum, Charles Eliot. *The Life and Public Services of Major-General Henry Warner Slocum*. Toledo: Slocum, 1913.

Smith, Donnal V. *Chase and Civil War Politics*. Columbus, Ohio: F.J. Heer, 1931.

———. "The Influence of the Foreign-Born in the Northwest in the Election of 1860." *MVHR* 19 (Sept. 1932), 192–204.

Smith, Elbert B. *Francis Preston Blair*. New York: Free Press, 1980.

Smith, Henry H., ed. *All the Republican National Conventions . . . Proceedings, Platforms, and Candidates*. Washington, D.C.: Robert Beall, 1896.

Smith, Theodore Clarke. *The Life and Letters of James Abram Garfield*. 2 vols. New Haven: Yale Univ. Press, 1925.

Smith, William Ernest. *The Francis Preston Blair Family in Politics*. New York: Macmillan, 1933.

Snyder, Louis L. *Roots of German Nationalism*. Bloomington: Indiana Univ. Press, 1978.

Sonthoff, Herbert. *Revolutionär—Soldat—Staatsmann: Der Deutsche und der Amerikaner, Carl Schurz*. Leipzig: Reklam, 1936.

Spael, Wilhelm. *Karl Schurz*. 2 vols. Essen: Fredebeul & Koenen, 1948, 1949.

Spielhagen, Friedrich. *Finder und Erfinder: Erinnerungen aus meinem Leben*. 2 vols. Leipzig: L. Staakmann, 1890.

Sproat, John G. *"The Best Men": Liberal Reformers in the Gilded Age*. New York: Oxford Univ. Press, 1968.

Stackpole, Edward. *From Cedar Mountain to Antietam, August–September 1862*. Harrisburg, Pa.: Stackpole, 1959.

Stampp, Kenneth M. *The Era of Reconstruction, 1865–1877*. New York: Knopf, 1965.

Stevenson, James H. *"Boots and Saddles:" A History of the First Volunteer Cavalry of the War Known as the First New York (Lincoln) Cavalry . . . .* Harrisburg, Pa.: Patriot Publishing 1879.

Stewart, Frank Mann. *The National Civil Service Reform League: History, Activities, and Problems*. Austin: Univ. of Texas Press, 1929.

Still, Baird. *Milwaukee: The History of a City*. Madison: State Historical Society of Wisconsin, 1948.

Stine, J. H. *History of the Army of the Potomac*. Philadelphia: J. B. Rogers, 1892.

Stoddard, Henry L. *As I Knew Them: Presidents and Politics From Grant to Coolidge*. New York: Harper, 1927.

Stollberg-Wernigerode, Otto Graf zu. *Deutschland und die Vereinigten Staaten im Zeitalter Bismarcks*. Berlin: Walter de Gruyter, 1933.

Stommel, Karl. *Das Kurkölnische Amt Lechenich: Seine Entstehung und seine Organisation*. Veröffentlichungen der Geschichts und Heimatsfreunde des Kreises Euskirchen, Series A, Pamphlet 7. Euskirchen, 1961.

Stone, Candace. *Dana and the Sun*. New York: Dodd, Mead, 1938.

Strodtmann, Adolph. *Gottfried Kinkel: Wahrheit ohne Dichtung . . . .* 2 vols. Hamburg: Hoffmann & Campe, 1851.

The Stranger's Guide. Around New York and its Vicinity. New York: W. H. Graham, 1853.

Straus, Oscar S. *Under Four Administrations: From Cleveland to Taft*. Boston: Houghton Mifflin, 1922.

Struve, Gustav. Diesseits und Jenseits des Oceans. Coburg: F. Streit, 1863.

Swart, Hannah Werwarth. *Margarethe Meyer Schurz*. Watertown, Wis.: Watertown Historical Society, 1967.

Swinton, William. *Campaigns of the Army of the Potomac*. New York: Charles P. Richardson, 1866.

Tansill, Charles Callan. *The Foreign Policy of Thomas F. Bayard, 1885–1897*. New York: Fordham Univ. Press, 1940.

———. *The United States and Santo Domingo, 1798–1873: A Chapter in Caribbean Diplomacy*. Baltimore: Johns Hopkins Univ. Press, 1938.

Taylor, Joe Gray. *Louisiana Reconstructed, 1863–1877*. Baton Rouge: Louisiana State Univ. Press, 1974.

Terzian, James P. *Defender of Human Rights: Carl Schurz*. New York: Messner, 1965.

Thomas, Benjamin P., and Hyman, Harold M. *Stanton: The Life and Times of Lincoln's Secretary of War*. New York: Knopf, 1962.

Thomson, A. M. *A Political History of Wisconsin.* Milwaukee: E. C. Williams, 1900.

Thoron, Ward, ed. *The Letters of Mrs. Henry Adams.* Boston: Little, Brown, 1936.

Tibbles, Thomas Henry. *Buckskin and Blanket Days: Memoirs of the Indians.* New York: Doubleday, 1957.

Tompkins, E. Berkeley. *Anti-Imperialism in the United States: The Great Debate, 1890-1920.* Philadelphia: Univ. of Pennsylvania Press, 1976.

Tonnelat, Ernest. "Les Allemands Aux États-Unis." *Revue de Paris* 13 (May, June 1906), 207–24, 564–82.

Tracy, J. L. *Tracy's Guide to Missouri and St. Louis.* St. Louis: R. P. Studly, 1871.

Trefousse, Hans L. *Ben Butler: The South Called Him Beast.* New York: Twayne, 1957.

———. *Benjamin Franklin Wade: Radical Republican from Ohio.* New York: Twayne, 1963.

———. "Carl Schurz, the South, and the Politics of Virtue," in Abraham S. Eisenstadt, et al., *Before Watergate: Problems of Corruption in American Society,* 99–116. Brooklyn, N.Y.: Brooklyn College Press, 1978.

———. "Carl Schurz's 1865 Southern Tour: A Reassessment." *Prospects* 2 (1976), 293–308.

———. *Impeachment of a President: Andrew Johnson, the Blacks, and Reconstruction.* Knoxville: Univ. of Tennessee Press, 1975.

———. *Lincoln's Decision for Emancipation,* ed. Harold M. Hyman. Philadelphia: Lippincott, 1975.

———. *The Radical Republicans: Lincoln's Vanguard for Racial Justice.* New York: Knopf, 1969.

Truax, Rhoda. *The Doctors Jacobi.* Boston: Little, Brown, 1952.

Tucker, Glenn. *Hancock the Superb.* Indianapolis: Bobbs-Merrill, 1960.

Tuttle, Charles. *An Illustrated History of the State of Wisconsin.* Madison: B. B. Russell, 1875.

Unger, Irwin. *The Greenback Era: A Social and Political History of American Finance, 1865-1879.* Princeton, N.J.: Princeton Univ. Press, 1969.

Utley, Robert M. *Frontier Regulars: The United States Army and the Indian, 1866-1890.* New York: Macmillan, 1973.

Valentin, Veit. *1848: Chapters of German History.* London: Allen & Unwin, 1940.

———. *Geschichte der deutschen Revolution von 1848–49.* 2 vols. Berlin: Ullstein, 1930.

Van Deusen, Glyndon. *Horace Greeley: Nineteenth Century Crusader.* New York: Hill & Wang, 1964.

Varnhagen von Ense, K. A. *See* Assing, Ludmilla.

The Venezuela Question: Report on the Subject by the Committee on Foreign Commerce and the Revenue Laws of the Chamber of Commerce of the State of New York Adopted by the Chamber January 2, 1896 . . . . New York: Chamber of Commerce, 1896.

Villard, Henry. *Memoirs of Henry Villard, Journalist and Financier, 1835–1900.* 2 vols. Boston: Houghton Mifflin, 1904.

Villard, Oswald Garrison. *Fighting Years: Memoirs of a Liberal Editor.* New York: Harcourt, Brace, 1939.

Violette, Eugene Morrow. *A History of Missouri.* Cape Girardeau: Ramfre Press, 1960.

Vocke, William. *Der Deutsche Soldat im Bürgerkriege: Vortrag . . . . vor der Northwestern University in Evansville am 5. Dec. 1895.* Chicago: Kolling & Klappenbach, n.d.

———. "Our German Soldiers." *Paper Read . . . Before the Commandery of the State of Illinois Military Order of the Loyal Legion.* Chicago: Dial Press, 1899.

Vulpius, Walter. "Carl Schurz, the Man and Friend: Personal Reminiscences." *American-German Review* 7 (Dec. 1940), 11.

Wainwright, Charles S. *See* Nevins, Allan.

Wall, Joseph Frazier. *Andrew Carnegie*. New York: Oxford Univ. Press, 1970.

Wallace, Sarah Agnes, and Gillespie, Frances Elma, eds. *The Journal of Benjamin Moran*. Chicago: Univ. of Chicago Press, 1949.

Warren, Charles. *The Supreme Court in United States History*. 2 vols. Boston: Little, Brown, 1926.

Watertown, Wisconsin Centennial, 1854–1954. N.d., n.p.

Watterson, Henry. *"Marse Henry": An Autobiography*. New York: Doran, 1919.

Webb, Ross A. *Benjamin Helm Bristow*. Lexington: Univ. Press of Kentucky, 1969.

Welch, Richard E., Jr. *George Frisbie Hoar and the Half-Breed Republicans*. Cambridge, Mass.: Harvard Univ. Press, 1971.

————. "Motives and Objectives of Anti-Imperialists, 1898." *Mid-America* 51 (Apr. 1969), 119–29.

————. *Response to Imperialism: The United States and the Philippine-American War, 1899–1902*. Chapel Hill: Univ. of North Carolina Press, 1979.

Welles, Gideon. *See* Beale, Howard K.

Wersich, Rüdiger, ed. *Carl Schurz: Revolutionär und Staatsmann, Sein Leben in Selbstzeugnissen, Bildern und Dokumenten*. Munich: Heinz Moos, 1979.

Wheeler, Everett P. *Sixty Years of American Life: Taylor to Roosevelt, 1850–1910*. New York: Dutton, 1917.

White, Andrew Dickinson. *Autobiography of Andrew Dickinson White.* 2 vols. New York: Century, 1905.

White, Horace. *The Life of Lyman Trumbull*. Boston: Houghton Mifflin, 1913.

White, Leonard. *The Republican Era: A Study in Administrative History, 1869–1901*. New York: Free Press, 1965.

White, William Allen. *Masks in a Pageant*. New York: Macmillan, 1928.

Whyte, William F. "Chronicles of Early Watertown." *Wisconsin Magazine of History* 4 (Mar. 1921), 287–314.

Wiegel, Mrs. C. W. "The Death of Ouray, Chief of the Utes." *The Colorado Magazine* 7 (Sept. 1930), 187–91.

Wiggers, Moritz. "Gottfried Kinkel's Befreiung." *Die Gartenlaube* (1863), 104–7, 120–24, 134–38, 152–55.

Willkie, Wendell. "There Were Giants in Those Days: The Story of Carl Schurz." *American-German Review* 9 (Dec. 1942), 4–5.

Williams, Charles Richard, ed. *Diary and Letters of Rutherford Birchard Hayes, 19th President of the United States*. 7 vols. Columbus: Ohio Archaeological and Historical Society, 1924.

Williams, Kenneth P. *Lincoln Finds a General: A Military Study of the Civil War*. 5 vols. New York: Macmillan, 1949–59.

Williams T. Harry, ed. *Hayes: The Diary of a President, 1875–1881*. New York: David McKay, 1964.

————. *Lincoln and His Generals*. New York: Grosset & Dunlap, 1952.

Winkler, Frederick C. *Letters of Frederick C. Winkler, 1862–1865*. Milwaukee: privately printed, 1963.

Wittke, Carl. "Carl Schurz and Rutherford B. Hayes." *Ohio Historical Quarterly* 65 (Oct. 1956), 337–55.

————. *The German Language Press in America*. Lexington: Univ. of Ky. Press, 1957.

————. *Refugees of Revolution: The German Forty-Eighters in America*. Philadelphia: Univ. of Pennsylvania Press, 1952.

Wolf, Simon. *The Presidents I Have Known from 1860 to 1910*. Washington: Byron & Adams, 1918.

Woodward, C. Vann. *Reunion and Reaction: The Compromise of 1877 and the End of Reconstruction.* Boston: Little, Brown, 1951.

Wright, Henry H. *A History of the Sixth Iowa Infantry.* Iowa City: State Historical Society of Iowa, 1923.

Young, Jesse Bowman. *The Battle of Gettysburg.* New York: Harper, 1913.

Zeek, Hans. "Kinkels Briefe aus Amerika 1851/52." *Die Neue Rundschau* 49 (1938), I, 600–14, II, 27–47.

Zucker, A. E., ed. *The Forty-Eighters: Political Refugees of the German Revolution of 1848.* New York: Columbia Univ. Press, 1950. Reprint: New York: Russell & Russell, 1967.

Zucker, Carl. "Carl Schurz's Escape Route from Rastatt." *American-German Review* 14 (Apr. 1948), 3–6.

Der Zug der Freischärler unter Kinkel, Schurz und Anneke behufs Plünderung des Zeughauses in Siegburg . . . . Bonn: P. Hanstein, 1886.

Index